FINANCIAL TIMES
MANAGEMENT

Knowledge   Skills   Understanding

Financ

deliver the knowledge,   fore the last date stamped below

enable students, managers a   eve their

ambitions, whatever their needs, wherever they are.

Financial Times Pitman Publishing, part of Financial Times
Management, is the leading publisher of books for practitioners
and students in business and finance, bringing cutting-edge
thinking and best practice to a global market.

To find out more about Financial Times Management and
Financial Times Pitman Publishing, visit our website at:

www.ftmanagement.com

MARKETING
Principles and Practice

THIRD EDITION

**Dennis Adcock, Ray Bradfield, Al Halborg
and Caroline Ross**

FINANCIAL TIMES
PITMAN PUBLISHING

LONDON · HONG KONG · JOHANNESBURG
MELBOURNE · SINGAPORE · WASHINGTON DC

FINANCIAL TIMES MANAGEMENT
128 Long Acre, London WC2E 9AN
Tel: +44 (0)171 447 2000
Fax: +44 (0)171 240 5771
Website: www.ftmanagement.com

A Division of Financial Times Professional Limited

First published in Great Britain in 1993
Second edition published 1995
Third edition published 1998

© Financial Times Professional Limited 1998

The right of Dennis Adcock, Ray Bradfield, Al Halborg and Caroline Ross
to be identified as Authors of this Work has been asserted by them in accordance
with the Copyright, Designs and Patents Act 1988.

ISBN 0 273 62798 8

British Library Cataloguing in Publication Data
A CIP catalogue record for this book can be obtained from the British Library.

10 9 8 7 6 5 4 3 2 1   92 05003 88

Typeset by Pantek Arts, Maidstone, Kent
Printed and bound in Great Britain by William Clowes Ltd, Beccles

The Publishers' policy is to use paper manufactured from sustainable forests.

658.8

Contents

Preface

It is with a lot of pleasure that we come to write the third edition of *Marketing: Principles and Practice*. The structure of the book has not changed dramatically, but in rewriting we have been able to include 15 new cases as well as significant chapters on Service Marketing and International Marketing – topics which all our students want to study in more depth. The final chapter which looks at Marketing in Action now has a case for each of the topics covered.

In addition, the colour plate section which you will find in the centre of this book has also been expanded. This means that there are 16 pages of examples of 'marketing in practice' for students to use.

This book is designed to give an introduction to the basis of Marketing for those students coming to this subject for the first time. However, it is complete enough to appeal both to those who study only one module on a modem mixed degree programme, as well as to provide a foundation for students who pursue the subject in more depth.

There are five main sections in the text:

- The first section is concerned with the role of marketing within its environment which encompasses macro-factors, competition and that most difficult uncontrollable variable which is how customers behave both individually and in organisations. This section is built on the exchange process and the understanding of benefits as affected by these environmental pressures.

  The need to understand such issues and how information helps marketing decisions leads into the second key section on the marketing offering.
- This section had been revised to stress the totality of the offering and to consider intangible aspects within the new chapter on services and relationships. Issues of quality, value and availability are all considered as part of the total offering.
- The third section looks at communication, both generally and the use of specific media. New communication could be through the internet and this is mentioned besides the more traditional media.
- All the issues of planning are brought together in the fourth section. This includes product policy, total marketing planning which is applied to existing products as well as new directions and new product development.
- The final section covers more general issues of detailed research and organising for marketing. It retains the chapter on ethics, but the Marketing in Action section has expanded to give a separate chapter on international issues and to give a wider range of examples in the practical Marketing in Action chapter. There are expanded appendices so that more direction is given to help students with informal research, which is often a part of projects but so often is lacking in methodology.

Dennis Adcock, Ray Bradfield, Al Halborg, Caroline Ross
Coventry, September 1997

Acknowledgements

All the authors are indebted to students at Coventry, Warwick and Southampton as well as the other universities who use the text and who have offered helpful and constructive criticism. In presenting the cases to enable discussion on the subject matter, many of the successful older cases have been updated and focused on current issues. More than half the cases are new, all cases have been tested and are offered to stimulate class discussion as well as helping to make the principles of marketing more relevant in practice.

There are a number of colour illustrations in the book, which are examples of marketing in practice. We are indebted to the agencies who help in this respect and we would urge all students to continue to study current media as well as articles in the marketing and national press. By considering these against the general principles as presented in this book it is possible to learn more of the subject which is so dynamic and so much fun.

In revising the text we have all relied on others to assist in typing, researching, revising and just putting up with us as we worked against publishing deadlines. Most important in this group are our respective partners, Marion, Peggy, Eileen and Ken. We thank them for their encouragement and their tolerance.

CHAPTER 1

What is Marketing?

Marketing: the action or business of bringing or sending to market.
Oxford English Dictionary

This marketing of supplies was the beginning ... of its prosperity.
Harper's Magazine (1984)

INTRODUCTION

As the 21st century approaches it is increasingly true to say that it is as difficult to avoid effective marketing as it is to avoid the effects of a physical phenomenon such as gravity. Whereas, gravity ensures anything we drop falls to the floor not the ceiling, it is through developing an understanding of marketing that for more than thirty years we have been offered an ever wider choice when meeting our needs and wants. This choice involves the food we eat for breakfast, the beverage we have with our breakfast, our choice of clothes and how we spend our time. It affects not only the products we choose, but also the place where we obtain these products and, in a subtle way, how we make these choices.

While one individual's choice of Crunchy Nut Corn Flakes for breakfast could be accidental, it is more likely to have been made partly as a result of past experiences and partly due to other factors which were relevant when the choice was made.

What are these other factors? When the choice was made it may have been because the only alternative was dry toast. However, the choice made was only available as a result of an earlier choice to purchase Crunchy Nut Corn Flakes rather than another brand of breakfast cereal. This choice involved the Crunchy Nut Corn Flakes being available where and when you did your shopping, in the quantity required, and at a price that was acceptable. Furthermore, this purchase involved accepting cereal for breakfast rather than, for instance, fruit, or doughnuts. This is clearly important to doughnut manufacturers who might significantly increase their sales if more people bought doughnuts rather than Crunchy Nut Corn Flakes for breakfast. How could this be achieved? What would it cost? Could this be paid for from the increased sales? Three typical questions which involve marketing issues.

THE PURPOSE OF MARKETING

In order to prosper, all business organisations have continuously to encourage potential customers to buy their products, and they must do this as efficiently as possible. This is central to all marketing activity. Marketing is thus not confined to advertising and selling, but covers everything related to what was once described as providing:

The right product, in the right place, at the right price, and at the right time.

What is right? From the marketing viewpoint it is right if it gets the desired response from the required number of potential customers, efficiently and ethically. As customers we expect to have a choice when we spend our money. We can also choose not to spend any money at all by deciding not to buy a product. When we do decide to buy, an exchange takes place. Money is exchanged for the chosen product and hopefully both parties will feel happy with their side of the bargain (Fig. 1.1). Usually, in addition to the actual money spent, it is necessary for the purchaser to invest time when making the decision to buy. This might involve visiting a shop or other selling outlet, studying catalogues and sometimes discussing the purchase with family or friends.

Inevitably a specific purchase also means the sacrifice of not being able to buy something else with the money spent (the opportunity cost of the purchase).

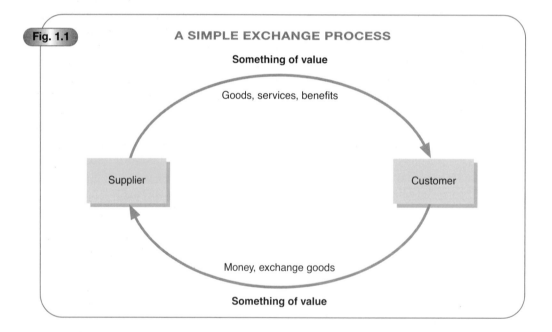

Fig. 1.1

A SIMPLE EXCHANGE PROCESS

Something of value

Goods, services, benefits

Supplier

Customer

Money, exchange goods

Something of value

MARKETING DEFINITIONS

It should be clear from the points already made that marketing involves an exchange process and this is central to one of the simplest accepted definitions of marketing which is:

Marketing is the study of exchange processes especially those associated with the provision of goods and services.

While clearly focused and concise, this definition provides no indication of the potential relevance and scope of the subject. This aspect is better addressed in the definition proposed by the celebrated American author of marketing textbooks, Philip Kotler:

Marketing is the human activity directed at satisfying needs and wants through an exchange process. (Kotler, 1980)

Since 1980 Kotler's definition has become developed:

Marketing is a social and managerial process by which individuals and groups obtain what they want and need through creating, offering, and exchanging products of value with others. (Kotler, 1991)

The major addition is the phrase 'of value', and as this is an important aspect of marketing, it will be explored fully in later chapters. There are many other useful and equally acceptable definitions. The one preferred by the British Chartered Institute of Marketing (CIM) is:

Marketing is the management process responsible for identifying, anticipating and satisfying customers' requirements profitably.

You can see that all of these definitions are relevant in the context of the selection of breakfast cereal. Both Kotler and CIM focus on the *profitable* exchange being for the supplier. The term *profitable* is not being used in the strict accounting sense, but rather as an indication of the importance of both parties having to benefit from the exchange.

As in all specialist subjects, marketing has allocated specific meanings to words which have general usage. The specialist terminology includes both single words such as *needs*, *wants*, and phrases such as *marketing offering*, *marketing mix* and *management process*. Within the context of marketing these words and phrases have specific meanings related to the concepts central to a proper understanding of the subject. You will in addition find, particularly in articles on the subject, other terms which have become part of the jargon associated with the subject.

THE EXCHANGE PROCESS

Economic prosperity and progress has depended upon the development of ways by which products can be exchanged between individuals and societies. At the simplest level this would be restricted to direct exchanges with near neighbours. To increase the opportunity to do this, and the variety of goods available, times and meeting places are established so people can gather to make exchanges. Typically these gatherings became known as fairs or markets. These allowed trade to expand over considerable distances as merchants took products from one market to another. Trade involving the direct exchange of goods is known as *barter* and depends upon individuals with complementary products finding one another. For an exchange to take place a person who has a pig and wants some wheat needs to find someone with wheat who wants a pig.

This difficulty is significantly reduced once a means of exchange has some general acceptance. This could be a valued product such as salt (paid to Roman soldiers and from which the word *salary* is derived), tea, precious stones, something made out of precious metal, or the tokens of value that we accept as money. The use of money allows the person to sell the pig on a day when there is someone wanting to buy a pig and buy the wheat on another day when there is someone wanting to sell wheat. It also allows very precise relative values to be placed on different products depending upon size, availability and demand. Thus, if there are fewer pigs available the person with the pig may find that what he receives in exchange for it will buy several bags of wheat. Alternatively, on another day, the person could find that to buy one bag of wheat it will be necessary to sell two pigs.

The demand and availability for some products such as wheat, or seasonal products such as vegetables, may well depend upon the weather, with the result that the price may vary significantly from month to month. Other products will not be affected in this way, which means that an accepted price for these products can become known by both sellers and buyers. This makes it unnecessary for a buyer to visit the market, as goods can be purchased at the accepted price through intermediaries or merchants.

As trade increases so does the number of markets and merchants. This provides individuals with opportunities to choose between many more potential suppliers. It also provides suppliers with opportunities to sell to many more potential customers. Inevitably this means suppliers and customers become increasingly separated: not only by physical distance and time, but also by culture and attitude. This separation is likely to reduce the benefits derived from the exchange. For the supplier this is because eventually income is reduced by the additional costs involved and for the purchaser as a result of reduced value being received. Marketing, by focusing on the exchange process, provides ways of analysing this process to maximise the benefit both parties gain from an exchange.

WHAT IS A MARKET?

At its most basic, a market could be considered to be a meeting place for making exchanges. As a result, markets can be places where it is accepted the relative value of different products are established. In practice, for this to happen reliably, markets need to have rules and procedures for their enforcement. This is the basis for the definition of a market used by economists.

Within the context of marketing, the word market is also used to mean all the individuals or organisations who are, or could be purchasers of a particular product. This use of the term can very often cause confusion. For instance, the UK car market could mean the 12 million existing car users, or more usually the 1.5 million or so new cars which are purchased in any one year. It is thus very important to use the word carefully so that its meaning is clear, and to ensure that you understand how it is being used when you come across it in your reading.

THE ORIGINS OF MARKETING

The technical developments of the first decades of this century provided great opportunities for businesses, since the demand for the many new products which became available at that time exceeded supply. These products included the equipment needed to supply electricity and telephones to every home, appliances such as vacuum cleaners, refrigerators and washing machines, radio receivers, and of course, motor vehicles. This demand provided business for companies manufacturing the tools and equipment needed to make these products and improved employment opportunities generally. This resulted in rapid economic growth which, although interrupted in Europe by World War I (1914–18), continued unabated in the USA.

Production capacity expanded and by the mid-1920s began to exceed demand. Customers for the first time found they were being offered a real choice by different manufacturers who responded by increasing their selling efforts. The benefits offered to the customer by the products began to be emphasised. Business had moved from the production era, when the main objective was to increase production, to the selling era, when the objective changed to increasing sales relative to the competition. Unfortunately, in the USA production continued to exceed sales in many markets, and this was one of the many factors which led to the economic crash of 1929 and the Great Depression that followed it.

The subsequent recovery was followed by World War II (1939–45), which meant that demand again exceeded supply until the mid-1950s. Then, as manufacturing grew worldwide it began to be realised by the managements of the most effective, mature companies in the USA, that the selling approach did not, in the long term, make suppliers more prosperous. They began to appreciate that to succeed in an increasingly competitive environment, it was essential to understand and respond to the needs of customers. As a result these companies began moving towards a marketing approach. To do this they began to apply the various concepts of marketing which had been developed at the University of Wisconsin and at the Harvard Business School since the early 1900s. As a result these ideas increasingly became an integral part of what was then known as modern management training.

By the early 1960s it was recognised that business in the UK was becoming increasingly uncompetitive by world standards. One of the reasons was believed to be the shortage of trained managers. The remedy was seen to be the introduction of formal management training courses like those which had been developed in the USA. Marketing was thus initially taught as part of these courses.

Subsequently, the competitive situation for businesses in the UK has become increasingly like that of the USA. As markets have become global, marketing has become even more important. Because of this the subject is increasingly being included in courses for engineers, designers and many others who are not training to be marketing specialists.

WHAT IS MARKETING?

While it could be argued that the definitions given earlier in this chapter fully answer this question, it is necessary to adopt a different approach to explain the different ways the term *marketing* is used. This involves recognising that, in practice, the term is used in four different ways. These are as an accepted business philosophy, as an organisational function, as a business concept and as a management function.

Marketing as a business philosophy

Marketing as a Business Philosophy recognises the importance of the customer and that businesses exist to serve customers rather than manufacture products. To be effective this philosophy must be accepted as being crucial in every part of an organisation. Peter Drucker once wrote, 'There is only one valid definition of business purpose: to create a customer.' At its simplest, if you do not have any customers for the product or service your organisation offers, then there is no reason for continuing existence.

This was recognised in 1776 by Adam Smith, the father of modern economics, who wrote:

> **Consumption is the sole end and purpose of all production and the interests of the product ought to be attended to only so far as it may be necessary for promoting those of the customer.**

Everyone in an organisation should be required to understand the final customer for their efforts, and thus to have a customer focus in their job. More recently N. W. (Red) Pope in a classic marketing article entitled 'Mickey Mouse Marketing' looked at the success of the Walt Disney organisation. Disney have a very positive attitude and have their own terminology to reflect this. At Disney, if your job involves you interfacing with the public (customers) in any way whatsoever, you are 'on stage'. If your work does not interface with the public, you are 'back-stage'. One is not better than the other. That is emphasised. No little insignificant jobs. It takes many people, doing many types of jobs, to 'put on the show'.

Disney know that the way to successful shows is centred on satisfying the paying public. The launch and initial results of EuroDisney seemed to show that this venture did not achieve this objective. Improvements have since been implemented although it may be some time before it can be established whether the resulting increased success has been achieved by returning to the fundamentals so valued by the late Walt Disney.

Marketing as an organisational function

Within all types of organisation it is generally considered good management practice to identify activities and responsibilities and allocate these within specific organisational functional areas such as production or accounting. For most organisations advertising, sales promotion and marketing research would be considered core marketing function activities, while other activities would be dependent upon the type of organisation. For example, within a retail organisation the buying function is likely to be classified as a marketing function whereas, in a manufacturing organisation it would normally may be considered a production function. Figure 1.2 shows the wide range of tasks which can be included within the marketing function. Some of these, like the core activities already mentioned, are sufficiently crucial to the function of marketing to warrant at least an individual chapter in this textbook. Others, however, may need more explanation. Buying has already been mentioned. Within all trading organisations the range of products offered to customers is likely to be of crucial importance to the success of the organisation. As it is the buyers who are responsible for making this selection it is logical to consider this as a marketing function within organisations of this type, for instance wholesalers, retailers and importers.

It is unusual for organisations to have the responsibility for two of the activities shown specifically assigned. Yet both can be of critical importance to an organisation in the marketing context. The first of these is *risk taking*. Many businesses involve the acceptance of risk. A simple example is the local greengrocer who goes to the market on Friday morning to purchase his stock for the weekend. During the summer he will

Fig. 1.2 THE OPERATIONAL FUNCTIONS OF MARKETING

need to purchase lettuces, tomatoes and the other salad produce. How much of each should he buy? It is important that he buys sufficient to meet the needs of his customers since, if he sells out there is always the possibility that a disappointed customer will be a lost customer. Equally he does not want to have so much left that some of it will have to be discarded. Since the amount sold is likely to depend upon the weather the decision will always involve risk. To reduce this risk he is likely to listen to the weather forecast before going to the market.

The second activity for which it is unusual for the responsibility to be allocated specifically is *standardisation*. At first sight this might be seen as having only a limited relevance to marketing. Yet the introduction of well-promoted standards have significantly contributed to the prosperity of many suppliers. Two very different examples would be the introduction of standardised sizes of eggs by the British Egg Marketing Board and the introduction of quality standards by the Japanese optical industry.

Marketing as a business concept

This third aspect of the term marketing relates to its use with respect to the insights that have resulted from the exchange process having been studied in detail and from many different points of view. From this study theories have been developed which are used to analyse the process of meeting customers needs and to determine how this may be improved. This has involved developing specific terminology to classify individual components of different types of need and ways that these can be met.

These concepts can be effectively used by all types of organisation. These include those which manufacture products such as were referred to by Adam Smith; those like the Disney organisation, whose main 'product' is not tangible since it is the enjoyable experience of visiting Disneyland; and organisations such as charities like Save the Children Fund. Their 'product' is the feeling you have after making a donation, so that even in this situation a real exchange is taking place between the giver and the charity.

Such examples illustrate the relevance of marketing to activities and products far-removed from breakfast cereals and the fmcg (fast moving consumer goods) sector which initially embraced the marketing concept. It is now accepted as being equally relevant to industrial and service industries of all types, the public sector and to voluntary organisations.

Marketing as a management function

The fourth aspect of marketing is its crucial role in ensuring that the activities of an organisation are clearly directed towards the principal objective of meeting the needs of customers effectively. This is the planning and co-ordinating role of marketing. This aspect of marketing was specifically identified in 1974 by the pioneering marketing author T. Levitt in *Marketing for Business Growth* in which he stated 'Marketing is not just a Business Function. It is a consolidating view of the whole business purpose.'

It is useful to separate this management aspect of marketing from the philosophy of marketing and the other functions of marketing, since it involves the allocation of resources as well as the co-ordination of effort so has to be carried out at a higher level within an organisation. It can indeed be argued, that Marketing as a Management Function, should always be the central task of the most senior management team whatever this might be called within any specific organisation.

UNDERSTANDING MARKETING AS A STUDENT

In recognising these four aspects of marketing it can be appreciated that any one of them can be the core theme of a basic text of marketing. A review of these will show that many use Marketing as a Management Function as the core theme. This approach assumes that marketing is primarily a planning activity and as a result has a number of disadvantages. This text seeks to avoid these by considering the four aspects of the subject in turn. Initially the philosophy of marketing will be explored in the terms of customers, their context and behaviour. Then the concepts of marketing will be introduced together with the related functions of marketing and finally the co-ordinating and planning aspects of marketing will be considered.

THE ORGANISATIONAL IMPLICATIONS OF MARKETING

If 'customers' are those that purchase, use, or consume a product or service, then clearly to be successful organisations need to develop and maintain relationships with a variety of different customers. Table 1.1 demonstrates that customers come in many different guises and may be described differently by organisations in different fields. The broad common factor is that they require special treatment from the provider. A customer-orientated approach can therefore apply equally to a food manufacturer or a public sector organisation.

Table 1.1 ● Who is the customer?

Buyer	Sponsor	Patient
Customer	Patron	Pupil
Consumer	Subscriber	Parent
User	Supporter	Motorist
Recipient	Member	Passenger
Adviser	Colleague	Guest
Client	Delegate	Accountant
Viewer	Tourist	Contractor
Reader	Shopper	Distributor
Listener	Householder	Agent
Lender	Taxpayer	Retailer
Banker	Resident	Stockist
Applicant	Ratepayer	Factor
Prospect	Voter	

Customer orientation has already been touched on – everyone in the organisation must aim to serve the customer, whether directly or indirectly. This is customer sovereignty: it places the customer effectively at the top of the organisation chart. The substance and credibility of this customer-centredness will daily be put to the test in all sorts of ways (e.g. how long to answer the telephone, promptness of delivery, product quality). The performance and integration of all these activities requires management and training. They cannot be left to chance.

Organisations which have adopted the marketing philosophy and are marketing orientated, will be consistently, over time, developing and improving their relationships with their customers. This requires a commitment to providing customer satisfaction, and the flexibility to respond to customer requirements and changes in the commercial, or other environment, in which the organisation operates.

THE MANAGEMENT IMPLICATIONS OF MARKETING

For managers, the application of marketing principles involves both how they operate as individuals and how they ensure the integration and co-ordination of activities within the organisation.

At the individual level, managers within organisations which are marketing-orientated regularly ask questions fundamental to the success of their organisation such as the following:

● Where are we now?
● Where do we want to get to?
● How do we get there?

Obviously the analysis of the organisation's current position is vital, but it is important to consider such issues for the future, rather than being focused on the past. This approach is shown in the following questions:

- Who are our existing/potential customers?
- What are their current and future needs?
- How can we satisfy these needs?
  - Can we offer a product/service the customer would value?
  - Can we communicate with customers?
  - Can we deliver a competitive product or service?
- Why should customers buy from us?

It is the responsibility of an organisation's management generally, and its marketing management specifically, to find answers to these questions, and thereby develop solutions to market needs, within the constraints of the organisation's resources and policies. Especially important is the final question, which recognises that customers in most markets have many products from which to choose.

To answer this question we need to first understand the environments in which all organisations operate (*see* Chapters 3 and 4). We also need to develop a basic knowledge of how people behave when making buying decisions (*see* Chapters 5 and 6).

At the organisational level, being marketing-orientated commits managers and their organisations to:

- a customer orientation;
- co-ordinated efforts by all parts of the organisation, and usually;
- return on investment, rather than sales volume.

Because of this, many writers have identified some of the key principles of successful marketing. For example, John Howard, an American marketer, proposes that a structured approach rests on six 'pillars' of good practice, which are outlined in Table 1.2. (Note: While most of Howard's 'pillars' or key principles have been mentioned already, the term 'market segmentation' may be unfamiliar. Basically this involves dividing a market into 'segments' or submarkets, for targeting and planning purposes. It will be discussed in detail in Chapter 7.)

Table 1.2 ● Howard's pillars of the marketing concept

The marketing concept

1 Generic product definition
2 Customer orientation
3 Marketing information
4 Market segmentation
5 Integrated marketing
6 Long-term viewpoint

(*Source*: Adapted from J. Howard, *Marketing Management, Analysis and Planning*, Irwin, 1963)

An alternative, though compatible, set of key principles is offered by Hugh Davidson, a British writer, who argues that successful marketing requires the application of POISE. That is, marketing should be:

P   Profitable
O   Offensive (rather than defensive)
I   Integrated
S   Strategic (= future-orientated)
E   Effective (it gets results)

The common thread in these observations, and those of other writers, is the recognition that marketing has to be consciously planned and integrated.

Co-ordination of effort will itself relate directly to management and the commitment of the organisation to marketing. Marketing management is essentially about the co-ordination of customer-directed activities. Particularly, good practice and competitive pressure should ensure that a customer focus prevails throughout the organisation. It must be present during each and every activity, rather than fall casualty to the sectional interests and biases of individuals or functional groups. For resource reasons too, marketing activities should be tightly and smoothly scheduled, without undue delays, cost-overruns or other problems that would affect profitability and competitiveness.

Organisationally, marketing involves a set of activities that has to be managed. The management process involved might be generalised as the following sequence:

1 Research and Information
2 Analysis   } Informed decisions
3 Plans and forecasts
4 Organisation and co-ordination   } Integration
5 Implementation
6 Control   } Responsiveness
7 Review   } Results – Orientation

The process might be viewed as a continuous cycle of managed activities, guided by key principles such as those presented by Howard and Davidson. The management task involves planning and co-ordinating the functions of marketing. These as already discussed from more familiar activities such as sales and advertising, to specialist fields such as merchandising, research, product development, distribution, and customer service.

In practice, these specialist activities will be planned and integrated within an organisation's marketing programme. The exact mix of activities will vary according to the demands of the target market, and will be the subject of major strategic decisions by marketing management.

There is a continuing debate about the relative merits of product management and market management. In the former, a product champion works to maximise objectives through the controllable variables available to the organisation. The latter focuses on a specific market or market segment and aims to offer the best mix of products to meet the requirement of this group. The merits of these different approaches will be discussed in more detail later, with respect to marketing organisation. There are also organisations with no formal marketing department, but to succeed in a dynamic market the key functions are performed either by specialists or by managers who intuitively understand market requirements. Also, everyone in an organisation needs to be aware of the importance of the customers of the organisation, which leads to the concept of part-time marketers, discussed in the next chapter.

CONCLUSION

From completing this chapter, you should have grasped a basic understanding of what marketing is. It should also be clear that this involves understanding a number of different aspects of the subject all of which centre upon the simple basic philosophy that customers are crucial to an organisation's success and this involves interacting with those customers and developing profitable exchanges with them over time. Tom Peters put profit into perspective:

> **Long-term profit equals revenue from continuously happy customer relationships minus cost.**

Marketing is therefore much more than selling, although some aspects of persuasion and influence are inevitably present. Satisfying customer needs over time, but not at any cost, is an ideal, but this requires that they are customers of your organisation, not your competitors. The obvious problem is that profit is required in any exchange, or at least a cost-effective use of resources. In addition there are wider ethical and moral issues which will be discussed later. Suffice it to say that business today is not sales at any cost. A prominent US businessman once suggested:

> **There is a new bottom line for business – social approval. Without it, economic victory be pyrrhic indeed.**

You might like to consider whether this is the true goal of a marketing-led organisation.

QUESTIONS

1 Describe in your own words the marketing concept.

2 How does marketing contribute to a company's prosperity?

3 What are the managerial tasks necessary in marketing?

4 From your own experience, name a company that you consider to be marketing-oriented. Justify your choice.

FURTHER READING

Davidson, J. H. (1972) *Offensive Marketing*, Cassell.
Drucker, P. (1968) *The Practice of Management*, Pan.
Howard, J. (1963) *Marketing Management, Analysis and Planning*, Irwin.
Kotler, P. (1991) *Marketing Management, Analysis, Planning Implementation and Control*, 7th Edn, Prentice-Hall.
Kotler, P. (1980) *Marketing Management*, 4th Edn, Prentice-Hall.
Levitt, T. (1974) *Marketing for Business Growth*.
Peters, T. (1988) *Thriving on Chaos*, Macmillan.
Pope, N. W. (Red) (1979) 'Mickey Mouse Marketing', *American Banker*, 25 July.
Smith, A. (1976) *The Wealth of Nations*.

CASE STUDY

The Cola wars

There is aggressive worldwide competition between the major suppliers of cola drinks. The 'weapons' used are all aspects of marketing aimed to make individual brands more desirable than competitors.

The UK market is worth £2.1 billion (1996) accounting for almost half of all carbonated soft drink sales. Although only 60 per cent of the population actually drink colas there are more men than women consumers, and the percentage of drinkers is much higher for the younger age groups when compared to the older age range. Thus the young are the main target market.

For many years Coca-Cola has been the leading brand, outselling Pepsi Cola by more than two to one in the UK and by four to one worldwide. A similar dominance was shown by Diet Coke over Diet Pepsi. However, a decade ago in the US, Pepsi gained significant market share as a result of the effective marketing campaign featuring the 'Pepsi challenge' which concentrated on the product taste. This led to the well documented launch of the ill-fated New Coke.

However Coca-Cola has now recovered and one of the secrets of its success is its widespread distribution coverage. Former Coke President Bob Woodward pledged 'to put Coke within an arm's reach of desire'. The emphasis on availability complements other aspects of the way Coke is offered.

More recently it is Pepsi that is changing the presentation of its product with Pepsi Max and project blue – the re-packaging of the product. However the re-launch is reported as not successful. Pepsi worldwide (excluding USA) made a loss of £16.8 million in the first quarter of 1997. In the UK volume was down 12.8 per cent in summer 1996. Although Max is performing well, the losses on the other two products (regular and Diet) have been a major problem.

Of course, it is not a straight fight between Coke and Pepsi. The launch of Sainsbury Cola in the UK coincided with a dramatic increase in Coke's advertising budget. This was further enhanced by the 1996 Olympic Games sponsorship in Coke's home city of Atlanta. There is also sponsorship of football in the UK prompting the slogan 'Eat football; sleep football; drink Coca-Cola'.

By contrast Virgin Cola has a very low marketing expenditure, but this brand has grabbed over 8 per cent of the static UK market in terms of volume.

Pepsi obviously has a lot to do to recover its position before challenging Coke. In France, where Coke has grown by 9 per cent, the Pepsi marketing Director, Michael Aidan, commented on a plan to test a new Pepsi taste by saying 'We are doing this because people are used to drinking Coke and we at Pepsi have not given them any real reason to switch.'

Tom Blackett of UK Interbrand says 'I don't think Pepsi will change the taste in just one of its markets, because it is a global brand and that would be a very unorthodox thing to do'.

Questions

Given the facts above, what differences do you identify in the UK market between Pepsi and its competitors?

Do you think these are the cause of the poor performance of Pepsi?

What changes do you think Pepsi could make to regain its position – the answer is not to spend more on advertising which has been tried, although you could discuss the benefits from association such as those when Pepsi sponsored international superstars Michael Jackson and the Spice Girls.

CHAPTER 2

Products, Services and Benefits

The times shown on this timetable are not the times when the trains will leave: rather they are the times before which the trains will not leave.

Indian train timetable

INTRODUCTION

In Chapter 1, marketing was described in terms of a profitable exchange between a buyer and a supplier. Both must be satisfied otherwise there will be little chance of further exchanges (repeat business) and also there is a good chance the dissatisfied buyer will tell friends, who in turn will be less willing to buy from that supplier in the future. This can be significant to the supplier since 'word of mouth' comment from someone you respect or trust has a significant influence on attitudes and hence action taken. Thus, positive comments can be far more beneficial than a series of TV commercials and negative ones can undo the effects of a brilliant promotional campaign. This will be discussed more fully in Chapter 15 'Promotional Planning'. Equally if the seller is dissatisfied it is likely that the product will be discontinued.

The opening quotation is an excellent example of not offering benefits that cannot be achieved. Train services in the UK are provided by the companies which have purchased franchises since privatisation. All of these companies have passenger's charters which are generally based on the one originally introduced by British Rail on 3 May 1992. These charters are statement of the companies' commitment to provide a high-quality service for all customers. They offer:

- a safe, punctual and reliable train service;
- clean stations and clean trains;
- friendly and efficient service;
- clear and up-to-date information;
- a fair and satisfactory response when things go wrong.

It would be interesting to compare the benefits offered by British railway franchise companies with the expectations of train passengers in India. A comparison of the resources employed might show how these franchise companies can avoid creating dissatisfied customers.

It is important that any product or service offered satisfies its customers by fulfilling the needs of those customers. However, it is equally important that there is no confusion regarding the benefits offered. The Indian train service may not fulfil all needs of train passengers in India, but, more importantly, it is very clear what is not being offered, so customers do not have hopes raised unrealistically. The best promotion in the world rarely sells a bad product twice. There is a logical progression from a person's need to travel, to a decision to travel by train. The individual product or service, such as the 9.10 from London to Birmingham, is just one individual 'product' offered to satisfy a potential demand.

PRODUCTS AND SERVICES

You will have already realised from the comments in this book that an important aspect of marketing is determining how suppliers can promote their products or services successfully to customers. In the context of marketing the word 'product' is used as a general term which covers any output from a supplier. Products and services are in this context considered interchangeable, since a service is only a product without a tangible core. We do not want to stray too far into jargon, so the difference between products and services is best illustrated by the following example:

EXAMPLE

I own a car. This obviously is a product, very tangible; I can touch it, wash and polish it and put petrol into it. I am very happy if it is reliable. I use it to get to work, and of course it is important that I get to work on time.

One day I could not start my car so I took a taxi to work. This made use of a service. I know I could also touch the taxi, but it is not the same as my own car. There is no tangible 'product' for me, and yet I derived the same benefit, Getting to work on time, albeit that in this case the service was rather more expensive.

Of course there are many reasons for owning a car, but I do not own it to leave it sitting on the drive for my neighbours to see. I own it to enable me to travel easily to work, to see friends, to do the shopping and many other things. Some people do not own cars but they have the same needs. They probably do not use taxis on a regular basis – although I know one elderly person who does. Most use other means of transport: buses, trains, bicycles, even walking. Figure 2.1 neatly summarises this.

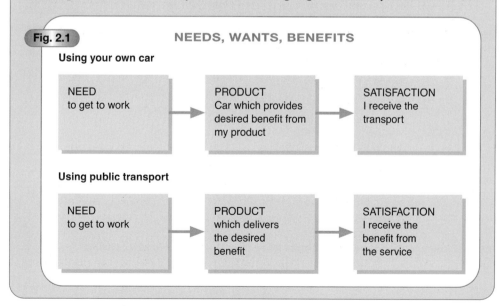

Fig. 2.1   **NEEDS, WANTS, BENEFITS**

Using your own car

| NEED to get to work | → | PRODUCT Car which provides desired benefit from my product | → | SATISFACTION I receive the transport |

Using public transport

| NEED to get to work | → | PRODUCT which delivers the desired benefit | → | SATISFACTION I receive the benefit from the service |

This example shows that the essential difference between a product and a service is ownership. This is not involved with respect to benefits received from services. One of the key roles of marketing is to identify customer needs and express these in terms of benefits required by customers and the product/service which can be provided by a supplier.

While occasionally marketing involves a new product which must be developed and launched successfully, most products already exist and are on sale. For these, the requirement is to develop sales and keep the product up-to-date.

For both new and existing products there are three stages of marketing:

1 Pre-consumption, when the goal is to create or manage expectations.
2 During consumption, with an aim of producing customer satisfaction.
3 After consumption, where the aim is to maintain or develop the relationship with customers, to ensure good reports and future repeat sales.

MARKETING MYOPIA

In a famous article published in 1960, Theodore Levitt, then a lecturer at the Harvard Business School, asked the key question that all organisations must answer, 'What business are we really in?'

Levitt gave examples of organisations that had failed to understand the benefits their customers derived from the product offered. In the case of the American railroads, for example, he argued:

> The railroads did not stop growing because the needs for passengers and freight transportation declined. That grew. The railroads are in trouble today, not because the need was filled by others (cars, trucks, airplanes, even telephones), but because it was not filled by the railroads themselves. They let others take customers away from them because they assumed themselves to be in the railroad business rather than in the transportation business. The reason they defined their industry incorrectly was because they were railroad-orientated; they were product-orientated not customer-orientated.

Later we will take this orientation further, from customer to total market orientation. Levitt's achievement was to get individual businesses to look at themselves from the

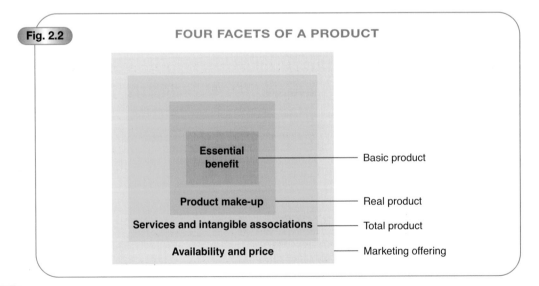

Fig. 2.2 FOUR FACETS OF A PRODUCT

Essential benefit ——— Basic product

Product make-up ——— Real product

Services and intangible associations ——— Total product

Availability and price ——— Marketing offering

Fig. 2.3 **THE CONTRAST BETWEEN EFFICIENCY AND EFFECTIVENESS**

	Inefficient	Efficient
Inefficient	Die quickly	Survive
Efficient	Die slowly	Thrive

(Adapted from R. Brown, 'Marketing – a function and philosophy', *Quarterly Review of Marketing*, Spring 1987)

customer's viewpoint and assess their offerings in terms of customer benefits. This includes not only the basic product but the added features and service which make up the total product that is effective in satisfying customers (*see* Fig. 2.2).

Effectiveness comes from meeting customer needs with the total product offered. Even a relatively inefficient company which is effective at creating and keeping customers will survive. Companies who fail to satisfy customers are basically ineffective, and they will not survive (Fig. 2.3).

TOTAL PRODUCTS AND MARKETING OFFERINGS

Even if we are able to answer Levitt's question, and we understand that airlines are substitutes for trains, and trains or taxis for private cars, we still only understand one facet of the total product concept. Again it may be best to start with an example:

EXAMPLE

A Mars Bar is a good example of a product widely accepted and as popular now as it ever was. The 1997 ingredients panel states that it contains:

> MILK CHOCOLATE, GLUCOSE SYRUP, SUGAR, SKIMMED MILK POWDER, HYDROGENATED VEGETABLE FAT, FAT-REDUCED COCOA POWDER, MILK FAT, MALT EXTRACT, LACTOSE, WHEY POWDER, SALT, FULL CREAM MILK POWDER, EGG WHITE, HYDROLYSED MILK PROTEIN, FLAVOURING. ON RARE OCCASIONS THIS PRODUCT MAY CONTAIN TRACES OF NUTS, MILK CHOCOLATE CONTAINS MILK SOLIDS 14% MINIMUM, VEGETABLE FAT, EMULSIFIER LECITHIN AND FLAVOURING

These are the ingredients we consume when we eat a Mars Bar. We are not told the actual proportion of chocolate to milk fat, but a clever food scientist could make an acceptable analysis, and, further, could probably make a good copy of a Mars Bar. The copy would offer a similar degree of enjoyment to anyone eating it.

▶

Some 20 years ago a rival confectionery firm (Cadbury's) did in fact develop a product called 'Aztec', which marketing research showed to be comparable to Mars in many ways. The product was launched, and as Cadbury's is a large company with a good reputation it was easily able to persuade retail shops to buy the product. The trouble was, that not enough consumers (members of the public) bought it from the retailers to make it a success. You have probably never heard of Aztec because Cadbury's stopped making it after only a short time. So why did Aztec fail against Mars in what is after all a very large market?

It was not the basic product – they were very similar. Nor was it the price or availability. It was the other features: brand name, packaging styling, quality, and most importantly image. We don't know if Mars is the 'taste of adventure', but there are certainly some psychological features which are part of a Mars Bar.

A total product will only be successful if customers are willing to buy it in preference to other products. For this to happen the product must be available when required and at a price considered acceptable. The term *Marketing Offering* is used to describe this combination of total product, availability and price. This is a useful concept since it allows all aspects of different marketing offerings to be compared from the viewpoint of the customer. Using this approach it is possible to explain why so many products succeed in spite of having prices which are higher than their main rivals. This is illustrated by the following examples:

1 Fruit and vegetables in the supermarket are more expensive than my local market. Is it convenience of location that people pay extra for?
2 People hire televisions when it is 'cheaper' to buy. Is it the convenient way of spreading expenditure or the after-sales service they value?
3 Company car purchasers buy from the Ford Motor Company and pay extra for 'Fordsure Cover'. Why do they pay the extra? Is it peace of mind they purchase with the extra warranty, or is perhaps the warranty an additional product which adds value to the basic product?
4 A local carpet supplier is not the cheapest, but they offer free fitting. Is this the reason they attract customers?

Perhaps you can think of other examples.

What is happening here is that products are being 'augmented' by additional features which are of value to customers. In this book we call the different levels of additions the 'basic product', the 'total product' and the 'marketing offering' to emphasise that it is the supplier who through investment and by using marketing skills can add value to the 'basic product'. It is this investment which makes a specific market offering different and attractive. Because of this a purchaser's decision to buy can depend more on the marketing offering than on the basic product, the total product or the price.

Visit your local supermarket and find a product that is offered both as a manufacturer's brand (e.g. Kelloggs, Maxwell House, Radox) and as a store's 'own label' product. Compare the product in every detail, design, pack size, price, value for money.

It is possible the 'own label' product offers a more cost-efficient option. But the other products must sell regularly or they would not be given shelf space. Why do you think there are still so many customers who buy these 'branded' products?

What characteristics do you think describes:

1 Purchasers of 'own label' products?
2 Purchasers of 'branded' products?

THINK BENEFITS

Marketing provides the interface between organisations and their customers. To do this it is essential that marketers think like customers so they can promote the customer needs to others within their organisation, as well as promoting the company and its products to potential customers.

You could say this is the task of a salesperson, and you would be right. Marketing, however, as has already been explained, encompasses in addition to direct selling, advertising, PR, packaging, and many other related areas. All of these factors contribute to developing the right product at the right price, available in the right place at the right time.

Without the customer focus resulting from being marketing-orientated, organisations inevitably tend to concentrate on developing the product with the objective of achieving customer acceptance. This is usually done by maximising its features and quality while minimising the price.

While there are few examples of this approach having led to long-term success, there are numerous examples of either short-term success or abject failure. One of the classic examples of the latter was the development of the Sinclair C5 electric vehicle as detailed in the example below:

EXAMPLE

The Sinclair C5 development

Sir Clive Sinclair is an entrepreneur and inventer who achieved a number of 'world firsts', including the executive pocket calculator (1972) and the microvision pocket TV (1977). He then went on to design and develop a range of low cost personal computers (including the very successful ZX Spectrum). Sir Clive is acknowledged as world-class inventor but has often demonstrated little understanding of marketing.

▶

He has openly admitted he does not value market research, believing that products should be developed and then a market created for them. His success with the ZX80 and ZX81 computers would at first sight seem to support this view. It is, however, contrary to the marketing approach, which recommends that consumers' needs and wants are first determined, and then a product developed which consumers believe fulfils their needs effectively. Products which customers do not see as meeting their needs fail as did the Sinclair C5.

The development of the C5 electric car can be traced back to 1973 when various ideas for electric vehicles were considered. The continuing energy crises of that period made the world more energy-conscious and in 1979 preliminary investigations were started into the possibility of a personal electric vehicle. This led to the development of the C5. This involved developing technology for manufacturing and joining very large plastic mouldings, a new type of electric motor and a new production facility. It was intended that it would provide low-cost personal transportation for journeys up to three miles. This was believed to be the average distance for which bicycles were used for journeys to work or to the shops. There is no reason to believe that the product was not suitable for this purpose. The difficulty arose when the potential customer faced the problem as to where a C5 could be stored both in the home and at the destination. Since it obviously took up much more space than a bicycle and needed an electrical supply from which the batteries could be charged. In addition, potential customers saw obvious problems when it rained and when faced with normal road hazards such as pot holes and drain covers. It may have had a potential market in areas with comprehensive provision for bicycles, as in Holland, Denmark and some parts of France, but this was not the case in the UK where the product was initially launched.

In failing to determine who could use the product and how could it be used, Sinclair failed to adequately define the potential customers for the product and thus it was deemed a failure.

ORIENTATION OF A BUSINESS

In view of the problems encountered when an organisation is product-orientated, it is important to understand the difference between this type of organisation and those which are sales-orientated or marketing-orientated.

These different approaches can be considered as stages along a progression from production through sales to marketing (*see* Fig. 2.4). At one end of the market we have companies that concentrate on producing what they think customers want. It is happening in many parts of the former USSR (now the CIS) today with companies that still have little competition. If there is little choice for customers then those customers might purchase a product that is not quite what they require, but is better than nothing at all. Certainly this attitude was prevalent in the UK nationalised industries, and even now the newly privatised local power and water companies leave consumers little choice for domestic supplies.

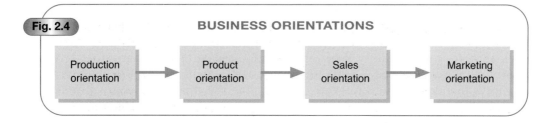

Fig. 2.4 — BUSINESS ORIENTATIONS

Production orientation → Product orientation → Sales orientation → Marketing orientation

You might consider that such organisations provide acceptable products, but it is interesting to see the changes in the services offered as a result of competition. As an example, consider how the service provided by British Telecom has changed since they have had to compete with Mercury and more recently with the telephone services offered by the cable television and mobile telephone service providers. As a result of this competition, customers are now offered itemised bills, credit card services with no surcharge, many additional free or low-cost services and cheaper international calls. Competition has also resulted in charges being imposed for directory enquiries, a service which previously had been free. However, this can also be considered evidence that British Telecom has become more aware of their customers' needs. They recognised that a free directory enquiries service meant its cost was shared among both those who used the service and those who did not. They also realised that with the introduction of competition their customers would be paying for providing numbers for users who would then place the call through one of their rivals.

Furthermore, research had shown that as the service was free, many directory enquiries were for local calls for which they provided a telephone directory. In charging for directory enquiries they were encouraging customers to use the directories provided and were shifting the cost from all customers to those who used the service. To reduce the need for the service further they publicised their policy of providing adjacent telephone directories at no charge for those customers who live at the border of a telephone directory area. Free directory enquiries were retained for blind customers who cannot use a telephone directory and in public telephones where the previous policy of providing telephone directories at considerable expense was discontinued. As a package, the decision to charge for directory enquiries should have been seen as being to the benefit of most domestic customers. The fact that many customers did not appreciate this, probably shows that when the charge was introduced British Telecom did not have the marketing skills or experience needed to ensure that most of their customers understood that they would benefit from the change.

PRODUCT ORIENTATION

Product orientation is often a characteristic of organisations which have developed specific skills or technologies. It often involves manufacturing products in large quantities in order to minimise the costs of production. For this reason product orientation often involves production orientation. Providing acceptable quality at the lowest price is seen by many organisations as the main objective. Very often the problems, such as dissatisfied customers, are easy to recognise but difficult to correct, particularly with service organisations involving dedicated staff. An example of this type could be a

National Health Service hospital where most of the customer (patient) complaints are about essentially peripheral aspects of the care, such as the food or the decor of the wards. In this example, the product is health care. As a result of having a product orientation resources are likely to be very much focused on the clinical treatment. As a result the budget allocated, e.g. for pharmaceuticals, might be adequate enough for expensive branded products to be used rather than the equivalent, cheaper, generic product. A more patient-centred approach might well have allocated some of the money to improve the food or the decor of the wards, both aspects of patient comfort which are likely to be more valued by patients and thereby aid recovery.

Generally where a product has mass appeal, product or production orientation within manufacturing organisations has the effect of providing initial success followed by a significant decline. There have been some classic examples of this, e.g. the Ford Motor Company of Detroit became the largest manufacturer of automobiles by developing the mass production process. This minimised the cost of production to the extent that no other manufacturer could offer a cheaper or better value car. In 1927 the company was producing 1.5 million cars per year, twice as many as its nearest rival General Motors. Yet during that year Ford were unable to sell the cars which were being made. Former loyal customers in the USA in ever-increasing numbers were choosing one of the more modern vehicles being offered by Ford's competitors. The situation became so serious that Ford were forced to close their production for 18 months until they could launch a new product. By this time, General Motors had successfully replaced Ford as market leader and Ford were never able to seriously challenge them again in the USA.

Forty-five years later this story repeated itself in Europe. By 1972 Volkswagen of West Germany had become the largest manufacturer of cars in Europe. Unlike Ford who had achieved this by offering lower prices, Volkswagen had achieved this by gaining a reputation for the superior quality and reliability of the single model they produced – the Beetle. But just like Ford had done in 1927, Volkswagen saw their most loyal customers choose competitors products rather than their own. The reason for this, was the rapid price increase in crude oil. This made petrol consumption of critical importance to potential customers and was the one feature for which the Volkswagen Beetle was considered inferior to its rivals. Volkswagen introduced a replacement, the Golf, more quickly than Ford had done in 1928, but at such considerable cost the survival of the company was put at risk.

There will always be examples of successful product-orientated companies. One regularly cited is Sony of Japan. The founder, Masaru Ibuka is, like Sir Clive Sinclair, a brilliant inventor and he has said that, 'Merchandising and marketing people cannot envisage a market that does not exist'. Both he and his commercially aware partner, Akio Morita, purposely go out to meet potential consumers. They both deliberately visit places where people gather. They talk about benefits. It might be unusual for a chairperson of a major international company to do market research, but it is claimed that is exactly how Morita found there was a need for a personal and portable tape player. He recognised a need, and in spite of scepticism from his marketing people proceeded to design the 'Walkman'. This success is well known, and has been paralleled in the now common personal CD-players and miniature televisions. Further research will, however, show that this approach has resulted in market failure of a number of Sony developments, in spite of the fact that they are technically superior to those offered by their competitors. One such product was the Betamax video recorder. This product tailed in the competition against the VHS system invented by JVC, mainly because it seems that JVC had a better understanding of the importance of the standardisation aspect of marketing. Unlike Sony, JVC actively encouraged other companies to adopt their system. Their agreement with companies in Taiwan and Korea prevented these companies from exporting their products for a number of years, while allowing them to manufacture and sell products in their domestic markets. Immediately the export ban expired these companies began exporting their products, and thus, the price of domestic video recorders dropped. Sony was unable to respond with their existing product and within months they were offering VHS recorders as these had become the accepted market standard.

This could suggest that like Ford, Volkswagen, Polaroid, ICI, Kodak, IBM and countless similar companies, it will not be long before Sony will no longer be cited as a successful product-orientated company.

PRODUCTION ORIENTATION

We produce excellent, well-designed, quality products which are great value for money. Customers are sure to want our products.

Product-orientated companies with potential mass markets very often become production-orientated. This makes them increasingly less able to respond when customers stop buying their products. Most respond to this situation by implementing vigorous sales and advertising campaigns. By doing this the company adopts a sales orientation.

SALES ORIENTATION

Sales orientation dictates that a business must aggressively promote its products. As the product already exists, sales staff are made responsible for identifying every potential customer. This does not mean that sales representatives are customer-orientated, as that would involve starting with customer needs and not the product.

The approach becomes 'We have a good product and in this competitive market we must push it hard to achieve our sales goals.'

The authors of this book have extensive experience of selling and do not want to be unfair to the thousands of good salespeople throughout industry. Good sales staff understand the benefits their products offer and use these 'selling points' to convince customers. They also understand competition, as they are at the 'sharp end' of business and often their pay includes an element of commission on actual sales.

The job case study below is reprinted from the *Association of Graduates Career Advisory Service Booklet* on selling as a career. Selling is described well in this case study, emphasising the various tasks involved. It is a logical development of and production orientation.

CASE STUDY
Job case study

Gary, a Plant Science graduate working for a major pharmaceutical company as a medical representative, got his job through a specialist agency. He describes his work thus:

'Within my own territory I have sole responsibility. I get a quarterly allowance for entertainment/meetings – how I spend this is up to me, but I am expected to get value for money.

'I have large quantities of prescription-only samples and free promotional material, which are also my responsibility. I also have a company car, film equipment, company stationery, etc. I work alone for most of the time. At the other times I am being field trained, attending sales meetings or being assisted by a colleague at a large promotional meeting.

'My working hours are not defined, but on average I leave the house at 7.30–8.00 am (later if working near home) and get back about 5.00–6.00 pm. I have an hour for lunch, flexible, but usually 1.00 till 2.00 pm. I work a five-day week, but may do meetings or attend exhibitions in the evenings or Saturdays, for which I get extra pay.

'I do not have to keep records of hours worked, it doesn't affect salary anyway. I spend Thursday evenings doing administration to be posted on Friday to my manager.

'The job is not a calling – we do it for the money. It is not a doddle, so there is a high drop-out rate. We are expected to be very smart at all times. Promotion is limitless – our managing director started as a rep – but it must be earned by success, and not time served.

'You need to get on with people, especially self-important ones, and to work on your own initiative. The ability to read minds is the most important asset possible. Being able to speak in public is essential, but it comes with practice anyway. You must be able to drive, and must have a clean licence when you start.

'Major satisfaction is rare, and only occurred once for me so far, when a doctor came up and thanked me for telling him about a drug because he saved someone's life with it. Most satisfaction comes from nice sales graphs with steep climbing lines on them, and therefore a healthier bank balance.'

Sales orientation can emphasise one of two approaches – a competitor focus or a customer focus. It may be enough to beat the competition. There are no prizes for being second in a sales negotiation. But if you win the contract, make the sale and see the sales graph rise, there is satisfaction as described in the case study.

Kenichi Ohmae introduced the concept of a competitive triangle. This considers that a customer can choose between a number of different, maybe even dissimilar, products or services. Each customer will choose the one that best meets his/her needs and reject the others. If this is accepted, it is enough that we offer a better match than our competitors (see Chapter 4 for more on the competitive triangle).

Unfortunately, companies which adopt a sales orientation inevitably find that this is only effective for a short time but involves significantly increased costs and so is successful only at the expense of the profitability of the organisation.

Customers' needs change over time, whether for industrial or consumer products. Maybe we have persuaded a customer to buy our product because it offered the best price or because of some high-pressure selling. Then, as soon as a product that is a better match for the customer's requirements comes on the market, they might drop us in favour of the new product. We have not earned much customer loyalty. If we have worked hard to develop our product to reflect customers' needs then they may not switch so readily. It is up to our company to be both competitor- and customer-orientated. This is called a *marketing orientation* (see Fig. 2.5).

To return to the words of Kenichi Ohmae:

Competitive realities are only what you test possible strategies against. You define what you want to do in terms of customers.

QUESTION

Which of these statements best describes a marketing orientation?

- I make what I can sell.
- I sell what I can make.

MARKETING ORIENTATION

We now should begin to understand the importance of marketing orientation and the crucial need to start with the customer in defining the business we are in. However, it is much more difficult to implant a marketing orientation in a company than it might seem. Marketing orientation does not occur because a company has a marketing department, or because the managing director says so. It occurs when the customer notices the difference. It only happens when all people in an organisation measure themselves in terms of the benefits offered to customers. It does not matter whether, in Disney language, you are 'on-stage' or 'back-stage' or, in marketing jargon, whether you are directly interfacing with a customer or not. In most organisations a whole range of people have contact with customers. This would include the telephone operator, delivery driver, repair mechanic, or invoice clerk, as well as the usual sales and marketing contacts.

There is a humorous training film entitled 'Who lost the sale?' which shows, among other events, a delivery truck with a company logo being driven badly and affecting a buyer who deals with that company.

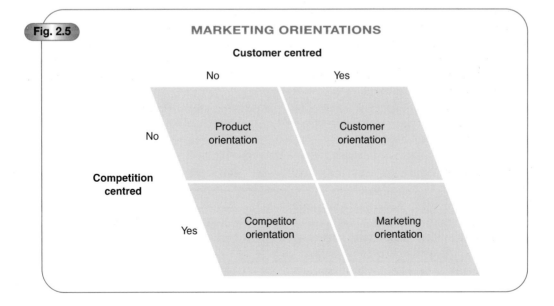

Fig. 2.5 MARKETING ORIENTATIONS

Many organisations are now running customer care programmes which include all members of staff. Those who are not directly involved in the marketing function can be called *part-time marketers* because they also have a key customer support role. Some organisations such as the Body Shop do not have any specific marketing staff, yet the company has been incredibly successful. Everyone is involved with customers and Anita Roddick, the founder, spends much of her time ensuring her products are right for her customers.

Customer relationships are particularly important if you are in a service organisation. We have already seen that one of the differences between a service and a product is the ownership of the core product. Another is that the production of the services takes place at the time of delivery. This was true with the taxi example. The taxi driver is not a marketer, but a taxi driver. In Coventry there are three or four major taxi firms, but because in the earlier example one particular firm gave prompt, efficient and cheerful service, when a taxi is next needed this will be remembered and that firm will get repeat business. This is a good example of a part-time marketer at work. A marketing-orientated organisation will be full of part-time marketers.

MARKETING IS NOT OPTIONAL

Many great business organisations have been built by entrepreneurs who have demonstrated or claimed that marketing has not made a significant contribution to their success. For some like Anita Roddick, it seems that their whole approach to business has so embraced the marketing concept, that it has been integral to their business. For others such as Henry Ford, Sir Clive Sinclair and Mr Masaru Ibuka, their businesses have grown within a market which has expanded fast enough to allow an increasing number of competitors to succeed.

Unfortunately, as has already been mentioned, history is not on the side of those who do not embrace the importance of marketing. Indeed it is one of the basic precepts of marketing that all products, at least in the form of marketing offerings, follow a predefined pattern of growth, maturity and decline. This is known as the Product Life Cycle.

It is illustrated by the diagram Fig. 2.6

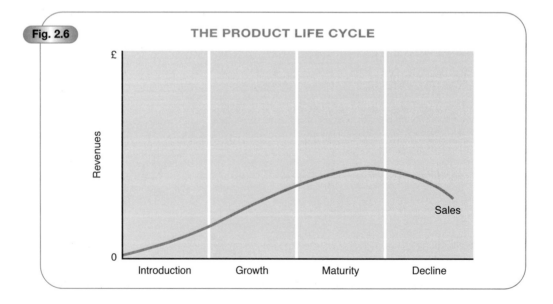

Fig. 2.6   THE PRODUCT LIFE CYCLE

This will be discussed in depth in Chapter 10 'Product – The Fundamental Marketing Concept'. Its relevance here, is that for most organisations, it is not until a product has reached the start of the decline stage that those aspects of business embraced by marketing become essential. At this point organisations which recognise this will usually adapt to address the problem and many will return to prosperity.

There are a number of products, such as the Mars Bar, which seem to contradict the concept of growth, maturity, and decline as defined by the Product Life Cycle. Again this will be discussed more fully in Chapter 10. At this stage it is sufficient to point out, that what is recognised as a Mars Bar is constantly changing. So while each of its different manifestations as a separate marketing offering has followed the pattern known as the Product Life Cycle, what is recognised as the Mars Bar at any stage seems to have contradicted it.

QUESTIONS

1 List some of the different manifestations of the Mars Bar.

2 List three other products which seem to contradict the concept of the Product Life Cycle and identify at least three manifestations of each.

CONCLUSION

In this chapter we have studied the differences between products and services. There are four levels of products. First, the basic core, which is not present in a service. Then the features which make up the Real and Total product of package and brand name. It is the role of marketing to make the basic core into a desirable product. This can be augmented by other features which add value to the product and differentiate it from competitors has a marketing offering.

In defining customer needs we have become aware of the benefits the customer receives from our product and our competitors' products. One famous quote by Theodore Levitt emphasised that:

Purchasing agents don't buy $\frac{1}{4}$-inch drills; they buy $\frac{1}{4}$-inch holes.

We don't know how many ways there are of making $\frac{1}{4}$-inch holes, but it is reasonable to suppose drills are not the only way. So we should define our market in terms of customer benefits. We can further expand this into the way we think about our products, as illustrated by Charles Revson of Revlon Cosmetics:

In the factory we make cosmetics; in the drug store we sell hope.

Marketing is about finding out what customers want, then producing, packaging and promoting it. If we do this successfully it will be easier (although never easy) to sell the product.

QUESTIONS

1 Revson asserted that cosmetic buyers were looking for 'hope'. Compile a list of the factors that might be important to a customer for cosmetics.

2 Select an advertisement which describes benefits rather than product features and comment on its effectiveness.

3 Brand names are shorthand for products and their benefits. What might the following brand names convey to their customers?
- Mars;
- Marlboro;
- Rolls-Royce;
- St Michael.

4 In what ways is it difficult to convey the benefits of a service compared to those from a product?

FURTHER READING

British Rail Passengers' Charter, May 1992.
Brown, R., 'Marketing – a function and a philosophy', *Quarterly Review of Marketing*, Spring 1987.
Kotler, P. and Armstrong, G. (1989) *Principles of Marketing*, 4th Edn, Prentice-Hall.
Levitt, T. (1960) 'Marketing myopia', *Harvard Business Review*.
Marks, A., 'Sinclair', *European Journal of Marketing*, January 1989.
Martin, P., 'How to succeed in business by really trying', *Sunday Times Magazine*, 5 November 1989.
Morita, A. (1986) *Made in Japan*, Dutton.
Ohmae Kenichi (1983) *The Mind of the Strategist*, Pan.
Slater, A. and Kolizeras, K., 'Graduate Careers Information Book' – Sales Careers Services Trust, 1988.

CASE STUDY
What went wrong?

Chamberlain Drop Forgings Plc

Chamberlains was founded one hundred years ago and in that time it established an international reputation for high-quality drop forgings. They proudly claim to have the ability to supply any type of forging in any quality and any quantity, although much of their output is high-volume runs for Midland automotive and engineering companies.

Business has been becoming more difficult for several years, and the increasing availability of Far East forgings at prices up to 50 per cent below Chamberlains has reduced both margins and volume. However, the company has responded by installing the latest technology and by using computer techniques to speed up diemaking, which is done in-house.

Nevertheless, Chamberlains are keen to respond to every new enquiry from any source. Early last year they were approached by Barry Barnes Engineering, a small recently established company based in Yorkshire.

A Chamberlain sales representative called on Mr Barnes the following week to discuss requirements, specifications and, most important, price. In spite of

the newness of the customer, Mr Barnes suggested he would require up to 10 000 forgings in a full year. He also asked for normal credit terms, which were granted after the usual bank references proved acceptable. An immediate trial order of 500 was telephoned through and Chamberlains were pleased to offer this new customer expedited delivery within 14 days.

The problems started when it came to delivering the order. Chamberlains driver arrived at 12.30 on Friday to find Barnes's warehouse closed, for lunch according to the notice. In fact the staff returned around 3.00 pm, having been celebrating the birthday of one of the employees. They were not very helpful and after a lot of argument the delivery driver unloaded the order, discovering the signature on the delivery notes was signed 'Mick the Mouse'.

No further orders were received for three months and to make things worse nor was any payment. When the sales representative contacted him, Mr Barnes apologised for the accounting problems of his company and immediately sent a cheque for the drop forgings, although he did not add on the delivery charge which is made on all orders under 1000. He wrote on the invoice that his total orders would exceed that, so he was not paying it. He also sent in another order for 500 forgings.

This order came at a time when Chamberlains were very busy with a major order for a European auto-assembler. The sales representative telephoned Mr Barnes, who was away, but his secretary said she was sure it would be fine to deliver the order in four weeks' time. It was only a fortnight later that Mr Barnes was on the telephone wanting to know where his order was. He also complained that the price quoted on the confirmation of the order was higher than last time, and had the cheek to ask if distribution costs had been added on to the unit prices.

The sales representative explained the telephone call to Mr Barnes's secretary, agreeing four weeks for the order, and pointed out that the rate quoted on the earlier order was on the basis of 10 000 units per year. He said current orders were nowhere near that level but offered a retrospective discount if they did indeed reach the figures discussed in the first meeting. He also told Mr Barnes that, as a gesture of goodwill, Chamberlains would write off the delivery charge for the first order, but in future orders less than 1000 would be subject to a charge. He reiterated that delivery would be possible in another two weeks' time.

Production of the Barnes order went to schedule, but when the distribution manager rang to arrange delivery a Barnes employee said they did not need them yet as there had been a hold-up from one of their customers, so could they be stored for a couple of months until Mr Barnes got in touch. Things got a little heated in this call, with a deal of bad language before the customer's employee put the phone down. When the sales representative called to speak to Mr Barnes it was discovered he was abroad for three weeks. However, promptly at 8.00 am on the day Mr Barnes returned to his office, the sales rep called and spoke about the order. He explained the deal he thought was agreed in the telephone call some five weeks earlier, agreeing delivery and other details. Obviously very upset, he was flabbergasted when Mr Barnes said if that was his attitude then Barnes did not want the order, and that anyway they had found a cheaper and more reliable source.

In spite of many subsequent attempts no further progress has been made and Mr Barnes refuses to answer any call from Chamberlains.

Questions

1 Mr Barnes' needs were clearly not fully met by the forgings supplied. What else did he need to be a satisfied customer?

2 How could Chamberlains have met these needs without incurring significant costs?

CHAPTER 3

The Marketing Environment

It is the everlasting and unchanging rule of this world that everything is created by a series of causes and conditions and everything disappears by the same rule; everything changes, nothing remains constant.

The teaching of Buddha

INTRODUCTION

Whenever an exchange takes place it does so within the context of the situation which prevails at that time. The parties making the exchange do so on the basis of their individual understanding of the prevailing situation. The traders selling ice cream at a large outdoor event such as the Notting Hill Carnival may decide to sell their ice cream at half the normal price if the afternoon becomes cold and wet. By doing this they are able to sell their products before they melt and those who like to eat ice cream regardless of the weather are encouraged to do so. The situation is likely to be very different for the traders selling hot drinks. They would see their business increase and to meet demand they may have to buy additional coffee and milk from the local shops regardless of price instead of from their normal cash and carry supplier.

In addition to the situation prevailing when the exchange takes place, there are many other factors which are likely to affect the exchange. For instance, if the individuals involved know one another as a result of having made exchanges on past occasions, they are likely to be more willing to give and accept information about the products they are offering for exchange. The man with a pig may be willing to agree to exchange it for fewer bags of grain to allow for it being a smaller pig than the one he last exchanged. On the other hand the person with the grain may be willing to increase the number of bags offered if he knows the quality of his grain is not as good as last time. Both still want a good deal, but because they know one another they are likely to see the benefit of being fair since dealing with someone who is known involves less risk than dealing with a stranger.

The need to deal with strangers increased with the growth and development of markets, so those involved in markets needed to introduce regulations to ensure that those coming to purchase at the market can trust in the market as a whole rather than individual traders. Markets as a result introduced customs and regulations which governed how trade should be conducted. With the introduction of money and universally accepted measures of length, weight and volume, these regulations involved such issues as the accuracy of the measures used by traders. The penalties for giving short measure became extremely harsh since to do so could significantly undermine the integrity of an established market. To further encourage good practice many of these regulations became nationally administrated laws.

THE OPEN MARKET

Both of the parties making an exchange are more likely to consider that the exchange has been beneficial when the exchange has been made within the context of what is known as an *Open Market*. This is a market which has all of the following characteristics:

1 Single homogeneous product.
2 Many buyers.
3 Many sellers.
4 Buyers and sellers have equal access to all available information relevant to the market.

An open market can only be established and continue when buyers and sellers agree to establish the rules necessary to maintain the four conditions set out above. This means that the product has to be clearly defined, that membership of the market as a buyer or seller has to be regulated and that rules relating to the availability of information are clearly established and regulated. Those markets which set the world price for commodities such as gold, oil, orange juice, wheat, or soya beans, as well as the major stock markets, all have rules which are intended to maintain the 'openness' of these markets. The penalties for infringing these rules are inevitably severe, since by their nature, these markets provide opportunities for speculation and indeed need to do so in order to continue as effective markets during times of difficulty.

For instance the demand for beer in the UK increases during a hot summer and is significantly depressed if the summer is cold and wet. This would reduce the demand for barley since this is an important ingredient of beer. Furthermore, after a cold wet summer brewers are likely to have unused stocks of the barley purchased in expectation of higher demand. As a result they are likely to postpone purchasing new supplies of barley. The farmer having taken in his crop is likely to need to sell some of it to at least to pay for the harvest. If his normal brewer customers are unwilling to buy barley he becomes dependent upon the speculators within the market who will purchase barley believing that because of the poor summer there will be a poor harvest and as a result the price will rise as time passes. Thus, the market is able to function in spite of there being low demand by the actual users of the product.

While there are many examples of open markets, these must be considered exceptions in the context of exchanges normally made by individuals. There are a number of reasons for this. First, products purchased are rarely homogeneous. Even potatoes vary by variety and packaging making comparison by the purchaser difficult. This frustrates the first condition of an open market. Generally the individual purchaser has a limited choice of supplier which frustrates the third condition of the open market. Third, purchasers rarely have as much information about the market as does the supplier which contravenes the fourth condition of an open market.

THE REGULATED MARKET

The regulations governing an Open Market are designed to ensure that it is able to operate as an open market with none of the participants having an advantage over the others. Regulated markets recognise that there is a lack of balance between the parties and therefore this type of market has rules which are intended to remedy this imbalance. Such regulations are laid out in the Sale of Goods Act which requires products offered to the general public to be fit for the purpose for which they were intended. Thus, the purchaser of a pair of gloves intended for washing up can expect them to be waterproof and have them replaced should those purchased leak.

All developed societies have similar regulations to regulate legal trade. It is therefore usual for manufacturing and trading organisations to have to comply with such regulations which effectively constitute one aspect of the environment in which an exchange, or trade in general, takes place. These factors are for this reason referred to as the environmental variables of marketing. The one already discussed is defined as the political or legal variable and there are three others. These are usually labled the Economic, Social and Technological variables (STEP). Since organisations have little influence over these environmental variables these four variables are generally referred to as uncontrollable variables. They contrast the variables such as product quality and price which can be determined by the organisation supplying a given product and because of this, these marketing activities or variables are known as the controllable variables. Figure 3.1 shows the relationship between these two types of variable.

THE MARKETING FUNCTION AND THE ENVIRONMENT

Marketing as a function is basically all about matching the offerings of the organisation to the outside world, in particular, the marketplace. Not surprisingly, many functions within marketing, such as selling, product development and market research,

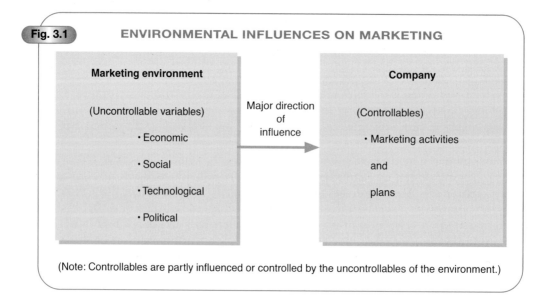

Fig. 3.1 ENVIRONMENTAL INFLUENCES ON MARKETING

Marketing environment		Company
(Uncontrollable variables)	Major direction of influence	(Controllables)
• Economic		• Marketing activities
• Social		and
• Technological		plans
• Political		

(Note: Controllables are partly influenced or controlled by the uncontrollables of the environment.)

concern themselves with issues, problems and opportunities outside the organisation, and focus on responding to outside events and circumstances. Indeed, Kotler identifies in this external role the need for marketers to develop an 'outside-in' perspective, an ability to work on external cues and stimuli to the profit of the whole organisation. Another marketing writer of note, John Howard, emphasises the strategic role of marketing as 'the function by which the firm responds to changes in its environment'.

Response and sensitivity to the environment remains one of the acid-test indicators of success or failure in business in general, and in marketing in particular. The annals of business history and new product development are littered with instances of companies that have lost touch with their markets, misinterpreted or ignored tell-tale signs of change, or become blinded by previous successes and driven by some corporate inertia. Theodore Levitt's example of the US railroads, and the case of the ill-fated C5 electric car, have already been discussed in Chapter 2. While other examples will be developed later in the text, readers might find it instructive to examine a company report, or columnist commentaries on company results, and consider the significant influence on company performance that environmental issues may wield.

At first sight it may seem difficult to see how companies cannot spot the environmental issues that affect their performance. After all, the environment is all about us, literally staring us in the face! Unfortunately, companies all too often become preoccupied with their day-to-day problems, and hard-pressed managers become engrossed in priorities and deadlines more squarely within their responsibility, than perhaps marginal changes outside. This is possibly one of the key difficulties with the external environment: it is outside the hubbub of today's business problems, and, excepting the rare instances of sudden change, it tends to present an all too comforting picture of at best gradual change; sudden changes are exceptional and, in any case, cannot be missed! The norm is generally a picture of incremental change over an extended period of time. It is this 'norm' that can prove deceptively dangerous, as the following commentary by Charlotte Villiers demonstrates:

> To look at British industry today is to be reminded of one simple, if rather brutal, analogy that top managers should take to heart: if you put a frog into a pan of cold water and turn on the heat, the frog will happily sit there without noticing the water is getting hot. The result, inevitably, is one boiled, dead frog. But if you drop a frog into some warm water, the frog realises immediately that it is too hot and jumps straight back out again.

The moral of this tale is simply that people do not notice incremental change going on around them until it is too late. Like the doomed frog, many businesses fail to notice what is happening in their environment until their fate is sealed.

THE DIMENSIONS OF THE ENVIRONMENT

In examining the environment in more detail, a basic model will be presented of different dimensions or levels of the environment, each more complex, distant and all-embracing than the previous one. A useful analogy would be to view the marketing environment as a series of subsets within sets, within an ultimate or universal set – the inner subsets are more accessible and familiar to the marketer, the outer sets more indistinct and vague, like a distant landscape. Figure 3.2 illustrates this multidimensional view.

Predictably, it is the more distant and complex dimensions of the wider environment (Level 4 in Fig. 3.2) that occasion most concern and problems among marketers, and therefore warrant more detailed coverage.

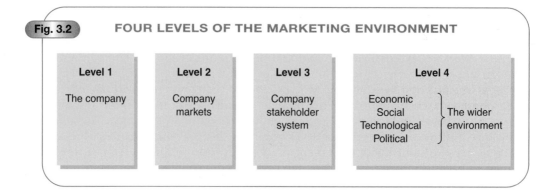

Fig. 3.2 FOUR LEVELS OF THE MARKETING ENVIRONMENT

Level 1	Level 2	Level 3	Level 4
The company	Company markets	Company stakeholder system	Economic / Social / Technological / Political — The wider environment

However, the nearer reaches of the marketing environment, Levels 1–3 in Fig. 3.2, are important elements of the everyday setting of marketing – Kotler refers to these collectively as the company's microenvironment. They are subject to many of the same external factors and the next chapter says some more about this aspect of marketing.

THE COMPANY SETTING (LEVEL 1)

Whether organised as a separate department or not, the marketing function operates within an organisational context, and is most effective when well managed, planned and resourced. Within marketing itself, subfunctions such as sales, advertising, research and promotion need to be co-ordinated to produce effective results. The marketing function must integrate with other functions such as production, engineering, purchasing, accounting and personnel. Close working relationships between marketing and functions such as R&D and production will be critical to key ventures, e.g. new product innovation, and will generally affect everyday performance indicators such as customer service. Within this 'inner environment', therefore, a wider role for marketing will be to communicate company-wide the market's requirements and their implications – an aspect of internal marketing. Marketers should be able to assess the organisation's strengths and limitations in major functional specialisms, since important policy issues such as product development and competitive strategy will depend heavily on the commercial exploitation of comparative advantage. Such internal 'audits' of relative strengths and weaknesses will often be routinely made in problem solving and planning, and will commonly be combined with information on the external situation, trends and events.

COMPANY MARKETS (LEVEL 2)

Many companies begin operations within one clearly defined market and develop, through market penetration, by servicing the market more efficiently and knowledgeably. Later growth, however, may depend on finding or developing new markets, and learning to service new types of customer with differing requirements. For other companies, multimarket operations may be entered into from the outset, as a conscious policy decision. Figure 3.3 presents a simplified view of the types of market that a company might choose to service.

Fig. 3.3   **A TYPOLOGY OF MARKETS**

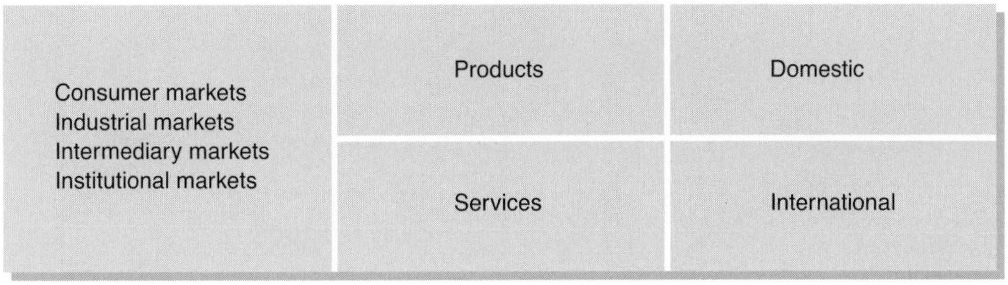

Consumer markets Industrial markets Intermediary markets Institutional markets	Products	Domestic
	Services	International

Although most of the terms used are self-explanatory, it is important to note that requirements may differ greatly between the market types, e.g. consumer markets usually involve many more customers, buying for various personal requirements, while industrial markets will involve a smaller number of professional buyers, sourcing for commercial reasons. Intermediary markets involve reseller organisations such as retailers, wholesalers and brokers, selling on to other buyers at a profit. The term 'institutional markets' denotes buyers within institutions such as schools, hospitals, dedicated associations and organisations (e.g. the Church), local authorities and central government. Buyers in such markets may operate through strict rules and procedures and by well-documented plans.

Clearly, the market environment within which a company chooses to operate will vary greatly according to market type. Even if specialising in one market, the company would need to conduct regular research and feedback exercises in order to monitor market changes and turning-points.

Last but not least, the competitors a company faces will vary according to the choice of market, or even the corner or sector of the market that it services – competitors are as much part of the market environment as customers.

THE STAKEHOLDER SYSTEM (LEVEL 3)

As the term implies, a company operates within the context of a network of interest groups, each of which has a particular relationship with the organisation, and often conflicting interests and motivations. Figure 3.4 illustrates the stakeholder system for a hypothetical company operating within the prescription medicines field.

Certainly part of this stakeholder system will be the participants in the company's *value chain*. The concept of the value chain, originated by Harvard Professor Michael Porter, models the vertical supply-market system within which a company seeks to fine-tune its performance in the interest of adding customer value and furthering corporate objectives. More detailed comment will be made on value chain analysis.

It should be stressed that the stakeholder system is a negotiated environment in which company relationships with different parties have to be carefully cultivated and managed. The company effectively has a series of publics – customers, shareholders, suppliers, employers, community bodies, etc. – with which it must maintain contact and ensure mutually productive relations. The marketing significance of this

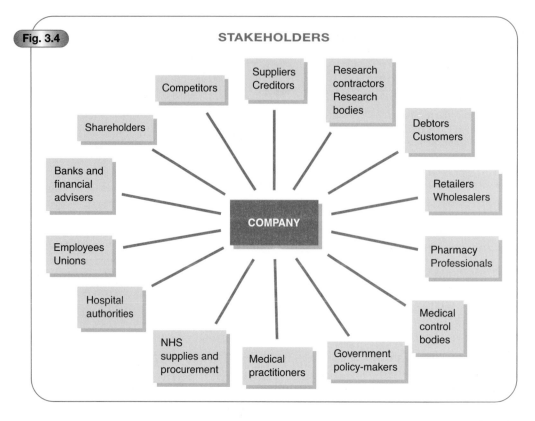

Fig. 3.4 STAKEHOLDERS

is that the state of these relationships can exert a powerful influence on success criteria such as brand image, product, acceptability, customer service, trade relations and company reputation.

A WIDER ENVIRONMENT (LEVEL 4)

In the wider environment, sometimes termed the macroenvironment, the company is faced by a complex set of uncontrollable variables that collectively shape its markets, its resources and the competitive climate, and that pose challenges and opportunities that may determine the success or failure of the company as a whole.

Figure 3.5 presents a simplified matrix of the four major sets of influence normally identified within the macroenvironment: social, technological, economic and political influences. These four broad categories are conventionally used as generalised headings, each of which encompasses a wide variety of variables, e.g. the social category includes factors at work in society in general, such as demographic and cultural influences. Further, the variables involved may work at different levels of aggregation – sectoral, regional, national and international – and they are likely to be interrelated across the four quadrants, e.g. changes in economic factors like investment may affect technological issues such as innovation (hence the arrows linking the quadrants). The letters denoting the four quadrants form the simple mnemonic STEP, often employed as a basic structure for STEP-analysis in outlining environmental forces relevant to business problems. A more detailed examination will now be made of these four sets of environmental influences.

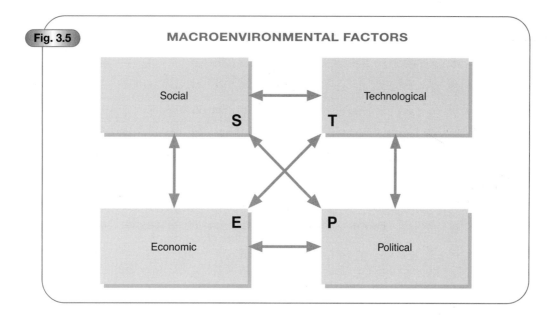

Fig. 3.5 MACROENVIRONMENTAL FACTORS

Social and cultural influences

Though sometimes difficult to pinpoint, these constitute, literally, the society-wide influences and changes that can affect the marketing environment. For convenience, they will be divided into two broad areas: demographic factors and cultural factors.

Demographic factors

These concern the population aggregates and patterns within a society – population size and make-up. While these factors change only slowly, and are statistically predictable, they nevertheless exert powerful effects on the volume and nature of demand for most products and services. Furthermore, they are the building-blocks of the patterns of lifestyle within a society, and constitute the circumstances in which consumers enact their commercial and social roles. Figure 3.6 presents a summary of the demographic variables of interest to marketers.

Some of these factors will have obvious influences on companies and services in particular markets: for example, the demand for baby-clothes, cots, nursery products, maternity and antenatal services will be directly correlated with birth-rate statistics. Not surprisingly, birth-rate will influence, with a time-lag, the demand for nursery facilities, primary education, toys and playthings, preschool clothes, and paediatric medicine. In like manner, an ageing population – a common phenomenon in industrialised countries – results in increased demand for age-related products and services such as sheltered accommodation, mobility aids, large-print books, preretirement counselling and geriatric nursing.

Other factors will exert influences that are less obvious and may vary geographically, or across social groups: especially over time, demographic factors will exhibit multiple influences that may present marketers with either opportunities or threats. An example of such temporal changes is given in Fig. 3.7, which shows the changes in UK beer and cider consumption over a 13-year period.

Fig. 3.6

DEMOGRAPHIC INFLUENCES ON MARKETS

	Population		
Data trends and projections	Size Growth rate	Age structure Birth/death-rates	Sex distribution Life expectancy
	Density	Location	Geographical/ regional shifts
	Household size Family size	Single/non-family households Marriage/divorce statistics	
	Income and wealth distribution	Working population	Educational participation
	Socio-economic groups	Occupation groups	Ethnic composition

Fig. 3.7

CHANGES IN UK BEER/CIDER CONSUMPTION

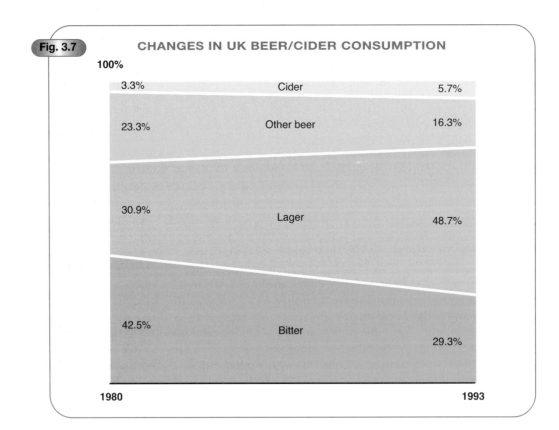

100%

	1980	1993
Cider	3.3%	5.7%
Other beer	23.3%	16.3%
Lager	30.9%	48.7%
Bitter	42.5%	29.3%

EXERCISE

Identify the major changes shown in Fig. 3.7 and comment on their likely or possible causes.

General demographic trends

Certainly in the UK and other industrial countries, recent years have witnessed major movements within the demographic landscape. It is worth noting that, though such changes appear general, and even international, they may not yet be described as irreversible. Some of the common factors in these demographic movements are:

1 *Population age distribution* Many countries have experienced in recent times a slowing in the birth-rate, after a period of high birth statistics in the 1950s and 1960s (the 'baby-boom' post-World War II period). This, combined with an extension of life expectancy related to medical, dietary and economic improvements, results in a rightward shift in the population profile – the classic symptoms of an ageing population. Some of these changes have far-reaching economic implications of interest to policy-makers, e.g. the increasing burden of the retired sector (even the 'super-old': 80 years and above) on social services, and the problems of the projected decline in the workforce pool – French government economic planners now view policy on this issue as a major priority.

2 *Household/family composition* In many countries there have been major changes in household and family size and make-up. Social and economic changes have led to later marriages, with fewer children. Workforce participation among married women has increased significantly, and many married women nowadays succeed in managing a return to work and career development after maternity breaks. Career couples, with no children, are now quite commonplace – indeed, they have been labelled by advertisers as 'Dinkies' (dual income, no kids), an advertising target group of some apparent interest!

Alongside these changes, the number of non-family households has increased substantially. Some of these households are made up of young careerist adults, or adults choosing singleness, while others represent adults that are divorced or widowed. If note is also taken of the growing number of single-parent families, it is hardly surprising that a researcher definition of 'head of household' is far from the straightforward matter it might have been thirty years ago. Significantly, these household changes have had a major effect on the pattern of demand for a wide range of everyday goods and services.

3 *Geographical shifts* Many 'post-industrial' societies, such as the UK and the US, have witnessed in recent years a major decline in traditional industrial regions and a parallel growth in 'new territory' regions based on service industries, e.g. the US Sunbelt and Silicon Valley phenomena. Other countries are experiencing similar movements of people and investment associated with rural depopulation and accelerated urbanisation and industrialisation. Though these phenomena are different, and may even coexist across regions within any one country, their economic and commercial impact may present common symptoms and problems. The marketer must reflect on the medium-term effects of such changes and consider how company development and investment plans are affected by them.

Cultural factors

Culture within any society is the complex of elements that reflect the society's beliefs and values, perceptions, preferences and behaviourial norms. These elements of culture express themselves in people's attitudes and behaviour, in their general lifestyle and in their working lives. Culture is therefore all-embracing and multidimensional, such that neat and exact definitions are difficult and elusive, and better left to specialists such as sociologists and anthropologists.

For the marketer, however, it is necessary to understand that culture will vary within and between societies, so that cultural norms may vary between countries, regions and culture groups or subcultures.

Within a society, culture may be most distinguishable by the prevalent core beliefs and values that people hold, which express themselves in family and friendship relations, in social conventions and rites, in social institutions and the social order itself. Such long-standing facets of culture change very slowly, as they are the product of family upbringing, the education system, national history and political development, religion, and a multiple of other influences such as aesthetic developments, communications and the media.

Below these prevailing core values may be identified a variety of secondary beliefs and values, which tend to be less durable, less universal and more situational. These may be tied in some way to core beliefs, but reflect the development of individual or group choices and feelings, e.g. a belief in education may be rooted in core values, whereas attitudes for or against private education will be an expression of secondary values and beliefs.

These secondary-level beliefs and values are therefore more likely to vary within society, to change over time, and be open to change and persuasion. Furthermore, they may be recognisable within the development of subcultures within a society. Subcultures develop in many ways and for different reasons, though they usually entail a grouping of people with common interests, experiences or motivations. Subcultures may therefore be associated with age groupings (the 'youth culture'), regional affiliations (Lancashire versus Yorkshire), religious or ethnic associations, or even situational facets of lifestyle (working mothers, single parents, students).

Secondary beliefs and values may sometimes exhibit society-wide changes over time, effecting a gradual change in a society's general orientation, e.g. in attitudes to work and leisure, an increased interest in self-development and choice, a growth in voluntary sector participation, ecological concern, consumerism, etc.

Environmental awareness is an interesting reflection of how society-wide concerns have delivered a powerful message to governments and business leaders. While the 'greening' of consumers has achieved comparable progress across a spread of international markets, the acceptance of 'green' consumerism in the UK was perhaps most notably marked by the 1988 publication of *The Green Consumer Guide* (Victor Gollancz), which recorded bestseller status and earned for its authors, John Elkington and Julia Hailes, a place in the United Nations Environmental Programme Global 500 Roll of Honour, announced on World Environment Day in June 1989. That the book market has sustained multiple reprints and a much-welcomed follow-up title, *The Green Consumer's Supermarket Shopping Guide*, testifies to the growing interest in 'green' products among the general public and, equally gratifying, among consumer goods manufacturers and retailing groups. Social responsibility and ethics in marketing is discussed further in Chapter 23.

EXERCISE

In June 1989 a MORI poll conducted in the UK showed that more than 18 million people – almost half the adult population – had within the survey period made at least one product purchase decision on the basis of environmental selection criteria.

1 As an individual consumer, note the most recent purchase you have made of an environment-friendly product, answer the following questions and be prepared to discuss your purchase in class:
  – Where did you buy the product?
  – What competing products were on display, and how did they compare on ecology-friendly terms?
  – Did 'going green' involve a price premium?
  – To what extent do you choose green products as a matter of principle?

2 As a student group, devise a simple checklist (twelve headings) by which to assess the 'green policy' of supermarkets. Between the group, visit five leading supermarket stores and apply the checklist you have developed. Analyse and present your group results in class.

Technological influences

Technology is the touchstone of economic progress, a leading source of competitive advantage commercially, and an indispensable part of everyday lifestyle for the modern consumer. Technology as a term is perhaps misleadingly general, as the technologies encompassed are highly disparate and may vary from the most apparently obscure improvement or technique to the substantive breakthroughs associated with quantum leaps in science and engineering. What cannot be denied is that technology is a major driving force for change, everywhere. Furthermore, technological change appears to be multiplicative, so that the rate of change increases. A simple illustration of this would be to consider the major changes that have taken place in the last twenty or more years – within the lifetime of the average business studies student – through innovations in the fields of information technology, biotechnology, fibre optics, aerospace and materials science. Though developments in these fields have followed different, sometimes faltering, paths, they have in some way combined to produce major changes and challenges, and to raise the commercial stakes of success and failure.

An earlier commentary on the commercial realities of technology was provided by Schumpeter, an American economist, who styled technology as a force for 'creative destruction', sweeping aside old products and their providers and replacing them with new competitors and technologies – a dynamic process that has been more recently expounded in the 'five forces' model of Michael Porter, another economist.

To illustrate the competitive force wielded by technology, it is worth observing that many manufacturers have been affected by technology development remote from their own field. Major sectors of the metalworking industry were made obsolete by the development of digital electronics. Weighing machines of all types, typewriters and cash registers are all examples of this.

For many companies, these technological changes have been difficult to detect, especially during periods of erratic economic growth which can conceal the real causes of falls in business activity. Developments in digital electronics have not only changed the form of products, but have also changed the way they are designed and manufactured. Computer-aided design not only permits more intricate designs, but also allows these to be manufactured without greatly increased costs. As a result, companies able to invest in these technologies have been able to introduce new products more quickly and competitively. These technologies have also enabled an increase in the variety of products available to the customer. For example, even low-cost items such as plastic patio chairs are available in dozens of styles.

Technology and research

An everyday marketing perspective on the effects of technology would be the growing consensus that product life cycles are becoming ever shorter – agreement on exact figures varies, though most marketers would reckon that as many as 80 per cent of products on today's market will have altogether disappeared within ten years. The corollary of this is that companies' sales and profits are becoming increasingly dependent on a managed succession of new product introductions. This, in turn, will hinge on success in the costly and speculative process of R&D and innovation (see example below).

While developments in leading-edge technologies and 'super science' may be associated with high-expenditure efforts in pure research, these high-visibility cases are by no means the standard route by which technology advances. Technology may often move incrementally and diagonally, through a chain process of linking developments, often 'authored' by competitor organisations that jostle for possession of the baton. (Sometimes final leadership position will be the result of a long and costly rivalry between competing systems – witness the confusing period of contention between JVC, Sony and Philips in the video-recorder market.) Furthermore, while commitment and investment is required in programmed research, even high-spending researcher companies (some pharmaceutical multinationals devote over 25 per cent of turnover to R&D) have found that high budgets alone are not the key to success. In managerial terms, research efforts need to be programmed, monitored for cost-effectiveness and directed towards market needs.

EXAMPLE

The cost of R&D

A fitting example of the cost of product development through R&D is provided by the case of Rolls-Royce Motor Cars. As recently as late August 1994, the world-famous car manufacturer, a subsidiary of UK engineering group Vickers, was being courted for a technology partnership by German auto rivals Mercedes and BMW. Commenting on the interest of Rolls-Royce in such collaboration, Rolls chief executive Sir Colin Chandler and Vickers chairman Sir Richard Lloyd stressed the need for a new core model to be jointly funded with a partner, in order to reduce the projected £200m development costs of such a venture.

The motives of the two German auto-groups are tied to their differing competitive circumstances. Mercedes-Benz, the vehicles subsidiary of Daimler-Benz, is reported to be determined to make good the recent losses on its troubled £88 000

▶

S-class limousine, launched as a rival to the Rolls-Royce standard model. Conversely, since its £800m acquisition of Rover in early 1994, BMW can already claim links with Rolls, since Rover produce body panels for Rolls-Royce. Further, BMW is said to be interested in involvement in co-developing prestige special-edition variants of Rolls-Royce and Bentley models.

Whatever the outcome of the partnership contest between the two German suitors, industry analysts are agreed that cost factors alone will lead Rolls into collaborative development for its new range of cars. Further, it has been speculated that such links might in future offer the strategic rationale for more ambitious arrangements such as merger or joint ownership.

Market needs represent the link between invention and innovation. While successful R&D outcomes might prove themselves in a new formulation, a product or process development, real success will not be achieved until users in the marketplace have adopted the new development. Technological progress therefore ultimately depends on a process of technology transfer and innovation, both of which involve commercialisation through an understanding of market needs. Here, then, is a critical role for marketing, to direct development efforts and facilitate their commercialisation.

Logically, market needs will be identified by research among customers – the market. Interestingly, this research does not have to be wholly esoteric or technical, as what is sought is an insight into the customer's problems and interests, rather than those of the technologist.

Perhaps the most telling illustration of this principle was provided by the Sony Corporation in developing the Walkman. In terms of technology sophistication, the Walkman formula was apparently basic and unexciting – the key element of its success was that it met a latent market need for a cheap, portable cassette-player, at the right moment in time. While Sony sales records doubtless catalogue the real success of the product, the hundreds of copycat versions that have been marketed worldwide are proof enough. Equally, follow-up Sony successes through the Watchman and the Discman are testimony to the market lead developed by the original product.

Market needs in other fields may be signalled by resource shortages, environmental problems and hazards, or the drive to reduce waste. Certainly, in the past, technology itself has presented environmental problems such as pollution and blighted landscapes that now require technological solutions. Given the recent awakening of international concern about the natural environment, it would be no exaggeration to assert that all organisations should consciously review their stance and performance in this regard.

Technology, then, is a major force for change for all organisations. Far-removed from the regulated atmosphere of the research laboratory, even the everyday High Street service firm must consider technology in the following terms:

- How will technological change affect our physical plant, equipment, work routines?
- How will it affect these issues for our customers, and what will this imply for our operations and offerings?
- How can we harness technology, or even take a lead role, in developing technology-based competitive advantage?

EXERCISE

Select one of the following service organisations and consider how technology (a) has affected the way the organisation operates, and (b) offers scope for future competitive advantage:

- solicitors' partnership;
- doctors' practice;
- travel agency;
- a high street bank.

The economic environment

The economy is a total system within which material and energy inputs are processed and converted to finished goods and services for distribution and final use. As all business organisations are part of the system, they have a direct interest in monitoring economic developments and guiding their policy decisions accordingly. Most performance-centred organisations incorporate economic data analysis into their business plans and marketing programmes. Often such information is collated as part of a formal Marketing Information System (MKIS).

The logic of this is that the current and projected events and trends in the economy – so-called macroeconomic variables – will likely affect the overall level of demand for goods and services, and related aggregates such as stock levels, prices, capacity utilisation and the like. In other markets, often tied to primary resource supplies and distribution, e.g. petroleum, companies make a practice of studying the microeconomic variables within their immediate market or sector.

While microeconomic factors will obviously vary for companies in different sectors, macroeconomic aggregates will present a common backcloth for all companies. Furthermore, as international communications and trade links develop, it is becoming more necessary to talk of the world economy – many Head Offices of large multinationals now operate around the clock, controlling operations across a spread of markets. While economic globalisation is being advanced through international and investment trade links, at the intermediate level regional trade blocs such as the EC, NAFTA, and ASEAN have superimposed a marked zoning influence within the trade statistics of many member countries. In the UK, for example, EC trade links now account for almost 60 per cent of overseas trade compared with a 30 per cent share in 1971. The aftermath of 1992 and the Single European Act provides a topical illustration of the realities of the economic environment for companies within both the UK and the wider European Community, since the free movement of goods, services and people is likely to pose major changes within national markets formerly assured as 'home territory'.

The economic environment is therefore a complex network of international, domestic and regional influences and dependencies that shape the market potential facing companies. Company performance itself will depend critically on the quality of preparation and decision making that is brought to bear on this potential.

Table 3.1 ● A typical databank reportage of major economic variables, showing a comparison between recent UK economic performance and that of selected competitors' countries

	France	Germany	Italy	Japan	UK	US
% Change GDP	2.1	1.9	2.9	1.4	2.5	2.0
% Change Retail price index	2.1	1.4	3.9	0.2	2.4	3.0
% Earnings rise	2.5	5.2	1.8	2.4	4.5	3.5
% Rate unemployed	10.7	8.8	9.7	3.2	8.6	5.3
% prime lending rate	3.7	3.3	9.1	0.5	5.9	5.3
Trade balance ($ bn)	33.5	1.5	62.6	10.1	−7.6	−127.3

Figures compiled July 1997 from latest available published annual statistics.

While cross-sectional data such as that shown in Table 3.1 may give a clue to current economic events, a firmer appraisal to underpin major decisions such as plant investment or international expansion would require methodical analysis of relevant indices, showing turning-points, trends and projections, with accompanying commentary and qualifications. Larger companies will retain in-house economists and planners for such purposes, or enlist the services of outsiders such as economic consultants, merchant bankers or venture capitalist organisations.

The significance of the economic data in Table 3.1 is that over time they will indicate major economic developments of direct interest to marketers and business people generally. Such 'economy-watching' may enable the vigilant company to respond in time to scenarios such as the following:

● *Recession* A downturn in economic activity of variable intensity. The diagnosis may range from a Chancellor's dismissive 'blip' or setback to a world recession. Usual indicators will be a fall or levelling in GNP (and GDP), industrial output, household income, consumer spending and investment expenditure, order-books and notified vacancies. Rises will be recorded in measures such as stocks, unemployment and company bankruptcies.

   As spending will be affected, market conditions become thin and more competitive. Though sales for some products and within certain income groups may be little affected, the general picture will be more difficult, while companies in some sectors (e.g. industrial components, machine tools, construction) may suffer heavier reversals through order cancellations, project postponements and stock depletion.

● *Recovery* The opposite of the above, again varying in intensity and time. Terms like boom, upturn and reflation will be used by economists. Marketers in some sectors will benefit from an early upturn in sales (their sales patterns may provide 'early indicators' of economic activity useful to forecasters, while other sectors, by contrast, may recover late ('lagging indicators'). Major upturns in economic activity may result in 'overheating', with higher costs and prices, import surges, bottlenecks and shortages, and failures through overtrading. Indicators such as investment and stock-levels may vary by sector and according to the 'investment climate'.

- *Inflation* Rising prices may be associated with buoyant conditions, demand growth and shortages. Although perverse combinations such as 'stagflation' (inflation and recession) are not unknown, severe inflation (hyperinflation, strato-inflation) may rock economic foundations and demand drastic policy remedies such as devaluation, tariffs and IMF assistance.

The scenarios above are rather simplistic and generalised, and by no means illustrate the real complexities to be met with in practice. More authoritative detail will be found in most economics textbooks. What these pictures do illustrate, though, is the way the economic 'isobars' may change and steepen, domestically and internationally. An added complication for the marketer will be the effect of government policy measures designed to stimulate or manage the economy. While these measures will vary by political preference and according to economic circumstance, they will usually entail manipulation of key instruments such as taxation and expenditure (fiscal policy), interest rates and credit (monetary policy) that will have obvious effects on markets. Furthermore, some industries may be subject to microeconomic measures, e.g. in respect of merger control or competition policy, investment or locational incentives. Companies engaged in international marketing will also need to respond to similar economic controls within their overseas markets. Finally, economic policies are likely in future to be more directly influenced by multilateral agencies and agreements (UN, GATT – General Agreement on Tariffs and Trade, etc.) and the expansion of common market blocs such as the EC.

The political and legal environment

Some aspects of political and legal environment were covered at the beginning of this chapter. However as an external marketing variable there are other equally important issues. The economic policies cited in the previous section are but one aspect of the political environment, which comprises the controls and checks instituted by central and local government, government agencies and quasi-official bodies. Also of relevance will be the growing influence of international laws and agreements, and at a more local level the activities of various professional and trade bodies, pressure groups and voluntary associations.

Such a regulatory environment may only appear to change slowly, and clear frameworks of rights and representations will usually exist. Nonetheless it is still necessary for marketers to be aware of the policy interpretations of the status quo, and to be attuned to the likely direction and nature of changes to the system. As company stakeholders may sometimes pursue particular interests and grievances through the 'political' system, it is in the interests of companies to frame policies that minimise stakeholder grievances and generally support a record of commercial good practice and social responsibility. In short, companies should seek to demonstrate good corporate citizenship by upholding the letter and the spirit of the law, and generally behaving in a responsible and responsive manner.

The marketing interpretation of such a stance would squarely equate with marketing excellence, and in practical terms might relate directly to a corporate mission statement that guides company activity from higher strategic issues, such as market choice, to everyday performance standards in respect of quality, service levels, customer protocol and the like.

While such autonomous standards of performance are to be commended, some markets and trades have developed general voluntary codes of conduct and control, supported and monitored by a central membership body. Practice within established professions such as medicine and accountancy has long been controlled by strict codes of professional behaviour. Likewise professionals within the Chartered Institute of Marketing have to abide by the Code of Practice.

Self-regulation aside, most governments have developed a body of legislation and enforcement frameworks in respect of industry and trade. In particular, the following areas of control are of direct concern to business:

1 Legislation in respect of monopoly and competition standards. In the UK, enforcement powers have in recent years been channelled particularly through the Office of Fair Trading and the Monopolies and Mergers Commission, both vested with wide competition reference powers. Statutory provisions in these matters derive from legislation such as the Fair Trading Act 1973, the Competition Act 1979, the Restrictive Practices Act 1976 and the Resale Prices Act 1977. As a full EC member, the UK is also subject to Community provisions in respect of these issues: in particular, Article 85 of the Treaty of Rome concerns practices hindering competition, and Article 86 of the Treaty addresses abuses of a dominant market position. Significantly, widening Treaty powers in this field are being proposed within Directives currently progressing through the Brussels chambers.

2 Measures to protect consumers, whether as groups (e.g. children, patients), individuals, as users of certain products and services (e.g. cigarettes, alcohol, gambling, food, drugs and medicines), or particularly as targets for business activities (mailshots, sales, promotion, etc.). In the UK the original provisions in consumer protection, founded in the law of contract and equity amendments to common law, have been supplemented significantly through legislation that is at least in part attributable to the growth of consumerism. Relevant legislation has included the Trades Descriptions Act 1973, the Consumer Credit Act 1974, the Supply of Goods (Implied Terms) Act 1973 and the Unfair Contract Terms Act 1977. A number of these statutes enhanced or introduced measures directly relating to marketing practices such as pricing claims, warranties, consumer information, product quality, and credit terms. Additionally, a welter of other measures relate to specific issues as diverse as branding (Trade Marks Act 1938), weights and measures (various Acts), food safety (Food and Drugs Act 1955 and revisions), product origin (Imported Goods Act 1972), promotional competitions (Lotteries and Amusements Act 1976), and inertia selling (Unsolicited Goods and Services Acts 1971 and 1975).

Additional to these provisions, government bodies exist with statutory and discretionary powers to control the business community in respect of a variety of other issues, from environmental protection and planning restrictions to commercial disclosure and public standards of decency. Figure 3.8 presents a collage of newspaper cuttings that illustrate the scope of such controls.

Fig. 3.8

COLLAGE OF NEWSPAPER ARTICLES

Rubber pact talks will aim to break price deadlock

Key rubber producing and consuming states will meet in Kuala Lumpur next week to try to break a deadlock over a new price-stabilisation pact, ... the meeting said,

Beijing may toughen line on N Korea

By Tony Walker in Beijing

China has given no official indication that it might be about to reconsider its refusal to countenance sanctions against North Korea over Pyongyang's resistance to International Atomic Energy Agency inspections of nuclear facilities.

But there is also no doubt that Beijing is viewing developments with increasing alarm, and may have decided to begin sending more pointed signals to Pyongyang that it cannot continue to defy international pressures.

In Hong Kong at the weekend, the Beijing-funded newspaper Ta Kung Pao provided the first hint that China might, if all else fails, fall into line with sanctions that would include an oil embargo. China w... cease all border ... article said.

China's oil exports ... Korea are critical to ... ued functioning of ... omy, and perhaps mo... tantly its war n... Chinese foodstuffs ... vital to a country s... from shortages of basi...

But, for the mom... seems more likely than ... will continue to insist ti... lomatic efforts be exh... before the internationa ... munity resorts to s--cti...

South Korea ha... with the North, s... of its sanctions w... ited without the ... of other nations.

South Korean ... indicated that S... resolution that ... economic embar... only if North F... offer a credible ... nuclear progra... line. "This f ... make it easie... take part in t... the official sai...

A condition... compatible w...

by US President Bill Clinton that Pyongyang could still head off sanctions.

In Beijing last week a foreign ministry spokesman said that, while China was very concerned about the issue, "we do not favour the resort to means that might sharpen the confrontation".

However, as the crisis deepens, it is becoming more difficult for Beijing to maintain that dialogue will yield positive benefits. In March, China headed off an earlier US attempt to promote a sanctions process in the United Nations Security Council, arguing that more time was needed to draw Pyongyang into discussion of the nuclear issue.

Two months have passe... without tangible proc... Indeed ...

Boards to be more accountable to members

Building societies given chance to widen services

By Alison Smith

Building societies will be able to offer a wider range of services but will also have to be more accountab'- to their members, under pla ... by the go... Setting ... Anthony ... nomic s... that the... intend to ... utory co... societie... instituti... "We ... sports ... shoot ... he said ... he was ... mutua ...

However, yesterday's announcement includes a requirement for societies' boards to inform their members at the next general meeting of any non-confidential takeover offers from organisations other than ... es.
fall... senic ... pow... er fro... fusing ... e gove... range o... can car... a to set ... te loans ... red on lan ... utting this ... Treasury's ...

nies offering a limited range of cover related to housing provision – buildings and contents insurance and mortgage payment protection. At present, there is a limit of 15 per cent on ... ety's stab... -

Call for tobacco events on TV to end

By Raymond Snoddy

The Commons national o... heritage committee yesterday leon said th... A s called for the phasing... sored by tobacco c... ion terrestrial televisi... han Mr Gerald Ka... st committee chair... w that the ITV com... or Channel 4 had dec... broadcast events sp... tobacco companies ... was "quite extraordi... the BBC continue ... so.

The corporation ha... will not enter into ... tracts for new even... tobacco sponsors. ... The committee ... mended that ... event ...

Yeltsin acts to curb financial advertising

By Leyla Boulton in Moscow

Russian President Boris Yeltsin has issued a long-awaited decree banning dishonest advertising, which has enabled crooked financiers to make fortunes at the expense of gullible investors.

Russian Information ... y said a decree at the ... nd, aimed primarily at ... agant promises made in ... nd newspaper advertise... s, prohibits companies ... promising specific levels ... ure dividend payments or ... antees of the future perfor... e of a given investment. ... e observers believe that ... seven decades of commu... propaganda TV viewers in ... sia's newly-developing mar... economy have proven vul... ... perceiving advertis...

promised to turn citizens' privatisation vouchers into "gold" was recently found to have defrauded investors of millions of dollars. Another suggested to investors they might make enough on a Rbs10,000 (£3.30) privatisation voucher to buy a house in Paris. Many small banks have attracted small savers with promises of astronomically high interest rates. But authorities say they have been powerless to stop television stations and newspapers from carrying advertising even months after it has been officially denounced as fraudulent.

From now on, businesses can only advertise actual dividend and interest rates they have paid in the past. The decree, to be enforced by Russia's anti-monopoly committee, obliges advertisers to withdraw within three days any advertising ... to violate the decree.

Eurotunnel to appeal over ferry duty-free

Eurotunnel, which runs trains through the Channel tunnel is to challenge a Europea... decision allowing ferry ... and airlines to c... ing duty-free sal ... Charles Batchelor ... e company intend ... in the next few ... for a judicial r... utumn of the I... on. It believes ... ales are worth ... its rivals and ... duty-free co... boost its tur... 170m up to 15... nnel said: ... to the ferrie... and we see ... on against ... free sales ...

OFT to investigate market-making

By John Gapper, Banking Editor

Sir Bryan Carsberg, director-general of fair trading, has launched a new inquiry into the practice of market-making on the London Stock Exchange, under which stockbroking firms buy and sell shares in publicly-quoted companies.

The Office of Fair Trading has market makers, bro-institutional investors comments on the arket-making, a sys-s not used by other tional exchanges. nquiry into market-ich relies on large riding liquidity by to sell or buy prices, was made in ured the system of ve effects. of market-making has helped London pre-eminent posi-because it guaran-the ability to sell stock of shares. ld yesterday the tandard re-exami-ea that had been ore, and had not by a particular rket-making had petitive.

ers to make excessive profits by fixing large margins between their bid and offer prices.

Other exchanges tend to use systems of an order-driven type, where offers to buy and sell blocks of shares at particular prices are posted on computer systems and matched centrally.

Pressure from the former director-general of fair trading, Sir Gordon Borrie, over the separation of brokers and jobbers, and minimum commissions, eventually led to the Big Bang deregulation of the City in 1986.

A subsequent inquiry into the privileges and obligations of market makers in 1988 found that the rules of market-making on the London Stock Exchange were "not significantly anti-competitive". Sir Gordon said after that inquiry the OFT might make a further assessment of market-making if there were representations to suggest that competitive circumstances had changed.

The stock exchange said it had been informed of the inquiry by its listed companies advisory committee, which had been contacted by the OFT. The OFT is asking for preliminary responses by the end of this month. The OFT may hold detailed talks with firms involved in market-making after that. It could refer the stock exchange to the Monopolies and Mergers Commission if dissatisfied at the outcome.

Philip Morris acts against Australian ban on advertising

By Nikki Tait in Sydney

Philip Morris, the US cigarettes, food, and brewing giant, yester... launched a High Court action ... king to overturn

Baby Bells open legal campaign

By Martin Dickson in New York

Four of America's "Baby Bell" local telephone companies yesterday launched a legal battle aimed at freeing them from a 10-year ban on competing in the long-distance telecommunications market and from manufacturing telecommunications equipment.

from the middle of last year. It will also phase out cigarette sponsorship of sporting events by the mid-1990s unless exemptions are obtained. Existing s... ship contracts were allo ... run their course.

When the legislation w... duced, federal health ... claimed that about 18, ... tralians died each ye ... tobacco-related diseases ... drain on health ... amounted to about ... (£3.3bn) a year. Some 2 ... of Australians are es... be smokers.

Philip Morris claim... day its decision to pro... lawsuit came last mo... tried to recall some ... cigarette lighters, ... thought to be faulty. ... Australian media gr... initially that they t... lish the recall aw... fear of breaching ... law. After a brief ... fied advertisem... accepted.

cigarette ... unds that ... freedom of ... e one of the ... US cigarette ... igate against ... s outside the ... the industry ... pressure from ... ne and in the ... :ket. ... said it filed a ... aim because the ... posed by the 1992 ... n Tobacco Adver- ... tion Act were "so ... that they deny it ... take part in debate ... public and social ... deny it the normal ... freedom of speech.

Call for tougher trademark bill likely

By Neil Buckley

Manufacturers of leading brands are vowing to continue their campaign for legislation to curb supermarket "lookalike" brands, in spite of their failure to get measures included in the trademarks bill, which has its third reading in the Commons today.

Several MPs are expected to call for tougher measures against lookalike brands, own-label products designed to resemble closely those of top manufacturers, but the bill is thought likely to be passed by

likely to focus apital by firms . and on wheth-ws market-mak-

EXERCISE

After studying the cuttings in Fig. 3.8, consult recent editions of the business press and collect a number of comparable photocopy stories. Prepare a brief presentation for discussion in class.

You may carry out the exercise as a group or individually – if as a group, more extensive reporting will be required, and evidence of group work.

Aside from direct action by government and regulatory bodies, companies have in the last 20 or more years had to recognise the increasingly strident concerns of consumerists and related environmental pressure groups and lobbyists. Consumer groups in particular have posed new challenges to marketers, especially through the publication of independent product quality and test information – in the UK, the Consumers' Association, publishers of *Which?*, now claims 7 million members. Through affiliation to BEUC (Bureau Européen des Unions de Consummateurs) it is connected with groups of similar strength in countries such as France and Germany.

CONCLUSION

The marketing environment comprises the playing-field upon which competitive marketing takes place. While some of the 'rules' of the playing-field may be common knowledge to all players, most 'game-plans' cannot be inspired wholly by mechanistic guidelines. The game is dynamic, and most moves are finally umpired by buyer preferences. Companies need to monitor and decide rational responses to changes in the environment in order to win their colours. The environment will almost invariably wield greater strength than a company can muster, so that pragmatic responses are generally more sensible than Canute-like gestures of defiance. Competitive management can benefit, within the rules, by good intelligence and planning and flexible execution – analysis and monitoring alone are not enough. This is perhaps best summarised by the old adage:

There are three types of companies: those who make things happen; those who watch things happen; and those who wonder what happened.

QUESTIONS

1 Taking any established product market, consider the various environmental changes that have influenced it over the last 15–20 years.

2 Develop a stakeholder map for a typical airline company, and comment on the conflicting interests that the various stakeholders might have in respect of the airline.

3 Consider the extent to which demographic changes are likely to influence the commercial success of (a) a supermarket chain, (b) a car manufacturer.

4 Many writers have proposed that the world is rapidly becoming a 'smaller place', as globalisation gathers pace. Consider how such a globalisation process will affect a company's market environment.

FURTHER READING

Howard, John (1976) *Marketing Management*, Irwin Dorsey.
Kotler, P. (1991) *Marketing Management: Analysis, Planning Implementation and Control*, Prentice-Hall.
Villiers, Charlotte, 'Boiled Frog Syndrome', *Management Today*, March 1989.

CASE STUDY
Can recycled money be used for garbage bins?

The Reserve Bank of Australia (RBA) is the central bank of Australia and is quietly but determinedly looking for business. The location for this growing business is a heavily guarded concrete fortress on the outskirts of Melbourne, where not only do they print Australian dollars, but also Thai bahts, Singapore dollars, Indonesian rupiahs and Kuwaiti dinars – in fact they specialise in turning out foreign banknotes and currently their printing presses are already producing as many foreign banknotes as Australian notes.

These banknotes all have one thing in common, they are made of plastic using patented technology which is promoted world-wide by the RBA and is intended to foil counterfeiters – it features a small transparent window which duplicators find hard to copy. The chief executive of the printing division of the bank, Robert Larkin is hopeful that this technology will be adopted internationally, it has been used in Australia since 1988. Prior to 1988 approximately 600 million local banknotes rolled off the RBA presses annually, now only 150 million Australian banknotes a year are produced. The problem that Robert Larkin is faced with, is that the RBA has become a victim of its own success. All Australian banknotes are printed on polymer not paper, and although a paper note can be worn out within months, a plastic note can last four years, thus the circulation life is much longer for the plastic note. The printing presses of the RBA are currently working well below capacity.

The RBA is now globetrotting for new business, trying to convince other major central banks to introduce the plastic note to their countries. Michael Beedle the printing division's sales manager stated that the bank has now liberated capacity for export opportunities – another way of saying that the bank wants to fill the excess capacity of their printing presses. A further statement pointed out that the industry in general is reluctant to move away from a 300 year old technology coupled with a reluctance to put plastic through the printing press. 'Significant numbers of countries have done or are currently undertaking trials on the plastic notes virtually around the world and printing presses do not need any modification to cope with the plastic notes', said Mr Larkin. In three years the RBA hopes that 75 per cent of the banknotes coming off its Melbourne presses will be for the export market. If however a country has a central bank that prints its own banknotes then the RBA is targeting them – it wants to sell them the blank polymer notes on which they can print their own designs. Fierce competition in this field is now developing with Canadian commercial printers Dura Note and Domtar Inc also making plastic banknotes, whilst the commercial paper banknote printers are actively guarding their livelihoods.

A British based company UCB Films Plc, a unit of Belgian chemicals, has set up an equal joint venture, Securency, to market the blank notes. RBA and UCB will divide the profits between them. It could prove to be a very profitable venture as they are interested in two of the most prized of all banknote printing jobs – the American dollar and the new Euro scheduled to come into circulation from 2002. Other big markets to aim for would be China and India. It would seem that the RBA has missed the boat with regard to the first Euro as it has already been planned for, but they will be actively seeking an interest in the next generation of the Euro. The American dollar bill represents 50 per cent of the manufacturing capability of the Federal Reserve, by introducing a polymer note the Federal Reserve would make massive savings. They may be persuaded by this cost argument, it is certain that RBA will be doing the best they can to convince them.

One voice of dissent reported in *The Economist* magazine was from a man who complained that he accidentally tumbled-dried an Australian note in the pocket of his jeans. 'The banknote I left in my jeans emerged shrunken and distorted,' he wrote.

These isolated incidents are unlikely to dissuade RBA who have another selling point for their product. In Australia, worn out banknotes are shredded and recycled to make, amongst other things – plastic garbage bins and flower pots.

Questions

Consider the following:

What will be the marketing environment implications of this new technology if it is accepted and implemented globally?

What, if any, will be the effect on paper manufacturers and their stakeholders?

(*Source*: Hong Kong Standard, 22 May 1997)

CHAPTER 4

The Competitive Environment

Not to resemble one's neighbour; that is everything.
Flaubert

INTRODUCTION

Some ten years ago there appeared in *Business Week* an article entitled 'Forget satisfying the consumer – Just outfox the other guy'. This neatly summarises some people's view of marketing. There are no rewards in telling your sales manager, 'I came second in the bid for the contract'; if you did not get the business it does not matter if you come second or twenty-second. The 1970s saw an emphasis on a strong customer focus within marketing organisations. In 1980 Michael Porter of the Harvard Business School published his key book, entitled *Competitive Strategy*, which was quickly followed by Kenichi Ohmae's *The Mind of the Strategist*. Both books have a brief that is wider than marketing *per se*, but both look at the importance of a competitor orientation for any organisation. They make the point that if you forget the competitive environment in which you operate, you could lose your business. This applies not just to private companies, but also the public services in the UK, where government legislation has introduced compulsory competitive tendering (CCT) for many local authority contracts.

Philip Kotler, a most prolific marketing author, also addressed competitive strategy when he jointly authored an article with Ravi Singh entitled 'Marketing warfare in the 1980s'. Interest in the parallels between military strategy and business has fascinated writers for a long time. Kotler and Singh suggested various attack and defence strategies which could help win a marketing conflict. These include several alternatives to the direct attack, since a direct assault rarely achieves victory – a view supported by a study of military history.

There are differences between war and business, however, and the Chairman of Electrolux was once reported to have said, 'Unlike the Military, Industry is always at war. If there is peace, they call it a cartel, and, as everyone knows, those are not allowed.'

The early 1980s also saw the publication of Peters and Waterman's book, *In Search of Excellence*. This focused on a survey of a number of then highly successful companies. Although this book says little on beating the competition, it does re-emphasise 'closeness to customers', and building stronger relationships, as one of the key principles of success. However, within this section they do suggest the art of 'nichemanship': 'finding a particular niche where you are better at something than anybody else'. This encapsulates getting ahead of the competition. In their research, Peters and Waterman found that 'a very large proportion of the surveyed companies were superb at dividing their customer base into numerous segments, so that they could provide tailored products and services'. The issues of how customers make buying decisions will be discussed in Chapters 5 and 6, and segmentation in Chapter 7. What this survey shows is that it may not be possible to win the competitive battle with all your potential customers, but it is possible to be the preferred product/service for a particular segment of the customer population.

In Search of Excellence dismisses the move to a more competitive focus, stating: 'The competitor issue is easily put to rest. The excellent companies clearly do more and better competitor analysis than the rest.' It is this ability to understand competitors and predict their actions which is vitally important to all marketing-orientated organisations.

Tom Peters redressed the lack of competitive emphasis in his later book, *Thriving on Chaos*, albeit in a chapter on 'Creative Swiping'. Here he advocates becoming obsessed with competitors – not just the major obvious competitors but all potential competitors. He suggests three tasks:

1 collect data on competitors;
2 update it regularly;
3 share it widely within the firm.

INDUSTRY STRUCTURE

The performance of an organisation will be influenced by the structure of the industry in which it operates because this will affect the level of competition in that market. Porter (1982) suggested that in addition to analysing what he calls 'jockeying for position' by obvious competitors, there are four other forces which affect the level of competition. These are:

- the bargaining power of suppliers;
- the bargaining power of customers;
- the threat of new entrants;
- the threat of substitute products or services.

If there is only a small number of key suppliers, perhaps controlling a key ingredient, or a small number of customers, then they can use this to squeeze profitability in an industry. There are other sources of power, but the factors which give rise to this power will change over time, so it is important to continually reassess the situation. As an example, some years ago Tesco supermarkets took over a small regional group called Hillards. The concentration of food retailers who are customers of food manufacturers thus increased. Companies who supplied Hillards but not Tesco were considered as potential suppliers to the wider group. However, since the Hillards stores were changed to Tesco layout, the predominant change was not in their favour. Certainly this was one example of a change in bargaining power for the food manufacturing industry in relation to its direct customers, the food retailers.

We could also look in detail at the food retailing industry itself. The customers here are families, students, housewives, and anyone who purchases food. While there are millions of customers they each spend only a small amount in relation to the turnover of a single large supermarket, let alone a company like Safeway or Tesco with total turnovers in excess of £6.5 billion.

An individual customer of Hillards might not like the Tesco store which replaced it. However, while all customers have a choice to purchase food wherever they like, the bargaining power of an individual is small and unlikely to affect Tesco's policy. In many cases the choice of supermarket is determined by location and not by the range of items on sale in a particular outlet. Therefore many customers who used the former Hillards store now use it in its 'Tesco' style. In defence of Tesco, it has to be said that during the 1980s Tesco managed very successfully to change its stores, which now attract increasing numbers of customers. However, for food manufacturers the problem is the bargaining power of the large retail groups, which encouraged *Marketing Magazine* to publish an article in 1987 entitled 'The five people who decide what we eat'. This referred to the buyers from the five largest grocery supermarkets who wield tremendous buying power in their decisions on which products to stock.

The threat of new entrants can also be studied in the context of food retailing. The 1990s have seen the large German retailer, Aldi, move into the UK, with a long-term plan to open 80 stores in the Midlands and North West. These new stores, with a distinct format, are already attracting customers, and since total food consumption is relatively static they must be winning customers from existing food retailers. Perhaps no obvious substitutes exist in food retailing, but in many industries new ways of applying benefits can be a significant threat. The subject of benefits and 'marketing myopia' were discussed in Chapter 2. From this you will already appreciate how an alternative way of delivering a customer benefit could alter the competitive environment in a dramatic way.

THE COMPETITIVE ENVIRONMENT

The competitive environment is likely to be of more immediate importance to marketers than the wider business environment discussed in Chapter 3. The different types of competitive environment can affect the way an organisation markets its products. At one extreme there are markets akin to what economists call 'perfect competition'. Here there are many small firms which are all too small to have an individual impact on price or performance norms. Usually it is easy to enter or leave such an industry, but the rewards are small due to the intense competition. In this market all firms have similar technologies and costs, and the product or service offered is almost impossible to distinguish from others. This is a very difficult marketplace, since there is no obvious reason why any buyer should choose any particular supplier other than on value and price.

At the other extreme is the monopoly market where only one supplier exists. The only decision faced by customers is to buy (or not to buy) the product. However, in practice, most markets lie somewhere in between these two extremes.

In creating reasons for customers to prefer one product over another, some form of competitive advantage is necessary. The study of competitors and the comparison of the strengths and weaknesses of competitor operations is very important in developing successful marketing plans. Marketing plans are also influenced by the stages of industrial development. In newly emergent industries such as video games, or new forms of entertainment, the emphasis is on developing customer awareness, as many will be first-time buyers. Growth markets still offer rewards for all competitors, but here the 'jockeying' for a favourable position really begins. As markets mature we find that:

- competition focuses on 'market share' and not market growth, and that;
- customers are usually experienced repeat-buyers who understand the product benefits and know something about the different offerings.

In mature markets there is also an emphasis on competition through modified or improved products, added value or operational efficiency. This becomes more intense as decline sets in, when excess production capacity is apparent and profits are falling. The concept of industry or demand life cycles can be linked to product life cycles, discussed in Chapter 11.

IDENTIFYING COMPETITORS

In order to develop a competitive marketing strategy it is vital that we decide who our competitors are. The most obvious competitors are other organisations which offer similar or identical products or services to the same customers as ours. However, the subject of substitute products and services highlights the indirect competitors, who also must be analysed.

Perhaps it is helpful to define five levels of competitors.

1 Direct competition.
2 Close competition.
3 Products of a similar nature.
4 Substitute products.
5 Indirect competition.

Direct competition

Perhaps we could see Pepsi Cola as a direct competitor to Coca-Cola. Both products offer similar products to the same general market. In this case the production methods employed are also very similar, although the actual formula for the basic cola essence is somewhat different in both companies since these products are in direct competition.

Close competition

Is Pepsi also a competitor to Tango orange drink? Both products offer similar benefits to similar consumers. The difference between orange and cola flavour is easier to recognise than the difference between Coca-Cola and Pepsi, but basically the products are substitutes for each other. In any analysis of drinks, all fizzy drinks need to be considered. Of course, it could be argued that other fizzy drinks include Perrier sparkling mineral water and champagne. Here we would be moving away from a strict interpretation of close competition.

Products of a similar nature

Perrier is a naturally sparkling mineral water from Southern France. The water comes up through a field of natural gas, hence the claim to be naturally sparkling as opposed to having added carbon dioxide, which is the case with Pepsi or other sparkling waters. However, it is the marketing decision to target Perrier at an adult market, rather than the younger age targeted by Pepsi, that makes Perrier less of a close competitor. Champagne also has an alternative way of producing the fizz. 'Methode Champenoise' is a secondary fermentation of the wine after it has been bottled. But again, it is not the different way of producing the bubbles, rather than positioning of the product, which makes it less relevant when considering competitors.

Substitute products

Is an ice cream a substitute for a fizzy drink? In some situations this is a reasonable choice. Marketers need to consider those products which can substitute in this way. The study of buyer behaviour is critical in deciding how wide such a study should go.

Indirect competition

Sometimes it is impossible to guess where competition is coming from. Any product that competes for the same buying power could be considered a competitor. If we consider a student surviving on a limited grant, could there sometimes be a choice between a Pepsi Cola and a newspaper? Perhaps here both are low-value items and the distinction is easily made. An article about the American motor cycle company, Harley Davidson, quoted a dealer as saying, 'We're competing against conservatories and swimming pools, not other (customised) bikes' (*Sunday Times*, 23 September 1990).

Another example was a decision by Boots The Chemist to reorganise its stores. The managing director of a company supplying dog biscuits to Boots was told his product would be discontinued even though it was selling well in the stores. The reason was an increase in the space allocated to audio and photographic products, and other 'high ticket' items. Pet foods were not contributing enough profit per square foot of store and were being completely phased out. This type of competition is almost impossible to assess although it could be said that the dog biscuit company really knew very little about the objectives and needs of the customer. Boots required profit from its shops and not dog biscuits to sell to its customers!

EXERCISE

The following products could be seen as competitors. Which level of competition is involved, and what attention do you think a marketing manager should give to analysing the competitive threat?

(a) A manufacturer of vinyl records when looking at vinyl records versus compact discs.
(b) A UK Rail Franchise Company considering the threat posed by coach travel.
(c) A flower shop considering the shop next door which sells fancy chocolate products.
(d) A Chinese restaurant looking at the range of pre-prepared Chinese meals available in a local supermarket.
(e) A large brewery company when considering home-brew kits.

You could also list other direct or indirect competitors for each of the examples above.

COMPETITOR ANALYSIS

The previous section should demonstrate that it is not always easy to identify who is your competitor for the purpose of understanding their strategies. Nevertheless, Tom Peters is right when suggesting, 'excellent companies do better competitor analysis'. The task is to understand the constraints restricting competitors and to predict competitor moves. The objective of this analysis is to find 'points of leverage' which can be used at minimum cost against competitors. It is not appropriate to collect data for its own sake – rather the analysis should focus on those essentials which can help take decisions on how to win in the marketplace.

It is not necessary at this stage to list the type of data collected in a competitor analysis. The need is specific to any particular set of competitors. It is, however, wider than the obvious marketing issues, and will include issues such as financial strength, operational efficiency and production capability, which could affect a competitor's market performance.

A typical evaluation process could follow the sequence below:

1 Evaluation of competitor objectives.
2 Evaluation of competitor's strategy.
3 Evaluation of competitor's success to date.
4 Evaluation of competitor's strengths and weaknesses.
5 Prediction of future competitor behaviour.

It is the future responses that are important for a marketer. However, many firms will behave in a consistent manner, so that studying past actions can help to predict how your competitors might react in the future, and this is of course vital when formulating your organisational plans.

Information on competitors will come from both formal research and informal information channels. The latter includes dialogue with customers, often conveyed in reports from sales staff, but also obtainable from suppliers or other third parties. Although unnecessary data is to be discouraged, an efficient marketing information system is appropriate. The assessment of information needs to be made by a marketing-orientated employer who understands the dynamics of the particular market.

THE COMPETITIVE TRIANGLE

Figure 4.1 is inspired by the work of Kenichi Ohmae. It is an excellent way of remembering that customers have choices. From the apex of the triangle customers can assess the different offerings of all companies and their competitors.

Obviously, customers will choose to do business with the company which best matches its requirements. Of course, the workings of customers' decision processes are not simple. These are discussed in the following chapters. Nevertheless, the match between the various offerings and particular customers, or groups of customers, should not be left to happen by chance. The role of marketers is to try to influence factors in such a way that their organisation's products or marketing offerings are chosen.

The object of this is to try to gain a sustainable advantage over competitors. Writing in the *Harvard Business Review* on this subject, Pankaj Ghemawat stated, 'For outstanding performance, a company has to beat the competition. The trouble is that the

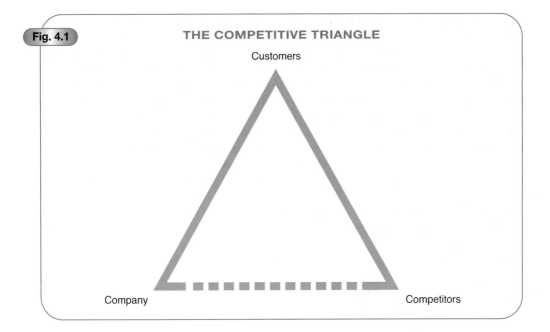

Fig. 4.1

THE COMPETITIVE TRIANGLE

Customers

Company   Competitors

competition has heard the same message.' He summarises three areas of potential advantage from cross-industry findings:

1 *Product innovation* Competitors secure detailed information on 70 per cent of all new products within a year of their development. Patenting usually fails to deter imitation. On average, imitation costs a third less than innovation and is a third quicker.
2 *Production* New processes are even harder to protect than new products. Incremental improvements to old processes are vulnerable too. If consultants are to be believed, 60 per cent to 90 per cent of all 'learning' ultimately diffuses to competitors. Production often blurs competitive advantage: recent studies show that unionised workers pocket two-thirds of the potential profits in US manufacturing.
3 *Marketing Non-price Instruments* are usually ascribed more potency than price changes, partly because they are harder to match. Rivals often react to a particular move, however, by adjusting their entire marketing mix. Such reactions tend to be intense; limited data on advertising suggest that the moves and countermoves frequently cancel out.

Nevertheless, Peters still suggests that the goal should be uniqueness. He advises: 'Uniqueness most often comes not from a breakthrough idea, but from the accumulation of thousands of tiny enhancements.'

In the early days of marketing it was suggested that organisations looked for the one Unique Selling Point (USP). In fact, as Peters points out, it is much more complex. Therefore, to achieve competitive advantage a marketer needs to be involved with the whole marketing offering, both inside and outside the organisation.

MEGA-MARKETING

Kotler suggested that competitive advantage could be gained by altering the external environment. This is undoubtedly possible, as exemplified by Pepsi bringing about the exclusion of Coca-Cola from India for more than a decade. The voluntary agreement limiting car imports from Japan to the UK is another example of reducing competition. However, the role of the EC Commissioner for Competition is specifically aimed at ensuring that no unfair competitive situations develop. Therefore, most organisations are open to the full power of competition and they have only the internal variables, controlled within their organisation, with which to achieve competitive advantage, as seen by customers outside the organisation.

CONCLUSION

The competitive environment is the most dynamic environment in which an organisation will operate. Other organisations, both nearby and remote, are also planning to offer their products or services, and are aware that success comes from improving on the existing offers. It is in this ever-changing arena that organisations have to strive for ongoing survival.

Companies can decide to try to lead developments and move faster than their rivals into new areas. This requires investment in Research and Development and a clear vision of the future. Other organisations will follow fast when new products or services are launched, hoping to improve on an idea with the benefit of seeing customers' reactions. However, laggard companies which react too late find that the market has already moved on.

The study of competitors' activities is vital. But it must be linked to a study of potential buyers, how those buyers behave now and how they are likely to behave in the future. This is the subject of the next chapter. It completes the study of the competitive triangle discussed here. It is necessary for marketers to study both customers and competitors. A focus on one alone is not enough, as it leaves the triangle incomplete. If there is a failure to appreciate the ever-changing competition, then the words of warning at the end of Chapter 3 will be even more relevant: 'There are those companies who wonder what happened.'

QUESTIONS

1 In a market of your choice, select two leading companies or brands and identify the means by which they compete with each other.

2 Do you think a marketer should take the advice:
'Never mind the customer, just outfox the competition'?

3 Why do customers still buy branded food products in supermarkets when the retailer's own label is often of similar quality and cheaper?

4 To what extent might competition come from unrelated markets in the form of a substitute product?

FURTHER READING

Brown, P. B., Buell, B., Davis, J. E. and Dreytack, K., 'Forget satisfying the customer', *Business Week*, 7 November 1985.

Ghemawhat, P., 'Sustainable advantage', *Harvard Business Review*, September–October 1986.

Kotler, P., 'Mega marketing', *Harvard Business Review*, 1986.

Kotler, P. (1991) *Marketing Management*, 7th Edn, Prentice-Hall.

Kotler, P. and Singh, R., 'Marketing warfare in the 1980s', *Journal of Business Strategy*, Winter 1981.

Ohmae, K. (1983) *The Mind of the Strategist*, Penguin.

Peters, T. (1988) *Thriving on Chaos*, Macmillan.

Porter, M. E. (1980) *Competitive Strategy*, The Free Press.

CASE STUDY
Wearport Docks Board

John Sampson has just been appointed to the newly created post of General Commercial Manager at the Wearport Docks Board. Working alongside the Board's General Operations Manager, he has been given a brief to halt and reverse the decline in traffic and profits that the port has been suffering in recent years.

In its heyday the busiest coal-port in the North East of England, Wearport is nowadays the typical example of a township suffering the problems of past dependence on basic industry. With the decline in output from the local coalfield, and a fall-off in employment and business in the marine engineering and foundry industries, the port's performance in recent years has mirrored the fortunes of the borough itself. The figures published by the Docks Board for 1997 are testimony to the very difficulties that have ushered in John Sampson's new post. While the port had long been a casualty to regional decline, the recent post recessionary shake-out has served to present new problems: in 1995 the bankruptcy of a major local customer, a steel stockholder, spelled the loss of 20 per cent in port traffic.

General changes in trade patterns in the years since EC membership have led to a steady shift southwards in UK port shipments, while major shipowners have responded to cost pressures by concentrating operations at the more efficient container ports (Table 4.1).

John Sampson has spent his first few weeks in office familiarising himself with the current position of the docks. Although the coal trade has been declining for some time, coal exports still account for some 30 per cent of the port's traffic volume. The balance is represented by a mix of general cargo business such as timber, grain, and animal feedstuff imports; and exports of scrap iron, chemicals, refractories and steelwork fabrications. Most traffic is on coastal or near-water routes to Holland, Germany, Scandinavia and Eastern Europe.

The port has two serviceable basins, given over to coal-handling and general cargo work respectively. A third dock, now disused through heavy silting, has at various times been the subject of abortive development plans by the Local Authority.

On pacing the weed-choked marshalling yard one evening, Sampson is struck by the picture of despair and disrepair that is evoked by the rusting crane derricks and corrugated store-sheds. He nevertheless feels that the port could better realise the potential left to it, given a more systematic and commercial approach to the management of its marketing efforts. In three weeks' time he has to present to the Board a situation report and a preliminary analysis of market opportunities, as a first input to the preparation of a formal Business Plan.

Question
Present your proposals on the investigations, analyses and preparations that John Sampson should treat as priorities during the next three weeks.

Table 4.1 ● Wearport Docks (Revenue Account – 1997 figures)

Traffic (m tonnes)	Revenue (£m)	Trading Profit/loss (£m)	Total workforce
1.85	7.4	2.6	220

CHAPTER 5

Buyer Behaviour

I do my thing, and you do your thing.
I am not in this world to live up to your expectations.
Fritz Perls

INTRODUCTION

It should be clear from the points made throughout the first four chapters, and especially in Chapter 2, that effective marketing involves focusing organisational activity on the needs of the potential customer. This requires an understanding of what determines these needs and how customers respond to them. Indeed, an appreciation of the factors which are most relevant in a decision to buy a particular product is likely to be crucial to the effectiveness of many, if not all, marketing decisions. This aspect of marketing comes within the scope of what is termed 'buyer behaviour'. The subject of buyer behaviour itself has developed to the extent where it is now conventional to study separately consumer buying behaviour, or consumer behaviour, and buying within an organisation, or organisational buyer behaviour. Following this convention, the present chapter will examine consumer buyer behaviour, and the next chapter will introduce organisational buyer behaviour.

SOME ISSUES IN BUYER BEHAVIOUR THEORY

The interested reader will find that there is a voluminous and growing body of literature and ongoing research on buyer behaviour, such that many universities offer whole modules and even degree specialisms based on the subject.

Though the initiation of much of the research has come from the development of marketing itself, valuable and varied combinations have been made by researchers from a number of other academic specialisms, ranging from economics and management theory to psychology, sociology and social anthropology. This multidisciplined approach is perhaps unsurprising, given the complexity of the field and the multiplicity of research questions that suggest themselves. By way of illustration, within the study of consumer behaviour marketers are interested in questions such as:

- How can models of buyer behaviour be of use to marketing practitioners?
- What are the major influences on purchase decisions?
- Do consumers pass through a sequence of decision stages?
- If so, do such stages apply equally to all purchase types, or all consumers?
- What is the relationship between needs, motivation and buying behaviour?
- How do attitudes affect buying behaviour, and is it necessary to achieve favourable attitude changes before buying takes place?
- How are attitudes formed, and to what extent are they modified, say, by marketing communications or buying experience?
- How and when do consumers seek and use information? How informed are consumers prior to purchasing?
- Is the purchase of a new product or brand approached as a different buying proposition?
- How do buyers evaluate the various alternatives facing them in their buying decisions?
- What is the nature and extent of loyalty among buyers, and how differently do loyal buyers approach their purchase decisions?
- What is the extent of individual versus group-influenced decision making among consumers?

This chapter will seek to provide at least an insight into the answers to such questions, while later sections of the book will return to some of the more specialist issues, such as the role of marketing communications.

THE SIMPLE BUYING DECISION PROCESS MODEL

The decision to buy a product, whether it be a soft drink or an item of clothing, involves responding to a stimulus. The decision to buy a soft drink may be as a result of being thirsty on a hot day or to be sociable having volunteered to be 'driver' for a night when out with friends at a country pub.

One approach to studying the buying decision process is to develop a model of it. The simplest way of doing this is to consider only the stimuli received by the person making the decision and the result – the person does or does not buy. This is a simple version of the classic stimulus–response model of behaviour which assumes that people will generally respond in some predictable way to a stimulus. The person making the decision is thus treated as a 'black box', which is a type of model generally accepted as useful for investigating complex systems which cannot be observed directly, such as the decision-making process of a buyer (*see* Fig. 5.1). It provides a framework which focuses on the inputs, the stimuli and the outcomes of the decision, but offers no insight as to why a decision was made. From elementary economics it might be expected that buying decisions would be made by logically comparing the available choices in terms of cost and value using criteria such as:

- economy of purchase or use;
- convenience;
- efficiency in operation or use;
- dependability in use;
- improvement in earnings (e.g. factory equipment).

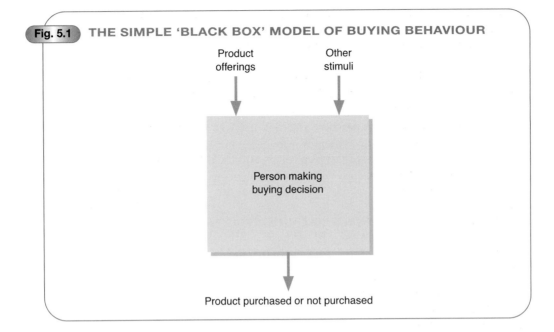

Fig. 5.1 THE SIMPLE 'BLACK BOX' MODEL OF BUYING BEHAVIOUR

Product offerings

Other stimuli

Person making buying decision

Product purchased or not purchased

A review of our own personal buying habits will show that in practice these factors are seldom considered and rarely of paramount importance when we make buying decisions.

EXERCISE

Think of a product you have purchased within the last week or so. Consider carefully why you chose that product. Write down as many reasons as you can to justify your purchase decision. When you have done this, list as many possible alternatives to the product purchased as you can. Remember that not to purchase anything is often an option.

Are you able to justify your choice against each of the alternatives you have listed solely in terms of the economic factors listed? Are there any other explanations? Refer back to your list of reasons as you read the rest of this chapter to see whether there might be a better explanation for your decision. Repeat the exercise for someone very different from yourself who might also have purchased the same product, and consider whether they might have different reasons for their purchase decision.

There are many reasons why economic criteria are ignored when making purchase decisions. Often the person making the decision does not have the necessary information or it is difficult to compare the different products on this basis alone.

THE PRINCIPAL BUYING DECISION VARIABLES

While it is not difficult to establish that buying decisions are not generally made on the basis of logical economic criteria, it is considerably more difficult to identify the factors or variables which do affect buying decisions. One reason is that many of these are dependent upon the person making the decision, and hence they are referred to as personal buying decision variables. These personal buying decision variables can be grouped under the following three categories:

1 Psychological variables.
2 Social influences variables.
3 Demographic variables.

In addition the influence of the purchase situation needs to be recognised; internal stimuli such as thirst or fatigue – the physiological variables – need to be separated from external stimuli such as the aroma of freshly brewed coffee, and the decision process separated from the variables. The basic relationships between these elements are summarised in Fig. 5.2.

THE BUYING DECISION PROCESS

The person who recognises a need effectively becomes a potential customer. It is the recognition of a need that creates a want. A person may be thirsty so will be in need of a drink, but this may be expressed as wanting a glass of champagne. The creation of a want involves a decision process which can involve some or all of the following seven stages:

1 Recognition of the need – this is a prerequisite of further action.
2 Choice of involvement level – how much time and effort does the need/want justify?

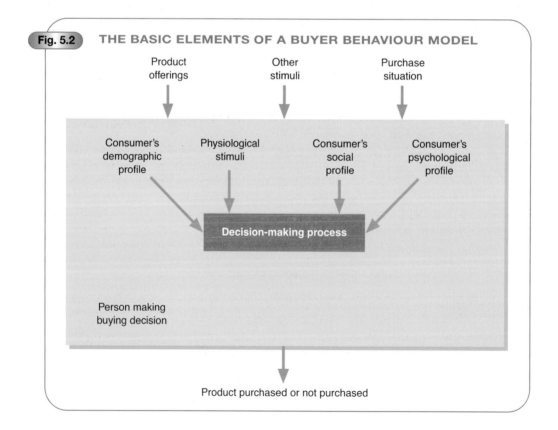

Fig. 5.2 THE BASIC ELEMENTS OF A BUYER BEHAVIOUR MODEL

Product offerings

Other stimuli

Purchase situation

Consumer's demographic profile

Physiological stimuli

Consumer's social profile

Consumer's psychological profile

Decision-making process

Person making buying decision

Product purchased or not purchased

3 Identification of alternatives.
4 Evaluation of alternatives.
5 Decision – choice made.
6 Action.
7 Post-purchase behaviour – need to resolve anxieties about choice made.

Most day-to-day purchases involve little or no risk in terms of being dissatisfied with the decision, so justify little time or effort. The choice is made on the basis of the immediately available information.

COMPLEX BUYING BEHAVIOUR

For very high-risk purchases buyers are likely to go through each stage of the decision-making process. This is termed 'complex buying behaviour' and is seldom adopted because of the time and trouble involved.

An example where this approach might be justified could be the purchase of a wedding present for someone overseas – in the US perhaps. Stage one comes with the engagement announcement. Because it is so far away the need to take extra time and trouble could well be accepted with little thought, whereas stage three might involve finding out how long parcel post takes by sea and air and the relative costs, whether the electrical supply is compatible, and whether a gift list is being circulated around other friends and family members. Possible alternatives might then be chosen on the basis of the amount of money available for the present. Stage five, the selection, could be made on the basis of ease of shipment and availability. Then, after the present has been purchased, stage seven might occur when it is being packed since if this is difficult the choice made may well seem less suitable than an alternative which could have been packed and shipped by the supplier.

INFORMATION SEARCH

The third stage of the process – information search – may involve starting from scratch, such as when the product is entirely new or is totally unfamiliar to the buyer. Obvious examples might be skis being purchased by the first-time skier or a hang glider by someone who has only tried the sport. This is, however, relatively uncommon. Most products are by their nature in some way associated with other products. Thus someone considering buying a new television is likely to consider the brand of their existing television favourably if it has been reliable: unfavourably otherwise. Perhaps the brand of their radio, music centre, CD player or other similar product would then be at least initially considered.

THE EVOKED SET

Those brands which initially come to mind when considering a purchase are referred to as the 'evoked set'. Clearly any brands which most people bring to mind in relation to certain types of product have a distinct advantage compared with other brands. It is the brands which are regularly within the evoked set of potential purchasers which set the standard that alternative products have to better if they are to be selected.

The concept of the evoked set was developed by Howard and Sheth as a result of their work on the development of a comprehensive buyer behaviour model.

EXERCISE

Most people considering buying a personal computer would include IBM as one of the possible brands. They might not actually evaluate this option, believing the IBM products would be too expensive, but the brand would be known. What other brands would you initially think of relative to personal computers? Repeat the exercise for another fairly specific product, for example a small inexpensive new car, breakfast cereal, or a soft drink. Compare your list with others considering the same products.

EVALUATION OF ALTERNATIVES

Stage four (evaluation of alternatives) is another important part of the process since it will inevitably depend upon making a comparison of only a few specific potential differences between the products. These are known as the *salient attributes*. Other differences are known as the *non-salient attributes*. Examples relevant to the choice of a motor vehicle might be the availability of fuel injection, a sun roof or electric windows. Other factors, such as more secure door-locking systems or low-level access to the boot, have until recently been considered non-salient attributes by most buyers. This is in spite of these features having significantly greater potential for saving inconvenience or injury than any of the attributes usually considered salient.

Studies have shown that there are many different evaluation procedures which are used when making buying decisions. This work has also shown that these tend to be complex since they involve comparing attributes within the context of brand beliefs and attitudes.

BELIEFS AND ATTITUDES

Other factors significant in the context of evaluating alternatives are the beliefs or attitudes held about the brands. Beliefs are perceptions of a brand which are based on explicit information. Attitudes are firmly held ideas which are often neither confirmed nor explicitly disproved by everyday information sources.

Attitudes are usually seen as multiplex, consisting of at least three elements :

(i) a knowledge (= cognitive) component;
(ii) a preference/liking (= affective) component; and
(iii) a *conative* element that drives the individual towards some behaviour or response.

The relationship between these components is the subject of ongoing research. From a marketing point of view, interest centres on the influence of *salient* attitudes, i.e. those of particular relevance to a purchase occasion, brand or marketing proposition. An interesting question concerns the extent to which salient attitudes, say to a brand offering, have to be favourable *before* a purchase decision can be made. Alternatively, it might be that favourable attitudes can be formed, and certainly reinforced, *after* the purchase decision, through use experience. In communications theory, these alternatives have been the focus of differing models of how communications may work, i.e. the *conversion* model v the *reinforcement* model. Both views of the communications process have validity, since research evidence indicates that the relationship between attitudes and behaviour is two-way, rather than unidirectional.

THE PURCHASE DECISION

Even when a decision to buy a particular product has been made, the purchase decision can be affected by unanticipated situational factors such as the cancellation of overtime working or because of the numerous other decisions often directly associated with the purchase: the vendor, the quantity, when and how to pay.

The quantity decision can often involve associated items such as batteries, film for cameras, tape for recording machines, etc., rather than the main item being purchased. Very often the supplier or the vendor removes the need to make these decisions by either including the essentials in the form of a prepackaged kit or by providing these as a discount on the price. The provision of the associated items as a kit can be considered a marketing strategy, whereas if they are provided as a form of discount this would be a selling strategy.

The timing decision is often linked to the payment decision, and the acceptance of credit cards has to a large extent reduced the importance of these decisions for many purchasers.

POST-PURCHASE BEHAVIOUR

The final stage of the complex buying process is post-purchase behaviour. Since it is seldom possible to make a fully rational purchase decision, it is hardly surprising that purchasers often doubt the wisdom of their choice when, finally, the purchase has been made. This leads to minor faults being found with the product itself or its features.

Recognising this, manufacturers have found it beneficial to aim some of their advertising directly at new owners to reassure them that they have made a wise decision. This approach is often used by motor vehicle and copier manufacturers: they have appreciated how important an influence existing users can be on potential customers. The provision of free telephone help-lines, call-out services and 'no quibble' return policies, such as those adopted by Marks & Spencer, are aimed specifically at overcoming this problem. It was also within this context that an increasing number of suppliers have recognised the importance of having good instruction manuals.

THE UTILISATION OF COMPLEX BUYING BEHAVIOUR

It would be logical to assume that complex buying behaviour is generally used for important purchases. Suppliers who believe this applies to their products tend to promote them on the basis of the features and benefits that are the result of the efforts and capabilities of their designers. This approach used to be seen in automobile catalogues which always included pictures of the engine and details of the technical features of the vehicle.

However, research showed that very few buyers have the knowledge necessary to appreciate the relative importance of this type of information and instead simply assume that competitive products are equivalent with regard to these features. This improved understanding of buyer behaviour can be seen in contemporary catalogues which seldom refer to these features. Instead, choice is focused specifically on acceptability for purpose (e.g. how many seats) and often to an even greater extent on the perceived prestige of the product. Promotion has also been increasingly focused on this aspect of the product.

DISSONANCE-REDUCING BUYING BEHAVIOUR

When buyers perceive commonplace products as being complex, they are likely to compensate for this by adopting a less involved style of buying behaviour. Usually this reduces the scope of any information search, which means the buying decision is often made from only a small range of the available products. The decision is made with the objective of limiting the possibility of being disappointed with the product. This is called 'dissonance-reducing buying behaviour'. It usually involves selecting a product on the basis of a few obvious, often new, features rather than on the basis of the features actually required. Domestic cookers are a very good example of a product for which this style of buying behaviour is typical. As a result, easily identified features such as automatic timers and light units are emphasised rather than basic performance or ease of use. Because of this, even comparatively low-cost, though useful, features such as thermostatically controlled hobs failed to gain general acceptance. Even more remarkable has been ready acceptance in the UK of 'built in' ovens which lack the separate grill which was an essential feature of the traditional British cooker. This is clear evidence that when purchased little or no consideration was given to the way the existing cooker was used.

Since the purchase choice is likely to be made from a limited range of products it is essential for sellers to promote their brands to ensure they are considered by as many people as possible. This is achieved by emphasising and promoting recognisable brand names. It also means that products that are subject to dissonance-reducing buying behaviour are likely to become increasingly standardised. This is because manufacturers will tend to focus their competitive effort on the features of the product which have the largest market share, rather than on those having the highest performance or most innovative features.

HABITUAL BUYING BEHAVIOUR

For most day-to-day purchases the process is even less involved since there is a whole range of products which are bought mainly as a result of habit. Newspapers, magazines, beverages, petrol and most food products are examples of products which are very often purchased on the basis of habitual buying behaviour.

VARIETY-SEEKING BUYING BEHAVIOUR

As an alternative to habitual buying behaviour most people adopt a less predictable approach to buying, at least for some of these low-value products. Usually these are products for which there is no clear preference either by the individual making the purchase or, more particularly, by the users of the product, e.g. the family. A typical example of a product in this category is breakfast cereal. Very often this is selected on the basis of buying an alternative to what was purchased on the previous occasion. Another example is the choice of magazine prior to an occasional train journey. Both of these are examples of variety-seeking buying behaviour.

This type of buying behaviour does not apply to high-value items except where the wealth of the individual is such that this would be a trivial purchase. Thus the ordinary car user who changes brand with every purchase is more likely to show dissonance-reducing buying behaviour, in which brand is of little importance, than variety-seeking buying behaviour.

THE PSYCHOLOGICAL FACTORS AFFECTING BUYING DECISIONS

Buying decisions which are made by individuals will inevitably, to at least some degree, be determined by the personality and experience of that individual. Within the context of buying behaviour, the areas of specific interest are those concerned with motivation, perception, learning, personality and attitudes.

Individual human behaviour has been studied since ancient times and systematically by psychologists, sociologists and other behavioural scientists for at least the past 100 years. Within the context of this work, theories have been developed to explain the behaviour of individuals and groups in specific situations such as the workplace. All of those listed as relevant to buyer behaviour are also likely to be studied within the context of human resource management and are therefore likely to be familiar to many readers.

MOTIVATION

In contrast to much of the early work on motivation which was concerned with deviant behaviour, Maslow's approach was to consider the factors concerned with the ultimate goal of 'self-actualisation' in terms of a hierarchy. He initially proposed that the individual would endeavour to meet the needs within each level sequentially. However, he recognised that in reality individuals would often be trying to meet the needs within different levels simultaneously. From the viewpoint of buyer behaviour the essential point of the theory is the realisation that there are different classes of need and the main focus of individuals will depend upon their individual circumstances.

The theory recognises that individuals have limited needs for existence. Thus, at the most basic level, human needs are physiological and concerned with sustenance (food and drink), recuperation (sleep) and procreation (sex). The theory then proposes that individuals who are able to satisfy these physiological needs will seek to make their situation more secure by trying to satisfy their 'safety' needs, which involve physical protection, ensuring continuity of supply of the basic physiological needs, and the physical well-being of health and fitness.

Individuals who have satisfied these second level 'safety' needs will then tend to focus upon satisfying what are defined as the 'social' needs – love, friendship, status and esteem. Again, once these seem to be satisfied the focus moves to what have been defined as the 'personal' needs – achievement, self-esteem, fun, freedom.

The fifth level represents self-actualisation. Maslow saw this as a goal which, for most people, was easily abandoned due to social pressures and other priorities. It provides a link with other self-actualisation theories but is considered of little relevance to buyer behaviour so is usually omitted in this context. The variety of needs defined by Maslow is usually summarised in what is known as the Maslow hierarchy of needs (*see* Fig. 5.3).

The different values attributed to the levels can be used when selecting product benefits. In particular, it has been found that effective advertising messages are often those which appeal to the most appropriate need level. For example, Procter & Gamble found the appeal 'Keeps your baby dry and happy' was more effective than 'Saves you time and trouble' during the initial promotion of their Pampers disposable nappies. In terms of the Maslow theory this can be explained on the basis that the first message appeals at a higher level (the social needs of the mother) than the second, which appeals at the physiological level (the need for rest).

EXERCISE

Take any newspaper colour supplement and see how many of the advertisements can be rated in terms of the Maslow need level to which they are designed to appeal. Clearly some cannot be graded on this basis since they are designed to provide information rather than draw attention to a need or want.

Since one of the main functions of marketing is to ensure that product offerings meet the needs of potential customers, it is clearly essential that great care is taken to understand as fully as possible what these needs are likely to be. Maslow's theory of

Fig. 5.3

THE MASLOW HIERARCHY OF NEEDS

Achievement
Self-esteem Fun Freedom

Personal needs

Friendship
Love Status Esteem

Social needs

Physical protection
Well-being Health Fitness

Safety needs

Sustenance
Recuperation Procreation

Physiological needs

motivation not only provides a framework which sometimes can be useful for doing this, but also shows that whereas needs can be defined relatively simply they are likely to be expressed as very much more complex and diverse wants.

Consider someone who is thirsty. If that person is climbing in the Pyrenees the need for a drink might be completely met by spring water drunk from cupped hands. To meet the same need while at the Ascot races the same person is likely to want to drink champagne from a crystal glass. The basic need is the same, but in the second case the want recognises the additional needs of meeting the expectations resulting from being part of a social group and perhaps the self-esteem that comes from doing the 'right' thing. The late Rajiv Gandhi earned great respect from the people of India by recognising that his need was the same as every villager and always drank the local water when travelling in rural areas.

The Maslow and other theories of motivation (such as Alderfer's ERG theory (Existence Relatedness and Growth Needs), which is an alternative to Maslow but one which accepts that a hierarchy might not exist, or Herzberg's two-factor theory) are well known and considered relevant in the context of both human resource management and marketing. They are useful for identifying categories and patterns of human needs yet can easily be used to justify the conclusion that 'everyone is different'. Indeed, this is the view taken in Schein's model of 'Complex man' which asserts that:

> Human needs fall into many categories and vary according to the stage of development and total life situation. These needs and motives will assume varying degrees of importance to each person creating some sort of hierarchy but this hierarchy is itself variable from person to person, from situation to situation and from one time to another.

While in itself it is of little help to someone trying to solve a specific marketing problem, this does provide a framework for analysing individual buyer behaviour.

PERCEPTION

Individuals literally receive, or sense, information through the five senses: sight, hearing, smell, touch and taste. Perception is the process by which this information is selected, organised and interpreted to produce messages and meanings. As a psychological process, perception is a key prerequisite for information processing and learning. As such, it is of interest to marketers for the influence it can have on consumer decision making generally, and on the way it can affect antecedent factors such as the reception and understanding of marketing communications.

Not surprisingly, as a person-specific psychological process, perceptions vary somewhat from person to person, even in relation to common stimuli (e.g. in marketing terms, a TV commercial). Psychologists attribute such individual differences in perception to the combined effect of three perpetual sub-processes: selective attention, selective distortion and selective retention.

● *Selective attention* refers to the means by which people make sense of a mass of stimuli by screening out less meaningful or relevant messages, and editing in stimuli that are somehow personally appropriate, attractive or noticeable (note that visual cues such as shape, colour and movement may have a role here, hence their interest to marketing communications specialists).

- *Selective distortion* describes the process by which, consistent with a particular and personal mind-set, individuals will distort information received in order to make it fit their preconceptions, existing beliefs and values.
- *Selective retention* refers to the tendency for people to retain or memorise only a selection of messages they receive. Usually this selection will be those that are personally meaningful, or deemed to be more supportive of their existing attitudes and beliefs, rather than information at variance with these (which may be distorted anyway by selective distortion).

These three sub-processes help to explain why perception can be highly selective: people see (or hear) what they want to see (or hear). Given such distortions, it is perhaps more understandable why marketing communications need to be well supported by research, and sometimes presented in bold, concentrated bursts in order to break through such perception barriers.

EXERCISE

Consult any magazine, journal or newspaper and identify a selection of advertisements that appear to be designed to counter, or exploit, perceptual distortions that may occur within the target group. Identify possible distortions, and the way the advertisements relate to these.

LEARNING

Learning refers to consistent changes in an individual's responses as a result of experience, or related changes in the context or pattern of personal memory. Most human behaviour is said to be the product of learning, and so it is highly probable that learning shapes much of the purchase and decision-making behaviour that consumers demonstrate. Like perception, learning involves information-processing, and is in turn a major influence on people's beliefs and attitudes.

Research into learning indicates the process of learning as dependent on factors such as stimuli, responses and reinforcement. Stimuli can be internal (e.g. a strong inner drive or need) or external (e.g. a cue such as an advertisement or display, or some associative reminder). Responses may be any action (e.g. purchase) or decision (e.g. a resolution or intention), whether positive or negative (e.g. non-purchase, postponement). Where responses are rewarded by positive feelings and experiences, reinforcement occurs.

This reward-reinforcement process learning theorists term operant conditioning, involving reward through a new stimulus or object (e.g. a free sample of a new product). Learning through reinforcement also occurs through classical conditioning (e.g. Pavlov's dogs), where positive associations are developed with an existing experience (the bell at feeding-time) e.g. the association effect of exciting music, visual effects, personality testimonies. So-called cognitive learning takes place without reinforcement, while vicarious learning involves learning through the experience, or example, of others. Clearly, learning is a highly complex process, still very much the subject of ongoing research. However, it is almost equally clear that learning, in various forms, may play a significant part in consumer behaviour, for example in the association-reinforcement effects of marketing communications (everything from packaging design to corporate communications efforts) on the 'supplier' side, or the effects of learning through product usage and conditioning, on the buyer side.

PERSONALITY

Personality is the unique psychological make-up of individuals that conditions their behaviour generally, and their responses to particular stimuli and situations. Over the years, researchers have developed a variety of measurement batteries, usually termed personality profile inventories, that measure an individual's personality characteristics (or traits), often calibrated along a two-pole scale, e.g. extrovert–introvert, sociable–nonsociable, dominant–subservient, etc.

A major complication with personality research derives from the often complex and confounding differences, and resultant disagreements, among the various schools of theory within the field. Psychoanalytic theory, still strongly associated with Freud, emphasises deep-seated impulses and influences through the unconscious mind. Trait theory, most notably associated with Jung's revisions of Freudian theory, lays emphasis on measuring personality factor (trait) combinations. Other schools of thought focus on social and environmental influences on the individual's personality – hence the continuing nature versus nurture debate in psychology. Some of the theoretical contributions to research have been piecemeal aspects of personality explanation, though useful in their own right, e.g. Maslow's concept of 'self-actualisation'.

An interesting and related concept, that of the 'self-concept', refers to the image people have of themselves, and in turn that which they would wish others to have of them; clearly, advertising themes appear to make various appeals to generalised portrayals of self-concept 'ideal' stereotypes. A comparable notion, that of 'brand personality', has for some time attracted the attentions of marketers and advertising specialists alike. Basically, the interest has lain in investing in a brand a set of associations, similar to the traits (characteristics) that make up a personality. Obviously, the brand associations selected for portrayal would need to be validated by prior research as salient and attractive, among sampled target group respondents. In summary, the detailed research studies into personality as a determinant of buyer behaviour have produced mixed results. While intuitively personality appears to have great potential influence on consumer behaviour, it does, almost by definition, pose major methodological problems in research. Indeed, some commentators (e.g. Lastovika *et al.*, 1988) argue that instrument error or measure unreliability may account for many of the non-significant research findings in the field, rather than absence of a real link with personality variables. As if by consolation, the more recent developments in psychographics, which borrow freely from personality constructs, do appear to promise results, especially through their linkage with product use and demographic variables.

DEMOGRAPHIC FACTORS

Buying decisions often depend upon a person's demographic profile. Within this any of the following variables can be relevant to an individual buying decision.

1 *Age* There are many needs which are age-dependent, for instance baby food for the very young; mobility aids for the very elderly.

2 *Stage in life cycle* Furniture purchases are likely to be more dependent upon stage in life cycle than age.
3 *Occupation* More formal clothing is probably purchased by white-collar workers.
4 *Economic circumstances* Many products are dependent upon perceived discretionary income, e.g records, theatre tickets, books.
5 *Lifestyle* This may increase the need for minor luxuries such as champagne as an alternative to, for instance, car ownership.

THE SOCIAL INFLUENCE VARIABLES

The following social factors will also affect buying decisions made by individuals:

1 *Family background* Political views, how education is valued, etc.
2 *Reference groups* Explained below, in terms of aspirational and dissociative reference groups.
3 *Roles and status* Relative to the product being considered.

The significance and the relevance of reference groups to buying behaviour varies widely according to the type of product being purchased; in particular, whether the product is a necessity or a luxury and whether the product is consumed in private or in public.

Primary reference groups are those groups to which the person is considered to be a full member. Of these the most important is likely to be the immediate family, groups of close friends and co-workers. Primary reference groups are of particular importance with respect to purchases which directly affect the other members of the group – for example, holidays.

Secondary reference groups are those within which contact is more formal and less continuous, such as those resulting from membership of professional associations, trades unions, religious organisations or as a result of where you live or work. Status within such groups is not necessarily automatic so purchases which may imply status within this type of group are likely to be affected by the expected attitude to the product selected. Menswear could, in general, be considered in this category.

Aspirational groups are those of which the purchaser would like to be considered a member. There is an implied association, however unrealistic, in owning the same brand of tennis racket as a favourite tennis star. The importance of this can be judged, at least in part, by the keenness with which manufacturers wish to sponsor these public heroes. In contrast, dissociative groups are those with which one would prefer not to be associated.

In addition to the factors already mentioned the impact of reference groups on an individual buying decision will depend to some extent on the degree of risk perceived in the purchase decision. This factor is also likely to affect the way by which the buying decision is reached.

Within the context of the family, as might be expected, the degree to which a buying decision is made by either a husband or wife as individuals or shared between the partners has been shown to depend upon the type of product involved. Research undertaken by Davis and Rigaux in Belgium suggested that the decision-making roles of husbands and wives could be classified as in Fig. 5.4.

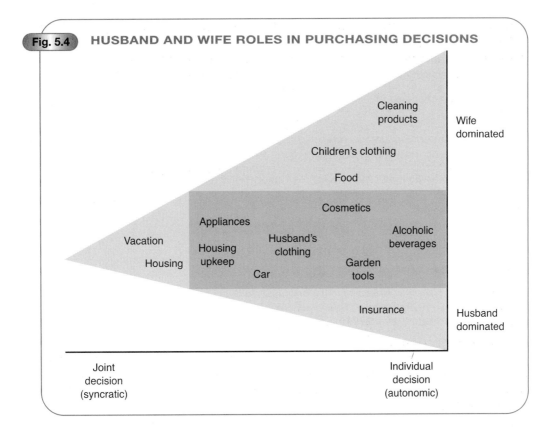

Fig. 5.4 HUSBAND AND WIFE ROLES IN PURCHASING DECISIONS

CONCLUSION

Buyer behaviour provides some valuable insights which can be applied usefully in many marketing situations. It also provides a framework, concepts and a vocabulary which can be used to analyse many marketing issues.

The complexity of the subject, however, is such that it cannot realistically be used prescriptively since it is likely to raise more questions than it answers. There is at least some circumstantial evidence to suggest that attempts have been made to apply these concepts in political campaigns both in the USA and the UK with little apparent success. This should not be seen to devalue the usefulness of the approach, but rather to emphasise the complexity of the marketplace and the need to make marketing decisions on the basis, at best, of an incomplete understanding of this evolving research field.

Readers interested in pursuing in more detail particular aspects of consumer behaviour are recommended to consult the specialist text on consumer psychology produced by Foxall and Goldsmith (1994), or the consumer behaviour texts of Chisnall (1994) or Engel, Blackwell and Miniard (1993).

QUESTIONS

1 Identify a product which is more appropriate to the 'self-esteem' needs as suggested by Maslow, rather than the more basic needs of a customer.

2 Consider a purchase you have made recently and identify the factors that influenced your decision to buy.

3 What do you consider is the role of consumer magazines such as *Which?* or *What Computer?* in influencing buyer behaviour?

4 How might a knowledge of buyer behaviour theory be of use within
(a) selling; and
(b) product design?

FURTHER READING

Assael, H. (1992) *Consumer Behaviour and Marketing Action*, PWS-Kent Publishing, Boston.

Chisnall, Peter M. (1994) *Consumer Behaviour*, 3rd Edn, McGraw-Hill, London.

Engel, J. F., Blackwell, R. D. and Miniard, P. W. (1993) *Consumer Behaviour*, 7th Edn, Dryden Press, Chicago.

Foxall, G. R. and Goldsmith, R. E. (1994) *Consumer Psychology for Marketing Managers*, Routledge, London and New York.

Lastovika, J. L. and Joachimsthaler, E. A., 'Improving the detection of personality-behaviour relationships in consumer research', *Journal of Consumer Research*, March 1988.

Peter, J. P. and Olson J. C. (1990) *Consumer Behaviour and Marketing Strategy*, 2nd Edn, Irwin, Homewood, Illinois.

Solomon, M. R. (1995) *Consumer Behaviour*, Allyn & Bacon, Boston.

CASE STUDY

Polar Electro Ltd

Polar Electro Ltd is a hi-tech electronics company located near the city of Oulu in Finland. It is the world's leading manufacturer of heart-rate monitoring, registering and evaluation equipment. The company was founded in 1977. The business idea of the company is based on many years of R&D. This research has led to numerous internationally patented inventions and new products covered by the POLAR trademark and design copyrights. Though the company still only employs some 200 full-time staff, in Finland and abroad, the sales of its monitoring products have shown impressive growth, especially in the prime markets of North America and Europe. Exports now go to over 30 countries, and the company has established sales offices in Germany and New York, with contract assembly operations in Hong Kong.

Marketing in target countries is generally handled by authorised importers and retailers, though in some major markets direct sales are also achieved through company-managed catalogue operations.

At first, the technology developed by Polar Electro Ltd was used as a means of optimising the quality and efficiency of athletics training. Due to continuous customer-orientated product development, the company now features a selection of heart monitoring products for everyone interested in physical exercise. Goal-orientated physical fitness enthusiasts can, for example, improve their marathon performance with the help of a heart-rate monitor. Weight reduction can be optimised through a combination of proper diet and regular exercise at the correct heart rate. The basic heart-rate monitor consists of two parts; a heart-rate transmitter worn on a belt around the chest and a watch-like monitor on the wrist. The measuring method is ECG accurate and the monitor itself is user friendly and suitable for any kind of exercise, including swimming.

The business rationale of Polar Electro Ltd is based on the idea that people want to be in a good physical condition, which leads to good mental health, too.

While marketing arrangements necessarily vary across national markets, company experience indicates that purchase behaviour within markets varies somewhat across buyer groups or user segments.

Questions

Given your understanding of the buyer behaviour process, consider the particular variables and influences that might affect buying behaviour, within any national market known to you. To what extent, for example, might perception, attitude formation and learning processes affect purchase behaviour among Polar Electro's product users? As a related question, what buyer groups or segments might be identified, and how might they vary in buyer behaviour terms?

(Written by Anna-Maija Lämsä, Oulu Business School, Oulu, Finland.)

CHAPTER 6

Organisational Buyer Behaviour

No man is an Iland, intire of itselfe; every man is
a peece of the Continent, a part of the maine.
John Donne

INTRODUCTION

As the term implies, organisational buyer behaviour is literally concerned with the processes involved in buying within the context of formal organisations. These organisations have a legal identity in their own right, and will usually have specific resources and procedures with which to conduct all activities within their remit. Specifically, buying and sourcing products and services will usually be managed as a separate activity in support of organisational objectives. A practical definition of organisational buying is:

> **The decision-making process by which formal organisations establish the need for purchased products and services, and identify, evaluate, and choose among alternative brands and suppliers.** (Kotler and Armstrong, 1995)

As the earlier history of marketing is more closely associated with consumer markets, it is perhaps not surprising that only in more recent times has an interest developed in analysing organisational buyer behaviour. Earlier contributions to the field were made by specialist writers on industrial buying, such as Fisher (1976) and Wilson (1968), and it is only more recently that the study has been redefined within the context of its essential 'organisational' focus, through an emphasis on analysing the decision-making dynamics of buying, as but one aspect of organisational activities. Indeed, there is still some confusion and ambiguity among marketing theorists in respect of the boundaries and elements of organisational buying behaviour, since some writers appear to 'fudge' the issue by wrongly using industrial buyer behaviour and organisational buyer behaviour interchangeably.

For semantic clarity, it will be proposed that industrial buyer behaviour be seen as a subset of organisational buyer behaviour.

Further, terms such as industrial marketing, business marketing and business-to-business marketing are best treated as somewhat separate, as particular marketing subfields, where usually the focus is on marketing/promotion activities undertaken by the supplier, as opposed to the distinct buyer focus that is central to the study of organisational buyer behaviour. The whole point of such a buyer focus is that it provides a means of improving our understanding of how the buying process works within organisations. In organisational settings, buying is often subject to different and more complex influences than is the case with consumer markets. The following section will examine some of these key differences.

SOME DISTINCTIVE CHARACTERISTICS OF ORGANISATIONAL BUYING

1 *Organisational purpose* Organisational buying is usually directly related to the ultimate purpose and objectives of the organisation itself. Buyers have to justify purchases in these terms, even in cases where organisational objectives appear to conflict, e.g. where profit motives are inconsistent with market service or innovation, say, at the level of a particular product or new initiative. Indeed, it is the resolution of such factors that often makes for the complexity of organisational buying situations, making for extended problem-solving routines, protracted negotiation and consultation procedures. Goods and services bought by organisations are therefore not selected for themselves or for personal gratification, as in consumer markets, but for their contribution to the wider delivery/production activity served by the organisation. In this sense, all purchases by the organisation are intermediate objects, inputs to an ultimate organisational purpose.

2 *Derived demand* Leading from the above characteristic, it follows that goods and services bought by organisations are subject to a derived demand, literally derived from the demand for the final products or services that they deliver. The implication of this relationship is more than academic, since in practice it makes for lagged and sometimes sudden changes in demand, in response to even moderate changes in the demand for final (= consumer) goods and services. This is the accelerator principle of macroeconomics, where, for example, a 5 per cent change in consumer shoe sales may be 'accelerated' back along the supply chain, leading perhaps to a 25 per cent fall-off in the raw materials orders placed by footwear manufacturers.

3 *Concentrated purchasing* Organisational purchases tend to be more concentrated, for a number of reasons. Formal requirements planning by organisations, combined with the management of stockholdings and careful administration of budgets, tends to make for discrete bundling of purchases and bulk-ordering against volume concessions. Larger industrial customers, though statistically in a minority, may dominate consumption in many markets for intermediate goods; while larger organisations generally tend still to display preferences for centralised purchasing and purchase approval policies.

4 *Direct dealings* As a generalisation, organisational buyers will more commonly deal direct with suppliers, rather than through intermediaries or third parties. Exceptions will be found, though, as in the case of multilayer wholesaler–retailer markets, industrial supply houses, and procurement agencies serving government bodies, such as the Crown Agents in the United Kingdom.

5 *Specialist activity* Increasingly, organisational buying has become more specialist, in parallel with the growth of purchasing itself as a professional management activity. Unlike consumer markets, therefore, organisational buying will usually be conducted, or at least assisted and directed, by full-time professionals, who are usually

up-to-date and well-informed on market, product and trading conditions, and not uncommonly are specialists in a particular product-market field. Moreover, where executives responsible for purchases are not themselves professionals, they will often be able to call on a range of expertise through professionals both within and outside the organisation.

In line with the specialist nature of organisational buying, there will usually be a degree of formalisation that ensures that professional and legal standards are adhered to (e.g. Health and Safety legislation provisions), and organisational policies and managerial controls are heeded.

6 *Multiple purchase influences* In common with many other managerial functions, buying within organisations tends to be an activity subject to group decision-making influences, across a number of interested parties, departments and functions within the organisation. While the principles of co-ordination and good communications would provide for some sharing of decisions, or at least consultation, other factors will also reinforce this. Of some significance will be the need to formally gain authority for purchases, while heavier expenditures or new ventures may represent major risks, which may be better shared, or assessed, through group consensus.

DIFFERENT ORGANISATION TYPES

Though organisational buyer behaviour is used as an umbrella term to cover buying within all organisations, it is both conventional and helpful to identify a general classification of organisational types that display broadly similar buying characteristics. Figure 6.1 presents such a typology.

It should be noted that the four broad types of organisation identified in Fig. 6.1 are general categories which could be further broken down into subcategories. For example, the first category could be subdivided into industrial manufacturers and primary producers, such as mining companies and agricultural producers. For simplicity, this subdivision has not been attempted. Notwithstanding this, some commentary on each of the categories will serve to show the diversity of buying behaviour to be met with in practice.

Industrial producers, typified by manufacturing companies, will usually display the most professional treatment of the buying task. Buyers, or purchasing executives, will usually be professionally trained and qualified, commonly working within a separate department, itself organised into specialist sections and tasks, e.g. dealing with specifications, contracts, quotations, forecasting, costing and progress-checking. Price and cost issues are likely to be less significant buying criteria on their own, since quality, performance and delivery issues are more likely to be seen as yardsticks of value. While for some manufacturers a concern for competitiveness and continuity of supplies will lead to the use of a number of suppliers, even for the same component (= multiple sourcing), other companies will seek competitive improvements through concentrating buying through fewer suppliers, or ultimately through one supplier (= single sourcing). Increasingly nowadays, the combination of cost competition, continuous quality improvement and quality standards accreditation (e.g. BS 5750, ISO 9000), and collaborative arrangements, has made for a dependence by manufacturers on fewer and closer supplier links. These circumstances have made for the conscious development of closer vertical links and partnership relationships between manufacturers and their chosen suppliers, under the banner of supply-chain management. Such strategies, inspired originally by the much-vaunted successes of Japanese companies, have centred on the application of systems thinking to achieve 'supply-chain integration' in order to eliminate waste and duplication, and reduce costs and delays within the supply chain.

To illustrate, the approach involves the application of a combination of methods such as electronic data interchange (EDI) for ordering, transport and invoice documentation, preplanned stock replenishment techniques, just-in-time (JIT) parts deliveries, and establishing joint user-supplier quality improvement teams. Properly managed, such partnership strategies promise key competitive advantages for each party. However, management of these relationships is by no means simple and uncomplicated, and demands a great deal of trust and information exchange. Indeed, a recent report based on research by UMIST and the management consultancy A. T. Kearney (1994) points to the risks and complications involved, proposing that companies customise relationships to different ends and different levels in the supply chain.

Among primary producers, agricultural producers will often have buying requirements that are subject to a range of outside influences, from government-supported subsidy schemes and financing-taxation concessions, to the various services offered by farming cooperatives and associations, agricultural merchants and advisory bodies. The cohesiveness that is often identified among farmers as a group may also act as a powerful word-of-mouth influence on equipment purchase and use, as more generally on farming practice.

Fig. 6.1 | A TYPOLOGY OF ORGANISATIONAL BUYERS

Organisational type	Examples	Common buying features
Industrial and producer organisations	Industrial manufacturers, agricultural producers	Quality delivery critical Specialist buyers Reciprocity Vertical linkages common
Commercial and reseller organisations	Retailers Wholesalers Banks and commercial services	Resale margins critical Discounts and volume deals Credit/financing terms Preferred suppliers Specialist buyers
Government and public sector organisations	Central government, municipal authorities	Strict budgetary controls Planned purchasing Competitive tendering Formalised procedures
Institutions	Colleges, hospitals, independent bodies	Budget constraints General management professionalising

Reseller organisations such as retailers and wholesalers will generally undertake purchases only for selling-on to an identified market. While they do not generally physically alter the products they handle, they will seek to add value through service. Aside from their stock-in-trade purchases of a range of products for resale, they will also make use of bought-in or contracted services (e.g. distribution, repair services), and will periodically undertake major capital investments for service enhancement, refurbishment, branch growth and resiting. Their purchase decisions in respect of traded goods will be dominated by commercial criteria such as bought-in costs and resale price, profitability (= margins), sales potential and related measures of commercial viability (e.g. stock turnover, sales per square metre, seasonality). Terms of trade (price, delivery, discounts) will be subject to hard negotiation and trade-off between competing suppliers, seeking to establish for the reseller an optimum market position that offers both profit potential and resale customer appeal. The larger retail organisations, with an increasingly dominant position in consumer markets, wield a formidable bargaining power that is matched only by the largest manufacturing suppliers. In recent years some of the more successful retail groups, such as Marks & Spencer and Sainsbury's, have taken the lead in developing stronger partnership links with preferred suppliers. Such a strategy bears comparison with the growth of partnering linkages among industrial manufacturers, noted earlier.

Government and public sector organisations probably exhibit the most formality in their buying behaviour. Certainly traditionally, their approaches to purchasing, as in all external dealings, have been highly conservative and slow-moving, often subject to labyrinthine red tape and committee stages, rules and procedures that call for the utmost perseverance on the part of would-be suppliers. However, there are signs that public sector purchasing is now becoming more professional and commercially driven, in response perhaps to the general containment of public sector expenditure almost everywhere, moves towards privatisation and the gradual professionalisation of public sector management itself.

Institutions such as colleges, hospitals, voluntary organisations and the like show through their buying behaviour many parallels with the public sector. Though difficult to generalise, it is probably true to say that purchasing has traditionally been a semi-formalised activity that is seen, as with many a managerial function, as subsidiary to the main purpose of the organisation. Again, as with government organisations, recent external influences and policy changes, such as funding constraints, reorganisations and changes in corporate status, have made purchasing both more professional and competitive, certainly within many western economies.

A MODEL OF ORGANISATIONAL BUYING BEHAVIOUR

A logical and useful approach to studying organisational buying behaviour is to employ a simplified model of the influences and processes involved. Though no model can realistically encompass all the complexities to be met across different organisational types and situations, modelling is certainly effective in 'mapping out' the more significant and typical factors at work within a field of study. As testimony to this, marketers have developed in recent years a number of both specialist and general models of organisational buying, some of which will be referred to later in the chapter. For present purposes Fig. 6.2 represents a simplified model of organisational buying.

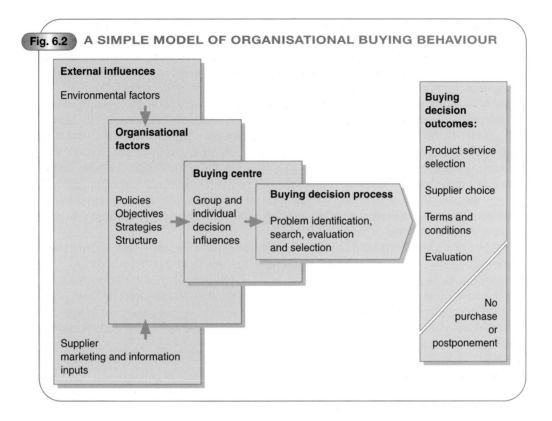

Fig. 6.2 A SIMPLE MODEL OF ORGANISATIONAL BUYING BEHAVIOUR

The model illustrated in Fig. 6.2 presents a flow-diagram representation of organisational buying behaviour, outlining the more readily recognised influences, decision sequences and outcomes involved. These will now be examined in further detail.

External influences

These consist of both the general environmental factors that affect buying behaviour, and those particular marketing contacts and information inputs that come from suppliers and prospective suppliers.

General environmental influences consist broadly of the STEP (Social, Technological, Economic, Political) factors that were identified as macroinfluences in Chapter 3. It is worth noting, though, that the effect of these influences on the *buying* function may be somewhat different from the pull they exert on the *marketing* side. The challenge for would-be suppliers is therefore to take account of such contrary effects, within the marketing programmes that they design for organisational buyers.

Social and cultural environmental influences are likely to affect organisational buying in more subtle and indirect ways, over time. For example, the nature of interpersonal dealings and relations, even in business settings, will gradually change as social norms change. However, some organisations, particularly government bodies and community-based organisations (such as schools and hospitals) are likely to work to a mission and purpose that is more explicitly concerned with social issues, values and norms, e.g. in respect of buying for a wider, more diverse customer base.

Technological factors are no less potent influences on purchasing behaviour within organisations than in other organisational functions. The classical example of technology changes affecting buying requirements would be the challenge facing manufacturers in keeping abreast of technology developments within their industry, and in seeking competitive improvements through technology-led solutions.

Manufacturing organisations with a serious policy commitment to innovation and to technology leadership, and related advances in quality and cost competitiveness, will usually be highly discriminating in their choice of suppliers, insisting that they keep pace in terms of these key issues. Once proved, such buying relationships may graduate further into more permanent partnerships and strategic alliances, offering the provision of mutual advantages through greater competitiveness and accelerated technology transfer, in both directions. Such strategies have now become integral to the search for global competitiveness in industries such as automobile manufacturing, aerospace and electronics.

Stuart (1991) and Dyer and Ouchi (1993) demonstrate the potential strategic and competitive benefits of such partnership approaches, while Magrath and Hardy (1994) consider the means by which companies might seek to develop such relationships. On a somewhat more cautionary note, though, Kalwani and Naryandas (1995) observe that the long-term benefits of such relationships may not be equally shared by the partners, given that major organisational buyers will often have a bargaining power advantage over individual suppliers.

On a perhaps more modest scale, it is interesting to note comparable buyer–supplier strategies being adopted by leading retailers, with the effect of 'locking in' suppliers through common technology, service and quality improvement standards.

Economic factors will have a powerful effect on purchasing behaviour within all organisations. Where major investment in facilities and plant are concerned, a number of economic criteria will be considered, including interest rates and financing charges, capacity lead-times and staff availability, cost inflation projections and other general indicators of the economic outlook. These factors will also influence everyday purchasing behaviour, certainly in terms of affecting general volumes of demand, budgetary limits, and the need for economy and added value.

Political and legal issues will also come into the picture, both directly and indirectly. Direct influences will be seen through the workings of legal restrictions, standards and codes of practice, e.g. in respect of competition law, professional and industrial standards and guidelines. These influences will affect organisations in the private and public sectors alike. Less directly, issues such as social responsibility, ecological awareness and public accountability will affect purchase behaviour, particularly within those organisations that are sufficiently far-sighted and politically aware to incorporate policy guidelines on such matters.

Marketing and information inputs

The purchasing and sourcing process depends heavily on collecting and assimilating various types of information, of direct and indirect relevance to the task in hand. Knowledge and updating on the environmental factors influencing buying will usually filter through to buyers through the organisation's policy and planning functions, through research and information specialists, professional and trade press sources, head office bulletins, consultancy reports and the like.

More specific information on particular procedures and services and the capabilities of prospective suppliers will come through the deliberate search efforts of buyers themselves, or through contact with supplier companies. For simplicity, these information inputs might be divided into supplier sources and third party sources, as illustrated in Fig. 6.3.

It should be noted that a number of the 'third party' information sources used by buyers will be in-house sources, involving key users and decision makers, budget-holders, technical advisers and the like. This underlines the significance of group buying decisions, and introduces the role of a buying centre or group, which will be examined in more detail shortly.

It should also be noted that information sources involve both personal and impersonal contacts. Unlike many consumer markets, organisational buying offers suppliers the opportunity to make effective use of personal contact with buyers, subject to staff and resource constraints. Given that word-of-mouth information sources will often be seen by buyers as more credible, suppliers will usually seek to ensure some regular personal contact with buyers, and other key influencers within the organisation.

Organisational Influences

Like any other managerial specialism or function, purchasing is subject to the organisation's general policies, objectives and strategies. As noted earlier, it is this tie that makes organisational buying more deliberate and specific than buying within consumer markets. While many of the major policies and objectives of an organisation may be very general and broad, they will nevertheless affect the buying task, for instance in respect of the need for cost-effectiveness, justification for returns on expenditure, and the standards of managerial performance to be expected. Further, particular policies may be followed that directly affect purchasing, e.g. 'Buy Local' preferences, multiple sourcing, buying policies to support small or local companies, and so forth.

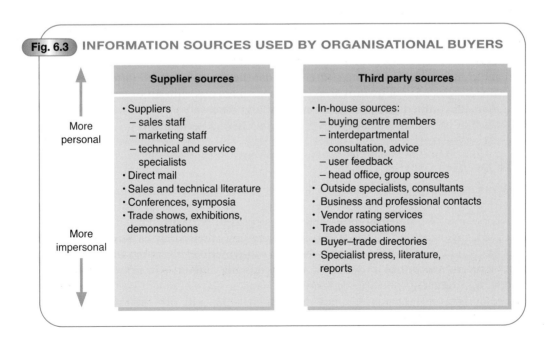

Fig. 6.3 INFORMATION SOURCES USED BY ORGANISATIONAL BUYERS

Supplier sources	Third party sources

• Suppliers
  – sales staff
  – marketing staff
  – technical and service
    specialists
• Direct mail
• Sales and technical literature
• Conferences, symposia
• Trade shows, exhibitions,
  demonstrations
	• In-house sources:
	  – buying centre members
	  – interdepartmental
	    consultation, advice
	  – user feedback
	  – head office, group sources
	• Outside specialists, consultants
	• Business and professional contacts
	• Vendor rating services
	• Trade associations
	• Buyer–trade directories
	• Specialist press, literature,
	  reports

More personal ↑

More impersonal ↓

Again, most of the apparently 'general' policies and objectives pursued by an organisation will inevitably have some impact on buying patterns, once incorporated into an annual business plan, with accompanying budgets, forecasts and deadlines. A prime example of such an effect would be the implications for buying from the planned development and launch of a new product or service offering. Effectively, such a venture would call for a specific launch plan, with budgets and target dates, for a number of functions, including buying.

Again, selected business growth or improvement strategies are likely to have direct influences on the buying task. For example, a total quality management strategy would probably have far-reaching implications for buying, from renewed supplier vetting and selection procedures to perhaps a total overhaul of all existing contracts, buying relationships and control procedures.

Indeed, the increasing adoption of quality certification systems such as ISO 9000 continues to exert a major influence on the whole supply chain, from purchasing to after-sales provision, across a spread of both manufacturing and service sectors. In terms of marketing, Ferguson (1996) demonstrates how suppliers can seek competitive advantage through quality registration, and additionally derive worthwhile efficiency gains through better business systems and organisational improvements.

Buying will also be affected by more everyday aspects of organisation such as the rules, systems and procedures employed within the task, staffing levels, departmental organisation and task division. In structural terms, the degree of centralisation imposed by top management may significantly affect the buying function. Centralised management policies will make for more formalised buying procedures that allow less buying autonomy below certain levels in the hierarchy. Obviously, supplier marketing and sales staff would need to be aware of such policies, and to plan their customer contacts accordingly.

Kohli (1989) proposes that, as a strategic response to the variability in such local circumstances, suppliers would be well advised to adopt a contingency approach throughout their marketing endeavours. A similar accommodation of situational factors is proposed by Patton (1996), who demonstrates through a US-based research study that vendor selection decisions within industrial buying can vary considerably according to the evaluative routines and models utilised, and across a range of contextual vehicles. St John and Young (1991) consider the extent to which differences in the agreed strategies of various functions and departments, within an organisation, may lead to major conflicts and problems generally, and especially in the context of 'shared' tasks such as particular (perhaps high profile) purchasing decisions.

The buying centre

Whether or not an organisation has a separate purchasing department, buying will to a greater or lesser extent represent a group-based task, the focus of multiple decision influences from a number of individuals and key executives within different functions across the organisation. Therefore, though purchasing officers may be involved in most purchases, and usually formally progress and implement final buying decisions, they will by no means control or dominate the key buying outcomes in respect of supplier selection, product specifications, terms and conditions. These will be the subject of shared decision making among a buying centre, the make-up of which will likely vary according to the type of purchase and the buying task itself. It is this variability, in group make-up and roles, that adds the essential dynamic to organisational buying, and that poses for suppliers a continuous challenge in their marketing efforts.

Buying centre membership may vary between and within purchase decisions, over time, and between different organisations. For example, a recent US study of different industrial companies found an average buying centre to consist of between 2.7 and 5.1 individuals (McWilliams, Naumann and Scott, 1992), though these limits may appear low if a broader range of influences were to be thoroughly considered.

Webster and Wind (1992), from their research work on organisational buying, identify five broad roles, and associated buying influences, within the buying centre, comprising:

1 *Users* – those using the product or service, perhaps administrative or operational staff, or their supervisors.
2 *Influencers* – those influencing key product attributes and criteria, or specifications, through perhaps technical expertise.
3 *Deciders* – those with the authority to select the product or supplier. For high-ticket purchases these are less likely to be purchasing executives alone.
4 *Gatekeepers* – those controlling and directing relevant information flows internally, and contact with outsiders such as suppliers. This role could be taken, or shared, by buyers, administrative, secretarial or technical staff.
5 *Buyers* – typically, purchasing executives charged with administering and progressing the buying task.

It should be stressed that these roles are not necessarily formal or assigned; rather they constitute the effective contribution of different individuals, which is often unplanned. It is another example of the reality of the informal organisation, and is perhaps a fitting reminder that organisations are social entities in which people inter-actions prevail.

It is worth noting that the decision authority within the buying centre may change according to the type of buying decision and task under consideration. Fisher (1976) proposed that decision leadership would be influenced by both product complexity and the commercial uncertainty of the purchase decision. He argued that, other things being equal, high product complexity would call for technologist lead roles, while high uncertainty would be a cue for leadership by policy-makers. Alternatively, a low rating on both criteria might leave decision making to purchasing executives, while a combination of complexity and uncertainly would make for multidisciplinary group decision making.

A more widely accepted framework is that originally proposed by Robinson, Faris and Wind (1967), identifying three different types of buying decisions, or 'buyclasses':

1 *New task* New purchase propositions where the organisation has no previous experience and therefore requiring careful search procedures, extended problem solving and shared decision making.
2 *Straight rebuy* Routine, low-risk, low-involvement repeat purchase decisions with standard information requirements and little shopping comparisons beyond working from a listing of predetermined 'vetted' suppliers. Here, the 'plurality' of the purchase decision may be minimal.
3 *Modified rebuy* A hybrid of the two previous situations, where, for example, there is a record of supplier experience and dealings, though product-design advances make for some re-examination of buying criteria, technical standards and the like. Here, new dimensions of the purchase decision, for instance design changes, may call for the involvement of relevant specialists such as engineers, technologists and accountants.

As noted before, membership of any buying centre may be a moving population, with individuals coming and going even during the life of one purchasing episode, while at any time there may be a number of overlapping centres or groups, dealing with different purchase requirements and tasks. Such a situation can make the supplier's marketing and selling task highly complex, since the target group for promotion and sales contact resembles a moving target. Staying on target demands of the supplier perseverance, up-to-date information and intelligence, and good communications abilities at different levels.

A further imponderable can be the dynamics of interaction within and across the buying group. While organisational goals and policies will be followed by all members of the group, *individual influences* will be evident, making for conflicts and delays, swings of direction and occasionally even wholesale revisions of the buying agenda.

As an illustration of these individual influences, certainly each 'active' member of the buying centre will behave differently according to their training and experience, their formal position and departmental agenda, as well as more subjective factors such as age, social background and personality. Psychological factors such as perception, motivation and attitudes (e.g. to risk) may therefore become as active in this context as they are within consumer buying situations. We could add yet a further layer of complexity by considering the *interplay* of these individual influences, through group deliberations involving occasional obstacles of personal chemistry, professional rivalry and even power politics.

As observed, some purchasing episodes will involve a number of functional specialists from across the organisation, which in turn introduces the dynamics of inter-departmental relations, and the territorial tensions and 'tribal' alignments that may exist, even within medium-sized single-sector companies. An interesting issue here is the extent to which purchasing tasks and decisions are devolved, as formal policy, to user functions or departments, formally centralised, or more informally shared through inter-disciplinary group working. Stuart (1991) comments on the need for effective teamwork within and across functional groups, in the interests of decision-making outcomes optimal to the whole organisation.

The buying decision process

Though a simplification, it is useful to envisage the buying decision-making process as a six-stage sequence, similar to the problem-solving framework sometimes applied to complex consumer purchases. The six stages comprise:

1 *Need identification* This can come through a number of channels, perhaps through an annual review/plan exercise, a sudden requirement for replacement, a new product, or as a by-product of another programme, such as a quality initiative. It can also come through outside influences, perhaps 'triggered' through successful supplier communication and presentation efforts, or through trade or professional sources, or some combination of these.

2 *Establishing specification* This is a logical refinement of the first stage, where relevant buying centre members such as users, or influencers in technical or development functions, jointly or separately provide information and guidance on the framing of a set of specifications that meet the needs identified. For more technical problems, a number of alternative designs and technologies may be considered before an agreed specification is produced.

3 *Search activity* This involves identifying possible products and suppliers that can meet the needs identified in the specification. Buyers are likely to undertake this search process, perhaps aided by other buying centre members such as gatekeepers. Search activities may range across contacting existing supplier 'accounts', new suppliers, perhaps on recommendation, working through information sources in trade directories, buyer guides, exhibitions, etc. Sometimes the process will be iterative, involving returning to and reworking the specification stage, perhaps in the light of new information or new perspectives on a solution. Such iterations may bring previous group participants back 'on-stage', or introduce new ones.

4 *Evaluation of alternatives* Identified suppliers and products will be evaluated, both in technical/operational terms, and in respect of price, delivery and capacity issues and service capabilities. A number of buying centre members will be involved in such evaluations, including purchase executives, technical and accounting staff.

5 *Selection and ordering* A natural follow-on from stage 4, involving choice of some supplier(s) and product(s) to meet the specification. Certainly for major purchases involving significant expenditure with high-risk and long-term commitments, this stage will likely be subject to formal approval, at director or committee level, supported by a comprehensive proposal outlining costs, investment 'payback' details, delivery, service and warranty arrangements and so forth. New task purchases, and some modified rebuy decisions, will also be subject to such formal authorisation. In these situations, the buying specialist's role will be more one of co-ordinating and administering, subject to the selections made by deciders. Obviously, straight rebuy situations will rarely involve such formal approval, nor all of the stages identified.

6 *Post-purchase monitoring* Here, product and supplier performance will be monitored and periodically reviewed, the need for future changes noted where necessary, and remedial action taken on particular problems, e.g. in delivery, quality, warranties. These activities will formally be the responsibility of buyers, assisted as necessary by user feedback and technical advice.

The above sequence of decision making is highly generalised, and would be much simpler for routinised repeat purchases, which probably account for many of the purchases made by the average purchase executive. In these situations, orders would be placed and confirmed by the buyer against standard sampling and inspection procedures, with much less involvement of other parties. However, for modified rebuys and new task situations, the above sequence may be understated, and the total activity may involve quite protracted meetings and face-to-face negotiations, involving many other buying group members.

Buying decision outcomes

Purchase decision outcomes will translate into orders and contracts specifying selected products and services, and their suppliers, with detailed terms and conditions in respect of price, discounts, delivery and service expectations.

Though straight purchases are most common, some transactions will involve non-ownership options such as lease or rental arrangements, which may be more appropriate in terms of capital outlay, tax advantages or budget planning. Where contracts are entered into, further decision variables would concern the contract period, trial or introductory periods, legal provisions for discontinuation, cost escalation and penalty factors, and precise details of service performance.

Finally, for a variety of reasons, the decision outcome may lead to non-purchase, total abandonment of a proposal, or at best postponement or a resolution to start afresh on a somewhat different proposition.

CONCLUSION

Clearly, organisational buying behaviour is a highly complex subject that defies total explanation through the kind of simple model that has been developed here. Nevertheless, modelling the process is a useful insight into the interactions involved. For a more detailed examination of some of the specialist models on the subject, the reader is referred to the theoretical and industrial buyer behaviour model of Sheth (1973), or the more empirical perceived-risk model developed by Newell (1977), or the general model of industrial buyer behaviour developed by Webster and Wind (1992).

QUESTIONS

1 Consider the possible differences in the way that buying decisions might be undertaken within (a) a small manufacturer; (b) a large multinational; (c) a local authority secondary school and (d) a private hospital.

2 Compare and contrast consumer buying behaviour with organisational buying behaviour.

3 For any company or organisation with which you are familiar, identify by occupation the people who might perform the following roles for a specific purchase: (i) gatekeeper; (ii) decider; (iii) influencer.

4 In what ways might risk affect organisational buying at the level of (a) the organisation and (b) the individual buyer?

5 Identify one major trend within organisational purchasing and consider its implications for marketing practitioners.

FURTHER READING

Dyer, J. H., Ouchi, W. G., 'Japanese-style partnerships: giving companies a competitive edge', *Sloan Management Review*, 1993, pp. 51–63.

Ferguson, W., 'The Impact of the ISO 9000 Series Standards on Industrial Marketing', *Industrial Marketing Management*, Vol. 25, No. 4, July 1996.

Fisher, L. (1976) *Industrial Marketing*, 2nd Edn, Business Books, London.

Kalwani, M., Naryandas, N., 'Long-term manufacturer-supplier relationships: do they pay off for supplier firms?', *Journal of Marketing*, Vol. 59, January 1995, pp. 1–16.

Kearney, A. T., 'Partnership or Power Play?' Report by A. T. Kearney, Management Consultants, July 1994.

Kohli, Ajay, 'Determinants of influence in organisational buying: a contingency approach', *Journal of Marketing*, July 1989.

Kotler, P. and Armstrong, G. (1995) *Principles of Marketing*, 4th Edn, Prentice-Hall.

Magrath, A. J., Hardy, K. G., 'Building Customer Partnerships', *Business Horizons*, pp. 24–27, Jan–Feb 1994.

McWilliams, R. D., Naumann, E. and Scott, S., 'Determining buyer centre size', *Industrial Marketing Management*, February 1992, pp. 43–49.

Newell, J., 'Industrial buyer behaviour', *European Journal of Marketing*, Vol. 11, No. 3, 1977.

Patton, W. E., 'Use of human judgement models in industrial buyers' vendor selection decisions', *Industrial Marketing Management*, Vol. 25, Issue 2, March 1996.

Robinson, P. J., Faris, C. W. and Wind, Y. (1967) *Industrial Buying and Creative Marketing*, Allyn & Bacon, Boston.

Sheth, J., 'A model of industrial buyer behaviour', *Journal of Marketing*, Vol. 37, No. 4, 1973.

St John, C. H., Young, S. T., 'The strategic consistency between purchasing and production', *International Journal of Purchasing and Materials Management*, Vol. 27, pp. 15–20, Spring 1991.

Stuart, F. I., 'Purchasing in a R & D environment: effective teamwork in business', *International Journal of Purchasing and Materials Management*, Vol. 27, pp. 29–34, Fall 1991.

Webster, F. E. and Wind, Y. (1992) *Organisational Buyer Behaviour*, Prentice-Hall, New Jersey.

Wilson, A. (1968) *The Assessment of Industrial Markets*, Cassell, London.

CASE STUDY
RBR Consultants

RBR Consultants is the recently-formed consultancy subsidiary of a long-established provincial accounting firm, Rollings, Bensham and Ratcliffe (RBR).

The parent company, RBR, operates from a Head Office base in Leeds, its place of origin, with three district practice offices, located in Manchester, Nottingham and Newcastle-upon-Tyne. While the firm has grown rapidly in recent years, it still does not count among the 'top ten' league, and it is still heavily dependent on a client base north of a line between the Severn and the Wash.

The desire of the senior partners to grow through development in the Home Counties and the South, has been a prime consideration in the formation and geographical location of the new management consultancy arm, RBR Consultants. Located on the M4 corridor in Reading (Berkshire), within easy distance of London and the South-East 'head office' belt, the new venture has been conceived as a means of taking the RBR 'flag' southwards, and in doing so capitalising on a rapidly expanding service market, consultancy. The early strategic rationale of the venture has been to offer management consultancy to new (and hopefully larger) corporate clients, who may subsequently be enlisted as accountancy clients by the main RBR organisation. Ultimately, therefore, the Reading office is destined to serve as a dual-purpose base, for consultancy and for the southward extension of the main accountancy practice.

Initially, a team of six RBR consultants will operate from the Reading office, nominally covering the whole country but treating the South as the prime target territory. The consultant team, which has just been selected, will comprise two individuals offering financial consultancy, three general business consultancy providers, and one marketing consultant. Two of the team – a marketer and a general management consultant – have been recruited from small consultancy firms, while the other four are RBR accountants on secondment from the parent base. In time, more consultants and specialisms will be taken on, depending on market growth.

Simon Herrington, the senior of the seconded accountants and the appointed manager of the consultancy team, has made an enthusiastic start in recruiting office staff, through a local secretarial bureau, and booking an early meeting with a Reading advertising agency, in his words: 'to loudly announce the arrival of RBR as the new kid on the block within the regional consultancy circuit'. Pointing to an estimated UK consultancy market worth in excess of £3000m in fees (based on RBR Leeds HQ estimates), he is quite optimistic about the prospects for RBR Consultants: 'It clearly looks like business is done in this market just like our home accounting field – clients are impressed with professionals that work to high standards. I'm sure all corporate 'buyers' the world over are discriminating and sensitive to quality and standards. Quite frankly, with the RBR name behind us we should be able to open a number of board-room doors'.

By contrast, Jane Harris, the newly recruited marketer on the consultant team, finds herself privately at odds with such sweeping generalisations. From her own first-hand experience in consultancy, she is convinced that client buying decisions are highly complex, and the product of dynamic interpersonal, interdepartmental and hierarchical influences and interactions within the client organisation. Furthermore, with recently increased competition from new entrants to the field [RBR is not a lone pioneer], she feels that winning client contracts now involves higher thresholds of performance and persistence, and certainly a keen understanding of the nuances of Organisational Buyer Behaviour.

Question

With reference to the above comments made by Jane Harris, consider the relevance of the principles of Organisational Buyer Behaviour theory to a company such as RBR Consultants.

CHAPTER 7

Customers, Market Segmentation and Targeting

Divide et Impera (Divide and rule)
Ancient political maxim cited by Machiavelli

INTRODUCTION

While marketing as a business philosophy makes the customer central to the objectives of an organisation, it is the concepts of marketing which have been developed from this philosophy which have made marketing so relevant to business and other organisations.

The marketing concepts provide the basic principles and framework within which appropriate decisions can be made by any supplier who wishes to ensure that exchanges made with consumers or customers are mutually beneficial. It is a basic precept of marketing that this must be the principal objective of any supplier who wishes to thrive in a dynamic competitive environment such as is usual today.

It is said, that a product is not sold until it has reached the ultimate consumer; in fact we could go further and say it is not sold until it is paid for and used by the final consumer. It is only then that there is any possibility of selling further products to that customer.

In the 1950s the pioneers of mass-marketing, multinational firms such as Procter & Gamble and Coca-Cola, had the power to sell large quantities of standardised goods to a 'homogeneous' mass market, using the promotional attraction of mass media (national press, and especially television). Even earlier, Henry Ford made his fortune by mass-marketing, offering his Model 'T' car in 'any colour as long as it is black'. Now things have changed in the marketplace. Coca-Cola now offer caffeine-free, diet, cherry and other variants which combine some or all of these attributes. Ford make cars from the Fiesta to the Granada in a host of finishes, colours and specifications. At a basic level this could be seen just as an increase in the variety of products offered, but of course the cause of this proliferation is to attempt to meet customer needs more precisely.

If marketing is the satisfying of the needs and wants of customers, then those wants must at least be established, even if they are found to be different for every single consumer. This fact recognises that customers do not always form a homogeneous group, nor are the demands of two, outwardly similar, people necessarily the same. However, you will remember that marketing really involves 'profitable or beneficial exchanges', so, as part of the marketing decision process, there must be a view on which customer groups are to be supplied. If different customers have different needs then why not offer them different products to meet those needs? And why not market those products in a way that appeals best to each particular group?

In Chapter 5 it was suggested that the buying decisions of consumers should be linked to relevant characteristics associated with individual buyers, e.g. baby foods are bought by new mothers, or business suits are purchased by white-collar workers. These examples already illustrate how some specific groups could be more likely to buy a particular product than another group. It is, of course, sometimes difficult to identify those people who prefer a red car rather than a black car, but these preferences certainly do exist.

WHO ARE OUR CUSTOMERS?

Before an organisation can make any decision associated with marketing a fundamental question must be answered: 'Who are our customers?'

One way to answer this question would be on the basis of Table 1.1 (see p. 9). This could well be a good initial approach, but it is unlikely to provide an answer which would be useful as the basis for making marketing decisions.

Another approach would be to use the behavioural criteria identified in Chapters 5 and 6 as being relevant to buyer decisions. The identifying of the different groups, and so subdividing the market into those groups which can be addressed by a specific marketing strategy, is termed segmentation. Its objective is to select from all possible potential customers those groups which are most likely to need and want to buy a product. The use of different marketing strategies for each distinct segment is known as target marketing, or differentiated marketing (see Fig. 7.1).

Each of these different strategies is likely to appeal to very different groups of customers. Consider the type of people who buy food in a delicatessen shop compared with those who regularly shop at a discount food store such as Kwiksave or Aldi. Even if some people use both outlets, the motivations for the visiting of such very different stores will enable those shoppers to be distinguished from those who visit only one of the outlet types mentioned.

This chapter looks at the identification of segments and the benefits of focusing on these segments. It also covers the criteria necessary for a segment to be useful to a marketer.

USEFUL SEGMENTATION

The basic principle of segmentation is very simple. It involves selecting the classification most appropriate to the groups of customers identified. The work involved in doing this is justified only if it can be used to improve marketing effectiveness. To meet this objective the resulting segments must be relevant to the purchase decision, and also capable of being reached by both distribution and communications with some measure of precision.

The traditional approach uses variables which can be described as geographic and/or demographic. Much of the data collected by the various UK media owners is quoted in terms of the socio-economic groupings shown in Table 7.1.

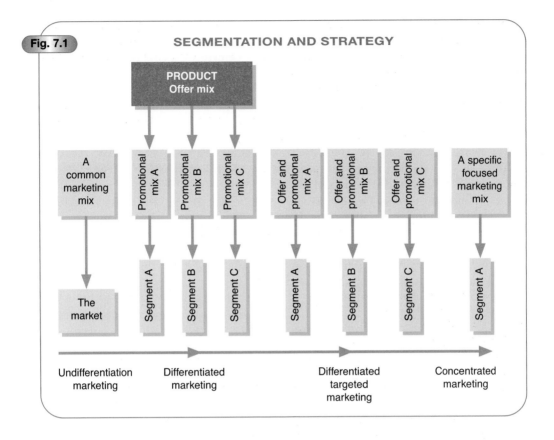

Fig. 7.1 SEGMENTATION AND STRATEGY

There are many potential problems when using a scale derived from the occupation of the 'head of the household' to determine how people behave. Anyway, the descriptions above are already outdated, using terms such as working class. The classification is also made less easy to use by the changing social order, for instance the move away from the traditional 'husband, wife and 2.4 children' household that prevailed when this classification was started. Now most homes contain either one or two people, and the traditional family group described above represents anything but a majority of homes.

Table 7.1 ● Market segmentation by socio-economic groupings

A	Upper Middle Class	High managerial/administrative/ professional, e.g. company director, or established doctor or solicitor
B	Middle Class	Intermediate managerial/administrative/or professional
C1	Lower Middle Class	Supervisory/clerical/junior managerial
C2	Skilled Working Class	Skilled manual workers
D	Working Class	Semi-skilled or unskilled workers
E	Pensioners, casual workers and others	

(*Source*: JICTAR)

A longitudinal study by Kirk McNulty looked at the changing face of UK society. He based his categories on the Maslow hierarchy discussed in Chapter 5. The study shows that his 'inner directed' groups are expanding as a percentage of the population, while other groups decrease.

Inner direction covers:

1 *Social resisters* Caring people; altruistic, green, and likely to join pressure groups.
2 *Experimentalists* Fun seekers, materialistic, pro-technology and individualistic.
3 *Self-explorers* Share social concerns, not materialistic, motivated by self-expression.

All these groups are defined in terms of Maslow's self-actualisation category. These groups make their own decisions and can afford to do so. As the size of these groups increase there will be more fragmentation of traditional markets, and more opportunities for marketing to ever smaller target groups.

Similar groups have been identified in the USA by studies such as the VALS (Values and LifeStyle) research. This classifies consumers on the basis of self-orientation and resources. It is a commercial classification which has proved very popular with major US advertising agencies (*see* Fig. 7.2).

The problems in finding a usable way of describing a segment do not mean that the concept of marketing segmentation is not useful. There are too many examples of successful target marketing which can be found. In fact the industrial product sector is a good example where the organisational characteristics (demographic and geographic, such as type of company, size, industry, etc.) can be successfully linked with personal characteristics of personnel who might be: users; influencers; buyers; deciders; or gate-keepers. By identifying how to reach a group of 'deciders' a positive marketing result can be achieved, as in the example below.

EXAMPLE

A campaign to communicate with the financial controllers of companies with large transport fleets was undertaken by a major tyre company. The company realised financial controllers were a key 'advisor' group and in some cases held the 'decider' role. They were primarily interested in the lowest total cost of operation, not just the cheapest tyre. They could be reached directly, and a campaign was directed at them, emphasising areas they considered important rather than issues important to the transport manager. It proved successful in boosting sales levels.

Returning to the consumer market, another useful set of segments is the ACORN grouping (A Classification Of Residential Neighbourhoods). This is a variation on traditional demographic descriptors, developed in a way that makes communication with this segment easy. It is sometimes termed geo-demographics, as it links postcodes (in Britain or other host countries) to the prime characteristics of the occupants of the households. In the UK a total of 38 groupings has been produced, so that a marketing organisation or other user can buy a list of all addresses in a particular category – say, all postcodes which have a majority of 'private flats with single pensioners' (category K38). A mail shot to this segment offering them a relevant product will have a greater

Fig. 7.2 VALUE AND LIFESTYLE CATEGORIES (SRI INTERNATIONAL)

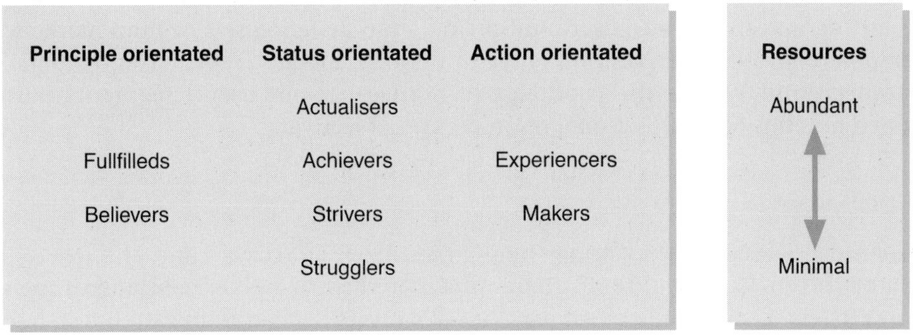

Principle orientated	Status orientated	Action orientated	Resources
	Actualisers		Abundant
Fullfilleds	Achievers	Experiencers	
Believers	Strivers	Makers	
	Strugglers		Minimal

success rate than a more random method of contacting this group. Alternatively, a company could collect all the addresses and postcodes of its customers. By analysing these against the ACORN database the predominant categories can be established and plans laid to communicate with other potential customers in the same categories.

Such an exercise can prove very rewarding, but it does not assume that all people in the same postcode groupings behave in the same way. Compare your family with your own neighbours. The use of ACORN does assume, and can demonstrate, that the probability of similarities exist. This is enough to make the database valuable to marketing managers. There are other rival databases such as MOSAIC, PINPOINT and PROFILES, offering similar services.

REQUIREMENTS FOR A USABLE SEGMENT

There is no limit to the numbers of ways a market may be segmented in particular circumstances, but to be useful a segment must be:

- definable;
- sizeable;
- reachable;
- relevant.

Definable

This means we must be able to describe the market segment, and for this the key characteristics of the segment should show a degree of homogeneity. The segment is of course a subset of a heterogeneous total market, because if the total market were homogeneous there would be no need for segmentation. It is also useful to be able to measure the market size and define the boundaries of the segment.

Sizeable

Is the segment large enough and can it produce the required turnover and profit for your organisation? This criterion depends on the particular organisation, as a minimum revenue of £10m for a brand sold by a large multinational might be required, while another company might find £0.5m an acceptable contribution to turnover. So size is relative, but organisations also need to make profits. Toffler suggests that markets are 'de-massifying' into ever-multiplying, ever-changing sets of mini-markets that demand a continually expanding range of options, models, types, sizes, colours, and customisations. That is the challenge of marketing, but useful segments must be assessed in terms of organisational resources and objectives.

Reachable

There must be a way of reaching the segment both effectively and efficiently. This includes the obvious physical distribution of a product, as well as communicating with customers via media or in a direct way. ACORN meets the communication test, but it is less easy to find a way of communicating with categories such as the 'experimentalists' or 'self-explorers' described by McNulty.

Relevant

This has already been mentioned as the most important test for any described segment. It cannot be considered in isolation from the other criteria as there is no point in describing a relevant segment which cannot be reached. Wilson (1994) introduces a number of criteria by which marketers may make the sometimes difficult choice between identified market segments. The criteria he outlines range from segment durability (or life cycle) and segment price level to customisation costs (including entry investment) and the extent of overlap or interdependency with other segments. On a somewhat different issue of segment selection, Reed (1996) observes that a number of companies are attempting to practice ever more accurate target marketing, even at the cost of customer deselection through screening criteria. While such approaches depend critically on data accuracy and marketing logic, they hold out the promise, if successful, of reducing costs, concentrating purchases and increasing the impact of promotions such as loyalty schemes.

The message of this section is that, although segmentation can be an effective marketing technique, it should be treated carefully. In the era of de-massification, organisations can easily appeal to segments which are too small to be viable or perhaps too costly to reach. While segmentation can help in the process of understanding customer similarities and differences, careless use could lead to the development of too many product variants, confusion of customers, and the failure to capitalise on the real opportunities that such a study of markets and their subsets offers.

SEGMENTATION VARIABLES

In order to describe segments there are two different approaches which can be used. The first concentrates on the characteristics of the buyer. Generally these are classified under one or a combination of the three categories:

- demographic;
- geographic;
- psychographic.

However, an alternative, but equally powerful, set of variables can be derived, offering a focus on how customers behave, and the benefits sought by those customers from a product or service. While benefits link closely with lifestyles and psychographics, they do warrant attention as a separate category for classification. So the other two categories are:

- benefit; and
- behaviourial segmentation.

Demographic segmentation

Demographics is the most widely used method of classification of marketing segments. It is the basis for the collection of many government statistics and the standard system used by the media industry. Pym Cornish of RSL, who is an acknowledged authority on demographics, wrote:

> Demographics are often thought of as consisting of no more than the dimensions of sex, age, social grade, region, and a few others that have traditionally been used as a standard market research variable in Britain. But society does not stand still. It has evolved; old generalisations about the family, such as that women look after the house and children while men earn the money, have become less and less true. Yet this does not mean that demographics have become less useful, only that the traditional classifications should be superseded by others that reflect the current structure of society more accurately.

So, based on Cornish's article, the traditional demographic bases are: gender, age, marital status, socio-economic classification and occupation. To these we must add descriptors such as family type and size, income levels, ethnic origin, education levels and stage in life cycle. The last factor was described in more detail in Cornish's article.

For industrial products there are equivalent demographic categories which can be used, such as industry type (SIC – Standard Industrial Codes), turnover and/or profit, numbers of employees, and numbers and types of customers.

Such demographic data are relatively easy to obtain. Every ten years in the UK there is a full census of the population, so that government statistics can be updated. This does not cover issues like lifestyle in great depth, but it does provide a good basis from which to start. Many organisations use census data as a basis for decisions on market potential. The type of information provided is called secondary data, in that it is collected for one purpose but it is then used for a secondary one. The sources of secondary data are discussed in Chapter 8 and Appendix 3. It cannot be stressed too often that the information collected must be relevant to the purchase decision.

The categories which are actually relevant can change, as in the example of Red Stripe lager. This Jamaican lager was originally imported into Britain from the Caribbean. Its price reflected the cost of importing, and it was primarily sold to areas with a high population of Jamaican origin. The brewers, Desnoes and Geddes, then arranged for the product to be brewed under licence in the UK. While they were very careful to maintain the distinctive quality of the lager, it was decided that the price could be modified, and there were opportunities for appealing to a wider number of drinkers. Hence ethnic origin is no longer such a relevant demographic variable for this product.

However, stage in the life cycle does affect consumption of beers and lagers. As people move through the stages of pre-family, family and post-family they change their drinking habits. Also, some people remain single, or form a relationship but do not marry or have any children. They, too, show changes in drinking according to life cycle. Life cycle is more powerful than age alone in this analysis, as it is able to include relative levels of disposable income and, equally important, leisure time, which a family with children finds is in short supply. Of course the traditional variables do help in describing segments as, for instance, men drink more beer than women, and there are differences identified by socio-economic groups (*see* Fig. 7.3). In order to describe their customers the major brewers use a combination of demographic data with other bases such as lifestyle (as distinct from life cycle, which is not the same).

One very full database which covers demographic profiles and also other bases is the TGI (Target Group Index), produced by the British Market Research Bureau. BMRB is a commercial organisation which carries out 3000 interviews every month and continually updates information on the several thousand brands and product categories covered. It offers purchasers of the index detailed demographic and lifestyle profiles of consumers. It also covers the media which reach the various segments, and is an invaluable source of information linking consumer product segments to the media usage. Geographic segmentation. This type of classification is often considered as another type of demographic variable. In some ways it is, and the development of geo-demographic bases such as ACORN prove this. Nevertheless it is an obvious grouping, and geographic variables can be considered separately. Issues, such as rural versus urban, warm versus cold, north versus south, all can be considered where appropriate. The consumption of sweet (sugar-based) products is greater in Scotland than in the rest of the UK. Is this perhaps useful information when planning a new confectionery product?

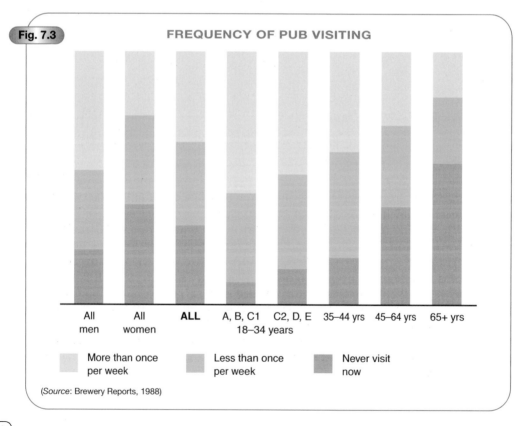

Fig. 7.3 FREQUENCY OF PUB VISITING

All men · All women · **ALL** · A, B, C1 · C2, D, E · 35–44 yrs · 45–64 yrs · 65+ yrs
18–34 years

More than once per week · Less than once per week · Never visit now

(*Source*: Brewery Reports, 1988)

There are also opportunities for the commercial market, such as planning new retail outlets. One company might look for a location in the key area bounded by outlets such as Marks & Spencer, Boots and W. H. Smith, which provides the greatest density of shoppers in many town centres. Another trader might base decisions on the number of suitable customers living within a specific radius or travelling a distance from the centre of a city. Both are dependent on geographic segmentation studies.

It might be appropriate to add a warning regarding large, apparently attractive segments. These naturally attract competitors and may not provide the anticipated level of business. There are many small shops serving a limited geographic area without direct competition and making a reasonable profit. If the business were located in the High Street of a major town, the competition would change the situation, such that although the numbers of potential customers is far greater, the actual custom may not be, and the increased costs involved would decrease profitability.

Psychographic and lifestyle segmentation

Psychographics seeks to classify people according to their personality traits. They are used more in relation to consumer products, but there is no reason why corporate interests, such as a measure of levels of social responsibility, could not be used when considering issues relevant to the segmenting of organisations. There is some debate over whether psychographics should be restricted to issues of sociability, self-reliance, assertiveness and other personality traits, or whether it should be widened to include lifestyles, which cover attitudes, interests and opinions. This book will follow the conclusions of Weinstein in considering psychographics to be a combination of personality traits and lifestyles. The bringing together of these factors from the two areas provides a more useful and robust segmentation base.

The use of lifestyle characteristics is attractive to the marketer for two reasons. First, it provides a simple link to the variables used in behavioural theory, e.g. attitudes, perception and social influences. Second, although lifestyles can change over time and over the life cycle of a person, there tends to be a consistency of action in selecting products and services which matches the 'persona' of a consumer at a particular period.

To establish psychographic characteristics, a series of questions are developed and respondents are asked to agree or disagree with statements such as: 'I like to do all my car maintenance' , 'Traditional home cooking is best', or 'I worry about environmental issues'. Thus scales are developed from a battery of questions, enabling a detailed picture of attitudes and lifestyle to be constructed. A fuller exposition of the market research procedures required to construct these segments can be found in most standard marketing research texts.

The results of a demographic analysis of whisky drinkers might show they are primarily: class – AB; sex – male; age – 45 plus. A lifestyle study of this category shows it is not homogeneous, and there are many other spirits consumed by the segment, but it could identify key attitudes of those who drink whisky rather than gin. This can then be applied to the product promotion (*see* Chapters 15 to 17).

In 1974, an early article on 'The concept and application of lifestyle segmentation' by Plummer identified the following list of subjects on which questions could be posed in lifestyle studies. This list shows the scope of such studies.

Activities	Interests	Opinions
Work	Family	Themselves
Hobbies	Home	Social issues
Social events	Job	Politics
Vacation	Community	Business
Entertainment	Recreation	Economics
Club membership	Fashion	Education
Community	Food	Products
Shopping	Media	Future
Sports	Achievements	Culture

In an interesting and practical application of psychographic segmentation, File and Prince (1996) analyse the influence of lifestyle, personal motivations and family circumstances on the purchasing attitudes and behaviour among the CEOs of industrial family businesses.

Benefit segmentation

The idea of segmentation on the basis of the benefit received is wholly consistent with the marketing concept. A motor car purchased as the main or only one for a family will provide a very different benefit from a company car supplied to a single employee, or a car purchased as a second car for a spouse. The benefits received are different and thus the actual car bought will be assessed by very different criteria. Using benefit segmentation these factors can be isolated and this information used to design appropriate products for each group.

In the USA there is a good example of a successful cost/focus strategy based on benefit segmentation, the US hotel chain, La Quinta, which offers a specific product for business travellers. La Quinta have above-average size rooms and good quality construction to ensure minimum external noise in any room. They provide a fast, efficient check-in/out system and certain business facilities required by travelling business people. They are conveniently located on major roads but do not offer restaurants or food service. There is always a 24-hour restaurant nearby if required, but not run by the hotel. La Quinta concentrate on providing a value package for a particular segment, mainly commercial travellers, who require facilities to do an evening's work after a day of meetings, but do not require on-site eating. A restaurant is expensive to run and so why provide it if the benefit it provides is not required? A similarly focused development in the UK is exemplified by the no frills, inexpensive tariff, overnight hotels being built by the Trust House group on sites close to their Little Chef restaurants.

Benefit segmentation depends on causal relationships rather than descriptive criteria of segment members. It is as applicable to industrial products or services as to consumer goods and services. In fact some products span these categories. For instance, a portable calculator could be a consumer item for use by a student, or an industrial product if used in an accounts office. An electrical maintenance service can be offered to a commercial organisation or a private home. A service situation such as this provides the maximum flexibility in target marketing, since each contact between supplier (electrician in this case) and customer is distinct, and the delivery of the service is inseparable from the production. Hence the supplier can provide a precise service to match the benefit required.

In other situations the product is not offered to a discrete segment. An aeroplane could contain passengers who have:

(a) bought tickets at full price;
(b) bought discount tickets in advance (APEX); or
(c) bought even cheaper standby tickets or 'bucket-shop' offers.

All groups receive the same prime benefit – air travel to their destination. But the problem regarding full-fare business travellers has been tackled by providing 'Club' or 'Business' class as distinct from 'economy' class. Nevertheless, some passengers buy full economy fares, others are discounted. The difference in benefits, such as ability to change times of travel if you hold a full-fare ticket, compared to the possibility of not travelling at all with a standby, illustrate the wider range of benefits which must be explored for the same marketing offering.

Benefit segmentation was popularised 25 years ago by Russell Haley, who studied the toothpaste market in the USA. He identified four groups (*see* Table 7.2). From such an analysis, it can be seen how different brands can be designed to meet each of the benefit segments identified above.

Table 7.2 ● **An example of benefit segmentation in the toothpaste market**

	Benefit required	*Other characteristics*
Sensory segment	Flavour + product appearance	Usually children
Social segment	Sound bright teeth	Outgoing and active, young (sometimes also smokers)
Worrier segment	Decay prevention	Heavy users, families
Independent segment	Low prices	Predominantly male, little loyalty, bought brand on offer

Behaviourial segmentation

A development of psychographic segmentation which concentrates on lifestyle and attitude is to study how people behave with respect to purchasing a particular product. The most obvious approach is to study usage rates and brand loyalty. Questions that can be answered include ones such as, 'How do heavy users differ from light users?', 'Can we isolate brand-loyal consumers?' If we can identify usage levels and link this to other segment criteria, then differentiated marketing strategies can be adopted for each group. Such groups could be:

- heavy users (say every day);
- medium users (maybe once a week);
- light users (say once a month);
- occasional users;
- non-users:
  - never used brand
  - lapsed users of brand.

Inevitably a version of the Pareto effect will apply. Perhaps eighty per cent of a company's sales will go to twenty per cent of its customers (heavy users). The temptation is to concentrate on these people, as they provide the bulk of the profitable sales. In fact, they need a marketing mix that retains and reinforces their custom. This will probably be very different from the message to occasional or light users, who may either purchase competitors' products or perhaps not use the product category very often.

Other behaviouristic criteria include:

- loyalty levels;
- purchase occasion;
- user status;
- readiness status.

Purchase occasion is an obvious discriminator with buying behaviour, and therefore should be considered when carrying out a segmentation study.

The behaviour of purchasers buying, say, beer or lager will vary between orders in a public house, occasional purchasing from an off-licence, or regular purchasing as part of a shopping trip. The same is true for an ice cream purchased during the interval in a theatre, where prices of more than £1 are not uncommon, and bulk purchase in a freezer centre where the same £1 could buy a box of 4 individual ice creams.

Dickson went further, linking purchase situation with benefits to fill what he termed 'person-situation: segmentation's missing link'. This work is just one example of linking criteria together to provide usable segmentation to assist marketing decisions.

Hahn et al. (1996) present their findings on a contemporary study of market segmentation based on brand loyalty and purchase behaviour within low-share products within a consumer market.

A direct marketing organisation subdivides its mailing list by what they term the 'customer pyramid' (see Fig. 7.4). The customer pyramid is one form of measure of readiness to buy, where each requires a different approach from the supplier. Another way of looking at readiness is the AIDA sequence discussed in Chapter 1. Customers need to progress from Awareness through Interest to Desire and Action. This progression could take time, and behaviour will be different for potential customers in different stages of this continuum.

TARGET MARKETING

The five principles of good marketing practice identified in Chapter 1 are: targeting; positioning; interacting; controlling; and monitoring relationships with customers.

Target marketing is the process of selecting one or more market segments and then developing a *product and offer* which is aimed specifically at those segments.

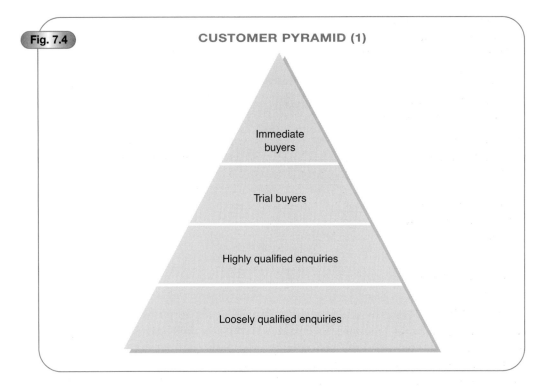

Fig. 7.4

CUSTOMER PYRAMID (1)

Immediate buyers

Trial buyers

Highly qualified enquiries

Loosely qualified enquiries

Once the target market segments have been identified, the key attitudes of those customers towards the product category should be determined. It is thus clearly essential to define market segments using appropriate criteria.

Writing in *Admap*, Adam Lury, the controversial Chairman of a UK advertising agency, stated, 'Demographics tell me nothing I want to know'. He argues that the world has changed fundamentally and it is no longer true that you can lump together all manual workers and consider their common wants. He gets very close to a 'product orientation' when he says, 'Brands and businesses must be themselves, and let consumers come to them by self-selection'.

As an example he cites the Body Shop as a company that set out what they believed in, and let customers come to them. This is, of course, a good example, but there are many unheard of examples of companies which are out of business because their products did not appeal to a sufficiently large segment of customers. Clearly there must be a link between the customers in the segment defined, their attitudes, and product wants. This is the basis of target marketing.

Target marketing is the link between segment selection and product positioning (*see* Fig. 7.5) which is discussed in Chapter 9. Target marketing is the opposite to undifferentiated marketing. This is where the same product is offered to the entire market. Undifferentiated offerings can succeed, but it is usually more effective to offer a variation of the product to suit each relevant market segment. This is especially true in global markets, where major differences of culture and history can also divide potential customers.

Fig. 7.5 TARGET MARKETING CONTINUUM

As an example, Mars, the chocolate company, feature only men in their promotional material in Saudi Arabia because of the Arab views on showing women. This is an example of differentiated marketing where the basic product is the same but the marketing mix is varied. Target marketing develops this further, including the total marketing mix with variations to the total product offered. Japanese car makers now claim they can personalise a car with regard to so many features that it is possible for every customer to buy a unique product. This could be the ultimate in personalisation, an extreme example of target marketing, and a long way from Henry Ford's bold claim of 'Any colour so long as it is black'. Using modern flexible manufacturing systems, an increasing number of suppliers will be able to define specific target market segments and interact with these ever more precisely.

Companies providing services have always been able to offer personalised products, since the provision of the service is inseparable from the production. Because of this, service products are inherently liable to variations depending upon the individual who actually provides the service. This is why service organisations such as banks, or the McDonalds fast-food restaurant chain, pay so much attention to supplying a standardised range of products. This approach helps to maintain consistency in the quality of service given, and to reduce the risk of the organisation's reputation being destroyed by a single incidence of poor service, as may happen if this attracts the attention of the media.

COMPETITIVE ADVANTAGE

The earlier chapters describe how customer needs and wants can change, making existing products obsolete. For example, a competitor may launch a new product which a particular group of customers find more attractive. Because of this, organisations must continuously revise their products or services to keep them relevant to the changing needs of customers.

This involves returning to the fundamental marketing questions:

- who are our existing and potential customers?;
- what are their current and future needs?;
- how do they judge value?;
- when and where can these customers be reached?

Those responsible for products already on the market need to continually ask these basic questions. For example, after being successfully developed on the 'pile it high, sell it cheap' philosophy of its founder, Sir Jack Cohen, the operation of the Tesco supermarket chain was reviewed when Sir Ian McLaurin became chairman. He changed the 'product' by radically revising the groceries and provisions stocked. He discontinued 'Green Shield' stamps and changed the pricing policy. He closed down many older stores and developed new, larger sites with much improved layout. The advertising featured food quality, especially fresh fruit, vegetables and meats. The new Tesco was aimed specifically at the 25–35 age group, seen as a relatively affluent sector of food shoppers. This strategy has succeeded. Tesco is now generally considered an equal rival to Sainsbury's both with respect to the quality of their products and the high market share achieved. This has resulted in a dramatic improvement in both sales and profits for the company. Developments such as these are going on all the time, and they show the importance of marketing that is sensitive to the external environment.

INTERNATIONAL SEGMENTATION

As global influences continue to exert themselves in marketing and in business generally, it is not entirely surprising that recent times have seen a growing interest in the international practice and potential of segmentation. Early interest in applying segmentation internationally tended to take the form of crude classification of overseas markets, *en masse*, as target markets to enter: rated as more or less prosperous, more or less accessible, expansionist and so forth. Alternatively, writers on international marketing dispensed with the segmentation issue by inviting international marketers to segment their overseas markets through generally the same approach and variables as within their home markets (e.g. usage, demographics, geography). Such a form of differentiated international marketing became associated with a multimarket strategy within international marketing.

From the mid-eighties onwards, interest was to develop in the whole issue of global marketing, and as a strategy concern within this, global segmentation. One approach to global segmentation has been based on identifying similar segments across markets, e.g. the youth market (*see* Feinberg (1989)), or the pre-retirement market (*see* Templeman *et al.*, 1989). Hassan and Blackwell (1994) review a number of other global approaches based on a variety of both conventional criteria (e.g. industrial structure, demographics) and less conventional, cluster-based analyses. An interesting intermediate form of international segmentation has developed in the guise of European segmentation. Of particular note, there has emerged a continuing stream of research studies on so-called 'Euro-consumers', usually based on geo-demographic variables (*see* Vandermerwe, 1992) or lifestyle typologies (e.g. Paitra, 1993).

CONCLUSION

The various alternative approaches to marketing segmentation have been described under the separate headings above. There should be no doubt that these bases are dependent on each other. Effective segmentation could make use of all of the categories, and will usually require a combination of more than one type. By combining the way market segments are analysed it is possible to understand them in great detail, and also to follow changes in the dynamics of those segments. This provides the framework which can be used to answer the question, 'Who is our customer?', and also the basis for identifying potential customers and effectively targeting marketing effort with the objective of developing new loyal customers.

QUESTIONS

1 How might you segment the market for
(a) motor cars; and (b) holidays

2 Segmentation leads on to differentiated marketing. How might a company avoid producing too many varieties of a product?

3 Do you think demographics alone are a useful way of segmenting the market for educational courses?

4 What variables do you think organisations should include in a marketing database to aid segmentation studies?

FURTHER READING

Advertising Association, *Advertising Association Pocket Book*, 1992.

Cornish, P., 'Demographics: not standing still', *Admap*, December 1990.

Dickson, P. R., 'Person – situation: segmentation's missing link', *Journal of Marketing*, 46, 1982.

Feinberg, A., 'The First Global Generation', *Adweek*, February 1989, pp. 18–27.

File, K. M. and Prince, R. A., 'A psychographic segmentation of industrial family businesses', *Industrial Marketing Management*, May 1996, Vol. 25, Issue 3.

Hahn, M., Kim, C. and Park, S., 'Identifying relevant market segments for low-shared foreign brands with co-occurrence information', *International Journal of Management*, June 1996, Vol. 12, No. 2, pp. 198–211.

Haley, R., 'Benefit segmentation: a decision-orientated research tool', *Journal of Marketing*, 32, July 1968.

Hassan, Salan S. and Blackwell, Roger D. (1994) *Global Marketing Perspectives and Cases*, Dryden Press, London, Chapters 4 & 5.

Lury, A., 'Demographics tell me nothing I want to know', *Admap*, December 1990.

McNulty, W. Kirk, 'UK change through a wide angle lens', *Futures*, 1985.

Mitchell, A. (1983) *The Nine American Lifestyles*, Macmillan, London.

Paitra, Jacques, 'The Euro-consumer, Myth or Reality?', printed as Reading 1.3 in *European Marketing*, Chris Halliburton and Reinhard Hünerberg, Addison-Wesley, 1993.

Plummer, J. T., 'The concept and application of lifestyle segmentation', *Journal of Marketing*, 38, January 1974.

Reed, David, 'Select Few', *Marketing Week*, March 1996, Vol. 19, Issue I, pp. 53–56.

Templeman, J., Wise, D., Last, E. and Evans, R., 'Grappling with the Graying of Europe', *Business Week*, March 1989.

Toffler, A. (1980) *The Third Wave*, London, Collins.

Vandermerwe, S. and L'Huillier, M., 'Euroconsumers in 1992', *Business Horizons*, January–February 1989, pp. 34–40.

Weinstein, A., (1987) *Market Segmentation*, Probus Publishing.

Wilson, Ian (1994) *Marketing Interfaces: Exploring the Marketing and Business Relationship*, Pitman Publishing, London.

CASE STUDY

Crown Sports

Following a takeover, an accountant friend of yours has been made redundant. He has decided to realise his ambition of running a sportswear retail shop. His redundancy payment (£25k) plus a loan guaranteed against his house will raise the £50 000 needed to purchase the business of Crown Sports. This business, started in 1959 by Charlie King after an undistinguished career as a professional footballer, trades from a 1000 sq ft shop about half a mile from the new Queen's Shopping Centre. Charlie is now 68 years old and is concerned that he is losing customers to the new Olympus shop in the shopping centre. In fact the Olympus shop seems to be doing about twice as much business compared to Crown Sports, and your friend has noticed that the typical Olympus customer is under 35, probably from social class A,B, or C1. These customers like a particular style in the layout of a shop and it is obvious Crown Sports is rather too old fashioned, although perhaps this more traditional layout is preferred by Crown's loyal customers which include parents buying for their children, and officials from several local sports clubs and kit sales to a number of local schools.

Crown Sports did, however, achieve a turnover of £300 000 in 1997 which after Charlie had drawn his salary of £16k, left a net margin of 2 per cent. Half the current turnover is in footwear with the rest split between equipment and clothes. Charlie has not specialised in any particular sport but rather covers the more popular ones, changing the emphasis depending on the relevant season, i.e. soccer/rugby in winter; cricket/tennis/golf in summer. He does, however, have a wide selection of footwear from such major manufacturers as Nike, Reebok, Fila, Puma and Hi Tec. There have been some past problems with Adidas who insisted on minimum order quantities which Mr King felt excessive, so currently no Adidas equipment is stocked.

Your friend believes he can improve the financial control of the business. The major trends all seem to indicate that sports activities are thriving and in spite of the demographic decline in the teenage market and recent curbs on consumer spending there is every chance of this market continuing to grow ahead of the rate of inflation. There is, however, continuing development of 'high technology' specialist equipment which could involve stocking more expensive items. Also major competition for retail sports equipment is coming from the growth of sports chain stores (e.g. Olympus, or JJB) and of buying groups (e.g. Inter Sport) who use their buying power to achieve significant deals which they advertise to attract customers.

Question

Before your friend acquires the business he needs to consider how he can develop it. He does not think he can compete on price with the likes of Olympus or specialist such as Footlocker but might be able to attract customers by specialising on particular parts of the market. Can you advise him on the marketing issues he should consider in this case?

CHAPTER 8

Marketing Information

*An advertiser (marketer) who ignores marketing research is as guilty
as a general who ignores the decodes of enemy signals.*
David Ogilvy

INTRODUCTION

The objectives of this chapter are to define marketing information, show how it can be relevant to decisions throughout an organisation, and in particular to those functions which are specifically concerned with marketing. It will cover information in its widest sense and the value of a marketing information system.

The overriding theme in this book, and every book on the subject of marketing, is that successful organisations meet the needs of their customers. It follows that managers are more likely to make good (rather than bad) marketing decisions if they understand the effect these decisions are likely to have on their organisation's customers. They can only do this if they understand who their customers are, the needs of these customers, and how these customers might respond to different marketing activities.

The importance of asking the question, 'who are our customers?' has been mentioned in previous chapters. Generally, it is an easy question to ask, but a difficult one to answer with any degree of precision. For example, a manufacturer of small cars might say that its customers are 'mostly young people who can only afford a small car'. This may be true, but is not very helpful in the marketing context. To be useful such information needs to classify these customers in more definite terms. This could be with regard to their occupation, the type of newspapers/magazines they read or any of the other segmentation variables discussed in Chapter 7. It would also be useful to know how large these groups are, what proportion of the group are existing customers, and what proportion are buying competitive products.

This is likely to be very important especially if different strategies are needed for existing customers who already own or use your product, and potential customers, who have yet to buy your product. Clearly the more we know about our existing and potential customers and how they feel about the products and services they buy, the better our marketing decisions will be.

SOURCES OF MARKETING INFORMATION

The information an organisation has about its market comes to it in a variety of ways, both formally and informally. All organisations have a fund of knowledge available both from the people who work for it and in the records accumulated over many years.

For example, any member of staff when reading through a technical magazine could notice an article about developments at a competitor's plant. Maybe this is to allow for a new product or to improve efficiency. If this information is passed to the appropriate department within the organisation it could be very useful. Although there can be a problem of an excess of such information, the most important issue is that all employees should know where to send such information. It would then be the responsibility of that department, usually marketing, to decide what to keep, what to check out properly, and what to ignore.

EXAMPLE

A failure to inform

A supplier of electrical components had noticed a sudden drop in the sales of one product. The marketing manager decided that he should consider reducing the price or increase the promotional activity to revive the line. He was supported in this by the sales director who was concerned by the effect the loss of sales was having on the commission earned by the sales team. Before deciding which action to take, the marketing manager decided to phone up a major customer to see if he could get any clue as to the reason for the lower sales. He was surprised by the customer telling him that a competitor had introduced a product of higher quality yet lower price some three months earlier. No one in the sales team had thought to report this, and the marketing manager admitted that for more than two months he had been working on the company's long-term plan so had not been out meeting customers. Why had the marketing manager not been informed about the launch of such a significant competitive product? A number of reasons were suggested by members of the sales force such as:

- 'I'm already working 12 hours a day trying to make a decent salary, I don't have time to pass on every bit of gossip.'
- 'I used to tell my boss everything, but the information was just ignored. My target was increased and I got no thanks for ringing in with information.'
- 'I phoned my Area Sales Manager, but he wasn't in so I left a message with his wife. Maybe she forgot to tell him.'
- 'I thought the Head Office always knew these things. That is the impression they give when you meet them.'

They obviously all got it wrong, and these comments show the company also has other problems. The serious one for the Marketing Department is the failure to have a proper system for capturing relevant information, and to reward those supplying it. A 'thank you' is usually sufficient – it does not have to be a financial incentive.

No organisation has complete knowledge about its markets, customers or competitors. At best it is like a mosaic or jigsaw, where the picture can still be clear, even though a large number of pieces are missing. Sometimes it would be helpful to acquire more information to make the picture clearer. However, information is often expensive so is only worth acquiring if it is likely to improve future marketing decisions. It must also be remembered that marketing information does not replace decision taking – it is at best an aid to help take better decisions. Therefore the purpose and value of information gathering must always be set against the cost of obtaining and processing that information.

Generally, the knowledge provided by marketing information changes over time. Thus, returning to our analogy of a mosaic, the colours of some pieces will fade over time. To revive the pattern, these pieces must be replaced as new ones become available. When information is used for marketing it must be current. Out of date information is likely to result in bad decisions. Again, like the pieces used to make a mosaic, marketing information has to be obtained from different sources and whenever possible alternative sources should be used to improve the overall reliability of the information collected.

Sources of marketing data

Useful marketing information can be obtained from any of the following sources:

- *Undirected observation* Informal, unstructured collection of information from any source. It includes casual reading of magazines and newspapers, meetings with contacts, TV reports and many other chance events.
- *Conditioned viewing* Formal searching but sometimes unstructured collection whereby a comprehensive search is made covering a specified range of publications. This can be done using an on-line database or a CD-rom. It could involve setting up a specific department to scan publications and extract interesting articles to circulate within the marketing management team.
- *Informal searching* A structured way of capturing vital information such as a system of receiving sales force reports. The information might present itself in an informal way but the system to ensure it reaches the relevant managers is structured.
- *Formal searching* This utilises formalised marketing research techniques. It is a specific study undertaken to fill in some of the gaps in the mosaic of information available. It involves the collation, analysis and presentation of appropriate, available and required data.

Research can be defined as the use of investigative techniques to discover non-trivial facts and insights which lead to an extension of knowledge.

There are well-established techniques for undertaking marketing research as a formal business activity and these are described in many specialist texts. Some of the more common are discussed in Chapter 21 and Appendices 4 and 5 at the end of this book.

THE NATURE OF ORGANISATIONAL INFORMATION

Before the essential characteristics of marketing information can be considered it is necessary to discuss organisational information generally and to establish how marketing information is a part of it. This involves appreciating that there are two distinct categories and three different types of organisational information. The two categories are labelled *tangible* and *intangible* and the three types are identified as *direct operational*, *indirect operational* and *marketing*.

Tangible and intangible organisational information

Evidence of tangible information can be seen throughout all types of organisation stored in filing cabinets, desk drawers, cardboard boxes in archives and on computer files. It is often classified by business function. Hence there will be files containing accounting information, personnel information, operational/production information, design information and so on. It is classified as *tangible* information as it can be seen and moved. This tangible information together with specific documents such as the 'Memorandum of Association' drawn up on the formation of a company, actually confirm the existence of an organisation as a functioning entity.

The tangible information within most organisations is impressive in terms of the space it occupies. However, this is because most of it is the stored record of past activities which has to be kept to comply with the legal and other regulations which apply to all organisations. Usually only a small proportion of the stored tangible information is actually needed for the day-to-day activities of the organisation. One reason for this is that, in addition to tangible information, organisations require procedures in order to operate effectively. It is by establishing procedures that organisations are able to benefit from the experience gained through past successes and avoid repeating past mistakes.

A simple example of such a procedure is the normal practice within all types of organisation to have every cheque signed by more than one person.

The procedures used within an organisation, and the routines which are used to implement these, are clearly types of organisational information. These are nonetheless examples of an entirely different type of information which cannot be separated from the individuals who use it. This is because it involves their individual skills, the approach these individuals have to their work and the relationships between them. Since such information cannot be seen or moved it is called *intangible* organisational information. While a feature of all organisations, its importance varies between organisations and between functional departments within organisations. It can be minimised by, for instance, developing comprehensive written procedures and requiring strict compliance by all members of the organisation.

TYPES OF ORGANISATIONAL INFORMATION

It is not only important to appreciate the difference between the two categories of organisational information already discussed, but it is essential to appreciate the fundamentally different characteristics of the three different types of organisational information. Just as all organisations cannot avoid having both categories of information, all organisations use all three types of information.

Direct operational information

Direct operational information is the information or knowledge an organisation needs to provide a service or manufacture a product. For example, it would be essential for a business set-up to provide treatment for sick or injured animals to have someone who has a knowledge of veterinary science. This is the direct operational information for a veterinary practice. It would essentially be the personal knowledge and skills of the qualified veterinary staff who work at the practice so would be intangible direct operational information. The practice will also maintain records of the animal owners who use the service and of the treatment given. It may also have purchased some specific reference books for use by these qualified members of staff. These are both examples of tangible direct operational information.

For a manufacturing organisation such as the manufacturer of leather coats in the example below there are clearly more examples of tangible direct operational information than there is for the veterinary practice, and the examples of intangible direct operational information will also be very different. What is important is that all of these examples have two common characteristics. First tangible and intangible direct operational information is specific to the service or product being offered. Second direct operation information has to be complete even though it may be tangible, intangible or a combination of both. For example the veterinary practice would not be able to offer a complete service if, for instance, none of the qualified staff had any knowledge of treating dogs. The situation is even worse for the manufacturer of leather jackets as is discussed in the example.

EXAMPLE

Direct operational information

To manufacture leather jackets requires an individual or group of people who not only have the information needed to design and manufacture leather jackets, but who also have the essential associated knowledge. This includes knowing where to obtain the leather and other materials used to manufacture leather jackets, the price which should be paid for these, and sources for the machinery and equipment needed to carry out the manufacturing process efficiently. Clearly if any aspect of this information is missing the organisation would not be able to product leather jackets. For example, if the organisation accepted an order for jackets with fluorescent orange zips but did not know of a supplier of these they would not be able to meet the order.

Indirect operational information

Being effective as an organisation involves more than simply manufacturing a product or providing a service. Each leather jacket manufactured (*see* the example on p. 116) has to be packed and shipped to the customer that ordered it. Thus, in addition to actually manufacturing leather jackets, the organisation has to produce delivery notes and invoices. Furthermore, information is required not only to deliver these items but also to keep track of them. This means producing monthly statements for each customer, and measuring the financial standing of the organisation. Information, again usually in the form of routines and procedures, is also needed to process orders received from customers, to place orders on suppliers, pay accounts, pay wages, meet the requirements for dealing with Value Added Tax, and similar tasks. This is just as essential as the direct operational information but is essentially common to all businesses. For this reason it is classified as *indirect* operational information.

Like direct operational information it can be either tangible or intangible and has to be complete for the organisation to function. Hence if for some reason the organisation did not have the information needed to determine the deductions which need to be made from employees' wages to cover income tax and National Insurance contributions its future would quickly be threatened. Unlike direct operational information, indirect operational information is not specific to the product or service being offered. Thus a wages clark who knows how to calculate tax and National Insurance contributions could work for either the veterinary practice or the leather jacket manufacturer.

MARKETING INFORMATION

In addition to direct and indirect operational information, organisations need a third type of information. This is the information which ensures the organisation actually produces and promotes products or services which are required by sufficient customers (or clients) to make the organisation viable. This is called *marketing information*. This can be defined as any information which is relevant to, or affects, the profitable exchange of a product/service between an organisation and its customers. It includes information on the market environment; customers and potential customers; competitors; distributors; and all aspects of promotion.

For the leather jacket manufacturer in the above example the essential marketing information required to trade successfully might include forecasts of future demand, a knowledge of customers' fashion trends, and perhaps information about other manufacturers who could be considered competitors.

There is an essential difference between direct and indirect operational information and marketing information. In order to accomplish the tasks to which an organisation exists it must have ALL of the direct and indirect operational information required. This is not the case with marketing information. Indeed all organisations have to operate with incomplete marketing information. What is important is that an organisation has the information which is essential for it to continue to meet the needs of its customers.

EXAMPLE

If the company manufacturing leather jackets considered in an earlier example received an enquiry from overseas asking them to quote for supplying 300 jackets in mixed sizes, and standard colour, they may well quote their standard price. If, when the order is received, it is clear that the required mix of sizes in this new market is different from that in the home market, the lack of this information could have resulted in a bad marketing decision being made. The required mix of sizes for the overseas market is a form of marketing information.

For production the problem is different. If an order for jackets is accepted without having patterns for some of the required sizes, they cannot be produced immediately. For production this information is essential.

EXERCISE

It was suggested in Chapter 1 that marketing could be seen as providing the right product, in the right place, at the right price and at the right time. Can you suggest what marketing information might be required to enable a toothpaste manufacturing company to achieve this?

Like other types of organisational information, marketing information can be either tangible or intangible. In many organisations there is little evidence of tangible marketing information. Furthermore, unlike tangible operational information, tangible marketing information is often dispersed within an organisation. Departments such as sales, design or advertising may have formal files. In addition, many managers are likely to have their own file labelled 'Competition' containing catalogues collected at an exhibition or other similar event.

Marketing information is also time-dependent so is often discarded when it is out of date since there is no legal requirement to store it. This can make it extremely difficult or even impossible to collate the information needed to show for instance long-term trends in market preferences.

Marketing as a business activity has developed as a result of recognising that the success of an organisation depends upon creating and retaining customers. In the short term these decisions are likely to be concerned with meeting the needs of customers efficiently. In the longer term they are likely to focus more on the organisation's need to respond to the ever-changing expectations of the users of its products and/or services.

EXAMPLE

Consider the problems facing someone wishing to open a restaurant. Their individual skill as a chef or their access to this skill is likely to determine the type of restaurant. Perhaps a high-class French restaurant, or maybe a Chinese take-away. If, in the intended location, there were already clearly too many Chinese restaurants it would be more sensible for a skilled Chinese chef to seek an alternative location rather than attempt to open a French restaurant. This and many of the associated operational decisions relating to the restaurant are likely to depend largely upon marketing information. For instance the relative sizes of the kitchen and dining areas, the equipment needed in the kitchen and the decor of the dining area will depend on the type of restaurant and the atmosphere which is

▶

considered best for successful operation. To be successful a high-class restaurant will require, at the very least, a greater investment in the dining area. It is accordingly essential for the owner to establish the likelihood of there being sufficient customers either in the area or willing to travel from adjacent areas who could afford the significantly higher prices which would be expected at a high-class restaurant. If not, it would be preferable to provide simpler fare, cater for many more people each day, and design the restaurant to suit.

All of these decisions involve judgement and require marketing information. To obtain this would involve, at the very least, visiting and spending time in the area. This could well involve investing time and money for travel and accommodation. It might involve the additional expense of employing someone locally to obtain the information required. To proceed without this marketing information would make any forecast of success for the venture somewhat unreasonable.

On another level the term 'getting close to the customer' can be a very sophisticated operation. Organisations such as Grattan Mail Order in the UK, and many international airlines and credit card companies have gained considerable competitive advantage by developing comprehensive customer databases. These are used to improve their understanding of consumer needs, and to support the development and marketing of new products. Grattan gather information on the personal characteristics and buying patterns of customers, as well as more general information on non-customers. They use this information to select prospects for sample mailings and to analyse the response to identify the specific characteristics of those who purchased. They then use the analysis to identify other customers with similar characteristics for a more general and usually very successful direct marketing offer.

Van Doren and Stickney (1990) demonstrate through case illustrations a useful 'how to' approach for developing a database for sales leads, utilising data sourced both in-house and externally, through commercial information brokers, software houses and on-line database vendors.

EXERCISE

Consider an enterprise with which you are familiar and itemise: (a) the operational knowledge likely to be necessary to produce the product or provide the service and (b) the marketing information necessary to implement this production knowledge successfully.

The collation of marketing information is generally more complicated in organisations which manufacture variations of a basic product. This is because the information of interest to those having to make marketing decisions is fundamentally different from that needed by manufacturing.

As a result of market analysis, the marketing department of a major car manufac-turer found that they were selling a lower proportion of 4-door cars, and therefore a higher proportion of 2–3-door cars, than their competition. Should they wish to investigate this further, they would need to look at the sales of this type of vehicle in terms of: the level of trim, e.g. L, GL, GTi, and so on; the size of engine; the type of gearbox; and even perhaps by colour. They might also want to know whether there were any regional variations in demand.

Although it might be expected that production would have records from which such information could be easily obtained, in practice their records may not show the detail required. For production purposes the information would be required in a different form. It could well show that of every 100 vehicles built, 50 have 1300 cc engines, 30 have 1600 cc engines and 20 have 1800 cc engines, and 50 have two doors, 30 have four doors and 20 are estates with five doors. From these com-ponents any combination of vehicle could be built and any minor variations in demand would be allowed for by adjusting the next batch accordingly. There is no reason why any records should be kept of how many 4-door cars have 1600 cc engines against either of the alternatives. Nor is there any reason for knowing whether the overall mix changes according to geographic region, or season or other factor. Thus, obtaining the information wanted by the marketing depart-ment would involve either having a separate system designed specifically to provide this information or analysing individual customer orders, invoices or shipping notes, which would inevitably be a tedious and error-prone process.

Indeed, it is because such data is often effectively unobtainable that many marketing decisions have to be made without adequate information or based on incorrect assump-tions. For instance, it may be logical to assume that since the estate version of the vehicle looks larger than any of the other models, most estates sold would have the larger engines. Equally, this could be entirely wrong since buyers of the estate model might consider it a utility vehicle and so rate its performance as relatively unimportant.

This example illustrates another important aspect of marketing information: its sheer volume. Most internal marketing information involves the collation of data from pro-duction or finance departments. This data must be measured against the tests of currency and relevance to the marketing decision being made. It is also very important that the data can be analysed in a way that is useful when making marketing decisions.

Marketing as a function can thus be critically dependent on information generated within the functional areas within the organisation. Karmarkar (1996) develops a per-suasive case for marketing information and research activities to be more closely integrated with parallel efforts in operations management, in the interests of cross-functional co-ordination and business strategy analysis. Similarly, Ratnatunga, Hooley and Pike (1992) review the practice of information integration between the marketing and finance functions, and the degree to which information exchange is affected by organisational factors. At a more strategic level, Bondro and Davis (1996) argue that the marketing function should seek to improve its own performance, and augment its strategic role, through a more active and deliberate involvement in the organisation's management information system.

CATEGORIES OF MARKETING INFORMATION

It is useful to classify marketing information in terms of the five main categories mentioned earlier. These respectively relate to:

1 The environment and market in which the product or service is produced, provided, supplied and used (termed the wider environment (level 4) in Chapter 3).
2 The target customers, clients, or users served by an organisation (and other key stakeholders).
3 Competitor information (*see* Chapter 4).
4 The product or service being provided.
5 How that product/service reaches and is communicated to the target customers.

The marketing environment

In Chapter 3 the various aspects of the marketing environment have been identified and discussed. Often, events which are likely to have an impact on an enterprise are seen, in the first instance, within the wider marketing or macroenvironment which comprises social, cultural, technological, economic, political and legal aspects.

Reports forecasting the macroenvironment are regularly published both for individual countries and for groups of countries such as the members of European Union. While many are expensive often an adequate summary can be obtained from a library or a report in the business or trade press. Many are also available through computerised business data services such as McCarthy's in the UK. These commercial reports while a good way of monitoring the wider environment should always be used with caution as their conclusions often appear to disagree significantly. Because of this it is important to understand the origin of any report used, always compare the information from a number of different sources and note the following warnings:

1 Many forecasts cover entire countries or industries and are not necessarily specific to the smaller sector or industry you may be studying.
2 Forecasts are based on historical data and specific assumptions, so they can have a wide margin for error.
3 Forecasts that conflict with 'common sense' should be carefully reviewed.
4 Forecasts will always be wrong.

The last warning is one of the 'fundamental laws' suggested by Flores and Whymark (1985) who also advise that:

> We should not forecast things that don't need to be forecast.

and

> The average of several simple methods often works best.

There are many specialist textbooks which cover the analysis of the marketing environment. Some are basic economics texts, but more specialist marketing references can be found in Palmer and Worthington (1992).

Over the last fifteen years, the use of scenarios has become an accepted method of evaluating the macroenvironment. A scenario is a qualitative description of the future and the approach involves developing a range of different scenarios each based on defined assumptions. Usually these include a 'most likely' scenario and a 'worst case' scenario. The use of scenarios was developed by the Royal Dutch Shell Company after the dramatic oil price movements in 1978. This technique has helped Shell and other organisations to study the likely effect of future plans in various different future situations.

Customer information

Customer information is central to the concept of marketing. Many existing businesses, especially those providing services, have direct contact with the people who use their service. For instance, hairdressers can judge from this direct contact whether their clientele is getting older and more prosperous or older and less prosperous. By consciously recognising such trends, hairdressers can maintain the future of their businesses either by ensuring that the service offered is changed to match the changing needs of the clientele or to attract another category of clientele. Customer information obtained through direct contact, although intangible, is likely to be the best available.

The management of larger organisations, even those who essentially provide services such as banks, can easily lose direct contact with their customers. To avoid this, managers need adequate tangible marketing information such as up-to-date customer satisfaction surveys. Without it, they will have no option but to make decisions based on the information, perhaps now out of date, they gained prior to becoming managers. The problem is even worse for the manufacturers of products. Very often these are sold through wholesale and retail intermediaries which means that managers could be making decisions without having any contact with their final customers and users.

Customer information can be either qualitative or quantitative. Qualitative information might involve opinions or reasons for a particular action. This can be as useful in the context of marketing decisions as quantitative facts such as that 8 out of 10 people buy a particular brand of cat food.

Information can be obtained as a one-off (*ad hoc*) study. It can also be tracked over a period of time, perhaps using a consumer panel to measure changes in behaviour.

An interesting and radical new approach to customer information and analysis, virtual shopping, has become available through ongoing development in computer modelling. Though methodologies can vary, a typical virtual shopping (or 'virtual store') experiment might involve having target consumers track their way, on screen, through a virtual shopping environment, or floor area, select products to buy, examine displays, record levels of interest and so forth. The virtual approach has obvious value in product development and testing settings. Research specialists and agencies, especially in the USA, are developing more comprehensive and integrated programmes (e.g. wish advertising exposure), and more dedicated applications such as for car showrooms and travel agencies. The results of two US validation studies on virtual shopping are discussed in detail in an informative article in the *Harvard Business Review* (March–April 1996).

At a more theoretical level, the whole field of computer modelling in marketing, and the related topic of market-based expert systems, is comprehensively covered within the authoritative text produced by Moutinho, Curry *et al.* (1996).

Competitor information

It is important to appreciate that the success of a product is dependent as much upon the alternatives available to a potential customer as upon the product itself. This was described earlier with respect to product/service benefits. It is the appreciation of these alternatives and the impact that they are likely to have on the acceptability of a product to the potential customer which often requires specific marketing information.

Most successful organisations will continually update a competitor profile of all their direct competitors. This will include what those competitors are doing, what products they are offering, as well as when, why and how they are performing and any other relevant information.

It should again be stressed that marketing is related to the future activities of an organisation and therefore it is important to develop a feel for what competitors are likely to do in the future. In his book *Managing for Marketing Excellence*, Ian Chaston suggests:

> Even in their analysis of existing competition, some marketers make insufficient use of information sources outside of standard market research studies. Marketeers could learn a valuable lesson from the financial community on the benefits of studying annual accounts and shareholder reports as a basis for appraising the capabilities of companies.
>
> Financial analysts also exploit other sources of information to gain a more complete picture of the future prospects for a company. These include the perspectives of supplier/intermediaries, publicity releases, announcement of capital investment programmes and recruitment advertising programmes. Given such a range of information it should be a danger signal to management if the marketing department only presents conclusions based on market share and customer surveys.

An interesting article under the heading 'How to Snoop on your Competitors' (*Fortune*, 14 May 1984) describes some highly questionable methods of obtaining information on competitors. It provides a real insight into the lengths to which some organisations go to get such data. Whether or not you approve of such practices they do go on, and they affect the whole image of marketing research. The article less controversially also suggests that:

> Competitive intelligence is a bits and pieces business ... much information you will find is inaccurate, irrelevant or stale and you must search hard to find golden nuggets. But, once you have 80% of the puzzle, you see things you didn't see when you had 20%.

Product/services information

Marketing information on products or services cannot be isolated from customers or competitors. Specifications can be compared but it is the degree to which an offering matches the future needs/wants of the customers which is of major importance to a marketer.

While it may be necessary to conduct a new product research study using blind (unbranded) tests it is essential that as far as possible the tests are applicable to the branded product to which the actual marketing decisions apply. Existing products can, of course, be assessed in direct comparative situations to evaluate how a product or service offering is perceived alongside competitive offerings with respect, for instance, to its acceptability in a specific situation. Indirect competition tends to be much more difficult to forecast. But very often it is not actually recognised until identified as a result of research initiated for instance as a result of significantly reduced sales of a product or group of products.

The development of the Sony Walkman as a new product, which has already been discussed in an earlier chapter, is an interesting example of a product which, at least for a time, affected the market for some apparently unrelated products. One example was the market for good quality pens. Both Walkmans and quality pens were similarly priced gift items for young people and were therefore competitors in the gift market. This is referred to, in Chapter 4, as indirect competition.

EXERCISE

Consider what impact the trend from hot to cold beverages is likely to have in the future. Are there any associated products which are likely to be affected by these changes?

Within this category of study will come the price of an offering. Price is very difficult to research when customers are not actually buying a product. However, actual prices of comparative products, and the differences between retail prices and trade prices, are matters of fact where information can be obtained.

Distribution and promotional information

Channels of distribution are described in Chapter 12. Since some products go through several intermediaries on their way to the final consumer, it is obviously important to learn as much as possible about the various intermediaries. Each is a customer of a supply organisation and has a key role in the promotion of products en route to the final consumers.

Decisions on distribution channels are critical to success, and once set up require careful monitoring. This area of trade research is often carried out as part of a continuous study by major research agencies such as the A. C. Neilsen organisation.

In terms of physical distribution across the entire supply chain, Wheatley (1996) illustrates the increasing role of sophisticated IT-based logistics systems and software solutions. These utilise technical developments such as those associated with barcoding, electronic point-of-sale (EPOS) and electronic data interchange (EDI). In short, growing competition, on the demand side, and technology developments, on the supply side, have encouraged manufacturers to focus on the competitive advantage which can be gained through improved delivery, response and service levels, while maintaining cost, productivity and quality targets.

The origins of marketing research are closely linked with those of advertising research. Perhaps because so much money is spent on consumer advertising this is still a key area of study. Most media providers have extensive information on readers/viewers. This allows careful targeting of marketing communications to a chosen segment. The information is usually made available to all potential advertisers. The effectiveness of advertisements is also studied in detail with most advertising agencies having good in-house research departments.

The value of good research when studying promotional effectiveness is well established and this may involve the use of some quite elaborate devices such as the pupilo-meter. This shows how the eye moves when an advert is being read. It is nonetheless very difficult to relate cause and effect in an advertising context. Measures such as awareness of product names and opportunities to see a particular advertisement are relatively easy to study. The problem arises in trying to relate these to sales volume changes. This is what prompted the now famous comment, sometimes attributed to Lord Leverhulme, 'I know half my advertising is wasted, but I don't know which half' (*see also* Chapter 14).

QUALITY OF INFORMATION

It will already be apparent that information requires to be *accurate* and *up to date* (current), but other criteria are equally important when considering the quality of data. The analogy of a mosaic can still be applied and while the mosaic is unlikely to be complete, a certain number of critical pieces are essential for the picture to be seen. Similarly it is essential to have the specific data needed to support any marketing decision. This means the information must be directly relevant, which is not always as easy as it sounds. For instance, government statistics often cover a large category of products, but if the decision only relates to one small specific subsegment it may not be possible to accurately separate this from the total data which could be misleading or irrelevant. It is essential that all data used is both valid and reliable.

Reliability is associated with data being consistent although coming from a number of independent sources or repeated measurements. When either different sources or measurements disagree, which often happens, the differences need to be evaluated to establish which information source should be used.

Validity is often an issue where data is obtained using a small sample in a formal market research survey. It refers to the extent to which the survey findings are in line with the research problem or hypothesis. Usually it is a measure of whether the findings can be extended to the whole population or the market being considered. This involves using appropriate statistical theory to establish confidence levels and is covered in most standard marketing research texts.

While there is no direct link between good decisions and good quality data, there is a real risk of poor decisions being taken if the information fails to be:

- reliable (accurate);
- valid;
- relevant;
- sufficient;
- current (up-to-date).

RAW DATA AND INFORMATION

In the examples given earlier in the chapter the individual intending to open a restaurant either had the marketing information needed, perhaps as a result of recent experience, or would have needed to acquire it. The gathering of required data must be separated from processing it into the marketing information which can be used for making marketing decisions. The data comprises the facts and other collected details from which things can be deduced, whereas the marketing information is the synthesis of that raw data. Much marketing information will comprise issues other than basic *facts*. A fact is a measurement of anything that actually exists or has existed.

An example of a fact is that our company sold 4000 units last month (tangible fact), or 8 out of 10 cat owners say that their cats prefer Whiskas Cat Food (intangible). However, for marketing decisions information is also needed on:

- what people know, true or false (*knowledge*);
- how customers perceive our product/service and other relevant attitudes or beliefs (*opinions*);
- what consumers intend to do, and the strength of those *intentions*;
- why people behave as they do (*motives*).

MARKETING INFORMATION SYSTEMS

Marketing information systems are really the frameworks used for managing, processing and accessing data. They can be simply a way of sharing information between key departments, but are more likely to be some form of integrated system using available information technology. The important issue is that the information from such a system is presented in a way that is useful for making marketing decisions.

Even in quite small companies they can involve large quantities of data. One apparently logical approach to the problem of extensive data is to develop, using computer technology, a system which stores and provides access to the information needed by those making marketing decisions. The term 'marketing information system' or MkIS is used to describe such a system. Such systems are generally discussed in the context of marketing information or marketing research. (It should be noted that the term MIS is commonly used for the somewhat more far-reaching 'management information system').

While it is essential for organisations to have systems by which marketing information can be stored, processed and accessed, it should be clear from the points made regarding the nature of information in general, and marketing information in particular, that such systems have fundamental limitations. At best the system can only handle such tangible and intangible information as is made available to it. There are three basic components of a good marketing information system:

1 Information acquired via market intelligence.
2 Information from operating data, often in database form.
3 Information library.

What an MkIS does is to bring together data from these sources, usually into a computerised database. If structured appropriately this should allow interrogation and linking of data accessed from a variety of sources. It is important for such systems to be basically designed by marketers rather than computer specialists as the form of the output can be critical to good decisions.

Market intelligence is all of the data available from the many external sources, some of which have already been mentioned in this chapter. It may have been acquired formally or informally but will usually be checked for reliability before it is entered into an MkIS.

Information from operating data, such as production or accounts, has been covered under the heading of operational information. It is usually different from marketing information as it is collected for very different reasons. Nevertheless, there is likely to be some marketing relevance in this data and that must input into the MkIS. It could perhaps contain the details of car production, 2-door versus 4-door, or various engine sizes ordered as in the earlier example. Certainly sales information drawn from invoices is very important and yet this needs to be presented in a way that might categorise customers by relevant market segment, or might show products purchased in as much detail as possible. It could take the form of a sophisticated customer database, such as those originally developed by major service companies for mail order business or airline reservations.

With advances in software design and IT generally, the development and use of both integrated and specialist databases has become increasingly commonplace. Networking and systems integration facilities allow companies to exchange, merge and cross-analyse data from databases within specialist functions (e.g. accounting and purchasing, or distribution/logistics and marketing), or to develop databases for common use within the organisation (e.g. on customers or suppliers). Equally, there has been a rapid expansion in the availability and use of on-line databases, capable of providing (by subscription, or usage fee) up-to-date information on a range of issues, from market aggregate statistics to target segment profiles and listings, information update summaries and so forth.

The information library is a collection of all the formal research gathered by an organisation that is still relevant and up to date. It might also include research surveys

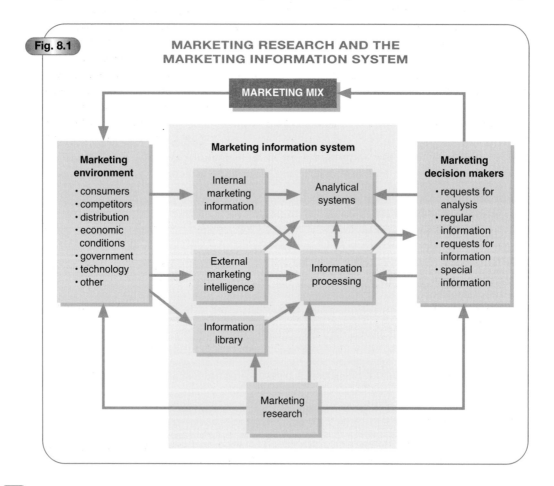

Fig. 8.1 MARKETING RESEARCH AND THE MARKETING INFORMATION SYSTEM

carried out by trade associations or by associated companies, as such reports are some-times available and they do add to knowledge. Thus the MkIS will contain a comprehensive collection of all relevant information which could help achieve better marketing decisions (*see* Fig. 8.1).

Computer-based systems are particularly useful for handling numerical information, but can provide only limited assistance when handling qualitative information based on descriptions and ideas. The need to address this problem has been recognised, and much work has been done to develop 'decision support systems' designed to provide the infor-mation needed for marketing decisions. No doubt the number of companies developing and using such systems will increase. The main benefit offered by such systems is likely to be the facilities they offer for accessing the available information. Because of the volume, complexity and time-dependent nature of marketing information, the provision of market-ing information will continue to be the specialist marketing activity of marketing research.

CONCLUSION

Marketing, no less than other functions, depends for its efficiency on the availability and utilisation of internal and external information. Information internal to the organ-isation may range far beyond data on marketing activities proper, and will include central and dispersed sources on operational tasks, procedures and routines throughout the company. In particular, information on production processes and stages may be critical to marketing success, as it will guide managers on the quality and capacity limi-tations of the organisation, product specifications and current commitments. Equally, the marketing information collected from customers and others in the marketplace will be critical as an input to the design and production functions. Any decision on what products are to be produced by an organisation must be made on the basis of cus-tomer considerations. It is the role of marketing in any organisation to ensure that this information is effectively disseminated within that organisation.

QUESTIONS

1 'Information is power.' Discuss this in relation to the cross-functional information flows necessary for good customer service.

2 Taking as an example any commercial product, consider the information sources that would shed light on changes in its market and economic environment.

3 Outline what you consider to be the characteristics of an effective marketing information system, and consider the means by which it might be designed and maintained.

4 Discuss the relationship between marketing information and marketing planning.

FURTHER READING

Besson, J. (1993) *Riding the Marketing Information Wave*, HBR S/O.
Birn, R. (1990) *The Effective Use of Marketing Research*, Kogan Page, London.
Boudra J. and Davis T.R., 'Marketing's role in cross-functional information management', *Industrial Marketing Management*, May 1996, Vol. 25, Issue 3 (pp. 187–195).

Chaston, I. (1990) *Managing for Marketing Excellence*, McGraw-Hill.

Flores, B. and Whymark, D., 'Forecasting "laws" for Management', *Business Horizon*, Vol. 28, No. 4, July 1985. *Harvard Business Review*, March/April 1996, Vol. 74, Issue 2 (p. 128 ff.).

Karmarkar, Uday S., 'Integrative Research in Marketing and Operations Management', *Journal of Marketing Research*, May 1996, Vol. 33, Issue 2 (p. 125 ff.).

Moutiuho Ref. Palmer, A. and Worthington, I. (1992) *The Business and Marketing Environment*, McGraw-Hill.

Ratnatunga, J., Hooley, G J. and Pike, R., 'Marketing Finance Interface', *European Journal of Marketing*, 1992.

Van Doren, D. C. and Stickney, T. A., 'How To Develop a Database for Sales Leads', *Industrial Marketing Management*, Issue 19 (pp. 201–208), 1990.

Wack, P., 'Scenarios: Shooting the Rapids', *Harvard Business Review*, Nov–Dec 1985.

Wheatley, Malcolm, 'IT drives the Chain', *Management Today*, November 1996 (p. 102 ff.).

CASE STUDY
Coventry Racquet Sport Centre

Coventry Racquet Sport Centre, now known locally as 'The Racquet Centre', opened in the early 1980s as the Grand Prix International Racquet Club and was positioned as an exclusive members-only indoor racquet centre offering:

- reception, bar, restaurant and changing facilities;
- eight indoor tennis courts;
- ten (indoor) badminton courts;
- eight (indoor) squash courts.

In less than a year the Centre was in difficulty and went into liquidation. The Centre was sold and reopened as the Ace Tennis Centre which also positioned itself as a membership facility although the membership fee was considerably reduced. But once again the Centre ran into financial difficulties and the receivers had to move in.

The current management bought the Centre in May 1985 and have sought to continually improve the quality of their service offering. Renamed as Coventry Racquet Sport Centre to identify more closely with the city, it was reopened as a 'pay as you play' centre with no membership fees. Initial marketing efforts were aimed internally at improving customer care to ensure that current users had good experiences and could spread the word that things had very much changed at the Centre. The 'new' Centre also advertised in the local press and obtained substantial publicity with a number of special events.

During the past decade a number of changes and additions have been made to both the physical facility and the programme of activities, including:

- addition of five outdoor tennis courts to counter the summer 'dip' in demand;
- converting one of the indoor tennis courts into five badminton courts;
- addition of large new facility to include an exercise room (20 m × 15 m), gym/fitness area (extensive range of equipment with qualified staff), and additional changing facilities;
- franchised sports shop;
- sauna/sunbed health area;
- aerobics and 'step' classes (using one of the tennis courts).

Current situation

The Racquet Centre has recently experienced a period of consolidation after the additions in the late 1980s. It offers 'pay as you play' in all activity areas with no official membership, although each sport has a variety of teams/clubs and leagues with named individuals as points of contact. The centre is currently advertised in the local press and on radio, targeting prospective and past users, and highlighting the 'pay as you play' philosophy and the general fitness (aerobics/gym) activities available as well as the racquet sports.

The Centre is currently experiencing healthy court usage in the main racquet sports with the 6.00–7.00 pm (Monday–Friday) courts being regularly oversubscribed. The other activity areas are also experiencing healthy demand during weekday evenings from 5.30 pm to 10.00 pm.

The Monday–Friday daytime usage in all areas is very poor, which is typical of many leisure facilities and the weekend use is slightly above the national average in each of the racquet sports – which still leaves substantial room for improvement. The outdoor tennis courts, which are multi-use surface and floodlit, are hardly used at all from November to April, the sauna and sunbeds are under-utilised, and the bar/restaurant takings are substantially below what could be achieved in a facility of this size with the current throughput (numbers of customers each day).

Available sources of internal data include:

- the booking sheets for each of the major racquet sports;
- the signing in sheets for aerobics and fitness area/gym;
- suggestion boxes situated at reception and in the bar.

The Centre is currently investigating the potential of a customer database for more targeted promotional activity. The Centre management is currently considering a variety of alternatives for improving profitability. They have already ruled out hiring facilities to local schools as this is not profitable and causes problems with facility misuse/abuse. There are between 15 000–20 000 students in the area at Coventry and Warwick Universities. Coventry is a city of some 300 000 people but is not over-supplied with facilities. Local price comparisons are shown below.

There is also much discussion about the corporate market, particularly for daytime use.

There is a Local rumour that a large leisure company has made an offer to buy the club with a view to completely renovating it and once again repositioning it as a private members club similar to other clubs they own.

Questions

1 What data could be available to the Racquet Centre, and how could this be developed into information useful to the marketing decisions that are being taken?

2 What information could be used by the large private leisure company in evaluating the purchase of the centre? Also what information would assist in assessing the feasibility of repositioning it as a members club?

Prices at Coventry Racquet Sport Centre and locally

	Mon–Fri off-peak 9.00–5.00 pm	Mon–Fri 5.00–11.00 pm and all weekends	Local competition
Tennis court	£10.00 per hour	£16.00 per hour	No local indoor facilities
Badminton court	£5.00 per hour	£8.00 per hour	Off-peak £2–3.00 Peak £4–5.00
Squash court	£3.50 per 40 mins	£5.00 per 40 mins	£100 membership + £3.00 per court
Aerobics/step	£3.00 per person	£4.00 per person	£3.00–£4.00 per person
Gym (per person)	£4.00 for each use	£4.50 for each use	£50 membership + £2.00 per use

(Case supplied by Jeff Clowes, Coventry Business School.)

CHAPTER 9

The Marketing Offering

O make harmonious mix.
Countess Pembroke, 1586

INTRODUCTION

In previous chapters this book has looked at the basic concept behind marketing which is to achieve a profitable, mutually beneficial, exchange with customers. It has covered those uncontrollable factors that can affect an exchange which are termed the marketing environment including competition. Of course one of the most uncontrollable elements is customer decision making, hence the need to study customer behaviour and to undertake market segmentation which enable a focus on an homogeneous group of customers. The analysis and understanding of these factors (*see* Chapters 3, 4, 5, 6 and 7) is important, but only if it helps to make better decisions in the marketing of a particular product or service. However no one should fail to realise their importance.

The next section of this book looks at those elements over which organisations have control and which are used to try to influence customers to choose one particular organisation in preference to another. These are generally termed the *marketing mix*. This description, which conjures up images of mixing together all the things that have a bearing on the '*supplier-customer*' relationship, was first published over 30 years ago by Neil Borden. His original marketing mix did include 4 external variables which we have already covered.

External factors in the original marketing mix

Customer buying behaviour
Trade behaviour
Competitors' position and behaviour
Government regulations

Borden's list of controllable internal variables had 12 specific factors.

Internal factors in the original marketing mix

Product policy	Promotions	Channels of distribution	Servicing
Pricing	Packaging	Personal selling	Physical handling
Branding	Display	Advertising	Fact finding and analysis

This list is not easy to remember and it should be obvious why Jerome McCarthy condensed the twelve items in Borden's original marketing mix into four major categories popularised the '4 Ps'.

The internal variables are therefore loosely grouped together under the headings of:

- Product ⎫
- Price ⎬ The offer mix
- Place ⎭
- Promotion } The promotional mix

You will note the distinction between what is offered, product price and place, and the promotion of that offer. This will be expanded in future chapters.

While the '4 Ps' is a useful framework, a vigorous debate has taken place over the last decade about the dangers of seeing marketing solely as the control of the '4 Ps'. In fact it is a trap that tends to make suppliers forget the needs of customers, as well as the importance of a mutually beneficial exchange. The '4 Ps' also ignores two key elements of the original mix – *Servicing* and *Physical handling*.

Because there is an attraction to the letter 'P', some authors on service marketing have suggested the addition of three other Ps:

- People
- Process
- Physical evidence

Others have suggested:

- Probe (research)
- Partition (segmentation)
- Position

All of these have good claims to be included in the marketing mix. The last being a key factor as it must be evaluated by the way a customer views a supply organisation.

It does not matter how many elements are included in the marketing mix. Neither is it important that all categories start with the letter 'P'. What is important is that these controllable factors are what is seen by the customers. They must be consistent one with another, and together they form the 'promise' of an offering being made to customers. The customers will judge the claims and benefits which comprise this 'promise' and will then decide how to behave in the light of the offering. The way marketing people describe the result of the promises is the concept of positioning which is discussed more fully later in this chapter. Whereas suppliers make promises through the various elements of the marketing mix, customers evaluate what they perceive and they consider the position of an offering in comparison to other competitive offerings.

> **Positioning is not what you do to a product; positioning is what you do to the mind of the prospect. (Ries and Trout, 1981)**

This quotation emphasises the fact that the most important issue is the perception and evaluation by the potential customers of *all* those things that are done in marketing a product.

This brings us to the simple and obvious fact that a product or service will not be purchased by a prospect or potential customer unless they are comfortable with the marketing offering. For the customer to reach this situation they must know:

(a) that it exists;

(b) where it can be purchased;

(c) that it is affordable; and most important

(d) that it is likely to meet the need for which it is required.

This introduces what within marketing can be referred to as the '4 As':

- Awareness
- Availability
- Affordability
- Acceptability

The Coca-Cola Company has been using the 'Availability, Affordability and Acceptability' as their test of strategy for many years. Of course Coca-Cola are clearly confident that most of the world is already aware of their product. Indeed in 1996 it was the second best-known brand in the world.

It follows that a supplier cannot expect to sell a product to a potential new customer until the following four conditions have been met. The supplier must thus ensure that the potential customer:

(a) is *aware* of the product's existence;

(b) finds the product to be *available* when it is needed;

(c) can *afford* to buy the product; and

(d) is willing to test its *acceptability*.

It further follows that the possibility of a sale is likely to be increased by any action taken by a supplier to improve the awareness, availability, acceptability or affordability of a product. All of this is involved in the task of marketing.

But how can this be accomplished? Returning to the original categories listed by Borden it is obvious:

- Awareness is affected by:
  Advertising
  Promotions
  Branding
  Display
  Personal selling.
- Availability is affected by:
  Channels of distribution
  Physical handling
- Affordability is affected by:
  Pricing
- Acceptability is affected by:
  Product policy
  Packaging
  Servicing

It will further be seen that each of these groups of variables can be conveniently summarised using the four categories: Product, Place, Price and Promotion, which are now universally accepted as the '4 Ps'. However, the full scope of the word *product* can be seen to embrace more than a physical product and this wider definition is very important in considering how the '4 Ps' should be interpreted. These issues will be discussed in more detail in later chapters.

It will be seen that the '4 Ps' completely mirror the '4 As' introduced earlier. Thus:

- Awareness is developed by Promotion;
- Availability by Place (used as a generic term for distribution);
- Affordability is a function of Price;
- Acceptability is of course determined by both the Product and the service.

These '4 Ps' which act as a reminder of the major components of the marketing mix, and are referred to as such in most marketing textbooks. Usually their order is reversed to rank them as they might be approached by the supplier (*see* Fig. 9.1). That is:

Product, Price, Place and Promotion.

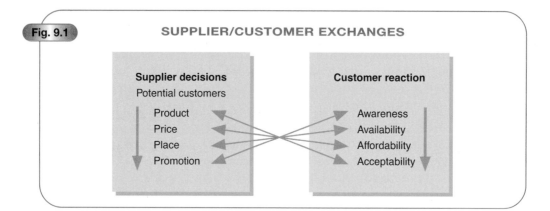

But marketers should consider all issues from a customer viewpoint. Consumers do not approach these factors in this order, so it is necessary to consider the consumer ordering, which is most likely to start with Awareness/Promotion when using these categories for functional marketing. In this way suppliers can fully understand the effect that each of these variables can have on the potential customer. Each of the components will be considered in detail in subsequent chapters.

It is equally important that the concept of a marketing mix is never seen in isolation. Its validity as a concept depends upon it always being considered in context. This means ensuring that every discussion of any element of the marketing mix 'product, price place or promotion' is always done within the context of a clearly defined exchange and a customer or market segment (*see* Fig. 9.2) as well as being evaluated relative to competitive offerings.

The variables a supplier can change are the '4 Ps' of their marketing mix. Those they have to monitor are the '4 As' of their customers and the '4 Ps' of their competition (*see* Fig. 9.3).

Competitors have an important influence on how customers respond to the marketing mix selected by a supplier. Customers are in the position to decide between competitive offerings, hence the importance of the question: 'WHY should customers

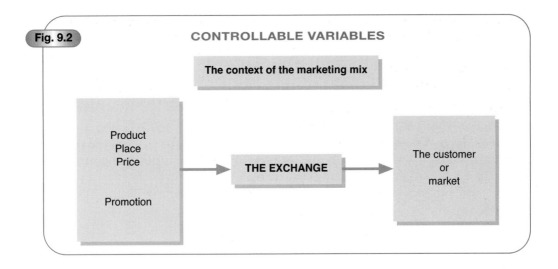

Fig. 9.2

CONTROLLABLE VARIABLES

The context of the marketing mix

Product
Place
Price

Promotion

THE EXCHANGE

The customer
or
market

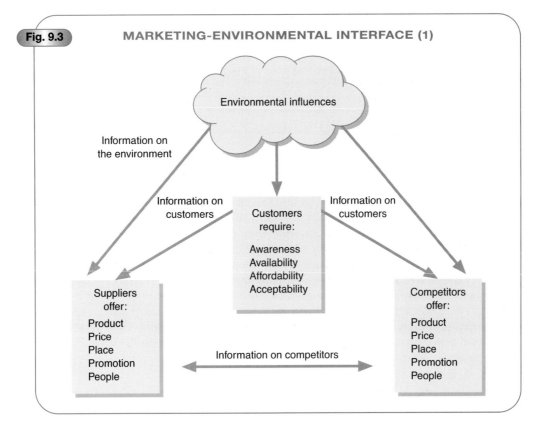

Fig. 9.3

MARKETING-ENVIRONMENTAL INTERFACE (1)

Environmental influences

Information on
the environment

Information on
customers

Information on
customers

Customers
require:

Awareness
Availability
Affordability
Acceptability

Suppliers
offer:

Product
Price
Place
Promotion
People

Information on competitors

Competitors
offer:

Product
Price
Place
Promotion
People

buy from us?' Newly established competitors can often benefit from changes in the environment, such as new technologies or new attitudes, by offering modified products before existing companies: 'WHY did Body Shop have such a success with environmentally friendly products when major competitors such as Boots failed to see the opportunity?' 'WHY were quartz/electronic watches from companies such as Casio able to take such a large share of the market before the Swiss watch industry fought back with Swatch?'

CUSTOMERS AS A BUSINESS ASSET

Peter Drucker, a well-known american writer on management, has said 'There is only one valid purpose of a business, that is to create and keep a customer.' All the marketing effort, both in terms of analysing markets for opportunities and planning a competitive mix, are aimed at creating customers.

The publisher McGraw-Hill once produced an advertisement with the following copy line:

I don't know you
I don't know your company
I don't know your product
I don't know what your company stands for
I don't know your company's customers
I don't know your company's record
I don't know your company's reputation

     Now, what do you want to sell to me?

This emphasises perfectly the need for customers to be aware of an offering before they will consider that offering. It also goes further by showing the importance of reputation as part of the decision-making process.

Ries and Trout offer the intriguing fact that the average supermarket carries 12 000 different products or brands on its shelves, yet an average college graduate has a speaking vocabulary of only 8000 words. As a comparison it does not follow logically, but these facts do indicate how difficult it is to achieve awareness of a product with so many different offerings being made on a regular basis. It also shows that availability can be a problem, but also it is very difficult to stand out in a very crowded marketplace. Supermarkets are an interesting example as they have limits on the amount of shelf space and constraints on the capacity of their cabinets. When introducing a new product it is invariably at the expense of another product which is withdrawn from sale.

A successful move to win customers directly from a competitor was the promotion by Diners Club which offered free membership to anyone sending them a cut-up American Express card. Not only did this take out the competition, it also freed Diners Club of the effort and expense of doing a credit check on applicants. They decided that anyone with an Amex card would also be likely to qualify for Diners Club.

The difficulty with winning customers from competitors is that your competitors do not like it, and will probably fight back. Diners Club did not gain any long-term sustainable advantage from their promotion. Writing on sustainable advantage, Pankaj Ghemawat said: 'All of your competitors may be stupid some of the time BUT you cannot count on them being stupid all of the time.'

Winning customers is not as simple as a game of chance which you sometimes win and sometimes lose. Sustainable advantage comes from all elements of the marketing mix. Of course, sometimes customers get tired of their regular brands and move to an alternative for a brief change. While valuable, these so-called change-of-pace sales rarely offer enough business for a viable product.

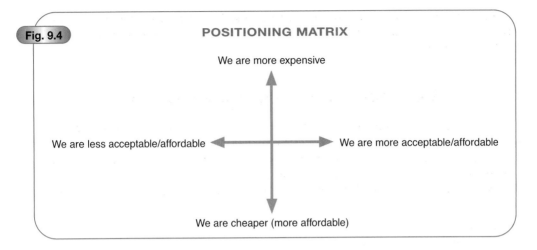

Fig. 9.4

POSITIONING MATRIX

We are more expensive

We are less acceptable/affordable ← → We are more acceptable/affordable

We are cheaper (more affordable)

It is often possible to plot competitive marketing offerings on a simple matrix such as the one in Fig. 9.4. The dimensions are those factors valued by customers, and in the figure these are the acceptability and affordability of an offering. The ideal position is to offer a more acceptable product at a more affordable price, as shown in the lower right quadrant of the Figure. Such a situation is rarely possible, it is more likely that any new offering will be in the more acceptable but also more expensive quadrant (top right), or in the less acceptable but cheaper one (bottom left). It is in these cases that customers have to make a value judgement, with a trade-off between features and price.

Once having gained a customer it is just as important to hang onto that customer and to trade on a regular basis.

There are various estimates about the cost of attracting new customers, but it is probably true that it costs on average up to five times more than the cost of retaining an existing customer. New business is the most expensive because it usually has to be won from a competitor. New customers, for whatever type of product, need to receive a disproportionate level of marketing input, which could include product design, promotion, personal selling or any other element from within the marketing mix.

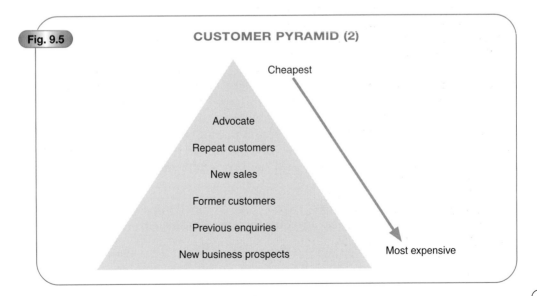

Fig. 9.5

CUSTOMER PYRAMID (2)

Cheapest

Advocate

Repeat customers

New sales

Former customers

Previous enquiries

New business prospects

Most expensive

Although a continuum can be constructed based on cost per customer, as shown in Fig. 9.5, it is often inappropriate to offer the same marketing message to all groups. The new business prospects are at a pre-transactional stage, which describes the period before any exchange takes place. Customers have to be persuaded about an intended purchase from a new supplier, and require reassurance that the offering is right for them. At the other end there are repeat sales either to loyal or occasional users, where the post-transactional stage exists. These customers may require confirmation that the purchase was right, and perhaps some encouragement to buy again. Repeat customers who become strong advocates also act as a source of new business because satisfied customers tell others and such endorsements are worth more than any advertisement.

Regular, loyal users are therefore extremely valuable to an organisation. At a time when many companies are valuing their brands as assets and incorporating these values into their balance sheets, it is a pity that no way can be found to put a value on loyal customers and include this also among the organisation's intangible assets. Of course the accountants do not treat customers as assets because most buyer–seller relationships are not contractual in a formal manner, but rely on the informal relationship between the two parties. However, it would be positive thinking for organisations to value their customer relationships even more than they value their other assets, and to devise measures to ensure they do not lose these valuable customers.

MARKETING OFFERINGS

It is the total marketing offering made to a potential customer that critically determines whether an exchange takes place or if that customer is lost.

The concept of the total product and its associated benefits was introduced in Chapter 2. The idea of a complete marketing offering is a development of this. It aims to focus a supplier on what is being offered to a specific customer. As conceived by McCarthy and Perrault (1990), the components of the marketing mix were seen to correlate with the Form, Time and Place components of value in its widest sense.

For many different types of products, suppliers have found that success has depended upon determining a particular target customer category or market segment, and then developing one specific offering to suit those needs precisely.

The actual offer that an organisation makes to its customers is called the offer mix. Thus, a marketing offering comprises all elements of the mix as below:

- the total product and/or service offered;
- the price including all discounts and deals; and
- the level of availability of the offering.

It would be naive to assume that marketing communication in the form of advertising and promotion does not play a significant role in making products seem acceptable. It obviously does. There are three major roles of communication, and different elements of the so-called promotional mix, and each can play a different part in achieving the best results regarding:

- creating awareness of the offering;
- a stimulus to purchase which can affect how an offer is evaluated;
- post-transactional reassurance.

Chapter 14 explores the process of communication and Chapters 15 to 18 explore the four traditional elements of the promotional mix which are: *paid advertising; public relations; sales promotion; and personal selling.* More recently, direct marketing, which includes direct mail and telemarketing, has developed to rival these elements. This development has enabled the promotional message to be targeted much more accurately, to reach the subsegments that are developing in many markets. Such 'micromarketing' is possible both in a tailored offering, such as a personalised new car, and in precise delivery of messages to the micromarket. Although the communication of the offer to target customers is a separate category its role in influencing the elements of the offer mix must not be ignored.

Customers will evaluate the offering using the tests of the '3 As' introduced earlier: acceptability, affordability and availability. These factors are discussed individually in more detail in Chapters 12 to 15. However, it must be remembered that a customer will evaluate the offer mix as a total package, trading off one element against another in making a buy/no-buy decision. Figure 9.6 illustrate how a product can be developed away from a commodity. The relative importance of all these factors will vary and depend both on the type of product and the particular customer involved. It is always a good discipline for marketers to try to put themselves in the position of a customer and try to see how a total offer can be assessed.

One obvious way of making an offer more acceptable is by the addition of service features to the core product. Service companies have always been able to achieve personalisation, as the delivery of the service is inseparable from the production. The delivered service is of course liable to variations, depending on who actually delivers the service. This is why service organisations such as McDonald's pay so much attention to the achievement of consistency in the quality of service given. This also introduces the requirement for all employees to value customers, which is discussed in the section on internal marketing in Chapter 11.

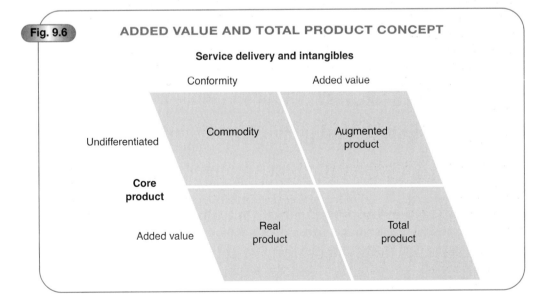

Fig. 9.6 · ADDED VALUE AND TOTAL PRODUCT CONCEPT

Think of a purchase you have made recently and note down the reasons why you bought the item under the '3 As' mentioned. When you have done that, think of an item or service that you did not buy and repeat the exercise.

The basis of the marketing concept is that organisations should match their offerings to the environment in which they are operating. Although it is sometimes possible to change how customers behave and their attitudes towards an offering by use of the controllable variables of marketing in particular, promotion, the perception customers have of a total offer is the critical test of an offering. This brings us to what is sometimes termed the positioning of a product or service.

Positioning starts with the choosing of a segment in which to compete (*see* Fig. 7.5). It goes further, in that an organisation could adopt a premium position or a low-cost position within that segment. Competitive position demands that an organisation considers what it is offering compared with competitors for the same target customers. It must choose a position which enables the organisation to answer the question, 'Why should customers buy from us?' This could mean differentiating the offering from competitors, by additional features or better availability perhaps. In his article 'Differentiation – of anything', Theodore Levitt wrote:

> There is no such thing as a commodity. All goods and services can be differentiated and usually are ... Everybody – whether producer, fabricator, seller, broker, agent, merchant – engages in a constant effort to distinguish his offering in his favour from all others.

Levitt goes on to consider the total product concept, which is discussed in the next chapter. It might be appropriate here to consider another view of the levels of an offering (*see* Fig. 2.2). That figure considered the way a product can be enhanced. Figure 9.6 is another way of representing the total product. Customers have to decide between two or more offerings from competing companies. Each communicates and promotes to the target group based on a strategy of who are those customers and what are we offering them (Product, Price and Distribution). All companies involved take a position, but the actual customers see any offering from a different perspective. It is further complicated by the macroenvironmental factors (PEST) discussed in Chapter 3. This is illustrated by Fig. 9.7.

POSITIONING

Positioning can be a confusing concept as there are two distinct approaches within marketing. One is market positioning which is an *a priori* activity. In this context it refers to the 'placing' of a product in that part of the market where it will be able to compete favourably with competitors' products. The other is based on the perception of customers regarding the product. This can be seen as a *post hoc* activity.

According to Wind 'a product's positioning is the place a product occupies in a given market, as perceived by the relevant group of customers; that group of customers is known as the target segment of the market.'

As can be seen the first approach considers the decisions taken by an organisation in putting together a competitive marketing mix, the second measures it by evaluating

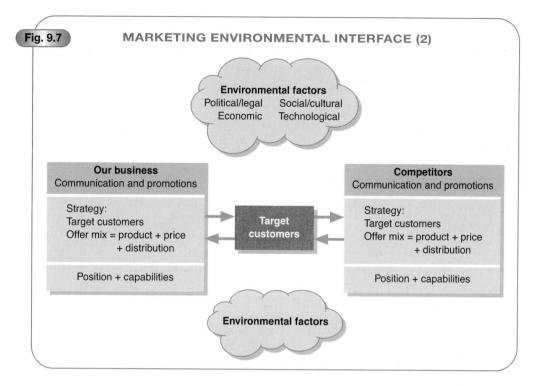

Fig. 9.7

MARKETING ENVIRONMENTAL INTERFACE (2)

Environmental factors
Political/legal   Social/cultural
Economic   Technological

Our business
Communication and promotions

Strategy:
Target customers
Offer mix = product + price
        + distribution

Position + capabilities

Target customers

Competitors
Communication and promotions

Strategy:
Target customers
Offer mix = product + price
        + distribution

Position + capabilities

Environmental factors

the way customers react. Customer reaction is the important issue, but it is the actual attributes and characteristics of a product offering which are controllable and will influence the perception of that product. It is necessary to consider those attributes of the total offering which make a product acceptable, affordable, and available to target customers. The process is shown in Fig. 9.8.

In studying the target segments it should be possible to identify those factors which potential customers see as desirable. There may be many such factors or only a few. Where a large number of factors are involved it is only by harnessing the power of computers that multidimensional models of the issues can be constructed. It is possible, however, to illustrate a simple positioning map (*see* Fig. 9.4 and Fig. 9.9) in two dimensions as long as it is realised there may be other key dimensions that customers value. Of course the importance of different factors varies, but this can also be accommodated.

A study of compact discs found factors such as: gives out a very good sound, enjoyable to play, and will not scratch, were rated much higher than: easy to store and can program the selections. This study was not aimed at specifically identifying attributes, but rather at seeking consistency in the information from respondents. Reliable and consistent methodology is a technical matter, but vital when developing attributes for use in positioning studies and gap analysis.

A positioning map for the US car market was published in the *Wall Street Journal*. The axes are reproduced in Fig. 9.9. You will see that they amalgamate several factors to enable a two-dimensional perceptual map to be produced. It will come as no surprise that Chrysler Motor Corporation research found customers placed BMW and Porsche in the top right quadrant; Toyota, Nissan and Volkswagen in the bottom right; with Cadillac and Mercedes in top left. Ford was considered as a single entity in bottom left, but if you considered the different models in Europe, it is likely the XR3i would be in a different place from the Orion.

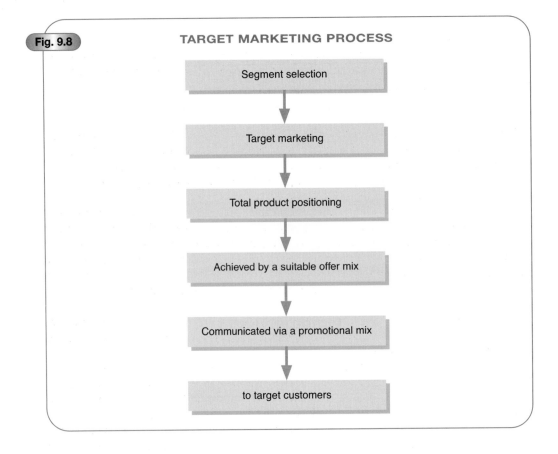

Fig. 9.8

TARGET MARKETING PROCESS

Segment selection

↓

Target marketing

↓

Total product positioning

↓

Achieved by a suitable offer mix

↓

Communicated via a promotional mix

↓

to target customers

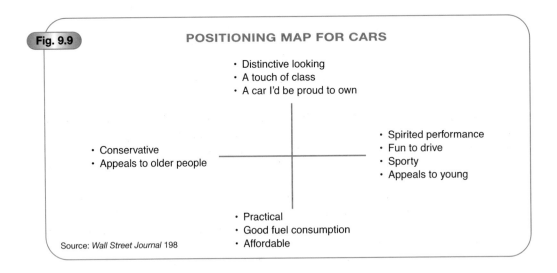

Fig. 9.9

POSITIONING MAP FOR CARS

- Distinctive looking
- A touch of class
- A car I'd be proud to own

- Conservative
- Appeals to older people

- Spirited performance
- Fun to drive
- Sporty
- Appeals to young

- Practical
- Good fuel consumption
- Affordable

Source: *Wall Street Journal* 198

You could suggest where to place some other car models with which you are familiar, but remember it is not your opinion that counts – it is the opinion of the customers in a particular target segment that is important.

For each segment, a number of ideal positions and desired levels of attributes will emerge. There will also be specific positions identified for competing brands. If you were designing a new product then the closer it is to the ideal mix of attributes, the better the chance of success. For an existing product it may be a strategy is necessary to try to change its position as perceived by potential customers.

When evaluating Positioning it is the attributes of an offering as interpreted by the chosen customers which are used in the buying decision process. These include rating of quality, value and the benefits that customer thinks a particular product offers. It is this perception which is critical, not the organisation's view of what it is offering. The role of marketing is to create a consistency between the offering and the appropriate customer perception. In this task there is a high degree of managing the expectations of the customer.

It is obviously possible to lose customers if a competitor makes a superior offering, but it is possible to win customers by positioning your product so that it is perceived to offer particularly desirable attributes.

US advertising men Ries and Trout describe this as repositioning your competitors. This actually means looking for a weakness in the competition's offering when compared with customer demands, and then to see if your strengths can be used to find an opening. If it is done in an effective way it could not only create awareness for your offering, but also develop a strong position for your product in its market. One of the examples Ries and Trout give is from the market for vodka in the USA. Pepsico ran an advertisement for their brand of imported vodka headed:

Most American Vodkas seem Russian
Samovar: made in Schenley, Pennsylvania
Smirnoff: made in Harford, Connecticut
Wolfschmidt: made in Lawrenceburg, Indiana

Stolichnaya is different. It is Russian.
Made in Leningrad, Russia.

This advertisement assumed the real thing was Russian-made vodka and it exposed the other brands with their pseudo-Russian names as frauds – a classic example of the repositioning of a brand and depositioning of the competition. (*Note*: The English vodka, Vladivar, made a virtue of its origins, used to advertising itself as the 'Vodka from Varrington'.)

This has now changed as, over the years, the whole play on 'Russia-ness' became irrelevant to potential customers, in comparison with other more important differentiators in the market. Smirnoff in the UK is the brand leader; the sophisticated one; the establishment. However, vodka is drunk predominantly by under 25s, so Vladivar repositioned itself to appeal to the young with a cheeky, irreverent style. An example of one of their outdoor posters with the 'play' on the word 'Vladi' is shown on one of the colour plates.

Another example of repositioning, is the way the holiday resort of Torbay (Torquay, Brixham and Paignton) halted the decline in visitors by rebranding the resort as the 'English Riviera'. South Devon has Britain's best climate in terms of sunshine hours and temperature, but ten years ago it was attracting a decreasing number of visitors. Visitors came primarily from northern England and were disproportionately from the lower socio-economic groups. The rebranding has created a new image of the area. It has had to be backed up by product improvements, as indicated in this quote from Maggie Corke, assistant Director of Torbay Tourist Board: 'If you call yourself a Riviera, you have to live up to it.'

This has meant redevelopment and new amenities. It is, however, the new position of the 'English Riviera' that is credited with the change in perception of the area and the halting of the decline in tourists.

Another attempt at repositioning an old product was the new image for the British Labour Party. The new position did not attract a sufficient number of voters to win the 1992 General Election. But there is no doubt that a change in the perception of the party has been achieved. The result of the 1997 election, and the overwhelming victory by the New Labour Party illustrates that it works.

All these examples involve changing the consumer's perception of an existing product for which there was a continuing customer demand. In every case what was considered acceptable or affordable was changed. This involved making changes to the controllable aspects of the marketing offering and thereby change the basis of customer evaluation of the product. Interestingly most changes were made to the product or its promotion, for these examples price was less relevant. 'Place' as an element of geographic location of Torbay is static but 'place' as one of the four marketing 'Ps' actually refers to channels between supplier and customer. It can be seen from these examples that 'place' is not a particularly controllable variable, especially outside the area of consumer and industrial products. In fact physical evidence, as mentioned earlier, is more important for Torbay, as this certainly shapes perception, while with a political party the people element is vital.

BRANDING

An important result of the way customers perceive an offering is the recognition of that offering as a brand. This is a substantive endorsement of all the activity that stems from the marketing offering, and is a distinct image which differentiates one offering from another. While the actual brand must be created and measured by the reaction of customers to a specific offering, companies build brands by the consistent way an offering is made to the marketplace. A strong brand and a strategy based on this is likely to prove very difficult for competitors to copy, and hence offer a real advantage over other offerings.

Branding is the practice of giving a distinctive identification – usually a name, symbol or design – to a product or range of products, and through usage and promotion establishing this identification in the marketplace. Products or product lines so identified are termed brands, and are the focus of marketing activity that is often referred to as brand strategy. The objective is to attract a group of customers who are 'brand loyal', in other words they purchase the brand regularly and resist switching to other competing brands.

The term brand in the marketing context refers to more than a readily recognisable name. It involves a product and a set of values. These values usually relate to the perceived quality of the product or to its value for money. Ford as a brand could be said to represent value for money whereas Ghia within the Ford range of products is intended to represent extra quality.

It is clear from this example that within the concept of brands there is a number of levels. At the highest level is the organisation, for example Ford, McDonald's or Coca-Cola. This is sometimes called the 'Umbrella' brand. At the second level there is what might be referred to as the sub-brand. Within this level would be names such as the Escort, Big Mac or Diet Coke.

Though distinctive symbols, corporate logos and packaging may accompany the brand, it will usually be most readily identified through a brand name. For legal purposes, brands and brand and product names have to be protected from unauthorised use by a trademark. An equivalent legal safeguard for less tangible properties such as literary and artistic works is the establishment of a copyright.

Branding has a long history, probably most commonly associated with the maker's stamps and hallmarks used by artisans through the ages. From a marketing perspective, branding has become more commonplace since the turn of the century, developing alongside the emergence of marketing itself. Brand names give products an identity among customers and intermediaries alike, distinguishing them from standard commodities, and particularly from competitor products. Brand names are adopted by customers as a shorthand identification of the product, and taken as an assurance of the general quality and characteristics of the product. Research studies employing 'blind' product tests, of branded versus unbranded and control products, repeatedly show respondents to have preferences for branded products, and a willingness to pay more for them. It is not surprising, therefore, that companies nowadays assign asset values to brand names, or that the owners of famous brand names such as Rolls-Royce or Coca-Cola go to great lengths to legally protect their properties.

It will be seen from these examples that brand names generally involve names which are:

- easy to remember;
- distinctive;
- easy to spell;
- easy to pronounce (ideally regardless of language).

Clearly the names already mentioned: Ford, Escort, McDonald's, and Coca-Cola conform to these requirements.

It takes a long time to create a distinctive name to which consumers relate positively. Once established a brand name becomes a valuable asset to the owner. Indeed the value is now sufficiently tangible for it to be included as a balance sheet item. Inevitably because of this major companies defend their brand names almost regardless of the legal costs involved.

The adoption of a suitable name for a product can have a profound effect on the products long-term success. The Japanese founders of Sony made up the name Sony on the basis of the English word sound as they initially saw their business in this sector of the electronics industry. Compaq, the computer company also adopted a carefully crafted brand name to epitomise the major feature of their original product; its relative compactness and portability. Clearly in both of these examples the name selected has outlasted the limited product orientation involved in the name's creation.

In many markets, brand names are used by buyers as convenient signposts during search and shopping behaviour, where favoured brands are mentally ranked at the top of a 'choice set' of contenders. Marketers will be concerned to maintain and develop such brand loyalty. Though branding has recently become more popular within industrial markets, the most well-known brands are still almost exclusively among consumer goods and service markets. In choosing brand names and developing a branding strategy, manufacturers may opt for:

1 Multiproduct brands, or 'umbrella' or 'family' brands, where the company uses one standard brand name, often the company name, for all its products, e.g. Heinz, Walkers, Colmans. Multiproduct branding can offer marketing economies where a favourable brand name carries across a whole product assortment, to the benefit of otherwise weaker products, and assisting in the acceptance of new products by consumers and intermediaries alike. Equally, a problem or failure in one product could work to the detriment of the whole brand 'family'.

2 Multibrand products involve a manufacturer assigning different brand names to different products, or even to various products within a product line. This practice is commonly seen in consumer good sectors such as biscuits, detergents, and cigarettes, where companies field a variety of products that are often individually developed and targeted at specific segments, or for particular uses or occasions. In other instances, less through design than circumstance, large manufacturer groups will find themselves with an extensive mix of competing brands, taken on board through a series of corporate acquisitions.

3 Retailer own brands predominately associated with consumer retail chains where 'own-label' brands have proved a useful source of supplementary business for some manufacturers (though some more brand-conscious companies have a deliberate policy of dismissing such ties as a threat to their brand franchise). Those entering own-brand contracts may value the extra sales involved, with little promotional outlay and at planned volumes and delivery dates, offering production economies through segments otherwise closed to them, or supplied by competitors. However, the cost of such business may be strict adherence to contract terms that include quality inspections, production-vetting and no-question returns policies, at prices that demand strict cost controls for often thin margins.

Indeed, aside from their commanding position in own-label contracting, leading supermarket groups have, through concentration, become so powerful in recent years that even large branded products manufacturers may have to make cost concessions to avoid the threat of their brands being 'delisted'.

EXERCISE

Visit a local supermarket and consider how much shelf space is allocated to the store's own label brands compared with the national manufacturer brands.

CUSTOMERS AND CONSUMERS

In this chapter the term 'customer' has been used to indicate the recipient of a product. In fact as the following example shows there can be more than one customer for such an offering.

Consider a manufacturer of chocolate confectionery countlines such as Mars Bars. This company needs, at the very least, to have individual product offerings which specifically address the needs of the wholesaler who receives the product in bulk from the factory, those of the retailer who displays the product to potential customers, and the consumer who buys the product as a snack or treat. Each of these are customers but each requires a different package of benefits. The final consumer will focus on an enjoyable, widely available, and reasonably priced product. The retailer wants a product which will attract people into the shop, look attractive when displayed, and give a good profit margin. It is also probable that supermarkets might need a different balance in their total offering from that required by the corner newsagent or station kiosk. One example of these different needs is that manufacturers of chocolate confectionery countlines introduced multipacks which are more relevant to the needs of grocery customers.

In addition to these separate requirements there is also a need to co-ordinate activities along a distribution chain. For instance television is an important tool in the promotion of this product. For a TV campaign to have maximum impact it is essential that the wholesaler be informed in time to ensure that adequate stocks are available, and the retailer perhaps given a special point-of-sale display to reinforce the television message.

The above example applies to a manufacturer who has decided to supply several different channels of distribution in order to gain the maximum sale of a product. However, such decisions also cost money. A smaller organisation than Mars might be faced with a choice between a number of different ways of reaching the final consumer.

COST OF PRODUCT MODIFICATIONS

All businesses need to consider both profit maximisation and risk assessment when balancing the cost considerations of what is to be offered with those of customer demand. Most changes to a marketing offering will usually cost money, and the elements of the marketing mix can be equated with headings used in Malcolm McDonald's components of cost model (*see* Fig. 9.10). This model can be used to assess the situation. The model shows that in addition to the production cost of a product, the supply organisation also has to cover the cost of distribution and promotion. Although organisations aim to create and keep customers they do not remain in business long if they fail to make a profit. Every additional cost incurred in improving the acceptability of an offering must be considered in respect of the extra revenue that such a change could produce. The message is one of sensibly assessing all components of an offering and concentrating on those which offer the best returns.

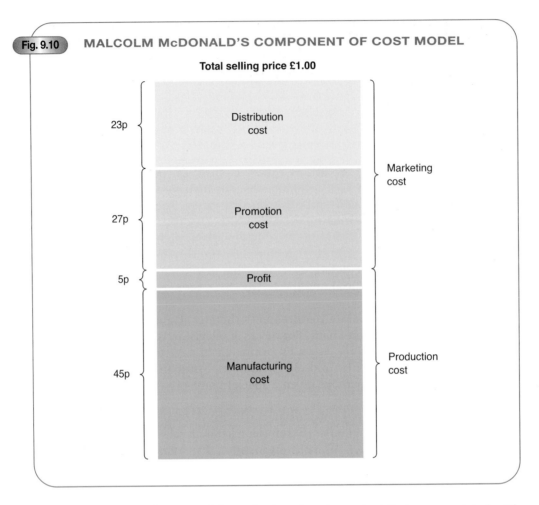

Fig. 9.10 MALCOLM McDONALD'S COMPONENT OF COST MODEL

Total selling price £1.00

- 23p — Distribution cost
- 27p — Promotion cost
- 5p — Profit
- 45p — Manufacturing cost

Marketing cost

Production cost

The component of cost model emphasises four important factors associated with marketing decisions which can easily be overlooked. First, it shows that the costs attributable to marketing functions are as much part of the total cost of supplying a product or service as those associated with actually producing the product or service. Second, just as the cost of production is made up of fixed and variable costs, so the costs of marketing can be classified under these headings. Third, the costs associated with the marketing elements can be at least in theory interchangeable. Lastly, the profit earned by a product can be increased by reducing the cost of any of the elements within the total cost.

CONCLUSION

In order for a company's marketing programmes to be successful, all of the factors in this chapter should be taken into account – from identification of the target market through to the positioning of the product. These are among the most important decisions that management will take with regards to the actual marketing strategy to be followed.

All of the elements of the marketing mix will have an important role to play. Further details of each of them will be unfolded in the following chapters. However, before putting marketing mix theories into practice, the objectives of the organisation must be taken into consideration. It is essential that these are identified and understood in order that management can target, position and generally market its products or services to the best of its ability.

Customers in western countries are offered far more products and services than they can afford or need. To be successful in such a competitive and dynamic situation requires marketers to understand their environment and to continually look for market advantage in the context of all the influences on the supplier–buyer relationship that they seek to build.

David Ogilvy, the Scottish-born founder of one of the world's largest advertising agencies, once said: 'Marketers who ignore marketing research are as guilty as generals who ignore intelligence reports during battle.' It is only after studying both customers and competitors in the ever-changing marketplace that decisions about the product offering can be made.

QUESTIONS

1 Using the matrix in Fig. 9.9, position six cars according to your perception. Compare this with another student and explain the differences.

2 Marks & Spencer is a very successful retail store group. How has it achieved a quality position in the marketplace?

3 If a company launches a new product, e.g. Mars ice cream, will customers naturally place it in a similar position to the original product, e.g. Mars Bar?

4 Consider how a product, such as a Ford Escort car, has changed since its launch. Why do you think this has happened?

FURTHER READING

Booms, B. and Bitner, M. J., 'Marketing strategies and organisation structures for service firms', in J. Donelly and W. George (Eds), *The Marketing of Services*, American Marketing Association, 1981, pp. 47–51, Chicago.

Borden, N., 'The concept of the marketing mix', *Journal of Advertising Research*, 1964.

Cowell, D. (1994) *The Marketing of Services*, 2nd Edn, Heinemann, Oxford.

Drucker P. (1968) *The Practice of Management*, Pan, London.

Ghemawat, P., 'Sustainable advantage', *Harvard Business Review*, September–October 1986.

Gronroos, C., 'Marketing orientated strategies in service businesses', *Finnish Journal of Business*, 4, 1979.

Levitt, T., 'Differentiation – of anything', *Harvard Business Review*, January–February 1980.

Lury, A., 'Demographics tell me nothing', *Admap*, December 1990.

McCarthy, E. J. and Perrault, W. D. (1990) *Basic Marketing*, Irwin, Illinois.

Palmer A. (1994) *Principles of Services Marketing*, McGraw-Hill, Maidenhead.

Piercy, N. (1992) *Marketing-led Strategic Change*, Butterworth Heinemann, Oxford.

Prince, M., 'How consistent is the information in positioning studies?' *Journal of Advertising Research*, June 1990.

Ries, A. and Trout, J. (1981) *Positioning the Battle for Your Mind*, McGraw-Hill, London.

Wind, Y., 'Going to market: new twists for some old tricks', *Wharton Magazine*, 4, 1980.

CASE STUDY

Plea for Blood Donors as Stocks Slump to 'Crisis Level'

For the third time in 5 years a dramatic appeal has been launched for more people to come forward to give blood as stocks again slump to less than one day's supply for the country's hospitals.

The National Blood Service have warned that supplies are at a 'critically low level', and have asked regular donors who may not have given recently: 'Please come back this week as next week may be too late.'

There is also a need for those who have never donated blood to become new donors. The UK Blood Transfusion Service has, in the past, been successful at developing its operations to meet the ever-increasing demand from hospitals for its products. However there are times when extra effort is required.

Although high profile appeals produce a good response in the short term, there are clearly issues which need to be dealt with on a longer timescale to ensure 'such a worrying situation' did not continue to occur again.

The BTS (Blood Transfusion Service) has begun to respond to this challenge and they now regularly advertise for donors. The use of advertising suggests that marketing concepts might provide a useful approach to analysing the problem.

Perhaps they need to start by asking who is their customer? At first sight the obvious answer would seem to be the users of their product: hospitals and patients requiring blood transfusions. However, another way of looking at the operation is to consider the donor as a customer. This then leads to the next question: what is the product or benefit exchanged between the BTS and the donor? It is tempting to suggest that it is a pint of blood exchanged for a cup of tea and, if needed, a packet of iron tablets which are given to donors at the end of their donation session. This, however, is supported by the provision of certificates to each donor and badges to recognise that a certain number of donations have been made. Perhaps the exchange involves blood for a 'done the right thing' feeling rather than for a cup of tea. Furthermore as all donors know, the pint of blood is not actually missed. So if that 'done the right thing' feeling was not exchanged for the blood donated what was it exchanged for? The answer is not a simple one, but it might involve the sacrifice of time by the donor.

One reason for the Blood Transfusion Service being less able to keep up with demand now is the declining number of the organisations large enough to co-operate with the BTS by providing facilities on site, thus allowing their employees to give blood during working hours. For these donors, the exchange had been a 'done the right thing' feeling in company time. This is often valued differently from personal time; if any waiting around was involved this was at least tolerated by the donors and often welcomed. Because of the reduction in company on-site giving, many of these donors were lost when the exchange started to require the time spent giving blood, and also the additional time spent travelling to and from a blood transfusion centre. To reduce the time involved meant introducing appointment systems and other approaches to ensure that the donor could see that what he or she was actually exchanging was treated as having value. It was not until this price element of the exchange had been addressed that steps could be taken which would ensure adequate supplies could be collected routinely.

Question

Consider the operations of the Blood Transfusion Service and suggest what is the product offering involved and how might the BTS develop this offering to appeal to the potential donors they require.

CHAPTER 10

Product – The Fundamental Marketing Concept

The product determines the upper limit of a supplier's profitability. The quality of the remaining components of the marketing mix determines the extent to which that potential is achieved.

INTRODUCTION

In the previous chapter the concept of a total marketing offering, sometimes called the marketing mix was introduced and discussed. In this chapter it is the product itself that will be considered in detail. As product offerings are the common factor linking any company and its customers, and as the product is the very framework around which other elements of the marketing mix are draped, decisions about product reach to the very centre of marketing strategy and management. The product will be an obvious focus of attention for all customers, and for all staff within a company. It will also, of course, be an object of interest to leading competitors, suppliers, potential customers, intermediaries and many others.

It is necessary to remember that the product is the part of the marketing mix which satisfies the fundamental customer need, but it is easy to confuse the basic product with the total product offering. While customers select from different product offerings rather than basic products, it is the basic product element which offers the eventual benefit and this has already been introduced in Chapter 2.

It has often been said that the 'quality of a product is remembered long after the price has been forgotten'. The point of this statement is that a product is purchased for a specific purpose and it will be continued to be judged by how well these functions are achieved even if this is a long time after the actual purchase.

EXAMPLE

Perhaps you own a calculator bought several years ago. Can you remember how much you paid for it? Even if you can, do you really think of the value for money aspect of the calculator? For many people the important issue is that you want to know it will continue to perform all the calculations you require. Is this your view?

WHAT IS A PRODUCT?

While the question is almost rhetorical, it is necessary to see the product from a market perspective, rather than in solely physical or company-centred terms – a mistake often made by production-dominated companies.

This is certainly reflected in one of the most useful definitions proposed by the American Marketing Association:

> **Anything which can be offered to a market for attention, acquisition or consumption including physical objects, services, personalities, organisations and desires.**

Our definition is more focused on what the customer perceives a product to be, so that a working definition might be:

> **Everything that the customer receives that is of value in terms of a perceived want, need or problem.**

Though rather broad and vague, such a definition allows that different customers will vary in their perception of their needs, wants and problems.

This could suggest that some products might appear to customers as better value or more attractive, for various reasons almost irrespective of producer intentions or objective measures of quality or product input. The result being that some product offerings will not be accepted by enough customers, and will fail commercially. Others may survive and continue to be marketed although in low volume and not necessarily producing many profits (so-called weaker or marginal products), while a few will gain commanding market shares as 'brand leaders' in their markets.

The term *product* applies not only to physical products, but also to services and other intangibles including causes and ideas. For example, the major charity organisations such as Oxfam and Save The Children are as actively involved in making product offerings as the ubiquitous widget manufacturer in the West Midlands! Even in the case of an everyday physical product such as washing-up liquid, there will be intangible extras and associations that are offered in addition to the basic product, for example the quality assurance of a known brand name and manufacturer source.

Simply stated, the marketer needs to view the product as a multidimensional offering, a mix of tangible features and intangible attributes together with an element of services, bundled around a basic or core benefit. This multi-layered view of the product is illustrated in Fig. 10.1.

The *basic product* represents the essential benefit on offer to the customer but expressed in a product form, e.g. an easily applied scuff-resistant shoe polish for children's shoes. The basic product could just as easily be a service such as the repairs carried out on a broken machine.

The *real product* will comprise the basic product plus an additional 'layer' of tangible features that make up the listed product or service, e.g. design and colour, packaging, quality specification, brand name. The *total product* will add to the listed product a number of intangible extras that augment the offering by adding utility through services (e.g. delivery, customer service), and perhaps subtle qualities and assurances of distinctive value to the customer.

It is probably worth noting that, in an era of increasing buyer sophistication and market competitiveness, marketing success is more likely to be achieved by those companies that manage to develop competitive advantage through original service

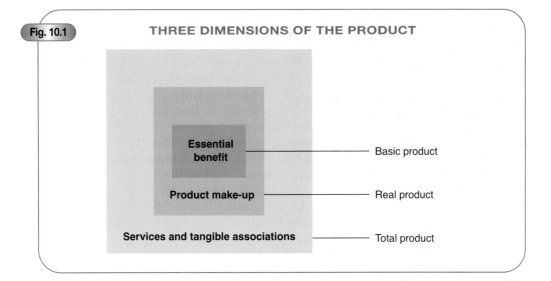

Fig. 10.1

THREE DIMENSIONS OF THE PRODUCT

Essential benefit —————— Basic product

Product make-up —————— Real product

Services and tangible associations —————— Total product

offerings and combinations associated with the 'penumbra' of the total product and the potential it offers for development and differentiation. Alternatively stated, the critical part of the value chain has shifted from the base product and the production process, to the wider product and the extended organisation that supports it.

Thus, if we consider the example of a farmer growing a seasonal crop, i.e. potatoes. A customer's purchase decision will involve a choice based on experience and information gained from many sources. At one level there could be a choice between a 50 kg sack of unwashed potatoes from the farm shop; or delivery at home from a mobile greengrocer with a van; or maybe a 5 kg bag of presorted and cleaned potatoes from a local supermarket. Each comes with a different level of added features and the acceptability of the purchase is likely to depend on the customer's particular requirement for such features, as well as the other elements in the total product offering. Some of these the farmer can control others he can't. This should illustrate the difficulty of separating the product from the product offering, a problem which is even greater when considering well-known branded manufactured products.

Although most of the accepted definitions of a product were probably intended to refer to the need-satisfying object or service component part of the product offering, in practice it will be seen that they apply equally to a product offering. Therefore the use of the word 'product' to cover the 'core' product, or perhaps the total product, or even the complete product offering, does mean that marketers must be extremely careful when using the term. It is critical that they should ensure understanding of the appropriate meaning of the word 'product' relevant to a specific given situation.

TYPES OF PRODUCT

There are a number of useful ways of classifying products. One of the most basic was introduced in Chapter 2 in the discussion regarding the different ways of making a journey. These included travelling in a car owned by the traveller, in a hired car, and by train, bus or plane. It was clear from this that the journey could be made by using purchased physical objects, i.e. the car, petrol and so on, or by purchasing the service offered by the car hire company or one of the organisations providing one of the alternative modes of transport.

This is an interesting example since although the use of a hire car or other transport provider involves purchasing a service, the use of the traveller's own car involves purchasing the essential physical objects (car and petrol) and in addition at least two mandatory service products. The first of these is vehicle insurance and the second is that offered by the Vehicle Licensing Authority which collects the Road Fund Licence Fee on behalf of the Government and issues the Road Fund Licence or tax disc. In addition, the car user will usually require other services such as those offered by garages who supply and service cars, sell petrol and provide toilet facilities.

Thus, while it would at first sight seem possible to separate products or product offerings into physical objects and services, in practice it is useful to see this as a continuum, with any specific product offering being either a service or a combination of a service and a physical object (*see* Fig. 10.2).

Another way in which products may be classified is by the type of customer. Some products such as heavy machinery, cooling towers, factories, ships and lorries are with few exceptions purchased by industrial organisations. Such products can then be classified as industrial products. Other products such as shoes, tea, visits to the cinema, cans of soft drink and so on are typically purchased for use or consumption by individuals. These products are accordingly generally classified as consumer products.

While industrial products are seldom purchased by individuals, most consumer products are also purchased for use within organisations. Thus hotels need to buy essentially the same food and household products as are purchased for use in the home. The difference is the quantities in which these products are typically purchased.

For instance, whereas toilet tissue might be purchased in packets of one to nine rolls for use in the home they could well be purchased by the 100 or 1000 rolls for a hotel or hotel chain.

Consumer products

It will be seen from Fig. 10.3 that consumer products are classified by how they meet the need for which they are purchased and by the way they are purchased rather than on the basis of the characteristics of the products themselves.

The three main categories of consumer product are consumables, durables and services. Consumables are those products which are used up in the process of satisfying the need for which they were purchased. Thus, a thirsty person who buys a bottle of Coca-Cola needs to drink the contents to benefit from that purchase.

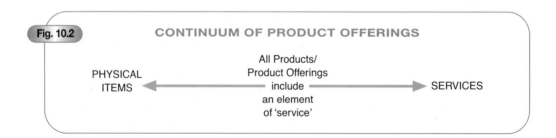

Fig. 10.2 — CONTINUUM OF PRODUCT OFFERINGS

PHYSICAL ITEMS ← All Products/ Product Offerings include an element of 'service' → SERVICES

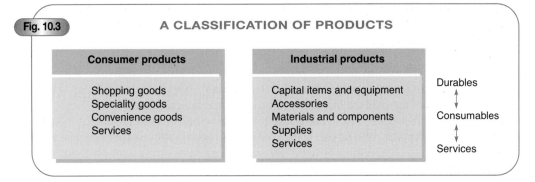

Fig. 10.3 · A CLASSIFICATION OF PRODUCTS

Consumable consumer products can be further divided into convenience goods and speciality goods.

- *Convenience goods* These represent the majority of frequently purchased consumer goods, bought with little effort or deliberation, e.g. newspapers, breakfast cereals, coffee, soap and cosmetics. The list includes all the classic mass-market products which can be purchased from any supermarket or corner shop. Much of the early development of marketing theory was aimed at the needs of these fmcg (fast moving consumer goods) products.

  It is often useful to further differentiate products within this category using the following subcategories: staples, impulse, and emergency. Staples are those products which are usually bought as part of an everyday shopping-list. Impulse goods are those purchased on sight without being considered previously, e.g. special offers or the chocolates, sweets and magazines sold at supermarket checkouts. Emergency goods are those consumable products for which buyers are likely to make a special visit to the shops when supplies run out or are low. Disposable nappies, milk, coffee, and cigarettes are all products likely to come within this category.

- *Speciality goods* These are consumable products which can only be purchased from specialist retailers and which consumers select deliberately. Examples are prescription medicines, alcoholic beverages, and hobby consumables including DIY products such as paint, photographic processing chemicals and artist supplies. In a second category would be food products purchased for a special occasion such as a dinner party, goods bought as a gift, and many cosmetics and personal care products.

Durables are purchased for the benefit they provide in themselves. Thus a bicycle purchased to take part in the London to Brighton cycle ride will, providing there are no mishaps, be essentially the same at the end of the journey as it was at the beginning or at any stage in between. Providing it is looked after it could be used year after year for the same purpose. Over time it will suffer from use until eventually it will need to be overhauled or discarded and replaced. It may then be considered to have come to the end of its useful life.

Consumer durable products can be further divided into the following three categories:

- *Shopping goods* These are those products which are usually selected after 'shopping around' to compare price, quality, specifications, design or colour. Clothes, white goods (washing machines, refrigerators, etc.), brown goods (television, stereo systems, etc.), furniture, and motor vehicles are typical of products in this category.

These are purchases made after considering the options available, and are often products where value for money is as important as the features themselves. Buyers generally exhibit dissonance-reducing buying behaviour when purchasing this type of product.

- *Speciality goods* These are generally products which are only available from a limited number of outlets. Car spares, textbooks, foreign maps, specialist tools, lamp shades and musical instruments are examples of products in this category.
- *Emergency durable goods* These are those products which buyers are likely to need without delay. Typical of this category would be replacement windscreens, exhausts and tyres.

The third main category of consumer products is consumer services. These are often part of the same offering with one of the categories above, but there are essential differences between services and the other two categories. These differences will be discussed in more detail in the section on services (*see* page 158).

Industrial products

Industrial products, sometimes termed business products, are products bought by organisations manufacturing or supplying products or providing services. Unlike consumer goods, they are bought not for their own sake or for personal consumption, but in order to contribute to an organisational objective. For the economist they are considered intermediate products or inputs, which means that the demand for this type of product will ultimately depend upon that of the final market being served by the organisation. This relationship is termed 'derived demand'. For this reason the markets for most types of industrial product are subject to greater fluctuations in demand and periodic cycles of activity than is usual for consumer products.

Figure 10.3 (*see* page 155) also identifies the major industrial product categories. It will be seen that these categories depend upon the relationship between the product and the purchasing organisation. Thus, depending upon the user, a computer may be classified either as a capital equipment item or as an accessory. The importance of recognising this difference will be seen in the detailed sections discussing these different categories:

- *Capital plant and equipment* This category includes those products which are required by an organisation to carry out the objective for which it exists and which thereby increase the organisation's revenue-generating capacity. Thus items of power station equipment such as boilers or turbine generator units come into this category for an electricity utility. A power press, transfer or assembly line would be within this category for a vehicle manufacturer. Similarly an airliner such as an Airbus A300 would be a capital item for an airline since it would enable this organisation to carry more passengers or freight and thus earn more revenue.
- *Accessories* These are also capital items but differ from plant and equipment in that accessories do not directly increase the capacity of the organisation to carry out the objective for which it exists or by which it generates revenue. Thus investment by a vehicle manufacture in electricity generating plant may be cost-effective but since it does not increase the organisation's capacity to manufacture vehicles it should be classed as an accessory. Likewise the airline purchasing a computer system to schedule passengers or a hanger in which to service their new Airbus A300s is investing in accessories not capital plant.

Recognising the difference between capital plant and equipment and accessories is important to suppliers since organisations purchasing capital plant and equipment tend to be extremely knowledgeable regarding their requirements. These requirements will thus, normally be specified very precisely and suppliers will be expected to comply with these specifications. Accessories, in contrast, although often involving items of similar value to capital plant and equipment, are generally specified less rigorously and the specifications are more likely to be changed on the recommendation of the supplier. Clearly, by correctly classifying a product from the customer's point of view as either plant and equipment or as an accessory, a supplier can make an offer which is more likely to meet the customer's actual requirements.

Both of these product categories normally involve carefully prepared production plans, design investigations and trials, protracted supplier discussions and negotiations. Marketing such products involves direct links with prospective purchasers, specialist-to-specialist technical contacts, presale service, and often contractual relationships extending far beyond the installation and commissioning stage.

In marketing terms, equipment markets will be characterised by the number of competing manufacturers who deal directly with their major corporate customers and specialist stockholding dealers who serve the market at large.

EXAMPLE

For a quarry supplying gravel to a construction site the purchase of a lorry would be classed as an accessory, whereas for a contract haulier it would be considered a capital equipment item. It can be through understanding the implications inherent in such classifications that products can be differentiated and competitive advantage created.

- *Materials and components* These represent the physical inputs to the production and delivery of the final product. This category includes raw materials, processed materials and components. Raw materials are often bought direct from domestic or overseas suppliers on long-term contracts. Processed materials such as chemical formulations, cloth or sheet steel are sourced either directly or through intermediaries as finished materials which are then used to manufacture the product being produced, for instance detergents, vehicle components or clothing. Contractual arrangements may be preferred by customers when justified by the volumes involved to ensure continuity of supply and quality standards. Promotional elements are unlikely to feature heavily in the marketing of materials, as standard grading systems may limit competition to differences in price, technical support and distribution arrangements.

  Components vary from standard items such as nuts, bolts and other fasteners, valves, pumps and switches, to more specialist customised items such as fabrications and subassemblies. While standard items may be bought in by volume-contract arrangements, or multiple-sourced distributors, key components and customised parts may be subject to individual contracts. Such subcontractor relationships increasingly involve close collaboration between customer and supplier. Following practices pioneered in Japan, increasingly this collaboration can include implementing JIT (just-in-time) systems, quality vetting programmes and single sourcing agreements.

● *Supplies (consumables)* Unlike materials and components which form part of the product produced by the organisation, supplies are those products which are used within the production process. These include the materials used in production such as lubricants, abrasives and cleaning materials, office sundries such as paperclips and note pads, and a whole miscellany of other items needed for various functions within the organisation such as the food supplied in the canteen and the refills needed to stock the vending machines. Generally these are standard, easily substituted, products purchased through intermediaries who often compete as much on the basis of the service provided as on price. Supplies generally fall into categories based on usage such as maintenance, repair, and operational items. This leads to the mnemonic MRO items which in some organisations is also the term for monthly re-order. Such items are not major cost items and are usually replenished regularly without much consideration of alternative products.

Services

Very few 'products' are purely 100 per cent service or 100 per cent tangible product. Usually they involve a mix of the two. In the previous chapter the three additional aspects of People, Process and Physical evidence were introduced. Also the added value matrix (Fig. 9.6 *see* page 140) which linked products and services is providing a unique offering. Kotler suggests there are four categories of 'products':

● a pure service;
● a major service with accompanying minor goods and services;
● a tangible good with accompanying service;
● a pure tangible product.

Sometimes customer services are subclassified as service products and product services.

1 *Service products* are those directly offered to individuals such as hairdressing, health care, transportation, education and insurance, a pure service or major service component.
2 *Product services* are those associated with a physical object such as car repairs, property repairs and plumbing services, each of these involving tangible goods.

Industrial and business service products can vary from those above where there is a legal requirement, such as accountants and civil aviation inspectors, to those providing peripheral services such as cleaners and the catering contractors who provide canteen services. Some industrial service companies provide an essentially financial benefit, as, for instance, the contract car leasing companies who are often the legal owners of the cars provided by employers to their employees. Such companies have developed the service offered so that for their customer organisations it is significantly cheaper to lease these cars than it would be to own them. It also allows the trading organisation to concentrate on its own core area of business leaving the car leasing in the hands of a specialist company.

However, Kotler's categories can apply and be used to enhance the benefit offered. For instance, servicing of key equipment and installations such as photocopiers or computers is often integral to the supply contract for the equipment. Pure services can be

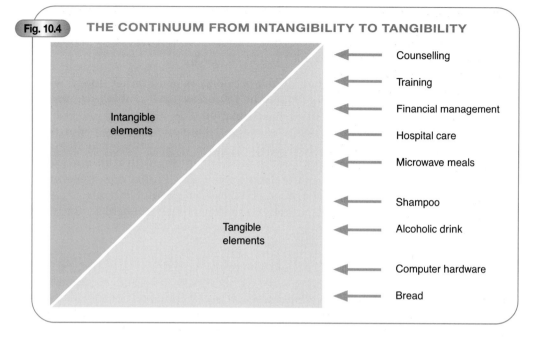

Fig. 10.4 THE CONTINUUM FROM INTANGIBILITY TO TANGIBILITY

exemplified by technological developments which have created new industrial markets for advisory services in specialist fields such as expert-systems software development.

Like vehicle leasing, haulage and distribution services are likely to involve contract arrangements. Other specialist business services such as market research, advertising or management consultancy are likely to be selected and managed by the relevant functional managers.

Earlier in this chapter products and services were placed in a continuum. It is possible to put products and services on this model to produce a continuum of tangibility (*see* Fig. 10.4).

While it is generally accepted that the marketing of services involves fully appreciating those characteristics which are fundamental to this type of product, and often also involves some element of a tangible product, it is useful to otherwise consider services as simply a specific product category. They are part of the total product offered to customers and can be a vital ingredient to gain advantage over competition.

There are some specific issues that must be considered when marketing services and these are discussed in the next chapter.

It is necessary at this point to introduce the concept of the product life cycle, to lay the groundwork for a more detailed examination of key issues in product policy, which will be covered later in Chapter 19.

THE PRODUCT LIFE CYCLE

The basic concept of a life cycle being an unavoidable feature of marketing was introduced in Chapter 2. This has over the years become an accepted part of marketing theory, providing a potentially valuable analytical and strategic tool. For this reason it is now appropriate to discuss this concept in greater detail. The basic life cycle pattern borrows heavily on the biological model of successive life stages, from gestation and birth, through adolescence to maturity and eventual demise. The marketing translation of this progression is illustrated in simple form in Fig. 10.5:

- *Introduction* In the immediate post-launch period sales build rather slowly, while financially the product has not recouped the resources put into its development, during what is strictly speaking a prior stage, gestation.
- *Growth* The product 'takes off', gaining market share and an early majority of buyers. Profits grow.
- *Maturity* For many products the longest period, beginning with continued sales growth that eventually slows as saturation approaches. Profits dip later in this period, as marketing outlays are stepped up to counter competitor entrants.
- *Decline* Sales may fall drastically, or the product may linger unhealthily for some time. Profits fall appreciably, giving way to, sometimes heavy, losses.

The generic product life cycle (PLC) model is commonly depicted as a bell-shaped curve, though variations are sometimes introduced to illustrate special cases, e.g. the inverted V-shape of a short-lived fad or novelty product, or the scalloped shape that might be associated with a fashion product adopted by 'waves' of followers. Individual products are accepted as each having a unique pattern, in terms of sales-profits volume, gradient, shape and duration. Long-standing brand-leader products are likely to show an extended 'maturity section' with variations, both up and down, these reflecting market trends, competitor activity and company marketing successes. In practice, of course, most veteran brands will have undergone major product and marketing changes over the years, if only to survive!

Over the course of the product life cycle, changes are likely to be registered in terms of market size and growth, customer types, and the dynamic interactions between company marketing strategies and those of competitors. These differences may both reflect and partly determine the successive stages within the cycle.

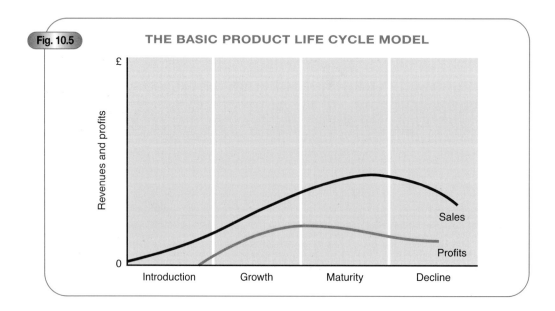

Fig. 10.5 THE BASIC PRODUCT LIFE CYCLE MODEL

Fig. 10.6 MARKETING IMPLICATIONS OF THE PRODUCT LIFE CYCLE

	Introduction	Growth	Maturity	Decline
Characteristics				
Sales	Low	Fast growth	Slow growth	Decline
Profits	Negligible	Peak levels	Declining	Low or zero
Cash flow	Negative	Moderate	High	Low
Customers	Innovative	Mass market	Mass market	Laggards
Competitors	Few	Growth	Numerous	Fewer
Responses				
Strategic focus	Expand market	Market penetration	Defend share	Productivity
Marketing expenditure	High	High (declining %)	Falling	Low
Marketing emphasis	Product awareness	Brand preference	Brand loyalty	Selective
Distribution	Patchy	Intensive	Intensive	Selective
Price	High	Lower	Lowest	Rising
Product	Basic	Improved	Differentiated	Rationalised

Marketing strategies over the cycle are difficult to summarise, though it might be possible to suggest that in the earlier period market development is the watchword, in the growth stage strategy becomes more offensive, while in later stages defensive and consolidation strategies predominate. A more detailed outline of strategy changes over the PLC has been presented by Doyle (1976) in his article 'The realities of the product life cycle', and appears in summary form in Fig. 10.6. For a fuller treatment, the reader would benefit by referring to the complete article, which has become a landmark in the literature (*see* Further Reading on page 169).

Extensions on life cycle analysis

From the earliest interest in the generalised 'product' life cycle, research has moved on to distinguish at least three distinct levels of aggregation: that for the product class (e.g. breakfast cereals), the product form (e.g. health-conscious cereals), and the specific product or brand (e.g. Alpen). Working at an analysis of three levels of market sales, it is possible to more realistically locate the position and prospects of one particular product or brand, and make strategic decisions in the light of market and sector trends, competition and general performance indicators.

Figure 10.7 illustrates such a three-level analysis, showing a scenario with three competitor brands. The picture is one of a product class until recently in slow decline, and a falling product life cycle within which Company B brand has long overtaken Company A brand, a product form competitor. More significantly, the arrival of Company C brand has introduced a new product form, which appears now to threaten the market sector for A and B, and add a new growth source to the total (product class) market. Clearly, Company B in particular will need to reassess its prospects, and perhaps modify its product or consider entering the 'new form' product market.

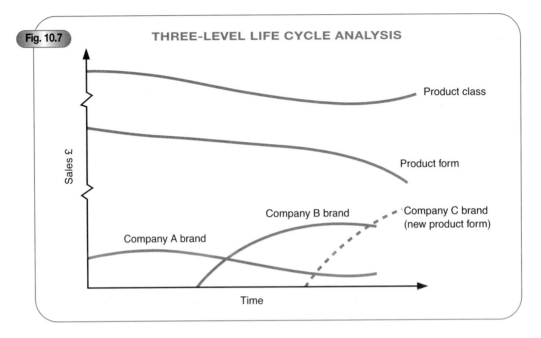

Fig. 10.7 THREE-LEVEL LIFE CYCLE ANALYSIS

Difficulties with PLC analysis

Companies sometimes create problems of their own making through an over-simplistic interpretation of the generalised PLC model. At any level of aggregation, PLC analysis can only provide a model or theoretical structure. It cannot offer a template against which to naively measure deviations from 'the norm', nor can it make prescriptions about the duration of phases or the requisite strategies to follow, nor defy the 'normal' pattern.

A common problem is the failure to apply and interpret the appropriate level of aggregation (brand, form or product class), or to seek understanding through comparison between levels. Research and information sources are sometimes inadequate for the expectations made of an analysis, while sometimes definitions employed, for example of competitors or substitutes, are inaccurate or subjective. Particularly at the brand life cycle level, difficulties are encountered in interpreting phase-to-phase movement or turning-points. While a large measure of subjective judgement is inevitable, it may be possible to approach such demarcation by studying evidence of saturation levels, general profits decline, industry over-capacity, or changes in market responsiveness to price or promotion. Notwithstanding, it would be more prudent to accept the inherent limitations of PLC analysis, and to use it as but one input within a wider auditing exercise.

Uses of PLC analysis

Used carefully and with the support of appropriate research, the PLC provides valuable insights into product strategy and market change. Mapping the path of both company and competitor brands, product form and general market sales, assists the company in reaching decisions about new product development or product modification, as shown in Fig. 10.7. Across the life of a product, PLC analysis might enable a company to

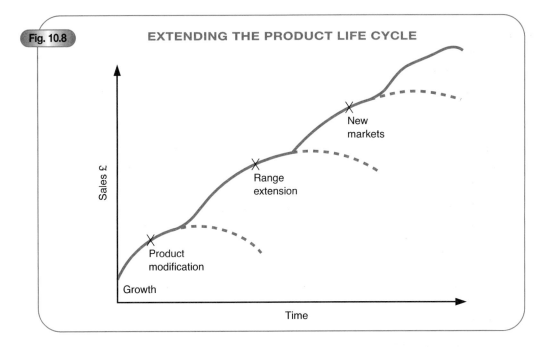

Fig. 10.8

EXTENDING THE PRODUCT LIFE CYCLE

better exploit product potential, and to avoid projected problems by well-timed strategy changes. Such a situation is illustrated in Fig. 10.8, where the company has managed to 'buck' the trend by timely changes in product strategy, so boosting the product's performance beyond the original projection.

There are differences in the opportunities at different stages of the PLC. Because of this those organisations who correctly appreciate their position can achieve a level of competitive advantage. In the growth stage there are likely to be fewer competitors, and the emphasis will be on growing the total market while making customers' aware of a specific offering. By the time the market growth has slowed and maturity reached there will be more competitors and the emphasis will be on the perceived benefits offered by each competing brand.

EXAMPLE

Extending the Product Life Cycle – the example of Persil

Whatever the washing need, there is a type of Persil to suit, be it conventional or concentrated; powder or liquid; biological or non-biological; specially formulated for colour fabrics; for use in a top-loading or front-loading washing machine.

Source: Lever Brothers Ltd Product information sheet

Persil was developed in 1909 by two Stuttgart professors, the name derived from Perborate and Silicate, two chemicals in the initial formula which enabled the product to be described as 'the amazing oxygen cleaner'.

The original Persil was a soap incorporating a bleaching agent. It was soon offered in powder form but this required to be stirred into a paste before adding to the washing. This 'new' way of washing was advertised as 'soap powder that would do away with the dolly rub and washboard and the labour of rubbing clothes'. Of course the whole method of washing was very different then to todays automatic washing machines.

The actual formulation has changed regularly over the years, although for 70 years Persil has remained purely a soap based product in spite of new competition from different types of detergents developed from 1950. The long-running slogan 'Persil washes whiter' helping to create a powerful position in the minds of consumers.

By 1968 the trend to front-loading washing machines had given rise to a need for low lathering washing powders. Although biological powders were being launched in the UK, the new product, Persil Automatic, was still soap based and it was marketed alongside the traditional product.

Persil did not add biological enzymes until 1983, relaunching as 'New System Persil'. However in 1984 they relaunched 'Original non-biological Persil' alongside the New System product. This illustrates the problems of moving too far away from the core values of an established product.

The last 10 years have seen many changes in this mature product as it utilised changes in available technology and sought to keep the offering competitive in a demanding marketplace.

1987   Persil available as a iiquid.
1990   Persil soap powder reformulated.
1991   Concentrated Persil powders and liquid launched.
1992   Further concentration as Persil Micro and Launch of Persil Colour.
1993   Launch of Persil Colour Liquid also Persil Eco-bag and tin.
1994   Persil Power, Pure and Colour new concentrated format.
1995   Persil Finesse, and New Generation Persil.
1996   Whole range reformulated and relaunched in new packaging.

Persil was once a single product, but there are now 13 different products in the Persil range in the UK, each targeted at a different customer segment. This does raise many problems about how to define a market with so many different varieties of a single brand.

In 1996 Persil UK sales were estimated as £185 million, with an advertising spend of £26.8 million giving it one of the highest advertising to sales ratios of any major product. Further study of this trend and of the activities of competitors with their product offerings will show how important it is to actively manage the total marketing mix at all stages of the product life cycle.

Note: Persil is marketed by Unilever in France and the UK. In Germany and much of the rest of Europe the brand is owned by Henkel. Such split ownership can cause problems in brand development.

PRODUCT DIFFERENTIATION AS A FUNDAMENTAL MARKETING CONCEPT

In the previous chapter, Thedore Levitt's famous quote about there being no such thing as a commodity was used. In his article about differentiation as a means of gaining competitive advantage, he refines the three-level concept of a product to explore those areas where advantage is possible. In particular, he uses the term 'expected product' to describe the minimum expectation of customers for a particular class of product. This is the basic product plus those other additions which are necessary to even be considered within the customer's evoked set. The expected product will, therefore, include some features in both the real and total product categories discussed earlier.

There are two further categories which are critical to marketing success. First the augmented product which an organisation offers to its customers, in the hope that the additional features, tangible and intangible, will be sufficient to achieve sales in a competitive marketplace. Levitt's augmented product is therefore the same as the total product offered by a supplier.

The second additional category is the potential product 'which consists of everything potentially feasible to attract and hold customers'. So while the total augmented product is the total of everything currently being offered, the potential product is only limited by a company's imagination. This category embraces anything that could be done both now and in the future as new technologies or other opportunities arise.

As already discussed, marketing takes place in a dynamic and ever-changing environment. It is therefore necessary to consider how a total product must change its formation over time to remain competitive. Raymond Corey in his classic book once said '... the form of a product is a variable, not a given, in developing market strategy. Products are planned and developed to serve markets.' This is especially true in the changing conditions in many markets. There is a continual migration between the various categories of the total and potential product.

One reason for this, is that customers become accustomed to a particular level of added value and therefore increase their expectations over time. This is possible as competitors see the augmentation of one company and move to copy it. For instance, there was a time when no UK Banks were open on Saturday. However, it was seen first that Building Societies were benefitting from Saturday opening so the National Westminster Bank started opening at these times. Now most Banks have some form of operation at a time convenient to many personal customers. This is an example of the move from augmented to expected in considering the 'product' offered by a Bank.

Now several banks are offering a 24-hour telephone banking service. This is linked to the Automatic Cash Dispenser (ATM) machines which are accessible outside normal bank hours. For many customers the services available through the use of technology is more than sufficient to meet their regular needs. The implications on employment in the banking sector are dramatic, with thousands of redundancies and many branch closures. However, it is the service to the customers rather than justification of traditional operations that is critical.

Of course, as competitors copy those features which once gave a single supplier a competitive advantage, then more has to be added to the total product to maintain an advantage in the marketplace. This means raiding the category of the potential product. It is for that reason that Fig. 10.9 has arrows from separating the different categories, as

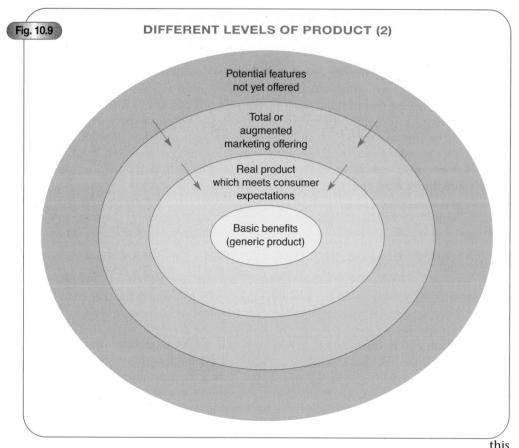

Fig. 10.9

DIFFERENT LEVELS OF PRODUCT (2)

Potential features
not yet offered

Total or
augmented
marketing offering

Real product
which meets consumer
expectations

Basic benefits
(generic product)

this
allows items in one of the outer rings to move in as the features which are expected and
therefore necessary change, and as those which are offered as part of the total product
are further augmented to retain an advantage over competition.

EXAMPLE

Häagen-Dazs

The Häagen-Dazs plants in France and the United States certainly produce ice
cream efficiently and operate with minimal workforce and carefully controlled
overheads. That is the style of a company owned by Grand Metropolitan plc.
However the trust of the Häagen-Dazs developments is not to lower prices. On the
contrary, since Grand Metropolitan acquired Pillsbury, which included Häagen-
Dazs – a luxury brand of ice cream sold in New York since the mid-1960s – their
efforts have been directed at enhancing its quality with luxurious and indulgent
ingredients. A few cents of Almond Crunch can put half a dollar on the list price.
Now sold in more than twenty major markets in Europe, Asia and the Americas, it
is an example of creativity in developing markets and widening margins.

PRODUCT POSITIONING

Positioning is a term sometimes used loosely among marketers. It has already been discussed in Chapter 9. Positioning can either refer to the company-wide strategic stance or 'mission' taken on where to do business, and with what competitive advantages, or it can be confined to a more tactical concern with how individual products are targeted and positioned within a particular market or segment. The former, policy-level positioning issue might better be termed strategic positioning or market positioning, though it is certainly in general terms relevant to product policy at the corporate level.

Product-level matters of positioning, product positioning proper, revolve around the way in which customers perceive a company product in relation to competitive products and/or their preferences and ideal product attributes. Both levels of positioning are related, and it may well be, that company experience of positioning, or repositioning one product may lead to major lessons and strategy changes that involve new product development, fundamental redesign exercises or product deletions, and decisive changes in marketing strategy.

Informed product positioning will depend on reliable research into the position of the product(s) in relation to competing products, and to 'ideal' attributes elicited from respondents. A first stage would be to identify, through experience or preliminary research, a listing of products or brands competing with those of the company, and then to isolate the major attributes or characteristics that customers hold to be significant in making purchase choices within the product field. A set of detailed ratings and rankings might then be obtained in relation to these attributes, across the named products, and against 'ideal' products that respondents are asked to envisage. Through such procedures a comprehensive set of research information should be generated, so that multidimensional comparisons may be made of competing products and ideal positions, usually with the aid of dedicated software packages. To illustrate the value of such an exercise, Fig. 10.10 shows a positioning 'map' of a hypothetical study of hotel groups, displayed for simplicity along two dimensions only.

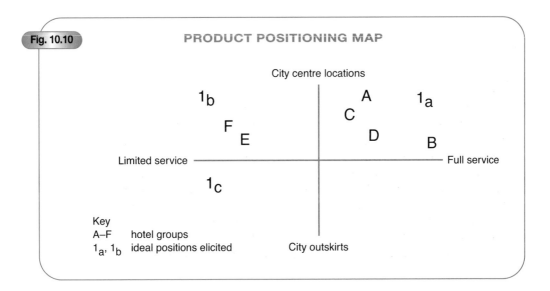

Fig. 10.10 PRODUCT POSITIONING MAP

From the positioning map it can be seen, that existing hotel groups have clustered themselves about the two upper ideal positions. Proximity to the ideals might imply that groups A and F are leaders in their respective segments – something to check against known business volume. It is significant that one ideal position (1c) is not catered for at all, perhaps revealing a market opportunity for 'basic board' overnight accommodation for short-stay travellers. Obviously, two-dimensional information on position and preferences should be supplemented by data on other attributes such as price, non-urban locations, accommodation style and the like. The mapped positions of course reflect only respondent perceptions, and it might be of value to check these. For example, Group D may have a number of out-of-town hotels, somehow not familiar to respondents, implying shortcomings in the company's communications programme.

THE QUALITY OF PRODUCTS

We cannot consider products or services without studying the topic of quality. Quality is one of those issues which everyone agrees is important but many find difficult to define. A quality product can embrace the meaning that the item offered, whether a food or other fmcg product or a car or a piece of industrial equipment, comes with very high specifications, added value benefits and top of the range characteristics, usually also at a premium price. However, it does not have to be defined in this way. A supermarket like Sainsbury's offers far less in terms of personal service and ambience when compared to the food Hall at Harrods in London, nevertheless within the chosen parameters both offer quality.

One useful approach to the issue of quality is to consider against the eight dimensions of quality proposed by David Garvin in his 1987 article in the *Harvard Business Review*. These are:

- *Performance* A product's primary operating characteristic.
- *Features* The 'bells and whistles', those characteristics that supplement basic functioning.
- *Conformance* The degree to which design of operating characteristics meets established standards.
- *Serviceability* Relating to the ease of maintenance.
- *Reliability* The probability of a product malfunctioning during a specified time period.
- *Durability* A measure of product life with both economic and technical dimensions.
- *Aesthetics* How a product looks, feels, sounds, tastes or smells – personal judgement comes in here.
- *Perceived quality* As consumers do not always have complete information to judge a product or service (amateur buyer), perception of quality, reputation or other intangibles are important in judging how customers rate your offering in their value equation.

It will be noticeable that Garvin's list progresses from the tangible characteristics and features of a product through the way a product performs to the perceived attributes which depend on customers making a value judgement.

These dimensions are a good starting point when considering the basis on which quality can be judged, a challenge for marketers is to reduce the dimensions to a manageable set selected as being relevant to the chosen customers. It will then be possible to achieve a better match between a supplier's offer and customer's requirements.

CONCLUSION

The product and product offering is often the logical starting point for any marketing analysis since it can be as useful to define customers and markets in terms of the type of products they buy. In turn, many product definitions depend upon the customer. However, the objective of marketing programmes is to achieve some measure of success in a given marketplace and in this, the aim is to differentiate one offering from another and thus win the competitive battle. Although the whole of the marketing mix is relevant at the time of most purchase decisions, it is the product itself, together with the service elements and added features, which is at the centre of the exchange. This is why we term products – the fundamental marketing concept. Products must be seen as complex combinations with many facets, and some of these have been explored in this chapter. Through the understanding of the various categories of products it is possible to understand more accurately how a customer might approach the purchase of that type of product. Also by appreciating the scope for changing total products it should stimulate creative thinking about the potential that the total product could achieve in a competitive context.

QUESTIONS

1 Suggest ways in which a car manufacturer could add to his product offering to provide a more attractive total product.

2 What is the total product offered by McDonald's hamburgers? How does this give them an advantage over their competitors?

3 'The brand is more important than the product'. Discuss.

4 Select a tangible product of your choice, then suggest ways in which it could be augmented by the addition of service elements.

5 Consider the value of product life cycle analysis for a specialist producer of business software packages.

6 'There is little a company can do with a product that is in the decline stage of the product life cycle'. Discuss.

7 What is the difference between a brand life cycle and a product class life cycle?

8 It has often been observed that the length of product life cycles is declining. What factors might lie behind such a phenomenon?

FURTHER READING

Ansoff, I. (1989) *Corporate Strategy*, Revised Edn, Penguin, Harmondsworth, Middlesex.
Boston Consulting Group (1971) 'The product portfolio', *Perspectives on Experience*.
Corey, E. R. (1991) *Industrial Marketing*, 4th Edn, Prentice-Hall, Englewood Cliffs, N.J.
Cram, T. (1994) *The Power of Relationship Marketing*, Pitman, London.
Doyle, P. (1976) 'The realities of the product life cycle', *Quarterly Review of Marketing*, Summer.
Drucker, P. F. (1973) *Management Tasks, Responsibilities and Practicalities*, Harper & Row, New York.

Garvin, D. A. (1987) 'Competing on the eight dimensions of quality', *Harvard Business Review*, Nov–Dec, pp. 101–109.

Levitt, T. (1980) 'Marketing success through the differentiation of anything', *Harvard Business Review*, Jan–Feb.

Palmer, A. (1994) *Principles of Services Marketing*, McGraw-Hill, Maidenhead.

Payne, A. (1993) *The Essence of Services Marketing*, Prentice-Hall, Hemel Hempstead.

Peters, T. and Waterman, R. (1982) *In Search of Excellence: Lessons from America's Best Run Companies*, Harper & Row, New York.

Ruskin, J. (1975) Unto this Last, MacDonald & Evans, Northcote House.

Shaw, G. B. (1956) *Man and Superman; A Comedy and A Philosophy*, Longman, Green & Co., London.

CASE STUDY
Sway Orchards Ltd

The owner of Sway Orchards Ltd, Jayne Powell recently inherited the company from her great aunt. On taking over she intended continuing the business as her great aunt had done by mainly selling the apples, pears and plums produced through the local market. Unfortunately she soon realised that although this resulted in a modest profit being achieved most years, the profit had been in decline for some years and it seemed realistic to expect this decline to continue if no changes were made.

Jayne knew that a number of fruit growers had successfully changed to other crops, however others were still prospering with traditional businesses very similar to her own. From her experience gained working in a number of successful businesses she realised that any changes would involve further investment as well as the acceptance of risk. Although she had some money which could be invested she saw no reason for doing this unless the risk could be minimised. She therefore decided to do some research to try to discover what options were feasible and if there was any approach which was more successful than the others. Her research discovered many different alternatives.

One producer she met had invested in a packing shed so that in addition to employing pickers to bring in the crop, he also employed additional people to grade and pack the fruit which could then be sold at higher (premium) prices. By doing this the farmer had invested both the capital needed for the building as well as the investing in boxes and other packing material, he also continued to incur additional labour costs involved with grading and packing the fruit. This farmer had been able to justify the cost of the packing shed because he had sufficient orchards for it to be used for nearly eight weeks each year and he was able to rent it out as storage during the winter. He admitted that initially he had arranged with other farmers in the area to pack and grade their products as well as his own, but it had only been practical to do this for small producers because it had been impossible to schedule packing his own fruit with that supplied from other large producers.

Another grower she visited did not have very extensive orchards but was situated on a main road. As a result what had started as a farm gate sales operation had developed into a full farm shop selling both produce from the orchards when this was in season together with a full range of other produce bought in from other local farms and markets.

She also met several growers who were running successful pick-your-own operations. These operations ranged from a basic shed, a set of scales and a notice alongside a main road to one where facilities for a family day out including mobile caterers, a bouncy castle and a funfair were provided. This latter also involved capital expenditure to provide for a large car parking area.

Jayne had located these operations by studying display advertisements in the attractions section of her local papers.

A farmer with orchards in the West Country had found that his profits were being reduced due to the rising transportation cost of getting his fruit to market. As a result he had invested in a commercial kitchen where he was making a range of farm produced preserves – jam, apple butter and other specialities. It seemed that this was possible as being remote he was able to employ adequate part-time staff whenever needed.

Another orchard owner in Suffolk had installed fruit pressing equipment to manufacture apple and pear juice. As a result he was buying in fruit from all of the neighbouring farms and had expanded to the extent that he was now able to supply one of the smaller supermarket chains with his premium grade product.

Unfortunately, for each of the successful operations she visited she saw another which was in every way similar except it was significantly less successful. In considering the different operations she could not decide the importance of the economies associated with the scale of each of the various operations. Would being a small producer make any of the costs more critical? For instance the cost of transportation will be greater if the quantity is less than a full lorry load. Of course the same speculation also applies to the other operations.

Jayne also worried about the investment costs associated with each type of offering. Some were one-off costs such as a building or a carpark, others were continuing costs, additional labour or regular advertising?

Questions

She began to wonder about the different examples of product offerings all derived from the same basic ingredients. She wanted to assess how well each matched the marketing environment, and what factors were critical to success in each of these operations?

What return could be expected from the investment and what were the risks associated with each approach? How could these risks be minimised?

CHAPTER 11

Intangible Products and Building Relationships that Last

He profits most who serves best.
Motto of International Rotary

INTRODUCTION

This chapter will consider three issues which have been the focus of much marketing attention in the 1990s. These are the marketing of service products, the internal marketing issues in achieving a satisfactory offering from an organisation, and the building of long-term relationships with customers. There have already been a number of references to these issues in previous chapters such as the description of 'Mickey Mouse' marketing and the wider aspects of the exchange process in Chapter 1, the discussion on benefits in Chapter 2, the service component of the total product concept in Chapter 10, and various sections on customer behaviour and keeping customers in other chapters. All these references will indicate that the topics are not confined to a discrete area of marketing, nor are they really new. The problem is, that as markets have grown and the organisations that serve them have become more complex, these issues which were once instinctive have been partially overlooked.

Before the industrial revolution, most trade was based on the understanding and interaction directly with customers. Because much of the business was direct and personal between a local supplier and customers, there was an obvious need to offer good service. It was also important to try to develop good ongoing relationships as an adjunct to the sale of such products as food, clothing, medicines and other items which required repeat orders. Most activity was at a local level and concentrated on individuals. These markets were dramatically affected by the move to mass markets, growth in manufacturing scale, mass communication and mass distribution channels. Marketing is a response to the increase in supply of all types of products, and the early marketing theory was indeed based on mass markets.

However, the element of service and personal contact in business exchanges has continued especially in the selling function. Organisations are just collections of individuals and in spite of work roles there are many individuals who meet, service, and in other ways interact with the customers of their organisation. When such dealings have been positive an ongoing relationship has developed between the employees of the supply organisation and the individuals with whom they do business.

What is a new development is the effort by those working in the so-called service industries to try to apply the principles of mass product marketing to their intangible offerings. There is also the development of technology which has enabled databases to be constructed, so that both product offerings and communications can be aimed much more precisely at individuals or small homogeneous groups. Putting these together has changed the way the principles are applied and modified marketing in thinking which is equally beneficial to fmcg marketers. The only difference from the local traders of the 18th century is that many of these 'personal' messages are today delivered by hi-tech information exchange products, such as computers, the Internet, fax machines or even the (old fashioned) telephone. There are many opportunities for returning to personalised marketing but many of these will be through the use of modern systems rather than direct personal contact.

Nevertheless, personal contact remains of the utmost importance, both in how it is performed and in the environment in which it takes place. The latter being very important as it represents the space where the customer actually meets a supplier. Close contact between the two parties brings both problems and opportunities, but the objective remains that of achieving an exchange offering which is *acceptable*, *affordable*, and *available*. Therefore the specific nature of services must be studied and a wider interpretation of the traditional components of product and place must be found.

THE MARKETING OF SERVICE PRODUCTS

The previous chapter discussed the concept of a total product which will usually have both tangible and intangible features. The question that has to be asked here is whether the marketing of a service product, or a product which is a major service with accompanying minor goods, is different from the marketing of tangible physical goods? The best answer will refer back to the basic idea of a mutually beneficial exchange, and the requirements for the proper application of the marketing concept as discussed in Chapter 1. It will be seen that the basic principles of marketing apply in all situations.

Kotler (1997) defines a service as: 'any act or performance that one party can offer to another that is essentially intangible and does not result in the ownership of anything. Its production may or may not be tied to a physical product.' This definition emphasises two key elements of a service:

1 *Intangibility* Services can rarely be experienced or tested in advance of the purchase.
2 *Lack of ownership* There is no aspect of ownership in a pure service.

There are three other distinctive features that must be considered:

3 *Inseparability* The fact that the production of a service takes place at the same time as its delivery.
4 *Perishability* Services cannot be stored or kept in a warehouse. Time is part of services and once that time has not been used then the service opportunity has gone.
5 *Variability* Because each delivery is unique there is no standardisation of output. The product and delivery depend on the two parties involved at the time of delivery.

Because of these issues there are likely to be some different actions and different emphases present when marketing a service product. However, as many total products have both a service component and a physical core the actions required to successfully market a service are likely to be similar to those required to market any total product.

Levitt (1976) observed that:

> The more technologically sophisticated the generic product (e.g cars and computers), the more dependant are its sales on the quality and availability of its accompanying customer services (e.g. display rooms, delivery, repairs and maintenance, application aids, operator training, installation advice, warranty fulfilment). In this sense, General Motors is probably more service intensive than manufacturing intensive. Without its service, its sales would shrivel.

Looking at the factors above in more detail will help to highlight the important actions necessary for good service marketing.

INTANGIBILITY

First is the issue of intangibility. This means the customer cannot be sure of what he/she is going to receive until after purchase. This increases the uncertainty of the purchase, and sometimes it is only after the purchase that a customer realises that the service was not what was expected. Of course, there are ways of reducing uncertainty; these come in two areas. First is previous experience or the recommendation of others which can be a powerful part of the decision making. But if there is no direct or indirect measure of previous satisfaction then a customer will look for other cues from the second category. These come in the form of attitude of the people involved, the ambience of the surroundings and the general reassurance of the way things seem to be carried out by a potential supplier, perhaps the speed of producing a quotation or the state of the supplier's premises. If these factors are positive then the uncertainty is reduced, but it can never be removed altogether because of the other issues such as the risk of variability which is covered below.

LACK OF OWNERSHIP

The next area which can cause concern is the fact that a pure service cannot be owned. All that can be acquired is the access to that service for a period of time. Of course such an exposure to the service should confer a benefit on the recipient. For instance, a rail journey is experienced from the point of departure to the destination and the benefit is arriving at a chosen location. But, after handing in the ticket, no tangible item remains. Similarly a student will receive knowledge from their teachers. This can be given an aura of tangibility by the handouts or textbooks purchased, but these are not the education and it is impossible to touch or feel the actual knowledge. These examples can give a clue as to the problem of the lack of ownership and some of the marketing activities that can be used to overcome them. An obvious issue is the physical extra such as textbooks or degree certificates to successful students. Perhaps guarantees for work done by a mechanic, or an impressive insurance policy document help. But a distinction must be made between the ownership of a physical symbol giving a right to receive a service and the service itself. A season ticket for your favourite football club gives you the right to attend all home matches and always sit in the same seat, however it gives no additional benefits and while you might enjoy the football you do not own the team.

INSEPARABILITY

The intangible product benefit in the case of a football match, is the enjoyment and entertainment experienced by watching the match actually take place. This leads on to the third important feature of any service product, i.e. the production of the service cannot be separated from the receipt – they take place at the same time and in the same place. There is an involvement between the provider and the recipient of the service so that the production and delivery cannot be separated. This opens up the question of how the quality of a service is judged at the time of delivery, and what a supplier can do to try to achieve a positive response. Sasser (1978) suggests that customers will initially assess the core benefit for the way it satisfies the substantive need for the service. This might be the requirement to be entertained by a football match, or the basic transport need provided by a train journey. However there are secondary attributes which are just as important to customers in evaluating the service. Sasser identified a number of these as:

- security (safety of the customer and his/her property);
- consistency;
- attitude;
- completeness;
- condition;
- availability; and
- timing.

Service providers compete by offering combinations of these attributes in order to meet the secondary needs better than the competitors. These can be seen as the augmented features of a service offering within the context of a total offering discussed in Chapters 9 and 10. From these attributes it is possible to see how the way the service is presented by the providers, and the environment within which it is provided are critical. This includes the comfort and cleanliness of a train, the attitude of employees who are in contact with the passengers and other issues which make a train journey a pleasure rather than something to be endured.

A service encounter occurs every time a customer interacts with a service organisation. Shostack suggested there are three types of encounters which can be experienced:

1 Face-to-face encounters.
2 Telephone encounters.
3 Remote encounters.

Remote encounters take place without any direct human contact such as an Automatic Teller Machine. With these it is the quality of the process or systems that is used to judge the quality of the service. But even when judging a process, and more specifically when reflecting on telephone or face-to-face encounters, it is the perception of the customer as to what was received, evaluated against what was expected that is the critical measure of quality and satisfaction. This perception could distort what was actually received as it depends on the value judgement of the customer. In most encounters the most vivid impression of a service occurs in the first few minutes of the encounter. These 'moments of truth' were described by Jan Carlzon, former Chief Executive Officer at Scandinavian Airways (SAS).

SAS is not a collection of material assets but the quality of the contact between an individual customer and the SAS (*front line*) employee who serve the customer directly.

Carlzon goes on to explain that each of SAS's 10 million customers come into contact with approximately five SAS employees. So there are 50 million contacts, yet each contact was averaging only 15 seconds at a time. He goes on to say:

SAS is thus created 50 million times a year, 15 seconds at a time. These 50 million 'moments of truth' are the moments that ultimately determine whether SAS will succeed or fail as a company. They are the moments when SAS must prove itself to its customers that it is the best alternative.

These contacts will be discussed later (*see* page 178) where the importance of personal contact in services is examined.

EXAMPLE

(Actual experience of one of the authors, November 1996)

In a Safeway supermarket the person in front of the checkout queue was wearing a Safeway uniform and obviously knew the till operator. They were chatting about common interests while the three customers behind had to wait to be served. Even though the encounter only took a few minutes it was obvious that other queues were moving while this one was not.

Question
What will be the effect on the others in that queue, and does it really matter that staff are seen to be served in front of other customers ?

Perishability

The next issue that separates services and tangible goods is that while goods can be produced ahead of the time required and stored until needed, this is impossible with a service. They cannot be prepared in advance for later exchanging with customers. This does not matter when demand can be controlled to take place at a constant rate, but it affects services where demand fluctuates. Such changes can be accommodated when demand for tangible goods varies, for instance a UK company making chocolate creme eggs used to make them throughout the year putting many into cold storage until the start of the Easter season when this product is much in demand. A service cannot be stored in this way so peaks of demand can be met only if additional staff are employed at the peak times. This is why supermarket checkouts are not fully staffed at periods of low business, but fully manned at busy times. But there has to be sufficient checkouts in the first place, and, therefore it is necessary to supplement the people with the necessary facilities for them to cope with the demand. Provision of these facilities is expensive and organisations have to decide the levels they are prepared to make available. The provision of extra facilities and staff during peak periods is a supply driven strategy of the sort which operation specialists will need to develop to deal with the problem.

It is also possible to try to reduce the extremes of high and low activity by marketing initiatives aimed at modifying demand, for instance the use of differential pricing. An example of this is the discounts offered to encourage rail users to use off-peak periods for travel. These are never more than partially successful. It is sometimes more appropriate to accept the problems and then try to benefit out of the situation by modifying the total product. For example, the famous London wax works museum Madame Tussauds expects long queues in the peak summer periods. To make the long waits more acceptable they hire entertainers such as jugglers and clowns to perform for those waiting. This has become as much a part of a visit to Tussauds as the museum itself. Another example is a hotel who offers an automatic checkout to approved business customers. This increases the benefit to those customers and reduces the demand on busy cashier staff at the peak period around 8.00 am when many guests want to settle the accounts and leave the hotel. There are innumerable creative marketing solutions to problems of uneven demand. However, the fact still remains that the time period over which a service is offered is the same time as when it is received; if a service is ready for a customer and no customer can be found then the service opportunity perishes for ever.

Variability

The final key difference to be considered by anyone involved in the marketing of a service, or a product with a service component, derives from the repetition of the service, i.e. it being a new production every time. Services can perhaps be likened to the performance of a play in the theatre. Each time it is performed there will be a different audience and the actors will have different feelings and moods with which to contend. So the services can vary at each performance, yet to those who receive the service, the people providing it on a specific occasion are the service. Sasser (1978) identified consistency and completeness as two issues in service quality. These are relevant every time a particular service is performed. The necessity for good staff training and motivation to provide a good service are obvious areas where attention can be focused. Marketing can play a part here both with ways of improving internal communications and by providing feedback from the marketplace on how customers react to particular offerings. However, Levitt (1981) suggested that: 'No matter how well trained or motivated, people make mistakes, forget, commit indiscretions, at times get hard to handle'. The fact is that much service delivery depends on people, or more often specifically on a single person who has the responsibility for delivering the service. This is true in a McDonald's fast-food outlet, as well as for a highly-trained dentist.

On the supply side, organisations look for systems to control the quality of the service, and sometimes try to find alternatives which are less dependent on people. Examples of this are Automatic Teller Machines (ATM) in Banks, or the use of barcodes on grocery products, so the supermarket operator does not have to enter prices into the till. Twenty years ago Levitt (1976) called this development the 'Industrialisation of Services', and his article gives further examples. However, it is as true today as when Levitt wrote his article that inconsistent service exists, and when that service falls below the standards acceptable to customers, those customers either complain, or more likely, do not return. Marketing should encourage customers to complain about poor service, as studies show that where a customer contacts the organisation and gets satis-factory response, that customer is far more likely to continue to use the service again. Most customers know that mistakes happen because no one is perfect. Complaints are also a very valuable source of marketing information about the service as perceived by the customers. In too many organisations the complaints department is controlled by the operations function or by some aspect of quality control. This should be consid-ered wrong, and the responsibility should be with the marketing function.

A SERVICES MARKETING MIX

While there are many factors which separate services from tangible products the principles of marketing are unchanged. A study of the factors considered above will show why the tra-ditional marketing mix was considered too restrictive for the planning of service delivery.

Perhaps the key difference, is the close contact between individual employees from supplier organisations and the individual customers. This leads to a re-evaluation of the traditional marketing mix, and in particular the definition of a product. The role of the people who participate in the delivery of the service is obviously vital, but so is the way a service is provided and the actual environment in which it is received. This is why Mary Jo Bitner with Bernard Booms have suggested an addition to the '4 Ps' of the marketing mix by the inclusion of People, Process, and Physical evidence. Bitner argues that these three 'new' elements should be included as separate parts of the marketing mix because they are within the control of the supply organisation in the same way as the original factors. These additional 'Ps' certainly highlight areas which can make an offering both *acceptable* and *available*.

THE IMPORTANCE OF PEOPLE TO SERVICE OFFERINGS

The nature of most service encounters requires direct personal contact. This leads to the view, that in many offerings the people providing the service *are* the service. This dependence was neatly described by one of the great advertising men, Leo Burnett, who said 'All our assets go down the elevator every evening'. It is the people who make the difference between good and bad service, and yet in many industries they are badly rewarded. This was highlighted by Schlessinger and Hesketh (1991) who found that average real wages fell in the service sector in the USA in the period 1979–1989, and further commented that 'for the most part these jobs are poorly paid, lead nowhere, and provide little if anything in the way of health, pension, or other benefits'. They concluded that in restaurants, hotels, grocery, department stores, building services supply and personnel that over 90 per cent of all jobs can be classified as '*truly dead-end jobs*'. Drucker highlighted this in his article 'The new productivity challenge' where he suggests the 'most pressing social challenge developed countries face is to raise the pro-ductivity of service workers'. He further throws doubt on whether 'capital' can replace the people as he concludes that in service work, the people are the 'tools' of produc-tion. However the motivation and training of people is crucial in service delivery, but their importance must be put into perspective. A simple mapping of the involvement of people against the relative cost of those people can be useful. (*See* Fig. 11.1.)

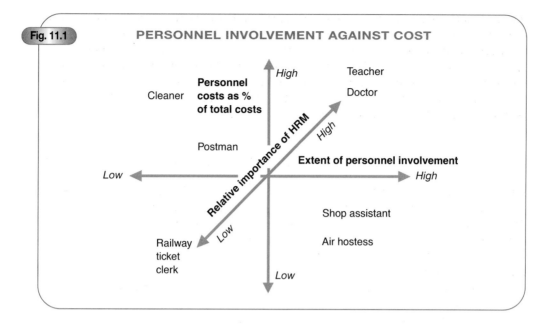

Fig. 11.1 PERSONNEL INVOLVEMENT AGAINST COST

This map can be used to highlight those areas where attention must be focused. For offerings in the top right quadrant such as hairdressing, or teaching, the emphasis is on the human resource activities. At the opposite side there are remote encounters and offerings where service plays a small part. Here the people are less important but can still make a difference during moment of truth encounters. This could be true when an aggressive bus driver tries to hurry passengers and drives off before some travellers have sat down. It could also be a situation when a telephone call to a company is answered by the receptionist. Robert Townsend in his classic book *Up the Organisation* gives the advice 'Call yourself up – when off on a business trip or a vacation, pretend you're a customer. Telephone some part of your organisation and ask for help. You'll run into some real horror shows. Don't blow up and ask for name, rank, and serial number – you're trying to correct, not punish ... Then try calling yourself up and see what indignities you've built into your own defenses.'

In addition to the two dimensions in Fig. 11.1, another factor which should be considered is the level of skill required by the person giving the service. Most of the jobs highlighted by Hesketh are low skill activities, however there are a number of skilled and complex services which are very different in nature. The role of a doctor or a lawyer are good examples. In these professional services there is a high degree of specific training but this tends to be related to the operation of that particular role rather than any training in how to interact with customers. It is often difficult to persuade a highly-qualified professional that they need to respond to patients and clients as customers, but there is competition in these areas as much as in other services and the way contact with customers is managed is equally important.

It is possible to split human resource management (HRM) into 'hard' and 'soft' categories. 'Hard' is measured in terms of efficiency and worker productivity, and is concerned with costs and financial measures. 'Soft' emphasises the role of employees as essential assets who must be encouraged and motivated in their jobs. It is these 'softer' qualitative issues which are reflected in the way customer contact is performed.

INTERNAL MARKETING

The direct link between an organisation and its customers is now being termed *external marketing*. The actual delivery of this, involving people, employees of the organisation, and their contact with customers, is termed interactive marketing. To complete the link there is the way an organisation treats, as well as how it motivates, its employees. This is generally referred to as internal marketing (*see* Fig. 11.2). Internal marketing has been defined by Christian Gronroos of the School of Economics and Business, Helsingfors, Finland, as:

> **To create an internal environment which supports customer-consciousness and sales-mindedness amongst all personnel within an organisation.**

Internal marketing also involves other functional disciplines, in particular HRM. Marketing specialists, however, should have both the research skills to identify employee needs and wants as internal customers of the organisation, and the communication skills to assist in meeting these needs effectively. More of the role of internal marketing will be discussed in Chapter 22.

If all aspects of Fig. 11.2 are positive, the organisation will offer excellent customer service. The opposite effect could come from the following vicious circle:

Company: The staff treat customers like rabble. 'They need a good talking to.'
Employees: 'If the company does not care about me, why should I bother?'
Customer: 'I'm not coming back.'

It is obvious that the way an offering is supplied to a customer is as much a part of the product offering as the product itself. Marketing must give as much attention to this area and get involved with internal marketing, otherwise all the other efforts in designing a competitive offering will be wasted.

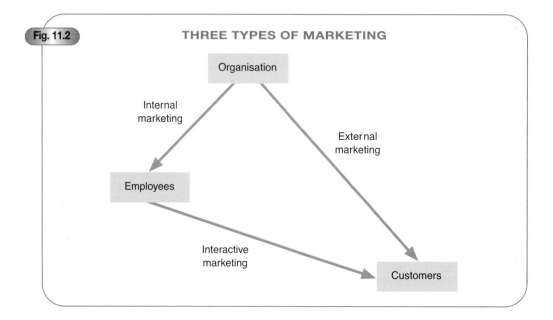

Fig. 11.2 **THREE TYPES OF MARKETING**

THE PROCESS OF SERVICE DELIVERY

To complement the people who deliver a service it is necessary to also consider the actual procedures and mechanisms involved in the delivery. There are all sorts of operational issues which directly affect customer's perception and level of satisfaction regarding a service. This could be the speed of an order being delivered in a fast-food restaurant or in an industrial setting, perhaps the ease of paying a bill, or any other issue regarding the way the service is received. Of course, where remote contact is present the process is paramount, but most services have some procedures which can make that service more or less *acceptable* to customers. When these procedures are unnecessarily complex and customers do not see any reason for the bureaucracy, then there is a natural tendency to reject the offering.

Some complex procedures have developed over time and, in some industries, all the organisations offering that service seem to follow the same methods. It can take an outside entrant into the market to find a way of providing the service which is easier for customers and thus giving an advantage over more established companies.

The food and clothing retailer, Marks & Spencer, have tried to capitalise on this by entering the pensions business. The extract from their publicity leaflet gives some idea of the claims they make:

> To live life to the full when you retire you need to take the right steps now. And all too often it is easier to put things off – even though the sooner you arrange a pension plan, the sooner you can start looking forward to a prosperous retirement.
>
> So, what if you could choose a pension designed to be simple, easy to understand and from a name you can trust?
>
> We have taken a new look at pensions, and cut out the jargon and the complicated forms, the salesmen and the pressure – making it easier for you to reach your own decision.

> (*Source*: Marks & Spencer Life Assurance Ltd.)

Technological developments are another factor that have also been utilised to make it easier for customers to make purchase decisions. For instance computerised ticketing and reservation systems used by airlines, or the use of credit cards to purchase from remote locations.

EXAMPLE

Computerised reservation systems

Sabre was the first CRS to be developed some forty years ago by its parent company American Airlines. It has computer terminals in 26 000 travel agencies in 184 countries. In addition to housing world airline information, it also services 200 hotel companies and 60 car hire firms. Its IBM computers are located in Tulsa, Oklahoma and process approximately 150 million travel requests per day.

Source: Sunday Times, 24 April 1994.

▶

The major development in the 1980s and 1990s has been the rapid switch to computerised reservation systems providing on-line reservation facilities to (travel) agents. The installation of such systems has been so costly that only principals carrying many thousands of customers each year could consider their installation, but continuing falls in the price of computer software and hardware have now made it possible for much smaller principals to consider automated reservation systems. Thomson Holidays' introduction of their 'TOPS' system, a low cost, user-friendly and extremely reliable reservation system, enabled that company to increase sales substantially and establish a huge lead over the rest of the inclusive tour business. Their later decision to abandon telephone sales entirely for their summer holiday programme, points the way to future developments and the need for all agents to be linked by VDU to principals' computer systems in order to survive.

In the airline world, the rapid development of computerised reservation systems has provided a new tool for the marketing manager. Originally seen merely as a method of controlling huge inventory speedily and efficiently, it soon became apparent that the way in which information was made available could radically improve sales potential.

. . .(initially) in the UK a *multi-access system*, known as Travicom was established. Financed principally by British Airways, this set out to operate a totally unbiased system on behalf of all the major carriers . . . In 1987 (the US systems) Sabre and Apollo became available in Europe, British Airways saw the need to operate on a larger scale, and reached agreement with other major carriers, initially within Europe, to commission a totally new system which could operate on a global scale. This system, Galileo, has merged with the US Apollo, to reinforce the global strength of this organisation. Travicom users and technology have been absorbed into the new system progressively.

Lufthansa and Air France have set up a different but parallel system, code-named Amadeus...Battle has now been joined to see which of these global reservation systems will become market leader.

Reservations technology is advancing at such a pace . . . Suffice it to say that these developments will have a profound effect on future distribution strategies, not least in terms of extending direct marketing opportunities. Airline tickets can be purchased in some countries from machines at airports, and this system is easily extended to the use of EFTPOS to pay for the ticket. Such expansion in direct selling, which threatens to cut out the retail agent, must be a further cause for concern among agents.

Source: *Marketing for Tourism* (1995) J. C. Holloway and C. Robinson, 3rd Edn., Addison Wesley Longman, pp. 147–8.

Reprinted by permission of Addison Wesley Longman Ltd.

Payne suggests two areas where processes should be given attention:

- as structural elements that help to achieve a position;
- as a way of achieving synergy between marketing and operations management in delivering a service.

The first involves issues such as the complexity of the process and the amount of individuality allowed to the person actually delivering the service.

The second ensures the actual operations are consistent with the claims and promises made to customers. In this second sense, the process of delivering a service can therefore be considered equivalent to the category of physical handling of a tangible good as in the original marketing mix presented by Borden.

PHYSICAL EVIDENCE

This category is the third of the additions proposed by Bitner for inclusion into a services marketing mix. She defines it as 'The environment in which the service is delivered and where the firm and customer interact, and any tangible components that facilitate performance or communication of the service'. Payne agrees on the two separate components of the category but suggests they are better considered under the more traditional heading of 'Product'. This perhaps says more about the restrictive nature of some interpretations of the marketing mix rather than any dispute over these controllable issues. There is agreement that the physical evidence must be consistent with the other elements in the mix and can greatly affect a customer's perception of the service offering.

Environmental factors

These are the locations in which a service is offered and consumed. The feel of the surroundings are particularly relevant when a customer visits a supplier's premises such as a bank, restaurant, or sports club.

Banks have traditionally used solid, large buildings which are supposed to reinforce the feeling of security for your money. Fast-food outlets are known to favour colour schemes which include red and yellow to give an impression of speed. Both colours and designs are also visible in the uniforms worn by employees. These complement the surroundings, and well-dressed staff are said to enhance images of efficiency with colours chosen to add to the message. It is really a form of packaging, but interpreted for intangible offerings.

Environmental elements can be used in many ways, in fact they can affect any of the customer's senses, including smell or sound, as well as sight. In retail supermarkets, the smell of freshly baked bread is promoted to enhance the environment, whereas the odour of fish is eliminated. Clothing stores aimed at young people play appropriate music, and also organise shops so that the target customers feel welcome. All these are examples of environmental evidence.

Physical clues

Two categories of services were introduced earlier; a pure service, and a service with accompanying minor goods. In fact to overcome some of the problems of *intangibility* and *lack of ownership*, it is quite common for providers of services to add some tangible features to the basic service. These could be a railway ticket, an insurance policy document, a holiday brochure, or a restaurant menu, none of which have much independent value by themselves. The use of the word 'clues' is important, as customers are often looking for information about the scope of the service and quality of the offering. A fully-illustrated travel brochure with pictures, temperature/climate information is useful, but this could be the expected product. Some tour companies enhance the offering by additional information based on customer comments and unambiguous fair trading promises. All these are clues presented in a way which could be considered as physical evidence; all are designed to reduce uncertainty. Since the objective of marketing is a satisfactory exchange then it is vital that these clues are used as part of the management of customer expectations. It is of course the actual offering which will be judged against these expectations. If it is perceived to meet or better expectations then the result is a satisfied customer. If not . . . the customer could be lost.

SERVICE PROMISES

Promises is another word beginning with 'P', and it could be considered the totality of the marketing mix encompassing all the claims made and benefits offered. Every element of the mix adds up to a total promise regarding the offering. Promises are obviously important in all categories of products, but in service industries the promises are critical because of the inseparability of the delivery of the service to customers. It is therefore critical to ensure that the promises made are realistic and that every employee involved in the delivery of a service is aware of those promises. If changes have to be made then the supplier should not hide such facts from customers, but they should keep customers informed of the situation and the implications discussed. It is not enough just to say 'sorry'. If a delivery is going to be late, tell customers as this defuses the anger and allows a strong relationship to develop. Of course, too many broken promises equals lost customers.

LONG-TERM RELATIONSHIPS

In Chapter 9 it was suggested that the purpose of an organisation is to 'create and retain' a customer. This is sometimes referred to as *customer catching* and *customer keeping*. The traditional marketing emphasis has been on the creation of an exchange rather than the retention of customers for future business. However, the first exchange with a particular customer might not be profitable because it could cost so much to find that customer and achieve the initial sale.

In addition, as further business progresses, future exchanges will be more profitable, primarily because of the fewer up-front costs but also exchanges with existing customers can benefit from past experiences. However, it is important not to lose any customer. Every lost customer costs money (profit) because in addition to the lost profit from future sales there is the cost of recruiting new replacement customers and the unquantifiable loss due to the failure to benefit from word-of-mouth recommendations from satisfied customers. Estimates vary but there is general agreement that it can cost five times as much to get an initial order as it is to obtain a repeat order from an established customer. The rationale for building relationships with customers is based on the long-term financial benefits that can accrue. It is based on two economic facts:

1 It is more expensive to obtain a new customer than to retain an existing customer.
2 The longer the period of the relationship, the more profitable the relationship becomes.

A useful analogy would be to consider a bucket full of water which has a small hole through which some of the liquid escapes. To keep the bucket full involves constant topping up. But the bigger the hole, the greater the loss of water, which in turn requires more effort and cost, and if it is too big then maybe total loss.

EXAMPLE

Research has shown that in America recruiting a new credit card customer can cost up to $50. This initial outlay will not be recovered until the customer has held a card for some 15 months.

Sasser (1978) suggests that retaining just 5 per cent more customers than normal can double profits. MBNA, an American credit card company, collected information from every lost customer. As a result they revised their products, amended their processes, and enhanced services. Their defection rate is one of the lowest in the industry and their profitability one of the highest.

Many organisations are now trying to calculate the *lifetime value* of their customers. It has been estimated that a new baby will require over £1000 of disposable nappies in the first year. Anyone who buys a newspaper every day could spend £10 000 in a lifetime, and most students will earn £1 million in their working life. These figures show the benefit that can derive from long-term relationships. As the quote below illustrates, the chosen supplier could obtain continuous business and be very hard to dislodge.

> We are not looking for new suppliers in any of our existing product areas. We have the suppliers we want and, unless something goes wrong with the relationship, we will not search for new suppliers. (A major retailer)

It is not always the case that long-term relationships are profitable. There are investments to be made in building relationships and these must be evaluated against the benefits expected. It is also possible to study the needs of customers and the possible relationships along a continuum. At one end there are customers constantly purchasing a particular category of product, but with low switching costs so it is relatively easy to change suppliers. At the other end, high switching costs mean changes are more difficult and will happen less often. Barbara Bund Jackson called the first 'always a share' and the second 'lost for good'. With the first a customer can have multiple suppliers and have a short-time horizon in relationships. Suppliers can always hope to get business and the established methods of transactional exchange marketing are appropriate. Marketers practising relationship marketing will try to move customers along to the other extreme by increasing switching costs. The risk is that if such an account is lost, it is lost for good along with the investment made in trying to develop the business.

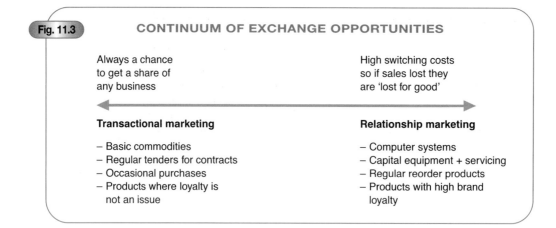

Fig. 11.3

CONTINUUM OF EXCHANGE OPPORTUNITIES

Always a chance to get a share of any business

High switching costs so if sales lost they are 'lost for good'

Transactional marketing

– Basic commodities
– Regular tenders for contracts
– Occasional purchases
– Products where loyalty is not an issue

Relationship marketing

– Computer systems
– Capital equipment + servicing
– Regular reorder products
– Products with high brand loyalty

STRATEGIES FOR CUSTOMER RETENTION

Building and maintaining long-term customer relationships involve a number of stages. These can be likened to the same stages in personal friendships, meeting, courtship, adjustments, and advancement. These mirror the stages of customer development introduced in Chapter 9.

Perhaps the most important issue in retaining customers is to refocus the marketing effort away from a single exchange onto the activities which will achieve a strong relationship.

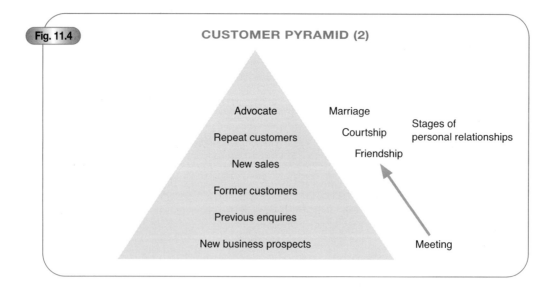

Fig. 11.4

CUSTOMER PYRAMID (2)

Advocate

Repeat customers

New sales

Former customers

Previous enquires

New business prospects

Marriage

Courtship

Friendship

Meeting

Stages of personal relationships

Table 11.1 ● **Differences between transactional and relationship marketing**

Exchange marketing	Relationship marketing
Importance on single sale	Importance of customer retention
Importance of product features	Importance of customer benefits
Short time scale	Longer time scale
Less emphasis on service	High customer service
Quality is concern of production	Quality is concern of all
Competitive commitment	High customer commitment
Persuasive communication	Regular customer communication

The issues in relationship marketing show how important it is to consider both the actual transaction and the period after the sale when the relationship can be strengthened. As time goes on, the benefits from any relationship can increase if both parties approach the interaction in a positive way. However, it is the perception of the advantages which is also important. Both the reality and the perception are reinforced by the ongoing contact between the parties based on some form of two-way communication.

Building good relationships concentrates on the softer issues of partnerships, more than the increasing of physical barriers to switching by customers. The latter are often resented. Strong relationships are ones which both parties enter into voluntarily, rather than because they have no choice. Enduring relationships provide an unique and sustained competitive advantage. It is difficult in a general book to give a full list of actual activities as there are many different individual contexts where relationships are developed. Buttle (1996) considers a dozen areas in more detail. These are:

- principal – agent
- manufacturer – retailer
- business to business
- financial adviser – client
- advertising agency – client
- charities – donors
- airlines – passengers
- retail banking – personal customers
- corporate banking – customers
- credit card operators
- hospitality
- internal company links

To these we could add many others such as Heinz customer clubs, Morgan Cars owners club, University Alumni Associations, and supermarket loyalty cards. In any specific situation there will be issues particular to that relationship.

Gronroos suggests 'that marketing can be considered as revolving around relationships, some of which are like single transactions, narrow in scope and not involving much or any social relationship (e.g. marketing soap or breakfast cereals). Other relationships, on the other hand, are broader in scope and may involve even substantial social contacts and be continuous and enduring in nature (e.g. marketing hospitality or financial services).'

The common issues in achieving strong relationships are:

- concern for the welfare of customers;
- adding benefits in the longer term;
- ongoing communications; and
- building trust and commitment between the parties.

Every contact between the supplier's organisation and the customer adds to the relationship. These contacts can be trading exchanges, or exchanges of information, or social exchanges. What is important is that all contacts should be mutually supporting. All should exhibit the issues above, and it is necessary for companies to monitor and plan all such exchanges across the whole organisation. This returns to the need for effective internal marketing, a subject that will be considered again in Chapter 22.

CONCLUSION

This chapter has considered a wide range of issues which are difficult to describe in hard factual ways, yet add greatly to the achievement of mutually satisfactory exchanges between supplier organisations and customers. For such exchanges to develop it is necessary to reconsider the company–consumer chain breaking it down into a series of exchanges such as below:

company ↔ employee ↔ intermediary ↔ customer ↔ consumer.

At each point there is a complex two-way contact, including the items of trade, information and social interactions. How these exchanges are managed by the suppliers and perceived by the recipients could lead to the building of trust and confidence, which will affect the development of a type of relationship. Although relationship marketing is a fairly recent academic theme, it has been around for a very long time and the applications are obvious as has been shown in this chapter.

It could be applied to segmentation with an emphasis on commitment to long-term relationships with high usage customers. It is very essential in complex industrial markets where multi-level contacts are common.

Relationship marketing is developing in fast-moving consumer markets, where developments in technology enable more accurate targeting of individual customers.

But it is in the area of services marketing that the growth in relationship marketing is most visible. The nature of services, in particular the direct contact between supplier and customer and also the issues which separate services from tangible goods, give rise to the need for good relationship marketing.

Of course many offerings are a combination of both services and tangible goods, therefore, the issues in this chapter are critical to all marketers.

QUESTIONS

1 Suggest a situation where investing in long-term relationships would not be the best choice.

2 Most services are distinguished by their intangibility, however it is often the perishability that gives the greatest problem. When a train leaves a station all unsold seats are redundant. What action could be taken to improve this situation?

3 How can the interactive contact between two individual people representing buyer and seller affect the delivery of a marketing offering?

4 The marketing mix is often confused with McCarthy's '4Ps'. A better way of considering marketing could be Product; Promises; People; and Perception. Discuss why these factors are important.

FURTHER READING

Booms, B. and Bitner, M. J. (1981) 'Marketing strategies and organisation structures for service firms', in J. Donelly and W. George (Eds), *The Marketing of Services*, American Marketing Association, pp. 47–51, Chicago.

Buttle, F. (1996) *Relationship Marketing* – Theory and Practice, Paul Chapman Publishing, London.

Carlzon, J. (1987) *Moments of Truth*, Ballinger, Cambridge, Mass.

Cowell, D. (1994) *The Marketing of Services,* 2nd Edn, Heinemann, Oxford.

Cram, Tony (1994) *The Power of Relationship Marketing*, Pitman Publishing, London.

Drucker, P. F. (1991) 'The new Productivity challenge', *Harvard Business Review*, Nov–Dec.

Gronroos, C. (1979) 'Marketing orientated strategies in service businesses', *Finnish Journal of Business*, 4.

Gronroos, C (1990) 'Relationship approach to the marketing function in service context: the marketing organisation interface', *Journal of Business Research*, Vol. 20, pp. 3–11.

Hales, M. G. (1995) 'Focusing on 15% of the pie', *Bank Marketing*, Vol. 27, No. 4.

Holloway, J. C. and Robinson, C. (1995) *Marketing for Tourism*, 3rd Edn, Longman, London.

Jackson, B. B. (1985) 'Build customer relationships that last', *Harvard Business Review*, Nov–Dec.

Levitt, T. (1976) 'The industrialisation of services', *Harvard Business Review*, Sept–Oct.

Levitt, T. (1981) 'Marketing intangible products and product intangibles', *Harvard Business Review*, May–June.

Palmer, A. (1994) *Principles of Services Marketing*, McGraw-Hill, Maidenhead.

Payne, A. (1993) *The Essence of Services Marketing*, Prentice-Hall, Hemel Hempstead.

Sasser, W. E., Olsen, R. P. and Wyckoff D. D. (1978) *Management of Service Operations*, Allyn & Bacon, Boston.

Schlessinger, L. A. and Hesketh, J. L. (1991) 'The service-driven service company', *Harvard Business Review*, Sept–Oct.

Shostack, G. L. (1987) 'Service positioning through structural change', *Journal of Marketing*, January, pp. 34–43.

Townsend, R. (1971) *Up the Organisation*, Michael Joseph.

Wall, M. (1996) Unpublished Student Report.

Zeithmal, V. A. and Bitner, M. J. (1996) *Service Marketing*, McGraw-Hill, Singapore.

Customer loyalty in the student banking market

Most new cheque accounts are unprofitable for the first three years. In the UK, to attract 150 000 new student/youth accounts could cost £3 million in advertising, and another £20 per head in incentives, mailings, literature, computer costs and administration. In early years, with high transaction levels and low balances, the business will be unprofitable. Profit comes with customer maturity, through higher income, higher balances, lending services, deposit products and insurance commissions. The proposition is only viable where the customer is retained. (*Tony Cram*, 1994)

The situation is perhaps even worse than the example suggests. Hales has shown that only 15 per cent of all Bank customers are ever profitable and suggests the focusing of efforts on these customers both for retention and additional product offerings.

The benefits for a Bank in targeting students as customers are said to be:

Students	Graduates
Grants received once a term	Ex-students usually get better paid jobs
(average credit balance higher than weekly paid customers)	
Simple needs	Many enter professions
Often high users of cash dispensers	New business acquisition connections
Opportunity to build relationship with parents	Likely to give opportunities for greater profit over lifetime.

While it is not always true that better educated customers will be tomorrow's high earners, there is sufficient proof that many high earners are graduates. The problem is that on average, it takes 7–9 years for the costs incurred while customers are students, to be recouped by the revenue after graduation.

A syndicated research study for the High Street Banks (Oct 1995) showed that 13 per cent of graduates switched their accounts after graduation, with the banks who take on the accounts benefiting by not incurring the earlier costs of student accounts. In fact the situation could be even worse as Melissa Wall found, in research for her undergraduate dissertation, that 16 per cent of final year students are contemplating changing, and a further 19 per cent intending to change after graduating because their Bank does not concentrate enough effort on the needs of prospective graduates. This related well to the higher figure in her survey which found almost 40 per cent of recent graduates had changed to Banks such as First Direct, rather than continue with the Bank they used while at College.

This loss of business is very expensive for the traditional Banks who offer student services. The most common reasons for choosing a particular bank for a student account were the cash and other incentives, or the fact that the student (or parents) already had an account at a particular Bank. This accounted for more than half of all students. When it comes to decisions of banking after graduation the continuation of an account seems to be less important. There are issues of the treatment received during the student period, the appreciation that post graduation needs will be very different, and the wish to leave overdrafts behind and start with a fresh account especially as debt is a serious concern for many recent graduates.

Most Banks claim they do try to contact students about graduate services, but less than a quarter of those interviewed by Miss Wall felt satisfied by the contact. One of the basic principles of marketing is that derived from understanding customers. As can be seen from this research these needs can change very dramatically at certain periods. Building strong relationships are a key part of long-term marketing, but these must take account of changes in customer requirements. If a customer focus is the critical success factor in marketing then the challenge is to get the right service to the right customer at the right price and at the right time.

Question
Considering the banking market suggest how Banks could effectively manage the relationships with potential graduates to retain many more accounts. Remember the level of investment already made in student banking and consider the additional investment required against the likely profit. In the light of your studies do you think Banks should continue to offer student accounts?

CHAPTER 12

Making Products Available

If you build mousetrap the world will beat a path to your door.
Ralph Waldo Emerson

INTRODUCTION

The above quote, by an American philosopher, is far from the truth in markets where supply exceeds demand. Obviously it is important to communicate with potential customers about your products, and the key benefits they offer. There are only a few products which customers will make the effort to seek out. For this to happen it has to be a product that the purchaser really values. These products, which potential customers would value, could be based on exclusivity, for example, a designer dress or an individually crafted piece of jewellery, or perhaps another type of 'aspirational' product. There are really very few products where customers will beat a path to your door. It is therefore very important that products are made readily available to customers. Marketing has already been described as 'making it easier for your customers to say yes'. Certainly the decision to purchase can be helped by making products available where potential customers can find them.

If the product required is specialised, or maybe one that needs to be made to an individual design as is common in industrial markets, then experienced purchasing officers will use all their skills to locate a potential supplier with the necessary abilities. Here they might 'beat a path to your door'. But this is unusual and this search is not necessarily going to find all organisations which can fulfil the requirements. It will be more likely to find those organisations which take positive action to develop channels linking them to potential customers.

The purchasing department must procure the right goods, at the right time, in the correct quantities, at the right price. The key decisions of the purchaser or the purchasing organisation regarding which goods to purchase will be taken to meet the objectives of the purchaser or the purchasing organisation. You might consider the role of a buyer for the Sainsbury organisation responsible for jams and marmalade, and how his or her actions would affect both a major supplier and a customer for this product.

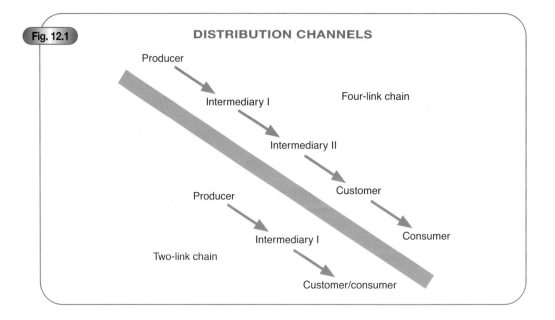

Fig. 12.1 DISTRIBUTION CHANNELS

Producer

Intermediary I

Four-link chain

Intermediary II

Customer

Producer

Intermediary I

Consumer

Two-link chain

Customer/consumer

The following example considers how to make products easily available to customers, and it might suggest a sales-based solution. It also highlights the fact that while Sainsbury's are a customer for Hartleys, the final consumer is in fact a customer of the retailer. The term 'trade marketing' is used regarding that part of the exchange process between supplier and intermediary. It is as important a marketing job as dealing with final consumers. The specific role of the intermediary will be discussed later in this chapter. This example also highlights what are called distribution channels (*see* Fig. 12.1), which are the links connecting (marketing) organisations and through which goods or services are transferred from the original producer to the final consumer.

EXAMPLE

Let's say that you were trying to purchase a jar of jam. You may go to your local grocer's shop. In the price list published by *The Grocer Magazine* there are 11 suppliers listed, but in an outlet of Sainsbury's visited in the winter of 1997, there were only the following six brands in stock:

Sainsbury's own label;
Robertsons;
Streamline;
Hartleys;
St Dalfour;
Meridian.

Hartleys was one of the brands not stocked by Sainsbury's in 1992. The problem Hartleys had was how to reach potential customers, especially those who did most of their shopping at Sainsbury's. Certainly few, if any, of these potential customers would have tried to visit the Hartleys factory in Cambridge. So Hartleys had to change Sainsbury's decision regarding the brands the supermarket group were prepared to stock, or find an alternative way of getting close to potential customers. By the summer of 1994, Sainsbury's were stocking Hartleys jams. Hartleys had obviously been successful in persuading Sainsbury's to change their decision. Likewise St Dalfour and Meridian are relative newcomers on the jam shelves at Sainsbury's, it will be interesting to see if they can keep shelf space against the competition.

Tesco stocks the following brands of jam: Tesco own label, Robertons, Streamline, Hartleys, St Dalfour, Meridian, and Bonne Mama. Perhaps Bonne Mama will also be successful in persuading Sainsbury's to stock their products in the future.

Distribution, when considered by a marketer, is not merely concerned with physical distribution. It covers:

- the choice of channels – direct or indirect;
- decisions on whether to use a single channel or several different (complementary) ones;
- decisions on how to make those channels available;
- decisions on building relationships with intermediaries;
- ownership and investment within the channels.

The problem of channel choice is not restricted to physical products alone, but can just as easily apply to a service. Consider a student insurance policy made available through an insurance broker, such as Endsleigh Insurance. It is covered in the '4 Ps' of marketing by the word 'place', but 'place' really does not describe all the elements involved in the task of making products easily available to customers. These include:

1 Bringing customers into contact with offered products/services.
2 Offering a sufficient choice to meet customers' needs.
3 Persuading customers to develop a favourable attitude to a particular product.
4 Maintaining adequate levels of sales both for your organisation, and if appropriate, for the intermediaries.
5 Providing appropriate services and information to help purchase decisions.
6 Maintaining an acceptable price, including the payments to members of the distribution channel.

SELECTION OF CHANNELS

The prime aim of any marketing decision relating to distribution channels is how to reach the relevant customers. This must be in the most appropriate way, given the following four major considerations:

1 Potential customers' requirements.
2 Your organisational resources.

3 Competitors' and distributors' actions.

4 Legal constraints.

Peter Chisnall wrote in his book, *Strategic Business Marketing:*

> Among the decisions then to be taken is the important one of how products will reach customers. Unless the channels of distribution are appropriate for the type of product and are efficiently operated, even intrinsically good products can end up as failures . . . it is worth spending a considerable amount of time and effort in evaluating alternative ways of ensuring that the channel eventually selected will make its full contribution to the marketing mix. Carelessly chosen methods of distribution may seriously damage the reputation of suppliers and also involve them in expensive litigation, if they seek to terminate agreements with distributors.

Established firms have well-defined channels. These channels often establish the norm for that particular market. While such channels will clearly differ from market to market, the channels themselves develop from the exchange between suppliers and customers. They then come to fit the needs of many customers and again become the expected norm. Such arrangements are usually of a long-term nature, and can prove a challenge to new entrants trying to break into the market.

Customer requirements

The choice of efficient distribution channels relies on a knowledge of a particular market. But, more specifically, it relies on the needs and wants of customers. It may not be possible to satisfy everything a particular customer wants, but that customer's decision is likely to be based on issues such as cost, convenience, and availability. We could look at the different ways in which varying types of food retailer might offer a particular food item for sale.

EXAMPLE

An out-of-town hypermarket might offer two different brands at a good price (especially if one is its own brand). The hypermarket will support it by long opening hours, including most outlets being open on Sundays. In fact the term 'place' does not just refer to the location as might be imagined, it also refers to such issues as opening hours, which are equally critical to availability and, therefore, to customer decisions.

The problems facing most customers are (a) travel to the hypermarket which could be difficult without a car, and (b) the queues at the checkout if you visit it at a peak period.

A town centre store such as Marks & Spencer will offer only its own brand, but it is likely to be slightly more expensive. Marks & Spencer trade on their quality position and not their price. The store might be more convenient to a customer shopping in a town centre, but that is not always so. Also, in some locations Marks & Spencer is not open especially late and some of their stores are not open on a Sunday.

A neighbourhood store, owner managed, but perhaps a member of a buying group like Spar, will have limited choice. They may stock just one branded product, offered for sale at its recommended retail price. Such a store could be near urban housing, and is likely to be open for even longer hours than the hypermarket.

The decision facing potential customers is how they rate the different elements of cost and convenience. The supplier of the food product will perhaps see no conflict in supplying all three types of retailers. The attempt by the supplier to obtain maximum coverage is termed intensive distribution. This is the strategy of giving the product the maximum exposure possible, so that it has the best chance of being found by a customer. However, the supplier is likely to put greatest effort into trying to develop the channel which offers the greatest return. In supplying a hypermarket it is likely that a direct approach will be used. But to supply the neighbourhood store they will probably supply in an indirect way via a wholesaler or Cash and Carry.

Opening times are relevant to the availability decision of customers, especially for such diverse organisations as public libraries and supermarkets. The restrictions on local authority budgets has been blamed for shorter library opening hours, as well as a more limited 'product' due to less spending on new books. However, the visible result is fewer books are being borrowed. It is possible to argue that the reason also has something to do with the ever-increasing presence of substitute products such as TV or video. While marketing is not a term used by many in the library service, the need to satisfy customers is still a key requirement. The use of mobile libraries over many years was one way libraries found of increasing availability. The reduction of opening hours in some towns is the opposite.

The maximum availability of food products, via all chosen channels, is desirable for the food supplier. If the product is not on sale when required then potential customers could buy an alternative (competitor's) food item. Here there could be an alternative for the customer but the supplier loses a sale. In the library example, a customer might be annoyed if the product was unavailable when required. That could influence future behaviour and decisions.

The situation is very different in an industrial setting for a specialist component required by a manufacturer. The production line could be brought to a halt if the component is not available when required. In the past, firms invested working capital in buffer stocks, but such costs are increasingly being reduced as companies change to sophisticated supply-chain systems such as JIT (just-in-time). This type of supply chain can only work if there is a close partnership between supplier and customer. Decisions by the customer on whether to source locally, or perhaps import cheaper components, would be determined by issues of convenience and availability. Hence such a situation provides an interesting challenge for the marketing department of a potential supplying company. For this reason knowledge of customers' behaviour is critical to decisions on suitable channels of distribution.

Organisational resources

The choice of channels has to be consistent with the needs and capabilities of the organisation as well as meeting the needs of customers. It might be considered necessary for a qualified person to install a more technical product such as a gas fire or a heavy duty machine. In this case suitable channels might be restricted to those where such a service is available. The producer could, of course, set up a network of wholly owned outlets.

This option is very expensive. It may be beyond the resources of a producer and it could also be an inefficient way of achieving the objectives.

An organisation will normally first make decisions on the market segments to which they want to offer their product. However, as has already been discussed, there is likely to be an ongoing need for market information to be fed back to the original supplier. In view of this, it could be decided to work with a particular type of channel which will facilitate the process. Many companies admit they are better off working through intermediaries because they can provide the resources to cover all the potential customers in a cost-effective way. In fact this is another reason why food manufacturers market via retailers rather than directly. In other cases intermediaries are in an excellent position with regards to customers. This is why certain life insurance and pension companies operate via solicitors, accountants or banks rather than recruiting large direct sales forces. The intermediary gives credibility to the product.

Imported products can also benefit from indirect channels, which is why French mineral water, Perrier, although owned by Nestlé, is distributed in the UK by Coca-Cola Schweppes beverages (CCSB). Both organisations benefit: Perrier from an efficient transport system, and CCSB's large professional sales force; CCSB by being able to include a very desirable product in their portfolio.

One problem arising from the use of intermediaries is that it almost invariably leads to some form of loss of control over the way markets are served. Obviously, it also involves lower margins, but this needs to be set against the costs of direct distribution, and the breadth of potential customers that any channel can achieve. Of course, if a manufacturer wants to reach regular customers of Marks & Spencer he cannot do it without losing his identity and control because he would have to supply an own-brand product. This now gives Marks & Spencer a very powerful position in part of the supply chain. Companies who successfully work with them, can gain very large sales by co-operating in this way.

Market considerations

The example above is also relevant when considering which channels are (a) suitable for customers, (b) acceptable to the organisation and (c) feasible within light of existing market conditions. Control of the distributive channels is a very effective barrier to entry in many markets. Even if it is possible to gain access to a general distributor alongside competitive products, it will not be enough if the distributor constantly recommends a competitor's product rather than your product.

An interesting phenomenon is that brands with small market shares suffer, in what Professor Ehrenburg calls, the 'Double Jeopardy Effect'. This is reflected by their customers being less loyal to that brand in regular purchases, hence emphasising the poor sales. This effect makes it very difficult for minor brands to compete effectively.

EXAMPLE

Opportunities do exist to develop sales in any market, as the example of Canon photocopiers shows. This was an effective market entry strategy. Rank Xerox used to dominate the UK photocopier market. They offered a range to meet almost every need. They supported this with a very large direct sales force and a national service network.

Canon broke this dominance by a strategy of producing reliable standardised machines which, although not as sophisticated, initially were cheaper. Canon offered their range through independent distributors who could undertake their own service requirements – a much cheaper operation than the Xerox sales and service teams.

Of course Rank Xerox have fought back and Canon have developed from their initial strategy. However, the role of alternative channels in Canon's market entry strategy was vital.

Another case where the use of alternative distribution channels was introduced to avoid direct competition with established products, is the way Avon cosmetics use thousands of direct sales agents rather than sell via retail outlets. Avon have a large turnover in the UK and make an excellent profit on their business.

Legal issues

The legal environment is important. There are obvious issues such as product liability laws, which affect all offerings. These restrictions vary from country to country. It is equally important to appreciate legal issues when developing channels for distribution. Key legislation such as the Sale of Goods Act puts responsibilities on retailers. In structuring the channels support must be given to the retailers (your customers) even if they are not the final consumers. Policies on returned stock, and replacing faulty goods, are a key element of distribution policy and customer service.

There are many laws restricting business. The legal environment relating to the customers (and the customers' customers) is part of the environment that must be considered when making products/services available.

TYPES OF DISTRIBUTION CHANNEL

Channels can be long or short, single or multiple (hybrid), and can achieve intensive, selective or exclusive distribution. The length of channel could have any number of intermediaries or be direct to customers (*see* Fig. 12.2).

EXERCISE

For each of the situations in Fig. 12.2 write down the advantages and disadvantages to the fruit farmer. The issues you are likely to consider are ones of control, cost, feedback, customer service and how likely it is that the supplier will achieve particular objectives.

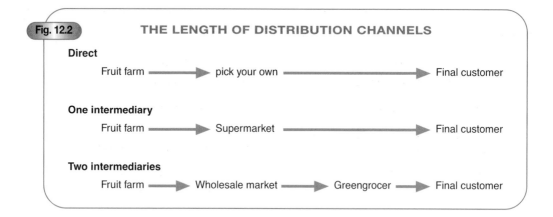

Fig. 12.2 THE LENGTH OF DISTRIBUTION CHANNELS

Direct

Fruit farm ⟶ pick your own ⟶ Final customer

One intermediary

Fruit farm ⟶ Supermarket ⟶ Final customer

Two intermediaries

Fruit farm ⟶ Wholesale market ⟶ Greengrocer ⟶ Final customer

Direct channels

A direct channel is said to exist when there are no intermediaries between the supply organisation and its customers. Such an arrangement could be:

Direct:

Insurance company   →   (own sales team)   →   Customers

Indirect:

General trader	→	mail order catalogue	→	Customers
Garden bulb supplier	→	direct mail leaflet	→	Customers
Clothing manufacturer	→	party plan	→	Customers
Library service	→	mobile library	→	Customers
Small bakery	→	own retail outlet	→	Customers

The last is also an example of vertical integration. In these examples the supplier will decide all aspects of the contact with the customer. This could include how often the salesperson should contact the customer or how frequently to send out a catalogue. In this type of direct channel there is no doubt who has control of the many decisions regarding the exchange. The situation is more complicated in indirect channels. There are many reasons for using direct channels, but equally there are a number of reasons why such channels are not always used. Some of these are listed in Fig. 12.3.

Indirect channels

The conventional channel structure is shown in Fig. 12.4. The roles of wholesaler and retailer could be filled by any of the intermediaries relevant to a particular market.

The links are important with a marketing exchange taking place at each stage. The link provided by negotiation is not necessarily formal, but it certainly takes place in the legal sense of an offer and acceptance.

It is important to realise the effect of the indirect nature of the channel, and the supply pipeline, on these indirect channels. One well-known British company launched its product into the USA with apparently great success. It more than met the year 1 estimates of sales. In year 2 sales did not increase, in fact they fell. On investigation it was found that many wholesalers had bought large quantities in the first year,

Fig. 12.3

'GOING DIRECT TO MARKET'

FOR	AGAINST
• Small market easily reached	• Wide geographic market spread
• Need to demonstrate a technical product	• Financial resources may be better used elsewere
• Inability to persuade intermediary to accept product	• Lack of retailing skills or know-how
• High intermediary profit margins	• Limited product range which is not economical for direct sales

being encouraged by attractive promotional deals. However, the retailers and consumers were not buying, and so the pipeline was blocked by large stocks of the old product. It was an expensive lesson as the British company attempted to sort out the problems. This example shows the importance of information and feedback from all parts of the distribution channel. It also illustrates the problem of loss of control that a supplier can have in an indirect channel.

Another common problem is the extent to which products are 'out-of-stock' at one level in a distribution chain. The longer the channel, the more difficult it is to cope with the variations of consumer demand. If a product is not available when required it could lead to a lost sale. This again emphasises the need for monitoring all levels of any indirect channel.

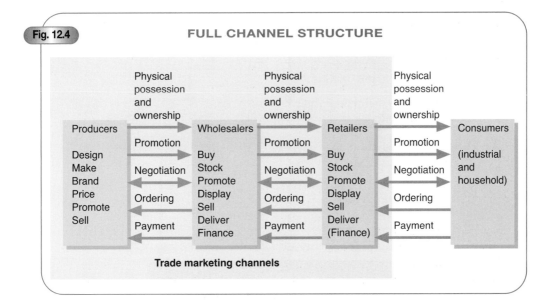

Fig. 12.4

FULL CHANNEL STRUCTURE

Hybrid channels

There is no reason why a supplier should stay with a single channel. Educational toy supplier, Early Learning, started with most sales via its mail order catalogue. It carefully monitored sales in large areas of population and, when it considered the time was appropriate, a retail outlet was opened in a secondary shopping area. Note that these areas were not in the prime High Street sites. It was considered customers would be prepared to seek out an Early Learning outlet because the company felt they offered a unique type of product. So it was decided there was no point in paying the highest retail rents for prime High Street sites. The catalogue still continued and sales justified both channels running alongside each other. Demand for the products offered has been such that some High Street sites have been opened in busy locations.

Figure 12.5 represents the channels used by a well-known UK confectionery company where maximum distribution (intensive) is vital for sales of impulse purchase items.

There can be problems with mixed channels, as the following example illustrates.

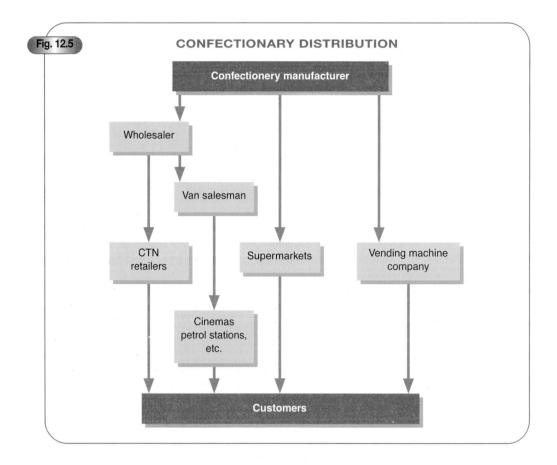

Fig. 12.5 CONFECTIONARY DISTRIBUTION

EXAMPLE

Wang Computers tried to base its distribution activities on a combination of its direct sales force, in conjunction with dealers.

In 1985 the company lowered the sales commission rates of its sales force for sales made jointly with dealers. Consequently, the rates for these sales were below those for sales made directly by the sales force without involving dealers. Inevitably Wang's own sales representatives began to compete with, rather than co-operate with, their resellers (retailers) – some Wang dealers even filed lawsuits because of this policy. Apparently it is now difficult for the company to re-establish its channel relationships as a residue of ill-will remains with the dealers towards the Wang direct sales operation. Obviously Wang failed to manage a workable hybrid channel strategy.

(*Note*: In August 1992, Wang filed for protection from bankruptcy in the USA.)

EXERCISE

Find out which channels are used by airlines to sell their tickets, you may be surprised by the diversity of outlets.

Intensive, selective and exclusive distribution

- Intensive distribution involves maximising the number of outlets where a product is available. This wide exposure means more opportunities to buy. It is typified by confectionery, soft drinks and other fmcgs (fast-moving consumer goods).
- Selective distribution is used where the choice of outlet or service offered is specifically relevant to the buying situation. Examples are electrical or photographic specialists who can offer professional advice or plumbers who can install purchases. However, this type of restricted distribution is becoming less common, with supermarkets and chemists, as well as department stores, offering ever wider ranges of household and electrical goods.
- Exclusive distribution is much more restrictive. In this case there is often only one exclusive company in any one geographic area. The major main dealers for motor cars come into this category but, in addition to sales, they offer service, repair and warranty facilities. They receive the benefit of exclusivity which reduces competition. It is likely that the relationship will be formalised with a legal contract including targets, and obligations on the distributor. In return for acting as the local distributor for Ford or BMW or Rover, the distributor could receive promotional help.

It is interesting to note that Daewoo Cars, relative newcomers to the British market, have chosen a different distribution strategy. Daewoo have chosen direct selling, hassle-free showrooms where customers are shown courtesy and are free to browse in peace. This approach combined with their aim of being the UK's most friendly and customer focused car company appears to be paying dividends in that, instead of meeting targets of gaining 1 per cent of the market within three years, they sold 18 000 cars in the first year, giving it a market share of 0.92 per cent, a very successful launch indeed. As yet other car manufacturers have not followed this lead.

THE ROLE OF INTERMEDIARIES

Many markets are subject to dynamic change and in some the functions of channel members are being modified. Nevertheless, the common roles of the intermediary remain important. The most basic role is to reach customers at a lower cost per unit than the supplier can achieve directly. Perhaps the role could include reaching the target in a more effective way, given the buying habits of customers. This could be achieved by simply buying in bulk from the supplier and selling individual items on to the customers. The supplier concentrates on production, and delivers in quantity to the intermediary who becomes the supplier's customer. The intermediary will obviously take a share of the profit from a product/service, but it might still benefit the supplier because the intermediary could well be responsible for:

- stockholding costs;
- transport and delivery to final customers;
- breaking bulk and consolidation of orders;
- providing local services such as display or service.

It is also possible that the supplier would be paid more quickly by the intermediary rather than the final customers. Certainly, use of intermediaries can reduce the number of transactions involved in reaching customers (*see* Fig. 12.6).

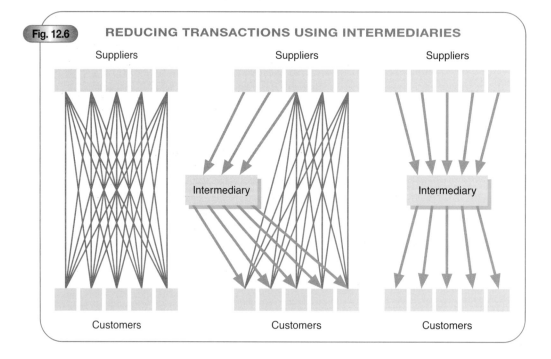

Fig. 12.6 REDUCING TRANSACTIONS USING INTERMEDIARIES

There are many different types of intermediary, such as those listed below. One key difference that should be noticed is whether the intermediary takes ownership for the products in transit as a merchant, rather than acting as an agent who just puts buyer and seller in contact:

1 *Agent* – primarily concerned in the identification, conduct and negotiation of sale of goods either direct or through intermediaries. Agents do not take title or ownership of goods, nor do they often become involved in the physical handling of goods.
2 *Merchant* – takes title (buys) and resells merchandise. Wholesalers and retailers are the two main types of merchant.
3 *Wholesaler* – buys and resells products to retailers and to major industrial institutions and commercial companies. Normally sells little directly to the consumer.
4 *Retailer* – a merchant dealing primarily with the final consumer.
5 *Dealer* – buys and resells merchandise at wholesale, retail or both. Thus dealers take ownership, are involved with stock, and usually have close market contacts within a particular area.
6 *Distributor* – often confused with dealer. More precisely, distributors are closer to the wholesaler role, often controlling independent dealers for retail distribution.
7 *Jobber* – a term widely used to designate a distributor or wholesaler. In the UK it usually carries the connotation of specialist knowledge or franchise with a particular market sector.
8 *Franchisee* – basically a licensing system under which the owner of a product or service grants an independent local operator the right to trade under the umbrella of the brand owner's name, offering the brand owner's product.

Recently much has been written about the power of food supermarket buyers in the selection of products. They are offered hundreds of new products every year and have room for only a small proportion on their shelves. Therefore the power of the buyer for the retail outlets is vital in deciding which products should be added to the range, which products should be delisted (deleted), and which will never be bought by that retailer, thus never becoming available to the customers of the shop. In these decisions a strong brand name can be an extremely powerful lever to persuade a major supermarket to stock a product. Once a relationship is formed it can be a long-term partnership. An article by Knox and White (1991) on the subject of fresh produce concluded:

> We have observed that these relationships are both highly interdependent and concentrated. Because of the increasing volume of high quality produce required by the retailer, they are obliged to work with a limited number of large suppliers who are capable of producing sufficient volume to meet these needs. As a consequence, there appears to be a reluctance to make rash changes in either supplier or retailer affiliation. Consequently, the average duration of a buyer–supplier relationship in the horticultural market was found to be about eight years.

Certainly channel choices are long term and the interdependence of the parties is obvious. But in some markets the intermediary may lead the marketing and promotional effort; in others it is the supplier (*see* Fig. 12.7).

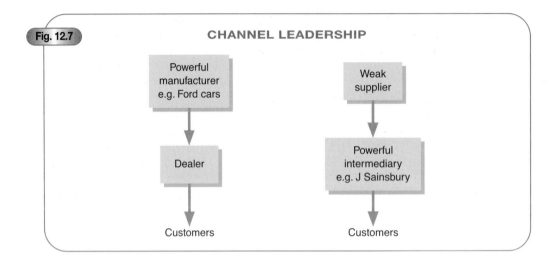

Fig. 12.7 CHANNEL LEADERSHIP

VERTICAL MARKETING SYSTEMS

The model of powerful suppliers or intermediaries competing for control of a distribution channel is now being challenged by what is termed vertical marketing systems (VMS). Certainly conflict can arise in a channel where channel members have their own distinct objectives which may not complement those of other channel members. Figure 12.8 suggests these differences.

The companies in Fig. 12.8 represent separate businesses, and each is seeking to maximise its own profits. The problem is that conflicting actions could reduce the effectiveness of the total system. But the companies are also interdependent, as the Knox and White study discussed. Hence it is really not sufficient to count intermedi-

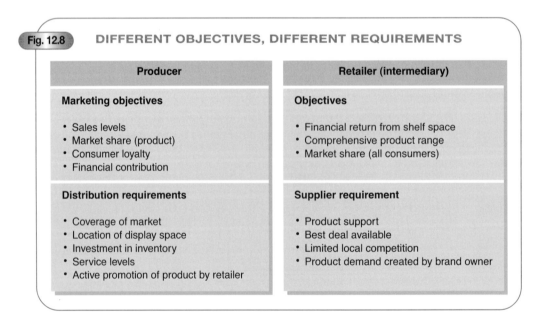

Fig. 12.8 DIFFERENT OBJECTIVES, DIFFERENT REQUIREMENTS

Producer	Retailer (intermediary)
Marketing objectives	**Objectives**
• Sales levels • Market share (product) • Consumer loyalty • Financial contribution	• Financial return from shelf space • Comprehensive product range • Market share (all consumers)
Distribution requirements	**Supplier requirement**
• Coverage of market • Location of display space • Investment in inventory • Service levels • Active promotion of product by retailer	• Product support • Best deal available • Limited local competition • Product demand created by brand owner

aries and measure/monitor members' performance. Not all channel systems have members who see themselves as part of a system. This does little to enhance the quality and effectiveness of service. The idea of a vertical marketing system is that producers and intermediaries make a serious attempt to co-ordinate the channel of which they form a part, and to eliminate conflict between individual members (*see* Fig. 12.9).

A survey of such relationships by Dawson and Shaw (1989) used a structured survey of 42 large British multiples and 60 suppliers in four very different product areas. Findings indicated that there are many examples of retailers and suppliers entering into long-term arrangements to do business together. Both parties invest heavily in the development of the relationship. It is interesting that 43 per cent of the retailers and 92 per cent of the manufacturers agreed that they preferred to remain with the same supplier/customer from year to year whenever possible. Factors acting to increase the stability of relationships included:

- a need for consistent quality;
- a need for a flexible response;
- joint product development work;
- specific delivery requirements.

Even if no formal VMS is developed it is still important to build strong relationships between channel members.

- Any manufacturer that can appeal to the channel partners' self-interest will find its influence over distributors or retailers probably higher than if its programmes are totally self-interested. This is providing benefits – the basis of marketing. For example, Levi Strauss jointly developed a computerised order processing-inventory management system with its retailers, the advantage of this being that retailers found themselves in a more favourable position in terms of profit. However, these information systems require closer partnerships. This has proved to be very well accepted by Levi wearers as well as retailers as there is an added benefit, a custom

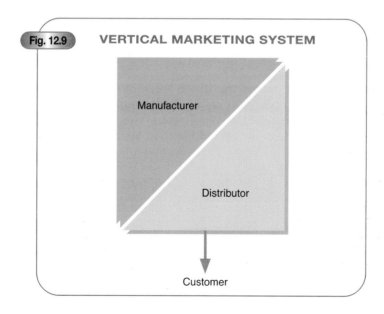

Fig. 12.9 **VERTICAL MARKETING SYSTEM**

Manufacturer

Distributor

Customer

made pair of jeans to fit perfectly can now be ordered – the information sent directly from the retailer to the manufacturer.

- Knowledge about the actual balance of power may be helpful to prevent wrong decisions with serious consequences. Attempts to drop the dealer network in order to sell directly from company-owned sales branches may end in a situation where former dealers join with competitors and successfully work against a manufacturer.
- Furthermore, channel arrangements should be based on adequate compensation. A distributor's response to a margin squeeze may be to cut back stocking levels to shift inventory-holding costs back to the manufacturer's side. In the long term this can only have negative effects on both parties.
- Manufacturers should be sensitive to the possibility of horizontal channel conflicts. These may be caused by increasing the number of outlets/intermediaries in an attempt to intensify distribution. Increased margins, for example, may be helpful to prevent such a conflict.
- The manufacturer's own sales force is a vital link to distributors. Training the sales force to support the distributors' sales forces may improve the overall channel performance.
- As a general guideline manufacturers should treat their channels of distribution as strategic assets.

VERTICAL INTEGRATION AND FRANCHISING

It will be apparent that there are two themes running through the subject of channel choice. First is the different operational roles of channel members at different levels in the system; the other is the co-operation and control of these different members within a total system.

To overcome the problems of control, the most obvious solution is for an organisation to combine the different levels in the distribution channel under a single ownership. Such an arrangement is usually called vertical integration, although now sometimes termed a corporate vertical marketing system. It is more costly for the supplier, but this can be offset by the higher revenue from not having to fund distributors' margins. Costs and control of distribution channels is illustrated in Fig. 12.10. Examples of this are the development of manufacturing units by the Cooperative Wholesale Society, or the way Laura Ashley, which started as a design and production operation, developed its own retail outlets.

An even longer integration was the Union International group run by the Vestey family. They combined companies to supply the Dewhurst Butchers chain which they owned. These included Weddel Meat Wholesalers, The British Beef Company (which also imported meat via the wholly owned Blue Star Shipping line), Thornhills Poultry (sold in 1987), Union Cold Storage (UCS) and many other related companies. For several decades the advantages were of great value. Now the increasing trend by consumers to buy less in traditional butchers and more in supermarkets and the general decrease in demand for beef has led to problems of such integrated companies which are difficult to solve. In fact none of the three companies have been particularly successful recently, although when they first developed vertically there were real advantages such as:

- economies of scale;
- savings in transaction costs;

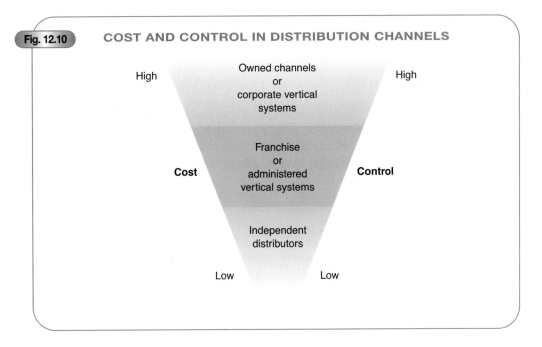

Fig. 12.10 COST AND CONTROL IN DISTRIBUTION CHANNELS

- close supplier relationships;
- barriers to entry;
- efficiency.

And for a time all companies performed very well. The problems have come in the dynamic, changing competitive world. The lack of flexibility, the stifling of competitive forces and the lack of focus by the organisations have been reflected in performance.

Laura Ashley plc has completely altered its business to concentrate on design and retailing, dramatically reducing its manufacturing operations in mid-Wales. CWS has been losing share to other food operations for many years; and Union International have been on the financial pages, although property was partly to blame for their problems.

Management guru, Tom Peters, advises companies to stick to the basic business which they are good at ('stick to your knitting'). This would suggest that companies who try to both manufacture and retail products could be spreading their activities too broadly.

One way of obtaining the advantages without all the problems is to use a franchise arrangement. It is often believed that franchising started in the USA; however, the concept is a development of the tied-house arrangement used by many British brewers, which has lasted for over 200 years. Strangely, this tied-house arrangement has been challenged as restrictive by the 1989 Monopolies Commission report on Beer and Brewing. At the same time as this report restricted the franchises available in beer retailing (public houses), other franchise arrangements covering such companies as Body Shop, Prontaprint, DynoRod and Benetton have been on the increase.

A franchise has a proven greater survival rate than other small businesses. It is therefore usually a better option for a small business person than starting a new business in an untried area. This is because the franchisor should have been through all the learning processes and expensive mistakes that can affect a new business. Franchisees find it easier to raise the necessary capital and they take on a tested formula. The advantage to the franchisor is that they can expand business with lower capital commitment, and yet gain highly motivated franchisees keen to benefit, and sharing both risks and rewards.

DISTRIBUTOR QUALITY AND SERVICE

Most intermediaries offer a level of service to add to the original supplier's product. Service organisations are dependent on people and processes, as considered earlier. The major problem is the level of commitment from employees in such service industries. A recent survey in the USA suggested over 80 per cent of employees in service industries are really in dead-end jobs. The problem that suppliers have in ensuring that the quality and service levels offered by their intermediaries is of a sufficiently high level is therefore a key element in channel decisions. We have already seen such solutions as franchising where the intermediary uses an agreed retail format controlled by the supplier, but this is not always a possible route. It is always very important for the supplier to find ways of achieving the right level of support for their product. When a distributor is offering their product as well as some competitor's products, then the supplier may have to offer incentives to the distributor's staff to get them to promote the supplier's offering. This can become a costly ever-increasing spiral. It is an area that will be of vital interest to the sales force responsible for ensuring that products are sold through the distributor rather than just to the distributor.

GETTING PRODUCTS INTO DISTRIBUTION: THE PUSH–PULL METHODS

There are two ways products get into a distribution channel. The first is through the efforts of a sales team to convince distributors to stock a product. Here a product is being *pushed* into the distribution channel. A good salesperson will not overload distributors with products, but will try to ensure the right level of product is available to meet requirements of the distributors' customers. To do this successfully a partnership needs to be created between salesperson and buyer. In some organisations the use of increasingly sophisticated electronic data and control systems could mean a product will not be purchased until it has been entered into a computer. The use of barcodes (article numbers seen on many products) means that purchases and sales can be tracked efficiently, and in some cases re-ordering of products is automatically controlled.

There is no point 'pushing' products into distribution if they do not move on to the final consumer. The customers can create demand, *pulling* products along a distribution chain. Perhaps you have wanted to buy a particular book, but found it not available in your local bookshop. By ordering it you create 'demand pull'. However, before you can initiate such a chain of events you will need to be aware of the existence of the required book. Perhaps your awareness came from advertising or a recommendation from one of your lecturers.

In practice most markets have a mixture of both 'push' and 'pull' techniques acting on the distribution chain. They are both necessary to keep the flow of products and services moving. At different stages in a product's life cycle there will be different emphasis on the balance between 'push' and 'pull'. You might like to consider the following examples in this context.

Example 1
A well-known national confectionery manufacturer such as Cadbury's when they launch a new product.

Example 2
The launch of Daewoo Cars into the British market using direct selling.

Example 3
Insurance policies specially designed for protection of students' possessions while in college/university halls of residence.

THE ROLE OF OVERSEAS AGENTS AND DISTRIBUTORS

The basic role of agents and distributors does not change in overseas markets; however, they are usually given more detailed consideration. Market entry is vital and the distances involved, together with cultural differences, mean a local intermediary is often beneficial. It is possible to set up a wholly owned channel, but agents and distributors are the most common in terms of numbers of exporters, although not always with larger volumes of goods. When volume gets high enough a supplier will be tempted to replace the agent with a corporate representation. However, to be fair to agents, and to get the best from their efforts, the partnership must be developed in an honest and open way.

An alternative arrangement, which is always worth consideration, is the joint venture or, even further, a strategic alliance. Such arrangements can be immensely beneficial, not only in one overseas market but, if well constructed, for the mutual development of both organisations.

PHYSICAL DISTRIBUTION MANAGEMENT

This chapter has described the vital role played by choice of effective distribution channels. However, this could all be wasted if the physical distribution of a product is not organised as efficiently as possible. It is also vital that the right level of customer service is achieved, hence the need to consider what an organisation is really capable of achieving. It is not subsidiary to the task of selling, nor is it purely a cost to be borne by an organisation. It is a key element in creating satisfied customers.

Peter Drucker (1973) suggested the difference between efficiency and effectiveness was that the former was 'doing things right' and the latter 'doing the right things'. If for the sake of efficiency you do not dispatch a delivery vehicle unless it has a 100 per cent full load, it could save costs. The delays involved with customers receiving the product late could lose sales and materially affect future business. The choice of levels and quality of service will be influenced by both what customers expect, and by what competitors are prepared to offer.

Physical distribution management is concerned with transportation, materials handling, packaging, warehousing (and locations of depots), inventory policy, stock control and order processing. It is not the role of this book to discuss such issues in depth. However, it is essential to understand how added value can be achieved through distribution policies and appreciate the necessity for a marketer to understand the role of logistics and physical distribution in the total product.

CONCLUSION

There are many ways of making a product available to potential customers. The marketing role is to identify the target market and to understand how the target customers make purchase decisions. This can then be translated into an 'availability' strategy that matches these requirements.

The decisions on channels are long term. If intermediaries are used, then the relationships developed between suppliers and distributors can be critical to the effectiveness of the channel.

It is the effectiveness of the availability strategy that should be the prime concern of marketers. Within this strategy, channel decisions can give a competitive edge, with one organisation reaching customers and gaining sales because its products reach customers in a more appropriate way than those from competitors. An example of this is Coca-Cola, the product is an impulse purchase product and, by being available in more outlets, Coke is able to outsell Pepsi.

Other types of products require different distribution strategies. What may be a suitable strategy for an industrial product may not be suitable for a consumer durable.

The one certainty is that it is unlikely that customers will 'beat a path to your door'. In a market with excess demand, availability strategies play a vital part.

QUESTIONS

1 Why might an organisation choose not to use an intermediary in its efforts to reach its customers?

2 In retailing, the '4Ps' of marketing are often said to be Place, Place, Place and Place. Explain why this might be said.

3 Suggest three products that might benefit from intensive distribution, and explain how this might be achieved.

4 What are the advantages of franchise distributors as opposed to other distributors?

5 Give as many examples as you can of products using the following distribution channels: intensive, selective and exclusive.

FURTHER READING

Chisnall, P. (1995) *Strategic Business Marketing*, Prentice-Hall, New York.

Dawson, J. A. and Shaw, S. A. (1989) 'The move to administered vertical marketing systems by British retailers', *European Journal of Marketing*, Vol. 23.

Drucker, P. (1973) *Management Tasks Responsibilities and Practices*, Harper & Row, New York.

Ehrenberg, A. S .C., Goodhardt, G. J. and Barwise, T. P. (1990) 'Double jeopardy revisited', *Journal of Marketing*, July.

Knox, S. D. and White, H. F. (1991) 'Retail buyers and their fresh produce suppliers', *European Journal of Marketing*, Vol. 25, Jan.

Marketing, IPA Advertising Effectiveness Awards 1996 Category One: New Launches.

CASE STUDY
Sway Orchards Ltd

Referring to the detail given at the end of Chapter 10 with respect to Sway Orchards. The owner Jayne Powell has now decided to evaluate the different ways in which she could make her products available to customers. Below she has started to list the benefits and risks which could be involved with each of the options. Can you help her by completing the list and deciding how significant each of the factors is likely to be when she reviews the various options.

Option 1(a): Continue to operate as at present selling fruit at wholesale prices to local market traders.

Factor	Benefits/risks
Low farm labour costs	
Low capital costs	
All crop sold irrespective of quality	
No outside damage to farm trees	
No promotional costs	
Can place beehives in orchard which assists pollination and provides additional revenue from honey	
LOW prices received from market traders	
Price varies considerably (no control)	
No knowledge of consumers nor consumers require-ments	
Totally dependent on a few traders	
Any more?	

Questions
You may add to the list but the key issue is to evaluate the effect of each factor and how important it is in the effective operation of the Sway Orchards business.

Option 1(b): Acquire a stall in the local market and use it for Sway produce so retail prices can be obtained rather than wholesale prices.

Factor	Benefits/risks

Option 2: Investing in a grading and packing operation in order to sell the better quality fruit pre-packed at a higher price through better outlets such as local supermarkets. Of course not all the fruit would meet the quality standards and blemished and damaged fruit would still have to be sold via markets or for pressing into juice by the local cider maker. Really bad fruit would be sold for animal feed in the same way as Sway Orchards.

Factor	Benefits/risks

Option 3: Set up a farm shop to sell to customers direct farm fresh fruit at prices which are better than the local market and can be controlled by the farmer, not the market traders.

Factor	Benefits/risks

Option 4: Run a 'Pick Your Own' operation at the farm.

Factor	Benefits/risks

Option 5: Further process the Sway fruit by setting up a small jam making plant, or fruit juice pressing operation.

Factor	Benefits/risks

CHAPTER 13

Price, Quality and Value

There is hardly anything in the World that some men cannot make a little worse and sell a little cheaper.
John Ruskin (1819–1900)

INTRODUCTION

In 1992 the inflation rate in Peru reached 1400 per cent per annum. Similar events occurred in Eastern Europe, as restrictions on the Russian rouble were removed. In the UK, we cannot contemplate prices doubling every month, but we can appreciate the problems it causes for both suppliers and customers. In some areas of Peru, people have so little faith in money that they rely on exchange of goods, such as chickens for clothes, and eggs for firewood. Their exchanges are dictated by the desirability of what is offered by the two parties. They have little to do with the cost of production.

Barter deals, also called *counter trade*, were commonly used in some controlled economies. An example is one international soft drinks firm selling drinks in Bulgaria, but receiving payment in soft fruit such as raspberries (used for jam making in another UK company) and Black Sea holidays. There were times in the past when barter was more common than it is now. By considering how it can be used, we are able to appreciate the value of products or services. This is known as the concept of 'affordability' described in Chapter 9.

Of course, the pricing of products must be put into context. Tickets for a concert by the band Oasis were being traded at over twice the face value. In fact price tickets were being advertised at more than £100 right up to the concert. At the same time, tickets for a long-running West End comedy show were on offer at half price at the Leicester Square ticket booth.

In this chapter we will look at the whole aspect of price, value and cost. There are different strategies where price can be used effectively within the marketing mix. These can vary as new products require different strategies from those appropriate to existing products. Also, different strategies are necessary for different market conditions, and at different stages of the product life cycle. There is no doubt that pricing decisions are vital for any organisation – after all it is the only element within the marketing mix which creates revenue for your organisation. Many companies are now finding that pricing lower than competitors is not the way to succeed, it generally leads to an eroding of profit levels and an inability to fund future growth projects. A balance must be made, the price must reflect the added value, and many companies now find that when they want to put prices up they must also change the product or service very slightly to help justify the increase and thus make it more acceptable to customers.

When it comes to low price as a strategy, it is as well to remember that anyone can give money away. Anyone can cut the price of their product, but price rarely offers a sustainable competitive advantage. If your competitor loses sales due to your price cut, then a similar price reduction redresses the balance. Of course, the customer gains in a price war at the expense of company profit. However, this can only continue while profit is still possible.

EXERCISE

If you live outside London, examine ways of travelling to London (if you live in London consider a journey to Birmingham). Write down five ways of travelling and find out the cost* of a return journey. Then explain the advantages and disadvantages of each type of journey and explain why they are all used by different groups of travellers:

e.g. Coach;
     Train (peak time);
     Train (off-peak saver travel);
     Hire car;
     Own car.

* *Note*: cost to you is the price charged by the supplier.

COMPONENTS OF A PRICE

It will be clear from the exercise above, that price has more components than the money actually charged. For instance, if you pay for your ticket by credit card rather than by cash, you have an extra few weeks before paying the account. This could benefit you in a number of ways, although British Rail pays the credit card company a small fee which adds to British Rail's costs. If you decide to drive to London you will have to include petrol and perhaps car parking charges, not to mention the problem of apportioning depreciation and tax/insurance. Alternatively, if you use a student travel card you get discount on your coach or train travel. There are other pricing situations where other components are involved. For instance, in many industrial situations the parties negotiate stage payments, and also additional benefits such as service levels, as part of the contract.

In deciding between alternatives, we should also cost the time required during the search for suitable products. In assessing benefits, time is also important. Compare the different times experienced in delivery. In our travel example, for instance, trains are faster than coaches; air freight is quicker than sea for overseas orders. A fleet car purchase manager will probably look at a lowest total cost model when deciding what to purchase. This could include: manufacturer's recommended price; discount offered; payment terms (when payments due); additional features offered (service deals or radio cassettes fitted free, for example); delivery terms; cost of use (routine maintenance and running costs); convenience; reliability; lifespan; and resale value of cars at the end of use by the fleet. In addition, such aspects as acceptability to users, image and other psychological issues, and affordability will be considered.

It will be apparent, from these various examples, that it is almost impossible to list all the elements which will be considered by a purchaser. You might like to think of a recent purchase, and write down all the costs incurred by you in the total purchase.

From a marketer's point of view, it is vital to understand the way a potential buyer is likely to behave. You can then offer the right deal to attract purchasers for your product. In the 1970s Japanese cars were offered with fitted car radios, while most UK companies made their customers pay (then £20) for a radio. The actual cost of fitting in the factory was only £2, so for a small extra cost customers received a real benefit. This was one reason for the attractiveness of the first Toyotas because the company realised that most purchasers fitted radios when buying a new car. This enhanced the Total Product.

THE ECONOMIST'S PRICE

In an economist's view of the marketplace, price is seen as the major factor determining the level of sales of a product. The theory suggests that demand for a product will rise dramatically if its price is reduced. The actual amount of change in demand is a factor of the 'elasticity' of the product (*see* Fig. 13.1).

The demand for a product is said to be inelastic if the quantity sold hardly varies in spite of a substantial price change. This can be the case where there are few substitutes available. Such a product is heating oil for an oil-fired central heating system. It is too

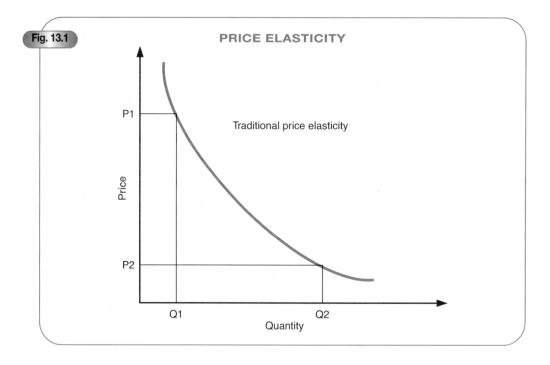

Fig. 13.1

PRICE ELASTICITY

Traditional price elasticity

expensive to replace the system with gas, and, in cold weather, heat is required for the home. Hence the heating oil is purchased when required in the cold weather. Price is less important than the temperature in assessing the volume to be sold in the UK. However, even this example is not completely straightforward. A study by a major oil company showed that householders in Germany, where they have larger domestic storage tanks installed, were very good at studying the oil market and buying when prices were low. In the UK, consumers generally purchase when the tank is nearly empty whatever the price, even though the difference of 1p/litre could mean £10 on a typical bill. So the UK market is more inelastic than the German market.

An elastic demand certainly occurs where a price rise is likely to frighten off a large number of customers, who either do not buy at all or purchase a substitute product.

$$\text{Price elasticity of demand} = \frac{\% \text{ change in quantity demanded}}{\% \text{ change in price}}$$

Of course, there are products which do not follow the basic economist's model. Perfume is an example – the more expensive a perfume is, the more it is generally desired. There are also products such as Stella Artois beer which have been advertised as 'Reassuringly expensive'. There are also prestige products, an example being Rolex watches which are in demand because of their exclusivity brought about by the high price and prestigious distribution outlets. Would volume increase if price was reduced or would consumers believe quality had also declined? More importantly, as profit is a multiplication of volume and margin, would total profit increase or reduce?

As times change so must companies adapt to the changing customer perception of products, Stella Artois found that with job security becoming scarce and house prices dropping in Britain, exclusivity of the product portrayed by price was inappropriate. They have found that their more recent television advertising message of 'people who appreciate good lager would give up anything for a pint of Stella Artios', to have much more impact. This has the effect of still portraying the brand as a premium product but attracting customers with different needs and motivations than the customers of the 1980s.

The traditional economist claims that prices should be set to maximise 'short-term' profits. This is said to be when 'marginal revenue', the increase in revenue for one extra unit of sale, is equivalent to 'marginal cost' of one extra unit of production. However, while this has a mathematical integrity, it fails to understand the marketing role of price in a competitive marketplace.

PRICE AND COMPETITION

One reason for changes in both volume and price is action by competitors. The basic demand curve assumes that all other facts remain constant, in reality they rarely do. At its simplest there can be a vicious circle as shown in Fig. 13.2.

It can easily be seen that such a competitive reaction, leading to a price war, would have a disastrous effect on an organisation. However, if you consider the situation from the point of view of one of your competitors, they do not want to lose sales because of your price cut. From your customers' position it all depends upon how they perceive value. This can be considered in the framework of buyer behaviour which is discussed in Chapter 5.

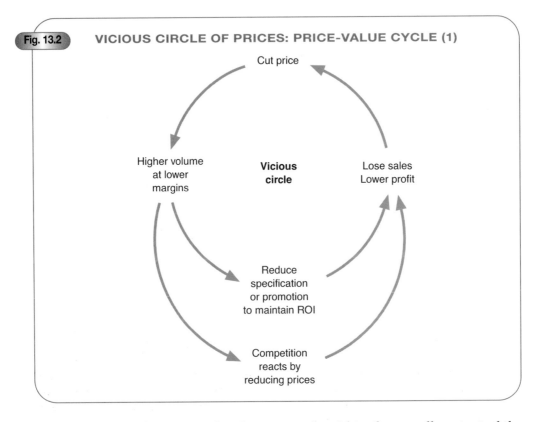

Fig. 13.2 — VICIOUS CIRCLE OF PRICES: PRICE-VALUE CYCLE (1)

It is important that pricing decisions are made within the overall context of the marketing mix. Products rarely offer directly equivalent features, and, in fact, it is one of the roles of marketers to find ways of differentiating their product. This could be achieved through offering additional levels of service, so the customer can decide to place a value on the total offering, rather than directly comparing identical products. In the customer's decision process, the perceived value is a function of required features, and the price paid. The object is to achieve a virtuous circle (see Fig. 13.3).

The level of competition varies from one product market to another. Some will have a large number of competing firms, others relatively few. Where there are many competitors, price (and other marketing) competition will be very severe. The other extreme is a monopoly, and perhaps that single supplier could fix his own price. The price set by a monopoly is, of course, modified by legislation and the Monopolies Commission.

In some competitive markets one or two companies emerge as leaders. The level of prices they charge can become the norm for the market. Smaller firms take their lead from these larger organisations without direct collusion, but most only move price when the leaders change. A study of the price of petrol will show how such a market operates.

To show that a competitive price does not always ensure a sale we could perhaps look at the fmcg (fast-moving consumer goods) market for a product such as instant coffee. Some shoppers search for low-priced brands, or own-label products, while others remain loyal to premium brands, such as Maxwell House or Nescafé. This could be because some consumers think these branded products to be better than the shop's own-label brands. However, they are not necessarily better, as companies such as Marks & Spencer or Sainsbury have very high-quality standards which they impose on

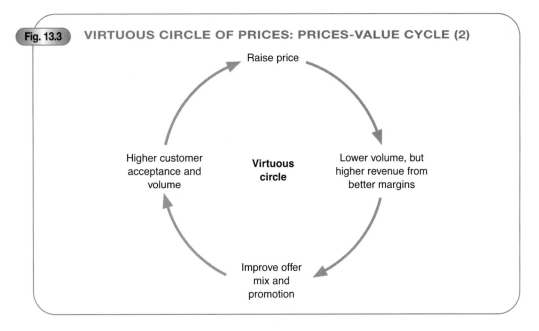

Fig. 13.3 VIRTUOUS CIRCLE OF PRICES: PRICES-VALUE CYCLE (2)

suppliers of their products, including instant coffee. There is no doubt about the good quality of Nescafé and other major brands of instant coffee, but even Nescafé offer different blends at different prices. Of course, another reason for the success of Nescafé is the marketing strength of the actual brand name. This will be discussed elsewhere, but the value of a brand name is being recognised by some companies who are valuing brand names and including the valuation on their balance sheets. The major accounting bodies also now realise the marketing value of brand names as an asset to a company. It is surprising, therefore, that in relation to the offering to the customers, there is still a blinkered view in many companies that prices must be based on costs.

PRICE AND COSTS

Decisions on price are of crucial importance to all organisations since, as stated already, it is the only element in the marketing mix which brings an input to the company. It is too important for price to be decided on some automatic formula based solely on cost; it is also too important to be left to accountants, or salespeople, or even marketing managers in isolation. Charles Dickens gave good Victorian advice when Mr Micawber, having been through a debtors prison, says to David Copperfield:

> Annual income twenty pounds, annual expenditure nineteen shillings and six pence, result happiness. Annual income twenty pounds, expenditure twenty pounds and six pence, result misery ... and in short you are for ever floored.

Of course, costs must be used to set a bottom line below which prices cannot go. Organisations can just as easily be floored if they spend more than they receive. But there can be a case for including a loss leader in a range, and using such products to develop customers while making profit on other items. The use of portfolio planning to ensure an overall profit for the company will be considered later.

Another area where low prices are justified can be the hope of high, extra sales reducing costs, so allowing profits. This could be possible in a new product situation. But price is still a marketing issue. The benefit of volume on costs is part of the total budget for a company. It is difficult to always make profits immediately upon launching a new product. In particular, development costs can be high and will probably take time to recover. The proper planning of profit-making and loss-making products is covered in marketing planning and control in Chapter 19.

A variety of cost-based formulas have been developed by organisations. The simplest version is to calculate the total cost, including all overheads, and add a set percentage for profit. This is known as 'cost-plus' pricing. This is justified on the basis that a satisfactory profit can always be achieved. But although this method seems straightforward, it does rely on the ways costs are calculated in an organisation, as well as reflecting any inefficiencies in operating that organisation. The biggest problem lies with allocating overheads since the basis for this allocation is, at best, arbitrary. Another area of uncertainty comes with the volume estimates, since the cost of producing 1000 units will be considerably different from producing 1 million units.

The biggest drawback with cost-plus pricing is that it takes no account of how customers might value a product, nor how competitors might price their version of the product. The National Health Service in the UK is currently suffering from this type of problem as different hospitals try to work out the price to charge for basic operations. The cost of a simple operation can vary dramatically across a number of hospitals. It is, of course, necessary to work out costs accurately to help efficient running of organisations. The message, however, must be:

Costs are about PRODUCTION
Prices are about VALUE

One important calculation relating cost, prices, and volume is the calculation of the so-called break-even point for a product. This can be explored in standard accounting texts and we will look at a sample break-even calculation here. Figure 13.4 illustrates the break-even point.

The break-even point is the level at which the cost of producing a product or service equals the revenue from selling it.

Assume a manufacturer has fixed costs of £1m. He sells his products at £3 each and the variable costs of manufacture and sale are £2. He will make £1 (£3 less £2) on every product sold. To 'break even' and to cover the fixed cost he will have to sell 1 million units.

To use break-even analysis effectively, it is necessary to calculate a break-even point for several alternative prices. However, great care must be taken in using break-even analysis as it does assume inelastic demand. This might be a fair assumption over a small change in price, but not over a large variation.

The calculation of break-even allows us to look at another cost-based pricing method called 'marginal cost pricing'. The marginal cost, or variable cost, of a product is the extra cost an organisation suffers in producing one more unit of that product – in our example above, £2 per unit. We could decide to add an agreed mark-up to this to determine our price. So if we suggest a 50 per cent mark-up then, given a £2 marginal cost, the mark-up will be £1, and the final price £3.

$$(£2 + (50\% @ £2)) = £2 + £1 = £3$$

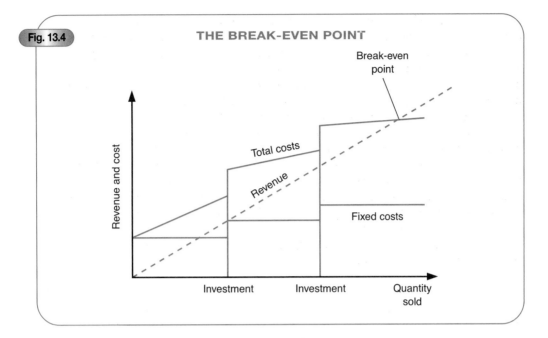

Fig. 13.4

THE BREAK-EVEN POINT

Break-even point

Total costs

Revenue

Fixed costs

Revenue and cost

Investment   Investment   Quantity sold

Some retailers use a version of this when calculating prices. However, experience, when dealing with companies like major High Street retailers, suggests they sometimes start with the price they want to sell at and then work back. As an example, suppose a retailer wishes to make a margin of 30 per cent and also wishes to sell a product at no more than 99 pence, then in this instance they might tell a supplier that they will pay no more than 69 pence for the item. This is only possible because of the strength of the large supermarkets, compared with some smaller companies who supply them. Marginal price deals are sometimes done, with selected customers, to stimulate demand, or to develop business with those chosen customers. The problem with marginal costing is that it only guarantees a gross profit per unit, but it does not guarantee a net profit from total sales.

John Winkler, a noted authority on pricing, states that if 'cost-plus pricing will generally keep you in business, marginal costing can easily put you out of it'. He goes on to suggest: 'Never do it if it will set a precedent for the long run with your biggest customers', 'Never do it if news of low price deals will spread in the market', 'Never do it if it commits you to extra capital cost in the short run, or long run', 'Never do it if it uses up scarce resources you need elsewhere', 'Never do it if you have to sacrifice some full profit business to fit it in', and 'Never delegate discretion on marginal pricing decisions down the line. Anyone can give products away, the aim of marketing is profitable business.'

Another perhaps dispiriting fact that John Winkler emphasises is that in today's economic climate it is extremely difficult to win any type of price increase. Companies that deal with Ford, Sainsbury and Rank Xerox expect suppliers costs to come down by at least 5 per cent every year and that cost reduction to be passed to them.

Although reducing prices can stimulate demand, it must be handled very carefully. Remembering the advice from Mr Micawber, say a car is priced at £10 000 and the manufacturer makes a gross profit of 18 per cent and net profit before tax of 7 per cent. If price is reduced by £1000 (just 10 per cent of reduction in price) we get the following effect.

Revenue	£10 000		£9 000	
Cost of goods	£8 200		£8 200	
Gross profit	£1 800	(18%)	£800	(8.9%)
Other costs	£1 100		£1 100	
Net profit before tax	£700	(7%)	(£300)	(loss of 3%)

It can be seen that a reduction of 10 per cent in price turns a healthy profit into a loss.

To conclude this section on costs, it should be clear that costs have a role in the determining of price. However, costs alone should not determine selling prices. The costs provide a bottom line to guide the pricing decision.

PRICE AND ORGANISATIONAL OBJECTIVES

Marketing decisions must be consistent with the total organisational objectives. Pricing decisions are just one of the marketing decisions. Obviously, if the organisation has a target return on investment, you can see the link to pricing. However, organisational objectives could be: 'Pile it high and sell it cheap', as coined by the founder of Tesco, Sir John Cohen. If your organisation has this latter objective all its operations must be designed to supply volume at low prices. More recently Tesco has changed its philosophy to compete more effectively with Sainsbury's. In the past few years price wars have broken out as both companies compete for the top slot in the supermarket league. In the run up to Christmas 1996 Tesco slashed prices on up to 400 lines to match competitors' prices while Sainsbury's Autumn Value 1996 campaign offered customers multi-buy and money off deals on 700 branded and own branded lines. Sainsbury's position has been encapsulated in the line, 'Good food costs less at Sainsbury's'. This slogan includes both price and quality in a statement of value directly related to customers.

EXAMPLE

Pricing a service

Two former secretaries have set up a secretarial and book-keeping service on a local trading estate. It offers basic services to the small companies on the estate. The major expense is the salaries of the two partners, and one employee, a word processing operator. Overheads include office rent and rates, and the maintenance of office equipment such as computers, fax machine, answerphone, etc. There is also the interest on the bank loan used to buy equipment. The organisation is really offering 'time' carrying out routine tasks. They calculate the overheads are £15 200 per annum, the employee is paid £6000 (including employee-related costs) and the two partners draw £1000 per month each. Total running costs for stationery, telephone bills, postage are a further £10 000 giving a total £55 200 per annum.

There are 230 working days per year if we eliminate weekends and holidays. But no one works at 100 per cent; 80 per cent is still good, so if we assume 184 days each (80% × 230) for the three productive workers there are 552 working days each year. To just break even they need to charge £100 per working day. What do you think they should charge clients?

PRICE AND QUALITY

The eight dimensions of quality proposed by David Garvin in a 1987 article in the *Harvard Business Review* are:

- *Performance* A product's primary operating characteristic;
- *Features* The 'bells and whistles', those characteristics that supplement basic functioning;
- *Reliability* The probability of a product malfunctioning during a specified time period;
- *Conformance* The degree to which design of operating characteristics meets established standards;
- *Durability* A measure of product life with both economic and technical dimensions;
- *Serviceability* Relating to the ease of maintenance;
- *Aesthetics* How a product looks, feels, sounds, tastes or smells – personal judgement comes in here;
- *Perceived quality* As consumers do not always have complete information to judge a product or service (amateur buyer), perception of quality, reputation or other intangibles are important in judging how customers rate your offering in their value equation.

You might offer your own measures of quality and how they help to add value to an offering. These dimensions, however, are a good basis for such discussions. Figure 13.5 shows a balance between quality of offerings and the benefits for an organisation.

There is a trade-off between price and quality at the basic level. To add features can cost money and this is not always recovered in profit in sales. However, the relationship is not that simple, and programmes such as zero defects are often very positive when assessing costs. But price should not be dependent on costs, but on customers' evaluation of value. Of course, some aspects of quality can increase this evaluation; others will not do so. The balance between quality and price should be considered in

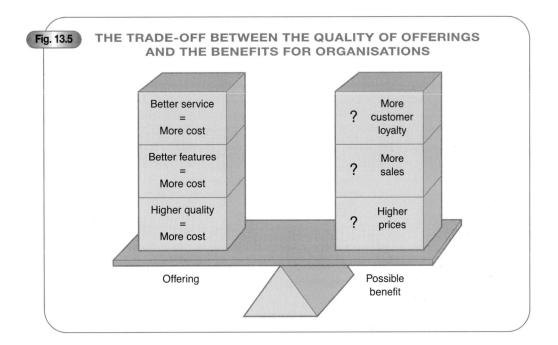

Fig. 13.5 THE TRADE-OFF BETWEEN THE QUALITY OF OFFERINGS AND THE BENEFITS FOR ORGANISATIONS

Better service = More cost

Better features = More cost

Higher quality = More cost

? More customer loyalty

? More sales

? Higher prices

Offering

Possible benefit

the context of profit, level of sales, and organisational positioning. It is not an easy equation but it is vital in an integrated marketing offering.

PRICING STRATEGIES

Figure 13.6 links the price to the quality of an offered product or service. Quality is a very difficult factor to measure. However, you should now realise that other elements of the marketing mix add to the 'quality' of value of the offering. It is useful to remind ourselves that: 'quality is remembered long after the price is forgotten.'

Premium pricing

A 'premium strategy' uses a high price, but gives good product/service in exchange. It is fair to customers, and, more importantly, customers see it as fair. This could include food bought from Marks & Spencer, or designer clothes, or a Jaguar car. We should remember that customers for consumer goods are often amateurs. They do not really know how to judge value. They build up a perception of such value, and sometimes use price to help establish levels of 'quality'. If you saw a new Jaguar car on offer at your local garage with a sign saying 'half-price offer' you might be suspicious about what you are being offered. If the offer were a Zil, which is a Russian luxury limousine, you might perhaps have less scepticism if it were offered at half price. But then you would worry about servicing and reliability.

An industrial buyer could have more knowledge of the technical characteristics of his purchases. In many cases tight specifications on the performance of machinery are used for buying in this area. But not all industrial purchases are professionally assessed, although no one should underestimate the ability of customers to assess value. Nevertheless, sometimes the benefits of a product need to be presented in a way that will help a buyer to make a buying decision. Remember, marketing is about making it easier for the customer to say 'yes'.

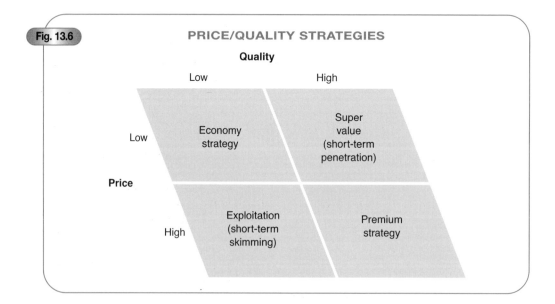

Fig. 13.6 PRICE/QUALITY STRATEGIES

In considering which car a company should use for its sales force, the car fleet manager mentioned at the beginning of this chapter might consider the lowest total cost over the life of 70 000 miles. It might be the resale value of a Ford Mondeo which gained it a superior rating to an equivalent car from another supplier. The car fleet buyer might be a professional, but might still require help to appreciate the total value of what is offered to him.

Even when evaluating relatively inexpensive products such as wood glue, some people view a higher price as a measure of the quality to expect from the product.

All the qualities of a Mercedes-Benz for £5,670

- - - - - - - - - - - - - - -

Hard to believe, isn't it? Fabled Mercedes-Benz refinement and peace of mind for the price of a run-of-the-mill volume car.

And the good news doesn't end there ....

Adapted from an advertisement for Mercedes-Benz seen in a local paper, March 1992

Penetration pricing

'Penetration' pricing is the name given to a strategy that deliberately starts offering 'super value'. This is done to gain a foothold in a market, using price as a major weapon. It could be because other products are already well established in the market, maybe at high prices. Alternatively, penetration pricing could be used as an attempt to gain a major share of a new market. It can also deter competitors who see no profit in the market.

As time goes on and the product is established, prices can be raised nearer market levels. Alternatively, the supplier's cost could come down as volume increases. In this case the consumer benefits by a continuation of the low prices (*see* example on page 224).

Penetration pricing must be used carefully as it is very difficult to raise prices to catch up with the market levels. There are many examples of products launched at a low price, but which lost significant sales volume when prices rose. It is sometimes possible to offer customers an initial discount to gain business provided you make it clear prices will rise later. Building societies have been offering discounted mortgages to first time buyers at reduced rates for the first twelve months, after that they rise to commercial rates and there is often a hefty penalty to repay should the borrower try to move the mortgage to another lender, or even make a lump sum repayment over and above that required for the monthly payment.

Economy price

'Economy' pricing is a deliberate strategy of low pricing. It could be that you are offering a 'no frills' product/service, with a price reflecting this. However, before such a product is launched, it is important to decide the position it will have in the marketplace. That position is how you want your customers to perceive it. A product that competes purely on price is vulnerable to attack from more established products.

This happened when Sir Freddie Laker launched his 'Sky Train' trans-Atlantic flights in the 1970s. Competitors such as British Airways, Pan Am, and others, reduced some of their prices. Laker found he could not sustain his flights profitably as passengers chose the most convenient of the cheap flights available. Laker went bankrupt, although later the receivers for his company claimed damages from other airlines. More recently 'Peoples Express', an American carrier, has also suffered from an unsustainable economy policy. It is perhaps not surprising that Richard Branson of Virgin Airlines has competed on customer service rather than a direct price war, and has attracted much publicity by accusing British Airways of a 'dirty tricks' campaign.

The Victorian philosopher John Ruskin (1819–1900) once said:

> It is unwise to pay too much, but it is unwise to pay too little. When you pay too much, you lose a little money, that is all. When you pay too little, you sometimes lose everything, because the thing you bought was incapable of doing the thing you bought it to do.

The common law of Business Balance prohibits paying a little and getting a lot. It can't be done. If you deal with the lowest bidder, it is as well to add something for the risk you run. And if you do that, you will have enough to pay for something better.

EXAMPLE

British motorcycles dominated the world market in the 1950s. In 1970 only 1 per cent of the UK market was 'made in Britain'. Honda, Yamaha, Kawasaki and Suzuki now supply over 90 per cent of the market. Honda first achieved recognition by taking the manufacturer's prize in the Isle of Man TT races in 1959. But their market entry was achieved with small motorcycles, sold at low prices that competitors could not match. In 1975 the Boston Consulting Group studied the industry worldwide on behalf of the British Government. Table 13.1 shows the production levels they found.

Table 13.1 ● Motorcycle production levels worldwide 1975

Country	Company	Output	Motorcycles per man/year
UK	BSA/Triumph	38 500	12
Italy	Motoguzzi	40 000	13
USA	Harley Davidson	50 000	15
Germany	BMW	25 000	20
Japan	Honda	2 000 000	280
Japan	Yamaha	1 000 000	200

While figures are not directly comparable, the high volume has dramatically reduced Honda's costs. They can make a good profit, and still retain their low prices. This lower price has now become the new normal level for pricing motorcycles, not only in the UK, but also worldwide. Recent developments in this market have shown the Triumph brand making a big comeback as they have just taken over the UK market leadership for superbikes from Honda. Demand has been such that potential customers have been willing to pay up to £1500 more than the selling price, meeting new proud owners at the factory gates. Triumph has increased production from around 2000 motorcycles a year at the beginning of the 90s to 15 000 in 1996.

Of course, there is legislation, such as the Sale of Goods Act, which demands that a product must be fit for the purpose for which it is sold. Nevertheless, Ruskin's point is taken sensibly from a customer's position, and all suppliers would do well to take heed of it.

Price skimming

We do not need to discuss 'exploitation' in detail. Customers won't pay if they don't think they are getting value. However there are times when high prices and large margins are appropriate. It is certainly easier to reduce prices than to raise them. A policy of 'price skimming' is often used for products at the introductory stage. Here the price is initially pitched high, which gives a good early cash flow to offset high development costs. If the product is new, and competition has not appeared, then customers might well pay a premium to acquire a product which is offering excellent features. The launch of many home computers showed this pattern. As competitors came into the market, and new features were added by the new entrants, prices dropped for all products. Another market with high margins is the drug market. The prescription drug market uses fairly cheap basic ingredients. The cost of developing medicines is high, and made even higher by the cost of testing, and gaining approval, from the regulatory bodies. The prices are high when new drugs are launched and they are protected by patents. When the patent runs out, 'generic' drugs come in to compete and prices fall. This official monopoly, based on the legal protection of a patent, is a reflection of the unique effort in developing a new drug. It is certainly justified by the costs involved.

Psychological pricing

'Psychological' pricing is designed to get customers to respond on an emotional, rather than rational, basis. It is most frequently seen in consumer markets, having less applicability in industrial markets. The most common is the use of prices such as 99 pence or £9.95 which can be seen in many retail outlets. We all know that 99 pence is £1.00 less 1 penny, and £9.95 is £10 less 5 pence. In recent years some companies such as Marks & Spencer have been phasing out this practice although it still remains widespread. You might like to consider why such prices are used.

In some markets companies are over-sensitive about price levels. Cadbury's were conscious of this with their bar chocolate. To maintain prices, as raw material costs rose, they reduced the thickness of the chocolate blocks. The result was thin chocolate bars.

Rowntrees spotted this and decided Cadbury's had gone too far. Rowntrees saw an opportunity for a chunky product, and so the Yorkie Bar was launched with great success.

Product line pricing

'Product-line' pricing is a strategy which involves all products offered. There may be a range of normal price points in a market. A supplier might decide to design a product suitable for all price levels, offering opportunities for a range of purchases. For instance, a basic Mars bar retails for about 27p, a multipack of five bars £1.05p (Tesco), and a multipack of ten snack size Mars bars at £1.55 (Tesco). The price points are 27p, £1.05p and £1.55. (These prices were correct in the summer of 1997. You should check the prices now, and see how each price level fits into the range of Mars products available.)

Pricing variations

'Off-peak' pricing and other variants, such as early booking discounts, stand-by prices and group discounts are used in particular circumstances. They are all well known in the travel trade but it is also appropriate to use different prices such as these in other industries. You could argue that an off-peak journey, say a rail journey to London one Tuesday afternoon, is not the same 'product' as one during the morning rush period. In the customer's eyes it is a different product. If you have to be in London by 9.00 am you cannot travel in the afternoon. Certainly, 'stand-by' prices represent a different product as there is no guarantee of travel. The opposite is an early booking price which not only ensures travel is reserved, but can offer the supplier a guarantee of the known demand.

PRICING IN INDUSTRIAL MARKETS

Industrial products can be ones purchased for resale, or they can be raw materials which are incorporated into manufactured products. Alternatively, they can be installations or consumables used in industrial operations. When dealing in this market, there are other considerations affecting all aspects of the marketing mix, including pricing strategies.

Consumables are the convenience goods of the industrial market. However, there is no need for fancy packaging to attract shoppers as in a supermarket. They therefore tend to have basic packing for protection, and can often be supplied in multiple packs. The price will reflect this. In addition, there may be a quantity discount, although this is more usual with raw materials. Certainly the business is usually done on credit, but it is common to offer discounts to customers who pay their invoice within (say) ten days.

Installations are more likely to be negotiated, with all the requirements costed to give a price specific to the customer's requirement. There is no role for psychological pricing, but it is common for the sales negotiators to be given some freedom in the price to be charged. In these types of negotiated situations the sales force can be rewarded according to profit achieved, and they certainly need to know the limits within which they can negotiate.

Raw materials will be regular purchases, and it is probably more important that suppliers are reliable. Customers will be prepared to pay a little extra to a known, and trusted, supplier rather than risk supply problems. Of course, a customer may operate a policy of dual sourcing so as to compare competition prices. If the supplier builds up a strong relationship with the customer, then a good exchange of information takes place, and prices are continually discussed along with other issues. There may be an annual contract between supplier and customer which confirms price for the whole year. The contract might have a rebate clause which allows for a discount if volume exceeds an agreed figure. As industrial markets are distinguished by smaller numbers of partners and larger orders, many of their contracts are individually negotiated and overriding discounts are built into the agreement.

Many of the above pricing methods are possible because industrial markets have much more direct contact between supplier and customer through the wide use of direct personal selling in these markets.

There is one very difficult area of industrial marketing where direct selling is not a factor. This is when suppliers are invited to submit a tender for a contract offered by a large customer, who may be a local authority or a government department. In this situation the customer specifies what they want, and asks a number of suppliers to submit a bid. In such a case it is necessary not only to carry out detailed costing on what is required, but also to have an appreciation of who else is bidding for the work. Here, a pricing strategy can be based on the knowledge of the competition, as well as how badly your organisation wants the contract. The final price is therefore a marketing decision, and not based solely on costs.

Such a situation being the 1996 bids received for the former British Rail franchises. Richard Branson's Virgin Group successfully bid for the Cross Country Rail franchise. This situation is also common in the oil and gas industry with competitors bidding for the exploration rights to designated geographical blocks.

DISTRIBUTOR PRICING

Many producers are not in direct contact with their customers. They will use indirect channels of distribution, perhaps via wholesalers or other intermediaries. No product is finally sold until it reaches the eventual consumer. So it is the final price to the final purchaser which is the measure of value.

You might have recently bought a birthday card for one of your friends, maybe paying, say, 99p in a card shop. This might seem expensive for a small piece of printed cardboard, and an envelope. Even if we know 17p is VAT charged by the government, it still seems a lot. But remember the printing company will probably have sold the card at 44p (excluding VAT) allowing the card shop to double the price. In this business 100 per cent mark-ups are usual, and can be justified by the relatively low turnover of individual designs. Also, as customers consider the purchase in relation to a more expensive present, the price is considered acceptable in spite of the retailer mark-up.

The problem many producers face is how to control the eventual selling price of their product. At one time it was possible to insist on the final selling price, but now this is not possible in most industries. Producers may suggest a recommended retail price (RRP) but that is all it is, a recommendation. Each member of the distribution chain will want to make some money from handling the product. It is therefore important for producers to understand the way distributors add margins so that they can judge the effect on the final selling price of any action taken further up the distributive chain.

PRICING AND ITS RELATION TO THE MARKETING MIX

In this chapter price has not been considered in isolation but as one key part of the marketing mix. The word *affordability* was used at an earlier point, but although this introduced the customer view it does not encompass the full area of value. The price is what is paid as part of the exchange process (*see* Fig. 13.7), being passed from customer to supplier either as money or in kind. What is received by the customer is the composite of the other elements of the marketing mix. This is an acceptable product, conveniently available so that the customer feels it is well worth the price asked. It is therefore essential that price is put into the wider context of the total marketing mix. If a product is made more attractive (added value by additional features), it makes that product more valuable to customers. Similarly, a service could be made more readily available and thus more valuable to customers. In this case it might be possible to raise prices to reflect the increase in value. Alternatively the enhanced value could lead to additional sales. The decision about additional features must be taken by managers who realise the way consumers measure value, and not simply by saying the additional features have increased costs hence prices must rise.

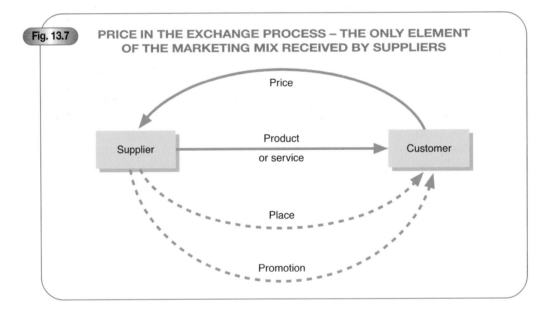

Fig. 13.7   **PRICE IN THE EXCHANGE PROCESS – THE ONLY ELEMENT OF THE MARKETING MIX RECEIVED BY SUPPLIERS**

Accountants are used to cost–benefit analysis in other parts of their work, but where price is concerned it is essential to do a cost–benefit analysis for the customer: cost to the customer being price from the supplier; benefit to the customer a measure of the quality of the offering.

PRICE AND THE PRODUCT LIFE CYCLE

In Chapter 2 you were introduced to the concept that a product develops through a 'product life cycle'. At different stages of this life cycle there are different competitive pressures, and differences in the way customers evaluate a product/service. For a new product (the first in the market) a 'skimming' policy could be appropriate. However, in a competitive, declining market with a mature product a different strategy is relevant.

Select a product you have bought in the last month. Decide where it is in its product life cycle. What is the range of prices for competitive products and where does the product you bought fit in?

Why do you think this is so?

What pricing strategy do you think the supplier is pursuing?

CONCLUSION – THE ART OF PRICING

Pricing is a management decision with a large marketing input. It also involves accountants, salespeople and probably the Managing Director. The objectives for the organisation will influence management policy. All organisations need to establish a framework within which to operate. This will provide the limits for their decisions. Figure 13.8 is quite useful in this respect.

The actual limits for the high and low points are still a matter of judgement, but the key points of competitors' prices can often be established to give reference points. But it is not always possible to establish the real price competitors charge as the 'price-list price' only tells part of the story. Winkler lists ten ways to 'increase' prices without increasing prices. These are:

1 Revise the discount structure.
2 Change the minimum order size.
3 Charge for delivery and special services.
4 Invoice for repairs on purchased equipment.

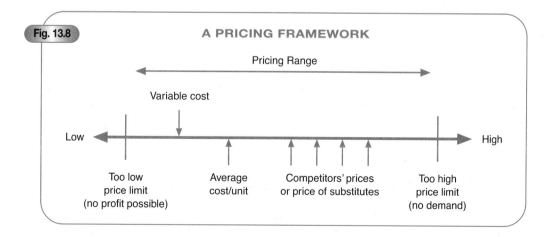

Fig. 13.8

A PRICING FRAMEWORK

5 Charge for engineering, installation, supervision.
6 Make customers pay for overtime required to get out rush orders.
7 Collect interest on overdue accounts.
8 Produce less of the lower margin models in the product line.
9 Write escalator clauses into contracts.
10 Change the physical characteristics of the product.

Obviously not all these are available in every market. However, the fact that such a list is possible shows how involved pricing decisions really are.

QUESTIONS

1 Some companies price a product at £9.99 or £19.99. What are the advantages and disadvantages of such prices?

2 Why do customers sometimes believe high prices indicate high-quality products?

3 Explain the reasons behind 'off-peak pricing'.

4 What are the drawbacks to using penetration pricing as the main strategy in entering a new market?

FURTHER READING

Boston Consulting Group (1975) *Strategy Alternatives for the British Motorcycle Industry*, HMSO.
Chartered Institute of Management Accountants, *Survey on Price*, 1988.
Garvin, D. A. (1987) 'Competing in the eight dimensions of quality', *Harvard Business Review*, Nov–Dec, pp. 99–101.
Griffiths, J. (1997) 'Motorcycles sales set to show strong growth', *Financial Times*, 7 April.
Lee, J. (1996) 'Sainbury's and Tesco square up for Price Battle', *Marketing*, 5 September.
Winkler, J. (1994) *Pricing in The Marketing Book*, Ed. M. J. Baker, Butterworth Heinemann, 3rd Edn, pp. 438–446, Oxford.
Winkler, J. (1996) 'Price Wise', *Management Accounting*, December.

CASE STUDY
St Thomas' Island Hotel

James Clarke had just completed his first year as Manager of the St Thomas' Island Hotel on the south coast of Cornwall. Although not on an island it was situated on a headland next to an excellent sandy beach with magnificent views of the coast and out to sea. It was also close to a local sailing centre where many boats were moored. For James this had been his first management job after a degree in Hotel Management and four years' experience with the Moat House Hotels group.

The hotel itself had recently been run by receivers after the previous owner had gone bankrupt. It had now been purchased by a Cornishman who was also a top London banker with romantic dreams of his birthplace but a hard-headed attitude to business. At the interview when James had been appointed the objectives had been made clear.

The hotel must break even in the first twelve months and go into profit thereafter. I am sure you will understand that if you fail to achieve this your position as Manager will not be tenable.

The hotel itself had 70 rooms all with en suite facilities. It had been owned by a number of different proprietors in the last ten years and each had added to the facilities without spoiling the front appearance of the hotel or the ten acres of woodland which it owned on the northern approach to the building. It had two tennis courts and a croquet lawn outside; a fitness room, sauna, and a billiards room in the west-wing extension, which also contained 50 of the bedrooms. The main building housed two excellent bars – the Pirates and the Swag – along with a restaurant capable of seating all guests at the same time.

John was now considering his first-year results where he had just met his target, but not because the occupancy rate was anywhere near break-even level. At the beginning of October when no guests were actually booked, a conference organiser had phoned having to relocate following a fire at one of the bigger hotels. All rooms full for seven days in October was a real bonus, but James had still felt it proper to charge in excess of the full room rate, especially since he had to hire in a marquee as a temporary conference hall. Luckily the weather had been kind and the event had gone very well.

The results for year one are shown below. Much of the bar profits were as a result of the conference delegates who did a lot of business in the bar.

Receipts	£	
11 500 room nights		
@ £45 per night (average)	517 500	(half board)
Conference one week		
@ £80 per night	39 200	(full board)
Bar profits	20 000	
Total	£576 700	

Expenses	
Staff and related costs	280 000
Food and drink	165 000
Utilities	
Building maintenance	80 000
Other supplies	
Advertising and brochures	15 000
Miscellaneous items	35 000
	£575 000

For next year James realises he cannot rely on a repeat conference. Anyway the hotel is not really equipped for such events. Recently, however, he has received a request from a national coach company for three months' block booking (May to July) at £2600 per night for up to 65 rooms, including dinner, breakfast and a packed lunch for all guests. While James is aware this will put his food bill up he hopes he will recoup some of the cost with increased bar profits. Although the £239 200 would be useful guaranteed revenue against only £190 000 taken during the same period in year one, James has some doubts.

Many of last year's guests had told him on leaving after their first stay at the hotel, how much they had enjoyed the hotel and the excellent service they had received. He even had a number of advance bookings from guests who wished to return during the spring and summer, and he wondered how they would react to sharing with a coach party. He would also need to achieve again the full bookings for August and Christmas, which contributed a quarter of year one's revenue. But he knew that there were also opportunities for growth as the figures on occupancy showed that from the end of October through to March the hotel was rarely more than 20 per cent full except for the Christmas period.

Question
James has until the end of the week to decide on the coach company contract. What would you advise him to do?

CHAPTER 14

Marketing Communications and Media

I know that half of what I spend on advertising is wasted;
but the trouble is I don't know which half.

INTRODUCTION

The above quote has been variously attributed to Lord Leverhulme, the first Chairman of Unilever, and John Wannamaker, the famous Philadelphia retailing magnate. While the comment was made specifically on advertising, it could just as easily apply to the wider-field of marketing communications, where precise answers and predictable results are as elusive as within advertising itself.

Notwithstanding this, companies and organisations have come to recognise the importance of communications as a means to achieving and making known their corporate objectives. Indeed, without good communications, both internally and externally, no organisation would be able to operate effectively.

This chapter considers the role of communications in marketing, within what is often referred to as the company's communications mix. There can be many objectives in marketing, such as launching a new product, promoting a brand or product range, or informing about the whole of a company's activities. In all of these there is a need to utilise some forms of communications. Basically, marketing communications involve enhancing or achieving awareness, better understanding, shared beliefs and meaning, and positive associations, attitudes and predispositions . . . in favour of the product, service or organisation that is being marketed.

While all business functions depend on some dissemination of information and communications with others, marketing activities are perhaps more people-centred than most, and are certainly more directly involved with key stakeholder groups such as customers, trade bodies, media commentators and the like. Obviously, relations with these stakeholder groups require a carefully planned and executed communications programme. Furthermore, as marketing effectiveness depends at least partly on non-marketing functions within a company, it follows that marketing communications may be affected by any of the company's dealings with the outside world. In reality, therefore, practically everything a company does will communicate something to its marketplace and its stakeholders. In turn, certain stakeholders such as distributors, contractors and service agents will need to be brought in as collaborators within a company's marketing communications activities.

A company's reputation and market standing may well be expressed through accounting convention as a 'goodwill' item within financial statements. In practice, the true worth of its reputation and image will be the outcome of how the company relates to and communicates with its various publics. A company's communications strategy is therefore of major significance to its survival and prosperity. This should be reflected in a co-ordinated programme of activities that presents a consistent picture to the world at large, while still accommodating the particular or local communication requirements of certain specialist groups or market sectors.

THE COMMUNICATION PROCESS

The communication process is the foundation of any relationship whether in the commercial or personal field, and it is on this that the success or failure of any relationship depends. A typical definition of communication would be:

> **The act of making known; intercourse by speech, correspondence, and messages.**

Communication is more than a message being sent. For communication to have taken place, it is necessary for the message that is received to have been understood in the way it was intended. This means that the sender of a message has to have a measure of response reaction to know whether communication has taken place. The response or feedback enables the sender to develop the message thereby ensuring that it is understood by the receiver. Communication is therefore a 'two-way' rather than a 'one-way' process.

It will be seen from the two-way communications process shown in Fig. 14.1 that the transfer of a message from a sender to a receiver involves a number of distinct

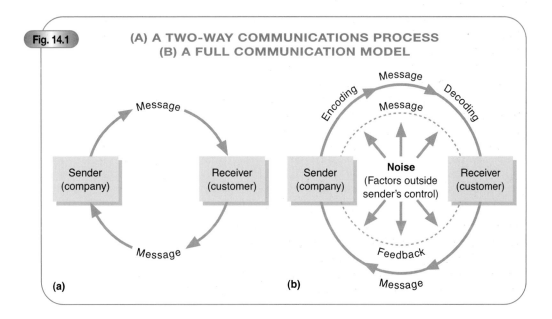

Fig. 14.1

(A) A TWO-WAY COMMUNICATIONS PROCESS
(B) A FULL COMMUNICATION MODEL

(a)

Message

Sender (company) → Message → Receiver (customer)

Message

(b)

Encoding — Message — Decoding

Message

Sender (company) — **Noise** (Factors outside sender's control) — Receiver (customer)

Feedback

Message

stages. Each of these provides an opportunity for the message to be altered from that originally intended. Furthermore, at each stage of the communication process the message can be affected by interference; for example a physical background sound, such as is normal in a disco, may make it impossible to hear what is said. This is often termed 'noise'. This could also be electronic interference on a telephone line or radio transmission which has the same effect. In the context of communications the term 'noise' has a wider meaning and is used to identify any extraneous factor which can affect the transfer of a message. This can even be extended to the effect of external factors on a consumers' attitude to spending.

It is perhaps easier to understand the communications process by considering how we as individuals respond when meeting someone for the first time. Generally, we are able to respond to the person appropriately without being aware of our response. We automatically note aspects of the person and assimilate unconsciously the information provided. For example, we note posture, gestures, facial expressions, eye movements, eye contact, the style and quality of clothing, and perhaps status symbols, such as jewellery. Such non-verbal messages are just as important in the communications process as the spoken message itself.

Usually when a person speaks, what they say is in keeping with the impression we have formed about them. Occasionally when this does not happen, such as when someone dressed casually speaks with unexpected authority, we are taken by surprise and as a result completely miss what was said. This is an example where the non-verbal messages can be considered to be 'noise' since they have had the same effect as the physical sound examples of noise given earlier, i.e. they have affected the transfer of the message. Noise can thus take many forms, all of which have the effect of drowning or distorting or distracting from the message being communicated.

Messages can also be distorted directly as a result of the processes involved in transmitting it from the sender to the receiver. The problem could lie with the sender, for instance

(i) The message may be incomplete because the sender may not have the full information that should be included in the message.

(ii) It may be vague because the sender may not know the precise words that should be used in some aspect of the message.

(iii) The sender may choose the wrong medium for sending the message: the telephone is used when a letter is needed; an item is described verbally when a drawing is needed.

These are examples where the message is distorted by the sender. It can also be distorted by the receiver. If a drawing is used to send the message the receiver will need to be able to interpret it. If words are used, the receiver will need to know what they mean. If the message is written, the writing needs to be intelligible.

In direct person-to-person communications the problems which arise as a result of the message not being heard or being distorted can easily be corrected as the communication progresses because the sender is able to revise the message according to the receiver's responses. By the nature of two-way communication this can be done even though these responses are, of course, subject to the same distortion and noise problems as the original message. In indirect communications it is not so easy as there is usually a time delay before feedback is received and thus before any clarification or revision is possible.

THE DYNAMICS OF MARKETING COMMUNICATIONS

Let us imagine that a message is to be sent to a potential group of customers and television is selected as the communication channel. For the message to be sent via television it must be first encoded in the form of words, pictures and images; it must then be broadcasted as television signals. Those signals will be received by every television tuned to that channel. The message will not, however, be the same on every television as the quality of the image and sound vary according to the quality of the television set and the reception for the message. As a result some of the people watching the television will receive essentially the original message, while others will receive something quite different. Those who decode the message may then either react to the message or just store it for future reference.

It is important to remember that each one of us is different. People differ psychologically and physiologically. They vary in intelligence, education, religious beliefs, social background and experience. These differences mean that different people receive and decode messages in different ways. As perception is known to be selective, individuals will perceive different messages. Further, situational factors (e.g. individual needs, lifestyle) may make the received messages either more or less relevant to the recipient. Indeed the workings of such intervening variables make two-way communication preferable to one-way communication.

COMMUNICATION OBJECTIVES

In general the objectives of communication will be derived from one of the three categories below:

- *Informing* Giving information, building awareness that a product/service exists, what the product does, where it can be obtained.
- *Persuading* Creating a favourable attitude, providing a stimulus to favour one brand over another, or one point of view against another.
- *Reinforcing* Dispelling doubts about an action already taken, building support/loyalty to a point of view or purchase, ensuring a good climate for future sales.

An equation can be developed, as shown in Fig. 14.2.

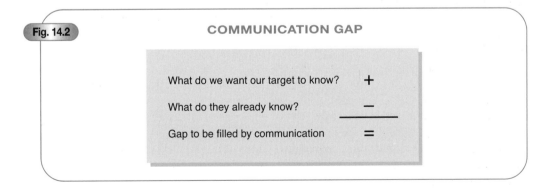

Fig. 14.2

COMMUNICATION GAP

What do we want our target to know?   +

What do they already know?   −

Gap to be filled by communication   =

The equation must be followed through before the implementation of communication plans are decided. The overall objectives can cover any of the main categories of informing, persuading or reassuring. The gap is the perceived difference with the actual situation. It is only by setting clear goals in this area, as in other parts of business, that successful execution can be assessed. One of the key studies in covering both objectives and assessment is the DAGMAR work by Russell Colley. This study was undertaken for the Advertising Research Foundation and an obvious but key conclusion was that in order to know how successful your advertising is you must first understand clearly the objectives you want to achieve. This may seem very basic, but it is surprising how often it is forgotten. There is a feeling that all advertising must be good, maybe akin to the show business dictum that it does not matter what critics write about you as long as they write something. DAGMAR stands for Defining Advertising Goals for Measured Advertising Results. However, in Colley's study he lists over 50 possible advertising objectives. A fuller discussion on the subject of feedback in marketing communications is included in Chapter 15 on promotional planning.

MARKETING COMMUNICATIONS MEDIA

One of the basics of communications is the selection of media to be used to transmit the communication to the target group. In general media can be split into two categories: personal and non-personal. Very often it happens that several different media need to be used in conjunction with each other in order to convey the message effectively.

If we imagine ourselves working in a large organisation, there are many methods of communication we can use internally: we may send a memorandum to another department and if after several days find that there has been no reply, back up the written word with a telephone call, thereby reinforcing our original message. In fact the repetition of messages is often appropriate in communicating information. However, it is important to know when the receivers of your message have heard enough. Some advertisements really irritate when seen for the twentieth or thirtieth time.

PERSONAL CHANNELS

Personal channels occur when there is an element of personal contact, that is, where one person, or even several people, take part in an exercise that communicates something to someone. A major advantage with personal channels of communication is that the content of the message can be fine-tuned to the particular receiver of the message. In this situation the communicator involved can gauge the reaction of the recipient, and depending on the feedback that is received, quickly amend the approach. There is obviously an increased chance that the content will be both properly heard and understood.

Perhaps you are a student who has to attend lectures and seminars. During these periods something is being conveyed to you. How much you learn is affected by 'noise' elements and interference discussed earlier. It could include how receptive you feel, how good the lecturer is, or even the quality of teaching materials such as slides and handouts.

Personal channels for marketing communications can include everything from telephone selling to office memos. The major areas of personal communications are:

- internal company communications;
- personal selling;
- personalised marketing – telesales/telemarketing, the Internet and direct mail;
- trade fairs and exhibitions.

Internal communication

Some people see communications as something done for outsiders. However, every part of an organisation is regularly in communication with other parts of the organisation. Most internal communication is of a personal nature, i.e. letters, memos, telephone calls, face-to-face meetings, presentations. Remember, the most potent method of communication is by word of mouth where colleagues, friends or family make personal recommendations to you. The desired result is to produce an offering acceptable to external customers. This is a situation where internal marketing is necessary. Remember, every employee is a potential part-time marketer and as such it is important that they have as deep a knowledge about the product as possible. The quality of internal communication will have a direct input on the effectiveness as well as the efficiency of an organisation and its marketing orientation.

Personal selling

The personal sales approach is the most direct and potent way of selling many products. It ranges from door-to-door insurance salespeople to assistants in your local department store. To be successful, salespeople must understand the use of body language, eye contact, and asking questions as well as being able to build a relationship with their clients. It is not about smart-talking salespeople who can talk their customers into submission. Rather, a good salesperson will use questions to discover needs and then show how their offerings fulfil those needs. Of course, atmosphere is important in creating the right conditions for a sale. Party-plan organisers, Tupperware, know this and are very successful at exploiting a social gathering for selling. However, personal selling can be a slow and expensive way of doing business. A less costly way is to adapt to what is called 'personalised selling'. This is not really personal (no body language!) but it is adaptable and individual. Chapter 18 covers selling in more detail.

Personalised marketing

(a) Telemarketing and the Internet

One advantage of telesales or telemarketing is that it is a much cheaper way of reaching the target audience than sending a salesperson to call and has been defined as 'the systematic use of the telephone as a communications channel between a company and its customers'. Such communications are common in industrial and other business-to-business situations, in particular those concerning regular repeat orders. For example, in the bakery trade it is common for the flour supplier to telephone the bakery: the order can then be noted and dispatched very quickly. A representative from the flour company would then only be required to call at infrequent intervals in order to maintain good customer relations.

For teleselling to succeed, the companies involved must try to make the approach as personal as possible. Normally the target market is well researched, even if it is only to make note of their prospective customers' names from the telephone directory. Using someone's name, even as a potential customer, makes the telephone call seem more friendly. It is thus more difficult to disregard immediately. If a company relies entirely on telesales there is a problem in that the salesperson rarely establishes a close personal relationship with the customer. However, skilled telemarketers are able to project their personalities over the telephone. The medium has to be used with care as some people view unsolicited telephone calls as intrusive. This subject is discussed further in Chapter 18.

The last few years have witnessed a tremendous growth in the use of the Internet as an effective media for communication. In some cases it is personalised and therefore direct, in other uses it is an indirect media. Simon Darling, currently *Interactive Marketing and Electronic Commerce Manager at Unilever*, was quoted as saying

> Any company worth its salt seeks aggressively to keep its eye on what's happening in the outside world and to find ways of turning these changes to profitable advantage. The possibilities that we see on the Internet today – such as search engines, online chat, sound and video delivery – are all ones that can be applied .... The challenge is to develop ideas, implement them rapidly and ensure that you get value for money from both new and existing applications.

EXERCISE

Identify a company web site on the Internet. What is the purpose of the site? Is it more likely to be found by casual surfers or are potential customers guided to it?

(b) Direct mail

When direct mail is sent using the names of the target customer personally, then it moves into the realm of a personalised communication. The ability to use a more personalised approach has come about due to the advanced technology afforded by computers.

Many people claim they are not influenced by 'junk mail'. However, a response rate of a few percentage points is often enough for a mailing to be considered a success. The economics of direct mail depend on the complexity of the actual item mailed, and the postage (which can be up to a third of the cost). The address list must be relevant to the offer, and the mailing itself must create attention. One company sent a mailing from Moscow. This not only dramatically reduced postage costs, but the letters from Russia created interest among recipients to the benefit of the sender. It is important, however, to ensure that the correct name/title of the proposed recipient is used, otherwise offense can be engendered and a potential customer lost.

The direct mail industry has set up a service, the Mailing Preference Service which offers consumers the possibility of either increasing or decreasing the volume of direct mail they receive. Direct mail is further discussed in Chapter 16.

Over the period of about one month note any direct mail correspondence that is sent direct to a named person within the household. Make a note of the accuracy of the printed name and address, and any code numbers that might indicate their source. Note also any immediate or likely response to the mailings. How effective did they prove?

Trade fairs and exhibitions

It has been said that if a salesperson visits a customer they have gone to sell. If the customer visits the supplier they have come to buy. The latter is a much stronger position for the supplier. A half-way situation is a trade fair or an exhibition. The advantage is that suppliers meet customers on neutral ground away from the formal office environment. The shows are generally industry- or trade-specific. Examples are the Smithfield Show and the Royal Show which are mainly for the farming and agricultural industries. However, the Royal Show, which is held annually, is more than a show for farmers. In June 1997 the Royal Show aimed at providing a family day out with such attractions as ostriches, a working bakery, the Royal Marines freefall parachute team, and the latest in jeeps and Jaguars alongside the tractors and combine harvesters. The advantage of such exhibitions is that the relaxed atmosphere can be very conducive to business. There are now many large exhibition centres throughout Britain, Europe and the rest of the world, which attract a large number of exhibitors, both home-based and from overseas, to regular events.

Exhibitions and trade shows give organisations the chance to show how they compare with their competitors, who are often present at the same event. The budget required to participate in such events can be substantial, so any involvement must be well planned, and probably communicated to potential customers in advance. Salespeople will always be in attendance to give advice, explain any complicated features, as well as trying to sell the product. New products are not only seen, but also tried and tested and compared to other similar products; but competitors are doing the same. Companies often use major exhibitions as an opportunity to launch new products. It can be important for a company to attend the major exhibitions in their product area so as to show all potential customers that it is still thriving in this particular market. In Britain, major exhibition centres include Earls Court, Olympia and the National Exhibition Centre. On a very much smaller and more localised scale this category could also include local craft fairs and perhaps could be extended to the popular 'car boot sale'.

List personal channels of communication which have been directed towards you recently. How did they differ in the effect they had upon you?

NON-PERSONAL CHANNELS

Non-personal channels of communication cover those situations where there is no personal contact involved. The communication is completely external to the audience. Non-personal channels include the use of one or more of the following channels of communication: commercial television; the press and other print media; radio; cinema; outdoor media; point-of-sale displays; and packaging.

Within these channels, techniques of advertising, publicity (PR), sponsorship, and sales promotion can be used. These are considered in Chapters 16 and 17.

Commercial television

This is the most important non-personal communication channel with very wide coverage to its audience. How many people come home from a day's work, have something to eat and then sit watching a television for the remainder of the evening? If they watch a commercial television station they will be subjected, during the course of an evening, to many commercial breaks, on which a large variety of products will be advertised. There may also be some exposure of products on the non-commercial channels, especially with sponsored sports events.

The television stations research in great detail the type of audience expected to watch each of their programmes. Similar detailed research is also carried out with regard to the other non-personal media and their audiences. For television it is to be expected that toys will be advertised during the period when children's programmes are screened, whereas products like cars might be featured in the evening, say around news bulletins.

Television does not offer lasting images, but it does combine sound and moving pictures in a very powerful way. Advertising, using television as the medium of communication, is considered one of the quickest ways of ensuring that your product is known to a wide audience. The technical terms coverage and OTS (opportunities to see) are used in advertising. Coverage is the percentage of the potential audience that is reached, OTS is the number of chances they have to see a particular advertisement.

In Britain 97 per cent of homes have a television set, and 50 per cent have two or more sets. The figures vary slightly for different European countries. In Norway 99 per cent of homes have television, whereas in Greece only 78 per cent have television. Major 'soap' serials get regular audiences of 10–20 million viewers in Britain, although specialist programmes such as 'gardening' are more relevant for particular products. The UK commercial television stations are regional. It is therefore possible to use geographic segmentation, as well as including other demographic and psychographic segmentation features related to programmes, when timing commercials.

In recent years satellite television has gained in popularity in Britain as the price of receiving equipment has fallen. The cable networks have increasingly drawn on the products of the satellite companies and the actual ownership of satellite dishes is increasing steadily.

An extension of television advertising is product placement. This is where the company pays the broadcaster a fee to ensure regular exposure of its product within the context of a specified programme. Any such exposure is felt to be beneficial. Television is such a powerful medium for images and associations that a saying has emerged in the industry: 'Television to sell, newspapers to tell'. This, of course, links to the objectives of a communication campaign.

The press

The press includes all forms of the following: newspapers both local and national; magazines; directories; and year books. If it is 'press to tell' the fact that twice as much is spent on newspaper and magazine advertising compared with commercial television will show the importance of the printed media.

Newspapers

The advertisements carried will obviously depend on whether the newspaper has national or local distribution. With local papers there is always a large section of classified advertisements. There are usually so many advertisements placed by the general public and small local firms that they are split up into different categories and displayed in groups.

EXERCISE

Find out how much it costs to advertise in your local newspapers. Is it much less than in a national newspaper?

There are a wide variety of daily newspapers on sale in Britain and the newspapers in general portray a wide spectrum of political views. To some extent it is possible to divide their readers into broad political and socio-economic groups. Most readers have a brand loyalty to the paper of their choice and will buy it each day. However, the loyalties may be changing as newspapers regularly use price promotions to increase sales. Other promotion tools being used include free papers, vouchers on Saturday for Sunday papers, and other tempting offers. These could well be discussed in any work on promotional offers covered in Chapter 15. The competition between newspapers is an example of aggressive marketing and it would be a good exercise to monitor the effect on circulation and profit. It would also be interesting to discover if the readership profiles of major newspapers have been changed by their promotional activity. Generally, however, it is possible to segment the readership and target specific groups with certain advertisements. Many newspapers have developed a strategy where specific days of the week are used regularly to advertise certain things on a larger scale, sometimes jobs, sometimes cars or perhaps property.

Almost 90 per cent of the population has access to a newspaper, but in order for the same advertisement to reach this population, a tremendous number of advertisements would have to be placed; that is why knowledge of the readership is so important. As a medium for target marketing it is very powerful.

There is a great deal of flexibility in newspaper advertising where the size of the advertisement, appearance, and colour, are a few of the variables available. Most of the national newspapers are produced with regional variations, and for advertisers this can be linked to a regional television campaign. Colour magazine supplements have been a bonus to advertisers and many newspapers now produce a good quality supplement.

In general, the public have a greater propensity to believe the written word. Certainly a lot of information can be given in a newspaper advertisement. A disadvantage with placing an advertisement in a newspaper is that it is likely to have a very short lifespan as newspapers tend to be read on the day they are published, and are then soon discarded.

Magazines

There are a great many magazines covering subjects which range from those covering topics of general interest to ones on highly specialist subjects. For practically any hobby or interest, it is possible to find some magazine which caters for those enthusiasts. There is an obvious link between a magazine and the lifestyle of its reader. It is therefore much easier for advertisers to be more selective by segmenting and targeting their audience through the use of magazines. For example, someone buying *Prima* magazine is likely to be interested in fashion, craft, knitting and beauty, and have far different interests from someone buying the *New Musical Express*, unless of course they have interest in both subjects.

Magazines do not suffer from the disadvantage of being discarded on the day they are published. Many are saved for several years by the people who buy them and are used as a source of reference. They may be passed from friend to friend until the copy is battered and torn, or they may be stacked in doctors' or dentists' waiting rooms. They are normally read and digested at a more leisurely pace than newspapers. *Vogue* claims that every copy is read by an average of eight people, so a circulation of 180 000 means a readership of almost 1.5 million people.

EXERCISE

List places where old copies of magazines are placed. Do many people have access to them? Are they read?

Many products can be enhanced by good quality colour advertisements and in magazines most advertisements for food products would fall into this category. High quality does mean high production costs but the results can be worth the expense.

EXERCISE

Find out the cost of advertising in your favourite magazine.

Directories and Year Books

Directories and year books range from the *Yellow Pages* directory to the *Daily Mail Year Book*, and would even include diaries promoted by a professional organisation. They include a tremendous amount of information and promote many different fields of interest. Despite being relatively inexpensive as a vehicle of communication, they can be highly effective. A local plumber having a large entry in the local *Yellow Pages* directory can win many customers. If the advertisement is good, and the plumber then proves to be a reliable worker for the customer who chose him from the directory, the plumber will be recommended to others and thus expand his business.

EXERCISE

Examine your local *Yellow Pages* directory. What size and kind of advertisements gain most attention?

Radio

Originally in the UK radio did not carry commercial advertising, and this is still true of the BBC. However, all radio is a media carrying communication messages, and even public service radio carries consumer interest programmes which influence potential purchasers. There are now many local and national commercial radio stations such as Virgin 1215, Classic FM and Atlantic 252. Many of these are very successful, increasing listeners at the expense of their non-commercial rivals. Radios are a major communication media for some 'captive' audiences, reaching car drivers as well as factory audio systems, also they are often just turned on, offering background sound in the home.

Radio commercials are much less expensive to produce than television commercials, but do not have the same advantages: there is no visual presentation, so only the aural senses are assailed. However, the medium is used by both local and national companies. Local organisations are able to target their message very precisely and at very reasonable costs.

The appeal of a radio commercial depends to a large extent on how the message is conveyed and it is not uncommon for famous personalities to lend their voice to the advertisement. Another recent development has been the sponsorship of programmes. Sometimes before a particular programme, the announcer will say, 'This programme is brought to you by courtesy of ... (a certain organisation)'. By hearing this announcement frequently it is easier to recall that organisation's name.

Radio messages are usually short-lived. They do not have the impact of television. Radio is sometimes described as 'noisy wallpaper'. Radio only accounts for just under 3 per cent of all advertising spending. Repetition is often necessary to create attention. But if the right message is developed it might have the same dramatic effect as, for example, Orson Welles' famous broadcast 'War of the Worlds', on US radio before World War II. The audience believed that the USA was being invaded from space and it was so realistic that it nearly caused a riot. But of course that was before the current dominance of television.

Cinema

As a vehicle of communication, cinema has had a chequered past in that its popularity has moved with the times. In Britain the cinema was very popular in the 1940s and 1950s, but its popularity waned in the 1960s and 1970s when audiences fell to an all-time low. There has been a recovery in audience figures in the last decade with the advent of the new multiplex screens. Advertising in the cinema has many of the same advantages of sound and moving pictures as television. Perhaps the cinema audience is slightly more captive. The majority of cinema goers tend to be in the age range 15 to 34 and it is therefore possible for precise target marketing to take place. As an advertising medium, cinema is popular with local businesses such as restaurants that are in relatively close proximity to the cinema.

Recently there has been a novel development in cinema advertising dubbed 'interactive cinema'. It involves a dialogue between a member of the audience (a paid actress) and the screen image. This, of course, is almost guaranteed to capture the interest of the rest of the audience.

EXERCISE

Next time you are at a cinema, note the type of advertising that is shown. Would the advertising vary from screen to screen if one was showing a Walt Disney film and another an Arnold Schwartzenegger film?

Outdoor media

Outdoor advertising can be a very effective channel of communication. It is also one of the cheapest, in terms of cost per thousand (CPT) of the adult population reached. Most of the adult population have the opportunity to see (OTS) posters every day. Not only does outdoor media include large posters, but also outdoor features such as parking meters and litter bins can act as host sites to advertisements. Every year more host sites seem to be discovered: carpark tickets are one example, with McDonald's using the back of carpark tickets to offer special prices on meals. Other outdoor hosts occasionally used are tethered balloons, perhaps on the site of a new shop or shopping area. Airships and aircraft with trailing banners have also been used, but they tend to be expensive to commission, and so do not enjoy tremendous popularity.

EXERCISE

What outdoor media other than posters are you aware of? How effective as channels of communication are they?

Transport advertising on the sides of buses has become very popular, and other commercial vehicles advertise company names and telephone numbers. However, advertising is not limited to the sides of larger vehicles. Taxis always have their telephone number displayed prominently, and now often feature advertisements for local firms pasted on to a convenient viewing position for the passengers to study. Other captive audiences are passengers in trains and aeroplanes.

EXERCISE

Study the advertisements on as many modes of transport as possible. Compare the variety of products which are advertised. Is there a common theme?

Go faster stripes by quattro.

As the quattro four wheel drive system offers the best possible grip through bends, at legal speeds, the only go faster stripes you'll need are on the side of the road.

Audi ⊙⊙⊙⊙
Vorsprung durch Technik

It is not always necessary to show a product in an advertisement. This advertisement is memorable because it makes you think about the benefits of the product which could be relevant to a potential customer. If it excites interest then the product name is strongly featured.

**AT DAEWOO YOU WON'T HAVE
COMMISSIONED SALESMEN AFTER YOU.**

That could be because we're the only car manufacturer to sell
direct. We're also the only car manufacturer that employs our own non-
commissioned customer advisers. Our staff don't make money by making
sales. Instead, they're there to greet you and answer any questions you may have.
You liked the idea of this, because in our first year alone we delivered over
18,000 Daewoos to you from our Motor Shows, Car Centres and Support
Centres. As well as not having commissioned sales staff we've also done away
with the hidden extras you find on most new cars. The fixed price you see on our
cars in the showroom, is the price you pay to put them on the road. Those
prices range from £8,795 to £12,995 for the 3, 4, or 5 door Nexia and
Espero Saloon. Take a look at the list and see what you get as
standard on every Daewoo 1.) 3 year/60,000 mile free
servicing including parts and labour. 2.) 3 year/60,000 mile
comprehensive warranty. 3.) 3 year Daewoo Total
AA Cover. 4.) 6 year anti-corrosion warranty.
5.) 30 day/1,000 mile money back or exchange
guarantee. 6.) Fixed purchase price
with no hidden extras. 7.) Delivery
included. 8.) Full tank of fuel.
9.) 12 months road
tax included.

10.) Air-conditioning included. 11.) Metallic paint included.
12.) Side impact protection. 13.) Electronic ABS.
14.) Driver's airbag. 15.) Power steering.
16.) Engine immobiliser. 17.) Security glass
etching. 18.) Mobile phone. 19.) Free courtesy
car. 20.) Pick up and return of your car for
service if needed. Mainland UK only. 21.) Free
customer helpline. Interested? With our
independent part exchange system there's also
never been a better time to have your car valued.
If you'd like to know where your nearest Daewoo
Showroom is call us free on 0800 666 222 or
write to Daewoo Cars Ltd, FREEPOST,
PO Box 401, Kent BR5 1BR.

*A car company that doesn't
have commissioned
salesmen?
That'll be the
Daewoo.*

✿ **DAEWOO**

Agency: Duckworth, Finn, Grubb & Waters

"Before eating, always let Häagen-Dazs

TEMPER

or soften for ten minutes. Only when allowed to

TEMPER

can the full flavour be appreciated."

Häagen-Dazs

Dedicated to Pleasure.

Daewoo (opposite) have revolutionised car retailing as Häagen-Dazs revolutionised ice cream. The Daewoo campaign was extremely successful in that the response to the freephone number generated a large and relevant database. The message is also different enough to promise benefits without hassle.

Häagen-Dazs (above) uses a more aspirational approach with strong copy in large letters, but in fact the total message is available if the full copy is read. Häagen-Dazs has created an image as the basis of its appeal.

THE CREAM OF MANCHESTER.

Boddingtons Draught Bitter. Brewed at the Strangeways Brewery since 1778.

It is essential that the packaging and the advertising work together, as it is the product which is bought at point of sale. Here we see the redesigned can for Boddingtons Draught Bitter, opposite Boddingtons 'the cream' advertising campaign.

The beer was relaunched by the Whitbread Beer Company in 1991 in a draught-flow can to ensure a creamy head when poured. The brand became strongly associated with the bright yellow can and even though the packaging of the product is not seen in the advertisement opposite, it still successfully communicates its message as a lighter bitter to a target audience of young lager drinkers.

Levi's jeans modelled
by original wearer.
Model : Josephine, 79, teacher, Colorado.
Item : 534 women's fit jeans.
Stylist : Simon Foxton.
Hair : Kevin Ryan.
Photographer : Nick Knight.

Agency: Bartle, Bogle & Hegarty. Photographer: Nick Knight

Segmentation is all very well. In fact, most people would suggest Levi's
were targeted at a younger age range. This advertisement dramatically
suggests that anyone can wear them, which is a different type of target
marketing.

Strong innovative packaging with good design is part of the offering. In fact it is the real message at the point of sale and deserves more attention than it sometimes gets. This particularly good example shows how Bacardi successfully reached a younger male audience in clubs, through a combination of modern graphics and unusual format.

Agency: Jones Knowles Ritchie Design

The above advertisement highlights the sad statistics regarding heart disease in the UK. The poster demonstrates how important it is for charities to take marketing seriously. They are hoping for donations in return for the donor feeling good.

Another example of captive audience advertising is on the London Underground. The tube stations have a very captive audience, and unless people want to study each other, the only entertainment available is the posters displayed on the station walls. Another similar example is where bus shelters play host to posters. Adshel bus shelters have been erected in many parts of the country. In return for supplying and providing maintenance of these bus shelters at no charge to the council, Adshel ask to be allowed to display a poster on them. A few years ago there was a large number of thefts from Adshel sites of posters advertising Sony Walkmans. On investigation it was found that students were removing the posters to use in their college rooms. Sony were said to be delighted because it both emphasised the attractiveness of the poster and provided additional advertising in student rooms. Adshel, faced with repair bills of up to £2000 per shelter, were not so pleased.

EXERCISE

Make a study of any bus shelters and the posters on them in your area. What posters are on them and are they Adshel shelters?

The positioning and site of the outdoor media is very important. The 1980s in particular saw a massive increase in poster popularity, the relatively low CPT being a contributing factor to this. There has also been a change in emphasis in the type of products advertised, away from alcohol and tobacco, to a more evenly balanced cross-section of products.

The size of the posters also varies, but there has been a concentrated effort by the advertising agencies to standardise the size of posters to ninety-six, forty-eight and six sheet size which increases impact and reduces production costs. There is also a move to increase poster illumination as they need to work after dark as well as during daylight. Mechanised posters which change picture are also on the increase.

The sites chosen to display posters are of paramount importance, the aim being for as many people as possible to see them. Sporting events are popular sites, especially if they are in areas which may be televised – such as Premier League football grounds. Competition for good sites is fierce and there is much creativity in discovering unusual sites where there could be an increasing impact from the advertisement. The use of electric scoreboards is an example of an unusual medium that is being used with success. Advertisements can also be found on supermarket trolleys, although this could also be considered a type of point-of-sale promotion.

The use of outdoor media can therefore be seen to be a dynamic and expanding vehicle of communication.

Point-of-sale displays

Advertising at or close to the 'point-of-sale' can prove to be a very effective vehicle of communication helping to influence a purchase decision at the precise point where and when decisions between product alternatives are being made. Often the material for point-of-sale displays is not only supplied by the producer of the products, but is also placed in position and restocked and generally looked after by a regular salesperson. But this is becoming much harder in the major supermarkets as they use their powerful position to control activities of suppliers, preferring instead to use their own material designed to be consistent with the store layout and colour schemes.

Point-of-sale material can include all or only a selection of the following: shelf edging; dummy packs; display packs; display stands; mobiles; and posters.

EXERCISE

In your local supermarket note the different kinds of point-of-sale material used.

Packaging

Packaging, which is sometimes called the Silent salesman, is the ultimate point-of-sale communication tool. It is a non-personal channel of communication, which has become an increasingly important part of the communications mix. Most grocery products are now purchased from a self-service supermarket, and so the need for good packaging has increased with the growth of self-selection. The packaging of a product involves the following functions:

1 Give protection.
2 Contain the product.
3 Be convenient.
4 Give information.
5 Have display advantages.
6 Convey any brand image.

Give protection – contain the product – be convenient

In order for the product to reach the consumer in perfect condition the packaging must offer basic protection. Protection is especially important when the product is very fragile, e.g. eggs. The protection must also safeguard against damage from rain, heat, cold – in fact against all the elements of the environment. This function relates more to the total product concept and quality of the offering rather than communications. However, just as a person's appearance is one of the initial communications in a personal situation, so the appearance of a package is an initial communication regarding a product.

As well as providing protection the packaging must contain the product – whether it is a bag of sugar or a bottle of wine or an aerosol deodorant. It would have been possible in the 1950s and 1960s to purchase four small nails loose from an ironmonger; today's consumer is more likely to find nails at the local DIY superstore and they are sold prepacked in tens. There are many different kinds of containers for products, e.g. toothpaste can either be in a tube or a pump dispenser. You might consider if this is really meeting the needs of the customers. Remember that the convenience of the packaging is important but it is the overall value to the customer that is paramount. Some products such as multipacks of drinks have been improved by having a ready-made handle attached, making it easier for the consumer to carry the product home.

Product tampering has become a threat, as happened with baby foods a few years ago where it was discovered that glass had been put into the food. The manufacturers' reaction was quickly to change the design of the baby food containers, so that it would be obvious if a jar of baby food had been opened. Manufacturers have spent much money and time in designing tamper-proof containers.

Other product factors could be the size of the package – it may be a carton of pot noodle or even individual tea bags or a small one-person portion of custard. Is the size of the package right for the consumer? Giant family packs of cereal or washing powder can be useful when large amounts of the product are used, but they are not so convenient if they don't fit on any of the shelves in the customer's kitchen. The product packaging should also be suitable for shelf display at the relevant retail outlet.

Packaging that is reusable has increased in importance with the growth of the 'green revolution'. Many products are now being designed so that when the original container is empty it can be filled again. This is common with many of the Body Shop products. With fabric conditioner it is also possible to buy refill packs. The original container for the fabric conditioner may be plastic and would cause a pollution problem when disposed of, whereas the carton container with the refill can be disposed of with much less harm to the environment.

Give information – have display advantages – convey brand images

Packaging now gives much more information about the product than was given a decade ago. It is now expected that the following information will be given as standard on food: ingredients, country of origin, sell-by date, calorific values and a barcode, which can be used both as a stock control and pricing mechanism. However, much of the information on packaging is to attract customers, even if some of it is to meet the legal requirements.

Packaging should have display advantages, especially if it is to be sold via intermediaries. It should be sufficiently attractive and eye-catching to interest the consumer as well as serve the needs of the members of the distribution chain.

One of the most important features of packaging is that it can convey the brand image. This has become easier with the advent of new processes and materials within the packaging industry, as more and more products are capable of being packaged. The last twenty years have seen an almost revolutionary change in packaging and distribution across many product ranges.

EXERCISE

Name five products of which the brands are easily recognised by the colour or shape of the packaging alone.

Packaging can be very important when a company is portraying a corporate image. They can use the same or similar designs and colours for all products and the packaging is constant over the whole product range.

Although packaging can carry out functions of protection, the communication and promotional aspects are of tremendous importance. It would be very dull indeed to go shopping and not be assailed by all the different colours, shapes and sizes of products in their various packaging. One of the reasons why Radion washing powder was so successful after its launch in Britain was that the packaging colours were so noticeable, being orange and lime green. This factor alongside the abysmal, old-fashioned television advertisements, assured it was noticed in the marketplace, and from this it became a successful product. However, it is not recommended that other companies follow this route to success with their products as it is a very dubious one.

NEW MEDIA

There are always new ideas on possible media, both personal and impersonal, which can be used to communicate with customers. You might have seen ads set into carpets in public places and even ones on the walls of very unlikely places. David Pugh from poster company Mills & Allen suggests

> Marketing Directors are finding themselves trapped in a vicious circle. On the one hand it is more and more difficult to keep abreast of all the changes in the media world, on the other hand the average marketer has less and less time to devote to the subject. These two pressures are pulling in opposite directions – while marketing departments are being compelled to improve on cost efficiency, the media choice continues to grow.

With the growth in media choice, the complex decisions on which media will achieve the communication objectives in the most effective manner becomes ever more difficult. Often media spending accounts for the greater part of the marketing budget, therefore marketing managers should give serious consideration to both traditional and unconventional media in their efforts to get their communications to inform, persuade, or reinforce an action relating to a chosen customer.

EXERCISE

Think of recent communications from organisations that have attracted your attention and made you more aware of that organisation. How did they do it?

CONCLUSION

Communications between an organisation and its stakeholders will take place in many ways. Such communications will affect potential customers, but only insofar as the actual way that the customer receives the message. It is therefore important to understand the process of communication and plan all communications to meet specific objectives. These will include the giving of information; persuading potential purchasers to buy; and reassuring existing customers. In order to benefit from communications, all parts of the process must be studied for effective encoding, allowance for 'noise', through to understanding, decoding and feedback in order to confirm the actual message received.

It is important that a company is aware of the channels of communication that it has at its disposal, and utilises them in the correct way. The medium chosen to convey the message must be appropriate. The appropriate medium depends very much on what the product or service is, and to whom it is targeted. If the product is of high value and aimed at the industrial market, a personal channel may be best – an example would be a fork-lift truck salesperson calling on a potential factory customer. However, if the product is of low value and aimed at the consumer market, a non-personal channel may be more effective. Television advertising is an expensive but very effective option. Word-of-mouth is another medium but one, of course, that cannot be controlled by the marketers. Other non-personal channels include the press, poster and radio and broadcasting.

We can therefore understand that a message must be sent via a channel from the organisation to the ultimate customer. This, however, is only half of the communication process. In order for it to function well it should also give a feedback, which we could perceive in the form of increased sales if the product were successful, or even decreased sales if the communication was bad and conveyed the wrong message. The feedback should be a definite reaction of some type to our message.

QUESTIONS

1 Think of a recent communication from an organisation that has attracted your attention. Explain how this has affected your views about that organisation.

2 What is meant by encoding? How might an advertising agency help an organisation to encode its messages?

3 What are the advantages of personal communications over non-personal communications?

4 Why is packaging sometimes called the silent salesman?

5 Why do large firms sometimes use a combination of media in their advertising campaigns? Illustrate your answer with examples.

6 Surf the Internet and find a company Website. Evaluate how this communicates and the content of the message. It is affected by any noise?

FURTHER READING

Abraham, M. and Lodish, L. (1996) 'Getting the most out of advertising and promotion', *Harvard Business Review*, May–June.

Colley, R. H. (1961) *Defining Advertising Goals for Measured Advertising Results*, New York Association of Advertisers.

Fill, C. (1995) *Marketing Communications*, Prentice-Hall, Hemel Hempstead.

Gilchrist, S. (1994) 'Discounters unmoved by ceasefire in store wars', *The Times*, Wednesday, 21 September.

Mueller, B. (1996) *International Advertising – communicating across cultures*, Wadsworth publishing/Thomson.

Rowell, R. (1994) 'Flattering to Deceive', *Marketing Business*, September.

Shimp, T. A. (1993) *Promotional Management and Marketing Communications*,3rd Edn, Dryden.

Smith, P. R. (1993) *Marketing Communications*, Kogan Page, London.

CASE STUDY
Panacea – launching a new band

Formed one year ago and all five members based in London, Panacea have brought together a variety of different influences to create their own unique and energetic sound. The band are regularly receiving recommendations in *Time Out* for their gigs at The Garage, Bull & Gate and The Monarch and have always had a great response from the audience.

Please listen to their first demo tape and find enclosed some photocopies of photos taken during and after their most recent gig at The Garage.'

This is a publicity letter sent by the band Panacea to record companies and the music press. The band play Industrial rock, writing all their own numbers. They see their music as similar to such bands as 3 Colours Red, Ministry, and Tool. The publicity package they use is similar to most bands, comprising

- PR brief;
- tickets for future concerts;
- photos of the band;
- demo tape.

As yet, they have had little reaction from this publicity mail shot although both Epic and Island Records have telephoned to register receipt of the material. The music press such as *New Musical Express* and *Melody Maker* (both owned by the same group), and specialist magazines like *Kerrang* and *Metal Hammer* have given no reviews.

Getting known in the music business is very tough. There are a large number of bands playing regularly in London, but those without a recording contract can do no more than break even at most events, as will be seen below.

Typically the band produces fliers (publicity leaflets) for gigs and, after expenses at the venue, receive no more than 50 per cent of the takings from customers showing the flier at the door. Panacea's first appearance at The Rock Garden netted £76 due to a large number of friends who attended. More recently audiences of over 100 have yielded only £28 between the five band members, and for their appearance at The Garage they received £67. Hardly a living wage!

They would like to make a CD to support the publicity and to sell at their concerts but the costs are high with a run of 500 likely to cost:

CD	$500 \times £1.80 = £900$
Sleeve	$500 \times £0.30 = £150$
Box	$500 \times £0.15 = £75$

Even if they do their own art work this is over £1000, which they are unable to find.

The influencers who could really enhance their music careers, and help them to get profitable gigs, are the record labels, particularly the more specialist labels, and the music press. Remember that the need is to stand out from all the other publicity on new bands, yet to achieve this within an affordable budget.

Question

How would you suggest that Panacea should attempt to communicate with these key influencers?

(*Note*: The name of the band in this case has been changed from the real name to avoid confusion. To our knowledge no band named Panacea exists, but should one be using this name the authors confirm the above case is not referring to that band.)

CHAPTER 15

Promotional Planning

*If you don't know where you are going you will probably
end up somewhere else.*
Laurence J Peter and Raymond Hull, *The Peter Principle*

INTRODUCTION

Promotional planning can be viewed as a sequential process aimed at deciding the strategies and necessary action plans to achieve communication objectives. The four elements of the promotional (or communication) mix are:

- Non-personal – 1 Advertising
  – 2 Publicity
  – 3 Sales promotion
- Personal – 4 Personal selling.

At some time every company will use one, or perhaps a combination, of the elements of the promotion mix. This will happen irrespective of whether it is production-, product-, selling- or marketing-orientated. The type of product or service offered by a company will have a bearing upon which elements are used. Of course, the budget which an organisation can afford to spend on promotions can influence decisions. The process is shown in Fig. 15.1.

The objectives of a promotion campaign were introduced in Chapter 14. They are very important; they are the targets that a company will wish to achieve with regard to the three possible groups of objectives:

- informing;
- persuading;
- reinforcing.

However, the long-run objective of promotions is not to inform, it is to encourage customers to purchase goods or to adopt ideas. When studying some advertisements it can be difficult to understand the logic behind the message, but effective promotions have usually been well researched, and they may appeal in some subconscious way that is not obvious to everyone. Alternatively, there will be occasions when a very amusing or eye-catching promotion fails to encourage any consumer behaviour. This should be discovered in routine marketing research which should track the usage of and attitude towards individual products.

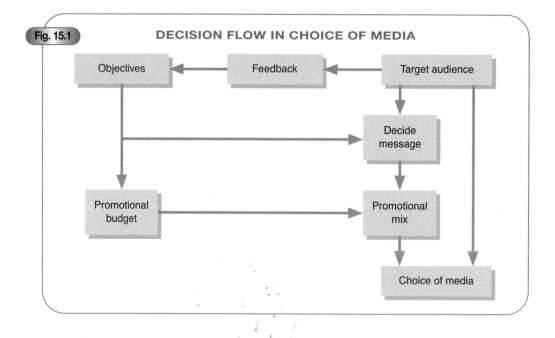

Fig. 15.1 — DECISION FLOW IN CHOICE OF MEDIA

It is only when the objectives have been analysed and decided upon that the company can set about deciding how best to achieve them. Objectives must be linked to the target audience, and, in particular, the stage they have reached in the purchase cycle. Informing is relevant to the pre-transactional stage (before a purchase), persuading equates to the transactional purchase period, and reinforcement can be necessary after a purchase (post-transactional).

Potential customers can go through these stages in deciding on a purchase. However, the objectives of communication could also refer to any of the pre-transactional stages a potential customer goes through before reaching the point where they make a purchase. Effectiveness of communication can then be judged against the customer's stage of development. The AIDA model was developed in the first part of the century when considering the psychology of selling. It reflects the stages prospects move through in the purchase cycle above:

Attention – Gain attention of the audience.
Interest – Kindle interest in the product/service on offer.
Desire – Arouse desire for your product above any desire for your competitor's product.
Action – The customer buys the product.

The usefulness of this model has been questioned in recent years. Other models such as Lavidge and Steiner (*see* Fig. 15.2) have been developed and it is now shown that AIDA is not robust when considering the success of advertising with all types of products. It will be possible in many instances for a product to create interest, perhaps by the very nature of the advertisement, but this in itself is not enough to create desire. Also AIDA does not cover the important post-transactional stage when further purchases are considered.

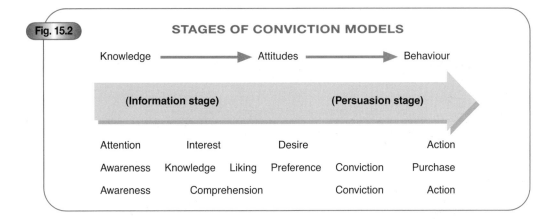

Fig. 15.2

STAGES OF CONVICTION MODELS

Knowledge ⟶ Attitudes ⟶ Behaviour

(Information stage)   (Persuasion stage)

Attention	Interest		Desire		Action
Awareness	Knowledge	Liking	Preference	Conviction	Purchase
Awareness	Comprehension			Conviction	Action

The more inexpensive and frequently bought products do not always require purchasers to go through all the stages of the model. For this type of repeat-purchase product, advertising covers only the reinforcement role of keeping the customer permanently aware of the value of the brand. Top-of-mind awareness for brands such as Mars have been reinforced by slogans such as, A Mars a day helps you work, rest and play. Shopping goods, which are more expensive and less frequently purchased, e.g. dishwashers or televisions, require more stages in the purchase decision. They may indeed require all the stages of the AIDA model. Nevertheless, a communication can be considered a success if it moves a potential customer from attention to interest, or from interest to desire.

It is possible to see an association in most of the alternate models which have been developed to show the progression of involvement. In general they can be classified under the three general headings of knowledge, attitudes and behaviour (*see* Fig. 15.2). The second line represents the AIDA model, the third line the six stages of the Lavidge and Steiner model and the bottom line shows the four steps described in the DAGMAR (Defining Advertising Goals for Measured Advertising Results) study. Other models can also be fitted into this progression. The starting point for different products will be different and so the measure of effectiveness requires a clear statement of the objectives within a specific context. At the pre-transactional stage the need could be for information such as: announcing a new product; explaining product features; describing available services; suggesting new uses; correcting false ideas; and informing of a price change. Here potential customers would probably be at the awareness or interest stage on the AIDA scale.

The transaction might not be an actual purchase of a product. It could be just the acceptance of a sales call. However, at the stage leading to the transaction the element of desire has to be developed and then extended into action. Persuasion is most important here and objectives could be arranging a sales appointment; enhancing company image; changing perception of product; building brand loyalty; stimulating a purchase decision; or encouraging brand switching.

In the post-transactional period the need is obviously for reinforcement and reminders. Major objectives could be reassuring that the purchase was right; maintaining top-of-mind awareness; or encouraging recommendations to friends. Within these objectives it is essential that goals are set so results can be measured as in the DAGMAR

Fig. 15.3

DAGMAR COMMUNICATION PROCESS

Enhance
communication
with:

Barriers to
communication:

	Unaware-ness	Aware-ness	Compre-hension	Conviction	Action or inaction	
Specificness Authority Impact Believability Relevancy Timeliness						Inertia Antipathy Incomprehension Memory lapse Competition Market Attrition (death etc.)

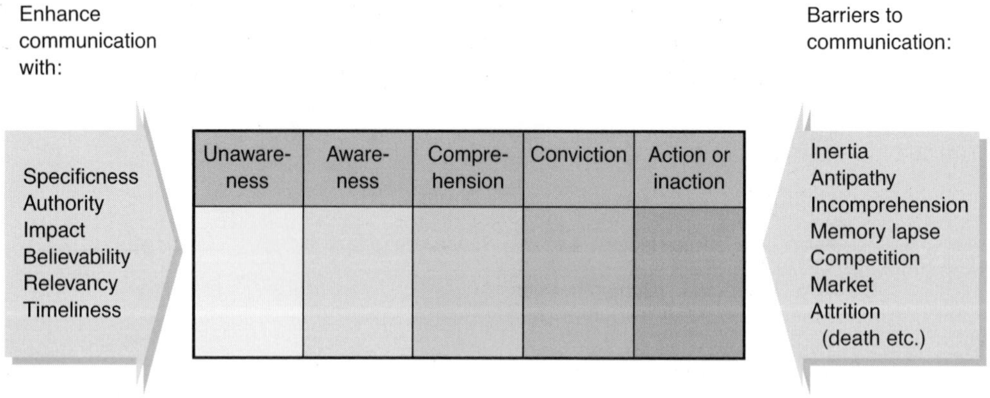

(*see* Chapter 14) process. In Fig. 15.3 it can be seen that as people are moved through the spectrum of the DAGMAR communication process they are encouraged by the factors on the left of the diagram and inhibited by the factors on the right. Each of the factors can have varying degrees of impact on potential consumers, depending upon the particular situation.

PROMOTION AS AN INVESTMENT

Promotional expenditure is not usually considered in the same category as research and development or training, but in considering the effect of various expenditures on the future of an organisation it is just as important. R&D can be seen as producing the products of the future, without which a company could struggle. Certainly these efforts need to be directed to meet the predicted requirements of target customers. But R&D is the investment in the offering side of the exchange process. Training, and the ever-increasing realisation of the benefits of customer-care programmes, concerns the delivery of the offering; a key ingredient in the long-term satisfying of customers.

Promotional expenditure should not be seen as a short-term effort to gain sales. Because there can be an immediate return from some types of promotion there is an assumption in some organisations that promotion should always be treated in this way. This forgets the full benefit of communication. It is an investment in the customers, hopefully creating positive attitudes towards an organisation or a product/service. Positioning has been described in the words of Ries and Trout as what happens in the mind of customers. Those authors are professional advertising executives, and they realise how communicating with customers is investing in the development of customers attitudes and beliefs.

A great deal of promotional investment is future orientated in exactly the same way as R&D and training. It should be treated in this way inside an organisation. If an organisation understands the exchange process, then they will appreciate how both sides of the exchange can be influenced by marketing action.

THE TARGET AUDIENCE

A promotion strategy developed by a company will aim to accomplish an improvement in the way that the company, and its goods and services, are perceived. In order to achieve this, some of the following stakeholder groups will be reached either directly or indirectly:

- specific target customers;
- the general public;
- present and potential distribution channel members;
- present and potential employees;
- suppliers of finance;
- present and potential shareholders.

It is possible that some communications could be seen by stakeholders who are not the prime target. This fall-out must be appreciated when placing advertisements. In addition, competitors often learn from advertisements. However, all communications must be aimed primarily at those publics identified in the marketing and promotional objectives. Precise targeting of the communication can both save money and ensure an effective response.

An audience of 10 million for a TV commercial could cost in excess of £150 000 for a single thirty-second spot. This is £15 per thousand viewers. For £42 000 you could buy the First mono full page appearing in all editions of the *Financial Times* with a circulation of over 300 000. This is £70 per thousand. On first appearance the TV is more expensive to buy but better value (CPT). But if all *FT* readers were in the target group, but only 10 per cent of the TV audience were acceptable targets, the equation changes. Of course it is not as easy as this. The TV programme reaches one million relevant people, which is five times that reached by the *FT*. If the object is to get coverage of the greatest number of target customers, then maybe the TV is still excellent value. But value, costs per thousand (CPT) and coverage all must be considered in the context of the most appropriate medium for the message. It is possible neither television nor press are really suitable to carry the message: it could be that a direct mail shot offers a more appropriate medium even if it is more expensive than either.

Therefore, marketing communicators must start with a clear view of the target group. But in particular they must decide both: how comprehensively the group is to be covered (coverage is the percentage of total target who are able to see a particular communication or series of communications); and what type of message and media is consistent with the communication objectives. Within the target group the role as user, decider or influencer will also have to be understood in order to develop a suitable campaign. This also enables the message to be developed at the right level and the selection of the most appropriate media to convey that message effectively to the chosen audience.

When considering promotion there can be two ways of creating demand. Products can be demanded by consumers who approach suppliers and pull the product through the distribution chain. The alternative is the traditional selling of products into distributors, thus pushing products towards the customers.

Pull strategy

A pull strategy is used by many companies. Basically, it is a strategy which by heavy use of advertising and promotion encourages consumers to demand the product. This strategy can be particularly successful when applied to goods which are sold through supermarkets or newsagents. Panini collector cards are an example at the start of the football season each year, as are British Airways Air Miles; the frequent flyer syndrome is part of airlines' marketing strategies to promote purchase of full and premium-priced tickets.

Occasionally there is a similar pull strategy when new magazines are launched, especially magazines of a specialist nature, such as *Do It Yourself* (DIY) or *Sewing and Knitting*, which by means of heavy advertising encourage consumers to demand that their local newsagents stock that particular magazine for them.

Push strategy

A push strategy works in the opposite direction to that of a pull strategy. It is the push from the producer to the distribution channel members and from them to the customer which increases demand for the product. Instead of aiming heavy advertising and promotional campaigns directly at the customer, the producer will specifically aim at the people and organisations selling the product to the final consumer. Examples of push strategy are very common in the industrial sector and also in the field of medicine. Medical sales representatives push products very strongly to doctors and back up this push with strong promotional measures. The doctors then prescribe the drugs to the patients who are ultimately the customer.

Avon, the cosmetics firm, is a well-known user of the push strategy. Salespeople call directly to the homes of customers to sell the products. Often companies will offer some kind of incentive to salespeople, to push their product more than their competitors products. This can occur with many different kinds of goods and services, from insurance to sports equipment.

It is difficult to measure the effect of either the push or pull strategy or to see how efficient they are. Many producers of goods and services do not want to take any chances and run both strategies simultaneously in order that they can reinforce any effect one or the other may be having. Figure 15.4 shows how the push strategy and the pull strategy differ.

PROMOTION FUNDING

An economist might suggest that promotional expenditure should be raised to the point where the marginal return from additional spend matches the marginal cost of that spend. However, this is not only impossible to measure, but it also forgets the long-term return of promotion. The benefits of a sustained campaign do not always come in the form of immediate results. A more appropriate plan is to set the expenditure based on objectives to be achieved and task to be done (*see* p. 257).

Some companies establish the amount of funds they feel able to allocate to promotion (affordable method). Others decide how much they need to spend separately on the various promotion tools, and then add the totals to arrive at a total promotion requirement. Whether a top-down or bottom-up approach is used, arriving at

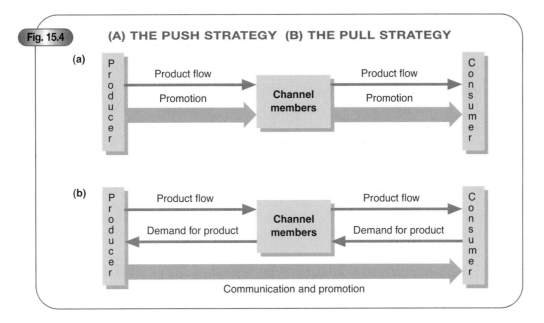

Fig. 15.4 — (A) THE PUSH STRATEGY (B) THE PULL STRATEGY

promotional budgets is a very inexact science. There are four major ways in which companies can calculate their total promotional budgets:

1 The objective and task method (zero-based budgeting).
2 The affordable method.
3 The percentage of sales method.
4 The competitive parity method.

However, for all its faults, the percentage of sales method is generally the one most commonly used. Crosier (1987) aggregated the results of a number of studies up to 1985 and found that the objective and task method was being used by 18 per cent of companies, the affordable method (or executive judgement) by 21 per cent, the percentage of sales or A/S (Advertising to Sales) ratio by 44 per cent and all other methods were being used by 17 per cent. There is no general model which allows sales increases to be forecast based on promotional spend. Therefore organisations choose methods of allocating budgets with which they feel comfortable.

The objective and task method

The objective and task method with its zero-base approach takes time to calculate and involves the setting of promotional objectives. It is closest to the real need within the promotional programme. The company decides what it would like to achieve with future promotions and works out several alternative ways of attaining these objectives. These will be costed and evaluated before the final decision about which approach to undertake is decided upon. This is a very logical process, but again is not without its disadvantages.

1 It is very difficult to determine the exact response to any particular expenditure on promotion. Although objectives have been set there is no guarantee that they will be met by following any one specific approach.

2 This method does not categorically take into consideration whether the company can afford to follow the objective and task method. The company may know the promotional objectives it wants to attain, and perhaps how to attain them, but is the company financially able to do it?

Unfortunately the method is rarely applied in its entirety.

The affordable method

The affordable method is very easy to understand and basically means that the company will spend on promotion what it thinks is reasonable and can afford. It is often based on either the previous year's spend, or what is available when the forecast revenue and required profit have been fixed. There is very little to commend this method except that the company is most unlikely to spend above its limits. The disadvantages far outweigh the advantages. Some of the disadvantages include the following:

- Any type of long-range planning is almost impossible. The company cannot guess exactly the funds that will be available in the future to spend on promotion.
- In times of recession or hardship for the company, very little will be able to be spent on promotion, and yet this is most likely to be the time when spending in this way would prove to be of most benefit.
- When the economy is especially buoyant or times are very good for the company, it is most likely to be able to afford to spend a lot more on promotion, but this is the very time when it may actually be possible to reduce spending on promotion and perhaps increase investment in an alternative, say, capital expenditure.
- In situations where the company is spending only what it can afford, it is likely that other departments in the company are also competing for these limited funds. This will cause the managers to have very little goodwill or harmony between themselves. Instead of all aiming for a common goal, the good of the company, they will be more likely to try to satisfy only their own personal empire-building or departmental goals.
- There is little opportunity to plan good promotional campaigns, i.e. making sure that the correct target audience is aimed for and using the correct media, message and promotional tool in general. The funds available under the affordable method can change from one day to the next depending on the activities of the company. Usually it is a reduction in the budget.

The percentage of sales method

Perhaps the classical approach, the percentage of sales method, is generally well liked by accountants as it is easy to calculate and therefore a precise amount can be allocated for promotion. A percentage of current yearly sales can be determined and this amount spent on the promotion mix, or a percentage of next year's forecasted sales can similarly be appropriated for this task. However, again, there are more disadvantages than advantages with this system.

1 There is no calculated theory to say what the percentage of sales should be. Whether a high or low percentage is correct, it is merely left to the discretion of management and may perhaps depend on how well the marketing manager can argue a case against, say, that of the finance manager.

2 If the percentage is fixed there is little opportunity to respond to any action by the competition or to any environmental demands that may arise. There is therefore the danger that valuable market share may be lost to a competitor should that competitor launch an aggressive promotional campaign which the firm cannot, because of lack of funds, respond to.

3 It is impossible to calculate what sales are won in relation to promotion spend if the spend always relates solely to the past or present sales figures.

4 Long-range planning for promotion over a period of more than a year is difficult to forecast. The budget is unlikely to remain at a similar level each year, unless the marketplace has remained fairly static.

The competitive parity method

The competitive parity method is where the amount allocated to be spent on the promotional mix is directly affected by how much is spent by competitors. It therefore aims to achieve a 'share of voice' similar to the company's market share. In fact there is some evidence to suggest that market shares are roughly in line with long-term share of advertising spend in some industries. However, this is not always so.

It is thought by those who engage in this method that the amount spent must be about right as it is almost an industrial norm. Organisations feel more comfortable not being the odd one out. But there are many abnormalities inherent with this approach.

1 All companies do not share the same objectives. Some companies may have the sole objective to become market leader, others may wish to become more profitable and although these are not mutually exclusive objectives, it is rare to be able to achieve both simultaneously.

2 It is suggested that this method diminishes the chance of promotional wars. But there is no logical reason to suppose that promotional fights will not happen. It is much more likely that all of the companies in direct competition, if they are all following the competitive parity method, will keep their spending patterns matching the others. This is likely to happen even if spending is at a much higher level than that which would exact a reasonable return.

3 The comparative parity method makes it less likely that a follower product could become a market leader. There are other aspects of the marketing mix to consider. Promotional activities cannot be considered on their own. But a challenger product is likely to require above parity promotional expenditure as part of its marketing mix.

THE PROMOTIONAL MESSAGE

Having decided on the communication objectives and the target audience, the next decision is the content of an effective message. This is necessary before deciding upon the balance of the promotional mix. The message has two components: content and mood. The content will reflect the requirement to communicate some particular information or relevant encouragement. This will be what the communicator hopes the receiver will do or consider following receipt of the message. The mood refers to the way the appeal is made to the target audience. Some moods are more appropriate than others for different types of message. Sometimes the mood is modified further when the medium is chosen and even when professional creative teams start to work on the actual advertisement. Relevant moods could be: rational, emotional, or moral.

It is here that a good knowledge of the personality traits and attitudes of the target audience can be invaluable. Use could be made of psychographic variables such as the activities, interests and opinions. Alternatively, the 'inner directed' groups suggested by McNulty and Kirk would show the rational to be self-explorers; the emotional to be experimentalists; and the moral to be social resisters. In some ways the credible emotional appeal is the most powerful. You can probably think of wholesome images shown to support Hovis bread, or the delight of the Andrex puppy, or the humour of Rowan Atkinson with respect to a well-known chargecard. Humour is not proven to be more powerful than rational appeals. In fact it can become boring very quickly once the joke is known. Nevertheless, it is an excellent attention-grabber and the need to gain attention is obviously the first need for an effective communication.

The AIDA sequence is critical here. The types of headlines which can grab attention must be consistent with the progression of the message. As already mentioned, it may not be necessary to take the target audience through all AIDA stages for a repeat purchase decision, but for the communication itself, all stages are relevant. Your communication must:

Grab ATTENTION
Excite INTEREST
Create DESIRE
Prompt ACTION

In terms of the total content the rule KISS (keep it simple – keep it short) is good to remember. Adding too many messages into one brief communication generally dilutes the effectiveness of the primary content. Do not let detail get in the way of a good strong message. And in internal communications a good summary on a couple of pages of A4 is often more effective than a complex report. If people want the details they will ask for them.

Pretesting of messages using specialised marketing research techniques is highly recommended. The research might study the format/layout of the advertisement. For instance, one technique tracks the movement of an eye across the page when reading an advertisement. This can be used to ensure the key messages are correctly positioned in the copy. However, the simplest techniques are just as important. Show the proposed advertisements, perhaps in rough form, to a sample of your audience and ask them what they make of the message.

PROMOTIONAL MIX DECISIONS

Consider your own personal communications – when do you send a letter or make a telephone call rather than calling on someone in person? How do you decide which is the best way to get your message across? A similar dilemma exists internally within an organisation. The decision to send a memo could be because it is more effective than a notice on the company notice board. But in another situation an article in the company newspaper could be more appropriate.

The same dilemma faces organisations in deciding between each of the promotion mix tools of advertising, publicity, sales promotion and personal selling. If there are only a small number of customers then perhaps a sales call is best. For mass markets there is a need to use mass media. Advertising is good at creating awareness and interest. Public relations can fulfil the same role as media advertising except there is a loss of control over what is published. This can be countered by the increased authority an editorial item might seem to have as opposed to an obvious advertisement. Sales promotion can be an immediate stimulus influencing a purchase but it can also be used effectively to encourage repeat purchase. Personal selling is expensive but very direct.

Depending on the type of product marketed, an organisation may wish to spend more on one of the promotion tools, say advertising, than another, say selling. Alternatively, an industrial machinery producer could find that personal selling is the most important tool, whereas a toy manufacturer may well be interested in media advertising and sales promotion. Usually the decision will be to concentrate on one element of the promotional mix for a specific objective but using the other elements in a consistent way to reinforce any message. It is not uncommon for a sales promotion to be featured in an advertising campaign, or for publicity activity using PR to complement main media advertising. There is of course a need for such campaigns to be co-ordinated to ensure the messages are actually consistent with each other.

In theory the choice of promotional tools should be determined by the task to be achieved. However the cost of television advertising can be extremely high and some organisations look for alternative ways to reach the target audience. Sometimes corporate advertising is used rather than promoting individual brands, and in other situations decisions are taken to experiment with unconventional media and this can be extremely successful.

The next two chapters discuss the merits of the major promotional methods. It is obvious that personal selling is a personal medium that offers direct contact with customers. The non-personal methods can be divided between advertising and publicity, which are indirect contact, and sales promotion which supports in a complementary way. Usually a mix of methods is used. This balances the push/pull requirements of reaching customers. Personal selling and sales promotion are very effective as 'push' techniques. The benefits of personal selling are that it is interactive, responsive and flexible. The drawback is that it can be very expensive. But selling should not be seen solely as a 'push' technique; it is also a major tool in developing long-term customer relationships and is part of the customer investment. Sales promotion can reinforce a position for a product or organisation if the promotion is well chosen. Money-off promotions can achieve significant short-term sales growth, but they do nothing for a brand's image. A link to a relevant celebrity could enhance a brand personality.

Advertising and publicity are definite investments. They may be indirect and non-personal, but they can be very intrusive. But for that to be achieved they must reach their target. The media is very overcrowded, and it was once suggested that we all receive over one thousand media advertising messages every day. Nevertheless, every reader of this book should be able to list a number of advertisements they remember well. These are ones that have been received.

The decision on how much to spend on each part of the promotional mix is a standard question, which does not have a standard answer. It really does all depend on the job to be done. It also depends on the budget. And it depends on the necessity of an advertisement or communication message to gain attention. If there is insufficient budget to gain attention using conventional media then any money spent is wasted. The overriding need is to deliver the message effectively. The budget allocated to any method should be judged on the basis of this task.

Problems of budget allocation arise more when organisations do not use the objective and task method of calculation. This 'bottom-up' approach allows a mix of promotional methods to be considered in an ideal context. The alternative 'top-down' approaches inevitably mean a compromise has to be made in the promotional mix allocation. The outcome of this is the mix of promotional methods illustrated in Fig. 15.5.

If heavy advertising can increase the size of a market then sometimes an organisation is faced with a version of the marketer's dilemma. If your company 'A' increases advertising, will the increased demand also benefit competitor 'B'? It certainly will if 'B' deploys extra salespeople. But if 'B' also advertises, the market could grow very fast and both companies will benefit if they can get the products to the customers. There are two other scenarios shown in the matrix in Fig. 15.6. How would you approach this problem?

PROMOTION AND THE DEMAND CURVE

Demand curve shifting to the right

Chapter 13 looked at how price and quantity define the demand curve. However, price changes only move demand along the demand curve. Promotional activities can help to shift the total demand curve, as well as sometimes changing its shape. Promotions can create a new environment in which buying decisions are made.

It is rare for organisations to have complete knowledge about their competitors plans. But companies need to make decisions for the future and to aim to gain competitive advantage for their offerings. Companies cannot gain sustainable advantage

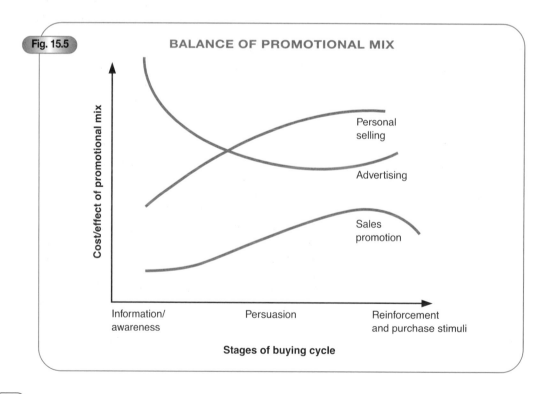

Fig. 15.5

BALANCE OF PROMOTIONAL MIX

Cost/effect of promotional mix

Personal selling

Advertising

Sales promotion

Information/ awareness

Persuasion

Reinforcement and purchase stimuli

Stages of buying cycle

Fig. 15.6 ADVERTISING/SALES DILEMMA

Company 'A'

	More advertising	More salespeople
Company 'B' — More advertising	Market grows fast. Both benefit in line with market share	Market grows. 'A' gains more than 'B'
Company 'B' — More sales-people	Market grows. 'B' gains more than 'A'	Market static. Both lose due to cost of sales staff

simply by decreasing the price. If price elasticity of demand existed, then more of the product would be bought if the price was lower, and if the price was increased, less of the product would be bought. This would only cause a movement along a demand curve, and not a complete shift of the demand curve. Also, competitors could soon follow to create the vicious circle described in Chapter 13.

It is possible to create or develop product differentiation by sustained promotional campaigns. This will produce a shift in the demand curve by changing the competitive situation. The movement will be easier to understand if we look at a few examples of products which have actually had a shift in their demand curves in recent years. One of the best British examples is the increase in healthy eating and organically produced food. Healthy eating has been promoted heavily on the back of government reports which are well exposed such as that of the Committee on the Medical Aspects of Health (COMA). The promotion has been supported by communications which range from leaflets in doctors' surgery waiting rooms, to articles in newspapers and advertisements on television. The increased awareness of the issues has caused a shift in the demand curve over a wide range of so-called healthy foods. Some examples are yoghurt, brown bread, muesli, and porridge, where the demand for the product has shown a marked increase. A similar pattern of activity and response occurred with vitamins when it was publicised that regular vitamin intake appeared to induce higher IQ ratings in children.

Porridge oats show a definite shift to the right in its demand curve over the last five years. In both Scotland and Northern Ireland porridge oats have always been a popular breakfast cereal, especially in winter. Even at other times of the day, porridge was used as a snack or as a good food that was filling, and helped keep one warm. Porridge has now become more popular in England, not because it was popular in Scotland, but purely because of the promotion. This concentrated on the facts that, if taken regularly, porridge oats could help lower the cholesterol level and bring down the risk of heart disease, a really effective benefit related to the product. The sales of porridge oats have risen. Whatever the answer, the demand curve for porridge has definitely shifted to the right. This is illustrated in Fig. 15.7.

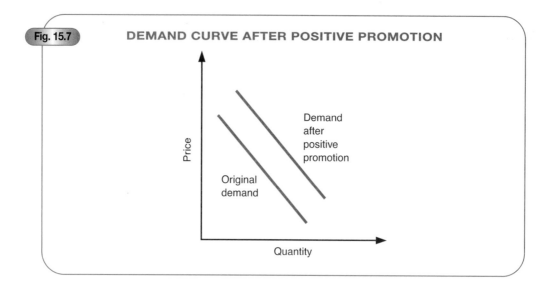

Fig. 15.7 DEMAND CURVE AFTER POSITIVE PROMOTION

These examples above show how good publicity can shift a demand curve to the right. It can, of course, move in the opposite direction when products are affected by bad publicity.

Demand curve shifting to the left

A recent example of a demand curve having a dramatic shift to the left can be seen by studying the demand for British beef. The problem follows the revelation that some cows had been infected with BSE or 'mad cow disease'. The situation became so serious that schools, colleges and hospitals took beef off their meal menus. Prices dropped and so did demand. Some farmers have faced financial ruin. The worldwide publicity about British 'mad cow disease' was so disturbing that the German Government campaigned to get a ban on the export of British beef to the EU countries. It would seem that BSE may have to be eradicated before British beef attains previously enjoyed levels of demand.

It is therefore evident that the demand curve can be caused to shift either to the left as an effect of bad publicity, or to the right after good publicity or promotion. A shift to the left is illustrated in Fig. 15.8.

The negative effect is not restricted to external events. There have been a number of cases where a promotional campaign had a negative effect on the perception or sales of a product. These include Hoover free flights, Fiat cars 'made by robots', Strand cigarette if you are alone! It must be remembered that one of the results of any promotion is to affect customer expectations. It is against these expectations that customers judge how satisfied they are with any product offering.

MEASURING EFFECTIVENESS

The communication is not always tested before it is used, although such an action is recommended. But after it has been used the strategy needs to be assessed and, if

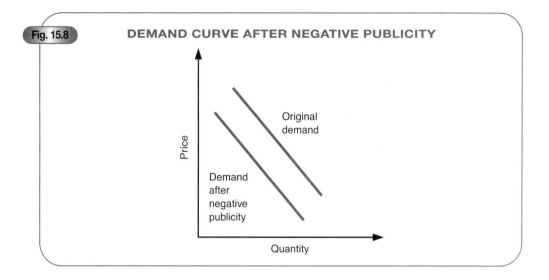

Fig. 15.8

DEMAND CURVE AFTER NEGATIVE PUBLICITY

required, refined. Two of the most common reasons given for why a promotional campaign should be monitored are:

- to show that the money has been well spent, and not wasted on something that is not worthwhile;
- to show that promotion has contributed to sales, that changes in demand were not just environmental factors.

Both are somewhat negative reasons. They do not measure up to the principles of the DAGMAR study which links feedback to clear communication objectives. Perhaps the problem is that so much of business is carefully controlled by capital payback periods and tangible purchases. Careful study will show that money spent on wages and salaries is not necessarily any more accountable than investment in promotions. But the fact remains that promotion is not directly related to sales in a one-to-one model. Promotion is an investment in customers' perceptions of products, but the return from such an investment is difficult to benchmark. When the judge in a notable pornography trial was asked to define 'pornography', he replied he could not define it but could point it out when he saw it. Good promotion has an element of this qualitative judgement about it, but the aim of feedback is to learn from your experience rather than develop a 'feel good' factor that the money was well spent.

Usually some form of attitudinal research or a continuous tracking study is carried out. Certainly 'benchmarks' can be established for targets such as level of unprompted awareness, level of message recall, stated brand preference and knowledge of facts included in the advertisement. These measures are mainly to do with measuring the effect of the communication. Even brand preference, as measured following a campaign, does not link precisely into actual sales. For many businesses the bottom line from their promotional investment is increased sales.

For the UK Government Health Education programme different objectives apply. These could be changing people's behaviour because of the risk of Aids. The research carried out following a major Aids campaign showed that the awareness of AIDS had exceeded the targets set. The worry was that few people said they had changed or were about to change their behaviour in spite of the new knowledge. If you look at the anti-smoking campaigns over many years it will be seen that behavioural changes happened very slowly, even though levels of knowledge had changed.

The problem is not how to give information, but how to persuade the target audience to act. Because of this it is usually inappropriate to measure the desired actions. It is more appropriate to measure against objectives related to the message. There are occasions where direct response is obvious. Say a charity advertises for donations to meet a particularly severe problem of malnutrition in Somalia. They can immediately measure donations and they do not worry if these are new gifts of money or donations which would otherwise have been made to an alternative charity. The short-term effect is easily quantified. There is also a long-term effect, for although the effect of a particular communication reduces with time, there will be some lasting subconscious residue which could mean you donate to 'Save the Children' again next time. This long-term shift is not so easily measured.

Work by Stephen King (1975) showed the gap between the desired action and the various ways of measuring advertising effectiveness. He suggested a scale of responses dependent on the task to be undertaken (*see* Fig. 15.9).

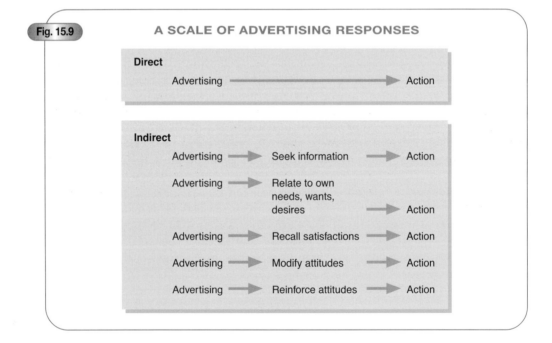

Fig. 15.9

A SCALE OF ADVERTISING RESPONSES

Direct

Advertising ⟶ Action

Indirect

Advertising ⟶ Seek information ⟶ Action

Advertising ⟶ Relate to own needs, wants, desires ⟶ Action

Advertising ⟶ Recall satisfactions ⟶ Action

Advertising ⟶ Modify attitudes ⟶ Action

Advertising ⟶ Reinforce attitudes ⟶ Action

In order to gauge the attitudes and behaviour of donors or customers it may be necessary to go to the customer to find out. This is an action promoted by Tom Peters, who regards it as essential. He states, 'Marketers should be in the field at least 25 per cent and preferably 50 per cent of their time.' You might sympathise with a charity worker who claimed they should not spend time with donors when there is other – 'more important' – work to do. But this confuses the different roles within a charity. The charity worker will benefit from the revenue achieved by the 'professional fundraisers', who could be seen as the marketing managers in the organisation. These fundraisers certainly do spend a great deal of time among potential donors.

Peters gives general advice suggesting all managers should go to the customer, look, listen and provide feedback. The need to listen is a necessary way of providing feedback on what has already been achieved. It is also a necessary preliminary to what still has to be achieved. Listening, like so many simple actions, is anything but simple. Peters advocates going out with a 'naive' mind set to gauge customers' reactions. He is incensed by statements like, 'we've got to communicate better with our customers'. On the face of it there is nothing wrong with the statement, but all too often it implies a one-way conversation. Have you ever heard a person in a foreign country trying to get a local to understand them? At each stage of confusion the foreigner speaks more loudly! It doesn't work. That is not communicating! To communicate you have to do it in the recipient's language. And it is all the better if it is relevant to the recipient's stage of development.

When listening you can ask limited questions, but ask them and then say no more and listen to the answer. You may not be able to listen to all of your potential customers, but the only way to measure need and effectiveness is to listen 'naively' to as many as you can. It is the relationship that an organisation builds through constant interaction with its customers and clients that is the measure required. Communication is the prime way of establishing this relationship but the requirement is for the contact to be two-way. If a two-way link is established then there will be no problems in measuring the effectiveness of communication.

CONCLUSION

This chapter has considered the planning of communications and the different elements in what is termed the **promotional mix**. The most important lesson from the material presented is that communications are vital as a link between an organisation and its customers. Those customers can be internal or external to the organisation. In all cases two-way communications are preferable. The goals for a communication must be well thought out before proceeding further.

However, in measuring the specific effect of a communication the measurement must be restricted to the communication's objectives and not to some more obtuse relationship. If good two-way communications are established with customers, other requirements for a satisfactory marketing exchange will be revealed.

QUESTIONS

1 What problems can be caused by trying to include a complex message into an advertisement?

2 How might an advertising budget be calculated for an organisation?

3 Why might an attention-grabbing advertisement fail to achieve its objectives?

4 Suggest a suitable situation for a 'pull' strategy as opposed to a 'push' strategy.

5 Demonstrate, using recent examples, how demand can be altered following publicity or promotion.

FURTHER READING

Brannan, T. (1995) *A Practical Guide to Integrated Marketing Communications*, Kogan Page, London.
Colley, R. H. (1961) *Defining Advertising Goals for Measured Advertising Results*, New York Association of Advertisers.
Crosier, K. (1987) 'Promotion', in *The Marketing Book*, ed. M. Baker, Heinemann, London.
Engel, J. F., Warshaw, M. R., Kinnear, T. C. (1994) *Promotional Strategy*, 8th Edn, Irwin.
Fill, C. (1995) *Marketing Communications*, Prentice-Hall, Hemel Hempstead.
Hart, N. (1995) *The Practice of Advertising*, 4th Edn, Heinemann/CIM.
King, S. (1975) 'Practical progress from a theory of advertising', *Admap*, October.
Lavidge, R. and Steiner, A. (1961) 'A model for predictive measurement of advertisement effectiveness', *Journal of Marketing*, October.
McNulty, W. Kirk (1985) 'UK change through a wide angle lens', *Futures*, London.
Peters, T. (1988) *Thriving on Chaos*, Macmillan, London.
Ries, A. and Trout, J. (1981) Positioning the Battle for Your Mind, McGraw-Hill, London.
Strong, E. K. (1925) *The Psychology of Selling*, McGraw-Hill, London.
Wilmshurst, J. (1993) *Below the Line Promotion*, Heinemann/CIM, London.

CASE STUDY
Mercia Glass

Mercia Glass is a small company just set up by John Wilson, a fifty-year-old glass-blower recently made redundant by a large Nuneaton glass manufacturer. Determined to make the best of the only opening available, John Wilson decided to put to practical use his £10 000 termination settlement by forming a business based on his extensive skills and experience in glass. With funding contributions from two other former glass-workers, now fellow directors, an initial investment of £25 000 has been supplemented by generous grant aid through the local Borough Industrial Office, and a low-rent first-year lease on a newly commissioned factory workshop at a Bedworth industrial estate. A further 'fitting-out' allowance from the Borough and bank borrowings for working capital have enabled the 'partners' to purchase suitable second-hand equipment and sufficient materials stock to provision them beyond their first six months of full operations.

The product line that the company will initially produce consists of a variety of hand-crafted glass ornaments and giftware, ranging from decorative blown flowers and frosted-glass fruits to stained-glass ashtrays and ships-in-bottles. Though other product ideas are under consideration, the opening range has been restricted to fifteen items, to simplify production start-up and offer a representative product mix for market launch. While no formal market research has been carried out, Wilson and his co-directors have met with largely enthusiastic comments on showing early product samples to friends and neighbours, and a number of local giftware retailers. In the business plans submitted to support their grant and loan applications, the three directors had anticipated they would confidently market all they produced through using local part-time 'party-selling' agents working on a commission basis. These arrangements appeared to produce no cause for comment from their financial sponsors, in spite of the £100 000 first-year sales target the company had subsequently committed itself to.

Now, two weeks before the planned commencement of trading, John Wilson has become concerned about the marketing side of the operation. Assisting part-time in planning the party-sales arrangements, his wife has confided to him the doubts that she now has about finding the right quantity and quality of party agents to move the planned volume of product. In considering the possibility of having to sell over an area wider than the Nuneaton/Coventry district, Wilson draws small comfort from the £800 provision for advertising that he recalls building into the Year one Marketing budget within the Business Plan. Though neither he nor his associates have any sales or customer-contact experience, he feels confident that the product range should almost 'sell itself', once the company has achieved entry within the market. He realises, however, that whatever marketing the company undertakes must be on a shoestring, or certainly based on efforts and arrangements not budgeted for within the original plan. In coming to this realisation, he also feels somewhat puzzled that the marketing section in the original plan had not attracted any critical comment within the vetting process following the company's grant and local applications.

Questions

Advise Mercia Glass on how to undertake the promotional side of the operation, given the obvious constraint of a limited budget.

In the face of the very real budget constraints within the Business Plan, propose and justify a number of new marketing activities that the company might undertake in order to support market entry.

Taking account of the circumstances of Mercia's grant and loan applications, what critical questions and tests do you think should have been applied to the Promotional section of the original Business Plan?

CHAPTER 16

Advertising and Direct Marketing

The great art of writing advertisements is the finding out a proper method to catch the reader's eye; without which a good thing may pass over unobserved, or be lost among commissions of bankrupt.

Addison, The Tatler, No. 224

INTRODUCTION

Advertising and direct marketing are two types of primary marketing communications but each uses different approaches. Both are controlled by the sender, who pays for the media used. Direct marketing differs from mass-media advertising by virtue of:

- the media used;
- the precise targeting of the customers;
- interaction with those customers.

In a recent interview, Philip Kotler suggested that 'the death knell for mass advertising is growing louder'. However, he sees a rapid growth in Europe of direct marketing as companies look for more precision in building their customer dialogue.

Such a prognosis is too radical. There will always be a role for mass-media advertising for mass-media products. There are also excellent 'one-way' media such as specialist magazines, and targeted television which uses media schedules chosen to maximise coverage of specific segments. Nevertheless, directly targeted messages are now very possible and so no organisation should ignore the full scope of communication techniques available.

Both media advertising and direct marketing can be considered as 'above the line' expenditure although the phrase predates direct marketing. 'Above the line' is a term still widely used in marketing which derives from the historical way advertising expenditure was treated in marketing budgets. Main media expenditure was shown 'above the line' because it represented actual expenditure, as opposed to sales promotion which was shown 'below the line', because much of the cost of such items came from a reduction in revenue, e.g. price cuts. Most advertisements run on behalf of a commercial organisation will be placed by an agency, who buy the space and pay the media owners. The agency then receives a commission from the media owners, but charge the full cost to the advertiser. It is not the same as placing a classified advertisement in your local newspaper where you would pay the media owner yourself. 'Above the line' is no longer specifically related to the accounting conventions, but the term is still widely used to encompass money spent for media coverage. As such it can apply to the total advertising and direct marketing expenditure.

Campaigns for 'above the line' expenditure are often planned as a whole, to achieve a regular series of messages about a company or a brand throughout a full year. However, the definition of PR from the Institute of Public Relations is 'the deliberate, planned, and sustained effort to establish and maintain mutual understanding between an organisation and its publics'. This definition is included here because it is important that not only publicity, but the total communications programme, is seen as a deliberate, planned and sustained effort. All the tools of the promotional mix should be used in a continuous effort to achieve the communication objectives of the organisation.

THE SCOPE OF ADVERTISING

Advertising has a very wide scope. When someone places a card in the local newsagent's window with an item for sale it is an advertisement. This can be contrasted with a major company's commercial shown on television. Each of these examples may be successful if they achieve their objectives, namely, moving potential customers closer to the point of purchase for a particular product or service.

Advertising is perhaps the first thing that people think about when considering marketing. You will already know that it comes at the end of the marketing process after a great deal of effort to ensure the marketing offer is worth promoting. However, it can be the most visible part of the marketing process. Main media advertising with multi-million budgets is undertaken by major consumer goods companies. These are only a small number of the total organisations who use advertising to communicate with their publics. For the major companies large amounts of money are involved. The impact of their advertising creates strong recall.

Advertising is a major part of their activities. For instance, Guinness have traditionally been high spenders. Guinness state that the reason for their spending is the need to promote their product more than other major brewers, as they do not own any pubs, unlike Ansells, Bass or Whitbread. So we can already see a relationship with other parts of the marketing mix, in this case the channels of distribution. Other high spenders that will immediately come to mind are companies like Procter & Gamble, Coca-Cola, Pepsi Cola and Cadbury. Their expenditures on advertising are important in maintaining a high profile for the various brands, thus keeping them firmly in the minds of consumers.

Other high spenders include financial institutions such as banks and insurance companies, as well as major High Street retailers like Boots, Debenhams, and Sainsbury. This reflects both the competition faced by these companies and the way retailers have taken the lead in many markets. Another major advertiser has been the Government, particularly in promoting the various new share issues, as state industries were sold to the general public. Promotional budgets of up to £10 million were allocated to individual privatisation campaigns. The result was not only the successful sales of shares, but also an increased awareness of share-owning in general among a wide spectrum of the British public.

It should be realised that advertising covers more than the persuading of a consumer to buy something. It is also a means of trying to influence behaviour and beliefs. This is the case with the following types of organisations:

- political parties;
- local authorities;
- charities;
- churches;
- pressure groups, such as Greenpeace.

Each of these organisations have a 'product' that they want to 'sell'. The advertising of their 'products', which could be their policies and beliefs, is how these organisations hope to influence and gain the support of the general public.

You will remember that the objectives of communication fall into the three categories:

- informing;
- persuading;
- reinforcing.

In general, media advertising is most effective when introducing new brands, or announcing modifications to existing brands. The research of Abraham and Lodish indicated that 59 per cent of new products received a positive impact from advertising, compared with 44 per cent of existing brands. The exact figures are not important, but advertising is much more effective at an early stage in the purchase cycle. When a product has lost its novelty factor, having been on the market for some time, consumers will have had time to make a balanced judgement about it. It is always difficult to change firmly held opinions and the advertising task therefore becomes more difficult. The objective of communication may change to one of trying to attract customers from different market segments; or perhaps introducing a new, improved version of the original product. Examples of changes to existing brands include a springfresh variant to Fairy Excel Plus, Right Guard launching an antiperspirant deodorant gel, and HP Bulmer launching Strongbow Smooth to the take-home market.

EXERCISE

Over the period of a few days make a note of any new products, or modifications to existing products, the advertising for which has been in magazines or on the television.

The stage of the product's life cycle will have a marked effect on the type of advertising and promotion that is carried out for a product. At the introductory stages of the product's life, advertisements are designed to create an awareness of the product. After the product has moved into the growth stage of the life cycle, building interest will be of paramount importance. Later, when competition becomes more intense, the benefits of the product, against those of competitors' products, will be stressed, and perhaps the emphasis will switch to other types of promotion, maybe sales promotion.

ADVERTISING CONSIDERATIONS

There are many factors which should be considered before advertising is undertaken. Advertisements should first be considered as part of the total communication process. The objectives, message, and likely budget could well have been determined. Decisions now have to be taken on the role of advertising as part of the promotional mix. Primarily it revolves around the balance between advertising and personal selling, as these are usually the elements where most money is committed. Often decisions will be taken on the basis of the previous year, rather than a proper objective and task evaluation. It is not easy to switch between personal selling and advertising, as salespeople are usually employees, with consequent rights. Even if an organisation does not employ a salesforce but uses commission agents, there is still the human problem of reductions. However, the cost/effectiveness of advertising reduces as customers move through the stages of the purchase cycle. This is also carried into a similar relationship with the stages of the product life cycle mentioned above. Advertising is more important at the early stages. Nevertheless, it is not advisable to stop all advertising in a competitive marketplace, as customers soon move on to new products.

Following a Monopolies Commission report into washing powders, both Lever Brothers and Procter & Gamble each stopped advertising one brand. The Commission claimed that advertising costs contributed to unacceptably high prices. For the chosen brands, advertising was stopped and prices lowered. The sales of both brands began to fall, and one of them has now disappeared altogether. This does not prove advertising works, as other factors were also at work, but it does warn against radical changes in advertising support.

Because salesforce costs are less directly variable than expenditure on advertising and other direct promotion, there tends to be more unplanned fluctuations in advertising budgets. Keith Crosier suggested that 65 per cent of promotional budgets are based on either the percentage of sales or the affordable methods. Both these methods are subject to fluctuations, and so when cuts come they fall on advertising rather than sales costs. This makes the effect even more pronounced.

To plan an advertising campaign the following must be considered:

1 The type of product or service offered;
2 The key benefit offered (why that product should be bought ahead of its competitors);
3 The objectives of the communication;
4 Who the target market consists of;
5 The advertising message and how it relates to other communication messages;
6 The amount to be spent on advertising within the context of the total communication spend;
7 The media chosen to carry the advertisement;
8 The prevailing marketing environment.

ADVERTISING CAMPAIGNS

The campaign planners will already know the answer as to who the target market is and what message is required. They need to decide when, where, and how they can reach that target in media terms. When, because timing is a key variable and advertising must be co-ordinated with other communication plans. Also, other marketing plans need integration, as there is no point in advertising heavily if there are not sufficient extra stocks available with distributors. Where and how is the media choice linked to the message. If the organisation is using a major advertising agency, they will have access to a wealth of statistics linking media to target groups, as defined by segmentation variables.

In organising for advertising very few organisations design their own advertisements. If they do, media facts are available from media owners, but these do not give comparative facts, nor are they able to link together a campaign using several media to calculate the total coverage. However, the range of skills required for advertising are better bought in from a specialist agency. You might be able to put together a good internal team with the necessary skills and, of course, doing it in-house can be seen as reducing costs, but does it really work out cheaper when considering the opportunity costs of staff time and the other risks involved in this specialist area? Another benefit from using a professional agency is that they are able to stand back and review your communications plans in an objective way. If you do not like the agency you are working with you can always change them. But agencies offer a service, and, as in all service marketing, interactions and the building up of personal relationships can be rewarding. Advertising agencies should become an extension of an organisation's own marketing department.

It is still important to have someone responsible for briefing the agency and approving plans. In small companies, dealing with local agencies, this can be done by the overworked marketing manager, who is trying to carry out all the marketing roles himself. Larger companies might use more than one agency and maybe even a specialist media buying service. These companies tend to have large advertising departments, not to produce advertising but to compare the different agency performances. Sometimes they get involved in media buying to ensure that the buying power of a major company like Cadbury Schweppes can be used to get good discounts across all its brand advertising.

The prima donnas of advertising agencies are rightly the creative talent. This is the key reason for using an agency, because an 'everyday product' has to be presented in a way that takes the target market through all its stages of attention, interest, desire and action. The very best agencies combine creative talent with first-rate business planning.

Coulson-Thomas, in his book *Marketing Communications*, suggests that on being told how much a client is prepared to pay, an agency will develop a media schedule giving details of which media should be used and why, how many insertions of what length should be made and so forth. In the case of a major campaign, an agency is likely to draw up a proposal which will set out campaign objectives and show how these can be furthered by sending certain messages along selected channels to priority identified target groups. A breakdown of the budget may also be given, showing how much is spent on creative development and on buying space and air time.

This seems to miss the point regarding objectives and integration. Advertising is not a function where a budget is stretched as much as possible and therefore a good brief and clear objectives are the most important issues. There will be a type of interactive process where media choice, message type and budget availability are continually studied against the coverage of the chosen target group. However, it is sometimes better to reduce coverage but present a full message with the preferred number of opportunities to see (OTS) for those reached, than to reduce OTS yet still try to reach everyone in the target.

The agency will try to answer the when, where, and how questions through a mixture of message presentation and media selection. The two are inextricably linked, as reflected in the saying that 'the medium is the message'.

ADVERTISING MESSAGES

The message will usually emphasise the key facts that an advertiser wants to communicate. This is part of the content described in the previous chapter. Sometimes there will be an attempt to find a unique selling proposition (USP) – something tangible or intangible that the brand can claim as its own. In some advertisements it is sufficient to just get over the brand name. This is sometimes forgotten in the creative enthusiasm. There have been some notable occasions when the recall of an advertisement was high, and the contribution of the actors involved was well received, but the recall of the brand was minimal. This does a lot for the actors but gives little return on the advertising investment. There have been a number of brands that have succeeded in gaining brand recall without using brand names. Cigarettes such as Silk Cut and Benson and Hedges Gold have achieved it, while in the past, Cadbury Smash ran successful advertisements without names. Where these succeeded was in the receiver having to work hard to understand the advertisement. Having worked out that the cut piece of purple silk represented the cigarette brand, the recall was stronger than if the brand name had been given and the receiver had not had to work it out. This is a clever approach to receivers but one that few brands dare risk. Another effective no-mention advertisement was just three words: 'Beanz meanz WHO?' You ought to be able to guess the brand.

It is often said that to be effective an advertisement must be read, understood, believed, remembered, and finally acted upon. This is a good list when developing and testing a suitable message. It is another variant of the AIDA progression already mentioned on several occasions. It leads into the question of repetition of messages. Do you remember a message on the first hearing, or does it take several repeats to really understand? For an advertiser there is no firm rule. Some messages for some audiences require a number of opportunities to see (OTS), others are remembered on the first showing. But the requirement needs to be established before the media planning stage, so the media schedule neither undershows nor over-exposes an advertisement.

An issue in campaign planning that is often ignored is the need for consistency in the messages offered. It is important for a brand to gain a suitable position in its market. The communication is part of the development of this position. Also, it is very difficult to change opinions held about a mature brand. It is, however, very easy to confuse customers through inconsistent messages. Sometimes a new marketing manager is appointed, and to create activity he/she changes the advertising. This might bring a new, fresh image to the product. It is acceptable if it is part of a well-thought-out campaign, but all too often it is confusing. If a new campaign ignores past messages and is inconsistent when placed alongside them, it has to work that much harder to achieve the desired result. A recent example is:

> Allied Domecq is relaunching its flagging sherry brand Harveys Luncheon Dry across the globe to woo a younger and more up-market customer. The dry sherry has been renamed Dune and repackaged in an elegant bottle to build up distribution in fashionable restaurant and retail outlets. The brand has also been made less dry. (*Marketing*, 10 April 1997)

One final point regarding the advertising message is its role in reinforcing a buying decision. If a customer has just bought a major product, then interest in that product category continues beyond the actual time of purchase. Advertisements featuring both the model purchased and competitive models will be studied with interest. Even if the real purpose of an advertisement is to persuade rather than reinforce, the high probability that recent purchasers will see it must be considered. The key benefits need to appeal to this group as well, as they can also influence future sales by their word-of-mouth endorsement of the product – a very useful addition to any marketing communication programme.

It is impossible to select word-of-mouth as a communication medium, although it is a very effective medium, and a supplier can hope everything else in the offer is sufficiently attractive to ensure good personal recommendation.

THE SELECTION OF MEDIA

Advertising revenue forms a large proportion of the income for most media owners, so they have to 'market' their 'product' to potential customers, agencies and advertisers. The benefit offered by the media is access to the relevant target customers, that is, the one the advertiser is trying to reach. To help identify the relevant groups the media owners supply very detailed profiles of their readers/viewers. The matching of these groups with the target audience has been greatly increased by the use of computers, and media planning is a very professional business.

Several years ago most advertising agencies offered a full service of account handling, research, planning, creative and media. Over the last fifteen years more specialists have developed, concentrating on just one of these functions. The most successful are creative hot-houses, and media planning specialists. If a company wished to do its own creative work it could still use a specialist agency to buy the media.

Decisions on media buying cover the right medium for the message, and then the interrelated question of frequency versus coverage, that is, how many opportunities to see against the percentage of the target market reached (covered) by the advertisement. The figures produced by the media planning packages are usually the averages. If an average OTS is 10 then that inevitably means some people see it on more occasions and some less. The ideal is never obtained. Also a highly concentrated campaign where there is an OTS of 10 over a period of a week or two will have a different result to one where the 10 OTS are spread out at one per month.

The vehicle for advertising is mass media. Each insertion of an advertisement in the chosen media is likely to be directed at a group of people and not an individual. As it is also one-way communication, there is an inevitable lag before any feedback can be obtained. Therefore there is rarely any opportunity to modify a campaign after it has been launched. Pretesting must involve both the message and the media as the two are inseparable in the actual campaign.

The choice between the different media will be taken based on the different strengths of each: that is, not only the ability to reach the target group efficiently, but the effective way in which that message is delivered. The issue of cost per thousand (CPT, a measure of media cost divided by audience) is only relevant when comparing two media of equal effectiveness. There have been times when TV airtime was so scarce that advertisers who had booked a spot were being bumped out by one offering a higher payment. There is a difference between a fixed-time TV spot during a specific programme, and buying a 'package' where the TV company guarantees a minimum number of rating points (a measure of audience used in television media). Some advertisements on the latter system will be at favourable times, others will be placed according to availability. The same is true of newspapers and magazines. A key position on the cover or facing a key editorial page will be sought as being better than other positions. Premium prices are charged for these positions compared with discounts for a 'run of paper' (i.e. where there happens to be space) position. The choice is therefore both the media used and the relevance of the timing or position in that media.

Lead-times are also important. Newspaper advertisements are quick to produce and can be very topical. Such advertisements appeared for Renault the day following Nigel Mansell winning the world drivers' championship. There are other examples that you could find. Lead-times for monthly magazines tend to be very long. Also in this category is space in the weekly Sunday newspaper colour magazines. Television also cannot be rushed, although the use of modern video rather than film means there are opportunities here. Although all these aspects are relevant, the key decision still is the one concerning 'the right media for the message'. This is an extension of the one liner, 'TV to sell, Press to tell'.

ADVERTISING AGENCIES

An advertising agency should be an extension of an organisation's marketing department. It can bring specific skills to the partnership, and these should enhance the ability of a company to get the most from its advertising. Agencies can be large, London-based, high-profile operations with international connections, or small, local but equally professional set-ups. The skills they have are related to communication in media. Since no two advertising problems are alike, each needs to be considered separately and in detail. Agencies can be what is termed 'full-service', offering all services to their clients. However, there is an increasing number of specialist agencies, concentrating on just one function.

As in any rewarding relationship, honesty and trust are needed to work towards the best solution. The agency skills are in projecting messages either visually or in words. The main functions in a full-service agency usually consist of the following:

1 A selection of creative teams comprising an art director and a copywriter, each team specialising in particular media. Agency reputations are often built on their creativity. These groups work closely with the production groups who translate approved creative ideas into finished commercials.
2 The account supervisor/director function, really a key account manager who builds and maintains the relationship in the same way as a sales manager might in another organisation. They also get involved with specialist areas such as advertising research, and other services directly relevant to the client relationship.
3 The media planning and buying function which contributes in this vital area.

The clients work directly with the account team, but there is no reason why they should not meet and help brief the other functions. However, clients should not try to do the agency's job. The way to be a good client is to give a clear brief, and, when evaluating work, to do so fairly but as a total package.

It must be remembered, however, that agencies are in business, and sometimes are very profitable. They started as agents for the media owners and that is the basis of the commission payments they receive when booking space. The Institute of Practitioners in Advertising recommend that contracts from full-service agencies should allow a 15 per cent net (17.65 per cent gross) margin on media. Even after the Office of Fair Trading ruling that the fixed 15 per cent standard rate commission represents a restrictive practice, many agencies still benefit from increased media spend by their clients. There are other elements of the promotional and marketing mix which compete for marketing investment, and sometimes agencies forget this. Some agencies do offer a range of additional marketing services alongside the advertising role. These could include marketing research, marketing planning, precision marketing/direct mail, publicity/PR, and sales promotion. At times these will be offered from the main agency, and sometimes from a separate agency in the same group. As with the basic agency relationship, a lot will depend on the interaction between the marketing manager for the client and the account supervisor in the agency. One client might feel comfortable with various services from a single group, others might use separate researchers or promotional groups.

The idea that a full-service agency can save the Marketing Director time has rightly been challenged. Certainly such one-stop-shop agencies should be able to offer a more integrated approach to client needs. But not all clients (advertisers) need to achieve this by buying from a single source. However well the agency is briefed, it is still an agency. The advertiser knows the product intimately and can assess the requirements. The different services can all be bought separately, but increasingly it is the media buying function which is being placed with a specialist. Figure 16.1 shows a traditional advertising agency structure. The extent that this industry has grown is highlighted in a Marketing Special Supplement which stated the following:

> It took the interplay of increased consumer wealth, technological progress which allowed the development of new media, and improved techniques of marketing and market research to transform the advertising industry from a minnow turning over £46m in 1926 to a colossus worth £8bn in 1996.

For other elements of the promotional mix such as direct marketing, publicity or sales promotion, there are both separate, independent agencies and members of large communications groups. The structure of creative, account handling, and delivery of message are still present in these agencies. They need to be judged as any supplier on the basis of their abilities. If an organisation decides to use an agency, then a proper briefing is appropriate.

Briefing an agency

This section refers primarily to briefing a specialist advertising agency. However, the issues can easily be adapted to cover any agency retained to advise on part or all of the communications mix. Before appointing an agency, it is necessary to go through a selection process. This can involve a competitive pitch, where several agencies are given the same brief and asked to present their plans. These presentations can be very elaborate and expensive for the participating agencies. Sometimes the client offers a payment to subsidise the agency costs, but for very large accounts agencies are prepared to invest, in the hope of landing a profitable account. There are some agencies who refuse to participate in this competition, preferring to let their past record indicate their abilities.

When briefing a new agency an advertiser has to give rather more background information than would be given to an incumbent agency which would already have the basic data. In his book, *Marketing*, David Mercer gives an excellent study on the process of developing advertising from a good brief. He states:

... the client's brief to the agency, and how it is translated within the agency, is the key determinant of a successful advertisement. No matter how brilliant the creative treatment, it will not succeed if it fails to meet the marketing objectives.

This obviously points to the need for a structured brief starting with clear objectives. Although the list below was given earlier in this chapter, it gives the key headings necessary for a good brief. Of course, item 7 – media – might be left to be discussed with the agency.

1 The type of product or service offered and issues from the elements of the offer mix such as channels of distribution and price/value.
2 The key benefit offered – the USP (why that product should be bought ahead of its competitors).
3 The objectives of the communication mix and the advertising role within it.
4 The target market profiled using the appropriate segmentation data.
5 The advertising message and how it relates to other communication messages.
6 The amount to be spent on advertising within the context of the total communication spend.
7 The media chosen to carry the advertising.
8 The prevailing marketing environment, including competition.

A brief will give details about all these issues and should also include any historical issue that could affect the responsiveness of the target group. It is also important to

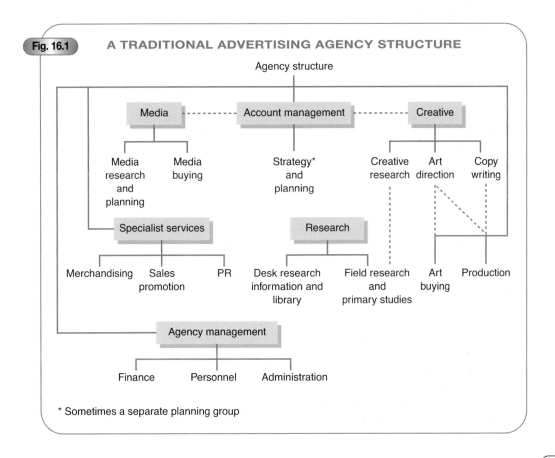

Fig. 16.1 **A TRADITIONAL ADVERTISING AGENCY STRUCTURE**

* Sometimes a separate planning group

share any up-to-date and relevant research data with the agency to ensure they are able to work as full partners.

The issue of budgets, mentioned earlier, is a tricky one. Certainly no company has an open cheque book and a guide can be given. However, if an organisation wishes to adopt the objective and task method of budgeting, the agency must be asked to draw up their recommendations aimed at meeting the objectives set for the advertising.

ADVERTISING EFFECTIVENESS

The subject of advertising effectiveness has been a contentious issue for a very long time. One study, undertaken by advertising man Alex Biel using the substantial PIMS database of over 3000 companies in USA and Europe, looked at comparative advertising to sales ratios related to market share. The results are shown in Table 16.1:

Table 16.1 ● Advertising effectiveness

Relative Ad/Sales compared to direct competitors	Average share of market (%)
Much less	14
Less	20
Equal	25
More	26
Much more	32

While these results could be simply reflecting the fact that major brands can afford to spend more on advertising than minor brands, the numbers and diversity of the firms investigated would suggest a correlation between advertising expenditure and market share. These results must be seen against research by Abraham and Lodish who concluded that only 46 per cent of the established brands they studied received a positive sales impact from advertising. The researchers found a higher figure of 59 per cent for new products, but of course we must remember that over a third of new products 'fail' so this figure perhaps refers to those new products that have 'succeeded'.

EXERCISE

Think of television advertisements which you have seen recently that have encouraged you or anyone in your household to take action by doing something or purchasing a particular product. What was it in the advertisement that really stimulated action? Was there already some prior knowledge or propensity to that action? What part did the advertisement play in the process?

DIRECT MARKETING AND PRECISION MARKETING

Direct marketing is the use of direct media to reach a target. There have always been opportunities to use direct mail, door-to-door and telephone communications. The actual media is wider than these but the growth in direct marketing has come about because of the:

- development of database marketing;
- proliferation of new products;
- multiplication of distribution channels;
- demassification of markets;
- decrease in the 'efficiency' of mass media.

These subjects are discussed in the excellent book by Rapp and Collins which used the term maxi-marketing. Maxi-marketing is the requirement of marketing to achieve:

- maximum efficient reach to target customers;
- maximum chance of marketing sales;
- maximum opportunity to develop relationships.

Direct marketing is much more personal than mass advertising, and so it can be a key part of the development of relationships with customers. In 1983 Levitt suggested that:

> the future will be a future of more and more intensified relationships, especially in industrial marketing, but also increasingly even in frequently purchased consumer goods.

Now, a decade later, relationship marketing is a reality.

Technology is developing fast in the area of communications, but so is the skill base to use it effectively. Jane Bird suggests that in the next five years there will be two types of company: those that use the computer as a marketing tool and those that face bankruptcy. This might be an over-exaggeration but harnessing the skills of 'database marketing' to the 'direct marketing media' is producing 'precision marketing'. The distinction between 'direct marketing' and 'database marketing' is well discussed by Keith Fletcher and his colleagues. They suggest Shaw and Stone's definition of database marketing as:

> an interactive approach to marketing communication, which uses individually addressable communications media (such as mail, telephone and the sales force) to: extend help to a company's target audience; stimulate their demand; and stay close to them by recording and keeping an electronic database memory of customers, prospects and all communications and commercial contacts, to help all future contacts.

The high-quality, computerised database must then be linked to direct response media, which includes everything from the so-called 'junk mail' to statement stuffers and electronic media. The advantages are:

- better targeting;
- powerful personal communications;
- flexibility;
- creative opportunities;
- controlled timing;
- controlled input.

Jane Bird describes a mailing to thousands of customers of the Nationwide Anglia Building Society. Obviously each letter is personalised to a named recipient. The additional element is that each letter offers a personalised offer based on detailed segmentation and geo-demographics. The mailing is therefore designed to give a different message to each different segment, so that this should be of much greater relevance than a circular sent to all customers.

The key to success in any communication is access to the audience, reaching the chosen target. However good the message, if it fails to reach its target recipient, it is wasted.

It used to be thought that a poor message reaching the right target could do some good – witness the general circulars and junk mail still in use. However, the wrong message can leave the relationship with the receiver if not neutral then actually harmed. The retaining of customers, and building of deep, profitable relationships can only be achieved if customers believe you know them and their needs. David Jones, formerly of Grattan Mail Order, said, 'You don't send a gardening catalogue to someone living in a high rise flat.' All mail order companies are developing sophisticated databases, and most importantly, they are continually refining them to keep them up to date. Figure 16.2 shows the types of media and the messages they give. The precision that direct marketing now offers is luring large firms such as Heinz and Lever Brothers, the UK arm of the Anglo-Dutch giant Unilever. Both firms see direct marketing as a more precise way to target individual consumers and have allocated large portions of their advertising budget to it.

The action of these two large companies is consistent with the view that manufacturers must become more aware of how important it is to strike a good balance between the advertising media they use. It has become obvious that television will be used more to build up brand awareness and company knowledge while direct marketing can be used to accurately pinpoint targeted consumers and gain immediate response.

Apart from the absolute precision afforded by direct marketing, other reasons why it is gaining in popularity, especially in America, is that the cost of advertising on television is very expensive, coupled with the fact that it is hard to calculate the cost-effectiveness of such television advertising. One solution is that an increasing number of firms are now experimenting with a form of direct marketing on television

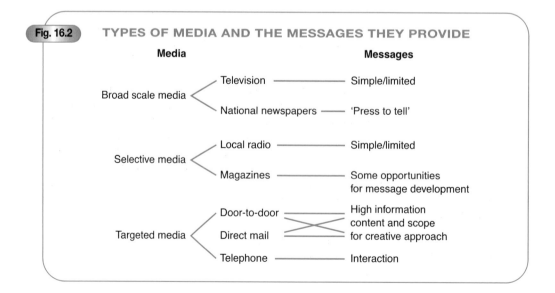

Fig. 16.2 TYPES OF MEDIA AND THE MESSAGES THEY PROVIDE

where advertisements are shown along with a freefone number that viewers can call to place orders for the product. In Britain on satellite/cable television such adverts are becoming commonplace; products recently advertised in this way include jewellery, kitchen knives and car polish.

When assessing media cost the role of 10 × applies. The following rule is a rough guide to costs.

1 Television can cost as little as £10 per thousand.
2 Magazines vary greatly but maybe cost £50 per thousand (5p each).
3 Direct mail is again ten times more expensive – £500 per thousand (50p per contact).
4 Telemarketing costs £5000 per thousand (£5 each contact).
5 Personal direct selling can be in excess of £50 per call.

However, it is not the cost that counts but the effectiveness. A telesales operation replacing regular weekly sales calls could save £45 per customer per call. But the sales call still produces more business so it is a real saving. On the other hand, if a well-targeted direct mail shot sent to a well-chosen segment brings more enquiries than from a magazine with a much larger circulation, there is a real gain. The gains are much greater and every reply adds information to the database, and can be used next time to improve the performance yet further. It is this constant development which really brings long-term gains in effective communications.

TARGETED MEDIA

Direct mail

The director of the European Direct Marketing Association (EDMA), Alena Hola, recently quoted in *Marketing Business* said, 'Some postal authorities do not seem to have grasped the fact that companies will only use direct mail if it is the most cost-effective, efficient and reliable tool available to sell their products.'

Technological change has become a threat to European postal authorities – the most lucrative customers have been seeking alternative ways of having their goods delivered. The fax machine is faster and less expensive than mail and is gaining in popularity as a new medium daily. Private carriers have also been gaining in popularity at the expense of the postal service. They have seen the opportunity to gain customers by offering extra services at no extra cost.

Some postal monopolies in Europe are being abolished in an effort to create a more efficient system. Sweden, whose postal monopoly was abolished in 1993, now has the most liberal postal system in Europe, with only 5 per cent of her mail sourced from individuals, the other 95 per cent coming either from business or direct mail.

Direct mail, despite having competition, has become more popular in recent years with over 2 billion items sent in the UK, and an expenditure of £945 million. In Britain the average household will receive about seven items of direct mail every month, but in other European countries this figure varies.

Mailing lists can come from various sources, for example:

● electoral register – geo-demographic selection;
● named subscribers to business magazines;
● companies classified by SIC code.

It is now possible to classify households by town, region, television area, type of property, lifestyle, income, spending habits, the drive time from retail outlets and even the number of pets, babies and plants in the house. This information revolution has led to direct marketing gaining customers as targeting can be very sophisticated. Whether this popularity will continue remains to be seen, but there is much ground to be covered by direct mail before much of Europe reaches the same levels of usage as the USA.

Telemarketing

As head of Direct Marketing and Sales Promotion at BT, Phil Mounsey has been quoted as saying, 'Telemarketing is the systematic use of the telephone to achieve business objectives in sales, customer care, market growth, promotions, market research, database building and cash flow management.'

QUESTIONS

1 Why was the 'Beanz Meanz WHO?' campaign so sucessful?

2 Explain the reason why it is said 'TV to sell, Press to tell'?

3 Why do organisations use direct marketing when it can cost a thousand times more than television for each person reached?

4 Why should an advertiser use an agency to create and place advertising?

FURTHER READING

Aakers, D.A and Myers, J.G., *Advertising Management*, 3rd Edn, Pretice Hall, 1987.
Advertising Association Marketing Pocket Book 1992, NTC Publications Ltd.
Beil, A.L., 'Strong brand – high spend', *Admap*, November 1990.
Bird, J., 'Pinpoint accuracy', *Marketing Business*, April 1992.
Boyd, P., 'Data Protection', *Marketing Business*, May 1992.
BT *Tele*marketing Handbook, 1993.
Coad, T., 'Can the EC Deliver Postal Harmony?', *Marketing Business*, February 1994.
Corstjens, J. (1990) *Strategic Advertising: A Practitioner's Handbook*, Heinemann, Oxford.
Coulson-Thomas, C.J., *Marketing Communications*, Heinemann, reprinted 1990.
Doyle, P. (1994) *Marketing Management and Strategy*, Prentice Hall International (UK) Ltd.
Fletcher, K, Wheeler, C. and Wright, J., 'The role and status of UK database marketing', *Quarterly Review of Marketing*, Autumn 1990.
Hart, N.A., *The Practice of Advertising*, Heinemann, 1990.
Howerd, W., *The Practice of Public Relations*, 3rd Edn, Heinemann, 1988.
Levitt, T., *The Marketing Imagination*, The Free Press, 1983.
Marketing, 30 June 1994.
Marketing, 14 July 1994.
Mazur, L, 'Silent Satisfaction', Interview with Philip Kotler, *Marketing Business*, December 1991.
Mercer, D, *Marketing*, Blackwell, 1992.
Miles, L, 'Going Solo', *Marketing Business*, June 1992.
Mueller, B. (1996) *International Advertising – Communicating Across Cultures*, Wadsworth Publishing/Thomson.
Oxley, M., *The Principles of Public Relations*, Kogan Page, 1989.
Rapps, S. and Collins, T., *Maxi-marketing*, McGraw-Hill, 1987.
Shaw, R. and Stone, M., *Database Marketing for Competitive Advantage*, Long Range Planning, 1987.
Wilmhurst, J, *The Fundamentals of Advertising*, Heinemann, 1985.

CASE STUDY

Giftworld Ltd

Giftworld Ltd are manufacturers of silverplated gifts and importers of other items to enlarge the range of products available to a wide range of customers. These customers ranged from a large supplier of thermal underwear who this year offered a small silverplated tray with their direct mailshots, through to many organisations who bought items to use as gifts for clients. In these latter cases Giftworld often used an in-house engraving facility to add the customer's name or logo to the gift so that it could be used as a key part of that customer's promotional plans.

Many regular customers place large orders at key occasions such as Christmas when over 60 per cent of all Giftworld's sales are made. Every February the company exhibits at the Birmingham International Spring Fair, held at the NEC which attracts over 90 000 trade visitors. This exhibition, together with advertisements in *Promotion and Incentive Magazine*, are the source of most new customer enquiries. However, many of the new customers only want gifts for Christmas, so there is an increasing problem of maintaining level of work for the rest of the year.

Over the last few years a silverplated 'Mother's Day' tray engraved 'For Mother' has been advertised in a number of consumer magazines and has proved successful both in the level of sales orders and because it fills the post-Christmas slack time in production, Mothering Sunday being in March. This product was the idea of one employee who remembered the immensely successful 'Coronation' tray unfortunately such high-profile events occur infrequently. Giftworld have also tried to market a 'wedding day' tray but this has proved less successful as weddings are not confined to one part of the year and the number of weddings has fallen to an all time low.

The problem Giftworld have is how to ensure they use their silverplating tank to its full capacity at the other times of the year. It is believed the mailshot by the thermal company will not be renewed in future years and so from March when the Mother's Day trays finish to September when production starts for Christmas orders there is the prospect of very little work, except low-value subcontracting orders.

When visiting this year's Frankfurt Gift Fair, the Sales Director established contacts with an Indian company which produces tea sets in brass ready to be finished by silverplating. These can be brought into the UK, plated and then sold as 'Made in the UK' because the final manufacturing process took place in England. The problem Giftworld have is that they do not have any sales contacts with companies who retail silverplated tea sets. The Giftworld name is not known in this market. The Indian supplier will only supply in full container loads, paid for in advance by irrevocable letter of credit. And there are only six months when the Giftworld silverplating operation is not fully used.

Question

You are recruited in the new role as Marketing Assistant reporting to the Sales Director. You have been asked to suggest what Giftworld should do with regards to the marketing and promotion of its products and potential new products.

CHAPTER 17

Publicity, Sales Promotion and Sponsorship

In every field of human endeavour, he that is first must perpetually live in the white light of publicity.

Theodore F. MacManus, 'The Penalty of Leadership'.
(*Saturday Evening Post*, 2 Jan 1915)

INTRODUCTION

This chapter brings together three separate elements of promotion. Publicity and sales promotion are part of the traditional promotional mix. Sponsorship is a form of promotion which must be viewed as an opportunity for publicity as well as a type of sales promotion. The expenditure on sponsorship has risen dramatically over the last decade but now organisations are trying to evaluate the return.

All these three forms of promotion are seen as effective but perhaps not excessively expensive. They all are difficult to evaluate and yet many case studies exist to show substantial benefits. It is therefore appropriate that this chapter considers all three ways of promoting an organisation or its products/services.

PUBLIC RELATIONS (PR) AND PUBLICITY

Advertising has been described as a primary method of communication which makes use of mass media. Publicity also uses mass media but the results are not directly controlled by the sender, and so it can be deemed a secondary communication for which no direct payment is made. This does not make publicity any less valuable, but it does mean it is sometimes harder to achieve a desired result.

Publicity is something that most people can recognise, but the recognition of publicity is often associated with famous people. Whatever well-known entertainers, politicians, or members of the royal family do in their private lives, it is soon reported in the press. It appears that publicity, in this sense, is strongest when it is regarding the personal lives of the people concerned. The general point is that any story has to appeal to the readers of the newspaper, otherwise it will not get printed. The same rule applies for any story which is not a 'paid-for advertisement', a point often forgotten by organisations. Any publicity item must contain issues of general interest to the readers or viewers, and not just to a particular organisation. Making a story relevant is one of the key skills of successful publicity specialists. The role of publicity, in a promotional budget, is to obtain positive and relevant mentions. These can be of most benefit if they are achieved to complement other promotional efforts. The definition of PR was given at the beginning of the last chapter, but will be repeated here:

PR is the deliberate, planned, and sustained effort to establish and maintain mutual understanding between an organisation and its publics.

Good media relations can also be of benefit to avoid unwelcome publicity. The best publicity specialists know the relevant newspaper editors well, so they are sometimes approached before an unfavourable story is published. In such a case it might be possible to mitigate the negative effects.

Publicity can be aimed at any of the stakeholder groups associated with an organisation. It is not restricted to customers, but can cover any of the other groups such as suppliers, employees, lenders, or the general public. The objectives of publicity can be any of the three roles of communication: informing, persuading or reinforcing.

In some situations there can be a direct link between advertising and publicity. Trade magazines will sometimes offer editorial coverage to a good advertiser, although the magazine will still retain editorial control. The issue of editorial freedom is very important to the major media. Editors and reporters would object strongly to any influence, whether to give positive mentions or suppress negative ones, from any organisation, even if it was a large purchaser of advertising space in a particular publication. Editorial opinion does carry more authority than 'paid-for advertising' because of the impartial nature of such comment. Some advertisers try to benefit from this by producing advertorials – adverts laid out in the same form as the editorial matter, with the heading 'advertising feature' written as small as allowed by the publication.

Areas of public relations activities

There are four major areas that can be relevant in achieving good public relations. These are:

- media relations;
- editorial and broadcast material;
- controlled communications;
- face-to-face events.

Media relations

Media relations involve taking news to the editors, taking editors to the news, creating relevant news stories and managing the news. Building good relationships with the media is obviously a benefit. The personal contact with editors is covered in the first two tasks above. The other two relate to the need to produce a regular supply of news items as part of the deliberate, planned and sustained publicity effort.

Editorial and broadcast material

Editorial and broadcast material is the 'product' of public relations. It covers press conferences, news releases, personal interviews, feature writing, case histories, press visits and journalist briefings. News releases and press conferences are the most commonly used methods of gaining publicity, but as you can see, there are many other techniques which can be used:

1 *Press conferences* A press conference is held in order to brief members of the media about a major news event. You might be familiar with these conferences being used by a political figure, or maybe by the police during an enquiry into a serious crime. The technique is equally applicable to PR for a company or product. Editors and feature writers receive many invitations to such events. They are, therefore, selective about which press conferences they choose to attend. The subject has to be particularly interesting or topical, or maybe the conference/presentation is attractive because it is held in an interesting location. The cider makers, H P Bulmer, used to own the steam engine, King George V. They used steam-train runs as a location for press conferences, and always found a willing audience.

2 *News releases* A news release is an item circulated to the media in the hope of getting it placed in a publication. It is the mainstay of publicity and, if published, can be of considerable value. Editorial matter is seen and read by more people than advertising in the same magazine or newspaper. The contents of an article also gain credibility by having the implied support of the publication. Whereas advertisements are seen for what they are, editorial comment is often considered objective and unbiased. The drawback of relying on publicity is that the editors decide what will be published and when it will appear. If a news release is set out in a way that is unsuitable for the publication, then it might be modified before insertion. This modification could change the balance and meaning of the release. The release could, of course, be rejected. Rejection is more likely with a major publication which is inundated with releases. Specialist journals, however, are often pleased to receive items about product successes, new contracts, innovations, export achievements or people in the industry. In some cases the specialist journals could be the best media to reach your target.

News releases are a 'one-way' communication, which do not give an opportunity for questions. Press conferences do give an opportunity for 'two-way' exchanges but only with the media editors, not with the eventual target audience. They are often used to support a news release where it is felt the story could be enhanced by contact.

Controlled communications

Controlled communications is the area of publicity material for company use. It includes annual reports, educational material, leaflets, audio-visual presentations, and any material that could be successfully placed to support organisational objectives. This low-cost material is a luxury for some organisations because of the time required to plan and prepare it. The benefits are even more difficult to measure than advertising or other main media publicity. But such channels should not be ignored. The less usual ways of reaching consumers could prove effective just because they offer a different approach.

Face-to-face events

These include other ways of reaching the chosen audience direct. Conferences, exhibitions, lectures, shopping centre events, demonstrations, open days, public visits and many more are examples of activities used to facilitate contact. The environment for such contact is a key ingredient. Then the event has to be structured to give the right level of interest, linked to the communication message, for the event to be considered worthwhile.

Exhibitions are an excellent way to present an organisation to its customers. They can be expensive, but can also be a simple, low-cost 'shell' construction. Whatever the cost, it is important to ensure that an exhibition is as effective as possible. This means being proactive in inviting visitors to your exhibition stand, rather than reactive, waiting for visitors to appear. The role of PR, as well as direct mail, in attracting visitors must not be ignored. The cost of such an exercise is only a small proportion of the cost of the exhibition as a whole, and usually is money well spent.

Financial and corporate PR

Financial PR has been given a separate section because it is a major area of importance to public 'quoted' companies. The share price of companies, and their financial credibility, cannot be separated from an organisation's trading success. The key measure with financial backers is confidence – the confidence the 'Money Men' have in the management of an organisation. This includes institutional investors, professional financial advisers and the financial media. It is naive to suggest an organisation is judged by its published performance. The role of financial PR is to directly influence the relevant individuals and institutions, and to develop good relationships with them. The media used are highly specialised, including the use of screen-based electronics news – the CNS (company news service) established by the Stock Exchange. Because this is so specialised it is perhaps outside the scope of this book.

In-house or agency?

The decision on whether to handle PR internally, or to appoint an agency, can depend on the way PR is perceived. In a small organisation it is often the Managing Director who takes control, but there are three other options: to train an existing manager to handle PR; to appoint professional PR staff; and to use an external agency. It is always possible to use a combination of these options to deal with the planned programme. However, there are always the unplanned events which have to be handled in-house. Just as every member of staff is a part-time marketer, so they are also all part-time PR people – anyone can accept an incoming enquiry from the media. In some 'sensitive' industries, for instance Nuclear Electric, there are nominated executives who are trained in dealing with tough media reporters, and all incoming enquiries are routed to these selected managers.

For the basic decision on in-house or agency PR the trade-off is between intimate knowledge of the company, its products and services, and the wide range of experience and objective advice from a PR consultancy. A compromise is often used whereby a small PR department, or just one nominated individual, works with an external agency, the agency being paid a retainer related to the task required.

The advantages and disadvantages of publicity

Advantages

Publicity should be an important but subtle part of the promotional mix, not just an adjunct to advertising. The most important advantages to be gained are:

● *Credibility* If the public are made aware of the benefits to be gained from a company's products from an independent source, and that source is not being paid by the company in question, then the credibility factor is that much greater.

- *Greater readership* When glancing through a newspaper it is seldom that a great deal of attention is primarily paid to advertisements. Much more attention is given to editorial or news sections. Similarly, people are more likely to divert attention from the television to do other things while the advertisements are being shown.

- *Contain more information* Publicity is able to impart more information to the public than advertisements can. A glance is all that is usually given to an advertisement, whereas publicity, when presented as news, is given more attention and is therefore able to contain much more detailed information.

- *Cost benefits* No direct payments are made to the media for publicity. There are obviously costs involved, but PR budgets are far less than those for advertising.

- *Speed* Publicity has an advantage of speed. Information on a major development can often be issued and reported in a short space of time. Publicity can also be flexible and reactive.

Disadvantages

Publicity is generally looked upon as being of benefit, but sometimes both companies, and famous personalities, wish that they could avoid publicity. If there is a major accident on the premises of a company, or an oil leak from one of the oil companies' installations offshore, that company will be on the receiving end of some very bad publicity. They can try to minimise this by breaking the news to the media themselves, and being as helpful as possible, but damage to their reputation will still be incurred.

- *Message distortion* A company has no control over what the media report about them. A press release, which a company hopes is reported in full, may in fact not be used at all, or may have only a small portion of it reported. If the publicity given is untrue or libellous, of course, the organisation will have recourse through the judicial system, but such action is expensive, and creates a difficult situation for the future. With good relations, and a good understanding of the type of release required, the risk of distortion can be dramatically reduced.

- *Repetition* With advertisements a company can ensure that there is frequency of the message. Publicity does not have this advantage and the message may only be given once, if at all.

INTRODUCTION TO SALES PROMOTION

Sales promotions have grown in importance during the last two decades. In part this has been a reaction to the ever-increasing cost of media advertising (higher than the rate of inflation); and in part it has been a reflection of the effectiveness of sales promotions in creating additional sales in a very direct manner. The Advertising Standards Authority's (ASA) Code of Sales Promotion defines sales promotion as:

> those Marketing techniques, which are used, usually on a temporary basis, to make goods and services more attractive to the consumer by providing some additional benefit whether in cash or in kind.

The code covers such forms of promotions as: premium offers of all kinds; reduced price and free offers; the distribution of vouchers, coupons, and samples; personality promotions; charity-linked promotions; and prize promotions of all types. In fact, almost any promotion that is not main media advertising or publicity can be grouped under the general heading of sales promotion.

The term 'below the line' is applied to sales promotion as opposed to 'above the line' for advertising. However, both sales promotion and advertising are key parts of the promotions mix. There was a time when advertising agencies were critical of the use of promotions. Now 'below the line' techniques have become increasingly sophisticated and effective; they are seen as an important complement to advertising. In fact, many campaigns use advertising to support promotions. Also promotional offers, while not slavishly following the 'above the line' theme, are often chosen to support the brand positioning.

There is a difference between promotions that really do benefit the promotional message and those that just bring forward sales to an earlier period. The latter is described by market research company Neilsen, as 'mortgaging' of future sales. This occurs if no overall sales increase is achieved. That is, the increase during the promotion is lost by lower than expected sales in following periods. Another criticism of sales promotion is that they can be easily copied by competitors. In this case a vicious circle, similar to a price war, can occur. A recent article on the cost of sales promotion by John Philip Jones said this vicious circle is described at Unilever as:

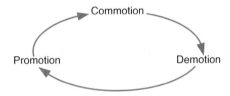

Jones considers the role of promotion in a large number of mature markets which exhibit what he calls the lack of market vitality, as growth rates decline. He suggests that if:

> after giving advertising every chance, there is no perceptible short- or long-term effect . . . [then] manufacturers should cut their losses. A brand can be maintained in effective distribution by a minimal level of promotional support and with only enough theme advertising to keep the brand name in front of the sales force and the retail trade. And sometimes no theme advertising at all.

The implicit objective that long-term profitability is the main aim, is fine. But there can be other marketing objectives. However, when products reach the later stages of their life cycles, the suggestion that some mature products should receive minimal support is a consistent marketing strategy. Doyle's article on the product life cycle and marketing strategy suggests marketing expenditure should be reduced. The emphasis should be on brand loyalty and the defence of market share. Within this, good sales promotion, rather than poorly thought-out short-term offers, do give an extra dimension. The problem is how to choose the right mix of promotions to meet the need of a given brand. To make some sense of the chaotic variety of sales promotions they have been grouped to reflect the target market:

- consumers;
- trade customers/intermediaries;
- sales force incentives.

Consumer promotions

Most sales promotions make one of the three ageless appeals: Save! Win! Free! There are several satellite appeals, too: Give! Now! Fun! Reassurance! The motivations appear to lie deep in the human psyche, and show themselves in many forms in our society:

- most people like a bargain;
- most people will jump at something for nothing;
- most people like to indulge some skill, or 'have a flutter'.

This was how Chris Petersen, an early practitioner of sales promotion, started a chapter of his book, *Sales Promotion in Action*. Although published in 1979 it captures the essence of consumer promotions. Of course, Petersen is talking about the various themes used in promotions. For a promotion to be suitable it must be consistent with the overall objectives of an organisation. These are often listed as:

1 *Extra sales volume* The original aim of sales promotion, it is usually short-term, but extra profitable sales is the ultimate aim of most commercial organisations.
2 *Point-of-sale impact* Linked to increased volume, this objective is to gain maximum exposure at the time of purchase and at the point of decision on whether and what to buy. The joint tasks of persuasion and reinforcement can be enhanced by effective point-of-sale promotion.
3 *Repeat purchase* The role of marketing as described in this book is building satisfying exchanges with customers. These will, hopefully, lead to increased levels of repeat purchase as well as gaining product advocates who will recommend a particular brand. Techniques such as collector schemes which build ongoing repeat business can lead to developments of future habits and loyalty.
4 *Sample purchase or product trial* One of the most difficult marketing jobs is to get people to try a new product, ranging from the test driving of a car to the sampling of a new chocolate bar. If a potential customer tries a product then at least they can evaluate the product properly. They might like it, or consider it is not as good as their current product. But trial is far superior as a basis of consumer judgement to ill-informed customers who have never tried the product.

Malcolm McDonald suggested a more structured classification based on direct versus indirect appeal, and whether the offer was based on money, goods or services (*see* Table 17.1).

Money-based consumer promotions

Money is the most widely acceptable type of offer but it suffers from the criticism of short-termism described by Jones. For instance, goods might not appeal, as not every purchaser wants the item offered. But, by offering 'money off' the purchaser is presumed to make a saving. They can, therefore, decide what to do with that saving, while the value of the product is enhanced. Money can be offered: directly as a price-cut; indirectly as a coupon linked to a product purchase; or as a money prize in a competition where proof of product purchase is required.

However, there are problems with both coupons and competitions. Some supermarket groups will accept coupons without the customer purchasing the relevant item. This negates much of the benefit from a coupon promotion. Competitions are controlled by the Lotteries and Amusement Act (1976), one of a number of legislative controls affecting sales promotions. Such laws can cause problems for ill-informed organisations.

Table 17.1 ● A classification of direct and indirect appeal of promotional materials

	Direct	Indirect
Money	Price reduction	Coupons Money equivalent Competitions
Goods	Free goods Premium goods Free gifts Trade-in offers	Stamps Coupons Vouchers Money equivalents Competitions
Services	Guarantees Group participation and events Special exhibitions and displays	Cooperative advertising Stamps Vouchers for services Event admission Competition

The four major problems of 'money off' promotions are:

1 They are expensive, with the reduction in revenue coming directly from profit.
2 A significant proportion of customers are 'price-off' buyers who buy only during the reductions.
3 Regular price reductions can damage the quality image of a product or company.
4 'Money-off' promotions are easily copied by competitors.

However, in a competitive marketplace, it can be difficult to resist competitive pressure. For example Marks & Spencer for many years refused to run 'money-off' sales. With the problems of retail volume they now compete with other major department stores running sales events.

'Money-off' schemes are appropriate in many situations such as to create sampling of products. In launching a new food product the first requirement is to get potential customers to try it. A coupon or reduced price will help to achieve this. These offers can also encourage possible multiple purchases. Another use of 'money off' is to bring purchases forward – for example, an early booking discount for holiday booking. In another context, however, the example below shows a problem with this type of promotion.

'Money-off' promotions are widely used, but perhaps they are the easiest promotion to criticise due to the obvious problems. Therefore, such promotions should be used very selectively, and certainly not be an automatic first-choice method.

Goods- or merchandise-based consumer offers

Value can be offered by goods and merchandise, without the same risk of damaging brand images. For example, free product (500 grammes extra free) costs relatively little to producers, and certainly does not change pricing structures. Also, merchandise can be bought in bulk at very heavy discounts. Consequently, excellent offers can be made either free or what is called 'self-liquidating' (i.e. at cost). By linking to purchases of the main brand then promotions can build brand loyalty and repeat purchase in a very direct way.

The fertilisers division of a major international chemical company used to encourage early purchase by offering an early purchase discount every year. Fertiliser is used primarily in the spring when it has maximum effect. One year sales were lagging so much that, in spite of the earlier price promotion for early orders, the company dropped prices dramatically during the season. Early purchasers were in fact worse off. Next year the early promotion was a disaster as customers had lost complete confidence in the company and its quality image. The fertiliser division never recovered from this effect.

It was suggested earlier that goods/merchandise might not appeal because the item offered might not be desired by the target customers. It is a risk, although it is possible to offer a range of items. One example of this is a choice from a catalogue offered by a major petrol company. The mechanics of the promotion is that sales are recorded in the form of points recorded on a swipe card. The points are then exchanged for a wide range of products, from a catalogue. This is just one attempt to offer value, and also to reduce the problem of restricted choice.

In considering how promotional offers influence behaviour, ask your student friends why they chose to open a bank account at a particular bank. It might be the convenient location of the branches, the overdraft limit, the fact that their families use that bank, or the promotional offer made. It could be that more than one issue influenced the decision, but it would be interesting to find out the role of the promotional offer.

EXERCISE

All major banks in Britain make offers to encourage students to open an account. Check the offers from leading banks. Do banks in other countries offer similar inducements? Ask a group of students to see what offers they value most.

The offers made by banks to attract students are often well chosen and very relevant to the needs of this group. The choice of offers is very important to the success of any promotion. You will be able to find evidence of this in many of your local retail outlets. However, sometimes the promotional offer can give problems which reflect badly on the product being promoted. Some years ago a brand of table jelly offered a 'free goldfish' as a promotion. Major problems resulted in dead fish being delivered to customers, and the resultant complaints affected the brand concerned. The Code of Sales Promotion Practice is particular on the subject of suitability of promotional products:

Promoters shall not offer promotional products which are of a nature likely to cause offence, or products which, in the context of the promotion, may reasonably be considered to be socially undesirable.

Particular care should be taken in the distribution of free samples to ensure that children or other particularly vulnerable groups are not harmed.

Consumers should not be led to over-estimate the quality or desirability of promotional products. Particular care should be exercised where the recipient has no opportunity to examine goods before taking delivery.

It might be interesting to find some current promotions and see how they adhere to the code.

Services as promotion

Promotions of this type are very varied: a guarantee, or a 'no-quibble' exchange are excellent in building strong positions in markets; new retail store openings, often featuring a major personality, can create high initial awareness; famous authors signing their books can draw large crowds; charity-linked promotions can show a brand as caring (for example, by linking with the Save the Children Fund). The scope is enormous. Events and sponsorship might be covered in part under this heading, although they also come under publicity. The subject of sponsorship cuts across all three areas of consumer, trade and sales force and so have been included in a separate section at the end of this chapter.

The benefit from services promotions is usually the provision of additional and specific benefits (added value), point-of-sale impact and enhanced product personalities. In many cases the benefits are qualitative and difficult to measure. But the effect they can have will usually last for longer than a short-term 'money-off' deal.

Industrial and trade promotions

This sector of business-to-business promotion can be subdivided into:

1 Industrial customers who are users of a product.
2 Trade intermediaries who sell the product on.

The first group will be receptive to some of the techniques discussed above under 'Consumer promotions'. However, the person who raises the sales order, in an industrial company, is not always the end user, nor necessarily the influencer of the purchase decision. It is therefore very important to understand the role and position of the person who could receive the promotional benefit. There is a problem of deciding what is fair promotion and what is bribery!

EXAMPLES

- An executive collects 'Air-miles' from his company travel trips. Should he use the benefits for company business or his next family holiday?
- A purchasing manager has placed a series of good orders with your organisation. You give that purchasing manager an expensive desk diary, embossed with your organisation logo. Is this good promotion?
- A purchasing manager has placed a series of good orders with your organisation. You are offering a free case of whisky for large orders. Should the purchasing manager receive the whisky for his personal consumption?

There are many other examples and they all start because the expenditure and purchase order is from the customer company, but the promotion is often received by an employee of that company. The Code of Sales Promotion practice states:

> No trade incentive which is directed towards employees should be such as to cause any conflict with their duty to their employer, or their obligations to give honest advice to the consumer.

Similar dilemmas are faced with respect to trade intermediaries. But where do you classify a meal purchased by a sales representative, who invites a buyer to that person's favourite (expensive) restaurant as a 'reward' for a particularly large order?

The ethical issues are brought into sharp focus because of the clash of people and their employing organisations. It is worth considering the type of promotional objectives a supplier organisation might have with respect to trade buyers. Writing about the promotion of durable products, Quelch *et al.* suggested objectives might be:

1 To persuade existing outlets to:
   – maintain existing floor/shelf space;
   – stock additional models or promotional versions;
   – provide additional floor/shelf space;
   – provide special displays and features;
   – increase inventories of a specific brand.
2 To persuade new outlets to stock a brand.
3 To insulate the trade from consumer-price negotiations at the point-of-purchase.
4 To insulate the trade from a temporary sales reduction that might be caused by an increase in price.
5 To compensate the trade when the traditional retail margins have been eroded by price competition.
6 To identify which items in a product range the dealer should push during particular periods.

While Quelch's article discussed durable products, this list could equally well apply to non-durable products. Petersen suggests the objectives of promoting to a retailer are:

- to gain, and/or to consolidate, distribution;
- to achieve required stock levels in outlets;
- to get display and other activity around the brand;
- to get noticed by the retailer.

All of these objectives can be satisfied by the category of 'push' techniques which typifies many sales promotions. The types of promotion aimed at an industrial or trade buyer can again be: money-based; goods/merchandise-based; or services-based. McDonald (1984) lists some specific techniques in his book, *Marketing Plans*. The detailed study of such techniques could be, however, the subject for a book in its own right.

Tailored promotions

Many organisations sell to a mix of different intermediaries. A 'tailored promotion' is a promotional offer that is made to a particular intermediary. It is a highly focused strategy, chosen to apply to a single customer, or small segment. The promotion is designed to meet the specific objectives the supplier might have towards that particular segment.

Such a promotion could be a general offer of the sort already discussed, such as a 'money-off' deal with a particular customer only. But this sort of deal can cause real friction with other customers, if they feel they are losing out. 'Tailored promotions' are most relevant to major customers, or ones that could be significant. For such outlets a promotion specifically designed for that outlet has a strong appeal. It could link a consumer promotion with trade incentives but still restrict the offer to a particular intermediary. The use of techniques which are wider than 'money-off' promotions with a particular intermediary has a definite appeal. For instance, a drinks company will run special events with individual public houses to promote new products. Alternatively, a cosmetics company could offer the services of a trained beauty consultant to a particular department store in return for extra sales.

Tailored promotions can involve a similar level of effort to national promotions. However, the return in sales could be higher and they can certainly be used to help build relationships with the intermediaries.

SPONSORSHIP

A promotional offer can be something tangible like 'money off' or a free gift. It can also be less tangible, for example in the form of an endorsement. Sporting equipment is often enhanced by the endorsement of a world-class performer, e.g. Nick Faldo Golf Clubs. Such products are able to sell at premium prices due to the association with a personality. The link here is direct and the benefit to the product is obvious. In return the personality will be paid for the endorsement.

From this point, it is a small jump to associating a personality with an unrelated product. The personality does not need to be a famous sportsperson, it could just as easily be Mr Men Yoghurts. The attraction of the character makes the product more acceptable to target consumers. The exchange process is apparent in both these situations with visible benefits to the products from the 'halo' effect of the association. It can also work effectively when a company name is displayed on sporting equipment, e.g. Benetton Formula One racing cars.

However, companies must also be aware that there can be a down side if the personality sponsored suffers some bad publicity; this in turn can be reflected on the product.

A definition of sponsorship might be:

Sponsorship takes place when a payment, either in financial or natural terms, is given in return for some consideration or benefit. Sponsorship should give benefit to both parties.

There are other definitions of sponsorship but many fail to grasp the exchange process and the WIIFM (what's in it for me?) factor. This definition includes endorsements and related product links, but the growth in sponsorship has come from deals linking all sorts of companies and brands to sport or the arts. Sport is generally thought to account for the major sponsorship expenditure; this includes the sponsorship of major events, teams and individual performers.

In 1994 an example of sponsorship at its best occurred in Lillehammer, Norway, in preparation for the Winter Olympics. The Olympic Committee were faced with preparing all that would be required to ensure that everything would be in place and working in time. The first step the Olympic Committee took was to prepare a detailed budget for the infrastructure and then to invite companies with environmental concerns to bid for the work.

There were two ways in which the companies could join this select group:

(a) Donate a large amount of cash which then gave the company the right to use the Olympic logo.

(b) Supply at budget level (or less) the infrastructure required, e.g. arenas (the balance between the company's bid and the budgeted amount in effect being the donation).

The companies who were successful gained the following advantages:

● the use of the Olympic logo for a four-year period;
● the status of being a successful company capable of completing a job on time and to a high standard;
● the right to invite 'guests' to the Olympics where transport was by accredited bus and hospitality was provided by the company in special accredited VIP tents with excellent facilities.

The high profile and reputation the 'sponsoring' companies gained from this will hold them in good stead with customers for many years. Customers will remember the special event and hospitality received and hopefully repay the company by placing orders with them in the future.

Sponsorship benefits

When considering sponsorship as part of a promotional campaign an organisation must assess the benefit they receive for the money spent. First must be the 'extra dimension' gained by association with a person or an event. The very act of sponsoring says something about a sponsor in a way no advertisement can. However, there are other positive advantages. Sponsorship can offer real opportunities for advertising or PR. In fact, one rule of thumb suggests a company shall spend as much again on publicity as they commit to the basic sponsorship. But the chance to gain publicity at a prearranged time can be very valuable. Media coverage, especially television, can be gained for products. This is only a small part of sponsorship, although it might be the area with which most people are familiar.

Sponsoring an event could give a company publicity but could also give them an opportunity to link to corporate hospitality. Inviting major customers to 'the company event' is much stronger than other events. Special ticket allowances are common practice. Promotional opportunities featuring the sponsor link can extend to merchandise, e.g. golf umbrellas. It will certainly be featured on event-related material. The link could go further so that key personalities meet customers or visit employees. Employee interest can also be enhanced if they have a team or event to follow. Again tickets can be used very effectively.

The key to successful sponsorship is to make it fun for all concerned; also to view sponsorship as a partnership which can yield benefits for a significant period of time, as was the case with the Norwegian Olympic Games 1994.

The future for sponsorship

The benefits from any sponsorship deal should be quantifiable. IBM sponsored the Atlanta Olympics, and is reported to have spent $40m (£26m) over a four-year period in almost two hundred countries, the payback was that it sold $540m (£346m) of product because of that spend. It has also been announced that IBM and MasterCard are planning to sponsor the Sydney Olympics, while MasterCard will also sponsor the World Cup in France in 1998.

The real future for successful sponsorship is for companies to undertake it only when they are able to integrate it into the marketing mix, without this the chances of a good payback to the sponsoring firm are very slim.

Sponsorship and promotional planning

Sponsorship should not be considered as a cheap alternative to media advertising. In most cases it is not done as a way to circumvent advertising restrictions. Sponsorship is not something to be offered to the first interesting project you are offered.

The first thing in all areas of promotion and communication is to sort out clear objectives. Sponsorship can become a link between all the elements of the promotion mix – advertising, publicity, sales promotion and selling. It provides a theme which can be exploited in many ways. However, sponsorship is expensive in terms of time, money and people. To benefit fully, an organisation must clearly know what it is trying to achieve and where it is now. If the aim is to enhance the corporate image, then first explore what is the current perception of your organisation and, also, of the intended sponsee. Then follow up by exploring if the link is credible. In fact some large companies, such as Siemens in Germany and Elf in France, take a more strategic long-term view with regard to sponsorship and have fully structured foundations in place to fund cultural, scientific or humanitarian works, enabling them to blaze a philanthropic trail in foreign markets.

One issue often forgotten is the effect of ending a sponsorship deal. The end can receive as much publicity as the commencement. The announcement that your company has decided not to renew a sponsorship needs to be handled well or the negative publicity could undo all the positive benefits previously achieved. But, perhaps the biggest risk with sponsorship is that it is a very difficult area to predict. It is difficult to forecast the level of media coverage. It is difficult to forecast the way an event or a personality will interact with a company or brand name. It is difficult to know if the target audience will see, and respond, to the sponsors. Nevertheless many organisations are prepared to take this 'risk' because the 'return' from successful sponsorship can be substantial.

CONCLUSION

Advertising is not the only way to promote a company or its products. All techniques need to be considered together in order to deliver a sustained and regular series of planned messages to target audiences. The objective of the communication element in a general marketing decision is derived from the overall marketing objectives. The delivery of the messages is a specialised function requiring highly skilled functional people. There are so many messages being broadcast that it is difficult to stand out from other communications. Creativity is needed to deliver a message that grabs attention and leads to action. Therefore no organisation should fail to consider the rich variety available with publicity, promotion and sponsorship.

QUESTIONS

1 How does corporate PR differ from publicity for a product?

2 What are the advantages and disadvantages of price-based sales promotions?

3 How might an organisation evaluate the success of a sales promotion?

4 Suggest a successful sponsorship, and explain why you consider it to be successful.

5 In what ways has the ending of a sponsorship affected the organisation?

FURTHER READING

Bend, D. (1994) 'Sponsors' sporting chance', *Marketing*, 7 July.

Bidlake, S. (1992) 'M&S in pricing U-turn', *Marketing*, 27 August.

British Code of Sales Promotion Practice, Advertising Standards Authority, Code of Advertising Practice (CAP) Committee, September 1984.

Curtis, J. (1997) 'Fear of the Unknown', *Marketing*, 6 February.

Howerd, W. (1988) *The Practice of Public Relations*, 3rd Edn, Heinemann, London.

Jones, J. P. (1990) 'The double jeopardy of sales promotion', *Harvard Business Review*, September–October.

McDonald, M. (1984) *Marketing Plans*, Heinemann, London.

Mercer, D. (1992) *Marketing*, Blackwell.

Miles, L. (1992) 'Going solo', *Marketing Business*, June.

Oxley, M. (1989) *The Principles of Public Relations*, Kogan Page, London.

Petersen, C. (1979) *Sales Promotion in Action*, Associated Business Press.

Quelch, J. A., Neslin, S. A. and Olson, L. B. (1987) 'Opportunities and risks of durable goods promotion', *Sloan Management Review*, Winter.

CASE STUDY

Sports sponsorship

The Rover Junior Tennis Initiative

Companies are increasingly seeing sport as a vehicle for promoting the name and personality of their products and organisation. In recent years the Rover Group have involved themselves in three main areas of sports sponsorship: ocean racing, golf and tennis.

Each sport is chosen for a variety of reasons, and in the case of Rover with a particular objective. The ocean racing is aimed at raising the profile and awareness of the brand on a European and international level. The golf sponsorship is targeted at local dealerships, who 'buy-in' to a particular package that leads to 'golf competition days' which can ultimately lead to paid golfing holidays abroad. The focus of this short case is on the Rover involvement with tennis.

The Rover Junior Tennis Initiative (Rover JTI) aims to find future champions by fostering British tennis talent at an early stage. The Rover JTI is a nationwide junior tennis development programme funded jointly by the Lawn Tennis Association (LTA) and Rover Cars. The scheme was launched at Wimbledon in 1990 under the directorship of Mark Cox.

Directed at the 10–16 age group, the scheme aims to raise the overall standard of tennis by specifically:

- targeting and selecting juniors (10–16 years) at a much younger age than previously;
- focusing on individual coaching as opposed to squads;
- creating a complete technical coaching, physical training and competitive tournament structure for each player, supported by an individual private coach.

The Rover JTI programme is aimed at the grass roots of talented players and represents an ongoing commitment. The Programme is reported to cost in total between £750 000 and £1 million per year and is funded jointly by the LTA and Rover. This money could have been spent on other sports or on more high profile 'one-off' tennis events such as the Stella Artois at Queens, though the company is reported to have expressed a preference for a sponsorship avenue with longer-term development potential, and firmly associated with youth and vitality. The company was also concerned to support an initiative that reflected and perhaps reinforced its marque values of tenacity, winning and leadership.

Question

Adopting the perspective of the corporate sponsor, what marketing returns or payoffs might be expected from this sponsorship scheme? How might such returns be projected, planned, monitored and evaluated?

(Case idea supplied by Jeff Clowes, Coventry University.)

CHAPTER 18

Selling

*I have heard of a man who had a mind to sell his house,
and therefore carried a piece of brick in his pocket, which he showed
as a pattern to encourage purchasers.*

Jonathan Swift (1667–1745)

INTRODUCTION

It is often easy to confuse selling and marketing. This is because the two disciplines are linked in many companies and sales marketing functions are easily found. But selling is not the same as marketing. It is, however, a key part of the marketing role and many of the skills of a good salesperson in understanding customers are required by good marketers.

The publicity material for a national sales training roadshow suggests that, 'No matter what business you are in, there are people out there waiting to buy. Lots of them. All you have to do is to find them before your competitors do.' There is nothing wrong with this statement if it is then developed into the full range of marketing activities as discussed in the previous chapters of this book. That is:

- identify target customers;
- discover needs;
- develop ways of fulfilling those needs.

Where it could go wrong is if the presenter lives up to one description as the Mohammed Ali of the selling profession. Selling is not a way of beating your opponents by having the biggest punch. Selling is:

- identifying target customers;
- discovering needs;
- matching offerings with needs.

This sequence is almost identical to the one above regarding marketing. Both have an element: 'find needs – fill them'. The differences are that marketing can usually work with all resources of a company, and aim to create satisfying exchanges with all potential customers. The offer mix of product, price and distribution can be planned by the marketer to be acceptable, affordable and available. In fact, a good marketing organisation will focus the entire company on its customers, with a medium- or long-term perspective.

Selling is more of a micro-relationship. The product is often given and restrictions on price and distribution can exist. The salesperson has less flexibility with the offer, and has to get sales now. But immediate sales are often made possible by existing relationships. What a salesperson must do is build on these personal relationships. They can do this by:

- augmenting product delivery in an appropriate way;
- creating a more receptive attitude from potential customers by using a combination of information and persuasion.

The idea of a sales orientation was introduced in Chapter 1. Direct selling is a widely used way of reaching individual customers and can be defined as:

> **the process of identifying potential customers, informing them of a company's offer mix, and finding a match between the benefits offered and customers' needs through personal communication.**

Selling is very much part of the communication mix. It is two-way and personal. This means salespeople have the maximum opportunity to find the connection between benefits and needs, and so to persuade the customer to change needs into wants.

Sales representatives are company advocates to the customer. But they can also be customer advocates whose detailed knowledge can be fed back to their company regarding future opportunities. Therefore, while selling is not marketing, it is wholly consistent with marketing. It is simply that part of marketing which deals with individual contacts with customers, and short-term achievement of sales with an existing offer mix.

THE SCOPE OF SELLING

To illustrate the major variations to be found within the sales occupation, Moncrief (1988) identified five distinct categories of industrial sales jobs, differing in terms of industrial setting and technical complexity, sales relationships and seniority. Taking still wider perspective of the sales field, Lidstone (1994) has proposed nine categories of sales position, ranging from inside order takers in retail outlets, 'missionary salespeople' undertaking more indirect sales-building duties, and technical salespeople selling industrial components and equipment, to highly skilled sales negotiators selling to specialist purchasing committees, senior executives and project terms.

Notwithstanding such diversity, it is likely that most proactive sales positions (excluding therefore more passive indoor selling) are likely to have in common the following key activities:

- prospecting or cold calling;
- selling;
- account maintenance and development.

Prospecting or cold calling

The role of these prospectors is to seek out new customers, establish contacts, and determine needs. They also need to identify the decision makers and influencers who must be convinced if a sale is to be made. These salespeople work in the early pre-transactional stage with a new customer.

The skills required in finding potential new customers are very different from building relationships with existing customers. It is much harder to persuade a customer to buy for the first time than to get a repeat order from a satisfied customer. This is because it involves an element of the unknown.

Even if the customer knows the company or product, they may have to be convinced to change from a competitive product. Prospectors have to deal with customers who say they are not interested. They have to move these potential customers into making a first appointment. Having achieved this, they must remember that they never get a second chance to make a first impression. This is why one group of potential customers – lapsed users and former customers – can be even more difficult to win back. Former customers already know your company and its products but have decided to trade with your competitors. It may be a simple evaluation of product features and price which a new offer mix would change. It may, however, be that your company let the customer down, gave poor service or somehow upset the relationship. Undoing the past can be much more difficult than starting from a situation where nothing is known.

Perhaps the most powerful weapon a prospector can use is personal recommendation. When contacting a new customer it can help if you can say that an existing customer suggested the contact. In some industries, such as life assurance, the salespeople are trained to follow up with existing customers to get recommendations to new prospects. Life assurance is a product that is not purchased regularly, so salespeople are always trying to find suitable new prospects who have reached the right stage in their life cycles to require the product.

Selling

This is the transactional stage. A customer could be:

- a 'hot prospect' – someone who is close to making a first purchase decision with your organisation;
- an occasional customer, who conducts limited business with you;
- a regular repeat customer; or
- an advocate who goes out of his or her way to trade with you.

The transactional stage is the most important as far as current performance is concerned because current sales are what keeps the organisation going. The process of making a sale is discussed later, because it is not solely the application of persuasive skills.

In some situations the customer comes to buy, for instance in a retail outlet or a visit to a manufacturer's factory. Here the salesperson has an advantage in that they are working in a familiar location. The disadvantage for retail sales staff is that they often have no knowledge of the potential customer, the customer background, or any previous history of a transaction with that particular customer. The salesperson has to find this out by suitable questioning.

In other situations, the sales representative or sales engineer can be visiting the customer. The seller will have researched the customer, have some knowledge of the customer needs and the previous history of transactions. But the customer will be on home territory. The salesperson has gone to sell. Issues such as the salespersons' attitudes, their beliefs in their products as well as their negotiation or persuasion skills are relevant in achieving success when selling. Chapter 2 included a short case study on the day of a travelling salesman. It will be apparent from this that the time spent actually face to face with a customer is comparatively short – sometimes less than 10 per cent of the salesperson's day. There are many other roles, like administration, that a salesperson needs to do. The need to make the contact time most effective is a critical role of a professional seller.

A good salesperson will have objectives for each individual customer. These objectives will lead to an individual strategy for the sales contact period with the customer. Such objectives could be:

- for a new customer/hot prospect – an objection that has to be overcome;
- for an occasional user – to discover why they are not regular customers and find ways of increasing sales frequency;
- for a regular customer – to introduce an additional product line to complement existing purchases.

The objectives and strategy should be thought out in advance, but the very nature of personal selling means that issues will be raised during a meeting that will require the plan to be modified. In this situation salespeople are on their own. They are the representatives of their organisation to the customer. They cannot continually refer back to Head Office for instructions, and so must fully understand the flexibility that they may have to vary the offer mix. They must beware that they do not make promises that cannot be kept, such as priority delivery dates. Of course they can make offers and promises that are possible. It is in this situation that a salesperson can be said to be at the sharp end of a company's operations.

Account maintenance and development

The building of relationships with customers is the key to future profitable sales. Therefore the process does not normally finish with a successful sale. Post-transactional activities start with successful, on time, delivery, but move through to many activities which forge strong relationships for the future. These could go as far as using computerised marketing, and even distribution data to track relationships. Such benefits can be part of what is now called direct marketing. It could mean establishing electronic links for future reordering such as that which links the production planning department of JCB excavators to its suppliers, to really produce 'just-in-time' ordering; or it could mean a simple note in a diary for a follow-up meeting. Figure 18.1 shows the continuum from a sale taken in a competitive market through to a close relationship, contractual link or dealing with an in-house supplier.

Losing customers is much easier than winning customers. The consulting firm Bain and Company has researched the situation, and concluded an increase of 2 per cent in the retention rate has the same effect on profits as cutting costs by 10 per cent – a worthwhile target. In cruder terms *Business Week* suggested:

> Smart selling means building relationships with customers, not just slam-dunking them on a single sale.

The elements of what is sometimes called relationship marketing were given by Christopher, Payne and Ballantyne as:

- focus on customer retention;
- orientation on product benefits;
- long timescale;

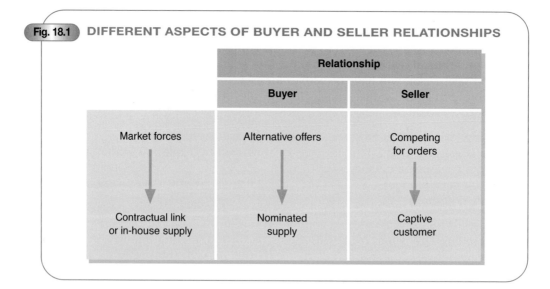

Fig. 18.1 DIFFERENT ASPECTS OF BUYER AND SELLER RELATIONSHIPS

- high customer service emphasis;
- high customer commitment;
- high customer contact;
- quality is the concern of all.

It can be seen that in the building of strong relationships there is a key role for personal salespeople.

THE PRINCIPLES OF SELLING

The role of a salesperson is often that of a solitary representative of an organisation, who visits other organisations. There are occasions and industries where team selling is appropriate (and, of course, there is the related issue of sales management), but many of the half million UK salespeople work alone. The different roles of selling were discussed in the previous section, but, for all groups, the principal role is to be an effective link between a supplier organisation and a potential customer.

The stereotype salesperson, depicted by Arthur Miller in his play *Death of a Salesman*, is a back-slapping, joke-telling individual who drops in each season to present products. This is still a reality in some industries and can be a relevant way of doing business in some instances. But, at a cost in excess of £50 for each sales call, it is a very expensive way of communicating with customers. There are many other ways of bringing products to the notice of customers.

The principle of personal selling is that personal contact is a very powerful way of communicating. Blake and Mouton, who are best known for their work on management and leadership styles, produced a grid for the two elements of the selling role – concern for the customer and concern for achieving the sale (*see* Fig. 18.2). Salespeople can fill all these roles. The relevant one for any particular situation is the one that matches the buying style of the customer.

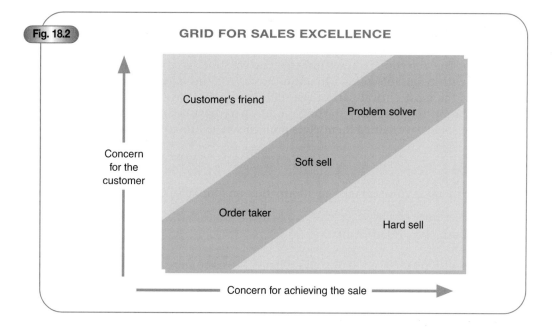

Fig. 18.2 — GRID FOR SALES EXCELLENCE

Customer's friend

Problem solver

Concern for the customer

Soft sell

Order taker

Hard sell

Concern for achieving the sale

The idea of a customer's friend could be: 'I want to understand the customer and respond to his feelings and interests so that he will like me.' It is the personal bond that leads him to purchase from me. This takes relationship marketing too far. However, it has more long-term opportunities than the hard sell: 'I'm in charge of the relationship and will pile on the pressure to get the customer to buy.' The hard sell approach may seem appropriate to a commission salesperson who only gets paid when a sale is made, but it can go against the basic principle of identifying a customer's needs and satisfying them.

Neither of these positions really reflect the principles of modern selling. The better positions lie along the shaded diagonal in Fig. 18.2, the actual position varying for different selling roles.

THE SELLING PROCESS

Selling is best thought of as a seven-stage process. The same process applies to prospectors, sellers and those responsible for future sales. In fact, there is no reason for all stages of the process to be the responsibility of a single individual, although it is often all carried out by one person. The stages of the selling process are:

- Research ⎫
- Objectives ⎬ preparation
- Problem identification ⎫
- Objections ⎬ negotiation
- Benefits ⎭
- Close ⎫
- Follow-up ⎬ relationships

The middle stages of problem identification (asking questions), meeting objections and explaining benefits do not take place in a formal sequential manner during sales contact. New objections can be raised, or questions asked, at any time during a negotiation. The objections often show that the customer is still interested in matching needs with a suitable offer. This middle stage is the negotiation/presentation period. It is the most critical part of the selling process. However, a well-researched solid foundation is a necessary starting point. There have been too many occasions where salespeople have caused themselves problems by failing to prepare properly.

Research

The research stage involves obtaining information on four key elements:

1 The product/offer mix.
2 Competitors, products/offer mixes.
3 The customers.
4 The relationship between the organisation and the customer.

The first item seems obvious but it relies on proper internal communications in an organisation, so the salesperson fully understands what is being offered. There have been times when a customer has seen details of a new product, maybe in a trade journal, before the salesperson. You can imagine the embarrassment this can cause when a customer tells you your business. It is also important for salespeople to know the constraints on how far they can negotiate. Buyers are well informed and this must not be underestimated. But the object is a win–win deal when both buyer and seller are satisfied. The limits need to be established well before negotiations start, hence the need for consistent and clear information.

Individual salespeople often learn a lot about their competitors and the directly competitive offerings being made. These individuals can, therefore, be a good source of such information, and they are able to utilise this knowledge in their selling. But organisations should not believe that all salespeople will have full information on all issues in their marketplace. Collection and dissipation of information on competitors to all salespeople can be linked to suggestions on how to counter the claims that competitors could be making.

The third element is again obvious but necessary. It is the studying of the prospect organisation, and this helps to reveal opportunities and threats which could arise. The customer should still know his own organisation better than the salesperson, but if there are plans for expansion, or contraction, or other developments, then prior knowledge can help in setting objectives, and in the face-to-face meeting. Additional information is obtained during the selling at the problem identification stage.

Prior knowledge is equally necessary for the relationship between suppliers and their customers. Maybe there have been problems in the past, or perhaps there are reasons above normal trading that bind the organisations together. All previous contacts will affect the relationship, so they must be known by the salesperson who can then decide a negotiating strategy with regard to such information.

Issues of power in negotiations can come from any size of organisation, but these can also come from the control of information itself. The sophisticated article number schemes, used by retailers, often give the retail trade more information than a salesperson on the product sold through these intermediaries. In dealing with intermediaries such as food retailers, the suppliers are at a disadvantage unless they can gather similar information.

Objectives

Setting objectives is necessary for businesses as a whole, and for individual negotiations. A strategy for a meeting with a customer will have objectives – let's say, for example, to get an order for 500 items, or to get machine X in the customer's plant for a test period, or to increase prices by 10 per cent and keep the business – but objectives must not be rigid. Selling is about negotiation. In the UK we rarely negotiate in private life. You are unlikely to succeed if you offer to pay 10 per cent less for your grocery bill when you reach the supermarket checkout. That is because the checkout operator has no power to negotiate. In other circumstances, in a retail store, it could work – try it! In some countries this type of bargaining is well established.

The requirement in setting objectives is to have an acceptable 'fall back' position of alternatives which could be offered; not just price but perhaps payment terms, or special after-sales service, or free merchandising help. Such alternatives can be introduced during the negotiation, if appropriate, with a view to making an offer that is acceptable to the customer. There will be other objectives for a meeting, such as to introduce a new product to an existing customer, or even to discover the names of potential new customers for existing products. These objectives are illustrated in Fig. 18.3 (derived from Ansoff's matrix).

Problem identification

Objectives are a necessary preparation for a sales contact, but when that contact actually takes place it is still necessary to re-establish the facts from the customer. It is obvious that a cold caller will need to ask questions to establish the needs a prospect may have. The same is also true of regular sales contacts because changes do happen and a sales presentation will fall flat if there has been a fundamental alteration in the needs of the customer's organisation.

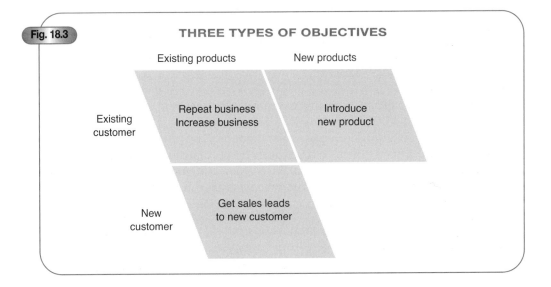

Fig. 18.3   **THREE TYPES OF OBJECTIVES**

	Existing products	New products
Existing customer	Repeat business / Increase business	Introduce new product
New customer	Get sales leads to new customer	

Questions need to be open-ended to allow customers to respond and to volunteer information that can be used in the subsequent presentation. Open questions are typically ones such as:

'In what way does this machine fail to meet your requirements?'
'What are the main reasons for your interest in this service?'

Closed questions, such as the ones below, do not give opportunities for enlargement:

'Does your company use a three-tonne press?'
'Who currently supplies this service?'

Questions should be used to identify problems. But they can also be used as a way of keeping control of the situation by dictating the agenda. The one question that should never be used, on an exhibition stand or in a retail store, is 'Can I help you?' The obvious response is, 'No, thank you'.

Objections

The experience of all the authors is that objections are a natural part of the sales process. They can come during the initial approach for a meeting right up to the point when the salesperson is trying to close the sale. If no objections are raised, even an experienced salesperson will worry that something unknown is wrong. Objections are not excuses but genuine statements of interests, while revealing some issue to be discussed further. Objections can highlight issues of direct importance to a buyer, but equally they can be false objections. In these cases the salesperson has to dig for the real problem. When dealing with objections it is essential that the salesperson does not take any objection personally. It is not a personal rejection and, if considered to be so, could be demoralising. Objections can be countered. Rebukes such as, 'I'm too busy to see you' can be countered by saying, 'Of course, I appreciate you are a busy person, but what I'd like to show you will only take ten minutes of your time'. This technique agrees with the prospect but then counters with a reasonable suggestion.

It is vital to respect the customer during negotiations. Do not interrupt and certainly do not argue with a prospect/customer: if there is an argument and the customer wins, the sale is probably lost; if the salesperson wins the argument, then the sale is definitely lost.

Benefits – the solution to the problem

It will be noticed that the sales process described here does not specifically include a sales presentation. That does not mean such presentations are not used. They are. The need is for the presentation or negotiation to address the customer's needs, and to describe the offer in terms of benefits as seen by that customer. An offer must be: acceptable, affordable and available. Since the customers are the judges of these factors, it is preferable to present the customers with benefits they can understand, not technical features that could confuse. Benefits can be described at two levels:

- the benefits offered by a particular product or service;
- the benefit of dealing with the salesperson's organisation.

The way to describe the benefits will come direct from customers and will use the customer's own language, something all successful salespeople are able to do. In the earlier questioning stage, the benefits required will be probed. Later in the meeting, the objections and other needs will be revealed. A good salesperson uses the customer's own words to describe why a particular product best fits that customer's requirement.

Closing

Closing is a word from sales jargon. It relates to the key requirement of closing the sale – getting the order, or meeting the objectives of the sales contact. To close, finish, bring to an end, conclude or complete is the last stage of a sales negotiation. But this is not a sudden action, at some prearranged time. It is a logical development that can take place at any time. Skilled salespeople look for signs, called buying signals, that the customer is ready to close. The body language is important in a personal sales situation, and it is often said that the whole period of contact is an attempt to bring the situation to a satisfactory close.

There are all sorts of devices for forcing a close, and successful salespeople have an instinct as to when they should use these. They know when to ask for an order, and then the golden rule is to shut up. By doing this, they do not talk themselves out of an order after the event. The use of silence is powerful in forcing customers to either accept the proposal or raise another objection. If a new objection is raised following an attempt to close (get an order), then the process of dealing with that objection, such as offering compensating benefits, is repeated. And then, perhaps, a new close can be attempted. A successful close might be the end of a particular sales contact but it is only the start of the next important stage – the follow-up.

Follow-up or after-sales service

It will come as no surprise to readers of this book that after-sales service is stressed. Of course, some delivery issues might be in the control of another department but, even if they let the customer down, it is the salesperson who has to visit the customer again next period. The salesperson is the real point of contact, and good after-sales service can mean increased business. It can also lead to contacts with new prospects. Poor service is likely to do the opposite.

Six things to avoid

Salespeople must carry out the various elements in the sales process effectively. However, there are six major mistakes that can be made even by successful salespeople:

1 Not following up quotations, enquiries or other promises quickly enough.
2 Making unrealistic promises to customers.
3 Overestimating their own ability to get a sale, and underestimating the competitor's ability.
4 Exaggerating the probability, size and profitability of future orders.
5 Underestimating a customer's potential.
6 Overselling a customer, so that the customer buys more than is needed now.

The first two factors are ones where there is no excuse. A good salesperson knows what is possible, and then deals with customers on that basis. The next two are more difficult. They stem from the necessary optimism and self-confidence required by a salesperson. In compiling sales forecasts from the estimates of sales forces, a usual precaution is to reduce such predictions by a little to allow for excess claims. The final two factors, underestimating potential and overselling, are major errors. It is difficult to identify when underestimating happens, but it obviously represents a lost opportunity. It is cheaper to get increased business from existing customers than from new customers, and hence the full potential of existing customers must be considered. The role of identifying problems by asking questions could be renamed identifying opportunities. For a salesperson every problem is a potential opportunity. But overselling is perhaps a worse mistake. In the continuous contact between supplier and customer, this represents an abuse. It will not help the building of trust so necessary in a good relationship.

CONTROL, MOTIVATION AND SALES MANAGEMENT

This section covers the two conflicting roles involved in managing a sales force: controlling activities while encouraging salespeople to do a better job.

Control ratios

The decision to use a sales force to communicate with customers is an expensive one. Even a small sales team can cost several million pounds every year. Therefore the expenditure should be treated as an investment, in just the same way as an investment in other communication media, or an investment in plant or equipment. There are alternative ways of reaching customers, but if the sales force is the way chosen, the sales performance must be controlled.

An investment needs to be monitored to ensure it is giving an adequate return; in this case the return will be measured in terms of sales made. However, there is no way of guaranteeing sales, and, in many organisations, salespeople do overestimate the probability of getting future orders. Unfortunately, when these orders are not forthcoming, it is often too late for the manager to take action to generate the required level of business. While sales orders are obviously required as an output, the measurement of sales level as the control is only one way to gauge selling success. In fact, sales levels are a resultant effect of the total selling operation. For instance, there should be a mixture of sales calls that produce the desired results, and some that do not. To assume all sales calls will produce orders is a mistake. Therefore it is important to measure elements of selling which can be considered the cause rather than the effect of sales performance.

In this context there are three key control ratios which could indicate how the business is developing. These are:

1 Call effectiveness.
2 Strike rate.
3 Prospecting success.

Call effectiveness measures the average return from a successful sales visit. It can be average sales revenue per order, or profit per order. Since the cost of a call is not very different (whether the order received is large or small), this measure can be used to show if too many small, perhaps unprofitable, calls are being made. Of course, it is also important to maintain the level of successful calls.

Strike rate measures the ratio of orders received to calls made, or sometimes orders received to quotations issued. It measures the productive level of the salesperson.

The third key measure involves new business, prospecting success, which obviously comes from new customers/prospects. If the customer group is not being renewed, there is a problem when an existing customer ceases to order. The measure can be expressed as numbers of new customers (who order for the first time) as a proportion of all prospect calls (where no order has yet been received). This measure reflects the difficulty in converting prospects into customers. It sometimes includes a measure of total calls as well.

These three ratios need to be linked to the total call rate to give a good measure of the effectiveness of individual salespeople. There are other ratios suggested in sales textbooks, but the controls covering how many calls a salesperson makes and how successful they are, on average, in each call, actually get closer to the cause of sales performance than the output of sales revenue.

Motivation

The management function is widely researched and many theories of motivation have been suggested. Motivation is particularly important with a sales force because of the scattered locations which could be involved, and the individual natures of most salespeople. This book is not the place to discuss the theories of human resource management (HRM) and psychology but a few relevant points can be made. Salespeople often work alone – regular, scheduled sales meetings, bringing people together, say once a month, can motivate individuals by group recognition and support. Salespeople tend to have a strong driving force. Stick-and-carrot techniques do not necessarily work well in this situation. The use of monetary rewards such as bonus payments and commission systems can prove effective means of directing supplementary efforts and acknowledging achievements, though the design and operation of such schemes is fraught with administrative difficulties and potential inequity. McAdams (1987) provides a useful review of reward systems, while in a similar vein, Murphy and Sohi (1995) propose a more informed approach to the use of one-off rewards and incentives such as sales contests. Of increased significance within a context of relationship marketing, the mutual benefits and motivations of teamwork have been re-examined by Cespedes, Doyle and Freedman (1989), while Cron (1988) stresses the career-related aspects of motivation at the individual level.

Figure 18.4 presents a basic theoretical model of motivation, though clearly the issue is highly conditional and dynamic, requiring great care and sensitivity on the part of sales managers and corporate management alike.

Sales management

As with motivation, there is little to separate sales management from general management. Stafford and Grant suggested the following format for successful sales management, but the same list could come from any management book and not refer to sales management at all:

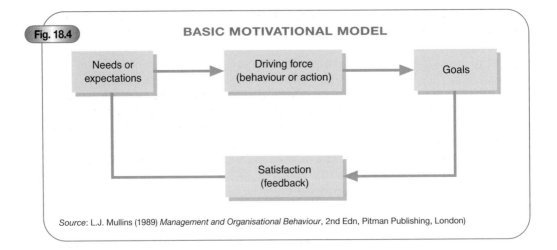

Fig. 18.4 BASIC MOTIVATIONAL MODEL

Needs or expectations → Driving force (behaviour or action) → Goals

Satisfaction (feedback)

Source: L.J. Mullins (1989) *Management and Organisational Behaviour*, 2nd Edn, Pitman Publishing, London)

1 Planning   The setting of objectives for the team.
2 Organisation   The strategy for achieving the objectives.
3 Recruitment   Selecting the right people to staff the sales organisation.
4 Training   Developing the skills required to get the job done.
5 Motivation   Getting the best result from the team.
6 Control   Ensuring the results conform to the plan.
7 Monitor   Setting up a feedback system.

Lancaster and Jobber emphasised recruitment and selection, motivation and training, and organisation and compensation as the key issues of the management of a sales force.

The size of a sales force

The sales force is an expensive resource, but the cost is not the prime consideration in determining size. The question must be: What is appropriate for the task to be tackled? Three techniques are described by Lancaster and Jobber. These are:

1 The workload approach.
2 The productivity approach.
3 The 'vaguely right' approach.

The workload approach recognises that there is only so much work any individual can tackle. If it is possible to calculate the number of customers, and frequency of calls, then this can be related to the workload and hence a size of sales force. But this may not be appropriate to develop new customers. The productivity approach looks at sales potential and costs to work out when the marginal return matches costs. The 'vaguely right' is much more scientific than it sounds but beyond the scope of this book.

Often sales forces are well established, which makes it difficult to increase or reduce the numbers employed. However, this really is short-sighted as the marketing environment could well be changing and the task required could differ over time. It does take time to train new salespeople, but this is happening all the time as salespeople are mobile in their careers. In any company up to 10 per cent of the sales force could leave every year. Hence, the level of investment in the sales force needs to be continually reviewed, and modifications can be accommodated as part of regular staff turnover.

The organisation of a sales force

The effectiveness of a sales force will be related to both the individual skills of the salespeople and the organisation chosen. For instance, it would be difficult to continually change sales territories if it is accepted that a key role of selling is to build good relationships with customers. Historically, field sales forces have been subdivided into geographical territories. Sometimes division goes even further, to have salespeople specialising with a small group of products, or a particular type of customer.

Geographical territories

Dividing the sales force into geographical territories allows a salesperson to become responsible for a certain geographical region. The territories should be organised in a way which makes the possible workload as similar as possible in each territory. The size of the territory should be such that little time is wasted in excessive travelling and all customers should be called upon frequently. This is known as 'the frequency of call rate'. A key advantage of a territorial design is continuity. Customers can get to know and trust the salesperson and administration can be kept simple.

Division by product

When the sales force is divided by product speciality, some salespeople are responsible for one group of products while others are responsible for different products. The main advantage of this method of sales force organisation is that the salespeople can concentrate on developing better product knowledge. A disadvantage is that costs may be duplicated if customers buy more than one of the firms products, because this would entail a visit by more than one salesperson.

Division by type of outlet

By using this type of organisation of a sales force, a supplier hopes to take advantage of the different skills that may be required when servicing different industries. This is quite common in the industrial sector where engineering firms may make components which can be used in several large industries. The salesperson will then try to become an expert in selling to one particular type of industry, by building up knowledge about the needs of that industry.

There is no universally right answer to sales force organisation. There can be intensive coverage and selective coverage in sales just as in channels of distribution. Life insurance salespeople could claim to be part of both the communications mix and distribution. A large national life insurance company could use intensive coverage even if it meant occasional conflicts when two salespeople contact the same prospect. Such conflicts would be inappropriate for a supplier of specialist machinery to industry; and it would be inefficient for a small bakery offering home delivery and using van salespeople. Here selective representation is the most relevant. But for one multiproduct company, organisation by products and customers meant some customers received multiple visits from sales representatives from the same company.

This example shows how sales organisation links to distribution for physical goods. In fact the whole marketing mix is interrelated, so any decision on a sales force or its organisation must be part of a totally integrated marketing plan and not taken solely for sales convenience.

EXAMPLE

At one time a survey by Cadbury Schweppes showed a single wholesaler received visits from Cadbury Confectionery, Cadbury Foods (Marvel, Smash, Biscuits), Typhoo Tea, Chivers-Hartley Jam and marmalade, Cadbury-Typhoo Catering Foods, Schweppes drinks, Jeyes disinfectants and Kenco coffee. Some of these calls were every week, some every month, but with eight separate representatives involved, then eight different relationships were being established. This situation has now changed as Cadbury Schweppes have sold several of these subsidiaries, but at the time the distribution of four of the companies was handled by a single delivery operation. Often this meant four separate deliveries, each week, to the same customer. Clearly a costly operation.

FUTURE TRENDS IN SELLING

When thinking of salespeople, there is a general image of company car, lunch allowance, stopping at good hotels, in fact a good life. But in practice the car doubles as an office, the lunch is often a rushed sandwich between calls and hotels are just boring. But selling can be a good life for those who enjoy meeting people. The problem is that much time is spent doing administration, driving, waiting and sorting out problems caused elsewhere in your organisation. Three trends need to be considered to conclude this section on selling:

1 Can new technology be used to make salespeople more effective in their profession?
2 Are there situations where direct personal selling is no longer cost-effective, and what happens in this case?
3 Are there changes in the structure of industries that mean the sales role must be redefined?

Selling is about meeting people, establishing relationships and communication. This cannot be replaced by modern technology but it can be helped by such developments. The aim is to improve effectiveness. For instance, mobile phones can keep salespeople in contact with their base. Entering orders into a portable computer is faster than writing an order. The orders can be downloaded automatically via telephone lines and the order directly input into the delivery schedule with minimal delay. Word processors can produce standard quotations twice as fast. Direct marketing databases can store much more information than a hand-written record card, and the information in the database can be analysed to help a salesperson target a customer more precisely. Increasingly, technology advances are making for greater speed, accuracy and administrative efficiency in both the core sales role and at the level of sales management and planning. In terms of software, recent developments have made quite commonplace the provision of tailored sales territory maps and routing systems, customer account and office administration systems, forecasting and modelling packages, and sophisticated contact management and direct marketing software. Overlapping such developments, rapid improvements in multi-media and communications technology have made themselves felt in state-of-the-art audio-visual facilities for sales presentations and business meetings, in interactive communications and research through the Internet and Intranet, and in a span of other innovations ranging from voice-activated foreign language translation software to multi-size video conferencing networks. Commenting on the extent to which such technological aids have been harnessed within the sales field, Rines (1995) has suggested that the art of selling is becoming more interface than face to face.

So many uses are being made of modern technology to improve preparation and the following up of sales calls. Even during the call a salesperson could show a video or use a small printer to print a personalised quotation. But there is a point when the use of such devices will get in the way of the personal contact and if this is the case they must be rejected.

A direct call by a salesperson could be replaced by a telephone call. This could save 90 per cent of the cost of the direct call. The loss of contact might not be critical, although there is evidence of both a reduction in sales received and more especially of information required for the future. Sometimes a successful hybrid system can be used, combining fewer sales visits with regular telesales contact. Another development mentioned earlier is direct computer-to-computer reordering links between customer and supplier. These can again be supplemented with infrequent direct sales contact.

In some organisations, and in some industries, suppliers have decided that the cost of sales staff is greater than the benefits. These are areas where the supplier lets customers choose for themselves. In the past this has happened with self-service retail stores replacing traditional service, self-service petrol-stations, cash and carry wholesalers replacing delivered wholesalers, and direct (mail order) insurance companies challenging traditional insurance brokers. The sensible rule is to continually reassess the investment in a sales force against the benefits received. Remember the alternatives available to reach and communicate with potential customers.

In some industries it is the customers and their needs that are changing. Not many years ago sales forces for major food manufacturers had several hundred people, each calling on a number of outlets. Now buying is centralised and a team approach is used with perhaps a senior sales account manager meeting a buying director, then account managers liaising with regional managers who control a number of stores, and, finally, maybe a part-time merchandiser visiting an individual outlet. In this situation there is a need to ensure excellent teamwork. Good communications between the various members of the sales team and an appropriate contact with the customer are essential.

The major sales force may not be used, but the senior account manager could have a role to negotiate sales. The account manager might ensure orders are placed and influence deliveries either direct to stores or to the retailer's central warehouse. The merchandiser is not a salesperson but efforts to improve product displays can ensure the product sells through the intermediary on to the eventual consumer. This type of multi-level contact can build very strong relationships, each at a relevant level. It is an example of assessing the task and answering the question, 'What is appropriate for the task?' The answer should cover all elements of marketing, but there is no reason that it must require a direct sales organisation.

CONCLUSION

This chapter has demonstrated the key role of personal selling as one way of reaching customers. While most selling activities are more immediate, or short-term, then marketing the skills of understanding customer needs are equally necessary. There are many levels to building personal relationships with customers and a successful salesperson will understand all of these.

Selling is not just the actual customer contact. It includes a great deal of preparation and follow-up. In these activities sales and marketing are closely related, and the people concerned need to work together.

Marketing managers have been described as representing the environment within the company as well as projecting the organisation out into its environment. To do this involves meeting customers. Salespeople are doing this all the time and can be a key part of such information channels. However, marketers must not leave it all to the sales force who have a key task of getting the sales required now to keep the company in business. In many companies the marketing or product managers will plan to accompany a sales visit or attend a sales meeting at least once a month. But more than this, marketing must ensure the sales force are always informed of decisions from inside the company that could affect the sales actions.

QUESTIONS

1 What is the difference between a salesperson involved in prospecting and a salesperson concentrating on account maintenance? Do you think these involve different skills?

2 Suggest some simple ways a salesperson can build a strong relationship with all customers even if that salesperson regularly contacts 500 such customers.

3 Why is preparation so important in the selling process?

4 How should a salesperson deal with objections raised by customers during a sales presentation?

FURTHER READING

Blake, R. and Mouton, J. (1970) *Grid for Sales Excellence*, McGraw-Hill.

Cespedes, Frank V., Doyle, Stephen and Freedman, Robert Jl (1989) 'Teamwork for Today's Selling', *Harvard Business Review*, March–April, Vol. 58.

Christopher, M., Payne, A. and Ballantyne, D. (1991) *Relationship Marketing*, Heinemann, London.

Cron, W. L. ex al (1988) 'The Influence of Career Stages on Components of Salesperson Motivation', *Journal of Marketing*, July, Vol. 52.

Lancaster, G. and Jobber, D. (1990) *Sales Techniques and Management*, 2nd Edn, Pitman, London.

Lidstone, John (1994) Chapter 19, 'The Marketing Book', ed. Michael J. Baker, 3rd Edn, Butterworth Heinemann, London.

McAdams, J. (1987) 'Rewarding Sales and Marketing Performance', *Management Review*, April, pp. 33–38.

McCall, J. B. and Warrington, J. B. (1984) *Marketing by Agreement*, Wiley, London.

Miller, Arthur (1949) Death of a Salesman, Penguin, London.

Moncrief, W. C. (1988), 'Five Types of Industrial Sales Jobs', *Industrial Marketing Management*, Vol. 17, pp. 161–7.

Mullins, L. J. (1989) *Management and Organisational Behaviour*, 2nd Edn, Pitman, London.

Murphy, William H. and Sohi, Ravipreet S. (1995) 'Salespersons' perceptions about sales contests: towards a greater understanding', *European Journal of Marketing*, Vol. 29, No. 13, pp. 42–67.

Power, C. and Driscoll, L. (1992) 'Smart selling', *Business Week*, 3 August.

Rines, Simon (1995) 'Forcing Change', *Marketing Week*, March.

Stafford, J. and Grant, C. (1986) *Effective Sales Management*, Heinemann, London.

Product recall and customer loyalty – a sales dilemma

The case of Vitasoy

Vitasoy and Vita are household names in Hong Kong; they are the brand names of Vitasoy International Holding Ltd. (referred to in the rest of the case as Vitasoy Ltd.). The company began operations in 1940 and was founded by Dr Lo Kwee-seong, whose mission was to provide the people of Hong Kong with cheap protein at a time when diseases of malnutrition like beriberi and pellagra were rampant.

Vitasoy began operations with a staff of about twenty employees and a capital investment of HK$25 000. The current operations are now staffed by a workforce of one thousand and the markets include Hong Kong, Macau, North America and about twenty others. The product line has been expanded to include, soya bean milk drinks, fruit juices, milk based drinks, teas, fresh milk and carbonated soft drinks. The company's revenue has grown to HK$1.25billion with a net profit of HK$122.3million.

Known as 'China's cow', soya is supposed to contain 40 per cent protein compared with about 18 per cent in meat or fish. The product concept was a nutritious, cheap and affordable drink. The production process had been very labour intensive but has become much more capital intensive – the basic process is to boil the soya beans in water to extract the goodness, filter off the solid waste, sweeten the liquid and bottle.

At the start of trading in 1940 the brand name Vitasoy was developed by combining the first two syllables of the words vitamin and soya bean. On the first day nine bottles were sold at six Hong Kong cents each. Growth in popularity depended upon word of mouth and the product as delivered fresh, door-to-door by boys on bicycles.

By the 1950s sales had soared and a large factory was established with the latest sterilization technology. This meant that refrigeration of Vitasoy in retail outlets was no longer necessary, and this combined with the introduction of the first Tetra-Brik Asceptic packaging instead of returnable bottles meant opportunities to sell in overseas markets. The market development began with a strategy of following the Hong Kong migrants but expanded into the health conscious locals. With its roots in health products, Vitasoy Ltd. was perfectly poised to cash in on the health conscious locals.

The era of diversification began in 1976. A range of fruit juices – orange, mango, guava and kalamansi – was launched under the brand name of Vita. Diversification continued with the introduction of carbonated drinks in the late 1970s. Growth continued with the establishment of new plants, and the company appeared to be going from strength to strength.

In 1995 things started to go seriously wrong for the company – a catalogue of the events is as follows:

May 1995 – October 24, 1995	Founder Dr Lo Kwee-seong died at the age of 85. Complaints of sour taste or kerosene like smell in soya milk products leads to recall of 12 million cartons. Vitasoy Ltd. carried out an immediate investigation into the matter after having received the complaint reported by a local newspaper. The findings indicated that the off-taste was caused by a fault in one of the steam filters during production.
December 28, 1995 – January 3, 1996	One complaint received about sour Malt Vitasoy. The management recalls 4000, 250ml, Malt Soya Milk packs with the same code. Three more complaints are received about the same product, which has been produced at the same factory but on a different production line. Vitasoy promises to step up monitoring of whole plant.
January 4, 1996	All seven paper pack lines at the production plant are closed. Eight million packs of all types of soya milk are recalled.
January 5, 1996	Two complaints are received about 250ml plain Vitasoy soya milk which has been produced at a different production plant. Management recalls another batch of 42 000 packs.
January 8, 1996	Three more complaints are received about 250ml plain Vitasoy soya milk.
January 9, 1996	The management decides to recall and destroy all 15 million packs of 28 types of carton drinks in all sizes and suspends all 13 production lines at one of the production plants. An additional 30 million packs in stock are also destroyed.

Due to the adverse publicity and general public interest the company employed a Swedish company to investigate the problems. The findings were as follows:

Equipment wear and tear and the possibility of human error may have been the likely causes that affected approximately 203 packs of Vitasoy Malt Soya Milk during a packaging materials changing operation at one of the plants. The probable causes for the sour taste were variations in machine performance and incomplete sterilization.

Questions

1 How will the sales teams deal with criticism regarding the product, and get sales targets back on track?

2 How should Vitasoy relaunch its products? Propose a marketing strategy explaining the reasons for your choice of strategy.

3 What is your opinion about the decisions of the Vitasoy management to implement a total product recall?

(Case supplied by Dr Thilaka S. Weerakoon, The Hong Kong Polytechnic University)

CHAPTER 19

Marketing Planning and Product Policy

'Would you tell me, please, which way I ought to go from here?'
'That depends a good deal on where you want to get to,' said the Cat.
Lewis Carroll, *Alice's Adventures in Wonderland*

INTRODUCTION

To be effective, marketing has to provide a means by which an organisation can focus its resources to meet the needs of their chosen customer efficiently. First, it is important to know where you are starting from. Second is the decision on where you wish to go in the future. Although objectives will doubtless be modified over time to reflect market dynamics, they should prove robust enough to guide key commercial decisions across the organisation, and should therefore lead on from much corporate soul-searching, analysis and preparation. There is an obvious link between these first two steps as it is difficult to set objectives in isolation of the starting position, so often these first two steps take place concurrently.

The outcome should be a commitment by the organisation to a deliberate policy on which markets to serve, with which products or offerings.

The third step is the planning of how to achieve these objectives, which will involve both the overall direction (strategy) and the efficient implementation of specific marketing tasks such as promotion, product development, distribution and other elements of the marketing mix.

Key decisions on product policy amount to a 'game-plan' to achieve a product-market match, thereby serving both market requirements and corporate objectives, for the present and into the future. The strategy will cover both the targeting and positioning of all offerings.

To achieve this could require the acquisition and allocation of investment resources such as those required for new product development and promotion. It also involves the co-ordination of marketing with all the other functions of the organisation.

Finally we need to know how to monitor our progress and ensure we arrive at our destination.

Stage 1   *Where are we starting from?*   The marketing audit.
Product range analysis

Stage 2   *Where do we want to be?*   Marketing objectives.
Targeting and positioning

Stage 3 *How do we get there?* Marketing mix strategies and resource allocation.

Stage 4 *How do we ensure we get there?* Control and feedback.

THE MARKETING PLANNING PROCESS

The marketing planning process has evolved to provide a framework for all four of these activities. For small organisations this is a straightforward process involving well-established stages and, if required, the production of a document, 'The Marketing Plan'. Often this can be used as the basis for negotiations with organisations such as banks which can provide start-up finance for a new venture or additional finance for expansion.

In many large organisations marketing planning has become an established formal procedure and part of the strategic planning process. In this context it is sometimes necessary to co-ordinate the marketing of a range of diverse products. This inevitably makes the process more complicated but potentially more beneficial. Also, in a number of organisations it has been found that the process itself has improved the level of co-operation between different business functions, and the involvement of the managers involved.

One approach which has been adopted by many organisations is to set overall objectives in a mission statement. This sets out the general purpose of an organisation and the values it aspires to while recognising the legitimate interests of other stakeholders such as customers, employees, suppliers and the communities in which the organisation operates. The mission statement is an important communication from an organisation and so it must also be seen as part of the overall marketing statement made by the company.

It is likely that the planning will be an iterative, rather than a sequential, process. When selecting a strategy to meet the chosen objectives there is a need to revisit those targets to assess both if they are really what is required as well as whether they are likely to be met. As a result, the objectives could be modified thereby requiring the strategy to be reconsidered. The process will be further complicated by the need to impose assumptions on both the objectives and strategy. These may involve estimations relating to data which is not available, the continuation or reversal of present trends, the timing of anticipated events and so on. The assumptions are often summarised as a forecast, which can then be used to develop a provisional budget. The budget can then be used as the basis for subsequent stages of the planning process.

It is essential that the assumptions upon which such a forecast is based are clearly stated since it will allow the forecast to be amended as the assumptions respond to any changes in the situation upon which they were based. The logic of this can easily be lost once the forecast has been buried within a carefully constructed budget and the outcome subjected to a variance analysis. While it is fundamental to the use of marketing budgets (we will return to it in the section on control), the impact resulting from having to revise assumptions can be minimised by the planning process (*see* Fig. 19.1).

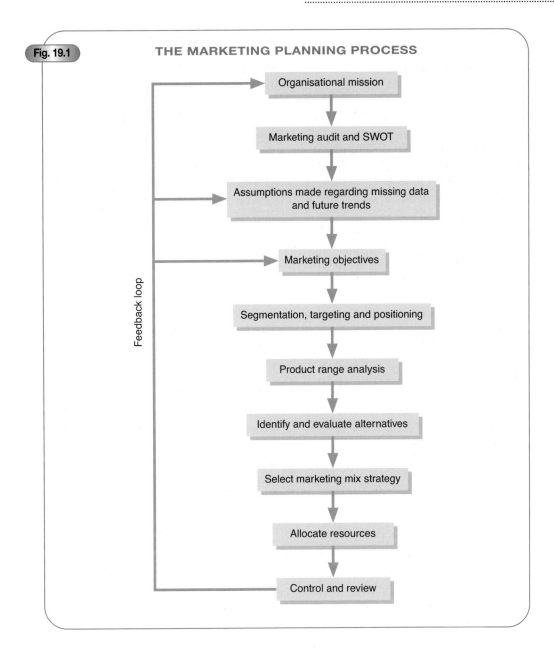

Fig. 19.1

THE MARKETING PLANNING PROCESS

Organisational mission

Marketing audit and SWOT

Assumptions made regarding missing data and future trends

Marketing objectives

Segmentation, targeting and positioning

Product range analysis

Identify and evaluate alternatives

Select marketing mix strategy

Allocate resources

Control and review

Feedback loop

THE MARKETING AUDIT

All the decisions in the planning process need to be set in the context of the skills and resources available to the organisation. This involves recognising what these are in comparison to the competition. While this is comparatively easy where the business is small, it is increasingly difficult as organisations become larger. The process is, however, the same and will cover the total organisation. Marketers are interested in those key elements of the wider business audit which involve marketing issues. This is usually termed the *marketing audit*.

A marketing audit has four major components which reflect the four levels of the marketing environment shown in Fig. 3.2. They are:

- the wider external environment, which was discussed in Chapter 3;
- the company stakeholder system;
- the markets in which the company operates, and the performances of the products in these markets;
- the review of resources and skills which are available to the organisation, and the systems and structure to deliver them.

All should focus on any changes, either current or expected, which are likely to affect the organisation or the markets it serves.

The external part of the marketing audit focuses on the uncontrollable macroenvironmental factors affecting the business. For many businesses the economic climate is of vital importance, so needs to be assessed critically. The technical and regulatory environments that affect the organisation, its markets and competitors also need to be at least discussed.

It should also include information which shows the size of the market in terms of both value and volume, and the trends in these. The position of the organisation should be compared with that of each significant competitor. The characteristics of the market should be defined and compared in terms of the range of products offered, their prices, distribution and promotion. In addition, the audit provides an opportunity for information gathered by the marketing research function, relevant to any aspect of the business, to be presented and its relevance assessed:

- **Macro-factors**
  Social and cultural influences
  Technological influences   } (STEP)
  Economic environment
  Political and legal environment
- **Micro-factors**
  Customers
  Competition
  Suppliers
  Other stakeholders

EXAMPLE ....

An example of a change which had direct marketing implications but which were ignored by a very significant number of organisations was the need to charge Value Added Tax on sales of many products. In most of these organisations the preparation of invoices was an accounting function and the need to collect VAT was considered a part of this. This resulted in many decisions which affected the way prices were presented being taken without considering the effect on customers. As a result many companies either disturbed cherished customer relationships or found that, having quoted VAT-inclusive prices, they lost business because their prices were then higher than those of competitors who were quoting prices excluding VAT.

The *stakeholder* audit covers the values and attitudes of those interest groups in this category. In particular it will concentrate on suppliers and customers.

The evaluation of all the product range in relation to customers and competitors is a key part of the audit. It covers both a wide look at the balance of the total product range offered and the individual elements of the marketing mix concentrating on how these meet customer needs and wants in a competitive context:

- product/services;
- price, quality, value;
- distribution;
- promotion and communication;
- interactions (people contact and processes).

Product performance is usefully compared to previous periods to establish short- and long-term trends, and the analysis needs to be sufficiently detailed to highlight relevant differences.

The final part of the audit involves an appreciation of what an organisation is capable of achieving and the systems it uses. It will cover the current situation with regard to the marketing research and information, personnel, planning and control systems, and product development.

Both the external and internal elements of the audit should be sufficiently thorough to show clearly how they relate to the business environment and future trends.

PRODUCT RANGE ANALYSIS

The product range, sometimes called the product portfolio or product mix, is the assortment of different products offered for sale by a company. Most established companies are multiproduct organisations which offer a mix of different products. New products will have been added over time as well as the introduction of variations on successful products. These will be to cater for new or different customer groups, to expand sales and profits, to become a more competitive and credible supplier in the market, or simply to spread commercial risk over a wider product mix. Growth in the product range may well be the chosen instrument of corporate growth, though the size (or length) of the mix will not guarantee success, and two similarly sized companies in the same market may have major differences in the number of products that they offer. Issues such as product line, width, depth and consistency are all relevant in a product range analysis. Figure 19.2 illustrates graphically the way in which 3M has grown over the years through product development.

- *Product line* A number of products that are related by being targeted to similar markets or for similar uses, or sold through similar outlets or on comparable terms, e.g. Procter & Gamble has a number of product offerings within its line of detergents, including famous names such as Tide, Bold, Oxydol and Dreft.

  A company's product mix can be measured in terms of size or length – the total number of products in the mix.
- *Width* The number of different product lines within the product mix. Thus, in addition to a sizeable detergent product line, Procter & Gamble also has toothpaste, shampoo, toilet soap and many other product lines.

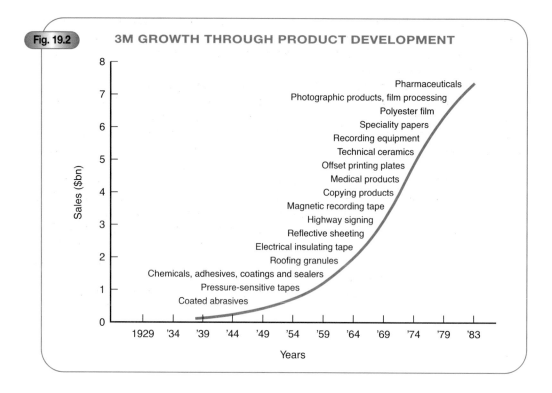

Fig. 19.2 **3M GROWTH THROUGH PRODUCT DEVELOPMENT**

- *Depth* The number of different versions offered within each product in a product line, e.g. a Procter & Gamble toilet soap may be offered in two sizes (regular, family) and three colours (pink, blue, white), giving the product line a depth measure of six. Obviously, depth will vary by product line, so for example a newly introduced soap may only be offered in one regular size, and one fragrance.
- *Consistency* This refers to the closeness of various product lines across the mix, in terms of production methods and materials, target markets, common distribution outlets and the like. It may not always be obvious how or why a company has an apparently disparate mix of products, e.g. 3M introduced Scotch masking tape after its abrasives customers in the motor trade voiced the need for such a product.

Both as a basis for longer-term decisions and for day-to-day marketing purposes companies need to monitor and analyse key performance indicators across their product range. Of critical concern will be indicators of product-market match, performance vis-à-vis leading competitors, identification of market opportunities and challenges, and some ongoing diagnosis/projection of each product's performance in terms of profitability, growth and resource usage. Such analysis will therefore range from the holistic (i.e. total range) level to a detailed focus on individual product items, pack-sizes and individual product variants. The information bases for these analyses will draw heavily on accounting and costing records and other internal control data, and company market research findings/information which is nowadays increasingly stored and accessed through marketing information system (MkIS).

Resourcing and accounting measures such as sales and profits express product performance in terms of internal common yardsticks that enable within- and across-range comparisons, which are vital to product planning and strategy. Figure 19.3 illustrates a more comprehensive list of measures by which a company might conduct an internal product audit, product by product.

The value of such an audit is that it presents an analysis of products across a common set of measures, so that anomalies and problems can be identified, examined and addressed. With accounting data alone, it is possible, for each major product, to present a 'mini' profit and loss account and balance sheet, to indicate financial performance. Certainly larger companies will treat leading products as separate profit centres, and sometimes organise them as product divisions or strategic business units.

A powerful facet of marketing planning is the recognition and exploitation of the dynamics within the product range – the extent to which products support each other, in marketing, resourcing or other terms. If it is a truism that company performance hinges on the product range, it is also to be expected that returns will vary according to the fine-tuning and management of resource-use against and within the range itself. In simple terms, there is a strategic dimension in the way that the product range is managed as a portfolio of (product) investments.

Figure 19.4 presents a simplified product range analysis for a hypothetical health-

---

Fig. 19.3

ACCOUNTING AND RESOURCE MEASURES OF PRODUCT PERFORMANCE

Measure	Measurements
Sales	Volume (units) Revenue (£000) Percentage of total (%) Ranking (1–n) Sales growth (% ± 12 months)
Profits	Total (£000) Gross margin % ROCE % Percentage of company profits (%) Ranking (1–n) Profits growth (% ± 12 months)
Costs	Total (£000) Unit cost £ Overhead allocation (£000) Fixed v variable cost (x:y)
Others	Investment (£000) Capital spending and recovery CASH flow (£000) Plant use Budget X Functions e.g. marketing, transport, service

care products manufacturer. Though simplistic and generalised, the analysis gives some insight into the strategic and managerial issues involved in product policy. In marketing terms, the company is fielding a spread of product lines (i.e. width), offering differing line choices (i.e. depth) to consumers. The sales and profits percentage figures indicate that the product lines make different contributions to company performance, while individual products within the lines themselves differ in their sales/profit profile. It is interesting to note that, even with a limited portfolio of twelve products, sales revenue contribution of individual products ranges from twenty to one per cent, while that for profits varies from eighteen to one per cent of the total.

Clearly, even with only two yardsticks, profits and sales, simple comparison shows that some products are performing better than others. While statistically this will always be the case, especially within extensive product ranges, companies need to understand why and how performance varies, as part of the overall product management and marketing process. For example, in Fig. 19.4, Product No. 4 may be facing severe market competition and production difficulties, while Product No. 11 may be a recent addition that has great profit potential, once it is established.

The above analysis is internal to an organisation. For a thorough marketing analysis

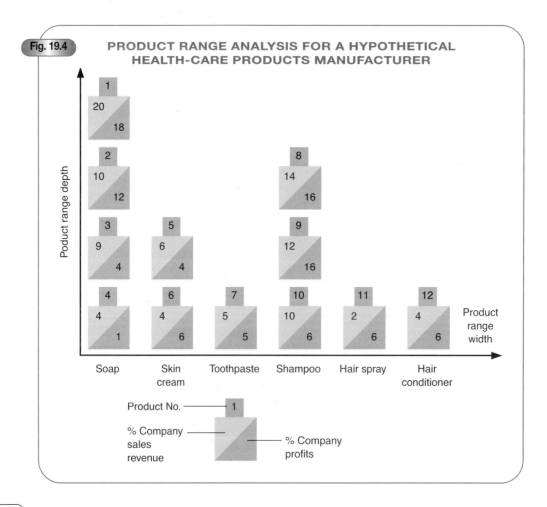

Fig. 19.4 **PRODUCT RANGE ANALYSIS FOR A HYPOTHETICAL HEALTH-CARE PRODUCTS MANUFACTURER**

of products, of course, financial information must be supplemented by external measures of how products perform within the competitive marketplace. Figure 19.5 illustrates the various measures of marketing performance that might be applied to products and product lines.

Various techniques of product range/portfolio analysis have been developed to assist this, usually based on a matrix (or grid) representation of the products/product divisions within the firm.

For competitive strength there is the Boston Consulting Group (BCG) matrix which uses memorable terms such as Cash cow, Star, Problem child and Dog. Figure 19.6 illustrates this popular approach. The matrix is based on two principal dimensions: relative market share (i.e. related to the nearest major competitors); and market growth (a proxy for life cycle development, and subject to interpretation). To apply the matrix, a company would plot its major products in the appropriate cells, positioning them, as in Fig. 19.6, by circles proportional to current (or projected) sales income. (*Note*: the technique makes reference to cash generation, which is a basic and definitive resource, rather than the possibly more nominal and conditional values that might measure profitability.) The analysis therefore attempts to describe the basic resource interdependencies of products within the portfolio. However, this matrix should be used with great care as it has major limitations due to its reliance on market share and market

---

Fig. 19.5   **MARKETING MEASURES OF PRODUCT PERFORMANCE**

- Sales and market share v. company target and v. leading competitors . . . current and historical
- Projected product sales potential
- Geographical sales – region, home v. export
- Sales pattern through year – seasonality, cyclicality
- Sales × market segment, e.g. age groups, income groups, etc.
- Product sales growth v. overall market/segment growth
- Age-maturity of product . . . life cycle features, trends
- Number of current buyers/users . . . and buyer profit (v. competition)
- Measures of product growth and success, e.g. purchase loyalty (v. competitors), repeat purchases, first-time buyers v. lapsed buyers
- Distribution measures – overall % market cover
  – stocking by outlet types
  – % full range stocking
- Quality measures, e.g. complaints, refunds and returns, late deliveries, damages and breakdowns, sales problems, lost orders and cancellations
- Awareness and recall measures of product/brand advertising and promotion
- Attitude/image/preference measures of product v. competition

growth as the only two dimensions in constructing it. Some high growth markets are really quite unattractive or very risky, e.g. the current personal computer hardware market. The value of the BCG matrix is that it gives some insight into the resource interdependencies that exist within the total product range, or within any mix of company initiatives (the technique could be applied to some effect in analysing a company's mix of export markets worldwide). It highlights in general terms the policy decisions necessary to maintain or change a company's position in respect of both individual product lines and the total product portfolio.

As an example, the hypothetical company in Fig. 19.6 would need to consider how Products 4 and 5 (problem children) can be promoted leftward by gaining market share. They also need to know which are the loss-makers and which the cash-earners among Products 6 to 10 (dogs), and how long Product 1 (the major cash cow) can be relied on to fund a possibly top-heavy array of less productive investments. Indeed, the company might well be advised to re-examine the criteria it uses to develop and manage product lines generally. As a qualification to the above, it should be stressed that no simple 2 × 2 matrix analysis will cope with the complexities and dynamics of product management and strategy to be expected in a large company setting. Certainly, there are major difficulties and risks in applying and over-interpreting formal analytical tools such as the BCG matrix.

While competing and more complex matrix approaches have been developed in recent years, notably by large multimarket companies such as General Electric and

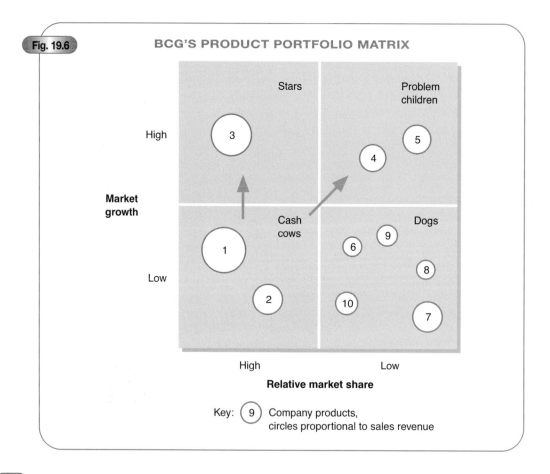

Fig. 19.6

BCG'S PRODUCT PORTFOLIO MATRIX

Key: (9) Company products, circles proportional to sales revenue

Shell International, the same advice applies: the basic merit of these techniques lies in the analytical skills and insight in producing the categories, rather than the development of standard prescriptions or panaceas. Other matrices have been proposed, such as the Directional Policy Matrix championed by McDonald (1993) and a development of the Hofer and Schendel matrix described by Rick Brown. This debate is beyond the scope of this book, but Brown's business screen is shown in Fig. 19.7.

This screen uses more dimensions than the Boston matrix in assessing market attractiveness and competitive capability. It is very helpful in considering options which an organisation might follow. These are discussed further in the strategy section later in this chapter. The decisions that could be available are:

- build for growth (Zone 1);
- hold position and use cash generated for new developments (Zone 2);
- harvest for cash recognising share decline (Zone 4);
- termination of real 'dogs' (Zone 5).

The most interesting products fall into the question mark zone 3 where the market is attractive but the organisation lacks real competitive strength. Here resolving the mar-

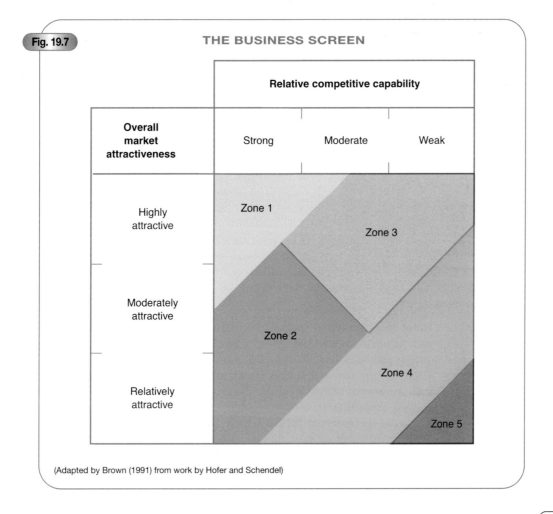

Fig. 19.7

THE BUSINESS SCREEN

Relative competitive capability

| Overall market attractiveness | Strong | Moderate | Weak |

Highly attractive — Zone 1, Zone 3

Moderately attractive — Zone 2

Relatively attractive — Zone 4, Zone 5

(Adapted by Brown (1991) from work by Hofer and Schendel)

keting direction depends on many factors but it is the area where marketing decisions to build, hold or harvest are most crucial.

MARKETING ANALYSIS

The audit process inevitably produces a great deal of data and information. Critical application of sales/profits and marketing measures to the product range will enable a company to identify those products that perform well, and those that patently under-perform. It can then make informed product policy decisions in respect of matters such as product improvement and modification, new product additions and replacements, and product withdrawals. It is probably no exaggeration to state that, even in the smallest of product ranges, products will differ in performance terms. Within larger product ranges, some products may have some common features that make for success or weakness in such a way that broad categories or types may be identifiable.

Peter Drucker, a well-known American management writer, has proposed a broad typology of products that encompasses the following categories:

1 Today's breadwinners (Cash Cows).
2 Yesterday's breadwinners (Dogs).
3 Tomorrow's breadwinners.
4 Others, referred to by such colourful terms as Cinderellas, also-rans, and investments in management ego (Stars).

While these descriptions are self-explanatory, if generalised they do indicate that company performance is closely linked to product offerings, and how these fare in a competitive market. There is also to be found in the writings of Drucker, and other management commentators, clear advice on how companies should plan and manage product policy through informed decision making following strategic analysis. Too often, managements launch products for the wrong motives (Drucker's 'investments in managerial ego'), or for the wrong market (product-market mismatch), or proceed to mis-allocate resources on 'lost cause' products rather than those with real potential (the Cinderella syndrome).

To plan effectively it is necessary to be very logical when analysing the data. An organisation must differentiate between those items which are likely to affect its performance significantly, from those which will have little effect. Treating the internal audit data separately from the external data allows the significant data to be classified under four headings:

- *Strengths*   These are the internal factors which are likely to enhance performance, such as having a well-trained sales force, efficient production and high-quality products.
- *Weaknesses*   These are the internal factors which are likely to inhibit performance, such as excessive capacity (high fixed costs), obsolete designs and long delivery schedules.
- *Opportunities* These are the external factors which favour the organisation, such as effective distributors, compliance with legislation, presence in growing market segments, security of supply of critical components or competitors being reorganised.

● *Threats*   These are the external factors which are likely to be to the organisation's disadvantage, such as strengthening currency making imported competition less expensive and exports more expensive, recently introduced competitive products, or substitutes able to offer comparable benefits to customers.

The selection of data in this way is known as a SWOT analysis as these are the initial letters of the classifications used. Its purpose is to provide a framework within which the selected information can be compared, the strengths can be developed to match the specific opportunities identified and those weaknesses for which there is a corresponding threat addressed.

However a good SWOT is not simply a listing of the key factors but a well-thought-out summary where the major strengths and weaknesses of greatest importance are highlighted.

There are several ways of reviewing the factors, but perhaps the easiest is to rank each on a scale of one (least important) to ten (most important). It is appropriate to concentrate efforts on the more important factors when planning future activity for any organisation.

The use of a SWOT analysis should not stop at the evaluation of the major factors. What is often overlooked is that combining these factors could point to distinct strategic choices. To focus on this a rearrangement into a TOWS (threats, opportunities, weaknesses and strengths) matrix is sometimes used. By highlighting the four strategy interactions below and allowing a time dimension the TOWS matrix helps both in the drawing up of marketing objectives and the formulation of strategy.

1 the WT strategy aimed to minimise both weaknesses and threats.
2 the WO strategy to minimise weaknesses and maximise opportunities.
3 the ST strategy based on the strengths of the organisation that can deal with threats from the environment.
4 the SO strategy which shows insight into possible actions that will build on the advantages available.

The full Tows Matrix was originally presented by Heinz Weihrich in 1982 and you should refer to the fuller account of its use in his original paper, it is illustrated in Fig. 19.8.

OBJECTIVES, STRATEGIES AND ASSUMPTIONS

From the SWOT/ TOWS analysis it should be possible to draw up marketing objectives which are consistent with the overall corporate objectives and the vision that might be set out in the mission statement. There will of course be financial and other operational objectives which also need to be internally consistent.

While a mission statement tends to be a general statement, objectives for any business, big or small, need to be specific to that business. For instance, say an entrepreneur wished to open a clothes shop in a town where there are already all the standard High Street retailers. Then he is likely to be more successful if his objective is framed to emphasise how his offering and shop will differ from the competitors' shops.

It is fundamental to effective planning that there has to be a goal to aim for. A good, and often used, analogy is that of a journey since the route can be planned only if the

Fig. 19.8	THE TOWS MATRIX	

Internal factors / External factors	Major internal STRENGTHS of high importance	Key internal WEAKNESSES of high importance
Key external OPPORTUNITIES	**S O strategies** Build and grow	**W O strategies** e.g. acquire resources (if possible) to allow opportunities to be taken
Major external THREATS	**S T strategies** Reassess strengths in relation to threats	**W T strategies** Real problems

starting point and the destination are both known. This does not go far enough since the real purpose of planning is to improve the effectiveness in achieving an agreed objective or task. When considering the journey this could be the reducing of the time taken to reach the destination. But, of course, to decide between the different options it is necessary that the objectives must be known. The situation tends to be more complicated in the social or business context since many, apparently sensible, objectives are not fixed, like a point on a map for example, but instead they are moving targets, such as being market leader. It is often difficult to formulate useful objectives even for commercial organisations where the basic objective is to increase asset value within acceptable levels of risk. It is even more difficult for other types of organisation.

EXERCISE

In a town there are already two record stores. One is a Virgin Records, centrally located and concentrating on chart music and videos. The other store has a preponderance of Classical and Jazz but also carries the current top hits. What opportunities would exist for an independent record store to be run by two former group musicians? And what objectives would you suggest are appropriate in this situation?

To be useful a marketing objective needs to have two basic components. The first is to specify what is to be achieved. This has to be realistic in both the light of present circumstances and past performance. The second is to state the time by which the objective is to be achieved. The objective needs to be stated in absolute terms. It is not sufficient to specify it in terms of a market share or previous growth. This is essential since otherwise there can be no comparison between actual performance and the objective set month by month or week by week. If the objective is found for some reason to be unrealistic, it should be amended as otherwise it will have no value as a goal.

A useful way of remembering this is to have SMART objectives which are:

Specific
Measurable
Achievable } What is to be achieved
Realistic
Time-based   When it is to be achieved

The next stage is to specify how the stated objectives are to be achieved in general rather than specific terms. This is an important step since it provides the structure within which the detailed steps involved can be selected and implemented. It may be that the most appropriate strategy is to build market share, or it may be more suitable to harvest by withdrawing from a product or market. There are, of course, several intermediate situations. A lot depends on the competitive strength of the organisation as compared with other organisations, but it is also important to consider how the different products/services offered by any one company support each other. Most companies will try to balance well-established and successful products with new products which need investment now in order to be the successes of the future.

The essentials of product policy

A company's product policy may not explicitly appear in any one policy document or statement, but will likely show itself in those major decisions of corporate and marketing strategy that involve product planning, future development and innovation. Product policy will therefore integrate closely with the organisation's mission statement and any ongoing re-evaluation of 'what business are we in?' Essentially, product policy will be concerned with:

1 Developing strategic guidelines that direct at once the marketing of existing products and the development of new products. While these guidelines will be associated with company-wide objectives such as profitability and growth-market share potential, they will also reflect corporate policy in respect of what is a desirable mix of product offerings. These guidelines will determine the overall strategic direction of the company in terms of product-market development, and will be the concern of senior management and marketing decision makers.

2 Translating these general guidelines into operational performance at the level of both individual products and the wider product mix. Specifically:

(a) For existing products, this will involve managing and monitoring the marketing of these products in respect of markets served, quality-performance indicators such as profitability and image, sales targets and competitive standing. These tasks will be the core of day-to-day marketing at the product level. While companies will vary in the way in which they staff and organise for these ongoing activities, it is not uncommon to find in larger companies a division of marketing responsibilities according to product lines or brands, by the employment of specialist product managers or brand managers, within the marketing department. (Though a more detailed examination of marketing organisation approaches will be made later, for present purposes it is enough to understand that each product or brand manager looks after the marketing and competitive 'health' of an allocated number of company products or brand ranges.) Product marketing represents the most obvious marketing tasks of the company on a day-by-day basis. While for many company products there will be a comfortable and familiar maintenance job to be done in managing a 'steady tiller' within the marketplace, there will occasionally be the need to engage in more radical changes in marketing plans, and in the very product itself. The dynamics of customer tastes, or the cut-and-thrust nature of competitive marketing or new product activity, may sometimes make it necessary to fundamentally change the marketing of certain products, to redesign and re-present them, perhaps for a different market, or even to delete them from the range.

(b) For reasons of extraneous factors such as competition or market change, or to serve corporate growth or diversification strategies, in due course new products will be added to the product range, and occasionally new offerings substituted for withdrawn products. While the arguments for a market-centred approach to new product development are nowadays accepted by most companies, the successful development and launch of new products involves the commitment of marketing resources to an integrated company-wide innovation effort. As with comparable activities such as product modification and relaunch, new product introduction and marketing involve effectively rebalancing the total product range, and reflect decisions on product policy made at the corporate level. Within such a market-centred approach to new product development, the role of the marketer will be to advise, inform and initiate product change, and to participate in a cross-disciplinary teamwork approach to development and commercialisation.

In summary, product policy represents a key area of corporate and operational decision making about the product offering, which involves marketing in supporting present products, effecting ongoing marketing changes to the product range, and commercialising new products, as part of a total corporate plan. In simple terms, it involves (i) managing and modifying existing products, and (ii) developing and establishing new products.

PRODUCT/MARKET STRATEGY

A major impetus of product policy will be the corporate objectives to be attained via a balanced product mix in all chosen markets. This reflects that the overall performance of the company is the sum total of that of its various product/service/market offerings. Product/market strategy will address the issue of how such corporate objectives are to be achieved, both at the level of the individual product and the total product range. Strategy implies purposeful, well-researched, well-planned and well-resourced activity. In product strategy terms, the research and planning foundation will depend heavily on the careful analysis and monitoring of existing products' performance, on market research and forecasting, competitive analysis, and a firm understanding of company marketing and resource strengths and limitations. Product/market strategy can take many forms and variants, at a number of levels, depending on market circumstances, company practices and the like. For simplicity, the present treatment will deal with only the major, more generic, strategy alternatives. It should be stressed that product strategy does not operate by product dimension alone as certainly market factors have to be considered in parallel.

A useful perspective on product strategy that reflects this product-market focus is the product-market scope matrix developed by Ansoff, illustrated in Fig. 19.9.

Four broad strategy alternatives are identified within the product-market scope matrix:

1 **Market penetration**
Basically the company follows the advice of Peters and Waterman in 'sticking to its knitting', competing with the same product types in existing markets. This might involve increasing sales to existing customers, finding new users within present markets, or taking market share from competitors through more effective marketing. It is an area where it is important to retain existing customers by building barriers to prevent competitors taking sales. In this sector there is a need to emphasise the building of strong relationships with customers, driving down transaction costs and thus adding value to the exchange.

2 **Market development**
Here the company offers the same products to new markets or segments. A classic example of this strategy was the case of Johnson and Johnson's Baby Powder, which the company successfully targeted to women purchasers when facing a projected fall-off in demand in the primary babycare market. Companies building export markets would also exemplify this strategy.

3 **Product development**
This entails the introduction of new products, aimed at the same target market. Here the company is exploiting its basic marketing strengths and familiarity with

Fig. 19.9

STRATEGY ALTERNATIVES WITHIN THE PRODUCT-MARKET SCOPE MATRIX

Markets	Products	
	Present	New
Present	★ 1 Market penetration	★★ 3 Product development
New	★★ 2 Market development	★★★★ 4 Diversification

(Key: ★ = indicative degree of risk in each strategy)

customers in order to widen its product offerings. New products are discussed further in Chapter 20.

4 Diversification

Here the company moves into both new markets and new product sectors, perhaps involving major changes in technology and marketing methods. As indicated in the risk star-rating (*) in Fig. 19.9, this strategy involves the greatest risk of the four strategies outlined. For this reason, companies will often seek to contain or reduce their risks in some way, for example by licensing in technology or products, buying products and market share through acquisitions, or building on some familiar experience, e.g. in distribution channels or supplier links. By way of qualification, it should be pointed out that the rewards of risk-taking through diversification may be proportionately higher, while it is a truism that without risk-takers pursuing such strategies, most really innovative products would never see the light of day.

The Ansoff matrix (Fig. 19.9) as a decision tool is a very effective way of considering marketing options. The direction an organisation might follow could include product development (*see* Chapter 20), market development, or possibly the risky business of diversification.

It is possible to modify the Ansoff matrix and this can be beneficial when considering the issues of what is a product and a new product in more depth. Gary Hamel replaces the term 'product' with his concept of 'core competencies' which are the skills an organisation possesses. This considerably widens the basis of existing products and allows for a customer focus to be applied to solving customer problems, as opposed to the supplier focus on producing products. The category of new products also needs to be reconsidered. Types of new products are discussed in Chapter 20, these range from simple product modifications which are introduced to keep a product offering relevant to developing customer needs, through application of existing technology or competencies to create 'new to the world' products. The latter are obviously more unpredictable and risky. New products can be stretched even further away from the safety of existing products to the possible new products which are not based on existing skills. Even if offered to existing customers there is a major risk inherent in mastering the skills required to produce the new product.

Derek Abell has argued that when changes in the market are only incremental, firms may successfully adapt themselves to the new situations. However, timing plays a vital role in all product and market modifications. There is only a limited window of opportunity between the market being receptive to a new development and the competitive activity or other changes which mean it is too late, this is especially true where market development involves major shifts in product offerings or in the target market. One of Abell's strategic windows is focused on the opportunity to use new technology to produce a new offering or modify a product. This can be seen in practice when studying the fast-moving consumer electronics market where it is absolutely vital to get the timing right.

Abell's other strategic windows are based on either the customer groups to be served or the customer needs to be served. The most obvious one involves the move to market in new segments and the development of new primary demand. Alternatively new channels could be exploited as in the move to out-of-town warehouses for companies such as Toys 'R' Us who redefined their industry.

Both of these could be placed in the area of market modifications in the product/market matrix. Of more interest is the fourth category where Abell suggests that it is possible to redefine a market, 'frequently, as markets evolve, the fundamental definition of the market changes in ways which increasingly disqualify some competitors while providing opportunities for others. The trend towards marketing "systems" of products as opposed to individual pieces of equipment provides many examples of this phenomenon.' Again returning to the IT market, the supply of systems based on supplying both computer hardware and software is a good example of this.

PRODUCT MIX DECISIONS

Decisions on the consistency and dimensions of the product mix will comprise key issues within a company's product policy, and will almost certainly involve senior management (i.e. corporate) decision makers, as well as functional specialists in the marketing department. Corporate sales growth and profit objectives may be served by, for example, increasing the width of the product mix (i.e. adding new product lines) and capitalising on the company's reputation, or a leading brand name, in a horizontal move to adjacent product markets. For example, the recent introduction of Persil washing-up liquid exploited the strength of the Persil brand name in the detergent sector.

Contributions to corporate growth objectives might equally be achieved through increasing the depth of the product mix, thereby gaining competitive advantage and market coverage, through reaching buyers with differing preferences, in other segments. For example, some time after the successful launch of Jif surface cleaner fluid, for bathrooms and kitchens, Lever introduced Lemon Jif, exploiting the favourable association of lemon-based ingredients with cleaning and grease-removing properties.

By the same token, some companies will, through careful product policy guidelines, resolve that the product range must retain a consistency and logic that should not be diluted by straying into unrelated product areas. Other companies, after mixed experiences with diversification into other product fields, will tighten up their product policy by rationalisation, withdrawing or selling off products outside their reconsolidated product base. Such product policy moves will be difficult, and possibly costly, and will involve higher-level corporate deliberations and decisions. They will hopefully return to product policy a thrust and focus, and free resources to concentrate on product markets where the company has known strengths. For example, among the many companies to have withdrawn from the computer market in recent years, Honeywell Inc. appears to have little cause for regret, having successfully grown since through a well-managed concentration in fields such as electronic components, controls and instrumentation.

While most large companies have some variety in their product range, they will usually seek a consistency in their total offering, reflecting their key strengths and competencies. As an example, Fig. 19.10 shows the product-market sales of Colgate-Palmolive, the US-controlled consumer products manufacturer. This long established company is probably best known for Colgate toothpaste and Palmolive soap, which are represented in the chart under the oral care and body care divisions respectively. While the company has 40 per cent of the world toothpaste market, it has a variety of product interests that range from household cleaners (e.g. Ajax) to mouthwash and other health-care products.

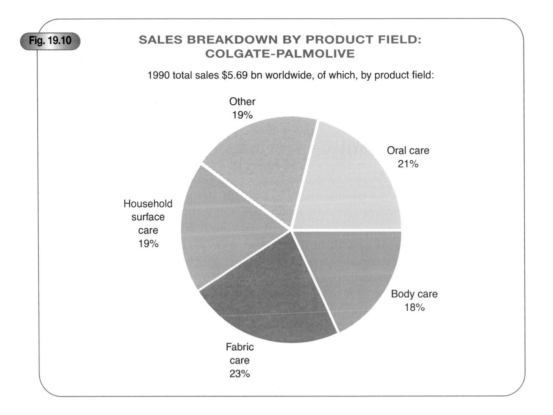

Fig. 19.10

**SALES BREAKDOWN BY PRODUCT FIELD:
COLGATE-PALMOLIVE**

1990 total sales $5.69 bn worldwide, of which, by product field:

Other
19%

Oral care
21%

Household
surface
care
19%

Body care
18%

Fabric
care
23%

MARKETING PROGRAMMES

With clearly defined objectives, a strategy for achieving these objectives selected and with a set of clearly defined assumptions, the next stage of the marketing planning process is the development of marketing programmes. The purpose of programmes is to specify the actions, responsibility, resources and schedule needed to achieve the stated objectives via the selected strategy. It will cover both marketing actions and the interfaces between the marketing function and other parts of the organisation which are essential to the achievement of the marketing task.

The simplest approach to programme development is to use the components of the marketing mix as a framework. This ensures that all essential tasks are covered and properly co-ordinated. It also ensures that the programmes are focused on the market segments which have been specified by the objectives and strategy statements.

By using this approach, it will be necessary to have separate programmes for each of the marketing mix elements which have been discussed in Chapters 10 to 18. There will also be programmes for the people and processes required to effectively deliver the offering. Depending upon the strategy these may be extensive or simple. For instance, where the strategy involves new products the programmes will be significantly more involved than if only minor product changes are considered necessary.

Generally the introduction of new products will also necessitate a co-ordinated programme of both making the product available and of promotion designed to create awareness of the new offering by potential users. This, as a result, might be considered as a single programme and separate from the general promotion programme. Often the complexity of the promotion programme for a new product launch will justify having a separate subprogramme for each of the four elements of the communication mix (advertising, public relations, sales promotion, and programme concerned with the personal selling aspects of promotion).

However most marketing programmes will relate to existing products. Use of product financial returns, portfolio analyses or research studies like the perceptual mapping exercise in Fig. 9.8 may highlight the need for a company to modify an offering to a greater or lesser extent. At one end of the spectrum such revision may entail no physical change to the product itself, but a repositioning job, perhaps through changing the marketing programme, the advertising strategy, or the platform or proposition on which the product is presented. Repositioning might require a redirection of the product to new target groups, perhaps for new uses or occasions. A now classic example of repositioning was the case of Lucozade, which was successfully remarketed from a remedial tonic drink to a leading 'soft' drink, targeted at younger health-conscious consumers.

Modification might take the form of other changes in marketing variables, such as price reductions or higher volume channels, in order to increase sales and market share. More fundamental changes to the product itself might be indicated, however. These could take the form of design face-lifts, to improve the product aesthetically and achieve a more contemporary image, as commonly happens with 'white goods' such as cookers and refrigerators, where such cosmetic changes are necessary to stay abreast of fashion trends. More radical still might be a complete redesign of the product, encompassing both bodywork restructuring, changes in functions and materials, and perhaps major changes in technology. While such a major product revision would entail the development of a new, second-generation or replacement product, it is a moot point at which level of revision a product modification has to be classified as a new product development strategy.

A practical issue in both product modification and replacement activities is the timing of the new product and the phase-out of the old, since decisions about production plant, old-model stock depletion and spares, and the promotion and selling-in of new models will need to be handled carefully to ensure a co-ordinated operation.

In addition to the programmes that can be directly related to the principal objectives there are likely to be some which address specific issues raised in the internal or external audit. The example of the introduction of a Value Added Tax (VAT) would justify having an individual programme since it affected the organisation's approach to pricing and invoicing, as well as revisions of the terms and conditions of sale.

Once the programmes have been detailed the total resources required for their implementation can be determined. Almost inevitably this will exceed the resources allocated in the budget developed from the initial objectives, strategy and assumptions. This will require an iterative process to reconcile the cost of the required programmes with the available resources, providing the opportunity to optimise these two factors. In doing so it is necessary to estimate the impact on the objective of each programme. The effect of both increasing and reducing the expenditure should be considered.

Consider the following example. An organisation estimates that on the basis of existing data the most likely effect of reducing advertising expenditure is to make the overall situation worse, because of the corresponding reduction in sales revenue. An increase in advertising could improve sales but would be more risky as the level of sales growth, as well as the time before such sales are achieved, is uncertain. However, if both a promotional push and an increase in direct sales effort are combined then the increase is more certain. If the results of the revised programmes are thought to be better then this could be the option chosen. As part of the reconciliation process, the effect that changing the assumptions would have should also be investigated so that the final plan has less risk and more potential of achieving the agreed objectives than any of the alternatives.

In carrying out this process it is inevitable that the underlying assumptions will have been fully evaluated and some innovative approaches considered. Usually the final plan will deviate only to a limited extent from the approach followed previously. The planning process should, however, ensure that a radical plan could be adopted if justified. Volvo provides an example of a company which responded appropriately to changing market conditions even though this required a significant revision of existing plans. By the early 1980s it had been expected that without a replacement for the ageing 240 series vehicle, the Volvo market share would be severely affected. A new vehicle was designed and the investment in a new production facility completed when it became clear that demand for the existing vehicle had revived. It was decided therefore to postpone the launch of the new vehicle in spite of the investment made. As a result, the 700 series vehicles were not launched for another two years with a corresponding extension to the expected life cycle of this model range.

STRATEGY FOR MARGINAL PRODUCTS

One of the major lessons of both portfolio analysis and PLC monitoring is that there are dynamic resource interdependencies among a company's product range. Simply stated, a company cannot afford to have too many loss-making or marginal products. Sooner or later, radical action will be called for, in the interests of the company as a whole. This is not to deny that some marginal products may be knowingly maintained for a time, in given circumstances, e.g. newly launched products in promising sectors, or older products performing a market-holding operation until a planned replacement issues off the assembly line.

Again, some products with specialist features or a strategic significance, perhaps among key customer groups, may be given a period of grace in which to be managed back to solvency. 'Special' products, sometimes heatedly defended by sales managers, might be repriced at 'special rates' in order to return profits. In other cases, a concentration strategy might enable the company to regroup product marketing activity about the strongest segments, or through the most viable channels.

Products identified through portfolio analysis as cash-earning dogs ('cash dogs') will be left alone while producing returns. More particularly, loss-making 'dog' products would require serious consideration. While loss-makers are known drains on company resources, it is often the case that their loss-making is under-recorded, since they may give rise to continued quality and other problems that take disproportionate managerial time, thereby indirectly affecting the prospects of more healthy products. For some of these products it may be possible to engineer a temporary break-even or small profit, through drastic cut-backs in support, increased prices, or both. Exceptionally, if the product sector generally is depressed, this might buy extra time within which some competitors might pull out, effecting a further, if temporary, improvement.

Sooner or later, though, decisions will have to be made to cut out the 'deadwood' products and eliminate the clutter in the range. Though statistically unproven, there is a consensus that the 80:20 rule operates as forcefully within product policy as elsewhere. Eighty per cent of the company's profits (or losses?) are attributable to 20 per cent of the products. The product deletion decision itself might take the form of an immediate discontinuation, or, more commonly, a planned phase-out over a short period to complete order commitments. Occasionally the product, its brand name or associated production facilities may be successfully sold to other interests, perhaps smaller concerns more able to cope with diminished volumes and margins.

MARKETING CONTROL

Marketing is really very simple in concept. The ideal offering (product or service) is described by the authors below:

> A perfect *product* is a combination of goods and services unique and impossible for actual or potential competitors to match, which solves a problem for a customer, or meets his or her need or desire, in a way which no other combinations of goods and services can do as well; and which can thereby generate a revenue stream, discounted at the company's cost of capital, more than adequate to pay the costs of its development and provision.

In most organisations survival depends upon positive cash flow but few are able to offer a perfect product. Good marketing is often the effective management of products and services which are far from perfect. Survival and future prospects can therefore depend upon the level of new business in the form of orders received. Accordingly, the level of new business is generally considered a critical measure of performance. Unfortunately, it tends to be somewhat volatile. It is subject to seasonal variations, changes in the economic climate and is affected by much talked about factors such as confidence. Because of such external factors it is often difficult to attribute sales changes to sales force activity alone.

It is tempting, therefore, to simply compare the figure week by week or month by month with the figure shown on the budget, and providing there is no negative variance, to assume all is well. There are two serious and related problems with this approach. First, there is an underlying assumption that the budgeted figure, having been agreed or accepted, should be seen as a benchmark against which actual performance can be measured. In manufacturing businesses this is often seen as realistic since production rates are seen to be also dependent upon assumptions being made. These, however, involve the reliability of the plant and equipment used, operator training, freedom from strikes and so on. Generally, deviations from an anticipated level of reliability can be traced back to a faulty repair or an incorrectly carried out maintenance procedure. The improvement in reliability depends upon these problems being identified and rectified. The marketing budget is very different, since the forecast is based on many more arbitrary factors. To consider it as a benchmark is akin to suggesting that the weather is unreliable because it is not as forecasted.

The second problem is that opportunities will be missed unless performance, as measured by new business, is judged in terms of the current situation rather than with the assumptions used to develop the forecast and budget. For instance, if the new business is more than forecast and production is limited, profit can be increased by either reducing expenditure on advertising, for example, or by increasing prices. These are, however, short-term approaches. More often sales being above budget is an indication that the market is expanding more quickly than expected. This is serious since if nothing is done to match this expansion market share will be lost. Many well-established companies have fallen into this trap. They have consistently exceeded their pessimistically set budgets while at the same time losing market share to competitors. This has two equally important implications. The first is that while production efficiency can be simply measured by output, new business cannot be used in the same way to measure marketing efficiency, unless it can be established that the assumptions, upon which the agreed budget was based, and the individual marketing programmes remain valid. There were periods when this may have been expected, but they were a long time ago. The modern experience is that situations can change rapidly and assumptions can become invalid just as quickly. The second implication is that to avoid these problems it is necessary to develop systems by which new business can be analysed in detail. The primary objective of the systems should be to discriminate between performance which can be attributed to factors external to the organisation and those which can be attributed to the implementation of the organisation's marketing programmes.

THE IMPLEMENTATION OF MARKETING PLANNING

Within an organisation the marketing planning process requires individuals who have a sound understanding of the principles of marketing. In particular, this has to be demonstrated by the commitment of senior management. Without this understanding the benefits of the planning process are perceived in terms of reducing uncertainty rather than as it should be, of increasing the ability of the organisation to respond to uncertainty.

As should be evident from the preceding section on control, the marketing plan should be at the centre of the performance measurement process. It should also provide the starting point whenever there is a need to respond to changes in external or internal circumstances which could affect the organisation, its customers, or the relationship between these.

When economic and technical situations are stable, marketing planning might easily become an annual task. In the turbulent economic and technical environment in which organisations must now compete it has to be a continuing process. It should be stressed, however, that this does not mean that programmes are changed month by month. If the planning has been done effectively, most, if not all, programmes will remain valid in spite of the assumptions upon which they were based. However, changing circumstances should be identified and analysed early enough to accommodate any needed modifications to the overall plan.

CONCLUSION

Marketing planning is the means by which well-organised companies bring together their marketing activities into a concerted action plan, ready for the market. A logical sequence will usually be followed in marketing planning, commencing with information gathering and analysis, combined with a marketing audit exercise involving issues and influences both within and outside the company. From the audit stage will be developed the marketing objectives to be addressed, while these in turn will largely direct the strategies to follow within the plan. Key assumptions made during the planning exercise need to be made explicit, as these will have some bearing on the flexibility and scope of the plan itself. Finally, no marketing plan will be complete without some provision for implementation, supporting organisation and control.

QUESTIONS

1 Taking any of the case studies in the text, develop a SWOT analysis to identify the major internal and external issues to be addressed.

2 What kind of market information would be necessary for marketing planning, and how might it be obtained?

3 Compare and contrast the marketing plan for an established product with that for a new product.

4 Consider the view that companies will derive as much benefit from the planning exercise as from the marketing plan itself.

FURTHER READING

Abell, D. 'Strategic windows', *Journal of Marketing*, Vol. 42, No. 3, 1978, pp. 56–62.

Ansoff, I. (1989) *Corporate Strategy*, Revised Edn, Penguin, Harmondsworth.

Boston Consulting Group (1971) 'The product portfolio', *Perspectives on Experience*, Boston.

Brown, R., 'Making the product portfolio a basis for action', *Long Range Planning*, Vol. 24, No. 1, 1991.

Doyle, P., 'The realities of the product life cycle', *Quarterly Review of Marketing*, Summer 1976.

Drucker, P. F., 'Managing for business effectiveness', *Harvard Business Review*, 41, May 1963.

Fifield, P. (1993) *Marketing Strategy*, Heinemann, Oxford.

Hamel, G. and Prahalad, C. K. (1994) *Competing for the Future*, Harvard Business Press, Boston.

Kotler, P. (1997) *Marketing Management: Analysis Planning and Control*, 7th Edn, Prentice-Hall, Implementation.

McDonald, M. H. B. (1995) *Marketing plans – and how to use them*, 3rd Edn, Heinemann.

McDonald, M. H. B. (1993) 'Portfolio analysis and Marketing Management', *Marketing Business*, May.

Peters, T. and Waterman, R. (1982) *In Search of Excellence: Lessons from America's Best Run Companies*, Harper & Row, New York.

Weihrich, H., 'The TOWS matrix – a tool for situational analysis', *Long Range Planning*, Vol. 15, No. 2, pp. 54–66, 1982.

CASE STUDY

Restaurant Kings, or just 'silly burgers'?

This was a headline of a UK newspaper article about McDonald's.

The problem is that McDonald's growth has relied on aggressive expansion in the number of outlets, rather than attracting new customers to existing outlets. In fact in 1996, outlet numbers increased by 6.4 per cent, turnover by 2.9 per cent, so actually turnover per outlet has dropped.

This is not how it used to be. Successful new initiatives such as Big Mac (1967), Egg McMuffin (1971), and Chicken McNuggets (1982) were all ideas from some of the 2000 plus franchise holders who own McDonald's outlets, all these boosted turnover. There is a view that these ideas are not encouraged as much today. Certainly the last few years have seen notable failures in the US such as McLean burgers (1992), and the 'adult orientated' Arch DeLuxe (1996) which was supported with a $100 million marketing support programme.

Major rival Burger King achieved a profitable link with Disney film's 'The Lion King' and other competitors have concentrated on enhancing quality with initiatives such as 'flame grilled' burgers, while McDonald's have apparently resorted to discount pricing, and 'feel-good' advertising. The 'Campaign 55' promotion, which was built on the tradition of 1955 when Ray Kroc founded the modern McDonald's, was cancelled prematurely. Under this promotion a Big Mac could be bought for 55 cents when purchased with fries and a drink, and customers received coupons for free product if orders failed to arrive

within 55 seconds. However, in the words of McDonald's vice president Richard Starmann, 'customer response over the first six weeks was not up to our expectations', also its US franchisees were failing to greet the promotion with the enthusiasm the Company had anticipated.

Worse, three successive failures in marketing initiatives/product launches has caused financial analysts to suggest that there is more wrong than just a few promotions, in fact 'Campaign 55' was supposed to be more than a promotion, it was planned to be used to motivate many levels of the Company and its operations. It is suggested that McDonald's have lost the focus on its core business of selling hamburgers, lurching from bad strategy to bad strategy and failing to understand its market. In particular the rapid expansion programme has seen cases of new restaurants opening within a mile of existing outlets leading to complaints from franchisees. There are also some suggestions that McDonald's products are perceived to be not as good as the competition's.

The newspaper article suggests that it is not obvious how McDonald's can recapture its pre-eminence. However with a brand name that is the best known worldwide, there is still a need for some 'McMagic' if the company is not to lose business to more focused rivals.

Question

What 'McMagic' marketing would you suggest could assist the company? Concentrate on actions related to good planning for the future rather than throwing money at the problem.

CHAPTER 20

Product Analysis and New Product Development

He that will not apply new remedies must expect new evils;
for time is the greatest innovator.
Francis Bacon

INTRODUCTION

New product development is a vital part of marketing policy for all companies and organisations, as it represents one of the key means by which corporate renewal is achieved, and a future secured. As it is a future-directed activity that affects the whole company and its commercial prospects, it follows that new product development should serve corporate objectives, and their expression through strategy. It will therefore be at the centre of much corporate deliberation and decision making, and in most well-managed companies it will be the focus of a planned development programme.

Marketers have a major role to play in new product development, for a number of reasons. First, product development is itself a material part of marketing strategy, and a route to both increased competitiveness and customer satisfaction. Second, marketers are, perhaps uniquely, in the position to direct and assist the development effort, through their market knowledge and research capability. Furthermore, it will be the role of the marketing function to launch and successfully commercialise the new products, once readied for market.

THE CASE FOR NEW PRODUCT DEVELOPMENT

The most obvious case for product development is the strategic need to innovate and change in response to, or preferably somewhat ahead of, market change. While companies will innovate at different speeds, and with varying success, some will appear more competitive and forward-thinking in their product development activities, and others more reactive and conservative. As in business generally, product development is an undertaking concerned with opportunity-seeking, but beset by risks – statistics vary, though conservative estimates would indicate that at least 50 per cent, and maybe 60 to 70 per cent, of new products fail within their launch year, while a high proportion of the remainder never become major successes. However, risk, and risk-taking, are necessary ingredients of the innovation process, as summarised in the adage: 'The biggest risk of all is to take no risks.'

In simple terms, one of the most telling implications of the product life cycle model is that a company must ensure that a succession of new products is coming on-stream, to cover the commercial ground lost through the demise of older products, at the other end of the life cycle. Certainly, the prospects would be rather weak for a company with a product range hemmed within the later stages of the life cycle. Appropriate to the biological analogy of the life cycle model itself, new product development can therefore be viewed as a form of plough-back, an investment for the future.

The growing body of research on new product development has shown that the rationale for product development will vary among companies, depending on factors such as market conditions and company performance. Among the strategic objectives that companies follow in their innovation programmes, the following are perhaps the most common:

1 To increase or defend market share. Given the evidence that market share has a strong association with profitability, through competitive mass and production economies, this rationale for innovation is closely tied to profit-seeking.
2 To develop or enter a future new market or segment, perhaps as a pre-emptive strategy to outpace competition.
3 To maintain a lead position as an innovator. While this objective is competition-related, those companies that operate in fast-changing technology fields, such as electronics, will find themselves almost carried along by a constant stream of product and process innovations.
4 To diversify into new product markets, as a strategic hedge against over-dependence on a limited product range: the classical 'third leg' strategy.
5 To exploit distribution strengths, to stimulate distribution channels, or to cement a firmer trading relationship with intermediaries.
6 To make productive use of slack resources, e.g. in sales or production capacity, or perhaps to remedy seasonal or cyclical dips in activity.
7 To exploit company experience in working with a new technology or new materials, or otherwise to commercialise spin-offs and by-products of the company's primary endeavours.

Whatever local policy guidelines companies set for themselves in product development terms, it has become a commonplace observation that dependence on new products for sales and profits growth is increasing steadily over time. Innovation-watchers might argue that the rate of change is multiplicative, making for a continual growth in product innovation. Such a view could certainly be supported by reference to factors such as the dismantling of trade barriers and the globalisation process, the convergence of technologies (e.g. telecommunications and computing), and the growing sophistication and innovativeness of customers generally.

TYPES OF NEW PRODUCTS

Product development represents a wide spectrum of activity, spanned at one end by the painstaking development of products and technologies through basic research programmes, and at the other extreme by the countless variations and improvements to existing products that are everyday features of 'busy' markets such as grocery products.

'Newness' is a relative term, and most products introduced to the marketplace are developments or variations on existing product formats. The norm for most markets will likely be a constant drip-feed of incremental product improvements, with the occasional 'splash' effect of a major product innovation that regroups the market and redirects technological development. In line with such a process, most major companies will subscribe to both ongoing product improvement and longer-term programmes of fundamental research. The variety of 'new' products to be met with will therefore encompass the following broad types:

1 *Major innovations* Products involving radical new combinations of technology, formulation or user benefits, with the potential to form entirely new markets and even whole industries – television, X-ray, the microprocessor and VCR technology would typify such innovations. By definition, such innovations are rare gems and not without major development and commercialisation risks, e.g. the build-up of a customer base can itself be a key issue, as instanced by the commercial difficulties of the Concorde supersonic aircraft joint venture.

2 *Product improvements* At one end of the scale, these products may represent major innovations in existing markets, with the potential to marginalise other competitors. A good example would be the succession of 'system' products that have effectively created new segments in markets as diverse as writing instruments, wet-shaving products, cameras and lawnmowers. In these and other markets (e.g. cars, washing machines) it is possible to trace a thread of development through to second- and third-generation products that consolidate updates in design and technology.

At the other end of this category would be the more everyday, marginal improvements and modifications that are regularly incorporated through features such as product redesign, repackaging, and formula and ingredient changes. A particular marketing variant on the improved product is the repositioned product, an existing product that is retargeted, often unchanged, to a new market or segment.

3 *Product additions* Products without major claims to innovation or novelty, usually imitations of current market leaders, or simply line extensions of product ranges that a company already markets successfully. Certainly below the brand leadership 'skyline' in the marketplace, most product entrants are likely to fall within this category. Not surprisingly, most product failures occur within the ranks of these 'me too' products. However, exceptionally it may happen that a largely imitative or indistinctive product, perhaps entered as a diversification move by an established company from another market, assumes market leadership through better marketing.

Note: A key point to make about new products is that 'newness', like beauty, is in the eye of the beholder – in marketing terms, customer perception is the ultimate judge of whether a product is new or not.

THE PRODUCT DEVELOPMENT PROCESS

The corporate setting

The development of any new product, or service, is usually a lengthy, costly and risky process. While 'lucky strike' discoveries of new products and formulations do happen, they are very much the exception to the general rule: 'success comes from 1 per cent inspiration and 99 per cent perspiration!'

Most companies will seek to create their own 'luck' by adopting a disciplined, commercially directed programme of new product development that follows key corporate objectives (market share, growth, profitability), and is consistent with whatever product policy guidelines these imply (as discussed in Chapter 11). Such a programme will depend for its success on a number of firm prerequisites:

1 An up-to-date summary, or shared understanding, of key corporate priorities for development.
2 Shared knowledge of company resources, capabilities and limitations.
3 Market, competitor and other external knowledge and information sources, e.g. for checking the commercial potential of projects.
4 Commitment to a base level of specialist resourcing, projected forward against target activities and projects.
5 A known and agreed set of procedures and decision criteria against which to assess and progress development projects.

In some companies these elements may be mirrored in corporate mission statements, annual plans and product policy guidelines, or even formally laid down in dedicated development or R&D plans. While over-formalisation may hinder rather than help, what is important is that at the appropriate levels in the company informed decisions are made and strategic criteria followed in respect of assessing and advancing development initiatives.

Stages in the product development process

While the gestation period for different products will doubtless vary according to technological complexity, resourcing issues, corporate priorities and the like, an attempt will be made to present a generalised sequence of the development process. Figure 20.1 illustrates a simple 'funnel' model of the process, in which new product ideas are initiated, screened, commercially assessed and progressed further, rejected or set aside for later reworking. The product development stages outlined in the model are examined in some detail below.

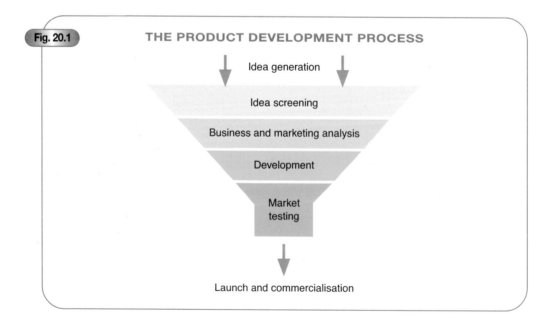

Fig. 20.1

THE PRODUCT DEVELOPMENT PROCESS

Idea generation

Idea screening

Business and marketing analysis

Development

Market testing

Launch and commercialisation

Idea generation

This stage, the logical beginning of product development, represents for most companies an ongoing effort of accumulating and generating development ideas, rather than a discrete once-and-for-all step or process. As worthwhile ideas are at a premium, a continuous effort is necessary to tap creativity from a number of sources.

The number of ideas necessary to support successful product development has been illustrated by research studies conducted by the US consulting firm Booz-Allen, Hamilton. In a landmark 1968 survey among American manufacturers it was estimated that 58 ideas were necessary to sustain a successful new product launch. This figure had been reduced to seven when the consultants conducted a duplicate survey in 1981, indicating that manufacturers had improved their development performance through stricter management and investment procedures. Even so, the research indicates that most product ideas fail to 'run the gauntlet' of successive stages and filters within the development process. Moreover, as no company can claim any monopoly on creativity, it would make sense to consider potential product ideas from a variety of sources.

Figure 20.2 presents a summary of idea sources available to a typical company. In most companies product ideas will come from both internal and external sources, though certainly in technology or science-led fields such as pharmaceuticals or electronics there will at any time be a feedstock of ideas and formula alternatives that stem directly from ongoing research programmes. Even in these cases, though, there is a strong case for drawing on problem 'cues' from users and customers, trade channels, competitor intelligence and sales force feedback. Without such market direction there is a danger that development efforts lose their focus and become directed solely by the forces of 'technology push'.

Fig. 20.2   NEW PRODUCT IDEA SOURCES AVAILABLE TO A COMPANY

Internal		External	
R&D Design	} Basic research	Competitors	– Imitation or improvement
Engineering Manufacture Purchasing	} Development and operations	Customers	– Trade customers, intermediaries, consumers Feedback, complaints, suggestions
Marketing Market research Sales personnel Customer service	} Market studies, analysis of previous research, product testing	Specialists	– Design houses, consultants, advertising and research agencies
Senior management		Others	– Suppliers Joint-venture partners, overseas contacts, licensing partners
Other sources – employee suggestions, interdepartmental efforts, e.g. brainstorming			

Whatever the product field, ideas for new products, and product improvements, can come from anywhere within the value chain, inside or outside the company. Within the company, multidisciplinary efforts, drawing on specialists from a number of departments, may prove especially effective. The logic of these approaches is that a more balanced spread of ideas may be generated, and that political or inter-departmental rivalry is reduced by eliminating the NIH ('not invented here') syndrome. Such teamwork efforts may take many forms, from the regular employment of creative techniques such as brainstorming, group problem solving and discussion sessions, to more permanent organisational mechanisms such as venture teams, 'think tanks' and new product committees.

Idea screening

Given a number of development ideas, it is necessary to put them through a standard screening method to select only those with apparent business and development prospects. This first-level screening will usually rate and compare ideas across a number of key factors held to be important in terms of company/product fit, such as compatibility with company technology and manufacturing capability, marketing resources, distribution channels, research/design capability and the like.

Figure 20.3 presents a simplified example of a rating sheet that might be used for comparing development ideas across such a screen of weighted factors. The score profile illustrated in the table is quite encouraging, though in practice most development ideas would score quite modestly, while still others would be rejected as too middle-of-the-

Fig. 20.3

DEVELOPMENT IDEA RATING SCREEN

Product selection criteria	(A) Weighting	(B) Criterion rating (1 2 3 4 5 6 7 8 9 10)	Weighted idea score (A × B)
Corporate objectives	4	9	36
Financial capability	4	9	36
Marketing compatibility (including export)	4	8	32
Relation to present products	3	8	24
R & D/Engineering	2	7	14
Manufacturing	2	9	18
Suppliers/sourcing	1	9	9
	20		169

Weighted key score: 0 – 89 poor; 90 – 139 fair: 140 + good.

road to justify retention – too high a 'pass-rate' might dilute development resources and prejudice the real potential winners. While the shortlist criteria and their weightings will vary from company to company, and over time, the important consideration is that a consistent and agreed set of benchmarks is used from the outset.

Business and market analysis

The development ideas that survive the initial screening illustrated in Fig. 20.3 will effectively enter a more rigorous series of checks and analysis within the next filter, as it is after this stage that 'green light' decisions will be made to authorise and commit costly resources to development projects.

The business and market analysis stage is concerned with establishing a viable commercial rationale for development products, as both a guide for development work and a first-level business planning statement. The assessments made will involve market and marketing investigations, financial projections and costing/scheduling estimates. These investigations are likely to be carried out by separate departmental specialists, though the final business assessment will depend on some information interchange between parties, e.g. sales estimates will be required to assess revenue/profit calculations.

The marketing information required within the business analysis will likely come from a combination of existing market data and previous research findings, frequently supplemented by specific qualitative research exercises designed to validate the market attractiveness of shortlisted product ideas. Usually the ideas will need to be translated into alternative product concepts, i.e. succinct statements of the essential dimensions, attributes and rationale of the proposed product, expressed in customer language. The most common means of concept testing is via group discussions, where a small number of potential customers are exposed to alternative concepts, sometimes supported by pack mock-ups or models, asked questions and led in discussion on issues such as concept acceptability, apparent uses and benefits, advantages over existing products and the like. The findings of such research, though highly tentative, give some early insight into customer reactions and perceptions, and usually a means of selecting the more viable concepts, together with the benefits to incorporate into their further development. Alongside existing market data, and information on matters such as buying and switching behaviour, it should be possible to estimate preliminary market and sales forecasts, as an input to financial assessment work.

The marketing assessment of a successful product concept is commonly summarised in an outline marketing rationale, which will include overall comment on market volume, target segments and product positioning, together with specific guidelines on product attributes and qualities, indicative price-bands, and performance targets versus likely competition. These latter details will serve as an early product specification and a development brief to be followed by R&D.

Business analysis of product ideas is likely to be expressed through financial reports, which will combine aggregates such as sales forecasts, investment requirements, functional outlays and costings, and profit projections. These broad indicators in turn may break down into detailed components such as investment appraisal/payback summaries over an assumed product life or depreciation period, direct–indirect cost structures and departmental estimates, pricing and break-even calculations, and other financial arithmetic necessary to compare the viability of alternative product proposals.

Development

The development stage proper is really a succession of overlapping activities, orchestrated as a teamwork effort. While in most companies the responsibility for development work will be located within the R&D department, or an equivalent function such as Design or Product Engineering, in practice a variety of inputs are needed from other functions in order to ensure that the final product or service is both marketable and commercially viable. Figure 20.4 illustrates the complexity of interfunctional working within the development stage.

In scientific sectors such as medicines, the development stage will be lengthy, and usually divided into subphases, starting with pure research in pursuit of chemical/physiological reactions, leading to a development stage proper, itself divided into laboratory and clinical phases. In other science-led or high-technology fields such as aerospace and electronics, development may be equally complex, speculative and costly. The scale of resourcing and effort at risk within the development stage therefore makes clear the case for co-ordinated teamwork, planning and controls.

In the interests of co-ordination many companies have adopted particular forms of organisation for product development. These will be discussed later in the chapter. As previously stated, marketers have a particular guidance role to play in product development, if only to ensure that customer realities remain a focus of the development task. The experience of many marketers is that R&D personnel, unsupported by market guidance, fall prey to a 'technology myopia', an interest in the (research) chase itself rather than the (marketplace) end product. During the development stage, therefore, mar-

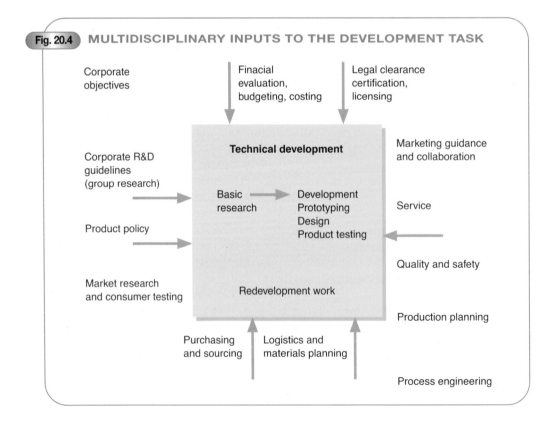

Fig. 20.4 MULTIDISCIPLINARY INPUTS TO THE DEVELOPMENT TASK

keters need to stay close to development staff, by ensuring for instance that prototypes are developed to market guidelines and assessed through customer research, and by generally advising on the maintenance of deadlines, cost, quality and design guidelines.

During the development period a succession of product tests will be made on a number of product formulations or prototypes in order to develop and 'fine-tune' a finished product ready for ultimate production and launch. For manufacturing planning purposes alone, varying tests will be made among alternatives in terms of materials specifications, design-performance configurations, production-assembly approaches and cost estimates, quality and safety assessments, supplier sourcing and the like. Logically, marketing specialists will need to stay abreast of these activities, and where necessary offer comment and advice on commercial and marketplace aspects of the decisions to be made.

Parallel to these 'internal' tests, there will usually be the need to subject successive product designs to customer tests, in order to check on market acceptability, decide on yet unresolved issues of product attributes (e.g. colour, materials, user controls, design aesthetics, minor design changes), or to make performance comparisons through in-use tests or trial placements.

A marketing-centred approach to development is therefore an iterative process, involving a dialogue with outside parties, primarily potential customers, and internally with various functional specialists within the organisation. It is worth stressing that both external and internal sides of the dialogue are critical. Furthermore, in today's competitive climate they are also interdependent. The increased zeal with which companies now embrace initiatives centred on Total Quality Improvement, just-in-time (JIT), design for assembly (DFA), and Simultaneous Engineering – to name but a few approaches that have gained a deserved respect within manufacturing and engineering – demonstrates that real market advantages can be won through internal improvements in production efficiency, quality and accelerated development.

Market testing

After the various product performance, functional and customer preference tests of the development phase, most companies will subject the, by now market-ready, product to a final assessment under market conditions, prior to full-scale launch. The objectives of doing this will be to reduce commercial risk by uncovering unforeseen product problems, fine-tuning the marketing and distribution programme, and making more accurate projections of sales, market performance and profitability.

The ultimate form of market test will be to conduct a formal test-marketing operation, usually in some test-market area(s) or town(s) chosen as representative of the total market area. Tests in TV regions, urban areas (e.g. London) and provincial cities are quite common for consumer goods. Test marketing would be undertaken as a scaled-down version of the intended national launch, involving similar advertising media and campaigns, distribution and sales cover, promotion and pricing elements of the marketing mix. Sometimes variations (e.g. in price, advertising intensity) may be tested in different test locations, in order to optimise the launch marketing mix, and to more accurately project sales volumes, purchaser profiles, buying volumes, first-time and repeat purchases. While marketing activity 'on the ground' will be most obvious in sales and advertising terms, the value of the test market will rest as firmly on the research conducted at trade and household level, through retail consumer audits, sales-force feedback and other sources. It may, for instance, prove necessary to buy in research in a control area outside the test market, in order to compare sales effects on competitor products, and to eliminate market-wide variations. Of particular interest to the marketer will be the recorded incidence of initial sales (penetration) and repeat sales (repurchase), which, together with purchase size, will indicate the likely success of the eventual full launch. Though generalised, the trial-repeat patterns set out in Table 20.1 would indicate varying degrees of success.

Limited market testing may be conducted instead of a full test-marketing operation, perhaps where:

- product and production variables have to be finalised well in advance, e.g. with cars and other durable manufactures;
- the product does not represent a major launch or commercial risk, e.g. as with a range addition or minor variation on a trusted formula; or where extensive previous in-development research assures confidence;
- competitive urgency may drive for an accelerated launch, or there may be the real risk of competitors spoiling test-market results (e.g. by underpricing, intensified sales and promotion), or the loss of competitive surprise, or even copycat products appearing;
- there are other factors involved, such as budget constraints, or a need for marketing information limited to restricted areas, e.g. brand-switching patterns, promotional effectiveness.

Limited marketing testing might take various forms, for example 'mini' test markets involving selected stores or a regional chain, where test products are 'placed' by the company for a period of time. In other cases, commercial market and research test services will be used, perhaps involving panels of households that are recruits to a shopping circle involving catalogue choice or home delivery. Comparable, though less strictly commercial, are the simulated 'shopping laboratories' operated by a number of research companies.

Market testing industrial products is usually conducted on a more controlled basis, for example through trial installation with selected customers, or through invitation to demonstration events, company showroom and test facilities and the like. Arguably, heavy investment industrial products are more likely to be developed through continuing contact with prospective customers, so that many of the 'grey areas' covered by test marketing may be already resolved.

Finally, it is worth noting that, with growing internationalisation, large global companies are increasingly conducting test-market operations in selected countries, prior to regional and international market launch operations.

Table 20.1 ● First-time and repeat sales combinations during test market

% Trial purchase	% Repeat purchase	Possible diagnosis
High	High	Marketing and product successful.
Low	High	Poor marketing threatens good product.
High	Low	Product unsatisfactory.
Low	Low	Both marketing and product unsatisfactory?

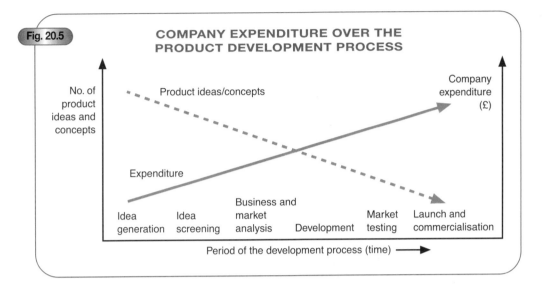

Fig. 20.5

COMPANY EXPENDITURE OVER THE PRODUCT DEVELOPMENT PROCESS

No. of product ideas and concepts

Product ideas/concepts

Company expenditure (£)

Expenditure

Idea generation — Idea screening — Business and market analysis — Development — Market testing — Launch and commercialisation

Period of the development process (time) ⟶

Launch and Commercialisation

This represents the end of the development process, and the full-scale introduction of the finished product to the marketplace. The resource costs and risks attending this stage are significant, as shown in the simple development-expenditure relationship outlined in Fig. 20.5. The commercial risks riding on any major launch justify the careful analyses, tests and preparations involved in the development process, and also the marketing professionalism required to support market entry. Competitive realities should ensure that the company makes objective decisions based on test-market results – even if the decision is to abort or delay product launch. Given a 'green light' decision to proceed, however, the company will still need to maximise the lessons of the test market, and ensure that launch activity proceeds methodically to the marketing plan developed. Given that production volumes will require scaling-up from the pilot plant levels of the test market, many companies will decide on a gradual 'rolling' launch region by region, or compromise by stock build-up to shorten the release period and increase launch impact. Critical to the success of the launch will be the monitoring of market research indicators, and generally the quality of managerial decisions taken on the basis of the controls built into the launch marketing plan.

Product adoption and diffusion

Of direct relevance to the process of new product development, segmentation and target marketing is the issue of how products are received and adopted on release to the marketplace. There is a consensus that new products penetrate or diffuse into the marketplace at differing rates, among different groups of buyers. The most notable theoretical contribution to this issue has been the work of the American researcher Everett Rogers who proposed that, at least in relative terms, first-time purchasers of new products could be classified according to the innovativeness of their adoption behaviour. Rogers presented the adoption behaviour of purchasers of a new product as a time-dependent phenomenon that could be plotted within a normal distribution curve, as illustrated in Fig. 20.6.

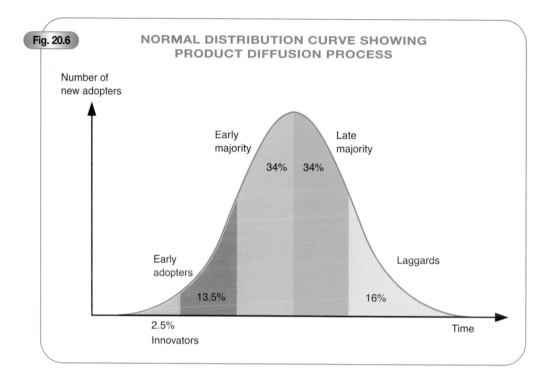

Fig. 20.6

NORMAL DISTRIBUTION CURVE SHOWING PRODUCT DIFFUSION PROCESS

The five adopter groupings statistically identified by this analysis might suggest that buyers vary somewhat in terms of innovativeness, openness to new propositions, conservatism, loyalty and related behaviourial dimensions. While there are a few research findings that indicate innovators to be younger, better educated, more cosmopolitan and open-minded, there has yet to emerge any set of general findings, or any reliable and practical indicator of innovativeness, that might help marketers in the obvious interest that they have in identifying and targeting these innovation-prone buyers.

ORGANISATION FOR NEW PRODUCT DEVELOPMENT

Of no small significance to the success of a company's innovation efforts will be the way in which it organises and manages the development effort. Research studies indicate that top management involvement and leadership are critical determinants of the 'entrepreneurship' shown by the whole organisation. Rigidity, bureaucratic rule-making, demarcation and inter-departmental conflict are major obstacles to success in new product development. In order to avoid these problems and to encourage team-work and co-ordination, progressive companies have evolved separate organisational arrangements for their innovation programmes. Figure 20.7 outlines a number of the more common organisational 'solutions' to be met with, though it should be stressed that structural preferences vary from company to company:

- The *Product Manager* system, commonly found in large consumer goods companies in particular, meets with mixed reports in terms of product development. The major reason for this is that product managers have enough pressing problems dealing with established products, so that, excepting more simple line extensions, new product development may suffer by comparison.

- The *New Product Manager* position has evolved from the product manager system, specifically to allow the full-time efforts in innovation that product managers rarely manage.
- *New Product Committees* are commonly used in large companies, usually for policy-making, review and product selection purposes, rather than full-time innovation management. Though composed of representatives of different functions, it may suffer the common committee malaise of bureaucracy, lethargy and political infighting.
- *The New Product Department* represents a more visible and dedicated solution for development than a new product committee, and will usually be headed by a senior manager experienced in product development, supported by a multidisciplinary team of specialists. Properly managed and resourced, such departments can be the driving force of innovation throughout the company.
- *Venture Groups* or teams represent a multifunctional task force grouping assigned to particular projects, or ventures. The efficacy of such a teamwork approach has been

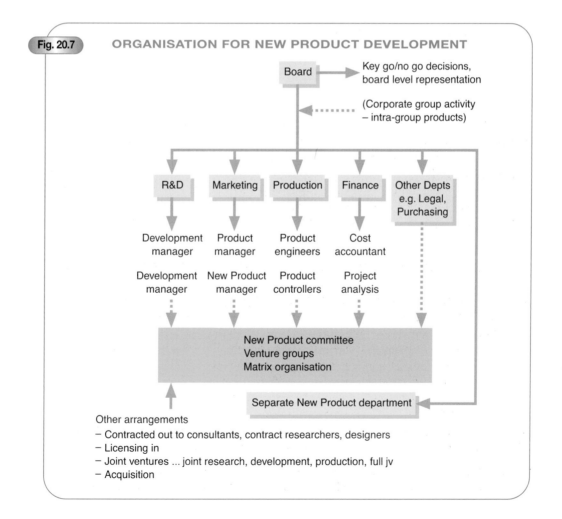

Fig. 20.7 ORGANISATION FOR NEW PRODUCT DEVELOPMENT

Board → Key go/no go decisions, board level representation

(Corporate group activity – intra-group products)

R&D	Marketing	Production	Finance	Other Depts e.g. Legal, Purchasing
Development manager	Product manager	Product engineers	Cost accountant	
Development manager	New Product manager	Product controllers	Project analysis	

New Product committee
Venture groups
Matrix organisation

Separate New Product department

Other arrangements
- Contracted out to consultants, contract researchers, designers
- Licensing in
- Joint ventures ... joint research, development, production, full jv
- Acquisition

confirmed by its major proponents, which include such large companies as Dow, Monsanto and 3M.

- The *Matrix Organisation* represents a radical company – or division-wide restructuring of staff and management in order to 'kick-start' innovation through improved communications, integration and working relationships. In simple terms, staff and functions are reorganised so that dual reporting relations impose closer collaboration across departmental boundaries.

While all these structures represent internal organisational mechanisms for new product developments, there remains a number of external sourcing avenues that companies use, for reasons of cost, or time-saving, or in order to 'import' creativity and innovation. In high-cost research environments such as proprietary medicines, licensing-in is a supplementary means of staying abreast of developments, or accelerated entry to new product sectors. Joint ventures and strategic alliances have the merit of risk-sharing and resource-pooling, and appear to be growing in popularity at the international level, especially in technology-led fields such as automobiles and aerospace.

CONCLUSION

New product development is of key strategic importance, as it represents the opportunity for a company to introduce 'fresh blood' into its products and services, and thereby strengthen and widen its opportunities in the marketplace.

Logically, from a marketing viewpoint, new product development should start with the identification of the needs and problems of customers, and the means to offer them enhanced performance and improvements over competitive offerings. Commercially, the innovation process generally is both costly and risky. Companies therefore need to adopt a managed approach to product development, ensuring informed decision making, co-ordinated efforts and effective returns on the investments involved. The marketing function has an important part to play in the general development process, and in the successful commercialisation of new products.

QUESTIONS

1 The 'right' organisation is often argued to be a critical factor in a successful programme of innovation. Comment on this view and evaluate the alternative means by which the product development function could be organised in a company manufacturing domestic and industrial refrigeration equipment.

2 'Test marketing is wasteful, inconclusive and unnecessary – if a new product is going to succeed, it is in the real market that success will be achieved.' Discuss.

3 Taking as a focus any recently launched new product, present in summary form a marketing rationale for its introduction, a broad view of its position relative to other products marketed by the company, and a brief listing of leading competitor products.

4 Consider the strategic role of new product development for a company operating within the service sector.

FURTHER READING

Booz-Allen, Hamilton (1982) *New Products Management for the 1980s*, Booz-Allen, Hamilton Inc.

Rogers, Everett M. (1983) *Diffusion of Innovations*, 3rd Edn, The Free Press.

Murray, J. A. and Driscoll, A. (1996) *Strategy and Process in Marketing*, Prentice-Hall.

Zeithaml,V. A. and Bitner, M. J. (1996) *Services Marketing*, McGraw-Hill.

CASE STUDY
Satin Gold

Michelle Graham sat in her office deep in thought. She had just received the latest Neilsen research figures on 'Satin Gold', the long established brand of bath oil which was the biggest contributor to her Company's revenue. The trend was clear, in spite of strong promotional support the brand was continuing in long-term decline. Over the past few years new competitive brands with more trendy images had nibbled into the market. There were also the new aromatic products which offered health enriching properties that now accounted for significant sales volumes, and of course there were the value for money own-label products in Boots as well as some major grocery stores.

It was obvious that fewer customers were buying 'Satin Gold' regularly, and the brand was not attracting new younger consumers.

Just over a year ago the company had launched a new product 'Bath Spice', which offered a powerful aroma and was packaged in a bright bulb shaped orange bottle. The product had been well received in home placement research tests, and seemed to be favoured by the younger age groups who were not attracted by the more mature image of 'Satin Gold'. However to launch 'Bath Spice' had involved some complex alterations to the production line and significant down time was experienced giving rise to stock shortages with both the new and the established products. For 'Bath Spice' this was particularly damaging as it led to the product not being available in key retail outlets at the time of the intensive launch advertising campaign. This was cited as one of the reasons why sales never achieved targets, and the product was withdrawn last month.

The problem with 'Satin Gold' remained. It was obvious that the slow loss of sales required some action if the Company was to maintain its sales and profit levels. At last weeks management meeting Ken Jones, the Production Director, had proposed installing a high speed automated packing line for 'Satin Gold'. By including a small redesign of the bottle this new line would reduce the cost of manufacture by 10 per cent which could be passed on to customers and help rekindle sales. He suggested the scheme would give a two year pay back on the capital expenditure which meets the company's financial requirements. However the new line would need to be located in the main building so the existing line would have to be taken out. The drawback of such a dedicated line was that all products packed by the company would have to use identical sized bottles but that was the price of efficiency.

Ken did have an alternative, but twice as expensive, that was a more flexible line that could handle a range of different bottle shapes without any loss of speed or increased labour. However this expenditure could not be justified on grounds of productivity gains from more efficient production.

The Finance Director leant his weight to the new dedicated filling line by saying, 'we don't need a sophisticated line; we have just tried a new product in a fancy bottle and it failed; customers can't be fooled by flashy shapes; it is only value for money that they understand so that's why we need to reduce our costs.'

Following the withdrawal of 'Bath Spice' a creative agency had been briefed to suggest the way forward. They had presented their initial ideas which involved testing three different products each in a different area of the country. Michelle reached across her desk to look at the proposals. The basic bath oil was not a problem, the technology of mixing a natural base with different essential oils, aromas and colours would also be no problem. The need to test the mixtures without using animals was in line with the comments made by young people during a number of qualitative focus groups, and that could be achieved. However the important part of the agency recommendations related to packaging. To achieve the excitement at the point of sale, the product had to be dramatic and all three proposals were based around packs which could not be accommodated on the proposed new production line. Michelle looked at the idea rating screen that she had drawn up and even scoring manufacturing at zero, the proposals totalled highly enough on all other criteria to make it look positive to proceed. The idea of comparing three different options instead of gambling on one single idea seemed realistic, but before taking the ideas into more detailed analysis and research it was going to be necessary to consider the issue of variations in packaging against the benefits of low price. Michelle knew she was in a difficult position as the marketing

department was being asked to resolve the future direction of the Company, yet if she could not accommodate the views of Finance and Production while achieving a new product offering acceptable to a carefully chosen target market, there would be just a steady decline in the sales of 'Satin Gold'.

Questions

1 What lessons can be learnt from the failure of Bath Spice?

2 How can Michelle try to make a success of any future new product launches?

CHAPTER 21

Research for Marketing

Managers make decisions: a good manager is one who makes good decisions. The basis of good decisions is having appropriate information available and using it effectively.

Peter Jackson

INTRODUCTION

In Chapter 8 marketing information was defined in the context of organisational information. It was compared with operational information and its importance to marketing decision making was discussed. This chapter introduces the formal approach to obtaining marketing information as a specific business activity or marketing function.

While as a marketing function this activity is generally known as marketing research there is no accepted definition of this term. This is in spite of many attempts having been made to define it both by the authors of the celebrated marketing textbooks and by the respected organisations involved in marketing. Of the many definitions offered one of the most straightforward is the one proposed in 1960 by the American Marketing Association. This defined marketing research as the:

> systematic gathering, recording, and analyzing of data about problems relating to the marketing of goods and services.

While satisfactory with regard to the basics, this definition ignored the important problem-solving and reporting aspects of marketing research as a business function. It was for this reason considered unsatisfactory by many authors, including Kotler, who in 1987 proposed the following definition. Marketing research:

> uses information to identify and define marketing opportunities and problems; generate, refine and evaluate marketing actions; monitor marketing performance; and improve understanding of marketing as a process. It communicates findings and their implications.

This satisfies the main criticisms made of the earlier definition, but ignores the more fundamental point made by Buzzell in 1963. In an article from the *Harvard Business Review*, he suggested it was the title 'marketing research' that was deceptive. In his opinion the function was in reality like military intelligence and the title 'marketing intelligence' would accordingly be more appropriate.

In spite of the logic of this argument the term marketing research continues to survive and, to confuse the situation further, is used by many authors interchangeably with the term 'market research'. This is unfortunate since, particularly in the UK, the term market research is accepted as the term used to define the specialist activities involved in applying the observational, survey and experimental social research techniques for marketing research applications. Accordingly market research may be usefully considered a specialist activity which is within the scope of the marketing research function rather than an alternative name for it.

MARKETING RESEARCH AS A MARKETING FUNCTION

Although within marketing-orientated organisations marketing research is generally considered a marketing function it is not unusual for it to be functionally distant from the other marketing functions identified in Chapter 1.

The most usual reason for this is the requirement for organisations to forecast sales revenues as part of the annual budgeting process. The importance of this activity can be seen from the following outline of the budgeting process taken from a standard accounting textbook:

1 State basic assumptions and company objectives.
2 Forecast general economic and industry conditions.
3 Develop detailed sales budgets, analysed suitably, e.g. between customers, products, areas, market sectors.
4 Prepare production budgets, including budgets for materials and labour, analysed between different products, locations, etc.
5 Prepare capital expenditure budgets.
6 Prepare cash budgets.
7 Combine all of the above into the master budget, the overall budgeted profit and loss account, balance sheet and cash flow statement.

(*Source:* M. W. Allen and D. R. Myddelton *Essential Management Accounting*)

This shows the validity of the whole budgeting process is dependent upon steps 2 and 3. For this reason many companies found that the benefits which were expected to result from adopting rigorous financial planning through the budgeting process could not be realised owing to discrepancies between forecast and actual sales. Many Marketing Research departments were formed with the single objective of improving the forecasting process and performance. While this is increasingly seen as only one of the functions of marketing research there are still many organisations for which it remains the most important function.

Among the organisations with this approach to marketing research are some which considered the development of a marketing research function to be in itself an adoption of marketing as a business philosophy. This was not only a fundamentally incorrect approach to marketing, but inevitably resulted in significant amounts of the information produced being of little value to the organisation.

It is interesting to note that this approach to marketing research can still be detected in commentaries relating to product success and failure. This is because, superficially, success can usually be attributed to the foresight and judgement of an organisation's management and a product or business failure to a lack of marketing research. More detailed investigations, however, are likely to be more revealing and show that usually successes are examples of the application of sound marketing principles whether by accident or design, and the failures are examples of these principles having been ignored. Accordingly, any suggestion that a product failure is due to a lack of marketing research is probably misleading since unless, by chance, any additional marketing research actually improved the overall understanding of the market it is unlikely to have prevented the failure.

TYPES OF MARKETING RESEARCH

There are four generally recognised approaches to classifying marketing research. The first of these relates to whether the research is routine when it is known as *continuous* or only undertaken when needed when it is known as *ad hoc*. The second approach differentiates the three basic sources of data – secondary internal, secondary external, and primary. These are discussed under 'Gather problem-specific data' later in the chapter. The third approach involves the essentially different types of data which might be obtained – quantitative or qualitative, and the fourth approach defines the different objectives for obtaining the information – exploratory, conclusive, descriptive or causal.

As will be seen in the paragraphs and sections which follow, these categories are interrelated rather than mutually exclusive, making the classification of marketing research activities in practice somewhat complicated.

Forms of research

Continuous marketing research

This involves collating marketing information, such as total sales by product variant or geographic region, on a routine basis so that it can be compared over time. This allows the performance of the marketing activities of an organisation to be monitored and, in particular, market trends determined. By definition, *continuous* marketing research is produced on a regular or periodic basis. It supplements existing marketing information and is usually presented as a memo or newsletter. Because of the cost and resources involved, *continuous* research should be limited to collecting information which is required for routine decisions or feedback and monitoring. It is an activity which needs to be kept in check since, with the advent of computer databases, it is comparatively easy to produce more data than can be used by the managers for whom it is produced.

Ad hoc *marketing research*

When research is required for a non-recurring purpose it is generally referred to as *ad hoc* research, as it is carried out only when actually required to assist a marketing decision. An example could be investigation of the viability of a new product, or the reasons behind a drop in sales. Usually the presentation of the research findings will be as a formal report. It is customary for such reports to be sufficiently comprehensive for the information presented to be of value to users who may have no relevant intangible marketing information on the subject. This is important since otherwise the value of the information provided is likely to depend more on the user's existing knowledge of the subject than on the quality of the marketing research.

In many organisations this type of research is seen as the main purpose of the marketing research department. However, this is generally misleading since, although the presentation of *continuous* research as a memo or newsletter may not be impressive, it is often used as the basis for much of the *ad hoc* research undertaken as well as routine feedback. For this reason it is important that *continuous* research information is produced in a form that allows detailed analysis, should this be required.

It is also inevitable that most marketing research textbooks focus mainly on *ad hoc* research. The reason for this is that *ad hoc* research involves a number of well-established stages and procedures. In contrast, since *continuous* research is a routine activity, most of these stages are only necessary when setting up the routine. In practice, most *continuous* research is, at least in part, subjected to the full research process from time to time as a result of being used in *ad hoc* research. In many organisations such research is also done when preparing the annual marketing planning reference document.

Types of data

Quantitative data

Any information which can be expressed using a numerical measure is considered quantitative. It includes not only numerical data, such as that obtained from internal sales and accounting records, but also the numerical aspects of other data, such as may be derived from questionnaires. It could also include studies of distribution levels, repeat purchase rates or even opinion polls regarding voting intentions. More than three-quarters of all marketing research data is classified as quantitative. Nearly all *continuous* marketing research comes within this category since usually it is undertaken to provide data for time series analysis.

Qualitative data

Qualitative research is concerned with information which is based on descriptions and shades of meaning rather than numerical analysis. It is commonly used in the early stages of *ad hoc* research studies. One popular source of qualitative data is that derived from small 'focus' group discussions. In general, it involves unstructured exploration or inductive problem-solving techniques which are beyond the scope of an introductory text such as this. Although in practice less than a quarter of the marketing research undertaken can be classified as qualitative, this category is much discussed both with regard to the methods used and resultant findings. It has resulted in the development of many concepts seen as useful in defining and categorising market segments, such as lifestyle.

Research objectives

Exploratory marketing research

The purpose of exploratory research is to identify the nature of a marketing problem in order to decide what issues should be measured or how best to undertake a study. It is used to indicate issues or to generate ideas or hypotheses. Since exploratory research is problem-orientated, it has always to be carried out as *ad hoc* research. Qualitative research techniques are often used in order to minimise the effect that the terms of reference might have on the research outcome.

Conclusive research

As has already been mentioned, research must be considered as an aid to marketing decisions and as such cannot replace this role. Conclusive research is aimed at providing the specific information needed by management to make a defined marketing decision. It might be used to test a hypothesis set up in advance of the data collection, but more likely it involves measuring the variables identified as relevant to a particular decision.

The *deductive* approach to problem solving can only be applied to problems where it is possible and practical to obtain data which is appropriate and reliable. For other problems, the alternative inductive approach to problem solving is generally more appropriate.

The *inductive* approach involves establishing concepts by identifying repeated patterns in the behaviour being observed. The validity of the applicability of these patterns is then verified by repeated empirical studies. The results obtained are generally stated as paradigms rather than laws since their application is subject to exception. This is the normal approach used for psychological work involved in, for instance, buyer behaviour studies. It would have been the approach used by Maslow to develop his hierarchical theory of motivation. It is also the basis used for qualitative marketing research. The implementation of this approach to problem solving requires specialist training and experience and is thus, like other qualitative research, beyond the scope of introductory texts such as this.

Descriptive marketing research

Descriptive research focuses on product performance, market size, trends, competitive strategies and market share. It is typically concerned with measuring or estimating variables and the frequency of their occurrence. Depending on the objective and context, this could be the result of either *continuous* or *ad hoc* research.

Causal marketing research

Causal research looks at the cause-and-effect relationships in an attempt to explain why things happen. For instance, whether loss of market share is due to the success of a direct competitor or the result of an indirect competitor's success in an associated market segment. Like exploratory research, causal research is usually undertaken on an *ad hoc* basis. Causal research is often more analytical than descriptive research and is intended to reveal the factors critical to the behaviour of consumers or, more generally, markets. It can thus involve using both quantitative and qualitative research techniques.

THE RESEARCH PROCESS

Marketing research was defined at the beginning of this chapter as the use of information, and the communication of findings and their implications. Much ongoing research is used to monitor situations, but, as stated earlier, there is an established, standard approach which can be termed the marketing research process. This comprises seven distinct stages. These are most obvious when setting up an *ad hoc* study, but are present in all studies. The relative importance of each stage will also vary according to the objective of the study. The seven stages are:

1 Define the problem.
2 Analyse the situation.
3 Establish objectives and agree cost–benefit parameters.

4 Gather problem-specific data.
5 Analyse the data to produce information relevant to the problem.
6 Prepare report.
7 Follow up to evaluate effectiveness of action taken.

In the following sections each of these stages are considered in detail.

Define the problem

Problem definition is often very difficult to complete objectively and, as the initial stage in the process, is all too easy to omit altogether. However, it is important both because it forces managers to think deeply about the reasons for collecting data, and to consider the value of information in the context of the decision to be made. Generally, an effective approach is to proceed on the basis of an initial definition of the problem and then to reconsider the definition after each of the subsequent stages has been completed. While this is good research practice, it has the significant disadvantage of being considered inefficient by many pragmatic business managers. It therefore generally needs to be used carefully to ensure the credibility of the study is not jeopardised.

Analyse the situation

An important characteristic of marketing research is that it is very common for the person who is initiating the research to have considerably more information about the subject at the start of the research process than the person who is to carry out the research. This information is likely to be a combination of day-to-day experience resulting from being involved with a particular market over many years and from receiving information produced by continuous research procedures on a regular basis. This can create commonly unforeseen difficulties for managers commissioning research studies. This is because unless the research brief clearly defines both the tangible and intangible information the manager already has, the context of the additional information required will not be properly understood. For this reason marketing research briefs should include a comprehensive analysis of the current situation especially when the work is to be done by a specialist outside organisation.

Establish objectives and agree cost–benefit parameters

It is important to establish objectives for the study to ensure that the research is properly focused, even when the problem has been adequately defined. Once the objectives for the study have been agreed, the essential methodology can be determined, and the likely cost of the research in terms of time and resources estimated. This is essential since it is very easy to agree market research study objectives which cannot be completed within the time or budget available. It is often necessary at this stage to decide whether it would be preferable for the study to be carried out by a specialist outside organisation such as a market research agency or by company staff. The decision made is likely to depend upon at least some of the following seven criteria:

1 Cost.
2 Project urgency.
3 Research expertise required.

4 Product or service knowledge necessary.
5 Objectivity.
6 Specialist resources required.
7 Confidentiality.

Sometimes the best solution is to use both internal and external personnel for different stages of the work. Whenever external personnel are involved a formal written brief should be prepared so their work can be costed and controlled. Not infrequently it is realised in the course of doing this that the benefit expected from the research will be offset by the time needed for it to be completed since time is often of the essence when considering marketing problems. For instance, delaying the launch of a new product in order to carry out research into the most suitable packaging could well cost more in terms of lost sales and product advantage than might be lost by the initial packaging not being ideally suited to the target market.

Gather problem-specific data

This should be carried out by considering data sources in order of the cheapest, most readily available information first, and only later, more expensive bespoke studies. There are three categories of data. These are defined by data source and discussed in the usual order in which they are accessed. While initially confusing it is important to remember that the first two of these are categories of secondary data. That is data from sources that already exist whereas it is the third of these categories which is considered primary data.

Secondary–internal data

Internal data is the information which is internal to an organisation and usually the starting point for data collection. It should provide a reliable source of up-to-date information immediately available within the organisation. It is thus essential it is fully utilised and can be drawn from:

- sales records;
- delivery and stock records;
- prices and quotations;
- sales promotion – price offers, etc.
- advertising – media and messages – size of budget;
- sales personnel's call reports and assessments of their effectiveness;
- past studies on marketing effectiveness.

In Chapter 8 the relevance of operating data was mentioned in the context of a marketing information system. Of particular interest in the context of marketing research is the time series data relating to orders received, products delivered, advertising expenditure, promotional campaigns, sales by customer or sales territory and so on. Sometimes the information required is available directly from routine reports giving continuous data. However, there are often occasions when it is insufficiently detailed in some way.

Much of the time series data will have been summarised, for instance as sales by day or week or month or even as quarterly or annual figures. Inevitably, detail is lost as the figures are summarised. Usually this is because the summaries are prepared primarily to provide managers with measures of financial efficiency. While such measures are essential in any business organisation, they are likely to use conventions set by the accounting requirements rather than the needs of marketing.

Traditionally, for manufacturing companies, financial efficiency has been seen as being largely dependent upon production efficiency. This orientation led to the development of the production-orientated costing systems which form the basis of modern management accounting practice. Cost accounting as a procedure involves considerable clerical routine and its automation was one of the earliest business applications of computer technology. Because of this, many costing systems retained their production orientation even when this was no longer justified. As a result, it is not uncommon to find that even sophisticated management accounting systems are unable to provide information in the form required for detailed marketing analysis. Fortunately, providing the basic information can be accessed, it is now usually possible to use a personal computer to extract and collate the information in the form required, although this can be surprisingly difficult and time consuming. Some of the inherent difficulties associated with internal data are illustrated in the following example.

EXAMPLE

Consider a company which manufactures plumbing fittings, e.g. taps, shower mixers, and so on. It is likely that for costing purposes weekly totals of shipments by product type (type A basin taps, type C bath taps and so on) would be adequate. For marketing purposes this information is likely to be needed not only by product type but also by type of customer (market segment) and geographic region. This is many times more information.

The problem becomes further complicated if the manufacturer decides to offer a range of products in sets – for instance, to house builders. In each set there could be two pairs of basin taps and one pair of bath taps and one kitchen mixer tap. To be attractive to the builder the set would be priced at less than the sum total of the individual items. For invoicing purposes the set would be treated as an individual product. To establish whether offering these sets increased sales sufficiently to cover the associated price reduction would require analysis of total sales by type of tap. This is likely to involve a significant amount of work and care to ensure that the items sold in the sets were not counted twice.

Although one of the principal objectives of collating internal marketing data is to monitor the performance of the organisation, in practice this information is of little value for making marketing decisions unless it can be compared with the market as a whole. For long-term success, organisations need to grow faster than the market during periods of growth and decline less rapidly than the market during periods of decline. In order to make these comparisons it is necessary to use data obtained from outside sources.

Secondary–external data

There is a plethora of external marketing data readily available if you know where to look for it. Some common sources are listed in Appendix 3. This section considers the use of secondary external data in detail since this is the main source of marketing data available to students.

Peter Jackson, in his excellent book *Desk Research*, states:

> ... many information needs can be met through desk research. This type of data collection is well within the practical scope of even a lone researcher and requires few additional, if any, resources. Arguably, if more or more and better desk research was undertaken, less field research would be needed and research budgets would be more effectively and efficiently spent.

The sources of secondary data available to desk researchers include newspapers, journals and magazines, directories of all sorts, on-line databases, government statistics and reports, company reports, surveys published by research organisations and others including trade associations. A fuller list and some useful addresses appear in Appendix 3.

Many industries have established trade associations and some of these, such as the Society of Motor Manufacturers and Traders, have become the principal source of marketing information relating to their industry. This, of course, is only possible when the members of the organisation agree that it is in their individual best interest to provide information to the organisation and contribute to the cost of its collation. Very often the information produced is only circulated to those companies which have fulfilled their obligation to supply information to the collating organisation. Of course, the validity of the information produced depends upon the proportion of the industry which is willing to contribute to and buy such services.

In the absence of specially collated industry data, more general data has to be used. Much of this is collated by government departments to measure the level of economic and industrial activity to determine the effectiveness of current economic policy. Some of these measures, such as the retail price index, have become newspaper headline news. Others are published quarterly in the Business Monitor series. Although companies are required to provide such information, many fail to do so within the time allowed. As a result, the published data inevitably includes estimates and amendments. Furthermore, its reliability is also affected by other important factors. These vary according to the industry concerned, although the following two examples may be considered typical.

First, to reduce the cost involved, data is not usually collected from companies which are small in terms of the number of people employed relative to the size of the industry as a whole. Instead, the totals for the industry are calculated by grossing up the data collected by a factor calculated to represent the output of the small companies. Because of this it is possible for market leaders of important market segments to be omitted from the figures.

Second, in order to maintain the confidentiality of the companies contributing information, product sectors with fewer than three contributors are combined with other product sectors. This, like the first example, has no effect on the overall industry totals, but can make segment totals meaningless.

Thus, although there are numerous sources of external data, the value must be assessed objectively because it was originally collected for purposes other than marketing research. Wherever possible the accuracy of secondary external data should be checked. One approach is to find other sources for the same data. However, a word of warning: it is not sufficient simply to show that several sources agree as sometimes this only shows that they all used the same original source. If it is not possible actually to check the accuracy of the information then an attempt should be made to put it into context.

Generally speaking, when external secondary data is used within an organisation it can be compared with relevant internal secondary data such as sales to a specific market segment. This is especially useful where the organisation is an important supplier with a major market share. For markets which are supplied by a large number of organisations none of which has a significant share it is sometimes possible to estimate either the total capacity on the basis of the use of a specific raw material.

Different approaches have to be used by students and organisations which, not being involved in a market, do not have access to relevant internal data. This may involve estimating market size on the basis of likely usage and the total number of potential customers. For instance, if information was required about the market for cash registers used in shops, garages, restaurants and so on, an estimate of the market could be made on the basis of the number of retail outlets within a town or the country, the average number of cash registers in each and how often these are replaced. The resulting figure would still be an estimate, but would nonetheless be useful as a check.

Another approach is to relate consumption to the population as a whole. Reliable population estimates are available for most developed countries since they are required as the basis for many government policies. Generally the population estimates are obtained by means of a census carried out every ten years. In the UK this was last done in 1991. The principal objective of a census is to measure variations in the population relating to the need for public services: schools, health care, law enforcement, and so on. In the UK the data shows the demographics of the population by area so can be used to estimate the potential demand for certain products or services. It can also be used as the basis for checking the likely validity of other secondary data.

EXAMPLE

Suppose you are looking for information regarding the market for jeans in the UK and you find an article in which it is stated that in the UK 47 million pairs of jeans are sold each year and the value of the market is £650 million. If the population of the UK is approximately 55 million and 10 per cent are children there would be about 50 million adults. This data would suggest that adults buy on average about one pair of jeans per year. Is this reasonable? It is quite likely that many students buy three or more pairs of jeans per year, but then the average student's parents possibly only buy on average one pair per year and the average student's grandparents probably buy none. Taking all this into account, what at least can be said is that while 47 million may or may not be correct, it is clearly not obviously incorrect.

How about the value? This suggests that the average price of a pair of jeans is less than £14. Is this likely to be right? A walk round any town centre looking in shop windows might show that there are jeans for sale at £14, but they are not branded and most jeans people are wearing seem to be branded. What does this mean? Either the article was using information which was wrong, or which was out of date, or there was a printing error. There are other possible explanations – the figure could be based on ex-works prices rather than the retail selling price, or on some other cost basis such as the value at which the goods were imported. Whatever the reason it is clear that the figure needs to be treated with caution and, if used because it is the only information available, its apparent shortcomings should at least be discussed.

The collation of relevant external data can involve continuously monitoring measures of national economic activity, such as the gross national product. Alternatively measures of business confidence, such as the Confederation of British Industry poll of investment intentions can be used. Generally, as with internal data, only measures which over time have been shown to be relevant should be monitored on a continuous basis. Information required to respond to specific marketing problems need only be collated on an *ad hoc* basis.

To return to Jackson's book he states:

> Desk research is a rather neglected part of market research. There are many source books providing references for marketing data ... but little is written on desk research as an activity and subject .... There is also little formal training given in desk research .... More often, the 'new boy' or 'new girl' is given a desk research project as a first task – but are left to their own devices and have to learn the basics of desk research as they go along. Part of the problem is that there is an erroneous assumption that anyone with even half an education will know how to build up an analysis of a market from library sources.

This warning applies equally to students. If you are to undertake a desk research project you would do well to refer to a book such as Jackson's before starting your study. Not all information is valid and it is much more important to learn how to evaluate the quality and reliability of data before making some basic mistakes.

Many marketing problems will only require analysis of either external secondary data or a combination of external secondary and internal data. In doing this it is always useful to try to check the validity of any external data used. In the jeans example this could involve at least a cursory visit to the shops to get some idea of the current price range for jeans. This simple example leads us to primary research which is the third category of marketing research data.

Primary data sources

Primary research is often referred to as field research, in contrast to the term desk research used above, to describe the collection of secondary data. Primary data is obtained by using one or more of the following four market research techniques:

- observation;
- surveys (interviews);
- projective methods;
- experimentation.

Details regarding the use and limitations of these techniques will be found in most of the recognised marketing research textbooks. There are also many others which are concerned with only one of these techniques. Since many students are required to conduct a questionnaire-based survey general guidelines for doing this are provided in Appendix 5.

We have already introduced, in Chapter 8, the issue of information quality. You will remember that to be of value marketing information must be:

- reliable/accurate;
- valid;
- relevant;
- sufficient;
- current/up-to-date.

It also needs to be understandable to whoever will be using the information. This is often a major challenge for the marketing researcher even though personal computers offer an extensive range of alternative methods of analysis and presentation. Ideally the method chosen should be simple and easily explained to the person who is to use the information.

The purpose of data analysis

In the context of marketing research it is important to appreciate the purpose and objective of data analysis is to produce relevant information from the available data. Accordingly this aspect of data analysis will be discussed in this section rather than the specific techniques which may be used. As an example, the use of one of these is introduced and explained in Appendix 4.

It needs to be stressed that the purpose of marketing research is to provide relevant information, not simply to present data. A primary necessity for useful information is that it can be understood without prior knowledge or interpretation. This involves analysing data and then putting it into context.

EXAMPLE

An example of context could be the fact that in 1960 a graduate engineer might have expected to start work as a trainee at £650 per year, while in 1996 that same graduate would expect to start at £12 000 per year. This is data. It could be presented as information by showing for instance that in 1960 a new Mini cost 75 per cent of a trainee graduate engineer's starting salary whereas in 1995 a new Mini (or equivalent) represented only 50 per cent of a similar graduate trainee engineer's starting salary. Another way would be to state that in 1960 £650 represented 3200 gallons of petrol whereas in 1996 £12 000 represented more than 4 500 gallons of petrol. Both of these comparisons would seem to show that the graduate engineer, as a trainee, is more highly valued in 1995 than in 1960. The fact is, in 1960, the graduate engineer was unlikely to find a better combination of salary and career prospects than that offered by becoming a graduate trainee engineer, whereas in 1996 graduates with the same degree could have increased their starting salary by 30 per cent or more by using their engineering degree as the basis for entering careers in finance or general management.

This example shows context in respect of relevant comparisons only, but many comparisons are possible and many are at best irrelevant and at worst misleading. It is hardly surprising that the following adage is so well known:

There are lies, damned lies and statistics.

There are many other issues emerging from the same data. For instance the Mini of 1960 was not only crude in comparison with the 1990s version, but it required more frequent servicing and was far less reliable. Because of product and specification changes such as these, market research analysis over extended time periods is often very difficult without specialist knowledge. This does not reduce the need to analyse any data presented but emphasises the importance of being careful when changing values are likely to be sufficiently significant to hide trends, especially in established markets. This is discussed fully with examples in Appendix 4.

The analysis of value data

Value data, whether collated from internal or external sources, can potentially be an extremely valuable source of marketing research information. It allows expenditure on different types of product to be combined and trends over long periods to be compared with leading indicators to establish relationships which can be used for forecasting. This type of analysis, however, needs to be done on a constant value basis as described in Appendix 4. The importance is recognised in many tables showing national economic statistics which include constant historical (e.g. 1995) values or a constant value index based on a specific year. This approach is convenient for those preparing the data as new data can be appended to that already published.

It is not, however, the best approach for presenting marketing information. It is inherently difficult to relate the values of even a few years ago to the present and even more difficult to do this with the accuracy needed to draw sensible conclusions. Thus, for business applications, it is very much better to present historic data in present value terms for discussion and analysis as explained in Appendix 4.

Thus, whenever using value data it should be done on the basis of the following three points. First, trends should be considered in both value and volume terms. Second, when considering monetary values it should be done in constant value terms and ideally using constant present-day values. Third, there are often trends which get hidden as figures are lumped together. It is often necessary to fully analyse the detailed figures to reveal actual happenings in the marketplace.

Prepare report

Unless the information is properly presented it is unlikely to meet the requirement of the person who requires the information. The report should show the objectives of the study, explain how the study was carried out, detail any assumptions made and present the findings of the study clearly. Data, whether directly applicable or as background information, is normally best presented in a series of separate appendices. Particular care needs to be taken with respect to the presentation of graphical information. The purpose of using graphics is to make the information easier to understand. It is useful to show trends and differences. Accordingly, it is usually inappropriate where trends are essentially static.

With the availability of modern computer presentation packages it is important to match the choice of diagram to the data being presented. Most packages include facilities for producing graphical data for use in presentations and these are generally unsuitable for written reports. In particular, any diagram which presents two-dimensional data in a three-dimensional format should be avoided. These often look smart, but usually make the data more difficult to interpret properly without explanation. This is not the purpose of a diagram. When in doubt the best guide is to follow the approach used in most basic textbooks, except where these use three-dimensional diagrams. Common sense is usually a sound guide.

Follow-up implementation

This stage need not be formal but should be conscientiously carried out since it provides opportunities to understand how the methods used in the investigation of the issues and the presentation of the 'marketing offering' could be improved on in future.

CONCLUSION

Marketing research means providing the information for decisions on marketing activities such as advertising, pricing and distribution. The approach used may vary in terms of research form (*continuous* versus *ad hoc*), data type (qualitative versus quantitative), or the research objectives (exploratory, conclusive, descriptive or causal), and the different data sources (secondary or primary).

Whatever the type of research, the demands of budget constraints, research rigour and timeliness will require a methodical, well-managed sequence to be followed, from the initial problem definition and objectives stage, through data collection and analysis, to presentation and reporting of findings.

Marketing information must be reliable, accurate, valid, relevant, sufficient, and up to date. It must also be available at an affordable cost. Further, it needs to be presented and communicated to the user in an understandable format. Statistical information, in particular, needs to be carefully handled, and presented consistently in terms of time series, measures and values.

QUESTIONS

1 'A problem well-defined is a problem half resolved.' Discuss.

2 Consider the distinctive advantages of continuous research, giving examples of the marketing questions that it might answer.

3 'Qualitative research has obvious value in the insights it can provide, but when over-used it can be distinctly misleading'. Discuss.

4 Should primary research only be carried out after considering secondary sources and finding the data from such sources to be inadequate?

5 Taking as an example the manufacturer of any leading consumer product, illustrate the variety of marketing decisions that might be better supported through the effective use of marketing research.

6 The orders for jeans grew in the early 1980s, falling back a little over the last ten years. A major UK manufacturer had, until recently, managed to resist this trend, keeping their volume sales constant in spite of increasing competitive activities. However, over the last six months sales have fallen by 10 per cent. The Managing Director wants a detailed market analysis to discover exactly what is happening in the marketplace. Suggest what will be studied as part of this analysis and recommend sources for obtaining the data, giving your reasons in each case.

7 Use the resources of your own library to find out the market shares and volume sales of the major soft drink brands available in the market. Look at the trends over several years

and suggest if there could be an opportunity for a new brand to enter the market, and if so which segment would seem to be the most attractive.

8 *Chamberlain Drop Forgings* (*see* p. 29).

At a recent Board meeting, while looking at some worrying trends in recent sales figures, the following views were expressed:

Sales Director: 'The main reasons behind our loss of sales are that our products are too expensive and not of sufficiently high quality to compete with imports.'

Production Director: 'The main reason behind our loss of sales are that we are not getting close enough to our customers to fully understand their needs. That is down to the sales department.'

Accounting Director: 'The main reasons behind our loss of sales are the economic environment and general recession, it really is not anyone's fault.'

You, a junior marketing researcher on placement from your college, have been asked to suggest how marketing research could help to resolve these differences. What suggestions would you make and what types of research would you be recommending?

9 Apart from studies to investigate the potential for new products, should marketing research be carried out primarily to investigate adverse changes and negative trends in the marketplace where an organisation is competing?

FURTHER READING

Chisnall, P. M. (1992) *Essentials of Marketing Research*, Prentice-Hall.
Crimp, M. (1985) *The Marketing Research Process*, 2nd Edn, Prentice-Hall.
Jackson, P. (1994) *Desk Research*, Kogan Page, London.
Kent, R. A. (1993) *Marketing Research in Action*, Routledge, London.
Moutinho, L. and Evans, M. (1992) *Applied Marketing Research*, Addison-Wesley.
Webb, J. R. (1992) *Understanding and Designing Marketing Research*, Academic Press.

CASE STUDY

Hairco Gmbh

Hairco corporation is a leading producer of hair dryers, crimpers, curlers, and other electrical hair styling products with sales in several European countries. Tanya Schlecht was very pleased to be recruited as product manager for hair dryers immediately after completing her business qualification at a German Fachoschule. She knew her ability to speak the three major European languages was a key factor in her appointment, but she also knew that the firm she had joined had a reputation for aggressive sales activity and the staff were judged by the results they achieved in meeting profit targets.

Hairco's current sales were around 500 000 hair dryers per year – all aimed at female buyers through department stores, discount electrical stores, and beauty shops. Large retail groups were regularly offered special deals but it was not clear how these were passed onto consumers. The promotional costs were just over 20 per cent of revenue, and this was spent on both main media and in support of in-store promotions. However there seemed to be little direct link between promotions and sales, and no attempt was made to test the effectiveness of different promotions. Tanya was also surprised to find very little data on the market for hair dryers, and only basic sales revenue data on outlets. Of course, Tanya knew the major competitors such as Braun, Phillips, and Pifco, but she had no idea as to how these companies were rated against Hairco by either retailers or consumers.

Tanya thought she could obtain some volume data quite cheaply from secondary sources, but she felt it was more important to understand why and when consumers bought hair dryers. She also hoped that if she could establish how they used the product she could influence product development for the future. She wanted to discover if consumers were loyal to a particular make or whether they bought mainly on price; also were there any differences between German, French and British consumers?

She had considered buying a few questions on an omnibus study to ask:

- When did you buy your current hair dryer?
- What make/model is it?
- Why did you choose this model?
- When do you think you will change it?
- What features does your current dryer lack?

However she knew that some of these were open-ended questions and therefore difficult to handle in a general questionnaire, but in getting answers to these questions Tanya felt she could direct the promotional spend more effectively as well as communicating the most appropriate message to potential target customers.

She therefore wondered what alternative ways were available to learn more about the product for which she had responsibility. She thought she could afford some 75 000 D Marks from her budget to obtain the much needed marketing information, so she asked a number of agencies to come to discuss what was possible. She now has to draw up a brief prior to the meeting with the agency giving details of what she hopes to achieve from the research.

Questions

1 Identify the different types of marketing information mentioned in the Case Study, e.g. Primary/Secondary; quantitive/qualitive.

2 Rank the different types of information identified relative to their importance with respect to Tanya's stated objectives.

3 Rank these different identified types of information relative to their cost of collation.

4 Compare costs for questions 2 and 3 and discuss.

CHAPTER 22

Organising
for Marketing

We trained hard but it seems that every time we were beginning to form into teams we would be reorganised. I was to learn later in life that we tend to meet any new situation by reorganising, and a wonderful method it can be for creating an illusion of progress, whilst producing confusion, inefficiency and demoralisation.

Gaius Petronius (AD 57)

INTRODUCTION

As the nature and role of marketing will vary among companies, so too will the resources involved and the approach adopted to marketing organisation. Exerting a particular influence on the way marketing is organised will be company policy on organisational issues such as centralisation, formalisation and management reporting, while a fundamental if general factor will be the level of market orientation shown by the company. While production-orientated companies are still to be found in large numbers in some sectors, writers such as Doyle have noted the prevalence of financially driven management, and the strategic risks that may attend it. Marketing management and organisation will be affected by both the strategic requirements of the external environment, and by a host of internal issues such as organisational culture, values and attitudes, management style, the company's own development pattern, ownership history and the like. Even within the same market, faced with similar problems, two similarly sized companies may therefore adopt totally different approaches to organising and resourcing their marketing function.

It should be stressed that the organisation chart itself can rarely be taken as an indicator of how serious or successful a company is in its marketing; market-leader companies such as the Body Shop, have built their success through entrepreneurial leadership rather than formal marketing appointments. Simply stated, a large marketing department bristling with specialists is not a sufficient nor, for some, a necessary condition for success. The organisation-wide imperative of the marketing message requires teamwork handling of customer issues across the company, so that functional specialisation without integration will be doomed to failure.

This necessary sharing and division of the marketing task may at least partly explain the differences companies show within the structure in the location of marketing tasks. Of course, dispersal may carry the risks of fragmentation, or, worse, may thwart the development of marketing in any recognisable form within the company. As part of a continuing research initiative concerning corporate marketing activity, Piercy found within a cross-industry sample that no more than 25 per cent of reporting companies claimed to have an integrated full-service marketing function, with the majority of companies having non-integrated provision in the form of either sales orientation, strategy servicing, or a limited staff advisory role. Problems commonly reported in the non-integrated provision ranged from under-resourcing, weak implementation and interfunctional conflict, to short-termism and a generally lower involvement of marketing in strategy.

Strategy matters play an important part in discussions of organisation, since on the one hand good strategy implementation depends on organisation, while on the other hand strategy formulation should be free of structural tramlines – structure should follow strategy, not vice versa. In the sections that follow a brief examination will be made of the different approaches companies use in organising for marketing.

ORGANISATIONAL STRUCTURES

Organisational structures without marketing

In many cases these will represent a less mature organisational form that predates the emergence and use of marketing proper. Commonly associated with traditional companies in stable markets, or with production-dominated organisations, this structure will likely follow a four-way functional division between the Production, Finance, Personnel and Sales departments, each with a separate chain of command, ultimately reporting to board level. Within such an organisation those activities that might otherwise be undertaken by a marketing department are likely to be subsumed within the four functional pillars of the structure, e.g. market feedback through the Sales department, forecasting and commercial analysis through financial planning, or through a nominated director. Though some market-related tasks are covered, it is unlikely that co-ordinated marketing will be performed to the standards achieved by, for example, marketing-led competitors. Of course, such an organisational approach may also be encountered within small developing companies where an enterprising founder and informal workings may make for success, even in the face of resource constraints.

In other circumstances, though more exceptionally, it may be that a well-established company has prospered without separately formalising the marketing activities that it does undertake, often to a high standard. It would therefore be inappropriate to style such a high-performing company as ineffective or lacking in market orientation.

The functional marketing structure

Where marketing first takes organisational roots in a company, it is most likely to be formally structured as a separate function. While it will represent a smaller department to start with, departmental status itself may come only after some intermediate phase of sales support, or a growing assortment of sub-activities lodging within various other departments. A common intermediate step will be the creation of a marketing section or subdepartment in parallel to the Sales department. Such an arrangement is likely to be sub-optimal, since it is unlikely to deliver integrated marketing, and may result in rivalry, rather than co-operation, between Sales and Marketing – indeed, cases where a long-established Sales department hinders or thwarts the development of marketing are not unknown.

The emergence and integration of marketing into one functional section or department is likely to come about as the level and complexity of previously dispersed activities increases, and as these new activities demand a co-ordination beyond the scope of previous organisational arrangements. The increase in marketing activities that prompts such a new structure will usually, in turn, be attributable to external changes such as increased competition or marketing maturity, or internal factors such as increasing promotional activity or a need for more market research or marketing planning support. A typical functionally organised marketing department is illustrated in Fig. 22.1. Essentially, the structure consists of an umbrella organisation that embraces both the sales function and the more recent marketing activities such as market research, sales promotion and advertising. Significantly, in the example shown, marketing has achieved representation at board level through the installation of a Marketing Director, though it should be stressed that such strategy-level participation is unfortunately by no means universal. Often it is a Sales and Marketing Director.

The major benefits of such a structure are that roles and reporting relationships are clearly defined, along conventional hierarchical lines, while specialisation is allowed without undue duplication or ambiguity. Activities requiring more horizontal integration can be accommodated by adding co-ordinator staff, e.g. new product development might demand such liaison, between market research and product planning, and through other departments such as R&D and Manufacturing. On the other hand, difficulties may arise if the organisation grows into a top-heavy hierarchy of specialists with strictly functional interests. Furthermore, frictions and inefficiencies may arise if increasing product and market diversification were to make heavily competing claims on the

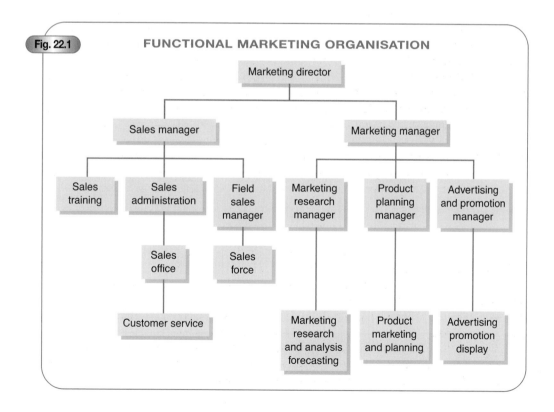

Fig. 22.1 FUNCTIONAL MARKETING ORGANISATION

core specialisms. Such a structure is therefore more appropriate to everyday marketing support of a relatively narrow product range, or within more stable market settings.

Product-based organisation

Originally adopted *en masse* in the 1950s and 1960s by international fmcg (fast-moving consumer goods) companies, this structure has since spread to other sectors such as industrial manufacturing, and more recently financial services. Essentially, a product marketing focus is introduced through the appointment of product (or brand) managers, responsible for the commercial health of some assigned product(s) or brand(s). Though often seen as a mini general manager for product marketing, the typical product manager will be of relatively junior status with little line authority over specialists either in marketing or elsewhere, so that effective working will rest heavily on persuasion and diplomacy, and hopefully the gradual assumption of expert power through demonstrated successes. Figure 22.2 depicts a typical product management organisation.

As shown in Fig. 22.2, product managers will often be organised in groups, under the responsibility of respective Product Group Managers, who are effectively marketing sub-managers at the level of a group of related products. The product manager is mainly a liaison post, achieving for a specified product the necessary co-ordination of support from marketing specialists (e.g. market research, advertising) and other func-

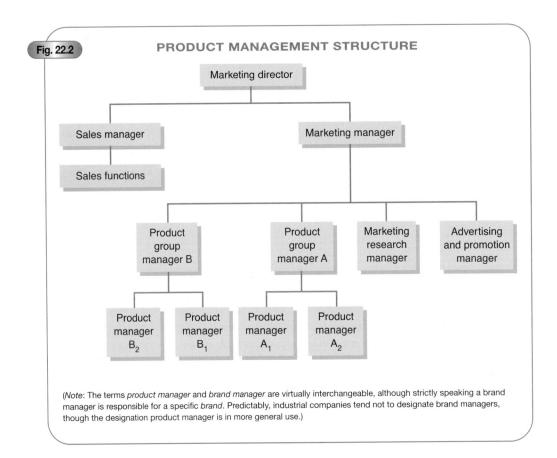

Fig. 22.2 PRODUCT MANAGEMENT STRUCTURE

(*Note:* The terms *product manager* and *brand manager* are virtually interchangeable, although strictly speaking a brand manager is responsible for a specific *brand*. Predictably, industrial companies tend not to designate brand managers, though the designation product manager is in more general use.)

tions alike. Product managers will usually be accountable for the financial and commercial health of their products, for product marketing planning and strategy, and for co-ordinating any necessary product development or modification activity.

Product management has a number of advantages as an organisational format. Certainly it guarantees a focus and specialisation of management expertise at the product/brand level, so that all the major products in the range get the benefit of a full-time champion dedicated solely to their well-being. In a multiproduct setting, product management therefore ensures a level of management attention that would not be feasible under a functionally based structure. As the product manager position entails extensive company-wide co-ordination duties, it also offers an excellent training ground for management; a fact that is often recognised in the recruitment policies of major companies.

Product management has a number of potential drawbacks, however, and it is probably true to say that companies are nowadays more critical and pragmatic in their attitude to this structure. Problems can arise in terms of reporting relationships and decision-making authority, while the healthy rivalry shown among product managers may develop into unproductive competition and conflict. Some companies have re-thought their organisations because of the overemphasis on product expertise at the expense of functional experience, or even market focus. Again, product managers may become preoccupied with existing products, to the detriment of new product development: to remedy this, some companies have introduced a hybrid position, the new product manager. In some markets, too, competitive conditions have demanded a change in orientation away from product strategy towards more operational issues, for example within trade marketing. Finally, it has been the experience of some companies that a product management system becomes increasingly costly and top-heavy, as new products are added and as original product appointments grow into teams through assistant managers, brand assistant positions and the like.

Market-based structures

The basic rationale for a market-based organisation is the need to give marketing attention to specific parts (e.g. groups, submarkets, segments) of the market. A popular version of this approach is the geographic division, where distinct regions or districts, or indeed countries or country blocs, are handled separately, perhaps in separate locations – industrial companies, for example, may have regional office bases that double as mini-headquarters, housing administration, sales, spares and service, marketing and showroom facilities. Where a product or service is actually provided at the local level, throughout the market, such regionalised organisation may be used for all functions, including marketing, e.g. utilities, retail chains, banking, franchise organisations. In some of these cases, a regional organisation may exist alongside a central or corporate support organisation, even for specialist functions such as marketing.

Where companies offer the same product to different customer groups, trades or industries, there may be a need to organise their marketing around these groupings, through the installation of market managers, or perhaps industry marketing groups or sections. Figure 22.3 illustrates a market-based organisation for a hypothetical manufacturer of cooking utensils. Not untypically, the example shown is a hybrid structure, where functions such as market research are shared by both market sectors. The sales function, though, has a regional or territory structure, commonly adopted in selling, whatever headquarters structure the company uses for its marketing base.

Fig. 22.3 MARKET-BASED ORGANISATION

The major advantage of a market-based structure is the specific focus it puts on customer requirements within different market sectors, and the flexibility and speed of response this affords. The major drawbacks of the structure centre on the resourcing issues of extra management layers, and the possible difficulties of co-ordination and communication associated with this. It may be worth noting that, while in principle the market-based structure is consistent with customer orientation, its practical value has been vindicated in research by Lynch, Hooley and Shepherd (1988) who found it to be a characteristic of a number of performance-centred British companies.

Composite or matrix structures

A matrix organisation is a grid-like structure along two (or more) dimensions, typically a dual combination of functions with certain business areas known as programmes or missions. The structure is commonly applied to meet the complex marketing requirements of a diversity in both products and markets, where a vigorous combination of functional, market and product expertise is required. As illustrated in Fig. 22.4, co-ordination within the organisation will be achieved by designated programme (or project) managers drawing as necessary on the expertise of specialists in marketing and other departments. In managerial terms, the programme team members involved have two formal reporting relationships, one to the programme manager and one to their own department head.

Different companies are likely to produce their own variations on the basic theme. For example, Du Pont, the US producer of synthetic fibres such as nylon and acetate,

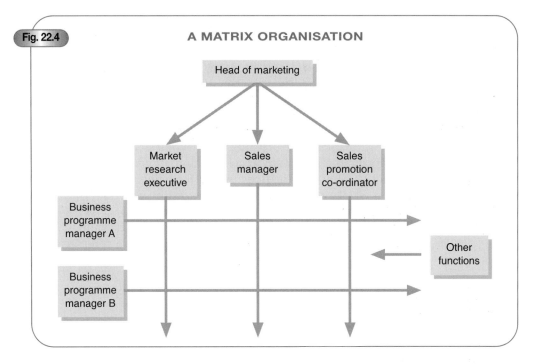

Fig. 22.4 A MATRIX ORGANISATION

organises around a product/market overlay system, where product managers work together with market managers, thus achieving for the company the advantages of both market and product expertise and experience. Other companies have adopted more modified versions of matrix structures, limited to perhaps strictly defined business units, or to particular activities such as new product development.

Note: the organisational aspects of new product development have already been covered in Chapter 20.

Having examined a number of common organisational approaches to marketing, it should be emphasised that in reality organisation structures will rarely take a simple or pure form, while certainly there is little merit in design elegance for its own sake. In an effort to get organised for new problems, to experiment for improvement, and to combine the advantages of different structures, many companies have adopted composite or matrix organisations.

A number of managerial benefits have been claimed for the matrix form of organisation. Certainly it promises greater co-ordination in settings that demand functional interdependence and busy information and communications flows, while the instituting of dual reporting allows more devolved decision making and thus faster and more flexible programming. Against these arguments, though, the experience of some companies confirms that matrix structures are no panacea, since they can create new problems in terms of resource costs, political arguments and other types of interdepartmental conflict.

Other organisational formats

Without attempting an exhaustive classification, the following organisational variants are worthy of brief mention:

- *Key account organisation*: a variation on market-based structuring, is common in consumer goods companies. Where major customers dominate a company's income, as with supermarket groups in the food sector, these are designated as key accounts or house accounts and given special marketing support through key account managers or groups. As such business will depend critically on negotiations and regular contacts with the customer's headquarters buying office, key account structures tend to be sales-dominated, and any associated marketing support sales-initiated.
- *Divisionalisation*: may take a number of forms, usually involving formal corporate restructuring, and even financial restructuring and devolution. Divisions may be based on broad product groups, geographical demarcation, or vertical divisions such as manufacturing-trading. Though usually employed for higher level strategic reasons, divisionalisation will have a direct effect on marketing organisation. Often, separate divisions will operate their own marketing functions, though dependence on some centralised corporate advisory or planning support is not uncommon.
- *Strategic Business Units (SBUs)*: are identifiable business areas within a company (usually product-market combinations) that are handled as separate profit centres. The treatment may be largely financial and strategic, though marketing and other functions are likely to be organised to service the SBUs. This format is therefore effectively a type of matrix organisation.
- *Group marketing*: as with corporate marketing support within a divisionalised structure, a group of associated companies may draw on a common head office marketing service, with or without their own function at subsidiary level. In overseas markets, where local subsidiaries may have to be established as legal entities, local sales and service operations may be supplemented by marketing support at parent company level, although larger subsidiaries in major markets may warrant their own marketing departments staffed by country nationals.

Conflict and co-operation between marketing and other functions

It is obvious that the effectiveness of any individual function, and ultimately the whole company, will depend on co-operation among the specialist staff themselves and with their counterparts in other functions across the company. This is perhaps more necessary still for a function such as marketing, which by its nature tends to be more intrusive and integrative. Indeed, a rough indicator of marketing orientation could be the extent of effective inter-disciplinary working on behalf of the customer.

In reality, many issues and influences may stand in the way of this ideal. As marketing is founded on a potent and purposeful philosophy, so other functions can claim their own professional standards and orientations, which may be at least partly at odds with a textbook marketing approach. Table 22.1 illustrates a number of issues that might present conflict or contention between marketing and other functions.

Many of these frictions will represent differences in attitude within different functions, and the apparently contrary aims to which they feel commitment. For example, the manufacturing – marketing relationship, examined in operational conflict terms by writers such as Shapiro, appears to owe some of its difficulties to the inner versus outer orientations that might be ascribed, as a generalisation albeit, to manufacturing versus marketing. The following anecdote, by the well-known designer Kenneth Grange, provides a telling insight into the deep-seated hostility that can surface within the marketing–production relationship:

Table 22.1 ● Potential conflicts between marketing and other functions

Function	Conflict source
Engineering	Marketers may request more customised components, while Engineering prefer more standardisation.
R&D	Marketers may show interest in applied research and development work, or become frustrated with laboratory over-runs in time or budget. R&D specialists may emphasise basic or pure research.
Purchasing	Purchasing specialists may make decisions on component specifications, cost, purchase volumes and delivery times at variance with the preferences of (product) marketing specialists, or occasionally with no consultation.
Manufacturing	Manufacturing may insist on metric accuracy in sales forecasting for planning purposes – regarded by marketers as unrealistic. Differences on issues such as production lead-times, model or component changes, order scheduling, fabrication methods, etc.
Finance/Accounting	Potential differences over prices and pricing methods, cost allocation, profitability targets, credit control, marketing budgets.

One of my abiding memories is of a boardroom in a large company where the capital costs needed for a new product were under examination. On that day I sat among the product team; design, development and production men, their various interests represented by a brilliant, hard-pressed chief engineer.

In the way those conversations go, a focus had been made on some detail; I think it was the value of prototype tooling. The fireworks started when the advertising director joined in. I then realised how deep was the contempt in which that urbane, witty and elegant man was held by my friend the production man. It seemed to me to point to a schism as serious as the management versus workforce, unions versus CBI that bedevils many industries.

In an interesting development of the interfunctional distance between Marketing and Manufacturing, St John and Hall (1991) identify a number of areas of interdependence, for instance in capacity planning and investment decisions, forecasting and scheduling, inventory and delivery responsiveness. Such interdependencies, if positively exploited, might present key influences on organisation and the means to inter-departmental relations. Equally, Payne (1988) stresses the quality of such intergroup co-ordination as a gangplank to real marketing orientation.

Inter-departmental conflicts of another sort, and certainly grievances, can be attributed to issues of ownership or territory – where within the organisation certain functions should be located, and under whose authority. Within the broad marketing area, subfunctions such as public relations, customer service, packaging and distribution can often be the centre of ongoing border skirmishes between marketing and other functional claimants. Certainly in some companies, the distribution area has recently witnessed such territorial rivalry, as it has merged with materials management to become an enhanced and independent logistics function.

Organisation structures should be robust enough to cope with such tensions, and to accommodate them at the everyday level through management control and co-ordination mechanisms, and ultimately through adaptation and evolution. In common with other functions, the marketing organisation should facilitate interfunctional co-ordination, and even conflict resolution, through the following mechanisms:

- explicit, rather than vague, organisational responsibilities and relationships;
- adequate support systems in key areas such as planning and information processing (information systems);
- inter-disciplinary liaison, planning, problem-solving and decision-making mechanisms such as meetings, committees, reports and audits;
- staffing solutions through liaison and co-ordination posts, joint undertakings through venture groups or task force activity, and a wider role for training and staff development.

Implicit in the above is the understanding that good internal communications will be a major source of improvement in inter-departmental relations, and general company effectiveness.

Some commentators have in recent years isolated the communications field, and related behavioural influences, as a key element of good management, within the company as well as outside. It is perhaps paradoxical that companies that spend literally millions on outside communications through their advertising agencies will sometimes baulk at the thought of serious expenditures within the field of internal communications. A lesson for marketers here is that, as communicators, they, of all people, should be sensitive to the communications process involved in their interactions with other functions. In particular, marketers should promote their plans and activities to ensure greater co-ordination and effectiveness or, to follow the advice of Nigel Piercy, they should practice internal marketing.

INTERNAL MARKETING

As outlined by its major British proponent, Nigel Piercy, internal marketing is nothing more nor less than the employment of marketing activities and approaches within the organisation, in order to gain support and necessary co-operation from other functions, key decision makers and general management, and all those contributing to the effective execution of marketing strategies. The emphasis given by Piercy is primarily on internal marketing in order to ensure success of a company's general marketing programme, though it is possible to see a wider role for internal marketing as an aid to any functional programme. Piercy argues that, both at the everyday level of marketing implementation, and to the end of a gradual culture change towards customer orientation, internal marketing has a contribution to make. He coins the general-purpose term Strategic Internal Marketing (SIM) to encompass all such endeavours. It is particularly instructive, and more appropriate, for marketers to follow an extract of this author's rationale for strategic internal marketing:

The silly thing is that it seems that the reality in many organizations is there is an explicit assumption that marketing plans and strategies will sell themselves to those in the company whose support and commitment are vital. When made explicit in this way, this is just as naive as making similar assumptions that, if they are good enough, our products will sell themselves to external customers. We have frequently been surprised that those same executives who have been trained and developed to cope with behavioural problems – like irrational behaviour by consumers and buyers, or the problems of managing power and conflict in the distribution channel, the need to communicate to buyers through a mix of communications vehicles and media, and trying to outguess competitors – have taken so long to arrive at the conclusion that these same issues have to be coped with inside the company.

The paradox is that we dismiss the better mousetrap syndrome for our external markets, but adopt exactly this approach in expecting managers and operatives, whose support we need, to make a beaten path to the marketing planner's office.

Piercy's advice is that, within the company, marketers should recognise the internal marketplace for their products and programmes, and respond to it by developing an internal marketing programme to support their programmes for the external marketplace. The internal marketing programme itself, therefore, should be produced alongside the primary external programme, and might mirror the external plan in its structure – internal target groups, intelligence and information sources, internal product features and benefits, promotional mechanisms, internal marketing objectives and strategies. For a more detailed outline of the process, the reader is referred to the author's original and persuasive exposition (*see* particularly pages 133–4 and Fig. 9.11).

ORGANISATION IN AN ERA OF 'NEW MARKETING'

Since the mid-90s key concerns have developed about the efficacy of what had become an organisational norm in the guise of 'marketing department marketing', and about some of its structural variants such as the product manager system. While some commentators question whether marketing had adapted sufficiently to issues such as buyer concentration, market competition and changes in marketing infrastructure, others point to the recovery of decision-making authority by parent companies, especially in parallel with trends towards globalisation and Euromarketing. Mitchell (1997) identifies also the influence of some of the managerial innovations of the early 90s such as de-layering, empowerment and multi-task teamworking, and especially the application of (business) process re-engineering (BPR). Under such BPR approaches, business functions, or departments, are subject to radical redesign, based on a fundamental review of their workings and interactions (=process), and especially the scope for flexible and improved customer interfaces. As an example of the kinds of reorganisation and re-shaping that might affect the marketing function, distinctions between sub-specialisms such as advertising, sales promotion and direct marketing may disappear or be dispersed across the whole business, 'shared' within newly-ordained processes such as Customer Relationship Management, brand experience delivery, reputation management. It is worth stressing that such reassignments of marketing are as yet confined to a number of pioneer companies such as Unipart, Xerox and IBM, mostly in the business-to-business field, while evidence contrary to such change indications certainly exists. As an example of the latter, a 1996 survey by the UK Chartered Institute of Marketing, based on a sample of 110 companies, concluded that marketing organisation was changing but slowly, and that the role of product/brand manager appeared as ubiquitous as ever. Nonetheless, there is a growing number of commentators who predict that the marketing function must change in response to the changes that are affecting organisations generally.

Interestingly, these changes correlate closely with the interfunctional dependencies propounded by Gummesson (1987) and other architects of the 'New Marketing'.

Recognition of the influence of internal marketing, outline above, is also quite consistent with the New Marketing model, which proposes de-emphasising formal marketing (department) demarcations, in favour of shared 'process' relationships with 'part-time marketers' across the organisation.

CONCLUSION

Marketing, no less than any other business function, needs to be managed, controlled and appropriately resourced. The organisation structure adopted for the marketing function will need to reflect and serve these managerial processes. Needless to say, it will also need to facilitate the effective execution of those marketing strategies required by the company's competitive position, and the general demands of the marketplace. As companies will vary in terms of resource strengths, market position and general policies on matters of management and planning, the approach taken to organising marketing will vary somewhat in practice.

Of perhaps equal importance will be the internal, social and political aspects of the company as an organisation, and the related need for internal marketing.

Suffice to say, marketers need to be aware of the dynamic and behavioural interactions that beset them within the organisation. As noted in numerous research studies, the people dimensions of the informal organisation may well become more significant than the line geometry of the formal organisation chart.

QUESTIONS

1 'The key ingredients of success are surely strategy and execution. Organisation changes amount to little more than rearranging the furniture.' Comment.

2 Argue the commercial case for a closer working relationship between marketing and the following specialisms:
   – purchasing;
   – accounting;
   – design;
   – credit control.

3 Consider the implications for marketing organisations of continuing growth in a company's overseas business.

4 Write a diary page account of the typical working day of a consumer goods product manager, indicating the variety of tasks undertaken and the interactions achieved with other functional specialists.

FURTHER READING

Chartered Institute of Marketing UK (CIM) (1996): *The Status of UK Product and Brand Management in the 1990s.*

Doyle, P., 'Marketing and the British chief executive', *Journal of Marketing Management,* Vol. 3, No. 2, 1987.

Gummesson, Evert, 'The new marketing – development long-term interactive relationships', *Long Range Planning*, Vol. 20, No.4 (1987), pp. 10–20.

Lynch, J. E., Hooley, G. J. and Shepherd, J., *The Effectiveness of British Marketing*, University of Bradford Management Centre, 1988.

Mitchell, Alan., 'Speeding up the Process', *Marketing Business*, March 1997, pp. 18–21.

Payne, Adrian F., 'Developing a marketing oriented organisation', *Business Horizons*, Vol. 31, No.3 (1988), pp. 46–53.

Piercy, N., 'The role and function of the Chief Marketing Executive and the Marketing Department', *Journal of Marketing Management*, Vol. 1, No. 3 (1986), pp. 265–290.

Piercy, N., (1990) *Market-led Strategic Change: Making Marketing Happen in Your Organisation*, HarperCollins Publishers (Chapter 10), London.

St John, C.H. and Hall, E.H. (1991) 'The Interdependency between Marketing and Manufacturing', *Industrial Marketing Management*, Vol. 20, pp. 223 ff.

Shapiro, Benson P., 'Can marketing and manufacturing coexist?', *Harvard Business Review*, Vol. 55, September–October 1977.

Wilson, I. (1994) *Marketing Interfaces,* Pitman Publishing, London.

CASE STUDY
Organising for marketing

The Chief Executive of a medium-sized metropolitan borough council in the West Midlands has recently obtained Council agreement to institute a phased introduction of Marketing within all functional departments across the borough.

The authority has a much-envied reputation for professional management and innovate approaches to training, staffing and organisation. Specifically, it has recorded successes in recent years in terms of competitive tendering programmes in leisure provision and technical services; customer awareness and image-building exercises in 'trading' sections; and business-interface functions such as economic development and business support services. In these areas, the piecemeal beginnings of a Marketing presence has developed, through staff training and new appointments, albeit at a rather junior level.

The Chief Executive and the Senior Officer Group have now resolved to take the process further, to a more widespread and fulsome adoption of Marketing across all specialist departments, over a four-year period. It is envisaged that, after a 16-month period of 'trialling' Marketing within a selected number of departments/sections, a boroughwide Marketing Programme will be introduced, under the management of a new post at Chief Officer level, supported by a small team of executive officers located within major departments.

Though yet to be formally confirmed, it is likely that the specialist areas for the trial period will be selected from the following:

1 Libraries and Information.
2 Education.
3 Leisure Services.
4 Tourism Development.
5 Social Services.

As a manager within one of these specialist functions, you have been invited to join a planning group to develop and commission a plan to integrate Marketing approaches within the trial period. Since you have undertaken some familiarisation training in Marketing as part of your college course, you are asked to bring to the first group meeting (next week) a preliminary view of how you suggest your area should organise for Marketing.

It is accepted that, within the trial period, some departments may be better placed than others to test-run a comprehensive Marketing Plan, however all are felt able to make a valuable contribution to the debate on how Marketing activities and approaches can be resourced, monitored and evaluated, and projected forward into Phase II.

Question
Assuming the role of a manager within one of the functional areas listed, develop a summarised outline of the scope you identify for marketing within your department.

CHAPTER 23

Consumerism, Ethics, and Social Responsibility

Right and wrong exist in the nature of things. Things are not right because they are commanded, nor wrong because they are prohibited.

R. G. Ingersoll, *The Ghosts*

INTRODUCTION

This chapter introduces some of the ethical issues which are inherent to the application of marketing principles and practice. First, it does this by considering how these have been promoted as issues as through co-ordinated consumer action, consumerism. The wider ethical issues are then introduced and finally the need for organisations to increasingly demonstrate 'social responsibility' is discussed. While all three of these issues are relevant to marketing in general, their relative importance will vary from culture to culture and from country to country. In each, this relative importance will depend upon factors such as the level of industrialisation, prosperity, and education. Accordingly the purpose of this chapter is to introduce some of these issues so that their importance can be appreciated by all those who work in organisations and are involved with marketing.

There is an obvious starting point for marketing and general behaviour, which is the need to obey the law. However, even this is not always easy as legislation varies between countries and what is acceptable in one situation is illegal in another. Going further and linking legal constraints to consumer sovereignty is not enough. Questions are raised about marketing techniques themselves. It is often suggested that these techniques artificially stimulate consumption so people buy and continue to buy products that are either unwanted, worth little or both. Marketing has to justify itself against these charges of encouraging materialism and the waste of scarce resources as portrayed by Vance Packard in his 1960 book, *The Waste Makers*.

CONSUMERISM

There is no single, agreed definition of consumerism. It is generally accepted as being any organised group pressure on behalf of customers or users of a product or service. This may be specific to an individual organisation such as a 'user group' or aimed at protecting consumers in general from organisations with which there can be exchange relationships. The objective of both is to influence organisational behaviour to the benefit of the consumer.

In exchanges with organisations individuals have little power. Consumerism is one response to redress the balance. One of the pioneers of its development was Ralph Nader who criticised the safety of automobiles in the USA in his book *Unsafe at Any Speed*. Since then the movement has grown into a powerful force. As a result customers are increasingly able to communicate with organisations with powerful collective voices when products or promotions are considered unacceptable.

The advertising used by organisations to promote product benefits to target consumer is intended to influence choice, and can do so especially if the product relates to the consumer's wants and needs. Consumers, however, expect to receive more than this, and this desire is sometimes encompassed in what is described as the 'Societal Marketing Concept'. This is where suppliers, in addition to trying to satisfy the needs and wants of consumers, are expected to at least maintain, if not improve, the well-being of society as a whole.

Furthermore, consumers are increasingly being given 'rights' and this trend needs to be appreciated by all marketers. Examples of this have been the development by the UK government of a Citizen's Charter which was then used as the basis for the 'Patient's Charter' for the National Health Service, the 'Passenger's Charter' for rail travellers, and various other customer-focused initiatives.

The real start of consumerism was in the USA. Even before Nader's book, President Kennedy highlighted the obligation that organisations owe their customers in his 'Consumer Bill of Rights'. This identified four basic consumer rights:

1 The right to safety.
2 The right to be informed.
3 The right to choose.
4 The right to be heard.

The idea of rights can be traced back to the 'inalienable rights' included in the US Declaration of Independence by Thomas Jefferson. The marketing profession of today must be aware of these rights and combine them where possible in any marketing plans for products and services. They form a good framework for considering all other associated issues.

Consumer rights

The right to safety

When a purchase is made, the consumer has the right to expect that it is safe to use. The product should be able to perform as promised and should not have false or misleading guarantees. This 'right' is in fact a minefield for the marketing profession. Products which were at one time regarded as safe have subsequently been found by research not to be so. There was a time when cigarettes were not regarded as being particularly harmful to health, sugar in foods was not highlighted in television advertising as being bad for teeth, and everyone was encouraged to 'go to work on an egg'.

Legislation which highlights 'product liability' has been introduced in several countries. This has forced suppliers to reassess their responsibility for the safety of their products. As a result many organisations have developed a positive approach to product safety. Since failure to do so often results in complicated legislation and it is obvious that marketers who fail to protect consumers do so at their peril.

The right to be informed

The right to be informed has far-reaching consequences: it encompasses false or misleading advertising, insufficient information about ingredients in products, insufficient information on product use and operating instructions, and information which is deceptive about pricing or credit terms. This negative approach to avoiding trouble is not sufficient. Marketers should take every opportunity to communicate with consumers and to inform them about the benefits and features of the product offered. It should be no protection to claim that consumers fail to read instructions. Marketers must develop effective communications between consumer and supplier. This 'right' also is crucial to customers having access to the information needed to effectively exercise the next right – the right to choose.

The right to choose

While the consumer's right to choose is central to the practice of marketing, this does involve trying to influence that choice. This is necessary, as in most western markets competition is encouraged, so this choice often involves comparing both different products and suppliers. This comparison can be effectively impossible if, for instance, similar products are not sold in standardised quantities. As a result some regulations have been introduced with this objective. However, it can be argued that such legislation restricts choice and is not considered important by customers. The fact that Sainsbury provide this information on shelf tickets whereas Tesco do not would seem to support this view.

The right to be heard

The right of free speech is present in all western countries. However, do organisations listen to consumers? In a well-focused marketing organisation such feedback should be encouraged, and it should be treated as a key input for the future. This right allows consumers to express their views after a purchase, especially if it is not satisfactory. When anything goes wrong with a purchase the customer should furthermore be able to expect complaints to be fairly and speedily dealt with.

In those markets where consumerism has been effective this is increasingly expected by consumers. Of course there will always be some unjustified complaints and others which, although justified, are not dealt with to the customer's satisfaction. This can often be minimised by using marketing principles to focus on the actual needs of customers.

Consumer groups

Consumerism is now often seen in terms of formally organised consumer groups created to represent the rights of buyers to specific sellers. Since the early groups often formed as a result of customers becoming dissatisfied with an individual or group of suppliers many were initially considered unwelcome by suppliers. It was, however, found that such groups can provide organisations with opportunities both to respond to customers' changing needs and develop improved relationships with their customers. Because of this developing a positive relationship with consumer groups is generally accepted as an important function of marketing. Six distinct types of consumer group can be identified:

1 Government-encouraged groups to monitor the behaviour of legalised monopolies, e.g. OFWAT, OFTEL (the offices set up by the UK government to regulate the water and telephone industries).

2 Independent groups campaigning for a change of product, such as the Campaign for Real Ale (CAMRA) in the UK which successfully persuaded UK brewers to continue brewing traditional types of beer.

3 Groups including some charities which campaign for legal restrictions to protect society. ASH (Action on Smoking and Health) and ROSPA (Royal Society for the Prevention of Accidents) are two examples. While some of these may be classified as pressure groups rather than consumer groups they need to be considered in the same category by a marketing function.

4 Groups formed after a major tragedy to influence future operating practices of organisations. Examples of such tragedies would be the Lockerbie Pan-Am air crash in Scotland, the Herald of Free Enterprise ferry accident at Zeebrugge and the Hillsborough football stadium disaster.

5 Commercial pressure groups. The Consumer's Association, Egon Ronay, and What Car? magazine are such enterprises.

6 Media campaigners such as Ann Robinson with the 'Watchdog' programme on UK television.

While some of these groups focus on trying to influence the government or organisations directly, others try to influence many groups and public opinion. An effective way of doing this is to have a 'national day' such as the national Non-Smoking Day promoted by ASH.

Consumerism and marketing

Consumer groups affect the marketing environment in which organisations operate. By working with such groups, organisations gain competitive advantage through the PR which can result. This can be particularly important for products subject to a wide range of customer taste, such as beer as was shown by the success achieved by the Campaign for Real Ale (CAMRA) consumer group.

Organisations need to understand the influence that even small consumer groups can have in reflecting consumer attitudes and in shaping demand. Failure to do so can provide significant advantages for competitors. In 1991 *The Times* reported:

> 'Stop drinking Nescafé for the sake of babies in Brazil', the General Synod of the Church of England told us this week. The General Synod had accepted a motion proposed by a pressure group Baby Milk Action. Their national coordinator, Patti Rundall, explained 'Nescafé is Nestlés highest profile brand, and the company can well afford to lose some of its market share without its affecting jobs.'

The campaigners claimed the action was justified as companies within the Nestlé group, were promoting bottle feeding in third world countries and thereby encouraging mothers to give up breast feeding so increasing the risk of disease. While Nestlé claimed that it was acting in accordance with a World Health Organisation code of 1981, the campaigners claimed it was breaching rules added to the code in 1986.

The point is that a top-selling Nestlé product had been targeted for consumer action as a result of promoting a different product (dried baby milk) in another country (Brazil).

Nestlé have now stopped this exporting; evidence of the impact that consumer pressure can have.

Campaigners do not necessarily measure effectiveness only in terms of policies reversed and products withdrawn. 'There is little doubt that numerically more boycotts fail than succeed', the magazine *The Ethical Consumer* said in 1992, adding: 'Even an "unsuccessful" boycott can be a useful campaigning tool.'

However, when the Avon cosmetics group announced in June 1989 that it was giving up animal-testing, a spokesman admitted that consumer boycotts had influenced the decision. A similar animal testing campaign against Boots The Chemist, has been less successful. The campaign is directed at Boots shops, but its targets include drug-testing by Boots Pharmaceuticals (Hill, 1991).

ETHICS

Ethics involve the application of moral principles to decisions made by individuals within an organisation. It is the study of what is 'right' in any activity, and is of course influenced by the collective values present in an organisation.

Ethical issues are inherently complicated. Inevitably they involve a number of individuals or groups and the situations to be resolved have no obviously right answer. Often ethical issues associated with marketing are further complicated by their relevance varying significantly between the groups involved.

EXAMPLE

All of the retailers in a small West Midlands village agreed that they would not sell fireworks provided one of the village organisations organised a 'Guy Fawkes' bonfire and fireworks display. As a result for more than ten years there had not been a single accident involving fireworks in the village. One of the shops was sold and the new owner having sold fireworks at his previous shop saw no reason to respect the agreement. In order not to lose customers the other similar shops followed suit. As a result at least in the short term the new shopkeeper lost goodwill. What are the ethical issues? What are the marketing and business issues? Who are the parties involved?

Ethics involve issues of human behaviour and human judgement applied in everyday situations. Kenneth Andrews in his US article 'Ethics in practice' started by saying:

As the 1990s overtake us, public interest in ethics is at a historic high. While the press calls attention to blatant derelictions on Wall Street, in the defense industry, and in the Pentagon, and to questionable activities in the White House, in the attorney general's office, and in Congress, observers wonder whether our society is sicker than usual. Probably not. The standards applied to corporate behaviour have risen over time, and that has raised the average rectitude of business persons and politicians both. It has been a long time since we could say with Mark Twain that we have the best Senate money can buy or agree with muckrakers like Upton Sinclair that our large companies are the fiefdoms of robber barons. But illegal and unethical behaviour persists, even as efforts to expose it often succeed in making its rewards short-lived.

Why is business ethics a problem that snares not just a few mature criminals, or crooks in the making, but a host of apparently good people who lead exemplary private lives while concealing information about dangerous products or systematically falsifying costs? Observation suggests that the problem of corporate ethics has three aspects: the development of the executive as a moral person; the influence of the corporation as a moral environment; and the actions needed to map a high road to economic and ethical performance – and to mount guardrails to keep corporate wayfarers on track.

One problem in business, especially consumer markets, is that customers are often not technical professionals. They do not have the skills to fully assess the products they are offered except in a general way of judging the fitness of that product for the purpose for which it was purchased. But does the average consumer know how much water can be 'added' to a frozen chicken? The Trading Standards officers do, but is it appropriate for employees or their companies to ensure the maximum levels or is this just good business practice?

In another industry, how expert is an individual in assessing different life assurance policies? There is again a regulator, the Securities and Investment Board (SIB) in the UK, but even with safeguards and periods after purchase when decisions can be changed, there are still opportunities for policies which pay the highest commission to be recommended more strongly than others.

When selling a house there is a legal restraint of caveat emptor – let the buyer beware. The ethical question for the seller is whether to just answer questions as asked or to volunteer information that might make a sale less likely. With regards choices made by individual executives to justify questionable conduct, Saul Gellerman suggests four 'rationalisations':

1 The activity is not 'really' illegal or immoral.
2 The activity is in the individual's, or the corporation's, best interest.
3 It will never be found out.
4 Because it helps the company, the company will condone it.

The decisions reflected here are all taken by individuals, but as suggested by Andrews, the influence of the corporation as a moral environment can put pressure on managers to act in a particular way. Andrews suggests that while an individual's initial values will come from family and school, most of the influence on ethical behaviour related to business 'will occur in the organisations in which people spend their lives'. Since many decisions are not clear-cut, it is the corporate influences which can determine the behaviour. In many cases behaviour is changed only as a result of a negative experience by a large enough group for it to be clear that something must be done. In this case we get:

Negative event
↓
Ethical view (what ought to be done)
↓
Code of behaviour

Such codes may be supported by law or enshrined in a voluntary agreement on appropriate industry practices. Because of this everyone involved with making marketing decisions needs to fully consider its ethical implications. In his book, *Beyond the Bottom Line*, Ted Tuleja asked the question, 'Can the good guys finish first?' His conclusion is one of hope that:

the corporate villains will fall by the wayside, leaving the finish line to those businesses that play the game hard, but fairly. As democracy and competition both increase, earning the public's goodwill will become less and less an ancillary preoccupation, and move ever more forcefully to the forefront of Managers' attention.

Ethical Marketing Concept

Companies, in order to be successful, must not only be able to sell a product or service, they need to be seen to adhere to high standards, both in the service offered and ethically. It appears that it may be the right time to move a stage higher than the Societal Marketing Concept, and introduce an Ethical Marketing Concept.

Individuals have their own standards of ethical behaviour and their own moral standards. Over the past decade some of these moral standards seem to have changed as circumstances alter, but the underlying beliefs tend to be more durable. A sense of what is fair permeates organisations as a result of their employees. There are exceptions to this fair play, and these should be the focus of the ethical concept. All employees are involved and need to accept responsibility for being ethical both with respect to the company itself and its customers. This involves being accurate when filing in expense claims, refusing to accept personal gifts at Christmas and many other day-to-day activities. It may involve the pricing of contracts where there are opportunities to make substantial profits from any subsequent amendments to the contract or through the supply of spare parts. Organisations have many opportunities to either promote or discourage ethical behaviour by their employees.

Other issues regarding the actual marketing of products also raise questions as to ethical standards. As an example: should a marketing manager suggest a bold flash on the front of his company's food product reading 'No added colours' and rely on consumers not reading the ingredients panel to see that while this claim is true there are many added flavourings?

There are other practices which although not illegal in themselves are aimed at gaining business regardless of what may be fair to customers. A code of conduct would be one way to encourage ethical marketing practices. This would effectively promote the Ethical Marketing Concept but it will be difficult to achieve within the context of the European Community. What is considered acceptable in one country may well be considered unacceptable in another.

Social responsibility

Corporate social responsibility is generally considered to be the 'duty' of an organisation to conduct its activities with due regard to the interest of society as a whole. While no definition is given for the term 'social responsibility' in Michael Baker's dictionary of marketing terms, this does give the following definition for a social responsibility audit:

> An evaluation or assessment of the policies and practices of an organisation to establish how and to what extent it is behaving in a socially responsible manner, e.g. in terms of employment practices, relationships with its local community, environmental protection, etc.

From this it can be seen that corporate social responsibility covers issues of interest to marketing as well as other business functions. However, anything that affects the way an organisation interacts with its stakeholders could be seen as a marketing issue.

Marketing has been defined in this book in terms of a satisfying exchange process between supplier and customer. The first part of this chapter shows that consumer groups can often demand more from organisations through organised pressure. It is perhaps appropriate that organisations attempt to achieve what Gordon Wills referred to when he said that efficiency and worth of marketing must be judged by what they do for society as a whole. An American Chief Executive Officer described this by saying:

> A new dimension must be observed – a new 'bottom line' for business really is 'social approval'. Without this, economic victory would be pyrrhic indeed.

Sutherland and Gross in their book, *Marketing in Action*, try to relate this new dimension to marketing in a definition of the boundaries of social marketing. Social marketing takes account of the consumer's need for wider satisfaction beyond just product satisfaction. In other words, consumers place a value on their quality of life as well as the quality of their possessions. In its wider context, social marketing refers to the study of markets and marketing in general within the social system as a whole.

This is not a tight definition, perhaps because the boundaries of social marketing have yet to be agreed. However social marketing can be seen as a direct reaction to consumerism. The question is whether it is enough to just react to consumerism or whether an organisation should go further in its relationship with its environment.

The Independent newspaper reported (on 14 July 1991) in an article by Matthew Fearnley:

> **Marketing: A green and caring image will help corporations promote their products in the Nineties. Companies find it pays to have a conscience.**
>
> The Body Shop is so well known for its unusual business methods that its latest scheme – the handing over of nearly half of its 40 UK shops to managers and staff in a five-year plan called Partnership – would not ordinarily attract much interest. But Anita Roddick's company is not alone in this kind of venture. Peterborough-based Thomas Cook is funding the building of a local hospital; Butlins is offering day visits for underprivileged children; and earlier this month Cadbury raised about £500 000 for young sufferers of cerebral palsy with its 'Strollerthon', which attracted 12 000 walkers. Kentucky Fried Chicken is operating with the Tidy Britain Group to remove litter and educate people on how to improve the environment, and ICI is turning redundant sites into nature reserves.
>
> 'During the Eighties value was placed on wealth creation. But now people judge companies by their effect on things within local communities,' says ICI spokesman Bob Mitchell.
>
> Two factors are accelerating the switch to corporate responsibility. First, according to work carried out by both the Henley Centre and Mori, there is a massive swing away from the attitudes of the Eighties. Greed is no longer good; ethics are in.
>
> Second, products are becoming increasingly similar. Wally Olins of the design group Wolf Olins explains: 'It's increasingly the case that only those companies as effective as the best in their industry will survive, which means products are getting closer and closer together. The only way to differentiate between them is emotionally rather than rationally.'

This debate often revolves around questions of cost and benefit with many authors rejecting actions that do not offer an immediate benefit to the organisation. One interesting counter to this is the glass company Pilkington. Two issues stand out in a paper by Tom Sorell. One is that in the 1950s the company succeeded in developing a new advanced manufacturing process – float glass. The development had been very expensive but instead of capitalising on the competitive advantages of the new process, Pilkington's licensed it to competitors. Lord Pilkington said:

> A great deal was said about ethics: that it was not our job to deliberately deny any existing glass competitor the opportunity of living in competition with us. I don't think we

were short-sighted or rapacious ... There was a great deal of investment worldwide in plate, and people needed to have time to write off this plant or convert over. The alternative was chaotic disruption of a great industry.

Of course, the company received over £400 million in royalties over the next 20 years, but it is unclear if the decision was really the best commercially. However, when Pilkington came to take over its largest competitor for car safety glass and to merge with the dominant Triplex company the Monopolies Commission declared it was 'satisfied that Pilkington was conscious of its responsibility, as a monopolist, to the public interest. This sense of responsibility may be associated to some extent with the long-established dominance of the Pilkington family within the business. There would, we think, have to be some quite unforeseen change ... before Pilkington would deliberately set out to exploit its position of strength at the expense of the public interest.'

So Pilkington exercised its market position in a responsible way. In 1986–7 a hostile takeover bid for Pilkington was launched by the BTR conglomerate. This is the second issue where Pilkington's used its latent goodwill as a 'responsible' company, in this case to defeat the bid. The chairman's report the following year stated:

> Our ability to demonstrate that it was possible to achieve world leadership in an industry, while maintaining that important balance between the interests of the shareholders, employees, and the wider community, was a powerful and convincing defence. Throughout the bid we were able to rely on the wholehearted support of our employees. This support gathered momentum and widened to all of the communities in which we work, to the media, and to all three political parties. I cannot recall a similar bid where such universal support was generated by a target company.

The Pilkington case involves issues of overall policy but does give an example of two unexpected paybacks from a history of benevolent action in its industry and within its home community in St Helens, Lancashire.

Consumers are now able to buy publications which 'inform the public about the social, environmental and ethical policies of companies' such as *Shopping for a Better World*, published by Kogan Page. More and more firms are introducing policies which will show them to be socially responsible.

Britain has been in the throes of an environmental awakening during the last decade. Environmentalism and subsequent consumer actions have developed as society has changed; the degree of social responsibility expected from firms has also dramatically increased. The marketing response to two of these issues will be covered in the next section.

Social responsibility and marketing

Earlier in this chapter we explained how some consumers, having become aware of the marketing concept, now expect more than products and services which satisfy their needs and wants. They look for the added bonus of the Societal Marketing Concept where the well-being of society is also catered for. The situation has now arisen where it has become impossible in some industries to produce what customers want, without an accompanying high cost in environmental terms.

The ozone layer

For more than a two decades scientists realised that the layer of ozone situated in the high atmosphere was becoming thinner. As a result the protection provided by this ozone layer against some of the sun's harmful ultraviolet radiation was also being reduced. This is important as this radiation is known to cause skin cancer. After much research a theory that the ozone layer was being damaged by chemicals known as chlorofluorocarbons (CFCs) gained wide acceptance. As a direct result the US government banned these chemicals for use as aerosol propellant. This was an important development because at that time a significant proportion of the CFCs released into the atmosphere was from that source.

Few other countries saw any need to follow the US example partly because their market for aerosols had not been anything like as significant and the industry as a whole seemed to be following the lead of the US manufacturers who dominated this market.

Furthermore, CFCs continued to be used in the production of insulation materials and as the circulating liquid (refrigerant) used in refrigerators and air conditioners. One reason for this being permitted was that there was no acceptable 'ozone friendly' alternative, and it took many years before one was developed. In the meantime CFCs continued to be manufactured and released into the atmosphere as very few countries introduced the legislation which would have been needed to regulate the disposal of old refrigerators, freezers and cars fitted with air conditioners.

Meanwhile, public concern has grown and manufacturers of suntan oil and moisturisers have found that they have more business as people become aware that they must protect their skin from harmful ultraviolet radiation. Women who formerly used pure moisturising lotion, are now asking for moisturising lotion with a sun protection factor. Suntan lotion is now produced with varying protection factors. This is a major change from the times when the lotion was perhaps just olive or coconut oil.

More recently some socially responsible companies have voluntarily tried to eliminate the use of CFCs and assist other companies to do the same. A few have been forced by consumer pressure to do so. Over the last few years most aerosols have been changed. Manufacturers have abandoned the use of CFCs and are actively using this fact as a selling point in their advertising campaigns. Unfortunately one of the most popular alternatives is also being condemned owing to it being classed as a 'greenhouse gas'. (*See* global warming.)

The problems associated with the use of CFCs have already provided both significant problems and opportunities with respect to marketing many different types of product. It will undoubtedly continue to be a significant marketing issue. To date it could be claimed that many of the opportunities were missed so hopefully the marketing world will address this problem more effectively in the future. It is becoming increasingly clear that both consumers and socially responsible companies will need to exercise what power they have effectively to bring about changes which are of long-term benefit to the environment.

Global warming

Packaging of goods uses up the raw material, wood, which is used for paper production. As there is a tremendous demand for paper the forests of the world are being depleted. Forests absorb carbon dioxide and emit oxygen, so reducing the harmful build-up of carbon dioxide in the upper atmosphere which leads to an increase in the earth's temperature. Although the majority of the general public do not want to return to the days when many products were not packaged, they expect companies to act in a socially responsible manner with regard to the type and amount of packaging used.

Significant improvements have been taken in the last few years, some firms even using their packaging policies as a selling point. Procter & Gamble have taken this one step further. Published on their Pampers nappies is the following information: 'Pulp: Made with care for the environment. The traditional chlorine bleaching process is not used. Pampers pulp is purified with an oxidation process. With smaller bags Pampers saves raw materials and energy: less packaging, less waste and fewer lorries for transport.'

Animal welfare

Some companies have used the fact that they are against animal testing in their marketing campaigns. One such company is The Body Shop, where leaflets explaining its policies are freely available to customers. An extract from one such leaflet states:

> The Body Shop never has, and never will, test ingredients or final products on animals or authorise such tests on its behalf. We adhere to BUAV'S five-year rule – every six months, our suppliers and manufacturers must sign a declaration stating that they are not testing our ingredients on animals and have not done so within the last five years. This dynamic policy is proving successful in changing the practices of suppliers and manufacturers who used to test on animals.

The Body Shop has tried to raise public awareness on the issue of animal testing and to this end has worked closely with the British Union for the Abolition of Vivisection.

Not only has the general public's attitude towards the testing of products and substances on animals changed, but also their attitude towards the killing of animals for their fur. Many businesses which dealt with the sale of fur coats no longer exist: the demand for such coats having almost disappeared in Britain. This is not the case in all European countries; in Scandinavia many people, both male and female, wear fur to combat the cold winters. For marketing purposes, it is most unlikely that interest will be revived in Britain for fur, such is the strength of public opinion against cruelty to animals. This has extended also to the trade in ivory, crocodile skin, etc.

Social responsibility towards animal welfare has developed to such an extent that companies such as ICI and Unilever carry out in-house research to try to find alternatives to testing products and substances on animals.

CONCLUSION

This chapter has considered the wider implications for marketing within the field of consumerism, ethics, and social responsibility. Certainly since the 1960s, the consumerism movement has gathered pace, making an impact on corporate behaviour in general, and marketing in particular. Most categories of products on sale in western markets have been affected by consumer groups making customers increasingly interested in quality, performance, value and related issues.

Ethics consider the morality of behaviour of individuals and groups that are party to decisions made within an organisation. Social responsibility encompasses arguably all activities, practices and policies through which a commercial organisation affects society at large and its interests.

While it is difficult to pass judgement on the multitude of 'grey' areas within corporate decision making and behaviour, it can be clearly demonstrated that there is now a society-wide concern for responsible corporate behaviour and moral standards in business decisions. Marketers, no less than other business specialists, need to embrace these challenges as a facet of their own professionalism.

QUESTIONS

1 Consider the view that consumerism would not have developed in the first place if marketers had been doing their job properly.

2 Obtain a copy of the mission statement of any organisation of your choice, and consider the extent to which it addresses the issues raised within this chapter.

3 What conflicts of morality and acceptable corporate behaviour might face a company operating across a spread of international markets?

4 Mention has been made of the NHS Patient's Charter. Working on your own experience as a student, what issues should be addressed within the Student's Charter?

FURTHER READING

Adams, R., Carrathers, J. and Fisher, C. (1991) *Shopping for a Better World*, Kogan Page, London.

Andrews, K., 'Ethics in practice', *Harvard Business Review*, September–October 1989.

Baker, M. (1990) *Dictionary of Marketing and Advertising*, 2nd Edn, Macmillan.

Fearnley, M., 'Companies find it pays to have a conscience', *The Independent on Sunday*, 14 July 1991.

Gellerman, S., 'Why "good" managers make bad ethical choices', *Harvard Business Review*, July–August 1986.

Hill, G., 'Those we have loved to hate', *The Times*, 19 July 1991.

Packard, V. (1960) *The Waste Makers*, Penguin, 1960.

Nader, R. (1965) *Unsafe at any Speed*, Grossman, New York.

Quinn, J. B. (1991) 'Pilkington Brothers Plc case study', in H. Mintzberg and J. B. Quinn, *The Strategy Process*, Prentice-Hall.

Sorrel, T. (1987) in Bowman and Asch, Readings in *Strategic Management*, Macmillan, London.

Sutherland, J. and Gross, N. (1991) *Marketing in Action*, Pitman, London.

Tuleja, T. (1987) *Beyond the Bottom Line*, Penguin.

Wills, G., 'Marketing's social dilemmas', *European Journal of Marketing*, Vol. 8, No.1, 1976.

CASE STUDY
Ethics in Packaging

Miss Margaret Knight now really has a problem. She is the product manager for solid deodorants at a leading manufacturer of personal care products and has just received a revised ethics policy document. The recently appointed Chief Executive Officer had a reputation for supporting ethical issues in business and was known to generally favour 'green' policies. The difficulty is that he is new to the personal care business having joined the organisation after a successful career in the health-care sector.

Margaret had been warned that the new policy made specific reference to the ethical issues of packaging. She now found it specifically stated that unnecessary packaging should be avoided and packaging should not be designed to deceive customers regarding what was being purchased. Margaret had hoped that the wording of this aspect of the policy would have allowed more room for interpretation.

The problem Margaret faces is due to the results of recently completed customer acceptance tests on a new range of products. These tests found that all of these products had been favourably accepted with regard to performance but required very creative packaging to be successful. There were three reasons for this. First, the product was much dryer than previous products so needed to be presented in a dispenser with a greater surface area than the current product range. Thus, if the volume of the container was to remain the same it would be shorter which would be undesirable for shelf display. Second, the product was far more economical in use so if each pack contained the same volume it is possible that sales would decline by 50 per cent or more. If the container size was

reduced to allow a genuine claim that the new product was 15 per cent more economical it would then become far smaller than competitive products which again had shelf space disadvantages. It would also appear to customers as providing reduced rather than increased value for money. Furthermore having tested a small pack it was found that customers found it inconvenient to use as it was easy to drop.

The preferred solution was to pack the product in a slightly larger container than the existing product to emphasise the improved economy, to use a different shape to emphasise that this was a new product not a variation of the existing product and to mount the product on a hollow plastic filler which would take up just over half of the pack volume. The draft marketing plan for the product had mentioned the potential for complaints with regard to the filler being used and a standard reply letter had been drafted. This emphasised the improved performance and economy of the new product and justified the filler on the basis that due to the properties of the new product this type of packaging reduced waste.

Margaret knew this was actually true, but had not been convinced that customers who complained would believe it. More immediately she wondered to what extent the proposed packaging might be considered as contravening the new ethics policy with respect to packaging.

Question

What are your views? Can you identify examples of other products which might be considered to be in contravention with the new ethics policy on packaging?

CHAPTER 24

International Marketing

Why the world's mine oyster,
which I with sword will open.
William Shakespeare,
***Merry Wives of Windsor*, Act I, Scene II.2.**

INTRODUCTION

Most business enterprises start life in the service of markets that are basically local or, at most, national in character. That this should be so is not difficult to understand. In all countries, whatever the state of economic development, there will be a ready 'home-grown' market for the community's basic and everyday requirements. With economic and technological advances, new opportunities will appear, to supply markets that are no longer confined to the potential of the home country. Indeed, strategically, it is a difficult if trite truism that 'the world is becoming a smaller place' as changes in technology, communications, economic alignments and political geography make for an internationalisation and convergence of markets. Such a 'globalisation' process is likely to affect marketing no less than other functions such as manufacturing, logistics or finance, or business in general. Nevertheless, it does not follow that globalisation has yet allowed companies to adopt standardised marketing approaches across international boundaries. In spite of the march of globalisation, there remain innumerable and significant environmental differences between markets across the globe. It is partly the enduring complexity of these environmental contrasts that underpins the case for international marketing as a legitimate specialism within its parent field.

THE INTERNATIONAL MARKET ENVIRONMENT

While it is quite positive to consider the similarities in environment between the firm's home market and prospective overseas markets, it is also good business sense to be wary of those environmental differences that can cause major problems if not heeded.

With increasing international experience, a company will develop an almost unconscious sensitivity and responsiveness to such issues. However, in the early stages of internationalisation, and certainly for those overseas markets that it first enters, a company would be well advised to adopt a systematic approach for investigating specific market environments.

Table 24.1 ● **How to assess environmental differences between markets**

Sector	Key elements
Economic	● National income and wealth ● Economic development, e.g. industrialisation ● International trade – volumes, trade patterns and partners — trade policies e.g. tariffs, quotas ● Economic and trade affiliations, e.g. EC, NAFTA (North American Free Trade Association) ● Economic and investment policies, e.g. taxes, incentives ● Financial and monetary issues, e.g. monetary policy, financial infrastructure, currency
Political-legal	● Type and stability of government ● Government policy and attitude to overseas companies and investors ● Framework and application of laws affecting marketing, e.g. competition, contract, agency law
Geographical	● Physical features – dimensions of country/ territory, topography and climatic conditions, resources ● Geocommercial – transport, infrastructure, population dispersion/ urbanisation, land-use
Technological	● Technological level – existing facilities and infrastructure, skills and training ● Development potential, e.g. joint venture potential, investment incentives
Social-cultural	● Demographic aspects, e.g. data on population age, ethnic, health, education, religious, lifestyle profiles ● Social – institutions, class influences ● Cultural – language, regional and customary factors; attitude to work, materialism, business protocol

Table 24.1 presents a framework for comparing differences in the market environment between countries. It should be stressed that this framework is not intended to be a checklist for 'auditing' purposes, while it certainly cannot be seen as exhaustive. Equally, it should be noted that :

(a) The less tangible and non-metric factors such as culture will often prove most durable, most troublesome and most unpredictable in international business.

(b) Within-market environmental differences can be equally challenging, especially in large diverse markets such as the US and India.

(c) There is an increasing dynamism and global interplay at work across the international marketplace which defies over-simplistic summaries or comparisons. Again, as Rowell (1994) and Hilton (1992) demonstrate in terms of the European Single Market, the same environmental spillover effects exist at sub-global, or regional levels.

COMPANY INTERNATIONALISATION

Companies involved in international business will tend to have different objectives, different orientations and different approaches to the market. While a gradation or scale of activity may not be clearly apparent, there will be a contrast to be seen in the roles and postures adopted by organisations in their dealings with overseas markets. At the one end of the spectrum will be the firm that scrambles around for overseas sales as a temporary stop-gap measure, to keep its machinery running or to export surplus or redundant stock. Such blow-hot-blow-cold courtships are not untypical of the attentions shown in foreign markets by the periodic exporter.

In another category entirely will be the company that plans to cultivate and exploit international opportunities to the mutual benefit of itself and its stakeholders. With a clearer view of some long-term future and a proven record of flexible marketing, such a 'global' company will identify as readily with the international market as with its country of origin.

Most companies actively engaged in international marketing will fit somewhere between these two examples, and research indicates that company internationalisation involves a dynamic process of experimentation, experience and development.

A particular research focus has centred on the process by which interesting overseas markets develop, or evolve, what initiates this and what factors promote the 'internationalisation process' (Anderson, 1993). A long-standing research question, of interest to academics and government policy-makers alike, concerns the process by which smaller firms enter export markets. One widely supported school of thought, holds that smaller firms go through 'stages' or phases of export learning and business development, such that eventually there is a firm commitment to overseas marketing – as opposed to exporting or overseas selling. While many branches of enquiry have developed within the internationalisation literature – for example on the relation between firm size and international readiness or maturity (*see* Bonaccorsi, 1992), it is worth mentioning that some commentators (e.g. Bell, 1995) view the internationalisation of firms in terms of anything but a stage-wise development process.

Table 24.2 presents a view of some different guises of international marketing, from export (sales) activity to the full-blown global marketing that is associated with the larger 'transnational' corporations.

Table 24.2 ● Variants on international marketing

Activity	Characteristics
Exporting/export sales	Sales-led push into export markets, often dominated by short-term objectives
Export marketing	Export sales and distribution, supported by HO-directed marketing support
International marketing operations	A marketing-led approach to international business, co-ordinated from company HQ. Some overseas supply, i.e. no longer wholly exports
Multinational marketing	Wherever viable, market-based marketing and operations, i.e. multimarket approaches tailored to local conditions
Global marketing	Marketing on a worldwide scale, strategically co-ordinated to exploit global markets or customer groups.

It should be noted, that the variants of international marketing depicted in Table 24.2 are somewhat generalised stereotypes, and that they do not claim to represent the international development path taken by all companies. In recent years, too, competing theories have emerged in terms of the commercial wisdom or appropriateness of different strategies and the possible trade-offs involved, e.g. in terms of home market v overseas market service levels.

DECISIONS WITHIN INTERNATIONAL MARKETING

On deciding to enter the international marketplace for the first time, or possibly considering adding new overseas markets, a company would do well to adopt a purposeful strategic approach, based on informed decisions. The major decision areas involved are outlined below.

1 Whether to market internationally?
2 Which markets to enter?
3 How to enter selected markets?
4 Marketing activities and strategy.
5 Organisation and management control.

Whether to market internationally?

This represents a critical decision, since it has major strategic implications. Many strategy-based arguments could be ranged in favour of international marketing. The list below presents a summary of the reasons that companies commonly cite for developing international markets:

- to gain more sales;
- as (strategic) market diversification;
- more profit potential overseas;
- to counter depressed or declining home market;
- to justify capacity increase, spread overheads;
- to follow key customers abroad;
- exploiting (new) products with world potential;
- exploiting improved company competitiveness;
- by invitation, through unsolicited business;
- market internationalisation 'pull';
- as spin-off from sourcing/supply links overseas.

Aside from the profit opportunities that do exist in selected markets, companies might be influenced by the need to strategically diversify their market base, to exploit a growing internationalisation in their prime market, or to capitalise on the overseas potential of new products or technologies. A classical marketing strategy might involve following key customers abroad – the stay-with-the-market strategy typified by leading international consultants, advertising agencies, insurance companies and other service-based organisations. More defensive strategies might involve efforts to counter seasonality or instability in the home market, or to justify capacity increases or seek scale economies.

Whatever strategic rationale a company may have for looking abroad, it would need to weigh up the 'downside' of the argument, the risks involved. It should be apparent from the earlier discussion that, in spite of accelerating globalisation, the business environment in many overseas markets will still be risky and unfamiliar in terms of economic and competitive conditions, legal factors, government policy and controls, and social and cultural influences on the marketplace. The list below illustrates some of the more common difficulties and risks that await the unwary entrant to the international arena:

- credit risk;
- cash flow problems;
- exchange rate fluctuations, currency upheavals;
- controls on profit repatriation;
- taxation problems;
- non-tariff barriers;
- political problems;
- legal traumas;
- bureaucracy;
- language and communications problems;
- cultural resistance;
- alien business culture.

While many of these difficulties can be minimised by careful research and good management, they nevertheless represent real potential pitfalls, even for the company seasoned in international business.

Which markets to enter?

No less than mainstream marketing itself, international marketing will likely be more successful through careful targeting within selected markets. Especially in the early days of internationalisation, a company would be better to restrict its attentions, and resources, to at most a few promising markets, and to treat these as a learning and trialling ground for hopefully more ambitious steps later.

Mindful of the risks inherent in overseas ventures, many companies will seek earlier custom, likely through export sales, in those few markets that may have produced interest, enquiries or unsolicited orders in the recent past, or perhaps where they have contacts for other purposes, such as sourcing. Often there will be a tendency to approach markets that are 'psychologically' nearer, perhaps through language, cultural or even geographical proximity, e.g. German companies may relate more readily to Austria or Switzerland, Swedish companies to other Scandinavian markets.

Such intuitive reasoning may well prove useful guidance to a company, but there may be a case for adopting a more rigorous and deliberate set of market selection criteria in order to objectively assess overseas opportunities in relation to company resources and capabilities. At its most basic there is a role for detailed SWOT (Strengths, Weaknesses, Opportunities, Threats) analysis approaches, while developments from this would lead to detailed research into market and competitor environments, albeit within a research budget constraint limited to a few selected 'shortlist' markets. Certainly within chosen target markets key entry and operating decisions will be better informed through market research efforts, perhaps involving a mix of secondary information sources and market-based primary research activities.

Marketing Research for international marketing should be employed at least as regularly as within the domestic market, though a number of studies (e.g. Brown and Cook, 1990) have shown that this is anything but the case, while even among companies using research, many do not engage in regular or consistent market research efforts, use detailed fieldwork methodologies or enlist the services of professional market research agencies. Of course, it is possible to be too purist in research terms, especially in those overseas markets where all sorts of practical difficulties and constraints enforce the need for pragmatism and compromise in conducting research.

In terms of desk research, even first-time exporters should find for most markets a variety of sources for general economic/commercial data, ranging from UN and World Bank statistics to data provided by banks, Chambers of Commerce, professional and academic bodies, directory publishers, the World Wide Web and the media. However, especially for less-developed overseas markets, the exporter is likely to be faced with a number of problems and pitfalls in terms of data accuracy and consistency, coverage and currency, and sometimes difficulties in comparability. Equally, language and translation errors can cause difficulties (e.g. with definitions and classification terms), while care and time may need to be taken in converting measures and monetary values and dealing with difficulties such as broken (interrupted) data sets or conflicting data from equally plausible sources.

Primary research in international markets can also involve major problems. In terms of methodology, and research design, shortfalls in secondary data may affect the availability and reliability of sampling frames and so rule out probability sampling; while issues of language, literacy and wider cultural constraints may strongly influence the type of questions asked, their scope and accuracy (e.g. scales) and the whole issue of questionnaire design and use. Culture may limit the availability of certain respondents (e.g. female consumers in Muslim countries), while even in general terms it will influence behavioural aspects of training and supervising research fieldworkers, the requirement for interviewer-respondent ethnic matching, and so forth. Of course, given that most primary research is customarily (and necessarily) completed by research agencies, most of these problems are of less direct concern to the international marketer. On using specialist agencies, though, a company would need to take care in appointing, briefing and dealing with a selected agency in order to ensure cost-effective, timely and reliable research outcomes.

How to enter selected markets?

Exactly how a company enters and supplies a foreign market has major influences on the extent to which it capitalises on market potential, and on the strategic control it allows itself over market development.

Usually the early phases of internationalisation will lead the company into limited resource commitments, often facilitated by using indirect channels of market entry, which offer advantages of both risk- and knowledge-sharing. Such indirect channels will involve the use of third parties, or intermediaries, that may be based either in the exporter's market or the overseas territory. A variety of such intermediary entry routes, and more direct servicing channels, are presented in Table 24.3.

Table 24.3 ● Market entry and servicing channels	
Indirect	*Direct*

● Home-based export agents, traders, and buying offices
● Overseas-based:
  – Agents
  – Distributors
	● Export sales, HQ-based selling
	● Overseas-based sales staff
	● Full-scale manufacturing and marketing overseas
	● Joint ventures:
	  – assembly, manufacture, full-scale joint venture
	  – licensing/franchising

In principle, a company might 'travel far' in export markets through trading on its own doorstep with export merchants in its home market, specialist 'export houses' perhaps specialising in certain trades or geographical markets, or with buying offices of overseas interests (e.g. department stores) based in the 'home' market. More commonly, companies will select and appoint foreign-based intermediaries such as agents or distributors, thereby at least achieving a closer representation at the market level. For practical purposes, it is worth pointing out that agents act 'on behalf' of the exporter (or legal 'principal'), while distributors buy and sell on their own behalf within the overseas market.

A common mistake made by exporters, is to hurriedly appoint agents or distributors within overseas markets and subsequently adopt a low profile, optimistically awaiting a flourish of orders from the newly-appointed intermediaries. In practice, to get the best out of any such third party approach, companies need to remain proactive and supportive from the very outset, taking care to treat the agent or distributor as a business partner and to develop an effective relationship based on responsive service and mutual respect (*see* Shipley *et al.*, 1989).

In the case of both an agency or distributor arrangement, the exporting company should select and recruit carefully, ensuring that the chosen intermediary has local market knowledge, credibility (including financial probity), customer contacts, sales coverage and market experience, and has those marketing facilities (e.g. storage, transport, administrative system, service and support back-up) necessary to both adequately address agreed sales volume targets and contribute to subsequent market development. Obviously, in both cases, the export company would be advised to 'appoint' from a shortlist, and after a market visit involving observations, meetings and negotiation discussions at first-hand. The legalities of a formal agreement should be treated as anything but a formality, since details on commission payments (for agents) or margins and allowances (for distributors) will necessarily relate to the duties and responsibilities expected of *both* parties, while these and other stipulations such as agreed products, territory coverage, competitive conflicts, contract duration and renewal arrangements will make for an effective working relationship, or alternatively occasion dissatisfaction and disputes, and even ultimately disengagement or litigation.

More direct representation in the overseas market will be achieved usually only by taking higher investments and risk. Obviously, the establishment of an overseas-based sales force, sales subsidiary or full-scale, full-service overseas subsidiary, would involve heavy investments that would only be justified by major market opportunities, likely

Kingston Environmental Laboratories

Based at Kingston-Upon-Hull, Humberside, Kingston Environmental Laboratories (KEL) is a private company, founded in 1970 by Dr Edmond Walker, a chemist formerly employed by Halifax Water Authority, now part of newly-incorporated Yorkshire Water Plc.

Since its inception, the company grew steadily for some fifteen years, undertaking water sampling and purification analysis work for a range of process industry manufacturers such as brewing and soft drinks manufacturers, food companies, pharmaceutical, textile and chemical manufacturers, to utilities corporations, local authorities and specialist government agencies. Since the early eighties, spurred by a growing national awareness of environmental standards, and increasingly stringent codes of conduct and legislation, company growth has accelerated rapidly.

Company turnover in 1996 topped £28m and pre-tax profits recorded a healthy £6.2m. Reflecting the changed nature of the company's business, in 1996 the traditional staple of water purity analysis laboratory work comprised some 55 per cent of this revenue figure, while the balance divided between a growing portfolio of research-funded projects (20 per cent), environmental consultancy contracts (17 per cent), and specialist laboratory equipment (8 per cent). The latter represents a recent (1991+) diversification into manufacturing/assembly, based on patented company know-how, through sub-contract supply links with hi-tech instrumentation manufacturers in both the UK, Scandinavia and mainland Europe. While most company business (88 per cent) is still conducted within the UK, the company's burgeoning management team found early on in the manufacturing initiative that there existed hungry European export markets for their innovative equipment, from a mix of science-based organisations and process industries similar to their UK customer profile.

The *ad hoc* direct sales arrangements that supported the early development of this export trade have since been replaced by the appointment of commission agents, based in Germany, France, Italy, Sweden and Holland, which collectively account for some 75 per cent of export business. Export orders from elsewhere in Europe, including occasional orders from Eastern Europe, and a growing number from other countries (including the US, South Africa and Australia), have so far been handled by direct market visits, where justified, or through catalogue-order transactions against cash payment.

At the company's 1997 Annual Review Meeting, Jack Mason, the appointee to the newly-created post of Business Development Manager, suggested to the company board that radical and new representation arrangements be devised to cover all the company's overseas interests. He argued that the agency network so far developed was only a partial and patchy coverage of the potentially vast export market, and that anyway, agency arrangements were not necessarily the best approach to marketing high-value products such as their specialist equipment line. Citing the home market, where a dedicated sales representative had recently been taken on, he argued that the company should consider 'upgrading' to locally-based sales representatives in leading markets. This, he argued, could also enable better local sourcing of environmental consultancy work, where recently the company had experienced a promising increase in enquiries.

Question

Consider the arguments put forward by Jack Mason, and review the alternative sales and marketing channels available to KEL, taking into account a possibly wider future overseas market for their products and services.

CHAPTER 25

Marketing in Action

The way to get things done is not to mind who gets the credit of doing them

Benjamin Jowitt

INTRODUCTION

This chapter is designed to look at marketing in particular situations. A large number of ideas and techniques have been discussed in the main body of this book, obviously not all are equally relevant in every application. To give some indication of the emphasis in several different contexts, the authors have drawn on their varying experience to look briefly at four areas:

● consumer product marketing;
● industrial marketing;
● services marketing;
● non-business marketing.

Five case studies covering these areas are presented at the end of the chapter.

CONSUMER MARKETING

Fast-moving consumer goods

The first serious development of marketing techniques was in the, so-called, fast-moving consumer goods (fmcg) markets of the USA. Companies such as Procter & Gamble became the 'universities' of marketing where people learnt the elements of the marketing mix and devised plans to win market share. As these marketers moved to other companies and other industries they took with them the skills of product development, and the ability to create unique selling propositions and effective promotions. These skills have been modified in other industries, but the emphasis on the marketing mix still remains in fast-moving consumer goods (fmcg) markets. The major objective in such markets is to build brand loyalty, as the products are typically low-value regular purchases such as food, drink, confectionery, household and health-care items, magazines, stationery and many others.

It was in one of these markets that Coca-Cola devised the tests of Acceptability, Affordability and Availability. This test is used in a wider context in this book, but for fmcg products the aim is to maximise all of the 'As' with the widest group of potential consumers. Information is continuously sought on product performance. This information comes in two basic forms, comparative data on market share and related issues from retailer and consumer panels, and acceptance/awareness data from tracking studies. It is such feedback that reveals small variations in performance and highlights trends which could require attention. These markets value the long-term investment to build brand names such as Mars, Kit Kat, Persil, Coke, Marlboro. Typically, main media are used and quite large advertising budgets (advertising/sales ratios can reach 10 per cent).

There have been a number of studies of the link between the share of grocery markets taken by retailers own brands and the advertising spent by manufacturers on their proprietary brands (*The Grocer* 28 March 1992, IGD Research Report 1995). In general there is a strong relationship with low spending categories, such as yoghurt and tea, having high penetration by own-label brands. Higher spending on toothpaste and pet food, has reduced the penetration. However, in conversation with a retail buyer, one of the authors was told it was too obvious to equate advertising spend and share. Product innovation and customer perception of product quality are also important. See the Müller case study at the end of this chapter.

One interesting development in the grocery market is the announcement by Migros, the large Swiss retailer, that it intends to launch Migros branded products into UK retailers. In this case you could ask what is an 'own-label' brand? Migros contend that they do not want to compete with UK supermarkets, but by selling Migros brands in Tesco or Sainsbury they will be bringing a new brand to the marketplace. It might be an 'own-brand' in Switzerland but in the UK maybe a brand is a brand is a brand.

Advertising is no guarantee of success and many years of investment are necessary to develop strong brands. However, fmcg marketing does involve large promotional budgets and a great deal of attention to communicating with the millions of customers for any product. Contact with these customers is, of necessity, non-personal and so sophisticated marketing research is used to obtain feedback.

Typically consumer goods companies will have large marketing departments covering all functional aspects of marketing such as advertising, marketing research and brand or product management. They will supplement this by use of agencies to provide specialist services including promotion and planning and new product development. The objective of fmcg marketing is to keep interest in the brands so that they remain relevant to customers, achieve high levels of awareness and become regular purchase items.

Table 25.1 ● **Estimates of own-label share of grocery markets**

	1990	1995
Toothpaste	5	8
Pet food	7	9
Tea	16	27
Yoghurt	42	27
Flour	50	40

One interesting issue is when fast-moving consumer goods become organisational (or industrial) goods. Most fmcg are sold through major supermarket groups such as Tesco or Sainsbury. These retail groups purchase in large quantities and the marketing of chocolate bars or frozen chickens to a supermarket has more to do with (organisational) industrial marketing, inter-company relationships, and meeting the profit objectives of the powerful retailer than it has to do with the taste of the food or positive consumer feedback.

Consumer durables

Unlike fmcg, consumer durables are less frequently purchased. Consumers have to be able to identify available products when they are considering the purchase of a durable product. In order to reach such customers communication is again vital.

Durables could be washing machines or cars or video recorders or classic clothing. As discussed in Chapter 10, most consumer durables would fall into one of two categories: shopping goods or speciality goods. If the former, then the marketing task is determined by the consumer and the need for useful comparative information. The usefulness will come from providing facts about the benefits that are valued by the customers and are the ones used to make decisions. An example of durable marketing can be seen by considering how car companies communicate with their customers. At one level you will see evocative advertisements for Ford or Volvo creating a glamour and a general position for the manufacturers, using television and other mass media. This is complemented by press advertisements giving other details and often the financial deals. Direct mail communication or sales promotion competitions are used to encourage customers to visit showrooms for the particular marque. Once in the showroom the actual cars are supported by technical information in brochures and from the direct sales staff.

Daewoo cars have used a more direct approach than is traditional in launching their range. The objective of the appeal to find people who felt let down by the motor trade not only yielded a great deal of information but also a very large database of customer names and contact addresses. In a crowded competitive market it is vital to offer customers a reason for buying – or more precisely a reason for buying again if dealing with an existing customer and a reason to switch for the customers buying from your competitors.

By studying car distributors it is possible to see a range of different techniques being used to bring a potential customer ever closer to the point of purchase. The integrated programmes of communication will be designed to both inform and persuade. Sometimes information is given in a direct way to compare one model with another and influence the comparisons of product suitability prior to actually seeing the product. The emphasis on information can be seen with many 'shopping' products.

Car dealers also reinforce decisions by direct communications with customers in the months and years after a sale. This is due to the period of time between the purchase and the need to replace the durable. Not only is there an emphasis on after-sales service but it is likely that other information on new models and other developments will be communicated to past customers. When the time comes for replacement the experience with the product will be very important in a customer's decision process. It was once said: 'The quality of a product is remembered long after the price is forgotten'. With durables it is certainly true that their performance is remembered rather than the purchase details. Therefore a consumer who has enjoyed excellent service from a product will remember that when the time comes for a replacement. The issue is a very personal one as exemplified by the differing experiences of two of the authors regarding cars.

One of the authors has a Vauxhall Cavalier, which was a former company car. It has already covered over 230 000 miles with few problems. However, it is nearing time for replacement and this person is convinced that a Vauxhall should be the next purchase. Another has a Vauxhall Astra which has proved unreliable at times and recently required a new engine. He has had a poorer experience so is not so keen on this make next time round.

In the case above, the importance of the channel of distribution is highlighted as it is the local distributor who gives the majority of after-sales service and can build a strong position for the future.

It must be remembered that durables are not only infrequent purchases, but they are also likely to involve substantial money. Issues of affordability are relevant, but perhaps value is a more important measure. Consumers do not necessarily buy the cheapest car or washing machine, but they buy the one that offers the features that they require. The features offered with a durable product will vary enormously. There is likely to be much more variety than for a non-durable product. These features form what we have called the 'total product', or some authors call the 'augmented product'. Some of these features are important only at the point of purchase, such as free road fund licence or a full tank of petrol for a car, or free fitting for a carpet or washing machine. These are really promotional additions sometimes described as the 'bells and whistles'. Other features are more substantive for the future, such as a sunroof in a car or special economy programme with a washing machine, or freeze-frame facility on a video recorder.

All features cost money to provide and not all features are valued by purchasers. Marketers responsible for consumer durables have to decide about such features in a diverse marketplace. The ability of Toyota Motors to produce customised cars, with personally chosen features, while producing volume cars, is one way marketing and production can combine to make a very attractive offering to customers.

Speciality goods are those where the exclusivity of the product is part of its appeal. A Jaguar or a Rolls-Royce car will be sold in small quantities at premium prices. While both these cars have many excellent features, it is the way potential owners aspire to own one that is equally important to the marketing task. A famous study of Morgan cars by Sir John Harvey Jones in his 'Troubleshooters' series recommended increasing production to capitalise on the long waiting list (over 2 years) for a new Morgan. This advice was rejected by Morgan as they believed the actual scarcity of the product was part of its appeal to customers.

ORGANISATIONAL MARKETING

In earlier chapters distinctions have been made between products which are purchased for use by individuals, such as a can of Coca-Cola, and products which are purchased by organisations. The point was further made that many of the products purchased by organisations are, like toilet tissue, the same as those purchased by consumers.

Furthermore, most products purchased by consumers have in their turn been purchased by wholesale and retail organisations before reaching the final consumer.

Organisational marketing involves those products which are used by organisations
in the course of their business. Accordingly it involves three different types of products. First, there is the capital equipment required in all types of organisation whether
engaged in manufacturing or providing a service. Second, there are products which
either as raw materials or finished components are used as part of the manufacturing
process, and third, there are those products which are used in the manufacturing
process, but do not become part of the final product.

Thus, the supply of the empty cans and bottles used by Coca-Cola to package their
product, the sugar and other ingredients used to manufacture the syrup, the com-
pressed carbon dioxide gas used to carbonate the drink and the material in which the
cans and bottles are subsequently packed are all examples of component industrial
products. In contrast the filter equipment used to process the water used in the drink,
the machinery used to fill and print the cans and bottles, the conveyors used to transport the packed cans to the dispatch area and the lorries used to deliver the product are
capital equipment and plant. The detergents used each day to clean the machinery are
examples of industrial supplies.

Like consumer marketing discussed earlier, organisational marketing involves optimising what is being offered to a potential buyer in terms of the product itself, the
price of the product, the availability of the product and the method by which the
potential customer is made aware of the product. Organisations differ from consumers
in a number of important ways. In particular there are fewer transactions and the value
of each is generally much higher. There are also similarities, especially, as with consumer marketing, the importance of understanding the need that the potential
customer wants the product to fulfil.

These needs depend upon a number of factors. In particular, the reason that an
organisational product is being purchased. Many issues affect this. For instance, the
expertise within an organisation develops as a result of experience. This means that the
routine purchases, particularly those which affect the final product, will be monitored
very carefully. As a result, it is likely that there will be a very good understanding of the
relative values of the products offered by different suppliers. As a result of this knowledge, it is quite likely that the preferred choice will not be the cheapest but the most
suitable offering, including such issues as reliability and quality of the supplier. For less
frequent purchases or those not directly concerned with the product being manufactured, it is likely that there will be less understanding of value and as a result a
tendency to consider price and specification as the main buying criteria.

It is the recognition that the buying criteria are likely to vary from organisation to
organisation that is the key to successful organisational marketing. This is, of course, a
form of market segmentation. Very often this segmentation involves not simply changing the product, but changing the level of service provided by the organisation. Even
suppliers of raw materials have found that by applying this approach not only can they
increase their share of the market but can at the same time improve their profitability.
What is required, is the recognition that different types of customers are willing to
accept different levels of service, and then finding a method by which this knowledge
can be applied. This may involve setting up a separate division which specialises in
supplying a specific segment of the market. Organisations adopting this approach usually have to overcome two problems. The first is that providing a different level of

service often is against the culture of the organisation and strongly resisted by the staff. This is best overcome by ensuring that the staff can see the advantages that the organisation will offer its customers. A second problem can be associated with this in that the old organisation is likely to compete with the new organisation, thereby putting at risk many of the potential advantages of the approach.

Where organisational products are ancillary to the production, such as might be the case with computers or delivery vehicles, it is possible that an organisation will buy on the reputation of the supplier rather than the suitability of the product. Hence the well-known adage, 'No one ever got fired for buying IBM!' It is for this reason that the creation of a brand within an industrial market can be so important. This involves, as it does in the consumer market, a single-minded approach to promotion. Also, like some sectors of the consumer market, it is necessary to create this brand awareness within a small specific market sector. Generally it is possible by using the technical press, not only for advertising but also for promoting the brand through consistent editorial coverage. This requires, for most companies operating in industrial markets, senior management commitment to public relations.

In Chapter 6 the issues of organisational buying behaviour were discussed. In many circumstances there will be an emphasis on personal selling and building long-term relationships with customers. Routine re-ordering is often carried out without a sales call, in fact some organisations use on-line computer re-ordering to replenish stock levels.

Where strong relationships exist it becomes very difficult for a new supplier to get any business. A well-known UK Purchasing Director once said:

> I have all the suppliers I need, and, unless one of them starts to let me down, I see no prospect of changing these arrangements.

This may be going too far as changes do take place but rarely is price the overriding stimuli, rather it is service levels which are critical. This is especially true with customers operating a JIT (just-in-time) policy for supplies. The best relationships are developed by *not* letting customers down. It is this area which is critical to success in Organisational Marketing.

SERVICE MARKETING

This book has emphasised marketing techniques irrespective of whether they are applied to tangible products or intangible services. The difference between products and services is irrelevant from a general viewpoint but there are some aspects of services that must be understood when involved in service marketing (*see* Chapter 11). At one level a service is a total product without a core.

Services can be offered to consumer markets, organisational markets, international markets, or be given in non-business situations. Therefore services can be seen as a subset of the marketing described in any of the other sections in this chapter. First and foremost, it is important to decide if the service could be described as a service product or a product service.

The term service product refers to a service which is a self-standing offering and therefore fits the view taken in this book of a service which can be considered under the general heading of product. Examples of service products could be:

- a plumber mending a broken pipe;
- an accountant auditing company accounts;
- a doctor visiting a sick patient;
- a taxi journey.

Product services are also subject to the distinctive factors introduced in Chapter 11 of intangibility, variability and perishability. However, because product services are attached directly to a product and are one of the added-value elements offered to augment that product, there is a feeling that some form of ownership could be present. Kotler describes product services as: 'Tangible goods with accompanying services'. He goes on to describe 'the offer which consists of a tangible good accompanied by one or more service to enhance its consumer appeal'.

The example given earlier related to two of the authors who both have a General Motors car. They have varying experiences, hence the variability of services received. The issue with product services is that the product is the fundamental core, car in the example or maybe a computer, and the service is an added element to increase the attractiveness of the offer. This is certainly the case when considering the service offered by the car salesman prior to and during the purchase period. The marketing emphasis at this time is then more on the product than on the accompanying service. In the post-purchase situation service becomes more important. The offer of an enhanced five-year 'parts & labour' warranty at a small extra charge is an example of a 'product service'. It is associated with the product although distinct from it. Maybe if the author who owns the Astra had such a 'product service' he could have benefited more from his total purchase.

With a 'service product' it is the service that dominates, although in this case a tangible product could be offered to enhance the service. This could be a meal supplied on an airflight or a prescription written by a doctor, or a guarantee from a builder.

NON-BUSINESS MARKETING

Just as marketing offers business organisations opportunities to be more successful so it has been realised that these same techniques could be applied with as great a benefit in non-business activities. This includes government organisations, providers of services such as the National Health Service, charities, and special interest groups such as political parties. The British Heart Foundation poster in the colour section shows the benefits of investing in heart research. This illustrates a benefit that a donor could acquire, but the donor actually receives nothing tangible, but the charity is able to use the donation to invest to achieve its objectives. It is not unusual for many of these organisations to be referred to as non-profit making organisations; this has the disadvantage of denying them the expectation that through prudent management their income might exceed their costs, thereby yielding a surplus which can be invested in improved facilities or services.

It is not after all the pursuit of such a surplus which is the principal characteristic which separates business from other types of organisation. The real difference is that the fundamental objective of a business is to increase the asset value of the owners at a rate which is commensurate with the risk involved. Even when businesses try to accommodate the interests of a wide range of stakeholders, this fundamental objective helps to focus the overall activity, since failure to meet this objective will ultimately lead to the organisation being disbanded or taken over.

One of the major benefits of applying marketing principles in the non-business context is that they provide effective alternatives to the financial surplus for measuring organisational performance. Examples of these can be seen in the various charters which have been implemented by the government in order to improve the accountability of organisations such as the National Health Service.

Another benefit of applying marketing principles in the non-business context is that it allows the often complicated transactions involved to be properly analysed. An example of where the failure to do this prevented an organisation from responding quickly enough to changing circumstances can be seen with regard to the Blood Transfusion Service. For many years this organisation depended to a significant extent upon the co-operation of the many manufacturing companies which regularly provided facilities for blood donor sessions. It provided the basis for ensuring both constancy of supply and the efficiency of the collection service. During the 1980s many of the companies which provided these facilities reduced the size of their workforce to such an extent that they no longer justified having their own blood donor sessions. The Blood Transfusion Service responded by expanding the number of local sessions they ran, only to find it was increasingly difficult to attract sufficient donors. What had not been appreciated was the actual cost incurred by the donor when giving blood. Time was a cost which had previously been 'paid' by the companies, who had not only provided the Blood Transfusion Service with the facilities it needed for the donor session, but had also allowed their employees to attend during working hours. It was not until the real cost to the donor was appreciated, and steps taken to minimise this by providing appointments and better information, that it was possible for the Service to bring demand and supply back into balance. (*See* case study Chapter 9.)

Another common problem faced by non-business organisations is that of multiple publics. Just as business organisations have a number of stakeholders such as customers and employees, so non-business organisations often have in addition to staff and clients, donors and volunteers. The exchanges involved between each of these groups and the organisation is likely to differ both with the frequency and degree of the commitment. As a result, the organisation has to be especially careful to ensure that any changes made to improve the effectiveness of one of these groups is acceptable to the others as well as to the public in general. This is one area where a lack of basic understanding of marketing has resulted in some very worthwhile charities losing support. By using dramatically strong adverts to improve the awareness of a charity and hopefully increase donations, a well-known charity actually upset both its staff and some existing supporters. Therefore by not taking proper account of the impact on the other groups upon which the organisation has to depend the result was negative not positive.

There are, then, a number of benefits to be derived by non-business organisations 'taking a leaf' from the marketing approach. In addition to the examples already cited, the following areas offer prime potential for improved effectiveness:

- *Market research* Is of no less relevance in non-profit organisations than in commercial companies. If non-profit bodies need to relate to and maintain a network of customers, users, sponsors and supporters, then market research techniques have a positive role to play in remaining *au fait* with trends and opportunities, and in identifying better ways of reaching and serving their various publics. On a general level, market research and analysis approaches will ensure that organisations do not lose sight of their wider environment.

- *Communications* Historically this has been a major problem in non-business organisations, for a variety of reasons. Large public sector bodies have often been perceived as aloof and impersonal, occasionally intimidating and uncaring, even among the very groups they were mandated to 'serve'. Better external communications, adopting more marketing-led approaches, hold the promise of communicating and achieving a closer match between provider and user, a more responsive service and a more positive perception of it. Internal communications, too, have often been hampered by zealously administrative approaches to management, certainly within public sector organisations. Recent changes in structure and formal reporting relationships within the public sector may yet serve to improve internal communications and open new possibilities in terms of internal marketing.

- *Price and value* A continuing dilemma for some non-business organisations, where funding and resourcing provisions may be formally separate from the 'market' and the user. The classic example would be central and local government activities, organised as statutory or local monopoly supply arrangements. In such circumstances, a customer or user focus may be all but totally absent, while notions of value and effectiveness may fall prey to the internal considerations of administrative convenience, producing sometimes a take-it-or-leave-it attitude among staff. The early attempts to establish customer charters, and a new-found interest in customer care and resource effectiveness, promise a radical if overdue re-think on issues such as market needs and the 'customer' perceptions of value and preference.

Not surprisingly, many of the larger non-business organisations, particularly in the public sector, have proved to be slow and resistant to change. For some, the introduction of competitive practices has had to be painfully imposed, through internal markets, market testing and compulsory competitive tendering. It would also be true to say that such resistance has been apparent among non-government organisations such as charities and educational establishments, where perhaps a major obstacle has been the ideological opposition to what for long was dismissed as the 'vulgarity' of commercialism and marketing.

While therefore the adoption of marketing techniques has had a faltering start, it can be asserted that they are now better accepted among non-business organisations. The final qualification that is needed, perhaps, is the observation that marketing in the non-business field, any more than in the private sector, cannot offer any panacea or instant solutions. Like all functions, it is only as good as the management that drives it.

CONCLUSION

This final chapter has tried to give a flavour of the richness of marketing in many different types of organisations. It will be realised, that the basic concept of an offer that is acceptable, affordable and available applies in all cases. It then needs to be promoted in the most appropriate way. It is not a question of placing advertisements all over the place, but deciding on a target market, deciding how to meet the needs, then finding an effective way of reaching the chosen customers.

The elements of the so-called marketing mix are important but the emphasis changes for different products/services and different situations. Understanding the exchange relationship is the key to marketing in all situations, and then resources and programmes can be devised to maximise the return.

1 In many consumer goods markets it is more important to encourage repeat purchases by loyal customers than to achieve a one-off sale. What techniques might be used to build loyalty and what other factors related to the total marketing offering could affect repeat purchase?

2 'Companies do not make purchases; they establish relationships' (Charles S. Goodman). Discuss the validity of this observation on industrial marketing.

3 'In service organisations, people come first.' Discuss this assertion in terms of the marketing concept.

4 Consider the potential value in adopting marketing techniques within a public sector organisation such as a public library.

CASE STUDY 1

Müller has cornered its market!

Apart from the irresistible pun on the brand's Crunch Corner, Fruit Corner and the new Candy Corner, it is also true that in the brand's 10 years in the UK yoghurt sector it has captured the leading position, achieving about one quarter of a market worth a total of £560m in 1996. At present this sector is growing at 6 per cent in value terms (5 per cent in volume).

In grocery outlets, where 50 per cent of the top 100 brands today are more than half a century old, and only seven have been launched in the last 10 years, Müller has now taken second place overall. So when Müller launches a new range, retailers take note.

Referring to the Candy Corner range, launched in Spring 1997, Managing Director Ken Wood said, 'We started selling-in at the back-end of 1996, and achieved almost 100 per cent listings. The trade reaction was favourable. I don't think we have ever had such a quick uptake in our history'.

The new range, inspired by American mousse-style pies – Lemon Meringue, Banoffee and Mississippi Mud, is packed in 150g split pots and priced in line with other Müller corner yoghurts despite their 'super-indulgent' nature. As they are different from anything else on the market, Müller decided they needed a new niche of their own. Wood said, 'I couldn't satisfy myself that these offerings fit in either Fruit Corner or Crunch, so we needed to devise a new segment. We would have been missing an opportunity if we had rationalised them into the other ranges'.

During the launch period, the new yoghurts were offered in triple packs containing all three flavours, but priced at the equivalent of two. Wood explains the rationale, 'We've found that to make a Müller product successful as soon as possible, we need trial'. The national TV support for all the 'corner' yoghurts followed up a few weeks after the launch.

Wood says the route to such success is not a secret. 'There are three cornerstones to our corporate philosophy: quality, innovation and support. I don't want to sound like a driven man but a lot of people talk about those things and very few actually do them.

'The innovation speaks for itself. We've revolutionised the yoghurt market in terms of pack format and quality. We spent £7m on support giving us over 57 per cent of share-of-voice in 1996. We're spending substantially more than anybody else.' In 1997 the ante will be upped to £8m.

UK yoghurt consumption is still well below continental levels, in Germany (where Müller originated in 1896) consumers eat twice as much as the Brits.

Wood implies that the better the quality, the greater the consumption. He adds that a little regard to quality may also make the chilled cabinet a better profit centre.

'There are a lot of lines that have no right to be in there. It's not rocket science, it's rate of sale times profit mix. On this criteria alone there are a number that should get thrown out.'

(*Source*: adapted from *The Grocer Magazine*, 1 February 1997.)

Questions

1 What were the reasons for Müllers' success?

2 Do you think these could lead to success for other consumer products?

Linley Engineering

Linley Engineering Services is a small Coventry company providing a range of subcontract metalwork and engineering services including welding, profile cutting, flamecutting, grinding and fabricating. It also undertakes intermittent contract fabrication of a range of trolleys, an outwork arrangement made five years ago with the trolley manufacturer, a Birmingham-based company specialising in palletisation and materials-handling systems. This work, never particularly profitable or reliable, has for the last two years amounted to no more than an occasional batch order from the Birmingham company, which is itself now troubled by recessionary difficulties.

In 1990 Linley had a monthly turnover of approximately £60 000 and had 22 employees. However, since that date it has suffered severely from the effects of the local recession in manufacturing, and has not markedly recovered in spite of a recent industrial upturn. It now has only ten employees and turnover has fallen to £28 000 per month. It has recorded a small loss in each of the last three years.

There are some 1100 accounts in the sales ledger but only 120 have been active during the last twelve months. Of these, ten accounts produce 70 per cent of the company's sales. Order sizes vary from 'one-off' jobs costing £100 to a long-standing contract worth £10 000 per month. Profits per job are known to vary somewhat, though the company has not succeeded in its periodic attempts to plan profits or purposefully provide for future growth.

Sales contacts are currently handled by the Managing Director, John Linley. Apart from a listing in a local trades directory the company spends no money on advertising or publicity. The company has a secretary/works accountant who costs all jobs and prepares estimates and quotations. Design, production and purchasing is handled by a production foreman, under the direction of John Linley.

In recent months John Linley has been giving serious thought to the strategic avenues open to the company, and especially to the possibilities that might exist in new product fields and markets. He believes that, if only for survival purposes, the company needs to move away from dependence on the depressed subcontract sector, and the 'metal-bashing' image that sticks to it. In particular, he feels that opportunities lie in the development and commercialisation of a credible range of company-manufactured products, supplied to the open market. In this way, he reasons, the company would be in more direct control of its own destiny.

To this end, he has resolved to make a careful assessment of the company's situation, its strengths and limitations. From this he means to develop a shortlist of possible new product ideas for the intended line of manufactured products.

Question

Advise John Linley on the issues and guiding principles he might consider in developing a plan for the design and commercialisation of any new product line.

CASE STUDY 3

QPR (Finland)

QPR is located in the city of Oulu in northern Finland. The company operates in the Oulu Technology Park (Technopolis) which is the first science park in the Nordic region. There are more than 100 companies in the Oulu Technology Park, mostly involved in hi-tech business.

QPR is a hi-tech company which creates new methods for business management and sells complete packages including written material, software and consultancy to companies. The company employs nine people. The turnover of the company is about £0.5 million and it is operating internationally. QPR co-operates with Swedish, Dutch, Swiss and Indian companies. One of QPR's corporate goals is to achieve substantial growth in sales through both the cultivation of these markets and the establishment of customers in new markets.

The most important program product of the company is called CostControl which is a software tool for the Net Management method. This method has been developed in QPR together with several companies, e.g. Nokia and ABB. The goal of this program is to increase the effectiveness and the use of cost information.

The CostControl project can vary depending on the customer and its needs. For example, in an industrial company one workshop is being converted in order to incorporate the lean management system. This workshop is aiming towards the minimization of stock and physical work room. With CostControl the customer can see the financial effects of this change. This type of change can be simulated before it is undertaken.

CostControl is a complex program which often requires managers to revise the way in which they view the costs of their business operations. Thus, the selling of the program requires several meetings with high-ranking executives. The price of CostControl starts at £5000 plus training and consulting fees. The majority of customers require consultancy in order to use CostControl effectively.

At the moment QPR is developing an international marketing team of four people, which takes care of market research in target countries and tries to market the Net Management method with CostControl to pilot customers. Different markets will be divided into segments for which a local partner is responsible. In important markets, it is possible to set up an office of their own. Partnerships could be formed with consulting companies, software distributors, or hardware suppliers. In addition it is important to get internationally known consultants as references.

Question

QPR want you to solve the following problem:

The value of a business deal is quite costly and requires a great deal of personal contact with a customer. Travel and communications expenses are high and, thus, sales costs are significant. How can QPR's marketing be made more cost effective without sacrificing effectiveness?

(Case supplied by Anna-Maija Lämsä, Oulu Business School, Oulu, Finland.)

Priestman Arts Centre

As a successful marketing executive with a national grocery chain, you have just embarked on a voluntary six-month secondment to a community arts project. Your salary increments and career progression have been guaranteed by your employers, who have a long-standing reputation for social work within a range of activities as diverse as wildfowl protection and arts sponsorship.

Your secondment assignment is to act as Marketing Consultant to the Priestman Arts Centre in Weardale, a large industrial town in the North-East of England. Now in its seventh year, the Centre operates within a somewhat broad brief of providing 'support and promotion of the Arts in general within and around the Borough of Weardale'. The Centre's well-appointed premises comprise two exhibition galleries, a 250-seat theatre with cafeteria, a flexible work studio accommodating a weaver-in-residence, and an Arts bookshop.

The Centre offers a programme that ranges from exhibitions of paintings, pottery and glassware to live performance events such as dance sketches and poetry readings, chamber music evenings and comedy playhouses. Though not strictly monitored, attendance figures tend to vary significantly. While a conventional painting exhibition might generate an encouraging through-traffic, other scheduled events such as music recitals may prove disappointing in spite of the performers' names.

The menu of activities on offer has recently been endangered by financial circumstances. For the coming year the Centre will suffer heavy cuts in its Arts Council Award and its Borough Council grant, both of which have been important supports in an otherwise loss-making picture. In the words of Miles Berenson, the Arts Centre Manager: 'This is a heavy blow. We've always made a policy of attracting the best events within the budget. This will be more difficult than ever now.'

Question

Within the terms of your 'appointment' as Marketing Consultant, you are expected to analyse the operations of the Centre and produce and activate a plan for its future marketing activities. As one preliminary step towards the plan, you are invited to comment and advise on product policy issues of relevance to the Centre, its activities and offerings.

Charities marketing

Leading aid charity Voluntary Services Overseas (VSO) is calling for direct action by British workers to help their counterparts in developing countries by switching to fairly traded products in their workplace.

Eighty per cent of the world's resources are consumed by 20 per cent of the world's population in rich countries. The VSO Week campaign aims to help 'Bridge the Gap' by asking people to think globally and act locally.

Buying fairly traded goods, including tea and coffee, helps ensure that farmers in the developing world get a decent wage and proper working conditions. Seventy billion cups of tea and 32 billion mugs of coffee are drunk in the UK each year, yet less than 10 per cent of the price paid goes to the local grower.

VSO is launching its Fair Trading Challenge by sending 100 000 'Bridge the Gap' postcards to UK employers to encourage them to adopt fairly traded products at work. People all over the UK will also be taking part in 'Bridge the Gap' events and activities during VSO Week.

VSO also launches the 'Bridge the Gap' challenge on-line at London's Global Cafe. It will be the first Internet cafe to take up the challenge at the start of VSO Week (July 1997) by serving Cafedirect fairly traded coffee to customers.

The charity will also publish a report into the impact of unfair trading practices on communities in the developing world – from the Caribbean's stricken banana trade to tea and coffee exports from sub-Saharan Africa.

VSO volunteers work with communities in 59 of the world's poorest countries to 'Bridge the Gap' by enabling local people to help themselves. They see the effects of unfair trade on the lives of their colleagues, from Asia to Africa and the Caribbean.

To receive a free 'Bridge the Gap' Action Pack, including postcards for your workplace, a copy of VSO's Fair Trade report and local event details, contact Roz Salik at VSO on 0181 780 2266, or check out VSO's website at http://www.oneworld.org/vso/.

Question

This is a press release issued by VSO. It is self explanatory, but you should evaluate it by asking if it will achieve the objectives:

- first to make people aware of the campaign;
- second to make them aware of the problem;
- third to get people (or some people) to actually take action.

APPENDIX 1

Glossary of Marketing Terms

Above the line A term applying to main media expenditure and its traditional accounting treatment. Now used for all costs of traditional media.

Acceptability A test of a product offering from a custom viewpoint.

ACORN (A Classification of Residential Neighbourhood) – a so-called, geo-demographic database of residential locality types. Commercially available from CACI.

***Ad hoc* research** Research which is conducted first hand on a one-off basis, for a particular research project.

Adoption Rate at which people accept and become users of a product. Often associated with the diffusion of innovation curve.

Advertisement A message from a person or an organisation to potential customers containing a specific message and in paid-for media space. Sometimes shortened by practitioners to 'ad' and by the general public to 'advert'.

Advertiser A client placing 'paid-for' advertising.

Advertising An element of the marketing mix involving the use of paid media.

Advertising agency An organisation which specialises in all forms of communication on behalf of clients.

Advertising campaign A planned approach to communication over a defined period of time.

Advertising media Communication channels such as radio, television, newspapers, magazines and posters.

Advertorial An advertisement written in an editorial style to attempt to give more credibility to the message.

Affordability A test of the value or price of an offering from a customer viewpoint.

Agent An individual or company acting in a sales capacity on behalf of a principal. An agent does not take ownership or handle the goods.

AIDA (Attention, Interest, Desire, Action) – A mnemonic used in advertising. First used by Strong in 1924. One of the hierarchy models.

Augmented Product *See* Marketing offering.

Availability A test of the convenience of obtaining an offering from a customer viewpoint.

Awareness A measure of the proportion of a target audience who have heard of a particular product or service. Can be measured on a 'prompted' or 'unprompted' basis.

Below the line Expenditure on promotional activities which traditionally reduces revenues or involves non-commission media.

BRAD (British Rate and Data) – The accepted tariff book of advertising in the EC.

Brand An article identified by a name, symbol, trade mark or characteristic which differentiates it from competitive offerings.

Break-even point Point at which the costs of production equal the revenue from selling.

Budget The amount of money allocated to performing a particular task.

Buyer behaviour The way in which customers act, and the steps taken in the purchase decision process.

Communication mix *See* Promotional mix.

Competitive advantage An element within a product offering that is particularly attractive to customers, and not offered by competitors.

Consumer The final user of a product or a service.

Consumer goods Products which are targeted at individuals in the general population, rather than at organisations.

Consumerism A movement which aims to change the actions of organisations in favour of particular groups.

Consumer panel A research method using a group of consumers who continuously report on their purchases over an extended period of time (*See* Panels).

Continuous research Research that is conducted regularly over an extended period of time, used to monitor trends in the marketplace.

Controllable factors *See* Marketing mix.

Convenience sample As the name implies, a research sampling technique using the most practical or convenient selection method to provide the necessary respondents.

Copy The written or broadcast words used in an advertisement.

Cost per thousand (CPT) Used in advertising as a measure of cost per thousand people viewing or reading the advertisement.

Cost plus pricing A pricing approach where an agreed percentage is added to the costs of a product.

Coverage The percentage of a selected target audience that have an opportunity to see a particular advertisement.

Customer In marketing it is generally anyone buying a product or service.

DAGMAR (Defining Advertising Goals for Measured Advertising Results) – An acronym for one of the hierarchy of effects models of advertising.

Decider Used in studying industrial buying as the person who makes the purchase decision, usually in a formal capacity.

Delphi method A forecasting technique using the opinions of a panel of experts to develop qualitative forecasts.

Demographic Information relating to broad population statistics, such as age, sex, income, education level or marital status.

Depth interviews A research technique involving detailed discussions with individual respondents to explore in detail issues such as motivation, beliefs, etc.

Derived demand The demand for a component or intermediate product dependent on the sale of the final good or service.

Desk research Research which uses existing sources of information, usually called secondary data.

Differentiated A separation of a total product from competitors. Can be a marketing mix unique to one supplier.

Differentiated marketing A marketing strategy which is making different offerings to each segment of a market.

Diffusion The rate at which new products move through various adoption categories.

Direct mail A form of below-the-line advertising where personalised letters are sent directly from the advertiser to potential customers.

Direct marketing An approach offering products without intermediaries where the supplier sells directly to customers.

Distribution channels Routes through which products go from the supplier to the consumer.

Distributor A person or organisation who distributes goods. Distributors take ownership from suppliers and are responsible for collecting payments.

Diversification A process of introducing new products into new markets unrelated to an organisation's current customers.

Elasticity Sensitivity of customer demand to changes in price.

Exclusive distribution A policy of organisations to restrict availability of products to a limited number of outlets.

Experiment A research approach which evaluates alternatives to identify the optimum mix.

Exploratory research A pilot marketing research used to review a problem in general forms before committing larger expenditure to the study.

Fast-moving consumer goods (fmcg) Regularly purchased products, usually of low value.

Field research Research which is conducted externally in a market, not using existing published sources.

Fieldwork The activity of gathering information in the marketplace.

Focus group A research technique where selected individuals are brought together to discuss their views and attitudes to a specific topic. Produces quantitative data.

Franchising A contractual relationship between a seller and an outlet which uses the seller's format, product and name.

Global brands Goods which can have universal appeal and are marketed in many countries with little modification to product or image.

Gross profit margin The difference between direct cost and selling price.

Group discussion *See* Focus group.

Hierarchy of needs A model of consumer behaviour suggested by A. Maslow.

Image The perceptions of a product, brand, or company by customers and consumers.

Industrial goods Products which are required by industrial organisations.

Intensive distribution ÊA policy of organisations to maximise the availability of products.

Intermediary A general name for a person who acts as a link in the flow of goods from a supplier to a final consumer.

Life cycle *See* product life cycle.

Likert scales Market research scales which use statements for respondents to indicate agreement or disagreement.

Loyalty (also brand loyalty) The extent to which customers repurchase a particular product or brand.

Macroenvironment The general external business environment in which a firm functions.

Market development A strategy of an organisation to increase sales by offering their existing product in new markets. Used by I. Ansoff in his famous matrix.

Market leader The organisation which has the greatest share of sales in a given market.

Market penetration A strategy of an organisation to increase sales by offering more of their existing products in their existing markets. Used by I. Ansoff in his famous matrix.

Market research The specialist Marketing Research activity of using observational, survey and experimental social research techniques for marketing applications.

Market segmentation The identifying of specific market segments in a marketplace, then developing different marketing offerings which will be attractive to each segment.

Market share The relative sales of a product in relation to the overall market sales. Can be measured in either sales value or sales volume.

Marketing audit A systematic appraisal of the strengths and weaknesses of a company in relation to its marketplace, and the evaluation of the opportunities and threats in that market.

Marketing concept The theories developed to analyse the process of meeting customer needs and determine how this can be improved.

Marketing environment The social, economical, legal, political, cultural, competitive and technological factors which affect an organisation and its marketing decision. *See* PEST.

Marketing information system Information which is relevant to the company's marketing operations, including marketing research, intelligence and market analysis. Often contained on computer databases.

Marketing mix The controllable elements of the marketing offering which can often be considered under the headings known as the 4Ps: product, price, place and promotion.

Marketing offering What actually is selected by a customer. Includes the core product or service plus the additional values provided by promotion, availability, brand, image, price etc.

Marketing orientation The focus of an organisation on customers to develop a relevant marketing offering.

Marketing planning The systematic process of analysing the environment and a company's resources. Then developing objectives and suitable strategies and action plans to meet those objectives. Also the feedback and control of such actions.

Marketing philosophy The recognition that organisations exist to meet the needs of their customers and that this should be the objective of every member of an organisation's staff.

Marketing research The collection of marketing information to improve marketing decisions. It is an aid to decision making but not a substitute for it.

Market research The application of the observational, survey and experimental social research techniques for marketing research applications.

Market strategy The long-term direction of an organisation relating to marketing actions and the interaction of controllable variables.

Mark-up A cost plus pricing technique.

MEAL (Media Expenditure Analysis Limited) A firm that collects and publishes information on major UK media use and cost by companies.

Media Channels of communication such as television, radio, newspapers, etc.

Media owners The controllers of media who try to encourage the use of their channel and often provide comprehensive data about readers and viewers.

Multi-stage sampling A market research technique often used in political sampling where several random samples are used to give a convenient sample, say, one street in one political ward in one constituency.

New product development The process of identifying, developing and evaluating new marketing offerings.

Niche A small discrete segment of a market which can be targeted with a distinct marketing strategy.

Non-price competition Other benefits such as warranties or additional features or merchandising which can give an offering a competitive advantage.

Objective In planning, a target to be achieved.

Objective and task method A method of establishing a promotional budget. It is based on the task to be achieved rather than money available. Good in theory but difficult in practice.

Observation (research) A research approach which involves evaluating customers' reactions and behaviour.

Offer mix The mix of product, price and availability offered to a customer. Not including the communication of that offer.

Omnibus survey A regular questionnaire-based field research survey with a large sample. Organisations can commission one or more questions to be asked; the survey includes questions from a number of different organisations.

OTS (opportunity to see) The average number of viewing occasions for a particular advertisement.

Panels (consumer panels) Groups of consumers who regularly monitor buying or usage information, often through keeping diary records.

Pareto effect The 80/20 rule. The largest proportion of sale, value or profit will often come from a small proportion of customers.

Perception The way a product or event or stimulus is received and evaluated by a cus-
(from psychology) tomer. The importance lies in the attempt to understand how people interpret messages.

Personal interview A research method where the researcher meets the respondent to carry out a survey.

Personal selling An element of the promotional mix, where a supplier uses representatives to visit customers.

PEST analysis (sometimes STEP) Elements of the macro, external environment, political/legal, economic, social/cultural and technological.

Place An element of the 4 Ps of the marketing mix. *See* Distribution.

Point-of-sale Usually in retail, the area where a retailer's customer buys a product supplied by that retailer.

Positioning, The establishing of factors valued by consumers in purchase decisions.
also product positioning Then the matching of product features to those factors.

Postal survey A research method which communicates with a respondent using a postal questionnaire.

Primary data Original data obtained from field research.

Product development A strategy of an organisation to increase sales by creating new products for existing markets used by I. Ansoff in his famous matrix (*see also* New product development).

Product life cycle The different stages through which a product develops over time. It covers development, birth (or introduction), growth, maturity and decline. The stage a product has reached in its life cycle will affect the marketing mix decisions which should be taken.

Product line A number of related products offered by a supplier, which often cover the needs of several different segments.

Product management The function responsible for the tactical and strategic planning of a company's existing and new products.

Product mix The total range of products or services that an organisation offers.

Product offering *See* Marketing offering.

Production orientation The focus of an organisation on to product quality and production capability. This differs from marketing orientation.

Promotion An element of the 4 Ps of the marketing mix, it covers the ways in which an organisation communicates with its market.

Promotional mix The elements of promotion enabling an organisation to communicate with its market. These include advertising, personal selling, sales promotion and publicity.

Prospecting The selling technique involved with identifying new customers.

Psychographics A base for segmentation derived from attitudes and behaviourial variables.

Publicity An element of the promotional mix. *See* Public relations.

Public relations A deliberate, planned and sustained effort to establish and maintain positive understanding between an organisation and its publics.

Pull strategy A marketing strategy in which the manufacturer promotes directly to the final customers, and hopes that they will demand the product from intermediaries. The product is then 'pulled' through the distribution channels by customer demand.

Push strategy A marketing strategy in which the manufacturer promotes to the intermediaries, who in turn promote to their customers. The product is therefore 'pushed' through the distribution channels by manufacturer and distributor effort.

Quantitative research Research which produces numerical data, often from large samples. This is sometimes called hard data.

Qualitative research Research which focuses on the options and feelings of customers and potential customers.

Questionnaire A prepared set of questions used to obtain information from a respondent.

Quota sample A sampling method where those questioned have to match a defined proportion on a number of attributes, e.g. gender, age, occupation.

Random sample A sampling method where everyone in the target population has an equal chance of being included.

Rate card The published cost of advertising media.

Recall *See* Awareness.

Research brief A structured document given to a research agency including background to the organisation, objectives of the research, limitations and objectives.

Respondent A person interviewed or contacted in a market research survey.

Retail audit The research undertaken in retail outlets involving checking invoices, delivery notes and sales records to determine the precise volume of goods sold. Results are often syndicated to several suppliers.

Sales call A visit made by a sales representative to a potential or existing customer.

Sales orientation The focus of an organisation on to customers with the aim of achieving short-term sales.

Sales promotion An element of the promotional mix. Techniques and incentives used to increase short-term sales.

Segment A grouping of customers who have common characteristics or features.

Shopping good Products which are considered purchases such as many consumer durables.

Skimming A pricing strategy where an organisation sells at a high price initially to maximise short-term profits.

Societal marketing Marketing which attempts to improve social benefit.

Socio-economic groups classification A grouping of the population according to the occupation of the head of the household: A, B, Cl, C2, D, E.

Speciality good Consumer goods for which customers are prepared or make an effort to acquire.

Sponsorship An element usually considered part of the promotional mix where money is linked to an event or a participant in an event.

Strategy An overall, long-term direction or approach which a company aims to follow, derived from the Greek words meaning to lead an army.

Stimulus A 'trigger' that starts a purchasing process.

SWOT analysis SWOT is an acronym for strengths and weaknesses, opportunities and threats. The 'SW' refer to internal resources of an organisation; the 'OT' to the macroenvironment.

Syndicated research Research conducted on behalf of more than one organisation. Such as: consumer panels, retails audits and omnibus studies.

Tactics The specific operational activities undertaken in support of an organisation's strategy.

Target market The segment of a market at which a marketing offering.

Test marketing The initial launching of a product into a limited area for a trial period to test its market acceptability prior to national sales.

Total Product *See* Marketing offering.

Trade press Published journals aimed at industrial and commercial readers.

TVR (Television Ratings) A measure of coverage representing 1 per cent of a potential television audience. Calculated by using panel research information.

Undifferentiated marketing A common marketing strategy aimed at the total market without modifications for specific segments.

Unique selling proposition (USP) A selling claim based on a distinctive product feature or unique element in the marketing mix.

Vertical marketing systems (VMS) The integration of operators at different levels of a distribution chain to offer a co-ordinated package.

Wholesaler An operation which buys products in bulk, reselling them in smaller quantities to retailers.

Width (of a product line) The variety and diversity of products offered in a product line.

The Use of Short Case Studies for Studying Marketing Principles and Practice

Most cases describe actual business situations although in some cases fictitious names are used. Many are based on real-life management problems, although sometimes the facts are modified to highlight particular situations. The problems described are very similar to those that are encountered daily by managers. There are many benefits from using cases.

1 Cases can cover a range of organisations and industries and thus provide a greater range than you are likely to experience in day-to-day management.
2 They help to build knowledge of a number of specific situations by dealing intensively with problems in each case.
3 In addition, cases and case discussions provide a focal point for an exchange of the lessons of experience. In discussing case situations, it is easy, often unconsciously, to draw from your different accumulated experiences, rules-of-thumb, or simple observations of events. This is to be encouraged in these cases. The discussion of cases provides a way of reassessing the lessons of experience, and gaining an increased measure of learning from them.
4 Cases also help to sharpen analytical skills. You need to work with both facts and figures to produce quantitative and qualitative evidence to support recommendations and decisions. These could be challenged both by your instructors and your colleagues. It is important that you learn to defend your arguments and to develop an ability to think and reason in a rigorous way.
5 Cases are obviously useful for developing sets of principles and concepts that can be applied in practice. Each case should be considered by itself. Out of each will come important concepts and approaches. Taken together, a series of cases should develop some key ideas that can then be applied in specific managerial situations.
6 Perhaps the most important skill to be gained from studying cases and case situations is learning to ask the right questions. This is a really critical business skill. 'Discussion questions' could be suggested by your instructor, but that does not pre-empt the task of identifying the key problems. You must always still ask yourself: 'What really are the problems here?' It is too easy to just rearrange the facts and figures without defining the real problems in the case.
7 Perhaps the greatest pedagogical benefit derived from the case studies is that they generate a high degree of involvement in the learning process. You will tend to learn the most from those things in which you are most deeply involved. It follows, too, that little can be learned from even the best cases without solid preparation.

There are, of course, major differences between cases and actual management. It is important to appreciate that:

- The 'facts' come in neatly written form. Managers in business rarely receive information in this way. Their knowledge usually comes through being in situ and via interactions with fellow managers, as well as memos, statistical reports; and even the external media.
- A case usually describes the situation at a single point in time. 'Real time' business problems are usually a continuing occurrence both in receipt and in implementation. It is not often that a manager can deal with one problem, put it away, then go on to the next 'case'.
- Any decision or recommendation made by students studying a case is just that – a recommendation. Students don't have the responsibility for implementing their decisions.
- A case is designed to fit a particular unit of study time. It will focus on certain categories of problems/marketing situations in order to explore them in more detail.

The marketing cases in this book are very short. They do not need great analysis. In fact they are really case-based examples. However, all will benefit from discussing the situations with other students. When studying them it might be helpful to follow the sequence below.

The first task is to read the case through quickly to put it into perspective. Initially the best preparation will come from working by yourself. Then, based on this, the next step is to decide whether the information is reliable. This will require a more thorough second reading, leading to an assessment of what is good or bad practice from the facts given. The aim is to try to isolate the real key problems which are there to be solved, or the lessons to be learnt.

It is best that you note down the problems to be tackled and the relevant areas for analysis. For example, if the problems are 'Should we introduce Product X? To whom should it be sold? What should be our advertising strategy?', the areas for analysis might include:

- trends in the marketplace;
- break-even analysis;
- buyer behaviour;
- segmentation;
- competition;
- communications needs.

The information in the case should be considered to see what links together. In particular it is necessary to see what helps the understanding of each area, and to draw some meaningful observations and conclusions. These may, in turn, provide the basis for answering the questions that have been suggested.

The purpose of individual preparation is to enhance the learning opportunities when discussing the case in class. The more familiar you are with the case facts and the more ideas you have about the case problems, the better prepared you will be to take in, react to, and learn from the ideas of others in a group discussion. Through interchanging ideas and constructive debate you will build analytical skills, develop judgement and gain conceptual understanding.

The next step is to present your arguments to other students and to listen to their views. This can be done in pairs, or in larger numbers, or in a seminar group. The purpose of the discussion of cases is to help refine, adjust and fill out your own thinking. It is not to develop a consensus or a 'group' position. In fact it is not necessary, or even desirable that you agree at this stage.

In a seminar you will usually be allowed to take the case where you wish. This is where you fully explore the issues and problems which you have identified. The seminar group is for you to express, support and defend your conclusions and recommendations. Most learning comes from controversy and discussion. The effective use of cases as a learning vehicle depends heavily on participation. This will benefit both your own education and the learning of all other students as well. The more you contribute, the more you will get from it. It is therefore a responsibility of every student to get involved.

Discussion in class is also not only an effective way for you to think rigorously, but it allows you to develop skill in communicating, in 'thinking on your feet' and in responding to questions under pressure. Expressing your own views, and defending them, are all part of a distinctive experience.

However important it is to express your views, listening is even more important. It's easy to become so preoccupied with what we think that our minds become closed to the thoughts of other participants in the discussion. In class, as well as in business, it is just as important to be open-minded and to be willing to shift positions when good arguments are presented.

The role of a seminar leader is to lead the discussion into a consideration of other areas that you may have missed, or even to require you to make a decision. At the end it is likely the discussions will be summarised to draw out the useful lessons and observations that come from class discussion comments, but please remember that there is no right answer in cases. The measure of your individual progress in any one case discussion is not based much on your own after-class assessment of whether your ideas were 'right'. Instead it is more useful to ask: 'How much did I take away from the discussion that I didn't know when I came in?'

Sources of Secondary Data

The following publications and many more can be found in the reference section of your local library or your closest university library. Librarians can often provide specific information via the telephone.

Annual publications of business information

- British Exports (Kompas)
- Contact Europe (Kompas)
- Croner's Reference Book for Exporters
- Directory of Directors
- Hambro's Guide to Company Information
- Kelly's Manufacturing and Merchants Yearbook
- Key British Enterprises
- Kompas – Separate directories for European countries
- Major Companies of Europe
- Sales and Marketing Software Handbook
- Stock Exchange Official Yearbook

Bibliographies

- Croner's A–Z Business Information in the UK
- Croner's A–Z Business Information in Europe
- Sources of European Business Information (University of Warwick)

Government statistics

- CSO Guide to Official Statistics, HMSO London
- Government Statistics: a brief guide to sources (free from Central Statistical Office)
- Business Monitors: industry data (free from CSO)
- CSO Annual Abstract of Statistics – Annual UK figures over 10-year periods; showing trends. More detailed and current data appear in
  - Monthly Digest of Statistics
  - Economic Trends (monthly)
  - Financial Statistics
  - Transport Statistics (annual), National Travel Survey
  - Family Spending
  - Social Trends
  - United Kingdom Balance of Payments
  - United Kingdom National Accounts

Abstracts and indexes

Abstracts contain short summaries of published articles. Indexes present listings of articles and information sources.

- Anbar management publications. Anbar appears in five separate editions, eight times per year:
  1. Accounting and data processing abstracts.
  2. Management services and production abstracts.
  3. Marketing and distribution abstracts.
  4. Personnel and training.
  5. Top management abstracts.
- Business Periodicals (monthly): mostly US coverage, some UK journal sources, good on financial and business matters.
- Economics titles/abstracts (fortnightly) – scope covers economics, business, trade markets.
- Research Index: 2-week intervals, quarterly volumes; academic management periodical and business press sources (company and industry sections).

Marketing problem and likely information sources

1 Customer requirement	– Customer contact
	– Bulletin/media
	– Government sources/agents
2 Market size	– Surveys/published information
	– Databases
3 Growth potential	– Market research political aspirations
4 Stability	– Political economic analyses
5 Competitors	– Database/contact/customer
6 Budgets	– Published data/agents/customer
7 Key players/influences	– Government agencies (DESO, FCO,etc.)
8 Funding/payment method	– Banking/Dun & Bradstreet/Government/previous
9 Inter-company	– Marketing contacts/corporate sources

Useful addresses

Some publishers of market research reports

Economist Intelligence Unit Ltd
15 Regent Street,
London W1A 1DW
Telephone 0171 830 1000

Euromonitor Plc
87–88 Turnmill Street,
London EC1M 5QU
Telephone 0171 251 8024

Key Note
Field House,
72 Oldfield Road, Hampton,
Middlesex TW12 2HQ
Telephone 0181 783 0755

Mintel International Group
18–19 Long Lane,
London EC1A 9HE
Telephone: 0171 606 4533

Selected trade and professional associations

Advertising Association
Abford House,
15 Wilton Road,
London WS1V 1NJ
Telephone: 0171 828 2771

Brewers' Society
42 Portman Square,
London W1H OBB
Telephone: 0171 486 4831

British Clothing Industry Association
British Apparel and Textile Centre,
7 Swallow Place,
London W1R 7AA
Telephone: 0171 408 0020

British Institute of Management
Cottingham Road,
Corby,
Northamptonshire, NN1 71FX
Telephone: 01536 20422

Building Employers' Confederation
82 New Cavendish Street,
London W1M 8AD
Telephone: 0171 580 5588

Chartered Institute of Marketing
Moor Hall, Cookham,
Maidenhead, SL6 9QH
Telephone 01628 524922

Food and Drink Federation
6 Catherine Street,
London WC2B 5JJ
Telephone: 0171 836 2460

Society of Motor Manufacturers and Traders
Forbes House,
Halkin Street,
London SW1X 7DS
Telephone: 0171 235 7000

Government statistical departments

Central Statistical Office
Great George Street,
London SW1P 3AQ
Telephone: 0171 270 6363/6364

Central Statistical Office Library
Government Buildings,
Cardiff Road,
Newport NP9 1XG
Telephone: 01633 81 2973

Department of Employment
Caxton House,
Tothill Street,
London SW1H 9NF
Telephone: 0171 273 6969

Office of Population Censuses and Surveys
St Catherine's House,
10 Kingsway WC2B 6JP
Telephone: 0171 396 2208/2243 (general enquiries and publication sales)

Office of Population Censuses and Surveys
Segensworth Road,
Titchfield, PO15 5RR
Telephone: 01329 813800 (detailed statistical information on the census)

The Analysis of Value Data

Value data, whether primary or collated from internal or external secondary sources, is essential for many aspects of marketing research. It allows expenditure on different types of product to be combined and trends over long periods to be compared with leading indicators to establish relationships which can be used when preparing forecasts. This type of analysis, however, needs to be done on a constant value basis. The importance is recognised in many tables showing national economic statistics which include constant historical (e.g. 1995) values or a constant value index based on a specific year. This approach is convenient for those preparing the data as new data can be appended to that already published.

This is not, however, the best approach for presenting marketing information. It is inherently difficult to relate the values of even a few years ago to the present, and even more difficult to do this with the accuracy needed to draw sensible conclusions. Thus, for marketing applications, it is very much better to present historic data in present value terms for discussion and analysis.

Example

From the data presented in the following table (which was based on industry sources but amended for illustration purposes) can anything be said about the market for biscuits in the UK?

The total UK biscuit market, 1993–96

	1993	1994	1995	1996
Sales £000 000 (RSP)				
Chocolate biscuits	348	371	433	504p
Other biscuits	779	788	816	817p
Total	1127	1159	1249	1321p
Sales volume (000 tonnes)				
Chocolate biscuits	138	142	160	179p
Other biscuits	455	452	456	451p
Total	593	594	616	630p
Average price £ per Kg (RSP)				
Chocolate biscuits	2.52	2.61	2.71	2.82p
Other biscuits	1.71	1.78	1.79	1.81p
All biscuits	1.90	1.95	2.03	2.07p

p = provisional

$$\text{Average price} = \frac{\text{Sales in £}}{\text{Volume in Kg}} \quad \text{hence} \quad \frac{348\,000\,000}{138\,000\,000} = £2.52/\text{kg}$$

The first point that should be made is that the market for chocolate biscuits is less than half that of plain biscuits in volume terms (000 tonnes), but is growing whereas that for plain biscuits seems to be essentially static. It would also appear that the market for both chocolate and other biscuits was growing both in terms of historic UK sterling values.

Another interesting point is that difference between the average price of chocolate and other biscuits is clearly sufficient to make the average for all biscuits essentially meaningless.

To analyse this data further it is necessary to use information taken from the retail price index to present this data in constant values. There are many sources for the Retail Price Index, the statistical data presented on one of the back pages of *The Economist* being as convenient as any. For many years there have been two versions of the Retail Price Index which are reported month by month as a news item. The first is usually referred to as the 'Headline' rate and includes the effect of changes in the mortgage interest rate whereas the alternative 'underlying' rate does not. There are also many other versions of the Retail Price Index since, depending on the source, it may be the figure at the end of each year, the figure at mid-year or the average for the year as a whole. In practice so long as one of these rates is used and all rates used are taken from one source the choice makes very little difference. This is because the differences are small compared with the overall effect.

There are also indices which specifically relate to fuel, food, durable goods, and so on. None of these should be used for calculating constant values although for specific products it can sometimes be useful to compare these with either the headline or underlying rates.

What would be the effect of adjusting the sales figures for biscuits to compensate for inflation? As an example, the calculations necessary to present these in constant 1997 values will be shown:

Year		1993	1994	1995	1996	1997
RPI % Increase		3.3	2.8	3.2	2.9	2.6
Year-on-year factor		1.033	1.028	1.032	1.029	1.026
Year-on-year adjustment		1.028	1.032	1.029	1.026	1.00
Cumulative adjustment		1.120	1.090	1.056	1.026	1.00
Sales constant 1997 £000 000 (RSP)						
Chocolate biscuits		390	404	457	517p	
Other biscuits		872	859	862	838p	
Total		1262	1263	1319	1355p	
					p = provisional	
Average price constant 1997 £ per Kg (RSP)						
Chocolate biscuits	2.82	2.85	2.86	2.89p		
Other biscuits	1.92	1.90	1.89	1.86p		

Note:

Year-on-year factor	=	(%RPI/100)+1
Year-on-year adjustment	=	1 for current year then Year-on-year factor for next year
Cumulative adjustment	=	1 for current year then Cumulative adjustment for next year × year-on-year adjustment for present year. Hence $1.00 \times 1.026 = 1.026$; $1.026 \times 1.029 = 1.056$ and so on.
Sales Constant 1997 £	=	Sales Historic × Cumulative adjustment. Hence $348 \times 1.120 = 390$
Average price 1997 £/Kg	=	$\dfrac{\text{Sales in 97£}}{\text{Volume in Kg}}$ hence
		$\dfrac{390\,000\,000}{138\,000\,000} = £2.82/\text{kg}$

It will be seen from these constant value figures that while the chocolate biscuit sector is growing in constant value terms, on the same basis the other sector is shrinking market.

It is noteworthy, that the constant value decline of other biscuits was not matched by the decline in volume, which is explained by the average price having also declined over the period studied. This would suggest that competition had increased in this sector or demand had shifted to either the lower priced brands or product varieties. Over the same period the average price of chocolate biscuits increased as might also be expected in a growing market.

This example demonstrates the importance of presenting time series data on a constant value basis since it reveals information about the market which otherwise is completely hidden. As with any secondary data, it would be sensible before formally presenting this data to attempt to validate it by comparing it with the present situation. At the simplest level this would involve visiting some supermarkets and comparing the price range for chocolate and other biscuits with the calculated 1997 average prices. Another simple but worthwhile check would be to compare the relative amount of shelf space devoted to the two types of biscuits since it would not be unreasonable to expect these to reflect the relative market sizes of the two products.

Questions

Here are some examples for practice. The data for each is based on industry sources but has been adjusted for illustrative purposes. Constant values should be calculated for the year when the calculations are being made. This will require establishing the retail price percentage changes for years subsequent to 1997. The following per cent changes can be used for previous years:

Changes in the Retail Price Index compared with previous year

Year	1991	1992	1993	1994	1995	1996	1997
RPI % INCREASE	5.8	3.9	3.3	2.8	3.2	2.9	2.6

1 As a recently appointed advertising agency marketing assistant you have been asked to review the current market for toasters. One of the agency's main clients is a toaster manufacturer and the account manager for that client obtained for you the market information shown in Table 1 below. He also provided the information Table 2 which can be used to verify the data analysed.

Table 1 The UK toaster market 1992–96

Year		1992	1993	1994	1995	1996
Sales value (£000 000):	Total	42	43	44	48	50 (est)
	Two slot	30.0	31.0	32.0	35.0	37.0 (est)
	Others	12.0	12.0	12.0	13.0	13.0 (est)
Sales volume (000 000 units):	Total	2.0	2.2	2.3	2.6	2.7 (est)
	Two slot	1.5	1.6	1.7	2.0	2.1 (est)
	Other	0.5	0.6	0.6	0.6	0.6 (est)

est= estimated   (Amended for illustrative purposes from industry estimates.)

Table 2 Average price of two slot and other toasters taken from consumer reports

Year	1991	1992	1993	1994	1995	1996
Two slot toasters (£each)		20.50		19.00		18.00
Other toasters (£each)	25.00		22.00		22.00	

Use this data to:

(a) Analyse the UK toaster market showing how this has changed using historic and constant current values for the period over which the available data has been collected.
(b) Comment on these changes or trends on the basis of your analysis.
(c) Discuss the validity of the data provided in the context of the case.

2 Assume you are the Sales and Marketing Manager of a small company which makes specialist chemicals used by manufacturers of shampoo. Your MD believes this market is beginning to decline but the market for conditioners is growing so wants to invested in developing products for the manufacturers of these products. Prepare a report on the UK shampoo and conditioner market using the following data:

The UK Shampoo and Conditioner Market 1991–94 (£000 000)

Year	1991	1992	1993	1994
Shampoo Sales value	210	220	229	241
Conditioner Sales Value	76	83	89	93

The UK Shampoo and Conditioner Market 1991–94 (Mn litres)

Year	1991	1992	1993	1994
Shampoo Sales Volume	74	79	82	85
Conditioner Sales Volume	43	47	51	52

(Amended for illustrative purposes from industry estimates.)

Average price of Shampoo and Conditioner taken from Consumer reports

Year	1991	1992	1993	1994	1995	1996
Shampoo £(historic) per litre		2.80		2.85		3.05
Conditioner £(historic) per litre		1.75		1.80		1.95

Use this data to:

(a) Analyse the UK market for shampoo and conditioners and show how this has changed using historic and constant current values for the period over which data has been collected.
(b) Comment on these changes or trends on the basis of your analysis.
(c) Discuss the validity of the data provided in the context of the case.

3 Jeans seem to continue to resist or adapt to fashion changes in the UK as can be seen from the following table:

Year	1982	1983	1984	1985	1986	1987
UK sales of jeans £m	460	490	540	610	740	820
UK sales of jeans (million pairs)	42.1	44.6	45.1	41.0	42.5	40.6

(a) What are the real trends in this market?
(b) Can you explain what may have happened in 1985?
(c) Does this data seem valid today?

Note: in addition to the percentage changes given above use:

Year	1982	1983	1984	1985	1986	1987	1988	1989	1990
RPI % change on previous year	8.5	4.6	5.0	5.5	3.9	4.9	7.8	7.6	10.4

4 Discuss the benefits and problems of using a computer spreadsheet program (such as Lotus 123) for the collation and analysis of secondary marketing research data.

Market Research Surveys

Surveys using questionnaires remain the most important of the four market research techniques for primary data collection even though the use of observational techniques has been developing rapidly for retail applications through the use of loyalty cards and barcode operated checkouts. Surveys can be used for both continuous and *ad hoc* research studies of all types. One well-known application of surveys are the polls used to monitor the voting intentions of the electorate and the relative popularity of the government and opposition. Usually such estimates are made on the basis of a sample of about 1000 potential voters and have an expected accuracy of +/– 3 per cent. This is remarkably good when one considers that in the UK this is a measure of the intentions of more that 40 million individuals voting in more than 600 separate constituencies.

Another important survey application is to monitor the standing of a major brand against its main competitors. Like all the major car manufacturers, Peugeot UK, for instance, interviews about 100 people regularly to find out how the name Peugeot and it's products are perceived with regard to characteristics such as value for money, economy, quality, performance, sportiness and so on. The results of such surveys are tracked using a moving average and the advertising emphasis changed if, for example, the advertising of an executive model had resulted in the perception of the brand in terms of value for money moving adversely relative to the competition.

Questionnaires can be used to obtain any of the following types of information:

1 Facts.
2 Knowledge.
3 Intentions.
4 Demographic characteristics.
5 Behaviour.
6 Opinions.
7 Attitudes.
8 Motivations.
9 Other psychological characteristics.
10 Lifestyle.

In the marketing context it is useful to seperate facts and knowledge. It should be possible to determine facts precisely for example 'Do you have with you now a phonecard which still has value?'. Knowledge is less straightforward since it is difficult to seperate a person's actual knowledge from their perception of this knowledge. Because of this, answers to a questions such as, 'Do you know about the Phonecard system?', are likely to depend on how complete the person answering believes his or her information to be on the subject.

It has also been recognised by the market research profession that its standing in the eyes of the public is important. In this respect the codes of conduct which have been adopted by both the Market Reasearch Society and the Industrial Market Reasearch

Society are significant. In particular these prohibit the use of market research as a method of screening potential customers. Sadly many doorstep sales personnel have found such an approach can be effective. This bad practice has often been responsible for the poor opinion many people have of market research.

In all types of survey, questionnaires are used to obtain the information required. These are structured which means the questions are answered in sequence often from a number of given alternatives. This allows a large number of respondents to be interviewed and their views recorded efficiently. So these views can be related to a more general population it is necessary to specify how each respondent is selected. This is then known as a formal survey. Structured questionnaires can also be used for informal or casual surveys such as those included with product guarantees and magazines.

For exploratory research or where the opinion of experts is required an informal survey using an unstructured questionnaire would normally be considered preferable. Unstructured questionnaires are designed to encourage the person being interviewed to talk about a number of specific issues associated with the subject being investigated. These may be covered in any order. Since the respondents interviewed for this type of survey will be limited to those who can be contacted, such surveys are known as informal surveys.

The validity of any information resulting from a survey is largely dependent upon two factors. The first is the design of the questionnaire and the second is the appropriateness of the respondents. Since the approach to both of these factors for a formal survey using a structured questionnaire is entirely different from that needed for an informal survey using an unstructured questionnaire these will be considered separately.

Formal surveys

In order to design a questionnaire, draft questions, and determine how respondents should be selected it is necessary to clearly establish:

1 The main purpose of the survey: its objective.
2 The specific information required.
3 Who will be providing this information.
4 Whether any of the required information might be considered sensitive or confidential?
5 How the questionnaire will be used: personal interview, telephone interview, or mail.

While it is generally relatively easy and indeed essential to provide specific responses to items 1 and 3 it is often necessary to reconsider the initial responses to the items 2 and 4. This is because unforeseen difficulties encountered during the design phase often provide opportunities to develop the scope of the survey. The response to item 5 depends upon the applicability of the advantages and disadvantages of each of these approaches for a specific survey. The main advantage of the personal interview is that it encourages the respondent to become more involved with the questions being asked which tends to ensure more considered responses especially to complicated questions. The main disadvantage of the personal interview is the time and cost involved.

The advantage of telephone interviewing is its speed and flexibility. By using a computer-based questionnaire, question responses can directly determine each subsequent question allowing specific issues to be investigated thoroughly. The main disadvantage of telephone interviewing is the difficulty of involving respondents. Many either answer the questions with the objective of terminating the interview or simply refuse. Response is also a major disadvantage of mail surveys.

Questionnaire design

Experience has shown that the effectiveness of questionnaires can be generally improved by following some well-established guidelines. These relate to layout, length and question order and to the essential functions of a questionnaire. These are:

- maintain the co-operation and involvement of the respondent;
- develop the confidence of the respondent;
- allow the respondent to develop answers;
- minimise bias;
- simplify the task of the interviewer; and
- minimise the difficulty of data collation and processing.

Since the questionnaire is the only tangible link between the person asking the questions and the person answering them, it is important that it is an effective means of communication. It therefore needs to appear at first glance straightforward, well-designed and not too long. As a general guide the length of questionnaires for trade surveys or for use 'in the street' should not exceed one typewritten side of A4; those for use on the doorstep, two typewritten sides of A4. Questionnaires for use in prearranged interviews can be longer since a good interviewer should be able to hold the attention of a respondent for an hour or more.

The layout first and foremost needs to be easy to use. A questionnaire should comprise six clearly defined blocks. The first should be the heading. This should contain a survey title in large enough print to be easily read by the respondent, even upside down; instructions to the interviewers, and the introductory statements the interviewers should use when introducing themselves to potential respondents.

Below this there should be four column blocks. The first should be narrow for the question numbers, the second wide enough for the questions, the third wide enough for the answers, and the fourth should be a narrow column for the answer codes.

Across the bottom of the sheet or the last sheet there should be a sixth block containing any questions needed to classify the questionnaire in terms of the location, time and date of the interview, the interviewer and any other relevant information such as weather conditions. It should also include a statement which reminds the interviewer to thank the respondent.

Initially draft those questions which focus on the main purpose of the survey and the other information required. The order in which the questions will be asked should then be considered.

The first two or three questions should be simple, interesting, positively confirm the purpose of the questionnaire and reassure the respondent by showing that the questionnaire will neither be difficult nor take longer than would be reasonable in the circumstances. They should be sufficiently factual and uncontroversial to allow respondents to gather their thoughts about the subject and should aim to develop trust between the interviewer and the respondent. This is important since it is through trust that respondents become involved and hence more likely to answer the questions candidly.

It is not unusual to find that none of the questions initially drafted can be used within the introduction and as a result questions relating to an associated issue need to be used. For instance in a survey regarding the acceptability of food additives questions about snack preferences may well provide an effective introduction.

There should be a logical development from one topic to the next which may involve adding questions to provide links. This approach allows the respondent to become involved with the objective of the questionnaire thereby encouraging accurate answers and a willingness to answer any sensitive questions which the respondent is more likely to accept as being necessary after having completed the majority of the questionnaire.

Question wording

Since the purpose of a questionnaire is to obtain accurate information, questions need to be worded to ensure, as far as possible, a truthful response. This is only possible if respondents:

- are able to understand the question;
- are able to provide the information requested;
- are willing to provide this information.

Does the question 'Do you have with you a phonecard?' meet these criteria? Can it be understood? This depends upon the person being asked the question understanding the term phonecard and if so, the interpretation which is applied to it. There are at least three possible interpretations. It could be the British Telecom Phonecard, or it could mean any phonecard, thereby including the BT card and others such as the French Telecarte, or it could even mean any card which can be used in a phone, which would include Access and Visa cards. There is enough choice here to produce a confusing result.

There is no reason to suspect that the second of the criteria would cause any problem. From a practical viewpoint anyone who believed that they had a card would probably get another if they found it had been lost or had no value when they next tried to use it. Likewise anyone who had one, but had forgotten would probably not remember to use it even when there was an opportunity to do so.

The willingness of the respondent to provide the information is, however, likely to depend upon the need for the information being understood and the respondent being confident that there is no other motive involved. Both of these factors are likely to depend to a significant extent upon the context of the question within the questionnaire and the context in which the questions are being asked.

Just as the effectiveness of questionnaires can be improved by complying with some well-established guidelines, so the wording of questions can be improved by adhering to some simple rules:

1 **Ask short, easy-to-understand questions.**
   Often these two requirements seem to be mutually conflicting. The need to be easily understood, however, should always be considered as more important than brevity. Often the easiest way to meet these apparently conflicting requirements is to ask two questions, the first being intended to assist the respondent rather than provide the required information.

2 **Use ordinary words.**
   Words should be easy for respondents to understand and this is best done by choosing words used in everyday speech. Generally, technical words should be avoided and, where possible, so should words which are not among the 1000 most common words in the English language.

3 **Avoid ambiguous words.**
   While the use of ordinary words is good practice, some words are difficult in that they have different meanings for different people, words such as regularly, often, normally, usually, sometimes, and occasionally are examples of words to avoid.

4 Avoid leading questions.

This requires extreme care both with regard to the wording of questions and the order in which they are asked. It is quite easy for respondents unconsciously to establish a pattern of answering. They are in effect, led on by the previous question. Sometimes this is simply because they are inquisitive about the questionnaire itself and want to avoid having it terminated as a result of giving negative responses.

Some subjects, especially those which have been advertised on the basis of their logic, are often assumed to have become accepted practice. Hence there are many people who, if asked the question: 'Do you use the *Yellow Pages* regularly?', are likely to respond 'Yes' even though they have not used it for months or even years. Further questions seeking to find out how often, are then likely to be answered vaguely or defensively thereby reducing any goodwill there may have been between the interviewer and respondent. One simple device which can be used to overcome this type of problem is to add 'or not' to the question. This reassures the respondent that a negative answer is just as acceptable as a positive one and avoids a situation which otherwise could have significantly reduced the reliability of all subsequent answers.

5 Ensure respondents are not given motives to lie.

This follows from the need to avoid leading questions. A typical example would be a question relating to something apparently peripheral to the stated purpose of the questionnaire for which it is easier to guess the answer than appear ignorant. It has to be emphasised that the purpose of a questionnaire is to obtain information not test the respondents' knowledge, memory or powers of deduction.

Basic guidelines such as these are surprisingly difficult to apply in practice, as can be seen by critically reviewing some of the questionnaires we receive either seeking market research information or for other purposes such as employment applications. The case study at the end of this chapter provides an opportunity to review a sadly not atypical example.

Rationalising the answers

The potential effectiveness of a questionnaire is affected by other factors in addition to the structure of the questionnaire and the wording of individual questions even though these are of prime importance. One of the most important of these other factors is the selection of a rational way by which the answer can be recorded. This determines the type of question used, affects the wording of the question and the number of questions required.

There are two considerations which need to be taken into account: first, 'What information is required?' and second, 'What information can I obtain most easily?' Consider a questionnaire concerning facilities used by students. One factor which could affect the choice of facilities might, for a number of reasons, be age. One approach would be simply to ask 'How old are you?' If asked at the end of a well-designed questionnaire which had developed trust between the interviewer and the respondent and which showed the question was relevant, it would generally get a truthful reply.

This is fine, but what could you do with this information? Divide it into categories such as <17, 17<18, 18<19, 19<20, 20<21, 21<22, 22<25, 25<35, 35<55, 55+. This would suggest that what is required is not the age of the respondent, but the age category of the respondent. The answer can be obtained by showing the respondent a card with each category identified by a code letter. This could safely be shown early in the questionnaire, thus allowing subsequent questions to be selected according to the age group of the respondent.

It is quite likely that nine data categories are more than necessary. In which case the question such as 'Are you under 25 or not?' may provide all the information required. If greater detail is required regarding those under 25 this could be a secondary question for those answering 'Yes' only.

These examples show the different types of answer that can be used to collate factual or demographic information and hence the five types of direct question:

1 **The open question** 'How old are you?'
2 **The closed dichotomous question**: 'Are you under 25?' (requiring a 'yes' or 'no' answer).
3 **The closed multiple choice single answer question**:

'Which age category are you in?' A = <17, B = 17<18, C = 18<19, D = 19<20, E = 20<21, F = 21<25, G = 25<35, H = 35<55, or I = 55+.

(The coded list can be offered to the respondent on a card.)

4 **The closed multiple choice multiple answer question**:

'Have you read any of the following marketing research books?'

Webb *Understanding and Designing MR*	Yes	No
Crimp *The MR process*	Yes	No
Crouch *MR for Managers*	Yes	No

5 **The closed multiple choice ranked answer question**:

'Please rank the following in terms of the greatest appeal in the way you prefer to spend Friday afternoons' (1 indicates your first choice)

Listening to an MR lecture	_____
Working on your own in a library	_____
At home listening to music	_____
On the train to London	_____

Of the ten different types of information listed on page 452 (in Chapter 21) only two, facts and demographic information, are likely to have unequivocal answers. For all of the others, the answer needs to be qualified in terms of degree. Even knowledge should be considered in this category, since as previously discussed, it can be influenced by people's beliefs and attitudes.

Returning to questions relating to phonecards. Assuming that for the purpose of the survey the type of card is important so the original question is changed to identify those who have BT Phonecards. How could the frequency this card is used be established?

There could be two aspects of this question. First is the perception of how frequently it is used. The second aspect is the respondent's perception of frequency. It is actually conceivable that some respondents would consider that once a week was frequent, whereas for others several times a day would be frequent and once a week infrequent. A respondent's perception in itself is often important, especially in marketing, since buying decisions can be strongly influenced by perceptions. Many different methods have been developed to measure the strength of feeling with regard to attitudes, beliefs and opinions. The following three are the most straightforward and are used frequently to measure strength of feeling using a direct question.

First, is the *non-comparative rating scale*. For example:

'How frequently do you use your BT Phonecard?'

5	4	3	2	1	0
Very frequently	Frequently	Sometimes	Occasionally	Seldom	Never

This is useful for measuring perceptions and first impressions and is used in situations where the overall confidence level needs to be investigated.

Where a more specific response is required, the *comparative rating scale* can be used. For example:

'When using a public phone how often do you use your BT Phonecard rather than coins?'

5	4	3	2	1
Always	Very often	About the same	Occasionally	Seldom

Often it is necessary to investigate a large number of potentially significant criteria or features in order to find the few that are critical. This can be done by wording each question so that the answers can be on a *agreement scale*. For example:

5	4	3	2	1
Agree strongly	Agree slightly	Neither agree nor disagree	Disagree slightly	Disagree strongly

This is known as the Likert scale since it was first proposed by Renis Likert in 1932. It will be noted that the non-comparative and comparative rating scales are variations of this basic approach.

With all these first three ways a table can be constructed with the questions in a left-hand column and the answer codes in an adjacent matrix. By this method it is possible to cover a large number of topics quickly and conveniently. The technique is particularly suitable where the questionnaire is being completed by an interviewer and the respondent has been handed a card showing the numbered answers. However, it is important, especially when used in questionnaires that will be completed by the respondent, that there is a random mix of favourable and unfavourable statements, otherwise the result is likely to be affected by respondents who continue to agree or disagree as much from the rhythm of ticking the boxes as from conviction.

The fourth style of questions is *semantic differential scale*. This uses two opposite statements instead of a single statement and the respondent is required to show a tendency towards one or other of the statements rather than to agree or disagree. The effectiveness of the measure depends upon choosing suitable opposing meanings which in practice can be difficult. An example of this approach would be:

'What are your opinions regarding the BT Phonecard? Please place a cross on the line at the point that best indicates your opinion.'

| Extremely expensive simple/available | Somewhat | Neither | Somewhat | Extremely cheap complicated/unavailable |

When considering the wording of questions it is useful to remember the following. Closed questions restrict answers, which make analysis easier but makes answering the questions more difficult. Dichotomous questions are the tightest category so are really only applicable for establishing a fact. When trying to probe motives or intentions then multiple answer or open questions are required. Open-ended questions invite unstructured answers which can be difficult to analyse and require sufficient space to be provided for the answer.

Malhotra suggests the following acronym:

W   who, what, when, where, why, and way;
O   ordinary words;
R   regularly, normally, usually, etc., should be avoided;
D   dual statements (positive and negative);
I   implicit alternatives and assumptions should be avoided;
N   non-leading and non-biasing questions;
G   generalisations and estimates should be avoided.

Reviewing the draft questionnaire

Having drafted a questionnaire it should be reviewed objectively with regard to the points already made and critically with respect to the essential functions of a questionnaire.

At this stage each question should be reviewed and the critical questions reviewed in detail. This involves especially considering the likelihood of the critical questions providing the information required. This will depend in part upon the type of information sought. There is no point in asking questions which the respondent is unable to answer. This can be avoided by using filter questions. Hence, before asking whether a person finds parking in the city centre difficult, it would generally be necessary to establish how the respondent came into the city centre on that particular day and whether or not this was a daily routine. Establishing that a respondent is able to answer a particular question is part way to ensuring that the question is answered accurately.

Sampling

Occasionally formal surveys involve a small total population such as might occur in an industrial market when all the potential customers for a particular product could be included in the survey. This is referred to as a census survey.

More usually this is not practical and surveys involve only a small proportion of the total population. This is then referred to as a sample survey. Using a sample has two specific advantages. First it is less costly than a census. Second it is faster, which in the marketing context is often of paramount importance.

Defining a satisfactory sample is a three stages process. The first of these is to define the target population. This is the total group about which information is required. It could be the female adult population of the country, it could be the Southampton Institute student population as a whole or it could be those members of it who have cars in Southampton. The latter is an example where the definition of the population could have a significant effect on the results of a survey since by limiting the population to students with cars in Southampton would eliminate any student who has a car, but does not have it in Southampton because of the difficulty and cost of parking.

The second stage is to specify how the sample will be selected and the third stage is to specify the sample size. Because of the inherent costs of undertaking market research, the most convenient satisfactory sample should be used.

Random and other types of samples

In order to estimate a population characteristic on the basis of a sample it is a fundamental requirement of statistics theory that a random sample is used. A random sample is defined as one in which a member of the population has an equal, non-zero chance of being included.

This is clearly not the case if the sample chosen is, for instance, a student class. It is equally not the case if every fifth student leaving the union bar is questioned since this would disqualify students who never visit the bar. If additional sites were chosen to overcome this problem say outside the library and outside the refectories, the chance of being interviewed would depend on how many of these facilities a student used. Samples of this type are called convenience samples.

The only theoretically sound approach to obtaining a random sample would be to randomly select the required number using, for example, student registration numbers. It would then be necessary to track down every one of these randomly selected individuals to find out how many were for instances referring to our previous example in possession of a valid BT Phonecard. Even in a reasonably compact area such as Southampton this would be very time consuming and potentially expensive. It also assumes that the list of student numbers can be accessed and is up to date.

Another approach would be to carry out the survey by, for instance, selecting a number of classes which include representatives from different types of course, different years of study, and in different subject areas. Then by including in the questionnaire questions relating to factors such as age, year of study, subject being studied, car ownership, and type of accommodation, the sample could be compared with the total student population of Southampton Institute with regard to these characteristics. If it was found from this comparison that the sample was similar to the population as a whole then it would not be unreasonable to assume that it was representative with respect to having BT Phonecards even though it was not a random sample.

Such an approach can also be used where the target population can be easily defined, e.g. Southampton city centre carpark users, but where there is no list from which a random selection can be made. Instead it would be necessary to attempt to obtain a representative sample by ensuring that interviews were carried out at a number of different sites and at different times of day. The representativeness of the sample could then be checked by asking each respondent the registration year letter of his or her vehicle, for instance, and then comparing the profile of the respondents with the profile of vehicles using the car parks. This could be obtained by observation. Another check might be the time of arrival and likely departure or length of stay which could be checked against the information which might be available from the equipment dispensing payment tickets. By comparing this information the representativeness of the sample could at least to some extent be verified or some allowance made with regard to any apparent bias.

This approach has been further refined by all of the established market research companies for specific applications such as forecasting national election results from comparatively small, non-random samples. These are known as a 'Quota Samples' and rely on the experience of the organisations using them. They are designed to make allowance for known characteristics of the survey population. Hence samples designed to predict election results will make due allowance for the fact the result will not be affected by any seats held by large majorities. Likewise allowance will be made for instance regarding older voters who are both more likely to vote and to vote as they did previously. By this approach it is possible to develop a critical sample rather than a typical or representative sample of the population. This is particularly useful where it is necessary to complete the survey quickly.

Readers requiring more information regarding the different types of sample used for market research surveys should refer to any of the standard textbooks on market research. This should, however, be done with caution as it is easy to unjustifiably attribute random sample properties to non-random samples without considering the implications of doing so.

Estimating a population characteristic

While it is feasible to establish a population characteristic such as possession of a BT Phonecard exactly for a small group of, say 20 individuals, this becomes increasingly more difficult as the size of the group increases.

EXAMPLE

If we wanted to know exactly how many Southampton Institute students have phonecards one way to do this would be to gather them all together in one place and count those who had cards and those without cards as they left. The accuracy of the result would depend upon the care with which the counting was carried out and the number of students who, due to illness or some other reason, could not attend. Thus, if it was found that at the time of the count there were 12 617 enroled students, 9463 had cards, 2771 did not have cards then it would appear that 383 did not attend. However it is quite likely that some of these were students who had recently left so should no longer have been counted as being enroled. For this reason not only is the total number of enroled in practice an estimate but the best that could be said having carried out the count is that of the estimated 12 617 students enroled between 9463 and 9 846 (9463 + 383) had cards and between 2771 and 3154 (2771 + 383) did not have cards. This means assuming the method of counting was totally accurate, card ownership could not be specified with 100 per cent certainty, more precisely than as being between 75 per cent and 78 per cent.

While it might be usual to assume that the ownership of phonecards in the above example, among those who did not attend would be similar to those who did, there is no justification for making this assumption without actual evidence. It is therefore preferable to allow for the possibility that they all may or may not have cards.

Furthermore, any method used to count those with and without cards would have some potential of error, so the precision with which card ownership could be stated with 100 per cent certainty would be accordingly reduced. Thus, if the counting error was estimated as being not greater than +/– 1 per cent, card ownership could not then be stated with 100 per cent certainty more precisely than being between 74 per cent and 79 per cent.

The 5 per cent difference between these is a measure of the precision of the measuring instrument used. This precision can only be improved by changing the measuring instrument, which could, for instance, involve tracking down some of the missing 383 students or by using a more accurate method of counting.

In most business situations measures based on 100 per cent certainty are neither necessary nor possible. Furthermore, the difficulties involved are clearly evident from the above example.

Let us consider a completely hypothetical reason as to why it might be useful to know the proportion of Southampton Institute students who have BT Phonecards. Imagine BT has developed a card-operated Internet access system for use in universities and colleges and wished to select those colleges where it was likely to be most successful. By installing a small number of systems on a trial basis, it might be possible to established that success depended on BT Phonecard ownership being in excess of say 40 per cent.

As with any business venture there are factors which affect success or failure which are outside the control of the organisation. Because of this it is accepted that some installations will be more successful than others and indeed that some will fail. Since it is estimated that two-thirds of new products fail, BT decide that initially they should aim for a 50 per cent installation success rate. That is, of every two systems installed one will be successful and the other, being unsuccessful, will have to be moved to another site.

Because of the other factors which were identified during the trials as contributing to success or failure it is decided that the risk due to insufficient card ownership should be limited to 5 per cent. That is, for every 20 card Internet access systems installed they would expect 10 to be successful and not more than 1 to be unsuccessful as a result of insufficient card ownership among the student population concerned.

This means that before installing a system in Southampton Institute they would need to be 95 per cent confident that not less than 40 per cent of the total Southampton Institute student population have BT Phonecards.

Since a 95 per cent confidence level is acceptable, a census such as the count described in the example which could provide a 100 per cent confidence level measurement is clearly unnecessary. Furthermore statistics theory provides a method for using a required confidence level to calculate the likely range for a specific population characteristic based on a measurement made using a random sample.

For instance, from a random sample of 100 male students it is possible to be 95 per cent confident that any male student between 1.75 and 1.85 metres in height will weigh between 50 and 90 kilograms.

When the same approach is applied to questions with a yes/no answer such as, 'Do you own a Walkman?', the result would be stated in the form that from the random sample used it is possible to be 95 per cent confident that from 74 per cent to 100 per cent of that population own a Walkman. It is also possible for both of these examples to calculate the range applicable for different confidence levels.

The only information needed to do this is the original sample data. Hence, if from a random sample of 40 students it was found that 21 had phonecards and 19 did not, this information could be used in the following formula to calculate the high low limits for the population from which the random sample was taken.

At a 68 per cent confidence level:

High 'Yes' limit (%)

$$\frac{Ny \times 100}{Ny + Nn} \quad + \quad \frac{50}{- \quad \sqrt{(Ny + Nn)}}$$

Low 'Yes' limit (%)

Substituting Ny = 21 and Nn = 19 we get:

High 'Yes' limit (%)

$$\frac{21 \times 100}{21 + 19} \quad + \quad \frac{50}{- \quad \sqrt{(21 + 19)}}$$

Low 'Yes' limit (%)

Calculating:

High 'Yes' limit (%)

$$\frac{2100}{40} \quad + \quad \frac{50}{- \quad \sqrt{(40)}}$$

Low 'Yes' limit (%)

High 'Yes' limit (%)   +   = 60.4
            52.5   7.9

Low 'Yes' limit (%)   −   = 44.6

Where the application requires a higher level of confidence than 68 per cent as in this example, it is a simple matter to recalculate the limits for either 95 or 99 per cent confidence levels as follows:

For 95 per cent confidence the:

High 'Yes' limit (%)   +   = 68.3
            52.5 2×7.9

Low 'Yes' limit (%)   −   = 36.7

For 99 per cent confidence the:

High 'Yes' limit (%)   +   = 76.2
            52.5 3×7.9

Low 'Yes' limit (%)   −   = 28.8

Thus, on the basis of this sample the requirement that at least 40 per cent of Southampton Institute students have BT Phonecards has been met at the 68 per cent confidence level but not at either the 95 per cent or 99 per cent confidence levels.

Since the assessment being undertaken is simple it would be little trouble to repeat the survey with another random sample of 120 students. The total random sample would then be 160. If we assume the proportions with and without cards remain exactly the same then of the 160 students, 84 would have BT Phonecards.

Thus, at a 68 per cent confidence level substituting Ny = 84 and Nn = 76 in the above formula, we get:

High 'Yes' limit (%)

$$\frac{84 \times 100}{84 + 76} \; + \; \frac{50}{\sqrt{(84 + 76)}} \; -$$

Low 'Yes' limit (%)

Calculating:

High 'Yes' limit (%)

$$\frac{8400}{160} \; + \; \frac{50}{\sqrt{(160)}} \; -$$

Low 'Yes' limit (%)

High 'Yes' limit (%)   52.5   +   3.95   = 56.5

Low 'Yes' limit (%)   −   = 48.5

For 95 per cent confidence the:

High 'Yes' limit (%)   52.5   + 3×3.95 = 60.4

Low 'Yes' limit (%)   −   = 44.6

And at the 99 per cent confidence level the:

High 'Yes' limit (%)   52.5   + 3×3.95 = 64.4

Low 'Yes' limit (%)   −   = 40.7

Thus, on the basis of this four-times larger sample, while the proportion within the sample has remained the same the requirement that at least 40 per cent own BT Phonecards at any one time has been met both at the 95 per cent and 99 per cent confidence levels. It should be noted that it was necessary to increase the sample size by a factor of four to reduce the difference between the high and low limits by a factor of two.

Sample size

Those readers who recognise that the formula used above is a specific application of the Central Limit Theorem as applied to proportions, will have no difficulty in developing a formula for calculating the minimum sample size needed to confirm or reject the proposition that a Phonecard Internet access system should be installed at Southampton Institute.

For the others, it will no doubt be sufficient to accept that this can be done using the following formula:

$$N = \frac{Z^2 \, p(1-p)}{E^2}$$

where N = sample size, Z = confidence factor constant (=1 for 68%, = 2 for 95% and 3 for 99%), p = proportion of 'Yes' answers and E = high/low limits/2

Thus, for: 95% confidence Z = 2, 50% proportion p = 0.5 and 20 % error E = 0.2/2

$$N = \frac{2^2\,(0.5 \times 0.5)}{0.1^2}$$

$$N = \frac{4 \times 0.25}{0.01}$$

$$N = 100$$

This demonstrates how important it is to understand not only what information is required but also how accurate it needs to be. The calculation of minimum sample size is based on the assumption that only half of the class possessed BT Phonecards, the worst case from the viewpoint of calculating sample size, and the error was twice the difference between half the class having cards and the minimum at which installation was considered viable. That is, 50–40 per cent at the 95 per cent confidence level.

Survey implementation

Having designed the questionnaire and defined the respondents, a limited number of questionnaires should be produced so that a pilot survey can be conducted. A pilot survey usually involves having ideally 50 or more (at the very least 20) questionnaires completed by experienced interviewers. It is important that the respondents for the pilot survey are selected in the same way as they will be for the full survey.

The purpose of the pilot study is to reveal any problems with regard to the order or wording of questions and the reply cards if these are used. Amendments are then made, and if extensive, another pilot conducted before producing the number of copies required for the full survey.

The next stage of the process involves distributing the questionnaires and having them completed. Where interviewers are to be used arrangements will need to be made for them to be briefed and possibly also trained. The completed questionnaires will then need to be collected, checked, coded and analysed. With the availability of market research analysis programmes such as SPSS, Marquis and Answers which can be run on personal computers the collation of the results is comparatively straightforward.

The interpretation of the collated results can, however, be surprisingly difficult and time consuming as the output produced by these programmes can be overwhelming. One of the easiest approaches to initially review the results is to use two blank questionnaires. On the first the actual response counts are written in against each answer while on the second the valid percentages are written in for each question. Doing this will both reveal some of the coding and inputting errors and provide a useful basis for subsequent more detailed analysis of the results. These will then need to be effectively presented in a report as discussed in Chapter 21.

Readers wishing to use statistical techniques for analysing market research data are also referred to the standard texts. Again, caution is advised since statistical analysis cannot improve the quality of the information being analysed or compensate for the limitations resulting from the use of a non-random sample or a poor questionnaire. It is important therefore to beware of false accuracy. There is no point calculating the high and low limits of a proportion which differ by 20 per cent to 0.1 per cent. In circumstances where the range is large it generally helps to think of the figures rounded to the nearest 5 per cent even though they might be specified for identification purposes to the nearest 1 per cent.

One of the main values of statistical analysis is to show the potential adequacy of information which is available. Thus whenever the results of a sample are used to estimate a population characteristic this should ALWAYS be done as it was for the possession of phone cards. That is with both the probability and range stated. This is essential since when this is done it is not unusual for the result to be clearly of little practical value.

Informal surveys

For students, an informal survey to establish the opinions of a defined group of 'experts' is often one of the most practical ways of obtaining primary information for final year projects and dissertations. They could for instance be used to determine the opinions of pub landlords and managers to the promotion and sale of alcopops or the need to provide additional entertainment to attract customers. This approach to obtaining primary data avoids many of the problems associated with conducting a formal survey using a structured questionnaire.

This does not mean that there are no difficulties associated with informal surveys but rather that these are different and generally more easily overcome or avoided within the context of an academic project.

Whereas structured questionnaires are designed to ensure subjects are covered in the order selected, unstructured questionnaires should provide the flexibility needed for the order to be at least partially controlled by the respondent. While the main purpose of an unstructured questionnaire is to provide a framework for the interview and to ensure all aspects of the subject are covered, it should be remembered that its functions are the same as those for a structured questionnaire. For this reason many of the same criteria apply.

The initial questions need to be straightforward and, as for a structured questionnaire, they should be simple, interesting, and positively confirm the purpose of the interview. They should also reassure the respondent by showing that the interview will neither be confrontational nor take longer than might be expected. Whereas with a structured questionnaire most of the questions used will be one of the forms of closed question, it is important to use open questions in an unstructured questionnaire. This format allows respondents to express more general views in the course of responding to each specific question. This is important especially since informal surveys are generally used to obtain the views of specifically selected individuals and having agreed to provide information they generally would like the opportunity to express their opinions rather than simply answer questions.

As a result it is quite likely that many questions, rather than by being asked directly, will be answered either in passing or by the interviewer guiding the topic being discussed. Where factual information is required, closed questions, as would be used for a structured questionnaire, can be used. These would normally be left until the other issues have been covered by which time adequate trust should have been established between the interviewer and the respondent.

It is not usually practical to pilot an unstructured questionnaire as is essential for a structured questionnaire. It is thus often necessary to revise the questionnaire during the course of the survey. This can be essential when a respondent raises an issue not included within the original questionnaire, but clearly important to the objectives of the survey. A question covering this can then be added to the questionnaire for subsequent respondents to answer. Occasionally the issue may be considered sufficiently important to justify trying to obtain the views of at least some respondents who were interviewed prior to the issue being raised. Generally this can be easily done by telephone providing the possibility that this may be necessary is mentioned during the original interview. Of course changes to the questionnaire involving deleting questions which are not providing the information expected are no problem.

Analysis of data resulting from unstructured questionnaires

Because mostly open questions are used in unstructured questionnaires the collation and analysis of the information obtained is likely to be difficult. The first problem is that interviewers have to note the essential points being made while asking specific questions, guiding the conversation and keeping track of which questions have been covered adequately. This task is made considerably easier if the respondent agrees to the interview being recorded. However there are many situations where this can limit what can be expected from the interview. Also when recording an interview it is usually helpful to have some additional general introductory questions to allow the respondent to get used to being recorded.

As soon as possible after the interview has been completed the notes or recording should be reviewed to determine the essential points made with respect to each question. These should then be written up as responses in the order used for the questionnaire rather than the order in which the issues were discussed. Points made, but not covered by an appropriate question should be added as responses to additional questions. If any of these are considered critical to the objectives of the study they should be added to the questionnaire to obtain responses from subsequent interviews.

By using this approach it is possible to compile directly comparable sets of responses from an informal survey. Their differences and similarities can then be identified, discussed and from this conclusions may be drawn. It would be normal for the final version of the unstructured questionnaire and the corresponding sets of responses to be included as appendices in a report using this data.

CASE STUDY

While seeking a permanent marketing-orientated job you accept a temporary post working in the planning office of a large regional hospital. You find on joining this office that your first task is to organise the piloting phase of a major survey to determine the expectations of young adults with respect to health care. As none of the existing staff have any knowledge of market research they were initially intending to use a questionnaire which had been drawn up by a previous temporary employee, but never used. You are given a copy of this questionnaire and realise it has numerous faults.

(a) Discuss how the order in which the questions are asked can affect the validity of the answers.
(b) Demonstrate a formal process for improving the wording of some of the badly worded questions.
(c) Comment on any other aspects of the questionnaire which ought to be revised before it is used.

REGIONAL HEALTH CARE SURVEY

1 Do you live in the Southampton area?　　　Yes/No　(If No terminate)

2 What is your Postcode? . . . .

3 What is your Name? . . . .

4 What is your Address? . . . .

5 What is your occupation? . . . .

6 Is this Full / Part time? . . . .

7 What is your household income level?

Below £5000	☐	£5000–£10 000	☐
£10 000–£15 000	☐	Over £15 000	☐

8 Are you Male/Female? . . . .　　　**9** What is your age? . . . .

10 Are you married?　Yes/No

11 Do you have children?　Yes/No

12 How often do you visit the doctor?　　Daily ☐　　Weekly ☐
　　　　　　　　　　　　　　　　　　　　　　Monthly ☐　　Yearly ☐　　Never ☐

13 How long have you been registered with your doctor?
　　<6 months ☐　　6–12 months ☐　　12–24 months ☐　　>24 months ☐

14 For the listed conditions what is the likelihood of you visiting your doctor?

	Always	Sometimes	Never
Coryza	☐	☐	☐
Otitis Media	☐	☐	☐
Pyrexia	☐	☐	☐
Coccydynia	☐	☐	☐

15 Would you be less likely to visit the doctor for these conditions if each visit　　cost £10
Yes/No

16 How often do you visit the dentist?　　Daily ☐　　Weekly ☐　　Monthly☐
　　　　　　　　　　　　　　　　　　　　　　Yearly ☐　　Never ☐

17 How long have you been registered with your dentist?
　　<6 months ☐　　6–12 months ☐　　12–24 months ☐　　>24 months ☐

18 Are you registered as a Private Patient   Yes/No

19 If you never visit the dentist – Why?

Too expensive ☐   Too much effort ☐   Teeth are fine ☐

Other, please state . . . .

20 Would you visit the dentist more often if treatment was free for students?   Yes/No

21 How would you rate the following treatment costs?

	Cheap	Reasonable	Expensive
Basic check-up £6	☐	☐	☐
One small filling £7	☐	☐	☐
Scale and polish £9	☐	☐	☐
Tooth extraction £10	☐	☐	☐

22 How often do you visit the pharmacist?   Daily ☐   Weekly ☐   Monthly ☐

Yearly ☐   Never ☐

23 Are you satisfied with the range of products offered?   Yes/No

If 'No' please explain . . . .

24 What percentage of these are food products? . . . .

25 Do you have a bank account?   Yes/No

26 Which Bank? . . . .

27 Which of these Credit Cards do you use?

Barclaycard ☐   Access ☐   Diners Card ☐   American Express ☐

28 What is your credit limit?   £ . . . .

1 Identify and discuss briefly the functions of a questionnaire.

2 Define the term random sample and discuss the advantages and disadvantages of using a random sample for a survey by personal interview.

3 Describe the term quota sample and discuss the advantages and disadvantages of using this type of sample for opinion and market research surveys.

4 Identify the different stages which normally are necessary when undertaking a full market research study and discuss the importance and the problems associated with each of these stages in the context of a study involving a specified product or service of your choice.

5 Explain briefly the difference between a random sample, convenience sample and quota sample.

Index